JENS OTTO JESPERSEN was born at Randers, Denmark, in
1860. In 1893 he was appointed professor at the University
of Copenhagen; during 1909-10 he lectured at Columbia
University in New York. His most important works, other
than the present volume, are *Progress in Language* (1894);
Phonetics (1897-99); *Growth and Structure of the English
Language* (1905, Prix Volney, 1906); and *Philosophy of
Grammar* (1924). He died in Denmark in 1943.

THE LANGUAGE LIBRARY

Edited by ERIC PARTRIDGE

LANGUAGE

ITS NATURE
DEVELOPMENT
AND ORIGIN

BY

OTTO JESPERSEN

The Norton Library
W · W · NORTON & COMPANY · INC ·
NEW YORK

FIRST PUBLISHED IN THE NORTON LIBRARY IN 1964 BY ARRANGEMENT
WITH THE MACMILLAN COMPANY

W. W. Norton & Company, Inc. is also the publisher of
The Norton Anthology of English Literature, edited by M. H.
Abrams, Robert M. Adams, David Daiches, E. Talbot Donaldson,
George H. Ford, Samuel Holt Monk, and Hallett Smith; *The Ameri-
can Tradition in Literature,* edited by Sculley Bradley, Richmond
Croom Beatty, and E. Hudson Long; *World Masterpieces,* edited
by Maynard Mack, Kenneth Douglas, Howard E. Hugo, Bernard
M. W. Knox, John C. McGalliard, P. M. Pasinetti, and René Wellek;
and the paperbound Norton Critical Editions—authoritative texts,
together with the leading critical interpretations, of *Adventures of
Huckleberry Finn, The Ambassadors, Crime and Punishment, Gul-
liver's Travels, Hamlet, Heart of Darkness, Henry IV, Part 1,
Madame Bovary, The Red Badge of Courage, The Scarlet Letter,* and
Wuthering Heights.

Printed in the United States of America

TO

VILHELM - THOMSEN

Glæde, når av andres mund
　　jeg hørte de tanker store,
Glæde over hvert et fund
　　jeg selv ved min forsken gjorde.

PREFACE

THE distinctive feature of the science of language as conceived nowadays is its historical character : a language or a word is no longer taken as something given once for all, but as a result of previous development and at the same time as the starting-point for subsequent development. This manner of viewing languages constitutes a decisive improvement on the way in which languages were dealt with in previous centuries, and it suffices to mention such words as ' evolution ' and ' Darwinism ' to show that linguistic research has in this respect been in full accordance with tendencies observed in many other branches of scientific work during the last hundred years. Still, it cannot be said that students of language have always and to the fullest extent made it clear to themselves what is the real essence of a language. Too often expressions are used which are nothing but metaphors—in many cases perfectly harmless metaphors, but in other cases metaphors that obscure the real facts of the matter. Language is frequently spoken of as a ' living organism ' ; we hear of the ' life ' of languages, of the ' birth ' of new languages and of the ' death ' of old languages, and the implication, though not always realized, is that a language is a living thing, something analogous to an animal or a plant. Yet a language evidently has no separate existence in the same way as a dog or a beech has, but is nothing but a function of certain living human beings. Language is activity, purposeful activity, and we should never lose sight of the speaking individuals and of their purpose in acting in this particular way. When people speak of the life of words—as in celebrated books with such titles as *La vie des mots*, or *Biographies of Words*—they do not always keep in view that a word has no ' life ' of its own : it exists only in so far as it is pronounced or heard or remembered by somebody, and this kind of existence cannot properly be compared with ' life ' in the original and proper sense of that word. The only unimpeachable definition of a word is that it is a human habit, an habitual act on the part of one human individual which has, or may have, the effect of evoking some idea in the mind of another individual. A word thus may be rightly compared with such an habitual act as taking off one's hat or raising one's fingers to one's cap : in both cases we have a certain set of muscular activities which, when seen or heard by somebody else, shows him what is passing in the mind of the original agent or what he desires to bring to the consciousness of the other man (or men). The act is individual, but the interpretation presupposes that the individual forms part of a community with analogous habits, and a language thus is seen to be one particular set of human customs of a well-defined social character.

It is indeed possible to speak of ' life ' in connexion with language even from this point of view, but it will be in a different sense from that in which the word was taken by the older school of linguistic science. I shall try to give a biological or biographical science of language, but it will be through sketching the linguistic biology or biography of the speaking individual. I shall give, therefore, a large part to the way in which a child learns his mother-tongue (Book II) : my conclusions there are chiefly based on the rich material I have collected during many years from direct observation of many Danish children, and particularly of my own boy, Frans (see my book *Nutid sprog hos börn og voxne*, Copenhagen, 1916). Unfortunately, I have not been able to make first-hand observations with regard to the speech of English children ; the English examples I quote are taken second-hand either from notes, for which I am obliged to English and American friends, or from books, chiefly by psychologists. I should be particularly happy if my remarks could induce some English or American linguist to take up a systematic study of the speech of children, or of one child. This study seems to me very fascinating indeed, and a linguist is sure to notice many things that would be passed by as uninteresting even by the closest observer among psychologists, but which may have some bearing on the life and development of language.

Another part of linguistic biology deals with the influence of the foreigner, and still another with the changes which the individual is apt independently to introduce into his speech even after he has fully acquired his mother-tongue. This naturally leads up to the question whether all these changes introduced by various individuals do, or do not, follow the same line of direction, and whether mankind has on the whole moved forward or not in linguistic matters. The conviction reached through a study of historically accessible periods of well-known languages is finally shown to throw some light on the disputed problem of the ultimate origin of human language.

Parts of my theory of sound-change, and especially my objections to the dogma of blind sound-laws, date back to my very first linguistic paper (1886) ; most of the chapters on Decay or Progress and parts of some of the following chapters, as well as the theory of the origin of speech, may be considered a new and revised edition of the general chapters of my *Progress in Language* (1894). Many of the ideas contained in this book thus are not new with me ; but even if a reader of my previous works may recognize things which he has seen before, I hope he will admit that they have been here worked up with much new material into something like a system, which forms a fairly comprehensive theory of linguistic development.

Still, I have not been able to compress into this volume the whole of my philosophy of speech. Considerations of space have obliged me to exclude the chapters I had first intended to write on the practical consequences of the ' energetic ' view of language which I have throughout maintained ; the estimation of linguistic phenomena implied in that view has bearings on such questions as these : What is to be considered ' correct ' or ' standard ' in matters of pronunciation, spelling, grammar and idiom ? Can (or should) individuals exert themselves to improve their mother-tongue by enriching it with new terms and by making it purer, more precise, more fit to express subtle shades of thought, more easy to handle in speech or in writing, etc. ? (A few hints on such questions may be found in my paper " Energetik der Sprache " in *Scientia*, 1914.) Is it possible to construct an artificial language on scientific prin-ciples for international use ? (On this question I may here briefly state my conviction that it is extremely important for the whole of mankind to have such a language, and that Ido is scientifically and practically very much superior to all previous attempts, Volapük, Esperanto, Idiom Neutral, Latin sine flexione, etc. But I have written more at length on that question elsewhere.) With regard to the system of grammar, the relation of grammar to logic, and grammatical categories and their definition, I must refer the reader to *Sprojets Logik* (Copenhagen, 1913), and to the first chapter of the second volume of my *Modern English Grammar* (Heidelberg, 1914), but I shall hope to deal with these questions more in detail in a future work, to be called, probably, *The Logic of Grammar*, of which some chapters have been ready in my drawers for some years and others are in active preparation.

I have prefixed to the theoretical chapters of this work a short survey of the history of the science of language in order to show how my problems have been previously treated. In this part (Book I) I have, as a matter of course, used the excellent works on the subject by Benfey, Raumer, Delbrück (*Einleitung in das Sprachstudium*, 1st ed., 1880 ; I did not see the 5th ed., 1908, till my own chapters on the history of linguistics were finished), Thomsen, Oertel and Pedersen. But I have in nearly every case gone to the sources themselves, and have, I think, found interesting things in some of the early books on linguistics that have been generally overlooked ; I have even pointed out some writers who had passed into undeserved oblivion. My intention has been on the whole to throw into relief the great lines of development rather than to give many details ; in judging the first part of my book it should also be borne in mind that its object primarily is to serve as an introduction to the problems dealt with in the rest of the book. Throughout I have tried to look at things with my own eyes, and accordingly my views on a great many points are different from those generally accepted ; it is my hope that an impartial observer will find that I have here and there succeeded in distributing light and shade more justly than my predecessors.

Wherever it has been necessary I have transcribed words phonetically according to the system of the *Association Phonétique Internationale*, though without going into too minute distinction of sounds, the object being, not to teach the exact pronunciation of various languages, but rather to bring out clearly the insufficiency of the ordinary spelling. The latter is given throughout in italics, while phonetic symbols have been inserted in brackets [ ]. I must ask the reader to forgive inconsistency in such matters as Greek accents, Old English marks of vowel-length, etc., which I have often omitted as of no importance for the purpose of this volume.

I must express here my gratitude to the directors of the Carlsbergfond for kind support of my work. I want to thank also Professor G. C. Moore Smith, of the University of Sheffield : not only has he sent me the manuscript of a translation of most of my *Nutidssprog*, which he had undertaken of his own accord and which served as the basis of Book II, but he has kindly gone through the whole of this volume, improving and correcting my English style in many passages. His friendship and the untiring interest he has always taken in my work have been extremely valuable to me for a great many years.

OTTO JESPERSEN.

UNIVERSITY OF COPENHAGEN,
June 1921.

CONTENTS

BOOK I

HISTORY OF LINGUISTIC SCIENCE

BOOK II

THE CHILD

BOOK III

THE INDIVIDUAL AND THE WORLD

BOOK IV

DEVELOPMENT OF LANGUAGE

ABBREVIATIONS OF BOOK TITLES, ETC.

Bally LV = Ch. Bally, *Le Langage et la Vie*, Genève 1913.
Benfey Gesch = Th. Benfey, *Geschichte der Sprachwissenschaft*, München 1869.
Bleek CG = W. H. I. Bleek, *Comparative Grammar of South African Languages*, London 1862–69.
Bloomfield SL = L. Bloomfield, *An Introduction to the Study of Language*, New York 1914.
Bopp C = F. Bopp, *Conjugationssystem der Sanskritsprache*, Frankfurt 1816.
    AC = *Analytical Comparison* (see ch. ii, § 6).
    VG = *Vergleichende Grammatik*, 2te Ausg., Berlin 1857.
Bréal M = M. Bréal, *Mélanges de Mythologie et de Linguistique*, Paris 1882.
Brugmann VG = K. Brugmann, *Grundriss der Vergleichenden Grammatik*, Strassburg 1886 ff., 2te Ausg., 1897 ff.
    KG = *Kurze Vergleichende Grammatik*, Strassburg 1904.
ChE = O. Jespersen, *Chapters on English*, London 1918.
Churchill B = W. Churchill, *Beach-la-Mar*, Washington 1911.
Curtius C = G. Curtius, *Zur Chronologie der indogerm. Sprachforschung*, Leipzig 1873.
    K = *Zur Kritik der neuesten Sprachforschung*, Leipzig 1885.
Dauzat V = A. Dauzat, *La Vie du Langage*, Paris 1910.
    Ph = *La Philosophie du Langage*, Paris 1912.
Delbrück E = B. Delbrück, *Einleitung in das Sprachstudium*, Leipzig 1880 ; 5te Aufl. 1908.
    Grfr = *Grundfragen der Sprachforschung*, Strassburg 1901.
E. = English.
EDD = J. Wright, *The English Dialect Dictionary*, Oxford 1898 ff.
ESt = *Englische Studien*.
Feist KI = S. Feist, *Kultur, Ausbreitung und Herkunft der Indogermanen*, Berlin 1913.
Fonetik = O. Jespersen, *Fonetik*, Copenhagen 1897.
Fr. = French.
Gabelentz Spr = G. v. d. Gabelentz, *Die Sprachwissenschaft*, Leipzig 1891.
    Gr = *Chinesische Grammatik*, Leipzig 1881.
Ginneken LP = J. v. Ginneken, *Principes de Linguistique Psychologique*, Amsterdam, Paris 1907.
Glenconner = P. Glenconner, *The Sayings of the Children*, Oxford 1918.
Gr. = Greek.
Greenough and Kittredge W = J. B. Greenough and G. L. Kittredge, *Words and their Ways in English Speech*, London 1902.
Grimm Gr. = J. Grimm, *Deutsche Grammatik*, 2te Ausg., Göttingen 1822.
    GDS = *Geschichte der deutschen Sprache*, 4te Aufl., Leipzig 1880.

GRM = *Germanisch-Romanische Monatsschrift.*

GS = O. Jespersen, *Growth and Structure of the English Language*, 3rd ed., Leipzig 1919.

Hilmer Sch = H. Hilmer, *Schallnachahmung, Wortschöpfung u. Bedeutungswandel*, Halle 1914.

Hirt GDS = H. Hirt, *Geschichte der deutschen Sprache*, München 1919.

    Idg = *Die Indogermanen*, Strassburg 1905-7.

Humboldt Versch = W. v. Humboldt, *Verschiedenheit des menschlichen Sprachbaues* (number of pages as in the original edition).

IF = *Indogermanische Forschungen.*

KZ = Kuhn's *Zeitschrift für vergleichende Sprachforschung.*

Lasch S = R. Lasch, *Sondersprachen u. ihre Entstehung*, Wien 1907.

LPh = O. Jespersen, *Lehrbuch der Phonetik*, 3te Aufl., Leipzig 1920.

Madvig 1857 = J. N. Madvig, *De grammatische Betegnelser*, Copenhagen 1857.

    Kl = *Kleine philologische Schriften*, Leipzig 1875.

ME. = Middle English.

MEG = O. Jespersen, *Modern English Grammar*, Heidelberg 1909, 1914.

Meillet DI = A. Meillet, *Les Dialectes Indo-Européens*, Paris 1908.

    Germ. = *Caractères généraux des Langues Germaniques*, Paris 1917.

    Gr = *Aperçu d'une Histoire de la Langue Grecque*, Paris 1913.

    LI = *Introduction à l'étude comp. des Langues Indo-Européennes*, 2e éd., Paris 1908.

Meinhof Ham = C. Meinhof, *Die hamitischen Sprachen*, Hamburg 1912.

    MSA = *Die moderne Sprachforschung in Afrika*, Berlin 1910.

Meringer L = R. Meringer, *Aus dem Leben der Sprache*, Berlin 1908.

Misteli = F. Misteli, *Charakteristik der haupts. Typen des Sprachbaues*, Berlin 1893.

MSL = *Mémoires de la Société de Linguistique de Paris.*

Fr. Müller Gr = Friedrich Müller, *Grundriss der Sprachwissenschaft*, Wien 1876 ff.

Max Müller Ch = F. Max Müller, *Chips from a German Workshop*, vol. iv, London 1875.

NED = *A New English Dictionary*, by Murray, etc., Oxford 1884 ff.

Noreen UL = A. Noreen, *Abriss der urgermanischen Lautlehre*, Strassburg 1894.

    VS = *Vårt Språk*, Lund 1903 ff.

Nyrop Gr = Kr. Nyrop, *Grammaire Historique de la Langue Française*, Copenhagen 1914 ff.

OE. = Old English (Anglo-Saxon).

Oertel = H. Oertel, *Lectures on the Study of Language*, New York 1901.

OFr. = Old French.

ON. = Old Norse.

Passy Ch = P. Passy, *Les Changements Phonétiques*, Paris 1890.

Paul P = H. Paul, *Prinzipien der Sprachgeschichte*, 4te Aufl., Halle 1909.

    Gr = *Grundriss der germanischen Philologie.*

PBB = *Beiträge zur Geschichte der deutschen Sprache* (Paul u. Braune).

Pedersen GKS = H. Pedersen, *Vergl. Grammatik der keltischen Sprachen*, Göttingen 1909.

PhG = O. Jespersen, *Phonetische Grundfragen*, Leipzig 1904.

Porzezinski Spr = V. Porzezinski, *Einleitung in die Sprachwissenschaft*, Leipzig 1910.

Progr. = O. Jespersen, *Progress in Language*, London 1894.

Rask P = R. Rask [Prisskrift] *Undersögelse om det gamle Nordiske Sprogs Oprindelse*, Copenhagen 1818.

SA = *Samlede Afhandlinger*, Copenhagen 1834.

Raumer Gesch = R. v. Raumer, *Geschichte der germanischen Philologie*, München 1870.

Ronjat = J. Ronjat, *Le Développement du Langage chez un Enfant Bilingue*, Paris 1913.

Sandfeld Jensen S = Kr. Sandfeld Jensen, *Sprogvidenskaben*, Copenhagen 1913.

Sprw = *Die Sprachwissenschaft*, Leipzig 1915.

Saussure LG = F. de Saussure, *Cours de Linguistique Générale*, Lausanne 1916.

Sayce P = A. H. Sayce, *Principles of Comparative Philology*, 2nd ed., London 1875.

S = *Introduction to the Science of Language*, London 1880.

Scherer GDS = W. Scherer, *Zur Geschichte der deutschen Sprache*, Berlin 1878.

Schleicher I, II = A. Schleicher, *Sprachvergleichende Untersuchungen*, I–II, Bonn 1848, 1850.

Bed. = *Die Bedeutung der Sprache*, Weimar 1865.

C = *Compendium der vergl. Grammatik*, 4te Aufl., Weimar 1876.

D = *Die deutsche Sprache*, Stuttgart 1860.

Darw. = *Die Darwinische Theorie und die Sprachwissenschaft*, Weimar 1873.

NV = *Nomen und Verbum*, Leipzig 1865.

Schuchardt SlD = H. Schuchardt, *Slawo-Deutsches u. Slawo-Italienisches*, Graz 1885.

KS = *Kreolische Studien* (Wien, Akademie).

Simonyi US = S. Simonyi, *Die Ungarische Sprache*, Strassburg 1907.

Skt. = Sanskrit.

Sommer Lat. = F. Sommer, *Handbuch der latein. Laut- und Formenlehre*, Heidelberg 1902.

Stern = Clara and William Stern, *Die Kindersprache*, Leipzig 1907.

Stoffel Int. = C. Stoffel, *Intensives and Down-toners*, Heidelberg 1901.

Streitberg Gesch = W. Streitberg, *Geschichte der indogerm. Sprachwissenschaft*, Strassburg 1917.

Urg = *Urgermanische Grammatik*, Heidelberg 1896.

Sturtevant LCh = E. H. Sturtevant, *Linguistic Change*, Chicago 1917.

Sütterlin WSG = L. Sütterlin, *Das Wesen der sprachlichen Gebilde*, Heidelberg 1902.

WW = *Werden und Wesen der Sprache*, Leipzig 1913.

Sweet CP = H. Sweet, *Collected Papers*, Oxford 1913.

H = *The History of Language*, London 1900.

PS = *The Practical Study of Languages*, London 1899.

Tegnér SM = E. Tegnér, *Språkets makt öfver tanken*, Stockholm 1880.

Verner = K. Verner, *Afhandlinger og Breve*, Copenhagen 1903.

Wechssler L = E. Wechssler, *Giebt es Lautgesetze?* Halle 1900.

Whitney G = W. D. Whitney, *Life and Growth of Language*, London 1875.

L = *Language and the Study of Language*, London 1868.

M = *Max Müller and the Science of Language*, New York 1892.

OLS = *Oriental and Linguistic Studies*, New York 1873-4.

Wundt S = W. Wundt, *Die Sprache*, Leipzig 1900.

PHONETIC SYMBOLS

ˈ stands before the stressed syllable.

· indicates length of the preceding sound.

[aˑ] as in *alms*.

[ai] as in *ice*.

[au] as in *house*.

[æ] as in *hat*.

[ei] as in *hate*.

[ε] as in *care* ; Fr. *tel*.

[ə] indistinct vowels.

[i] as in *fill* ; Fr. qu*i*.

[iˑ] as in *feel* ; Fr. *fille*.

[o] as in Fr. *seau*.

[ou] as in *so*.

[ɔ] open *o*-sounds.

[u] as in *full* ; Fr. *fou*.

[uˑ] as in *fool* ; Fr. *épouse*.

[y] as in Fr. v*u*.

[ʌ] as in *cut*.

[ø] as in Fr. *feu*.

[œ] as in Fr. *sœur*.

[~] French nasalization.

[c] as in G. *ich*.

[x] as in G., Sc. lo*ch*.

[ð] as in *this*.

[j] as in *you*.

[þ] as in *thick*.

[ʃ] as in *she*.

[ʒ] as in mea*s*ure.

['] in Russian palatalization, in Danish glottal stop.

16

BOOK I

HISTORY OF LINGUISTIC SCIENCE

CHAPTER I

BEFORE 1800

§ 1. Antiquity. § 2. Middle Ages and Renaissance. § 3. Eighteenth-century Speculation. Herder. § 4. Jenisch.

I.—§ 1. Antiquity.

THE science of language began, tentatively and approximately, when the minds of men first turned to problems like these : How is it that people do not speak everywhere the same language ? How were words first created ? What is the relation between a name and the thing it stands for ? Why is such and such a person, or such and such a thing, called *this* and not *that* ? The first answers to these questions, like primitive answers to other riddles of the universe, were largely theological : God, or one particular god, had created language, or God led all animals to the first man in order that he might give them names. Thus in the Old Testament the diversity of languages is explained as a punishment from God for man's crimes and presumption. These were great and general problems, but the minds of the early Jews were also occupied with smaller and more particular problems of language, as when etymological interpretations were given of such personal names as were not immediately self-explanatory.

The same predilection for etymology, and a similar primitive kind of etymology, based entirely on a more or less accidental similarity of sound and easily satisfied with any fanciful connexion in sense, is found abundantly in Greek writers and in their Latin imitators. But to the speculative minds of Greek thinkers the problem that proved most attractive was the general and abstract one, Are words natural and necessary expressions of the notions underlying them, or are they merely arbitrary and conventional signs for notions that might have been equally well expressed by any other sounds ? Endless discussions were carried on about this question, as we see particularly from Plato's *Kratylos*, and no very definite result was arrived at, nor could any be expected so long as one language only formed the basis of the discussion—even in our own days, after a century of comparative philology, the question still remains an open one. In Greece, the two catch-words *phúsei* (by nature) and *thései* (by convention) for centuries divided philosophers and grammarians into two camps, while some, like Sokrates in Plato's dialogue, though admitting that in language as actually existing there was no natural connexion between word and thing, still wished that an ideal language might be created in which words and things would be tied together in a perfectly rational way—thus paving the way for Bishop Wilkins and other modern constructors of philosophical languages.

Such abstract and *a priori* speculations, however stimulating and clever, hardly deserve the name of science, as this term is understood nowadays. Science presupposes careful observation and systematic classification of facts, and of that in the old Greek writers on language we find very little. The earliest masters in linguistic observation and classification were the old Indian grammarians. The language of the old sacred hymns had become in many points obsolete, but religion required that not one iota of these revered texts should be altered, and a scrupulous oral tradition kept them unchanged from generation to generation in every minute particular. This led to a wonderfully exact analysis of speech sounds, in which every detail of articulation was carefully described, and to a no less admirable analysis of grammatical forms, which were arranged systematically and described in a concise and highly ingenious, though artificial, terminology. The whole manner of treatment was entirely different from the methods of Western grammarians, and when the works of Panini and other Sanskrit grammarians were first made known to Europeans in the nineteenth century, they profoundly influenced our own linguistic science, as witnessed, among other things, by the fact that some of the Indian technical terms are still extensively used, for instance those describing various kinds of compound nouns.

In Europe grammatical science was slowly and laboriously developed in Greece and later in Rome. Aristotle laid the foundation of the division of words into " parts of speech " and introduced the notion of case (*ptôsis*). His work in this connexion was continued by the Stoics, many of whose grammatical distinctions and terms are still in use, the latter in their Latin dress, which embodies some curious mistakes, as when *genikḗ*, "the case of kind or species," was rendered *genitivus*, as if it meant "the case of origin," or, worse still, when *aitiatikḗ*, " the case of object," was rendered *accusativus*, as if from *aitiáomai*, 'I accuse.' In later times the philological school of Alexandria was particularly important, the object of research being the interpretation of the old poets, whose language was no longer instantly intelligible. Details of flexion and of the meaning of words were described and referred to the two categories of analogy or regularity and anomaly or irregularity, but real insight into the nature of language made very little progress either with the Alexandrians or with their Roman inheritors, and etymology still remained in the childlike stage.

I.—§ 2. Middle Ages and Renaissance.

Nor did linguistic science advance in the Middle Ages. The chief thing then was learning Latin as the common language of the Church and of what little there was of civilization generally; but Latin was not studied in a scientific spirit, and the various vernacular languages, which one by one blossomed out into languages of literature, even less so.

The Renaissance in so far brought about a change in this, as it widened the horizon, especially by introducing the study of Greek. It also favoured grammatical studies through the stress it laid on correct Latin as represented in the best period of classical literature : it now became the ambition of humanists in all countries to write Latin like Cicero. In the following centuries we witness a constantly deepening interest in the various living languages of Europe, owing to the growing importance of native literatures and to increasing facilities of international traffic and communication in general. The most important factor here was, of course, the invention of printing, which rendered it incomparably more easy than formerly to obtain the means of studying foreign languages. It should be noted also that in those times the prevalent theological interest made it a much more common thing than nowadays for ordinary scholars to have some knowledge of Hebrew as the original language of the Old Testament. The acquaintance with a language so different in type from those spoken in Europe in many ways stimulated the interest in linguistic studies, though on the other hand it proved a fruitful source of error, because the position of the Semitic family of languages was not yet understood, and because Hebrew was thought to be the language spoken in Paradise, and therefore imagined to be the language from which all other languages were descended. All kinds of fanciful similarities between Hebrew and European languages were taken as proofs of the origin of the latter ; every imaginable permutation of sounds (or rather of letters) was looked upon as possible so long as there was a slight connexion in the sense of the two words compared, and however incredible it may seem nowadays, the fact that Hebrew was written from right to left, while we in our writing proceed from left to right, was considered justification enough for the most violent transposition of letters in etymological explanations. And yet all these flighty and whimsical comparisons served perhaps in some measure to pave the way for a more systematic treatment of etymology through collecting vast stores of words from which sober and critical minds might select those instances of indubitable connexion on which a sound science of etymology could eventually be constructed.

The discovery and publication of texts in the old Gothonic (Germanic) languages, especially Wulfila's Gothic translation of the Bible, compared with which Old English (Anglo-Saxon), Old German and Old Icelandic texts were of less, though by no means of despicable, account, paved the way for historical treatment of this important group of languages in the seventeenth and eighteenth centuries. But on the whole, the interest in the history of languages in those days was small, and linguistic thinkers thought it more urgent to establish vast treasuries of languages as actually spoken than to follow the development of any one language from century to century. Thus we see that the great philosopher Leibniz, who took much interest in linguistic pursuits and to whom we owe many judicious utterances on the possibility of a universal language, instigated Peter the Great to have vocabularies and specimens collected of all the various languages of his vast empire. To this initiative taken by Leibniz, and to the great personal interest that the Empress Catherine II took in these studies, we owe, directly or indirectly, the great repertories of all languages then known, first Pallas's *Linguarum totius orbis vocabularia comparativa* (1786–87), then Hervas's *Catálogo de las lenguas de las naziones conocidas* (1800–5), and finally Adelung's *Mithridates oder allgemeine Sprachenkunde* (1806–17). In spite of their inevitable shortcomings, their uncritical and unequal treatment of many languages, the preponderance of lexical over grammatical information, and the use of biblical texts as their sole connected illustrations, these great works exercised a mighty influence on the linguistic thought and research of the time, and contributed very much to the birth of the linguistic science of the nineteenth century. It should not be forgotten, moreover, that Hervas was one of the first to recognize the superior importance of grammar to vocabulary for deciding questions of relationship between languages.

It will be well here to consider the manner in which languages and the teaching of languages were generally viewed during the centuries preceding the rise of Comparative Linguistics. The chief language taught was Latin ; the first and in many cases the only grammar with which scholars came into contact was Latin grammar. No wonder therefore that grammar and Latin grammar came in the minds of most people to be synonyms. Latin grammar played an enormous rôle in the schools, to the exclusion of many subjects (the pupil's own native language, science, history, etc.)

which we are now beginning to think more essential for the education of the young. The traditional term for 'secondary school'
was in England 'grammar school' and in Denmark 'latinskole,'
and the reason for both expressions was obviously the same.
Here, however, we are concerned with this privileged position of
Latin grammar only in so far as it influenced the treatment of
languages in general. It did so in more ways than one.

Latin was a language with a wealth of flexional forms, and
in describing other languages the same categories as were found
in Latin were applied as a matter of course, even where there was
nothing in these other languages which really corresponded to what
was found in Latin. In English and Danish grammars paradigms
of noun declension were given with such cases as accusative, dative
and ablative, in spite of the fact that no separate forms for these
cases had existed for centuries. All languages were indiscriminately
saddled with the elaborate Latin system of tenses and moods in
the verbs, and by means of such Procrustean methods the actual
facts of many languages were distorted and misrepresented.
Discriminations which had no foundation in reality were nevertheless insisted on, while discriminations which happened to be
non-existent in Latin were apt to be overlooked. The mischief
consequent on this unfortunate method of measuring all grammar
after the pattern of Latin grammar has not even yet completely
disappeared, and it is even now difficult to find a single grammar
of any language that is not here and there influenced by the
Latin bias.

Latin was chiefly taught as a written language (witness the
totally different manner in which Latin was pronounced in
the different countries, the consequence being that as early as the
sixteenth century French and English scholars were unable to
understand each other's spoken Latin). This led to the almost
exclusive occupation with letters instead of sounds. The fact
that all language is primarily spoken and only secondarily written
down, that the real life of language is in the mouth and ear and
not in the pen and eye, was overlooked, to the detriment of a real
understanding of the essence of language and linguistic development ; and very often where the spoken form of a language was
accessible scholars contented themselves with a reading knowledge.
In spite of many efforts, some of which go back to the sixteenth
century, but which did not become really powerful till the rise
of modern phonetics in the nineteenth century, the fundamental
significance of spoken as opposed to written language has not
yet been fully appreciated by all linguists. There are still too
many writers on philological questions who have evidently never
tried to think in sounds instead of thinking in letters and symbols,

and who would probably be sorely puzzled if they were to pronounce all the forms that come so glibly to their pens. What
Sweet wrote in 1877 in the preface to his *Handbook of Phonetics*
is perhaps less true now than it was then, but it still contains some
elements of truth. "Many instances," he said, "might be quoted
of the way in which important philological facts and laws have
been passed over or misrepresented through the observer's want
of phonetic training. Schleicher's failing to observe the Lithuanian accents, or even to comprehend them when pointed out by
Kurschat, is a striking instance." But there can be no doubt
that the way in which Latin has been for centuries made the
basis of all linguistic instruction is largely responsible for the
preponderance of eye-philology to ear-philology in the history of
our science.

We next come to a point which to my mind is very important,
because it concerns something which has had, and has justly had,
enduring effects on the manner in which language, and especially
grammar, is viewed and taught to this day. What was the object
of teaching Latin in the Middle Ages and later ? Certainly not
the purely scientific one of imparting knowledge for knowledge's
own sake, apart from any practical use or advantage, simply in
order to widen the spiritual horizon and to obtain the joy of pure
intellectual understanding. For such a purpose some people with
scientific leanings may here and there take up the study of some
out-of-the-way African or American idiom. But the reasons for
teaching and learning Latin were not so idealistic. Latin was
not even taught and learnt solely with the purpose of opening the
doors to the old classical or to the more recent religious literature
in that language, but chiefly, and in the first instance, because
Latin was a practical and highly important means of communication
between educated people. One had to learn not only to read
Latin, but also to write Latin, if one wanted to maintain no matter
how humble a position in the republic of learning or in the hier-
archy of the Church. Consequently, grammar was not (even
primarily) the science of how words were inflected and how forms
were used by the old Romans, but chiefly and essentially the
art of inflecting words and of using the forms yourself, if you
wanted to write correct Latin. This you must say, and these
faults you must avoid—such were the lessons imparted in the
schools. Grammar was not a set of facts observed but of rules to
be observed, and of paradigms, i.e. of patterns, to be followed.
Sometimes this character of grammatical instruction is expressly
indicated in the form of the precepts given, as in such memorial
verses as this : "Tolle *-me, -mi, -mu, -mis*, Si declinare *domus* vis ! "
In other words, grammar was *prescriptive* rather than *descriptive*.

The current definition of grammar, therefore, was " ars bene dicendi et bene scribendi," " l'art de bien dire et de bien écrire," the art of speaking and writing correctly.   J. C. Scaliger said, " Grammatici unus finis est recte loqui."   To attain to correct diction (' good grammar ') and to avoid faulty diction (' bad grammar '), such were the two objects of grammatical teaching. Now, the same point of view, in which the two elements of ' art ' and of ' correctness ' entered so largely, was applied not only to Latin, but to other languages as well, when the various vernaculars came to be treated grammatically.

The vocabulary, too, was treated from the same point of view. This is especially evident in the case of the dictionaries issued by the French and Italian Academies.   They differ from dictionaries as now usually compiled in being not collections of all and any words their authors could get hold of within the limits of the language concerned, but in being selections of words deserving the recommendations of the best arbiters of taste and therefore fit to be used in the highest literature by even the most elegant or fastidious writers.   Dictionaries thus understood were less descriptions of actual usage than prescriptions for the best usage of words.

The normative way of viewing language is fraught with some great dangers which can only be avoided through a comprehensive knowledge of the historic development of languages and of the general conditions of linguistic psychology.   Otherwise, the tendency everywhere is to draw too narrow limits for what is allowable or correct.   In many cases one form, or one construction, only is recognized, even where two or more are found in actual speech ; the question which is to be selected as the only good form comes to be decided too often by individual fancy or predilection, where no scientific tests can yet be applied, and thus a form may often be proscribed which from a less narrow point of view might have appeared just as good as, or even better than, the one preferred in the official grammar or dictionary.   In other instances, where two forms were recognized, the grammarian wanted to give rules for their discrimination, and sometimes on the basis of a totally inadequate induction he would establish nice distinctions not really warranted by actual usage—distinctions which subsequent generations had to learn at school with the sweat of their brows and which were often considered most important in spite of their intrinsic insignificance.   Such unreal or half-real subtle distinctions are the besetting sin of French grammarians from the ' grand siècle ' onwards, while they have played a much less considerable part in England, where people have been on the whole more inclined to let things slide as best they may on the

'laissez faire' principle, and where no Academy was ever established to regulate language. But even in English rules are not
unfrequently given in schools and in newspaper offices which are
based on narrow views and hasty generalizations. Because a
preposition at the end of a sentence may in some instances be
clumsy or unwieldy, this is no reason why a final preposition should
always and under all circumstances be considered a grave error.
But it is of course easier for the schoolmaster to give an absolute
and inviolable rule once and for all than to study carefully all
the various considerations that might render a qualification
desirable. If the ordinary books on *Common Faults in Writing
and Speaking English* and similar works in other languages have
not even now assimilated the teachings of Comparative and
Historic Linguistics, it is no wonder that the grammarians of the
seventeenth and eighteenth centuries, with whom we are here
concerned, should be in many ways guided by narrow and
insufficient views on what ought to determine correctness of speech.

Here also the importance given to the study of Latin was
sometimes harmful ; too much was settled by a reference to Latin
rules, even where the modern languages really followed rules of
their own that were opposed to those of Latin. The learning of
Latin grammar was supposed to be, and to some extent really
was, a schooling in logic, as the strict observance of the rules of
any foreign language is bound to be ; but the consequence of this
was that when questions of grammatical correctness were to be
settled, too much importance was often given to purely logical
considerations, and scholars were sometimes apt to determine
what was to be called ' logical ' in language according to whether
it was or was not in conformity with Latin usage. This disposition,
joined with the unavoidable conservatism of mankind, and more
particularly of teachers, would in many ways prove a hindrance
to natural developments in a living speech. But we must again
take up the thread of the history of linguistic theory.

I.—§ 3. Eighteenth-century Speculation. Herder.

The problem of a natural origin of language exercised some of
the best-known thinkers of the eighteenth century. Rousseau
imagined the first men setting themselves more or less deliberately
to frame a language by an agreement similar to (or forming part
of) the *contrat social* which according to him was the basis of all
social order. There is here the obvious difficulty of imagining
how primitive men who had been previously without any speech
came to feel the want of language, and how they could agree on
what sound was to represent what idea without having already

some means of communication. Rousseau's whole manner of putting and of viewing the problem is evidently too crude to be of any real importance in the history of linguistic science.

Condillac is much more sensible when he tries to imagine how a speechless man and a speechless woman might be led quite naturally to acquire something like language, starting with instinctive cries and violent gestures called forth by strong emotions. Such cries would come to be associated with elementary feelings, and new sounds might come to indicate various objects if produced repeatedly in connexion with gestures showing what objects the speaker wanted to call attention to. If these two first speaking beings had as yet very little power to vary their sounds, their child would have a more flexible tongue, and would therefore be able to, and be impelled to, produce some new sounds, the meaning of which his parents would guess at, and which they in their turn would imitate ; thus gradually a greater and greater number of words would come into existence, generation after generation working painfully to enrich and develop what had been already acquired, until it finally became a real language.

The profoundest thinker on these problems in the eighteenth century was Johann Gottfried Herder, who, though he did little or nothing in the way of scientific research, yet prepared the rise of linguistic science. In his prize essay on the *Origin of Language* (1772) Herder first vigorously and successfully attacks the orthodox view of his age—a view which had been recently upheld very emphatically by one Süssmilch—that language could not have been invented by man, but was a direct gift from God. One of Herder's strongest arguments is that if language had been framed by God and by Him instilled into the mind of man, we should expect it to be much more logical, much more imbued with pure reason than it is as an actual matter of fact. Much in all existing languages is so chaotic and ill-arranged that it could not be God's work, but must come from the hand of man. On the other hand, Herder does not think that language was really 'invented' by man—although this was the word used by the Berlin Academy when opening the competition in which Herder's essay gained the prize. Language was not deliberately framed by man, but sprang of necessity from his innermost nature ; the genesis of language according to him is due to an impulse similar to that of the mature embryo pressing to be born. Man, in the same way as all animals, gives vent to his feelings in tones, but this is not enough ; it is impossible to trace the origin of human language to these emotional cries alone. However much they may be refined and fixed, without understanding they can never become human, conscious language. Man differs from brute animals not in degree or in the addition of

new powers, but in a totally different direction and development
of all powers. Man's inferiority to animals in strength and sureness
of instinct is compensated by his wider sphere of attention ; the
whole disposition of his mind as an unanalysable entity constitutes
the impassable barrier between him and the lower animals. Man,
then, shows conscious reflexion when among the ocean of sensations that rush into his soul through all the senses he singles out
one wave and arrests it, as when, seeing a lamb, he looks for a distinguishing mark and finds it in the bleating, so that next time
when he recognizes the same animal he imitates the sound of
bleating, and thereby creates a name for that animal. Thus the
lamb to him is ' the bleater,' and nouns are created from verbs,
whereas, according to Herder, if language had been the creation
of God it would inversely have begun with nouns, as that would
have been the logically ideal order of procedure. Another characteristic trait of primitive languages is the crossing of various
shades of feeling and the necessity of expressing thoughts through
strong, bold metaphors, presenting the most motley picture.
" The genetic cause lies in the poverty of the human mind and
in the flowing together of the emotions of a primitive human
being." Another consequence is the wealth of synonyms in
primitive language ; " alongside of real poverty it has the most
unnecessary superfluity."

When Herder here speaks of primitive or ' original ' languages,
he is thinking of Oriental languages, and especially of Hebrew.
" We should never forget," says Edward Sapir,[1] " that Herder's
time-perspective was necessarily very different from ours. While
we unconcernedly take tens or even hundreds of thousands of
years in which to allow the products of human civilization to
develop, Herder was still compelled to operate with the less than
six thousand years that orthodoxy stingily doled out. To us the
two or three thousand years that separate our language from the
Old Testament Hebrew seems a negligible quantity, when speculating on the origin of language in general ; to Herder, however,
the Hebrew and the Greek of Homer seemed to be appreciably
nearer the oldest conditions than our vernaculars—hence his
exaggeration of their *ursprünglichkeit*."

Herder's chief influence on the science of speech, to my mind,
is not derived directly from the ideas contained in his essay on
the actual origin of speech, but rather indirectly through the
whole of his life's work. He had a very strong sense of the value
of everything that had grown naturally (das naturwüchsige) ; he
prepared the minds of his countrymen for the manysided recep-

[1] See his essay on Herder's " Ursprung der sprache " in *Modern Philology*,
5. 117 (1907).

tiveness of the Romanticists, who translated and admired the
popular poetry of a great many countries, which had hitherto been
terræ incognitæ ; and he was one of the first to draw attention to
the great national value of his own country's medieval literature
and its folklore, and thus was one of the spiritual ancestors of
Grimm. He sees the close connexion that exists between language
and primitive poetry, or that kind of spontaneous singing that
characterizes the childhood or youth of mankind, and which is
totally distinct from the artificial poetry of later ages. But to
him each language is not only the instrument of literature, but
itself literature and poetry. A nation speaks its soul in the words
it uses. Herder admires his own mother-tongue, which to him
is perhaps inferior to Greek, but superior to its neighbours. The
combinations of consonants give it a certain measured pace ; it
does not rush forward, but walks with the firm carriage of a
German. The nice gradation of vowels mitigates the force of
the consonants, and the numerous spirants make the German
speech pleasant and endearing. Its syllables are rich and firm,
its phrases are stately, and its idiomatic expressions are emphatic
and serious. Still in some ways the present German language is
degenerate if compared with that of Luther, and still more with
that of the Suabian Emperors, and much therefore remains to be
done in the way of disinterring and revivifying the powerful
expressions now lost. Through ideas like these Herder not only
exercised a strong influence on Goethe and the Romanticists,
but also gave impulses to the linguistic studies of the following
generation, and caused many younger men to turn from the
well-worn classics to fields of research previously neglected.

I.—§ 4. Jenisch.

Where questions of correct language or of the best usage are
dealt with, or where different languages are compared with regard
to their efficiency or beauty, as is done very often, though more
often in dilettante conversation or in casual remarks in literary
works than in scientific linguistic disquisitions, it is no far cry to
the question, What would an ideal language be like ? But such
is the matter-of-factness of modern scientific thought, that probably
no scientific Academy in our own days would think of doing what
the Berlin Academy did in 1794 when it offered a prize for the
best essay on the ideal of a perfect language and a comparison of
the best-known languages of Europe as tested by the standard
of such an ideal. A Berlin pastor, D. Jenisch, won the prize, and
in 1796 brought out his book under the title *Philosophisch-kritische
vergleichung und würdigung von vierzehn ältern und neuern sprachen*

Europens—a book which is even now well worth reading, the more so because its subject has been all but completely neglected in the hundred and twenty years that have since intervened. In the Introduction the author has the following passage, which might be taken as the motto of Wilhelm v. Humboldt, Steinthal, Finck and Byrne, who do not, however, seem to have been inspired by Jenisch : " In language the whole intellectual and moral essence of a man is to some extent revealed. ' Speak, and you are ' is rightly said by the Oriental. The language of the natural man is savage and rude, that of the cultured man is elegant and polished. As the Greek was subtle in thought and sensuously refined in feeling—as the Roman was serious and practical rather than speculative—as the Frenchman is popular and sociable— as the Briton is profound and the German philosophic—so are also the languages of each of these nations."

Jenisch then goes on to say that language as the organ for communicating our ideas and feelings accomplishes its end if it represents idea and feeling according to the actual want or need of the mind at the given moment. We have to examine in each case the following essential qualities of the languages compared, (1) richness, (2) energy or emphasis, (3) clearness, and (4) euphony. Under the head of richness we are concerned not only with the number of words, first for material objects, then for spiritual and abstract notions, but also with the ease with which new words can be formed (lexikalische bildsamkeit). The energy of a language is shown in its lexicon and in its grammar (simplicity of grammatical structure, absence of articles, etc.), but also in " the characteristic energy of the nation and its original writers." Clearness and definiteness in the same way are shown in vocabulary and grammar, especially in a regular and natural syntax. Euphony, finally, depends not only on the selection of consonants and vowels utilized in the language, but on their harmonious combination, the general impression of the language being more important than any details capable of being analysed.

These, then, are the criteria by which Greek and Latin and a number of living languages are compared and judged. The author displays great learning and a sound practical knowledge of many languages, and his remarks on the advantages and shortcomings of these are on the whole judicious, though often perhaps too much stress is laid on the literary merits of great writers, which have really no intrinsic connexion with the value of a language as such. It depends to a great extent on accidental circumstances whether a language has been or has not been used in elevated literature, and its merits should be estimated, so far as this is possible, independently of the perfection of its literature. Jenisch's prejudice

in that respect is shown, for instance, when he says (p. 36) that
the endeavours of Hickes are entirely futile, when he tries to make
out regular declensions and conjugations in the barbarous language
of Wulfila's translation of the Bible. But otherwise Jenisch is
singularly free from prejudices, as shown by a great number of
passages in which other languages are praised at the expense of
his own. Thus, on p. 396, he declares German to be the most
repellent contrast to that most supple modern language, French,
on account of its unnatural word-order, its eternally trailing
article, its want of participial constructions, and its interminable
auxiliaries (as in 'ich werde geliebt werden, ich würde geliebt
worden sein,' etc.), with the frequent separation of these auxiliaries
from the main verb through extraneous intermediate words, all
of which gives to German something incredibly awkward, which
to the reader appears as lengthy and diffuse and to the writer as
inconvenient and intractable. It is not often that we find an
author appraising his own language with such severe impartiality,
and I have given the passage also to show what kind of problems
confront the man who wishes to compare the relative value of
languages as wholes. Jenisch's view here forms a striking contrast
to Herder's appreciation of their common mother-tongue.

Jenisch's book does not seem to have been widely read by
nineteenth-century scholars, who took up totally different problems.
Those few who read it were perhaps inclined to say with S. Lefmann
(see his book on Franz Bopp, Nachtrag, 1897, p. xi) that it is difficult to decide which was the greater fool, the one who put this
problem or the one who tried to answer it. This attitude, however,
towards problems of valuation in the matter of languages is
neither just nor wise, though it is perhaps easy to see how students
of comparative grammar were by the very nature of their study
led to look down upon those who compared languages from the
point of view of æsthetic or literary merits. Anyhow, it seems to
me no small merit to have been the first to treat such problems
as these, which are generally answered in an off-hand way
according to a loose general judgement, so as to put them on a
scientific footing by examining in detail what it is that makes us
more or less instinctively prefer one language, or one turn or expression in a language, and thus lay the foundation of that inductive
æsthetic theory of language which has still to be developed in a
truly scientific spirit.

CHAPTER II

BEGINNING OF NINETEENTH CENTURY

§ 1. Introduction. Sanskrit. § 2. Friedrich von Schlegel. § 3. Rasmus
Rask. § 4. Jacob Grimm. § 5. The Sound Shift. § 6. Franz Bopp.
§ 7. Bopp continued. § 8. Wilhelm von Humboldt. § 9. Grimm
once more.

II.—§ 1. Introduction. Sanskrit.

THE nineteenth century witnessed an enormous growth and
development of the science of language, which in some respects
came to present features totally unknown to previous centuries.
The horizon was widened ; more and more languages were described,
studied and examined, many of them for their own sake, as they
had no important literature. Everywhere a deeper insight was
gained into the structures even of such languages as had been
for centuries objects of study ; a more comprehensive and more
incisive classification of languages was obtained with a deeper
understanding of their mutual relationships, and at the same time
linguistic forms were not only described and analysed, but also
explained, their genesis being traced as far back as historical
evidence allowed, if not sometimes further. Instead of contenting
itself with stating when and where a form existed and how it looked
and was employed, linguistic science now also began to ask why
it had taken that definite shape, and thus passed from a purely
descriptive to an explanatory science.

The chief innovation of the beginning of the nineteenth century
was the historical point of view. On the whole, it must be said
that it was reserved for that century to apply the notion of history
to other things than wars and the vicissitudes of dynasties, and
thus to discover the idea of development or evolution as pervading
the whole universe. This brought about a vast change in the
science of language, as in other sciences. Instead of looking at such
a language as Latin as one fixed point, and instead of aiming at
fixing another language, such as French, in one classical form,
the new science viewed both as being in constant flux, as growing,
as moving, as continually changing. It cried aloud like Heraclitus

" Pánta reî," and like Galileo " Eppur si muove."   And lo ! the
better this historical point of view was applied, the more secrets
languages seemed to unveil, and the more light seemed also to be
thrown on objects outside the proper sphere of language, such as
ethnology and the early history of mankind at large and of
particular countries.

It is often said that it was the discovery of Sanskrit that was
the real turning-point in the history of linguistics, and there is
some truth in this assertion, though we shall see on the one hand
that Sanskrit was not in itself enough to give to those who studied
it the true insight into the essence of language and linguistic science,
and on the other hand that real genius enabled at least one man
to grasp essential truths about the relationships and development
of languages even without a knowledge of Sanskrit.   Still, it must
be said that the first acquaintance with this language gave a mighty
impulse to linguistic studies and exerted a lasting influence on
the way in which most European languages were viewed by scholars,
and it will therefore be necessary here briefly to sketch the history
of these studies.   India was very little known in Europe till the
mighty struggle between the French and the English for the mastery
of its wealth excited a wide interest also in its ancient culture.
It was but natural that on this intellectual domain, too, the French
and the English should at first be rivals and that we should find
both nations represented in the pioneers of Sanskrit scholarship.
The French Jesuit missionary Cœurdoux as early as 1767 sent to
the French Institut a memoir in which he called attention to the
similarity of many Sanskrit words with Latin, and even compared
the flexion of the present indicative and subjunctive of Sanskrit
asmi, ' I am,' with the corresponding forms of Latin grammar.
Unfortunately, however, his work was not printed till forty years
later, when the same discovery had been announced independently
by others.   The next scholar to be mentioned in this connexion
is Sir William Jones, who in 1796 uttered the following memorable
words, which have often been quoted in books on the history of
linguistics : " The Sanscrit language, whatever be its antiquity,
is of a wonderful structure ; more perfect than the Greek, more
copious than the Latin and more exquisitely refined than either ;
yet bearing to both of them a stronger affinity, both in the roots
of verbs and in the forms of grammar, than could possibly have
been produced by accident ; so strong, indeed, that no philologer
could examine them all three without believing them to have
sprung from some common source, which, perhaps, no longer
exists.   There is a similar reason, though not quite so forcible, for
supposing that both the Gothic and the Celtic . . . had the same
origin with the Sanscrit ; and the old Persian might be added to

the same family." Sir W. Jones, however, did nothing to carry out in detail the comparison thus inaugurated, and it was reserved for younger men to follow up the clue he had given.

II.—§ 2. Friedrich von Schlegel.

One of the books that exercised a great influence on the development of linguistic science in the beginning of the nineteenth century was Friedrich von Schlegel's *Ueber die sprache und weisheit der Indier* (1808). Schlegel had studied Sanskrit for some years in Paris, and in his romantic enthusiasm he hoped that the study of the old Indian books would bring about a revolution in European thought similar to that produced in the Renaissance through the revival of the study of Greek. We are here concerned exclusively with his linguistic theories, but to his mind they were inseparable from Indian religion and philosophy, or rather religious and philosophic poetry. He is struck by the similarity between Sanskrit and the best-known European languages, and gives quite a number of words from Sanskrit found with scarcely any change in German, Greek and Latin. He repudiates the idea that these similarities might be accidental or due to borrowings on the side of the Indians, saying expressly that the proof of original relationship between these languages, as well as of the greater age of Sanskrit, lies in the far-reaching correspondences in the whole grammatical structure of these as opposed to many other languages. In this connexion it is noticeable that he is the first to speak of 'comparative grammar' (p. 28), but, like Moses, he only looks into this promised land without entering it. Indeed, his method of comparison precludes him from being the founder of the new science, for he says himself (p. 6) that he will refrain from stating any rules for change or substitution of letters (sounds), and require complete identity of the words used as proofs of the descent of languages. He adds that in other cases, "where intermediate stages are historically demonstrable, we may derive *giorno* from *dies*, and when Spanish so often has *h* for Latin *f*, or Latin *p* very often becomes *f* in the German form of the same word, and *c* not rarely becomes *h* [by the way, an interesting foreshadowing of one part of the discovery of the Germanic sound-shifting], then this may be the foundation of analogical conclusions with regard to other less evident instances." If he had followed up this idea by establishing similar 'sound-laws,' as we now say, between Sanskrit and other languages, he would have been many years ahead of his time; as it is, his comparisons are those of a dilettante, and he sometimes falls into the pitfalls of accidental similarities while overlooking the real correspondences. He is also led astray by the idea of a particularly close relationship between Persian and German, an idea which at that time was widely spread[1]—we find it in Jenisch and even in Bopp's first book.

Schlegel is not afraid of surveying the whole world of human languages ; he divides them into two classes, one comprising Sanskrit and its congeners, and the second all other languages. In the former he finds organic growth of the roots as shown by their capability of inner change or, as he terms it, ' flexion,' while in the latter class everything is effected by the addition of affixes (prefixes and suffixes). In Greek he admits that it would be possible to believe in the possibility of the grammatical endings (bildungssylben) having arisen from particles and auxiliary words amalgamated into the word itself, but in Sanskrit even the last semblance of this possibility disappears, and it becomes necessary to confess that the structure of the language is formed in a thoroughly organic way through flexion, i.e. inner changes and modifications of the radical sound, and not composed merely mechanically by the addition of words and particles. He admits, however, that affixes in some other languages have brought about something that resembles real flexion. On the whole he finds that the movement of grammatical art and perfection (der gang der bloss grammatischen kunst und ausbildung, p. 56) goes in opposite directions in the two species of languages. In the organic languages, which represent the highest state, the beauty and art of their structure is apt to be lost through indolence ; and German as well as Romanic and modern Indian languages show this degeneracy when compared with the earlier forms of the same languages. In the affix languages, on the other hand, we see that the beginnings are completely artless, but the ' art ' in them grows more and more perfect the more the affixes are fused with the main word.

As to the question of the ultimate origin of language, Schlegel thinks that the diversity of linguistic structure points to different beginnings. While some languages, such as Manchu, are so interwoven with onomatopœia that imitation of natural sounds must have played the greatest rôle in their formation, this is by no means the case in other languages, and the perfection of the oldest organic or flexional languages, such as Sanskrit, shows that they cannot be derived from merely animal sounds ; indeed, they form an additional proof, if any such were needed, that men did not everywhere start from a brutish state, but that the clearest and intensest reason existed from the very first beginning. On all these points Schlegel's ideas foreshadow views that are found in later works ; and it is probable that his fame as a writer outside the philological field gave to his linguistic speculations a notoriety which his often

[1] It dates back to Vulcanius, 1597 ; see Streitberg, IF 35. 182.

loose and superficial reasonings would not otherwise have acquired for them.

Schlegel's bipartition of the languages of the world carries in it the germ of a tripartition. On the lowest stage of his second class he places Chinese, in which, as he acknowledges, the particles denoting secondary sense modifications consist in monosyllables that are completely independent of the actual word. It is clear that from Schlegel's own point of view we cannot here properly speak of ' affixes,' and thus Chinese really, though Schlegel himself does not say so, falls outside his affix languages and forms a class by itself. On the other hand, his arguments for reckoning Semitic languages among affix languages are very weak, and he seems also somewhat inclined to say that much in their structure resembles real flexion. If we introduce these two changes into his system, we arrive at the threefold division found in slightly different shapes in most subsequent works on general linguistics, the first to give it being perhaps Schlegel's brother, A. W. Schlegel, who speaks of (1) les langues sans aucune structure grammaticale— under which misleading term he understands Chinese with its unchangeable monosyllabic words ; (2) les langues qui emploient des affixes ; (3) les langues à inflexions.

Like his brother, A. W. Schlegel places the flexional languages highest and thinks them alone ' organic.' On the other hand, he subdivides flexional languages into two classes, synthetic and analytic, the latter using personal pronouns and auxiliaries in the conjugation of verbs, prepositions to supply the want of cases, and adverbs to express the degrees of comparison. While the origin of the synthetic languages loses itself in the darkness of ages, the analytic languages have been created in modern times ; all those that we know are due to the decomposition of synthetic languages. These remarks on the division of languages are found in the Introduction to the book *Observations sur la langue et la littérature provençale* (1818) and are thus primarily meant to account for the contrast between synthetic Latin and analytic Romanic.

II.—§ 3. Rasmus Rask.

We now come to the three greatest names among the initiators of linguistic science in the beginning of the nineteenth century. If we give them in their alphabetical order, Bopp, Grimm and Rask, we also give them in the order of merit in which most subsequent historians have placed them. The works that constitute their first claims to the title of founder of the new science came in close succession, Bopp's *Conjugationssystem* in 1816, Rask's *Undersøgelse* in 1818, and the first volume of Grimm's *Grammatik* in

1819. While Bopp is entirely independent of the two others, we shall see that Grimm was deeply influenced by Rask, and as the latter's contributions to our science began some years before his chief work just mentioned (which had also been finished in manuscript in 1814, thus two years before Bopp's *Conjugationssystem*), the best order in which to deal with the three men will perhaps be to take Rask first, then to mention Grimm, who in some ways was his pupil, and finally to treat of Bopp : in this way we shall also be enabled to see Bopp in close relation with the subsequent development of Comparative Grammar, on which he, and not Rask, exerted the strongest influence.

Born in a peasant's hut in the heart of Denmark in 1787, Rasmus Rask was a grammarian from his boyhood. When a copy of the *Heimskringla* was given him as a school prize, he at once, without any grammar or dictionary, set about establishing paradigms, and so, before he left school, acquired proficiency in Icelandic, as well as in many other languages. At the University of Copenhagen he continued in the same course, constantly widened his linguistic horizon and penetrated into the grammatical structure of the most diverse languages. Icelandic (Old Norse), however, remained his favourite study, and it filled him with enthusiasm and national pride that " our ancestors had such an excellent language," the excellency being measured chiefly by the full flexional system which Icelandic shared with the classical tongues, partly also by the pure, unmixed state of the Icelandic vocabulary. His first book (1811) was an Icelandic grammar, an admirable production when we consider the meagre work done previously in this field. With great lucidity he reduces the intricate forms of the language into a consistent system, and his penetrating insight into the essence of language is seen when he explains the vowel changes, which we now comprise under the name of mutation or umlaut, as due to the approximation of the vowel of the stem to that of the ending, at that time a totally new point of view. This we gather from Grimm's review, in which Rask's explanation is said to be " more astute than true " (" mehr scharfsinnig als wahr," *Kleinere schriften*, 7. 515). Rask even sees the reason of the change in the plural *blöð* as against the singular *blað* in the former having once ended in -*u*, which has since disappeared. This is, so far as I know, the first inference ever drawn to a prehistoric state of language.

In 1814, during a prolonged stay in Iceland, Rask sent down to Copenhagen his most important work, the prize essay on the origin of the Old Norse language (*Undersøgelse om det gamle nordiske eller islandske sprogs oprindelse*) which for various reasons was not printed till 1818. If it had been published when it was finished, and especially if it had been printed in a language better known than Danish, Rask might well have been styled the founder of the modern science of language, for his work contains the best exposition of the true method of linguistic research written in the first half of the nineteenth century and applies this method to the solution of a long series of important questions. Only one part of it was ever translated into another language, and this was unfortunately buried in an appendix to Vater's *Vergleichungstafeln*, 1822. Yet Rask's work even now repays careful perusal, and I shall therefore give a brief résumé of its principal contents.

Language according to Rask is our principal means of finding out anything about the history of nations before the existence of written documents, for though everything may change in religion, customs, laws and institutions, language generally remains, if not unchanged, yet recognizable even after thousands of years. But in order to find out anything about the relationship of a language we must proceed methodically and examine its whole structure instead of comparing mere details ; what is here of prime importance is the grammatical system, because words are very often taken over from one language to another, but very rarely grammatical forms. The capital error in most of what has been written on this subject is that this important point has been overlooked. That language which has the most complicated grammar is nearest to the source ; however mixed a language may be, it belongs to the same family as another if it has the most essential, most material and indispensable words in common with it ; pronouns and numerals are in this respect most decisive. If in such words there are so many points of agreement between two languages that it is possible to frame rules for the transitions of letters (in other passages Rask more correctly says sounds) from the one language to the other, there is a fundamental kinship between the two languages, more particularly if there are corresponding similarities in their structure and constitution. This is a most important thesis, and Rask supplements it by saying that transitions of sounds are naturally dependent on their organ and manner of production.

Next Rask proceeds to apply these principles to his task of finding out the origin of the Old Icelandic language. He describes its position in the ' Gothic ' (Gothonic, Germanic) group and then looks round to find congeners elsewhere. He rapidly discards Greenlandic and Basque as being too remote in grammar and vocabulary ; with regard to Keltic languages he hesitates, but finally decides in favour of denying relationship. (He was soon to see his error in this ; see below.) Next he deals at some length with Finnic and Lapp, and comes to the conclusion that the similarities are due to loans rather than to original kinship. But when he comes to the Slavonic languages his utterances have a different ring, for he is here able to disclose so many similarities in fundamentals that he ranges these languages witnin the same great family as Icelandic. The same is true with regard to Lithuanian and Lettic, which are here for the first time correctly placed as an independent sub-family, though closely akin to Slavonic. The comparisons with Latin, and especially with Greek, are even more detailed ; and Rask in these chapters really presents us with a succinct, but on the whole marvellously correct, comparative grammar of Gothonic, Slavonic, Lithuanian, Latin and Greek, besides examining numerous lexical correspondences. He does not yet know any of the related Asiatic languages, but throws out the hint that Persian and Indian may be the remote source of Icelandic through Greek. Greek he considers to be the ' source ' or ' root ' of the Gothonic languages, though he expresses himself with a degree of uncertainty which forestalls the correct notion that these languages have all of them sprung from the same extinct and unknown language. This view is very clearly expressed in a letter he wrote from St. Petersburg in the same year in which his *Undersøgelse* was published ; he here says : " I divide our family of languages in this way : the Indian (Dekanic, Hindostanic), Iranic (Persian, Armenian, Ossetic), Thracian (Greek and Latin), Sarmatian (Lettic and Slavonic), Gothic (Germanic and Skandinavian) and Keltic (Britannic and Gaelic) tribes " (SA 2. 281, dated June 11, 1818).

This is the fullest and clearest account of the relationships of our family of languages found for many years, and Rask showed true genius in the way in which he saw what languages belonged together and how they were related. About the same time he gave a classification of the Finno-Ugrian family of languages which is pronounced by such living authorities on these languages as Vilhelm Thomsen and Emil Setälä to be superior to most later attempts. When travelling in India he recognized the true position of Zend, about which previous scholars had held the most erroneous views, and his survey of the languages of India and Persia was thought valuable enough in 1863 to be printed from his manuscript, forty years after it was written. He was also the first to see that the Dravidian (by him called Malabaric) languages were totally different from Sanskrit. In his short essay on Zend (1826) he also incidentally gave the correct value of two letters in the first cuneiform writing, and thus made an important contribution towards the final deciphering of these inscriptions.

His long tour (1816–23) through Sweden, Finland, Russia, the Caucasus, Persia and India was spent in the most intense study of a great variety of languages, but unfortunately brought on the illness and disappointments which, together with economic anxieties, marred the rest of his short life.

When Rask died in 1832 he had written a great number of grammars of single languages, all of them remarkable for their accuracy in details and clear systematic treatment, more particularly of morphology, and some of them breaking new ground ; besides his Icelandic grammar already mentioned, his Anglo-Saxon, Frisian and Lapp grammars should be specially named. Historical grammar in the strict sense is perhaps not his forte, though in a remarkable essay of the year 1815 he explains historically a great many features of Danish grammar, and in his Spanish and Italian grammars he in some respects forestalls Diez's historical explanations. But in some points he stuck to erroneous views, a notable instance being his system of old Gothonic ' long vowels,' which was reared on the assumption that modern Icelandic pronunciation reflects the pronunciation of primitive times, while it is really a recent development, as Grimm saw from a comparison of all the old languages. With regard to consonants, however, Rask was the clearer-sighted of the two, and throughout he had this immense advantage over most of the comparative linguists of his age, that he had studied a great many languages at first hand with native speakers, while the others knew languages chiefly or exclusively through the medium of books and manuscripts. In no work of that period, or even of a much later time, are found so many first-hand observations of living speech as in Rask's *Retskrivningslære.* Handicapped though he was in many ways, by poverty and illness and by the fact that he wrote in a language so little known as Danish, Rasmus Rask, through his wide outlook, his critical sagacity and aversion to all fanciful theorizing, stands out as one of the foremost leaders of linguistic science.[1]

II.—§ 4. Jacob Grimm.

Jacob Grimm's career was totally different from Rask's. Born in 1785 as the son of a lawyer, he himself studied law and came under the influence of Savigny, whose view of legal institutions as the outcome of gradual development in intimate connexion with popular tradition and the whole intellectual and moral life of the

---

[1] I have given a life of Rask and an appraisement of his work in the small volume *Rasmus Rask* (Copenhagen, Gyldendal, 1918). See also Vilh. Thomsen, *Samlede afhandlinger*, 1. 47 ff. and 125 ff. A good and full account of Rask's work is found in Raumer, *Gesch.* ; cf. also Paul, *Gr.* Recent short appreciations of his genius may be read in Trombetti, *Come si fa la critica*, 1907, p. 41, Meillet, LI, p. 415, Hirt, Idg, pp. 74 and 578.

people appealed strongly to the young man's imagination. But
he was drawn even more to that study of old German popular
poetry which then began to be the fashion, thanks to Tieck and
other Romanticists ; and when he was in Paris to assist Savigny
with his historico-legal research, the old German manuscripts in
the Bibliothèque nationale nourished his enthusiasm for the
poetical treasures of the Middle Ages. He became a librarian
and brought out his first book, *Ueber den altdeutschen meistergesang*
(1811). At the same time, with his brother Wilhelm as constant
companion and fellow-worker, he began collecting popular traditions, of which he published a first instalment in his famous *Kinder-
und hausmärchen* (1812 ff.), a work whose learned notes and comparisons may be said to have laid the foundation of the science of
folklore. Language at first had only a subordinate interest to
him, and when he tried his hand at etymology, he indulged in the
wildest guesses, according to the method (or want of method) of
previous centuries. A. W. Schlegel's criticism of his early attempts
in this field, and still more Rask's example, opened Grimm's eyes
to the necessity of a stricter method, and he soon threw himself
with great energy into a painstaking and exact study of the oldest
stages of the German language and its congeners. In his review
(1812) of Rask's Icelandic grammar he writes : " Each individuality,
even in the world of languages, should be respected as sacred ;
it is desirable that even the smallest and most despised dialect
should be left only to itself and to its own nature and in nowise
subjected to violence, because it is sure to have some secret advantages over the greatest and most highly valued language." Here
we meet with that valuation of the hitherto overlooked popular
dialects which sprang from the Romanticists' interest in the
' people ' and everything it had produced. Much valuable
linguistic work was directly inspired by this feeling and by conscious opposition to the old philology, that occupied itself exclusively with the two classical languages and the upper-class
literature embodied in them. As Scherer expresses it (*Jacob
Grimm*, 2te ausg., Berlin, 1885, p. 152) : " The brothers Grimm
applied to the old national literature and to popular traditions
the old philological virtue of exactitude, which had up to then
been bestowed solely on Greek and Roman classics and on the Bible.
They extended the field of strict philology, as they extended the
field of recognized poetry. They discarded the aristocratic narrowmindedness with which philologists looked down on unwritten
tradition, on popular ballads, legends, fairy tales, superstition,
nursery rimes. . . . In the hands of the two Grimms philology
became national and popular ; and at the same time a pattern was
created for the scientific study of all the peoples of the earth and

for a comparative investigation of the entire mental life of mankind, of which written literature is nothing but a small epitome."

But though Grimm thus broke loose from the traditions of classical philology, he still carried with him one relic of it, namely the standard by which the merits of different languages were measured. " In reading carefully the old Gothonic (altdeutschen) sources, I was every day discovering forms and perfections which we generally envy the Greeks and Romans when we consider the present condition of our language.". . . " Six hundred years ago every rustic knew, that is to say practised daily, perfections and niceties in the German language of which the best grammarians nowadays do not even dream ; in the poetry of Wolfram von Eschenbach and of Hartmann von Aue, who had never heard of declension and conjugation, nay who perhaps did not even know how to read and write, many differences in the flexion and use of nouns and verbs are still nicely and unerringly observed, which we have gradually to rediscover in learned guise, but dare not reintroduce, for language ever follows its inalterable course."

Grimm then sets about writing his great historical and com parative *Deutsche Grammatik*, taking the term ' deutsch ' in its widest and hardly justifiable sense of what is now ordinarily called Germanic and which is in this work called Gothonic. The first volume appeared in 1819, and in the preface we see that he was quite clear that he was breaking new ground and introducing a new method of looking at grammar. He speaks of previous German grammars and says expressly that he does not want his to be ranged with them. He charges them with unspeakable pedantry ; they wanted to dogmatize magisterially, while to Grimm language, like everything natural and moral, is an unconscious and unnoticed secret which is implanted in us in youth. Every German therefore who speaks his language naturally, i.e. untaught, may call himself his own living grammar and leave all school-masters' rules alone. Grimm accordingly has no wish to prescribe anything, but to observe what has grown naturally, and very appropriately he dedicates his work to Savigny, who has taught him how institutions grow in the life of a nation. In the new preface to the second edition there are also some noteworthy indications of the changed attitude. " I am hostile to general logical notions in grammar ; they conduce apparently to strict-ness and solidity of definition, but hamper observation, which I take to be the soul of linguistic science. : . . As my starting-point was to trace the never-resting (unstillstehende) element of our language which changes with time and place, it became necessary for me to admit one dialect after the other, and I could not even forbear to glance at those foreign languages that are ultimately related with ours."

Here we have the first clear programme of that historical school which has since then been the dominating one in linguistics. But as language according to this new point of view was constantly changing and developing, so also, during these years, were Grimm's own ideas. And the man who then exercised the greatest influence on him was Rasmus Rask. When Grimm wrote the first edition of his *Grammatik* (1819), he knew nothing of Rask but the Icelandic grammar, but just before finishing his own volume Rask's prize essay reached him, and in the preface he at once speaks of it in the highest terms of praise, as he does also in several letters of this period ; he is equally enthusiastic about Rask's Anglo-Saxon grammar and the Swedish edition of his Icelandic grammar, neither of which reached him till after his own first volume had been printed off. The consequence was that instead of going on to the second volume, Grimm entirely recast the first volume and brought it out in a new shape in 1822. The chief innovation was the phonology or, as he calls it, " Erstes buch. Von den buchstaben," which was entirely absent in 1819, but now ran to 595 pages.

II.—§ 5. The Sound Shift.

This first book in the 1822 volume contains much, perhaps most, of what constitutes Grimm's fame as a grammarian, notably his exposition of the ' sound shift ' (lautverschiebung), which it has been customary in England since Max Müller to term ' Grimm's Law.' If any one man is to give his name to this law, a better name would be ' Rask's Law,' for all these transitions, Lat. Gr. $p = f$, $t = þ$ (*th*), $k = h$, etc., are enumerated in Rask's *Undersøgelse*, p. 168, which Grimm knew before he wrote a single word about the sound shift.

Now, it is interesting to compare the two scholars' treatment of these transitions. The sober-minded, matter-of-fact Rask contents himself with a bare statement of the facts, with just enough well-chosen examples to establish the correspondence ; the way in which he arranges the sounds shows that he saw their parallelism clearly enough, though he did not attempt to bring everything under one single formula, any more than he tried to explain why these sounds had changed.[1] Grimm multiplies the examples and

---

[1] Only in one subordinate point did Rask make a mistake ($b = b$), which is all the more venial as there are extremely few examples of this sound. Bredsdorff (*Aarsagerne*, 1821, p. 21) evidently had the law from Rask, and gives it in the comprehensive formula which Paul (Gr. 1. 86) misses in Rask and gives as Grimm's meritorious improvement on Rask. "The Germanic

then systematizes the whole process in one formula so as to comprise also the 'second shift' found in High German alone—a shift well known to Rask, though treated by him in a different place (p. 68 f.). Grimm's formula looks thus :

Greek	p	b	f	t	d	th	k	g	ch
Gothic	f	p	b	th	t	d	h	k	g
High G.	b(v)f	p		d	z	t	g	ch	k,

which may be expressed generally thus, that tenuis (T) becomes aspirate (A) and then media (M), etc., or, tabulated :

Greek	T	M	A
Gothic	A	T	M
High G.	M	A	T.

For this Grimm would of course have deserved great credit, because a comprehensive formula is more scientific than a rough statement of facts—*if* the formula had been correct ; but unfortunately it is not so. In the first place, it breaks down in the very first instance, for there is no media in High German corresponding to Gr. *p* and Gothic *f* (cf. *poús, fotus, fuss,* etc.) ; secondly, High German has *h* just as Gothic has, corresponding to Greek *k* (cf. *kardía, hairto, herz,* etc.), and where it has *g*, Gothic has also *g* in accordance with rules unknown to Grimm and not explained till long afterwards (by Verner). But the worst thing is that the whole specious generalization produces the impression of regularity and uniformity only through the highly unscientific use of the word ' aspirate,' which is made to cover such phonetically disparate things as (1) combination of stop with following *h*, (2) combination of stop with following fricative, *pf, ts* written *z*, (3) voiceless fricative, *f, s* in G. *das*, (4) voiced fricative, *v*, ð written *th*, and (5) *h*. Grimm rejoiced in his formula, giving as it does three chronological stages in each of the three subdivisions (tenuis, media, aspirate) of each of the three classes of consonants (labial, dental, ' guttural '). This evidently took hold of his fancy through the mystic power of the number three, which he elsewhere (Gesch 1. 191, cf. 241) finds pervading language generally : three original vowels, *a, i, u*, three genders, three numbers (singular, dual, plural), three persons, three ' voices ' (genera : active, middle, passive), three tenses (present, preterit, future), three declensions through *a, i, u*. As there is here an element of mysticism, so is there also in Grimm's highflown

family has most often aspirates where Greek has tenues, tenues where it has mediæ, and again mediæ where it has aspirates, e.g. *fod*, Gr. *pous* ; *horn*, Gr. *keras* ; Þrír, Gr. *treis* ; *padde*, Gr. *batrakhos* ; *kone*, Gr. *gunē* ; *ti*, Gr. *deka* ; *bœrer*, Gr. *pherō* ; *galde*, Gr. *kholē* ; *dør*, Gr. *thura*.'' To the word ' horn ' was appended a foot-note to the effect that *h* without doubt here originally was the German *ch*-sound. This was one year before Grimm stated his law !

explanation of the whole process from pretended popular psychology, which is full of the cloudiest romanticism. "When once the language had made the first step and had rid itself of the organic basis of its sounds, it was hardly possible for it to escape the second step and not to arrive at the third stage,[1] through which this development was perfected. . . . It is impossible not to admire the instinct by which the linguistic spirit (sprachgeist) carried this out to the end. A great many sounds got out of joint, but they always knew how to arrange themselves in a different place and to find the new application of the old law. I am not saying that the shift happened without any detriment, nay from one point of view the sound shift appears to me as a barbarous aberration, from which other more quiet nations abstained, but which is connected with the violent progress and craving for freedom which was found in Germany in the beginning of the Middle Ages and which initiated the transformation of Europe. The Germans pressed forward even in the matter of the innermost sounds of their language," etc., with remarks on intellectual progress and on victorious and ruling races. Grimm further says that "die dritte stufe des verschobnen lauts den kreislauf abschliesse und nach ihr ein neuer ansatz zur abweichung wieder von vorn anheben müsse. Doch eben weil der sprachgeist seinen lauf vollbracht hat, scheint er nicht wieder neu beginnen zu wollen" (GDS 1. 292 f., 299). It would be difficult to attach any clear ideas to these words.

Grimm's idea of a 'kreislauf' is caused by the notion that the two shifts, separated by several centuries, represent one continued movement, while the High German shift of the eighth century has really no more to do with the primitive Gothonic shift, which took place probably some time before Christ, than has, for instance, the Danish shift in words like *gribe*, *bide*, *bage*, from *gripœ*, *bitœ*, *bakœ* (about 1400), or the still more recent transition in Danish through which stressed *t* in *tid*, *tyve*, etc., sounds nearly like [ts], as in HG. *zeit*. There cannot possibly be any causal nexus between such transitions, separated chronologically by long periods, with just as little change in the pronunciation of these consonants as there has been in English.[2]

---

[1] The muddling of the negatives is Grimm's, not the translator's.

[2] I am therefore surprised to find that in a recent article (*Am. Journ. of Philol.* 39. 415, 1918) Collitz praises Grimm's view in preference to Rask's because he saw "an inherent connexion between the various processes of the shifting," which were "subdivisions of one great law in which the formula T : A : M may be used to illustrate the shifting (in a single language) of three different groups of consonants and the result of a double or threefold shifting (in three different languages) of a single group of consonants. This great law was unknown to Rask." Collitz recognizes that "Grimm's law will hold good only if we accept the term 'aspirate' in the broad sense in which

Grimm was anything but a phonetician, and sometimes says things which nowadays cannot but produce a smile, as when he says (Gr 1. 3) "in our word *schrift*, for instance, we express eight sounds through seven signs, for *f* stands for *ph* "; thus he earnestly believes that *sch* contains three sounds, *s* and the 'aspirate' *ch=c+h*! Yet through the irony of fate it was on the history of sounds that Grimm exercised the strongest influence. As in other parts of his grammar, so also in the "theory of letters" he gave fuller word lists than people had been accustomed to, and this opened the eyes of scholars to the great regularity reigning in this department of linguistic development. Though in his own etymological practice he was far from the strict idea of 'phonetic law' that played such a prominent rôle in later times, he thus paved the way for it. He speaks of law at any rate in connexion with the consonant shift, and there recognizes that it serves to curb wild etymologies and becomes a test for them (Gesch 291). The consonant shift thus became *the* law in linguistics, and because it affected a great many words known to everybody, and in a new and surprising way associated well-known Latin or Greek words with words of one's own mother-tongue, it became popularly the keystone of a new wonderful science.

Grimm coined several of the terms now generally used in linguistics; thus *umlaut* and *ablaut*, 'strong' and 'weak' declensions and conjugations. As to the first, we have seen that it was Rask who first understood and who taught Grimm the cause of this phenomenon, which in English has often been designated by the German term, while Sweet calls it 'mutation' and others better 'infection.' With regard to 'ablaut' (Sweet: gradation, best perhaps in English apophony), Rask termed it 'omlyd,' a word which he never applied to Grimm's 'umlaut,' thus keeping the two kinds of vowel change as strictly apart as Grimm does. Apophony was first discovered in that class of verbs which Grimm called 'strong'; he was fascinated by the commutation of the vowels in *springe, sprang, gesprungen*, and sees in it, as in *bimbambum*, something mystic and admirable, characteristic of the old German spirit. He was thus blind to the correspondences found in other languages, and his theory led him astray in the second volume, in which he constructed imaginary verbal roots to explain apophony wherever it was found outside the verbs.

it is employed by J. Grimm"—but 'broad' here means 'wrong' or 'unscientific.' There is no *kreislauf* in the case of initial *k = h*; only in a few of the nine series do we find three distinct stages (as in *tres, three, drei*); here we have in Danish three stages, of which the third is a reversal to the first (*tre*); in E. *mother* we have five stages : *t*, þ, ð, *d*, (OE. *modor*) and again ð. Is there an "inherent connexion between the various processes of this shifting" too?

Though Grimm, as we have seen, was by his principles and whole tendency averse to prescribing laws for a language, he is sometimes carried away by his love for mediæval German, as when he gives as the correct nominative form *der boge*, though everybody for centuries had said *der bogen*. In the same way many of his followers would apply the historical method to questions of correctness of speech, and would discard the forms evolved in later times in favour of previously existing forms which were looked upon as more ' organic.'

It will not be necessary here to speak of the imposing work done by Grimm in the rest of his long life, chiefly spent as a professor in Berlin. But in contrast to the ordinary view I must say that what appears to me as most likely to endure is his work on syntax, contained in the fourth volume of his grammar and in monographs. Here his enormous learning, his close power of observation, and his historical method stand him in good stead, and there is much good sense and freedom from that kind of metaphysical systematism which was triumphant in contemporaneous work on classical syntax. His services in this field are the more interesting because he did not himself seem to set much store by these studies and even said that syntax was half outside the scope of grammar. This utterance belongs to a later period than that of the birth of historical and comparative linguistics, and we shall have to revert to it after sketching the work of the third great founder of this science, to whom we shall now turn.

II.—§ 6. Franz Bopp.

The third, by some accounted the greatest, among the founders of modern linguistic science was Franz Bopp. His life was uneventful. At the age of twenty-one (he was born in 1791) he went to Paris to study Oriental languages, and soon concentrated his attention on Sanskrit. His first book, from which it is customary in Germany to date the birth of Comparative Philology, appeared in 1816, while he was still in Paris, under the title *Ueber des conjugationssystem der sanskritsprache in vergleichung mit jenem der griechischen, lateinischen, persischen und germanischen sprache*, but the latter part of the small volume was taken up with translations from Sanskrit, and for a long time he was just as much a Sanskrit scholar, editing and translating Sanskrit texts, as a comparative grammarian. He showed himself in the latter character in several papers read before the Berlin Academy, after he had been made a professor there in 1822, and especially in his famous *Vergleichende grammatik des sanskrit, send, armenischen, griechischen, lateinischen, litauischen, altslawischen, gotischen und deutschen*, the first edition of which was published between 1833 and 1849, the second in 1857, and the third in 1868. Bopp died in 1867.

Of Bopp's *Conjugationssystem* a revised, rearranged and greatly improved English translation came out in 1820 under the title *Analytical Comparison of the Sanskrit, Greek, Latin and Teutonic Languages*. This was reprinted with a good introduction by F. Techmer in his *Internationale zeitschrift für allgem. sprachwissenschaft IV* (1888), and in the following remarks I shall quote this (abbreviated AC) instead of, or alongside of, the German original (abbreviated C).

Bopp's chief aim (and in this he was characteristically different from Rask) was to find out the ultimate origin of grammatical forms. He follows his quest by the aid of Sanskrit forms, though he does not consider these as the ultimate forms themselves : " I do not believe that the Greek, Latin, and other European languages are to be considered as derived from the Sanskrit in the state in which we find it in Indian books ; I feel rather inclined to consider them altogether as subsequent variations of one original tongue, which, however, the Sanskrit has preserved more perfect than its kindred dialects. But whilst therefore the language of the Brahmans more frequently enables us to conjecture the primitive form of the Greek and Latin languages than what we discover in the oldest authors and monuments, the latter on their side also may not unfrequently elucidate the Sanskrit grammar " (AC3). Herein subsequent research has certainly borne out Bopp's view.

After finding out by a comparison of the grammatical forms of Sanskrit, Greek, etc., which of these forms were identical and what were their oldest shapes, he tries to investigate the ultimate origin of these forms. This he takes to be a comparatively easy consequence of the first task, but he was here too much under the influence of the philosophical grammar then in vogue. Gottfried Hermann (*De emendanda ratione Græcæ grammaticæ*, 1801), on purely logical grounds, distinguishes three things as necessary elements of each sentence, the subject, the predicate, and the copula joining the first two elements together ; as the power of the verb is to attribute the predicate to the subject, there is really only one verb, namely the verb *to be*. Bopp's teacher in Paris, Silvestre de Sacy, says the same thing, and Bopp repeats : " A verb, in the most restricted meaning of the term, is that part of speech by which a subject is connected with its attribute. According to this definition it would appear that there can exist only one verb, namely, the substantive verb, in Latin *esse* ; in English, *to be*. . . . Languages of a structure similar to that of the Greek, Latin, etc., can express by one verb of this kind a whole logical proposition, in which, however, that part of speech which expresses the connexion of the subject with its attribute, which is the characteristic function of the verb, is generally entirely omitted or understood. The Latin verb *dat* expresses the proposition ' he gives,' or ' he is giving ' : the letter *t*, indicating the third person, is the subject, *da* expresses the attribute of giving, and the grammatical *copula* is understood. In the verb *potest*, the latter is expressed, and *potest* unites in itself the three essential parts of speech, *t* being the subject, *es* the copula, and *pot* the attribute."

Starting from this logical conception of grammar, Bopp is inclined to find everywhere the ' substantive verb ' *to be* in its two Sanskrit forms *as* and *bhu* as an integral part of verbal forms. He is not the first to think that terminations, which are now in-separable parts of a verb, were originally independent words; thus Horne Tooke (in *Epea pteroenta*, 1786, ii. 429) expressly says that " All those common terminations in any language . . . are them-selves separate words with distinct meanings," and explains, for instance, Latin *ibo* from *i*, ' go ' + *b*, ' will,' from Greek *boúl-(omai)* + *o* ' I,' from *ego*. Bopp's explanations are similar to this, though they do not imply such violent shortenings as that of *boúl-(omai)* to *b*. He finds the root Sanskrit *as*, ' to be,' in Latin perfects like *scrip-s-i*, in Greek aorists like *e-tup-s-a* and in futures like *tup-s-o*. That the same addition thus indicates different tenses does not trouble Bopp greatly ; he explains Lat. *fueram* from *fu* + *es* + *am*, etc., and says that the root *fu* " contains, properly, nothing to indi-cate past time, but the usage of language having supplied the want of an adequate inflexion, *fui* received the sense of a perfect, and *fu-eram*, which would be nothing more than an imperfect, that of a pluperfect, and after the same manner *fu-ero* signifies ' I shall have been,' instead of ' I shall be ' " (AC 57). All Latin verbal endings containing *r* are thus explained as being ultimately formed with the substantive verb (*ama-rem*, etc.) ; thus among others the infinitives *fac-ere*, *ed-ere*, as well as *esse*, *posse* : " *E* is properly, in Latin, the termination of a simple infinitive active ; and the root *Es* produced anciently *ese*, by adding *e* ; the *s* having afterwards been doubled, we have *esse*. This termination *e* answers to the Greek infinitive in *ai*, *eînai* . . ." (AC 58).

If Bopp found a master-key to many of the verbal endings in the Sanskrit root *es*, he found a key to many others in the other root of the verb ' to be,' Sanskrit *bhu*. He finds it in the Latin imperfect *da-bam*, as well as in the future *da-bo*, the relation between which is the same as that between *er-am* and *er-o*. " *Bo*, *bis*, *bit* has a striking similarity with the Anglo-Saxon *beo*, *bys*, *byth*, the future tense of the verb substantive, a similarity which cannot be considered as merely accidental." [Here neither the form nor the function of the Anglo-Saxon is stated quite correctly.] But the ending in Latin *ama-vi* is also referred to the same root; for the change of the *b* into *v* we are referred to Italian *amava*, from Lat. *amabam*; thus also *fui* is for *fuvi* and *potui* is for *pot-vi*: "languages manifest a constant effort to combine heterogeneous materials in such a manner as to offer to the ear or eye one perfect whole, like a statue executed by a skilful artist, that wears the appearance of a figure hewn out of one piece of marble" (AC 60).

The following may be taken as a fair specimen of the method followed in these first attempts to account for the origin of flexional forms: "The Latin passive forms *amat-ur*, *amant-ur*, would, in some measure, conform to this mode of joining the verb substantive, if the *r* was also the result of a permutation of an original *s*; and this appears not quite incredible, if we compare the second person *ama-ris* with the third *amat-ur*. Either in one or the other there must be a transposition of letters, to which the Latin language is particularly addicted. If *ama-ris*, which might have been produced from *ama-sis*, has preserved the original order of letters, then *ama-tur* must be the transposition of *ama-rut* or *ama-sut*, and *ama-ntur* that of *ama-runt* or *ama-sunt*. If this be the case, the origin of the Latin passive can be accounted for, and although differing from that of the Sanskrit, Greek, and Gothic languages, it is not produced by the invention of a new grammatical form. It becomes clear, also, why many verbs, with a passive form, have an active signification; because there is no reason why the addition of the verb substantive should necessarily produce a passive sense. There is another way of explaining *ama-ris*, if it really stands for *ama-sis*; the *s* may be the radical consonant of the reflex pronoun *se*. The introduction of this pronoun would be particularly adapted to form the middle voice, which expresses the reflexion of the action upon the actor; but the Greek language exemplifies the facility with which the peculiar signification of the middle voice passes into that of the passive." The reasoning in the beginning of this passage (the only one contained in C) carries us back to a pre-scientific atmosphere, of which there are few or no traces in Rask's writings; the latter explanation (added in AC) was preferred by Bopp himself in later works, and was for many years accepted as the correct one, until scholars found a passive in *r* in Keltic, where the transition from *s* to *r* is not found as it is in Latin; and as the closely corresponding forms in Keltic and Italic must obviously be explained in the same way, the hypothesis of a composition with *se* was generally abandoned. Bopp's partiality for the abstract verb is seen clearly when he explains the Icelandic passive in *-st* from *s* = *es* (C 132); here Rask and Grimm saw the correct and obvious explanation.

Among the other explanations given first by Bopp must be mentioned the Latin second person of the passive voice -*mini*, as in *ama-mini*, which he takes to be the nominative masculine plural of a participle corresponding to Greek -*menos* and found in a different form in Lat. *alumnus* (AC 51). This explanation is still widely accepted, though not by everybody.

With regard to the preterit of what Grimm was later to term the 'weak' verbs, Bopp vacillates between different explanations. In C 118 he thinks the *t* or *d* is identical with the ending of the participle, in which the case endings were omitted and supplanted by personal endings ; the syllable *ed* after *d* [in Gothic *sok-id-edum* ; ' Greek,' p. 119, must be a misprint for Gothic] is nothing but an accidental addition. But on p. 151 he sees in *sokidedun, sokidedi*, a connexion of *sok* with the preterit of the verb *Tun*, as if the Germans were to say *suchetaten, suchetäte* ; he compares the English use of *did* (*did seek*), and thinks the verb used is G. *tun*, Goth. *tanjan*. The theory of composition is here restricted to those forms that contain two *d's*, i.e. the plural indicative and the subjunctive. In the English edition this twofold explanation is repeated with some additions : *d* or *t* as in Gothic *sok-i-da* and *oh-ta* originates from a participle found in Sanskr. *tyak-ta, likh-i-ta*, Lat. -*tus*, Gr. -*tós* ; this suffix generally has a passive sense, but in neuter verbs an active sense, and therefore would naturally serve to form a preterit tense with an active signification. He finds a proof of the connexion between this preterit and the participle in the fact that only such verbs as have this ending in the participle form their preterit by means of a dental, while the others (the 'strong' verbs, as Grimm afterwards termed them) have a participle in *an* and reduplication or a change of vowel in the preterit ; and Bopp compares the Greek aorist passive *etúphth-ēn, edóth-ēn*, which he conceives may proceed from the participle *tuphth-eís, doth-eís* (AC 37 ff.). This suggestion seems to have been commonly overlooked or abandoned, while the other explanation, from *dedi* as in English *did seek*, which Bopp gives p. 49 for the subjunctive and the indicative plural, was accepted by Grimm as the explanation of all the forms, even of those containing only one dental ; in later works Bopp agreed with Grimm and thus gave up the first part of his original explanation. The *did* explanation had been given already by D. von Stade (d. 1718, see Collitz, *Das schwache präteritum*, p. 1) ; Rask (P 270, not mentioned by Collitz) says : " Whence this *d* or *t* has come is not easy to tell, as it is not found in Latin and Greek, but as it is evident from the Icelandic grammar that it is closely connected with the past participle and is also found in the preterit subjunctive, it seems clear that it must have been an old characteristic of the past tense in every mood, but was lost in Greek when the above-mentioned participles in *tos* disappeared from the verbs " (cf. Ch. XIX § 12).

With regard to the vowels, Bopp in AC has the interesting theory that it is only through a defect in the alphabet that Sanskrit appears to have *a* in so many places ; he believes that the spoken language had often " the short Italian *e* and *o*," where *a* was written. " If this was the case, we can give a reason why, in words common to the Sanskrit and Greek, the Indian *akāra* [that is, short *a*] so often corresponds to ε and *o*, as, for instance, *asti*, he is, ἐστί ; *patis*, husband, πόσις ; *ambaras*, sky, ὄμβρος, rain, etc." Later, unfortunately, Bopp came under the influence of Grimm, who, as we saw, on speculative grounds admitted in the primitive language only the three vowels *a, i, u,* and Bopp and his followers went on believing that the Sanskrit *a* represented the original state of language, until the discovery of the ' palatal law ' (about 1880) showed (what Bopp's occasional remark might otherwise easily have led up to, if he had not himself discarded it) that the Greek tripartition into *a, e, o* represented really a more original state of things.

II.—§ 7. Bopp continued.

In a chapter on the roots in AC (not found in C), Bopp contrasts the structure of Semitic roots and of our own ; in Semitic languages roots must consist of three letters, neither more nor less, and thus generally contain two syllables, while in Sanskrit, Greek, etc., the character of the root " is not to be determined by the number of letters, but by that of the syllables, of which they contain only one " ; thus a root like *i*, ' to go,' would be unthinkable in Arabic. The consequence of this structure of the roots is that the inner changes which play such a large part in expressing grammatical modifications in Semitic languages must be much more restricted in our family of languages. These changes were what F. Schlegel termed flexions and what Bopp himself, two years before (C 7), had named " the truly organic way " of expressing relation and mentioned as a wonderful flexibility found in an extraordinary degree in Sanskrit, by the side of which composition with the verb ' to be ' is found only occasionally. Now, however, in 1820, Bopp repudiates Schlegel's and his own previous assumption that ' flexion ' was characteristic of Sanskrit in contradistinction to other languages in which grammatical modifications were expressed by the addition of suffixes. On the contrary, while holding that both methods are employed in all languages, Chinese perhaps alone excepted, he now thinks that it is the suffix method which is prevalent in Sanskrit, and that " the only real inflexions . . . possible in a language, whose elements are monosyllables, are the change of their vowels and the repetition of their radical consonants, otherwise called reduplication." It will be seen that Bopp here avoids both the onesidedness found in Schlegel's division of languages and the other onesidedness which we shall encounter in later theories, according to which *all* grammatical elements are originally independent subordinate roots added to the main root.

In his *Vocalismus* (1827, reprinted 1836) Bopp opposes Grimm's theory that the changes for which Grimm had introduced the term *ablaut* were due to psychological causes; in other words, possessed an inner meaning from the very outset. Bopp inclined to a mechanical explanation [1] and thought them dependent on the weight of the endings, as shown by the contrast between Sanskr. *vēda*, Goth. *vait*, Gr. *oîda* and the plural, respectively *vidima, vitum, idmen*. In this instance Bopp is in closer agreement than Grimm with the majority of younger scholars, who see in apophony (ablaut) an originally non-significant change brought about mechanically by phonetic conditions, though they do not find these in the ' weight ' of the ending, but in the primeval accent : the accentuation of Sanskrit was not known to Bopp when he wrote his essay.

The personal endings of the verbs had already been identified with the corresponding pronouns by Scheidius (1790) and Rask (P 258) ; Bopp adopts the same view, only reproaching Scheidius for thinking exclusively of the nominative forms of the pronouns.

It thus appears that in his early work Bopp deals with a great many general problems, but his treatment is suggestive rather than exhaustive or decisive, for there are too many errors in details and his whole method is open to serious criticism. A modern reader is astonished to see the facility with which violent changes of sounds, omissions and transpositions of consonants, etc., are gratuitously accepted. Bopp never reflected as deeply as Rask did on what constitutes linguistic kinship, hence in C he accepts the common belief that Persian was related more closely to German than to Sanskrit, and in later life he tried to establish a relationship between the Malayo-Polynesian and the Indo-European languages. But in spite of all this it must be recognized that in his long laborious life he accomplished an enormous amount of highly meritorious work, not only in Sanskrit philology, but also in comparative grammar, in which he gradually freed himself of his worst methodical errors. He was constantly widening his range of vision, taking into consideration more and more cognate languages. The ingenious way in which he explained the curious Keltic shiftings in initial

---

[1] Probably under the influence of Humboldt, who wrote to him (September 1826) : "Absichtlich grammatisch ist gewiss kein vokalwechsel."

consonants (which had so puzzled Rask as to make him doubt of a connexion of these languages with our family, but which Bopp showed to be dependent on a lost final sound of the preceding word) definitely and irrefutably established the position of those languages. Among other things that might be credited to his genius, I shall select his explanation of the various declensional classes as determined by the final sound of the stem. But it is not part of my plan to go into many details ; suffice it to say that Bopp's great *Vergleichende grammatik* served for long years as the best, or really the only, exposition of the new science, and vastly contributed not only to elucidate obscure points, but also to make comparative grammar as popular as it is possible for such a necessarily abstruse science to be.

In Bopp's *Vergleichende grammatik* (1. § 108) he gives his classification of languages in general. He rejects Fr. Schlegel's bipartition, but his growing tendency to explain everything in Aryan grammar, even the inner changes of Sanskrit roots, by mechanical causes makes him modify A. W. Schlegel's tripartition and place our family of languages with the second instead of the third class. His three classes are therefore as follows : I. Languages without roots proper and without the power of composition, and thus without organism or grammar ; to this class belongs Chinese, in which most grammatical relations are only to be recognized by the position of the words. II. Languages with monosyllabic roots, capable of composition and acquiring their organism, their grammar, nearly exclusively in this way ; the main principle of word formation is the connexion of verbal and pronominal roots. To this class belong the Indo-European languages, but also all languages not comprised under the first or the third class. III. Languages with disyllabic roots and three necessary consonants as sole bearers of the signification of the word. This class includes only the Semitic languages. Grammatical forms are here created not only by means of composition, as in the second class, but also by inner modification of the roots.

It will be seen that Bopp here expressly avoids both expressions 'agglutination' and 'flexion,' the former because it had been used of languages contrasted with Aryan, while Bopp wanted to show the essential identity of the two classes ; the latter because it had been invested with much obscurity on account of Fr. Schlegel's use of it to signify inner modification only. According to Schlegel, only such instances as English *drink / drank / drunk* are pure flexion, while German *trink-e / trank / ge-trunk-en,* and still more Greek *leip-ō / e-lip-on / le-loip-a,* besides an element of 'flexion' contain also affixed elements. It is clear that no language can use 'flexion' (in Schlegel's sense) exclusively, and consequently this cannot be made a principle on which to erect a classification of languages generally. Schlegel's use of the term 'flexion' seems to have been dropped by all subsequent writers, who use it so as to include what is actually found in the grammar of such languages as Sanskrit and Greek, comprising under it inner and outer modifications, but of course not requiring both in the same form.

In view of the later development of our science, it is worthy of notice that neither in the brothers Schlegel nor in Bopp do we yet meet with the idea that the classes set up are not only a distribution of the languages found side by side in the world at this time, but also represent so many stages in historical development ; indeed, Bopp's definitions are framed so as positively to exclude any development from his Class II to Class III, as the character of the underlying roots is quite heterogeneous. On the other hand, Bopp's tendency to explain Aryan endings from originally independent roots paved the way for the theory of isolation, agglutination and flexion as three successive stages of the same language.

In his first work (C 56) Bopp had already hinted that in the earliest period known to us languages had already outlived their most perfect state and were in a process of decay ; and in his review of Grimm (1827) he repeats this : " We perceive them in a condition in which they may indeed be progressive syntactically, but have, as far as grammar is concerned, lost more or less of what belonged to the perfect structure, in which the separate members stand in exact relation to each other and in which everything derived has still a visible and unimpaired connexion with its source " (Voc. 2). We shall see kindred ideas in Humboldt and Schleicher.

To sum up : Bopp set about discovering the ultimate origin of flexional elements, but instead of that he discovered Comparative Grammar—" à peu près comme Christophe Colomb a découvert l'Amérique en cherchant la route des Indes," as A. Meillet puts it (LI 413). A countryman of Rask may be forgiven for pushing the French scholar's brilliant comparison still further : in the same way as Norsemen from Iceland had discovered America before Columbus, without imagining that they were finding the way to India, just so Rasmus Rask through his Icelandic studies had discovered Comparative Grammar before Bopp, without needing to take the circuitous route through Sanskrit.

II.—§ 8. Wilhelm von Humboldt.

This will be the proper place to mention one of the profoundest thinkers in the domain of linguistics, Wilhelm von Humboldt (1767–1835), who, while playing an important part in the political world, found time to study a great many languages and to think deeply on many problems connected with philology and ethnography.[1]

In numerous works, the most important of which, *Ueber die Kawisprache auf der Insel Jawa*, with the famous introduction "Ueber die Verschiedenheit des menschlichen Sprachbaues und ihren Einfluss auf die geistige Entwickelung des Menschengeschlechts," was published posthumously in 1836–40, Humboldt developed his linguistic philosophy, of which it is not easy to give a succinct idea, as it is largely couched in a most abstruse style; it is not surprising that his admirer and follower, Heymann Steinthal, in a series of books, gave as many different interpretations of Humboldt's thoughts, each purporting to be more correct than its predecessors. Still, I believe the following may be found to be a tolerably fair rendering of some of Humboldt's ideas.

He rightly insists on the importance of seeing in language a continued activity. Language is not a substance or a finished work, but action (Sie selbst ist kein werk, *ergon*, sondern eine tätigkeit, *energeia*). Language therefore cannot be defined except genetically. It is the ever-repeated labour of the mind to utilize articulated sounds to express thoughts. Strictly speaking, this is a definition of each separate act of speech; but truly and essentially a language must be looked upon as the totality of such acts.

---

[1] Humboldt's relation to Bopp's general ideas is worth studying; see his letters to Bopp, printed as Nachtrag to S. Lefman's *Franz Bopp, sein leben und seine wissenschaft* (Berlin, 1897). He is (p. 5) on the whole of Bopp's opinion that flexions have arisen through agglutination of syllables, the independent meaning of which was lost; still, he is not certain that all flexion can be explained in that way, and especially doubts it in the case of 'umlaut,' under which term he here certainly includes 'ablaut,' as seen by his reference (p. 12) to Greek future *stalô* from *stéllō*; he adds that "some flexions are at the same time so insignificant and so widely spread in languages that I should be inclined to call them original; for example, our *i* of the dative and *m* of the same case, both of which by their sharper sound seem intended to call attention to the peculiar nature of this case, which does not, like the other cases, denote a simple, but a double relation" (repeated p. 10). Humboldt doubts Bopp's identification of the temporal augment with the *a* privativum. He says (p. 14) that cases often originate from prepositions, as in American languages and in Basque, and that he has always explained our genitive, as in G. *manne-s*, as a remnant of *aus*. This is evidently wrong, as the *s* of *aus* is a special High German development from *t*, while the *s* of the genitive is also found in languages which do not share in this development of *t*. But the remark is interesting because, apart from the historical proof to the contrary which we happen to possess in this case, the derivation is no whit worse than many of the explanations resorted to by adherents of the agglutinative theory. But Humboldt goes on to say that in Greek and Latin he is not prepared to maintain that one single case is to be explained in this way. Humboldt probably had some influence on Bopp's view of the weak preterit, for he is skeptical with regard to the *did* explanation and inclines to connect the ending with the participle in *t*.

For the words and rules, which according to our ordinary notions make up a language, exist really only in the act of connected speech. The breaking up of language into words and rules is nothing but a dead product of our bungling scientific analysis (Versch 41). Nothing in language is static, everything is dynamic. Language has nowhere any abiding place, not even in writing ; its dead part must continually be re-created in the mind ; in order to exist it must be spoken or understood, and so pass in its entirety into the subject (ib. 63).

Humboldt speaks continually of languages as more perfect or less perfect. Yet "no language should be condemned or depreciated, not even that of the most savage tribe, for each language is a picture of the original aptitude for language " (Versch 304). In another place he speaks about special excellencies even of languages that cannot in themselves be recognized as superlatively good instruments of thought. Undoubtedly Chinese of the old style carries with it an impressive dignity through the immediate succession of nothing but momentous notions ; it acquires a simple greatness because it throws away all unnecessary accessory elements and thus, as it were, takes flight to pure thinking. Malay is rightly praised for its ease and the great simplicity of its constructions. The Semitic languages retain an admirable art in the nice discrimination of sense assigned to many shades of vowels. Basque possesses a particular vigour, dependent on the briefness and boldness of expression imparted by the structure of its words and by their combination. Delaware and other American languages express in one word a number of ideas for which we should require many words. The human mind is always capable of producing something admirable, however one-sided it may be ; such special points decide nothing with regard to the rank of languages (Versch 189 f.). We have here, as indeed continually in Humboldt, a valuation of languages with many brilliant remarks, but on the whole we miss the concrete details abounding in Jenisch's work. Humboldt, as it were, lifts us to a higher plane, where the air may be purer, but where it is also thinner and not seldom cloudier as well.

According to Humboldt, each separate language, even the most despised dialect, should be looked upon as an organic whole, different from all the rest and expressing the individuality of the people speaking it ; it is characteristic of one nation's psyche, and indicates the peculiar way in which that nation attempts to realize the ideal of speech. As a language is thus symbolic of the national character of those who speak it, very much in each language had its origin in a symbolic representation of the notion it stands for ; there is a natural nexus between certain sounds and certain general ideas, and consequently we often find similar sounds used for the same, or nearly the same, idea in languages not otherwise related to one another.

Humboldt is opposed to the idea of 'general' or 'universal' grammar as understood in his time ; instead of this purely deductive grammar he would found an inductive general grammar, based upon the comparison of the different ways in which the same grammatical notion was actually expressed in a variety of languages. He set the example in his paper on the Dual. His own studies covered a variety of languages ; but his works do not give us many actual concrete facts from the languages he had studied ; he was more interested in abstract reasonings on language in general than in details.

In an important paper, *Ueber das Entstehen der grammatischen Formen und ihren Einfluss auf die Ideenentwickelung* (1822), he says that language at first denotes only objects, leaving it to the hearer to understand or guess at (hinzudenken) their connexion. By and by the word-order becomes fixed, and some words lose their independent use and sound, so that in the second stage we see grammatical relations denoted through word-order and through words vacillating between material and formal significations. Gradually these become affixes, but the connexion is not yet firm, the joints are still visible, the result being an aggregate, not yet a unit. Thus in the third stage we have something analogous to form, but not real form. This is achieved in the fourth stage, where the word is *one*, only modified in its grammatical relations through the flexional sound ; each word belongs to one definite part of speech, and form-words have no longer any disturbing material signification, but are pure expressions of relation. Such words as Lat. *amavit* and Greek *epoíēsas* are truly grammatical forms in contradistinction to such combinations of words and syllables as are found in cruder languages, because we have here a fusion into one whole, which causes the signification of the parts to be forgotten and joins them firmly under one accent. Though Humboldt thus thinks flexion developed out of agglutination, he distinctly repudiates the idea of a gradual development and rather inclines to something like a sudden crystallization (see especially Steinthal's ed., p. 585).

Humboldt's position with regard to the classification of languages is interesting. In his works we continually meet with the terms agglutination [1] and flexion by the side of a new term, 'incorporation.' This he finds in full bloom in many American languages, such as Mexican, where the object may be inserted into the verbal form between the element indicating person and the

[1] Humboldt seems to be the inventor of this term (1821; see Streitberg, IF 35. 191).

root. Now, Humboldt says that besides Chinese, which has no grammatical form, there are three possible forms of languages, the flexional, the agglutinative and the incorporating, but he adds that all languages contain one or more of these forms (Versch 301). He tends to deny the existence of any exclusively agglutinative or exclusively flexional language, as the two principles are generally commingled (132). Flexion is the only method that gives to the word the true inner firmness and at the same time distributes the parts of the sentence according to the necessary interlacing of thoughts, and thus undoubtedly represents the pure principle of linguistic structure. Now, the question is, what language carries out this method in the most consistent way ? True perfection may not be found in any one language : in the Semitic languages we find flexion in its most genuine shape, united with the most refined symbolism, only it is not pursued consistently in all parts of the language, but restricted by more or less accidental laws. On the other hand, in the Sanskritic languages the compact unity of every word saves flexion from any suspicion of agglutination ; it pervades all parts of the language and rules it in the highest freedom (Versch 188). Compared with incorporation and with the method of loose juxtaposition without any real word-unity, flexion appears as an intuitive principle born of true linguistic genius (ib.). Between Sanskrit and Chinese, as the two opposed poles of linguistic structure, each of them perfect in the consistent following one principle, we may place all the remaining languages (ib. 326). But the languages called agglutinative have nothing in common except just the negative trait that they are neither isolating nor flexional. The structural diversities of human languages are so great that they make one despair of a fully comprehensive classification (ib. 330).

According to Humboldt, language is in continued development under the influence of the changing mental power of its speakers. In this development there are naturally two definite periods, one in which the creative instinct of speech is still growing and active, and another in which a seeming stagnation begins and then an appreciable decline of that creative instinct. Still, the period of decline may initiate new principles of life and new successful changes in a language (Versch 184). In the form-creating period nations are occupied more with the language than with its purpose, i.e. with what it is meant to signify. They struggle to express thought, and this craving in connexion with the inspiring feeling of success produces and sustains the creative power of language (ib. 191). In the second period we witness a wearing-off of the flexional forms. This is found less in languages reputed crude or rough than in refined ones. Language is exposed to the most violent changes when the human mind is most active, for then it considers too careful an observation of the modifications of sound as superfluous. To this may be added a want of perception of the poetic charm inherent in the sound. Thus it is the transition from a more sensuous to a more intellectual mood that works changes in a language. In other cases less noble causes are at work. Rougher organs and less sensitive ears are productive of indifference to the principle of harmony, and finally a prevalent practical trend may bring about abbreviations and omissions of all kinds in its contempt for everything that is not strictly necessary for the purpose of being understood. While in the first period the elements still recall their origin to man's consciousness, there is an æsthetic pleasure in developing the instrument of mental activity ; but in the second period language serves only the practical needs of life. In this way such a language as English may reduce its forms so as to resemble the structure of Chinese ; but there will always remain traces of the old flexions ; and English is no more incapable of high excellences than German (Versch 282–6). What these are Humboldt, however, does not tell us.

II.—§ 9. Grimm Once More.

Humboldt here foreshadowed and probably influenced ideas to which Jacob Grimm gave expression in two essays written in his old age and which it will be necessary here to touch upon. In the essay on the pedantry of the German language (*Ueber das pedantische in der deutschen sprache*, 1847), Grimm says that he has so often praised his mother-tongue that he has acquired the right once in a while to blame it. If pedantry had not existed already, Germans would have invented it ; it is the shadowy side of one of their virtues, painstaking accuracy and loyalty. Grimm's essay is an attempt at estimating a language, but on the whole it is less comprehensive and less deep than that of Jenisch. Grimm finds fault with such things as the ceremoniousness with which princes are spoken to and spoken of (*Durchlauchtigster, allerhöchstderselbe*), and the use of the pronoun *Sie* in the third person plural in addressing a single person ; he speaks of the clumsiness of the auxiliaries for the passive, the past and the future, and of the word-order which makes the Frenchman cry impatiently "J'attends le verbe." He blames the use of capitals for substantives and other peculiarities of German spelling, but gives no general statement of the principles on which the comparative valuation of different languages should be based, though in many passages we see that he places the old stages of the language very much higher than the language of his own day.

The essay on the origin of language (1851) is much more important, and may be said to contain the mature expression of all Grimm's thoughts on the philosophy of language. Unfortunately, much of it is couched in that high-flown poetical style which may be partly a consequence of Grimm's having approached the exact study of language through the less exact studies of popular poetry and folklore ; this style is not conducive to clear ideas, and therefore renders the task of the reporter very difficult indeed. Grimm at some length argues against the possibility of language having been either created by God when he created man or having been revealed by God to man after his creation. The very imperfections and changeability of language speak against its divine origin. Language as gradually developed must be the work of man himself, and therein is different from the immutable cries and songs of the lower creation. Nature and natural instinct have no history, but mankind has. Man and woman were created as grown-up and marriageable beings, and there must have been created at once more than one couple, for if there had been only one couple, there would have been the possibility that the one mother had borne only sons or only daughters, further procreation being thus rendered impossible (!), not to mention the moral objections to marriages between brother and sister. How these once created beings, human in every respect except in language, were able to begin talking and to find themselves understood, Grimm does not really tell us ; he uses such expressions as 'inventors' of words, but apart from the symbolical value of some sounds, such as *l* and *r*, he thinks that the connexion of word and sense was quite arbitrary. On the other hand, he can tell us a great deal about the first stage of human speech : it contained only the three vowels *a, i, u*, and only few consonant groups ; every word was a monosyllable, and abstract notions were at first absent. The existence in all (?) old languages of masculine and feminine flexions must be due to the influence of women on the formation of language. Through the distinction of genders Grimm says that regularity and clearness were suddenly brought about in everything concerning the noun as by a most happy stroke of fortune. Endings to indicate person, number, tense and mood originated in added pronouns and auxiliary words, which at first were loosely joined to the root, but later coalesced with it. Besides, reduplication was used to indicate the past ; and after the absorption of the reduplicational syllable the same effect was obtained in German through apophony. All nouns presuppose verbs, whose material sense was applied to the designation of things, as when G. *hahn* (' cock ') was thus called from an extinct verb *hanan,* corresponding to Lat. *canere,* ' to sing.'

In what Grimm says about the development of language it is easy to trace the influence of Humboldt's ideas, though they are worked out with great originality. He discerns three stages, the last two alone being accessible to us through historical documents. In the first period we have the creation and growing of roots and words, in the second the flourishing of a perfect flexion, and in the third a tendency to thoughts, which leads to the giving up of flexion as not yet (?) satisfactory. They may be compared to leaf, blossom and fruit, " the beauty of human speech did not bloom in its beginning, but in its middle period ; its ripest fruits will not be gathered till some time in the future." He thus sums up his theory of the three stages : " Language in its earliest form was melodious, but diffuse and straggling ; in its middle form it was full of intense poetical vigour ; in our own days it seeks to remedy the diminution of beauty by the harmony of the whole, and is more effective though it has inferior means." In most places Grimm still speaks of the downward course of linguistic development ; all the oldest languages of our family " show a rich, pleasant and admirable perfection of form, in which all material and spiritual elements have vividly interpenetrated each other," while in the later developments of the same languages the inner power and subtlety of flexion has generally been given up and destroyed, though partly replaced by external means and auxiliary words. On the whole, then, the history of language discloses a descent from a period of perfection to a less perfect condition. This is the point of view that we meet with in nearly all linguists ; but there is a new note when Grimm begins vaguely and dimly to see that the loss of flexional forms is sometimes compensated by other things that may be equally valuable or even more valuable ; and he even, without elaborate arguments, contradicts his own main contention when he says that " human language is retrogressive only apparently and in particular points, but looked upon as a whole it is progressive, and its intrinsic force is continually increasing." He instances the English language, which by sheer making havoc of all old phonetic laws and by the loss of all flexions has acquired a great force and power, such as is found perhaps in no other human language. Its wonderfully happy structure resulted from the marriage of the two noblest languages of Europe ; therefore it was a fit vehicle for the greatest poet of modern times, and may justly claim the right to be called a world's language ; like the English people, it seems destined to reign in future even more than now in all parts of the earth. This enthusiastic panegyric forms a striking contrast to what the next great German scholar with whom we have to deal, Schleicher, says about the same language, which to him shows only " how rapidly the language of a nation important both in history and literature can decline " (II. 231).

CHAPTER III

MIDDLE OF NINETEENTH CENTURY

§ 1. After Bopp and Grimm. § 2. K. M. Rapp. § 3. J. H. Bredsdorff.
§ 4. August Schleicher. § 5. Classification of Languages. § 6. Reconstruction. § 7. Curtius, Madvig and Specialists. § 8. Max Müller and
Whitney.

III.—§ 1. After Bopp and Grimm.

BOPP and Grimm exercised an enormous influence on linguistic
thought and linguistic research in Germany and other countries.
Long even before their death we see a host of successors following
in the main the lines laid down in their work, and thus directly
and indirectly they determined the development of this science
for a long time. Through their efforts so much new light had
been shed on a number of linguistic phenomena that these took
a quite different aspect from that which they had presented to the
previous generation ; most of what had been written about etymology and kindred subjects in the eighteenth century seemed to the
new school utterly antiquated, mere fanciful vagaries of incom-
petent blunderers, whereas now scholars had found firm ground
on which to raise a magnificent structure of solid science. This
feeling was especially due to the undoubted recognition of one
great family of languages to which the vast majority of European
languages, as well as some of the most important Asiatic languages,
belonged : here we had one firmly established fact of the greatest
magnitude, which at once put an end to all the earlier whimsical
attempts to connect Latin and Greek words with Hebrew roots.
As for the name of that family of languages, Rask hesitated between
different names, ' European,' ' Sarmatic ' and finally ' Japhetic '
(as a counterpart of the Semitic and the Hamitic languages) ;
Bopp at first had no comprehensive name, and on the title-page
of his *Vergl. grammatik* contents himself with enumerating the
chief languages described, but in the work itself he says that he
prefers the name ' Indo-European,' which has also found wide
acceptance, though more in France, England and Skandinavia
than in Germany. Humboldt for a long while said ' Sanskritic,'
but later he adopted ' Indo-Germanic,' and this has been the gener
ally recognized name used in Germany, in spite of Bopp's protest
who said that ' Indo-klassisch ' would be more to the point ; ' Indo-

Keltic' has also been proposed as designating the family through its two extreme members to the East and West. But all these compound names are clumsy without being completely pertinent, and it seems therefore much better to use the short and convenient term 'the Aryan languages': Aryan being the oldest name by which any members of the family designated themselves (in India and Persia).[1]

Thanks to the labours of Bopp and Grimm and their co-workers and followers, we see also a change in the status of the study of languages. Formerly this was chiefly a handmaiden to philology —but as this word is often in English used in a sense unknown to other languages and really objectionable, namely as a synonym of (comparative) study of languages, it will be necessary first to say a few words about the terminology of our science. In this book I shall use the word 'philology' in its continental sense, which is often rendered in English by the vague word 'scholarship,' meaning thereby the study of the specific culture of one nation ; thus we speak of Latin philology, Greek philology, Icelandic philology, etc. The word 'linguist,' on the other hand, is not infrequently used in the sense of one who has merely a practical knowledge of some foreign language ; but I think I am in accordance with a growing number of scholars in England and America if I call such a man a 'practical linguist' and apply the word 'linguist' by itself to the scientific student of language (or of languages) ; 'linguistics' then becomes a shorter and more convenient name for what is also called the science of language (or of languages).

Now that the reader understands the sense in which I take these two terms, I may go on to say that the beginning of the nineteenth century witnessed a growing differentiation between philology and linguistics in consequence of the new method introduced by comparative and by historical grammar ; it was nothing less than a completely new way of looking at the facts of language and trying to trace their origin. While to the philologist the Greek or Latin language, etc., was only a means to an end, to the linguist it was an end in itself. The former saw in it a valuable, and in fact an indispensable, means of gaining a first-hand knowledge of the literature which was his chief concern, but the linguist cared not for the literature as such, but studied languages for their own sake, and might even turn to languages destitute of literature because they were able to throw some light on the life of language in general or on forms in related languages. The philologist as such would not think of studying the Gothic of Wulfila, as a know-

---

[1] It has been objected to the use of Aryan in this wide sense that the name is also used in the restricted sense of Indian + Iranic ; but no separate name is needed for that small group other than Indo-Iranic.

ledge of that language gives access only to a translation of parts of the Bible, the ideas of which can be studied much better else-where ; but to the linguist Gothic was extremely valuable. The differentiation, of course, is not an absolute one ; besides being linguists in the new sense, Rask was an Icelandic philologist, Bopp a Sanskrit philologist, and Grimm a German philologist ; but the tendency towards the emancipation of linguistics was very strong in them, and some of their pupils were pure linguists and did no work in philology.

In breaking away from philology and claiming for linguistics the rank of a new and independent science, the partisans of the new doctrine were apt to think that not only had they discovered a new method, but that the object of their study was different from that of the philologists, even when they were both concerned with language. While the philologist looked upon language as part of the culture of some nation, the linguist looked upon it as a natural object ; and when in the beginning of the nineteenth cen-tury philosophers began to divide all sciences into the two sharply separated classes of mental and natural sciences (geistes- und naturwissenschaften), linguists would often reckon their science among the latter. There was in this a certain amount of pride or boastfulness, for on account of the rapid rise and splendid achievements of the natural sciences at that time, it began to be a matter of common belief that they were superior to, and were pos-sessed of a more scientific method than, the other class—the same view that finds an expression in the ordinary English usage, according to which ' science ' means natural science and the other domains of human knowledge are termed the ' arts ' or the ' humanities.'

We see the new point of view in occasional utterances of the pioneers of linguistic science. Rask expressly says that " Language is a natural object and its study resembles natural history " (SA 2. 502) ; but when he repeats the same sentence (in *Retskrivn-ingslære*, 8) it appears that he is thinking of language as opposed to the more artificial writing, and the contrast is not between mental and natural science, but between art and nature, between what can and what cannot be consciously modified by man—it is really a different question.

Bopp, in his review of Grimm (1827, reprinted *Vocalismus*, 1836, p. 1), says : " Languages are to be considered organic natural bodies, which are formed according to fixed laws, develop as pos-sessing an inner principle of life, and gradually die out because they do not understand themselves any longer [!], and therefore cast off or mutilate their members or forms, which were at first significant, but gradually have become more of an extrinsic mass.

. . . It is not possible to determine how long languages may preserve their full vigour of life and of procreation," etc. This is highly figurative language which should not be taken at its face value ; but expressions like these, and the constant use of such words as ' organic ' and ' inorganic ' in speaking of formations in languages, and ' organism ' of the whole language, would tend to widen the gulf between the philological and the linguistic point of view. Bopp himself never consistently followed the naturalistic way of looking at language, but in § 4 of this chapter we shall see that Schleicher was not afraid of going to extremes and building up a consistent natural science of language.

The cleavage between philology and linguistics did not take place without arousing warm feeling. Classical scholars disliked the intrusion of Sanskrit everywhere ; they did not know that language and did not see the use of it. They resented the way in which the new science wanted to reconstruct Latin and Greek grammar and to substitute new explanations for those which had always been accepted. Those Sanskritists chatted of guna and vrddhi and other barbaric terms, and even ventured to talk of a locative case in Latin, as if the number of cases had not been settled once for all long ago ! [1]

Classicists were no doubt perfectly right when they reproached comparativists for their neglect of syntax, which to them was the most important part of grammar ; they were also in some measure right when they maintained that linguists to a great extent contented themselves with a superficial knowledge of the languages compared, which they studied more in grammars and glossaries than in living texts, and sometimes they would even exult when they found proof of this in solecisms in Bopp's Latin translations from Sanskrit, and even on the title-page of *Glossarium Sanscritum a Franzisco Bopp*. Classical scholars also looked askance at the growing interest in the changes of sounds, or, as it was then usual to say, of letters. But when they were apt here to quote the scriptural phrase about the letter that killeth, while the spirit giveth life, they overlooked the fact that Nature has rendered it impossible for anyone to penetrate to the mind of anyone else except through its outer manifestations, and that it is consequently impossible to get at the spirit of a language except through its sounds : phonology must therefore form the necessary basis and prerequisite of the scientific study of any group of languages. Still, it cannot be denied that sometimes comparative phonology was treated in such a mechanical way as partly to dehumanize the study of language.

[1] In Lefmann's book on Bopp, pp. 292 and 299, there are some interesting quotations on this point.

When we look back at this period in the history of linguistics, there are certain tendencies and characteristics that cannot fail to catch our attention. First we must mention the prominence given to Sanskrit, which was thought to be the unavoidable requirement of every comparative linguist. In explaining anything in any of the cognate languages the etymologist always turned first to Sanskrit words and Sanskrit forms. This standpoint is found even much later, for instance in Max Müller's *Inaugural Address* (1868, Ch. 19) : "Sanskrit certainly forms the only sound foundation of Comparative Philology, and it will always remain the only safe guide through all its intricacies. A comparative philologist without a knowledge of Sanskrit is like an astronomer without a knowledge of mathematics." A linguist of a later generation may be excused for agreeing rather with Ellis, who says (*Transact. Philol. Soc.*, 1873–4, 21) : "Almost in our own days came the discovery of Sanskrit, and philology proper began—but, alas ! at the wrong end. Now, here I run great danger of being misunderstood. Although for a scientific sifting of the nature of language I presume to think that beginning at Sanskrit was unfortunate, yet I freely admit that, had that language not been brought into Europe . . . our knowledge of language would have been in a poor condition indeed. . . . We are under the greatest obligations to those distinguished men who have undertaken to unravel its secrets and to show its connexion with the languages of Europe. Yet I must repeat that for the pure science of language, to begin with Sanskrit was as much beginning at the wrong end as it would have been to commence zoology with palæontology—the relations of life with the bones of the dead."

Next, Bopp and his nearest successors were chiefly occupied with finding likenesses between the languages treated and discovering things that united them. This was quite natural in the first stage of the new science, but sometimes led to one-sidedness, the characteristic individuality of each language being lost sight of, while forms from many countries and many times were mixed up in a hotch-potch. Rask, on account of his whole mental equipment, was less liable to this danger than most of his contemporaries ; but Pott was evidently right when he warned his fellow-students that their comparative linguistics should be supplemented by separative linguistics (*Zählmethode*, 229), as it has been to a great extent in recent years.

Still another feature of the linguistic science of those days is the almost exclusive occupation of the student with dead languages. It was quite natural that the earliest comparativists should first give their attention to the oldest stages of the languages compared, since these alone enabled them to prove the essential kinship between the different members of the great Aryan family. In Grimm's grammar nearly all the space is taken up with Gothic, Old High German, Old Norse, etc., and comparatively little is said about recent developments of the same languages. In Bopp's comparative grammar classical Greek and Latin are, of course, treated carefully, but Modern Greek and the Romanic languages are not mentioned (thus also in Schleicher's *Compendium* and in Brugmann's *Grammar*), such later developments being left to specialists who were more or less considered to be outside the sphere of Comparative Linguistics and even of the science of language in general, though it would have been a much more correct view to include them in both, and though much more could really be learnt of the life of language from these studies than from comparisons made in the spirit of Bopp.

The earlier stages of different languages, which were compared by linguists, were, of course, accessible only through the medium of writing ; we have seen that the early linguists spoke constantly of letters and not of sounds. But this vitiated their whole outlook on languages. These were scarcely ever studied at first-hand, and neither in Bopp nor in Grimm nor in Pott or Benfey do we find such first-hand observations of living spoken languages as play a great rôle in the writings of Rask and impart an atmosphere of soundness to his whole manner of looking at languages. If languages were called natural objects, they were not yet studied as such or by truly naturalistic methods.

When living dialects were studied, the interest constantly centred round the archaic traits in them ; every survival of an old form, every trace of old sounds that had been dropped in the standard speech, was greeted with enthusiasm, and the significance of these old characteristics greatly exaggerated, the general impression being that popular dialects were always much more conservative than the speech of educated people. It was reserved for a much later time to prove that this view is completely erroneous, and that popular dialects, in spite of many archaic details, are on the whole further developed than the various standard languages with their stronger tradition and literary reminiscences.

III.—§ 2. K. M. Rapp.

It was from this archæological point of view only that Grimm encouraged the study of dialects, but he expressly advised students not to carry the research too far in the direction of discriminating minutiæ of sounds, because these had little bearing on the history of language as he understood it. In this connexion we may

mention an episode in the history of early linguistics that is sympto-
matic. K. M. Rapp brought out his *Versuch einer Physiologie
der Sprache nebst historischer Entwickelung der abendländischen
Idiome nach physiologischen Grundsätzen* in four volumes (1836,
1839, 1840, 1841). A physiological examination into the nature
and classification of speech sounds was to serve only as the basis
of the historical part, the grandiose plan of which was to find out
how Greek, Latin and Gothic sounded, and then to pursue the
destinies of these sound systems through the Middle Ages (Byzan-
tine Greek, Old Provençal, Old French, Old Norse, Anglo-Saxon, Old
High German) to the present time (Modern Greek, Italian, Spanish,
etc., down to Low and High German, with different dialects).
To carry out this plan Rapp was equipped with no small knowledge
of the earlier stages of these languages and a not contemptible
first-hand observation of living languages. He relates how from
his childhood he had a " morbidly sharpened ear for all acoustic
impressions " ; he had early observed the difference between
dialectal and educated speech and taken an interest in foreign
languages, such as French, Italian and English. He visited Denmark, and there made the acquaintance of and became the pupil
of Rask ; he often speaks of him and his works in terms of the
greatest admiration. After his return he took up the study of
Jacob Grimm ; but though he speaks always very warmly about
the other parts of Grimm's work, Grimm's phonology disappointed
him. " Grimm's theory of letters I devoured with a ravenous
appetite for all the new things I had to learn from it, but also with
heartburning on account of the equally numerous things that
warred against the whole of my previous research with regard to
the nature of speech sounds ; fascinated though I was by what
I read, it thus made me incredibly miserable." He set to his
great task with enthusiasm, led by the conviction that " the historical material gives here only one side of the truth, and that the
living language in all its branches that have never been committed
to writing forms the other and equally important side which is
still far from being satisfactorily investigated." It is easy to
understand that Rapp came into conflict with Grimm's *Buch-
stabenlehre*, that had been based exclusively on written forms,
and Rapp was not afraid of expressing his unorthodox views in
what he himself terms " a violent and arrogating tone." No
wonder, therefore, that his book fell into disgrace with the leaders
of linguistics in Germany, who noticed its errors and mistakes,
which were indeed numerous and conspicuous, rather than the new
and sane ideas it contained. Rapp's work is extrrordinarily little
known ; in Raumer's *Geschichte der germani*x*chen Philologie* and
similar works it is not even mentioned, and when I disinterred it

from undeserved oblivion in my *Fonetik* (1897, p. 35 ; cf. *Die neueren Sprachen*, vol. xiii, 1904) it was utterly unknown to the German phoneticians of my acquaintance. Yet not only are its phonetic observations [1] deserving of praise, but still more its whole plan, based as it is on a thorough comprehension of the mutual relations of sounds and writing, which led Rapp to use phonetic transcription throughout, even in connected specimens both of living and dead languages ; that this is really the only way in which it is possible to obtain a comprehensive and living understanding of the sound-system of any language (as well as to get a clear perception of the extent of one's own ignorance of it !) has not yet been generally recognized. The science of language would have made swifter and steadier progress if Grimm and his successors had been able to assimilate the main thoughts of Rapp.

III.—§ 3. J. H. Bredsdorff.

Another (and still earlier) work that was overlooked at the time was the little pamphlet *Om Aarsagerne til Sprogenes Forandringer* (1821) by the Dane J. H. Bredsdorff. Bopp and Grimm never really asked themselves the fundamental question, How is it that language changes : what are the driving forces that lead in course of time to such far-reaching differences as those we find between Sanskrit and Latin, or between Latin and French ? Now, this is exactly the question that Bredsdorff treats in his masterly pamphlet. Like Rapp, he was a very good phonetician; but in the pamphlet that concerns us here he speaks not only of phonetic but of other linguistic changes as well. These he refers to the following causes, which he illustrates with well-chosen examples : (1) Mishearing and misunderstanding ; (2) misrecollection ; (3) imperfection of organs ; (4) indolence : to this he inclines to refer nine-tenths of all those changes in the pronunciation of a language that are not due to foreign influences ; (5) tendency towards analogy : here he gives instances from the speech of children and explains by analogy such phenomena as the extension of *s* to all genitives, etc. ; (6) the desire to be distinct ; (7) the need of expressing new ideas. He recognizes that there are changes that cannot be brought under any of these explanations, e.g. the Gothonic sound shift (cf. above, p. 43 note), and he emphasizes the many ways in which foreign nations or foreign languages may influence a language. Bredsdorff's explanations may not always be correct ;

---

[1] For example, the correct appreciation of Scandinavian *o* sounds and especially the recognition of syllables without any vowel, for instance, in G. *mittel*, *schmeicheln*, E. *heaven*, *little*; this important truth was unnoticed by linguists till Sievers in 1876 called attention to it and Brugmann in 1877 used it in a famous article.

but what constitutes the deep originality of his little book is the
way in which linguistic changes are always regarded in terms of
human activity, chiefly of a psychological character. Here he was
head and shoulders above his contemporaries ; in fact, most of
Bredsdorff's ideas, such as the power of analogy, were the same
that sixty years later had to fight so hard to be recognized by
the leading linguists of that time.[1]

III.—§ 4. August Schleicher.

In Rapp, and even more in Bredsdorff, we get a whiff of the
scientific atmosphere of a much later time ; but most of the linguists
of the twenties and following decades (among whom A. F. Pott
deserves to be specially named) moved in essentially the same
grooves as Bopp and Grimm, and it will not be necessary here to
deal in detail with their work.

August Schleicher (1821–68) in many ways marks the cul-
mination of the first period of Comparative Linguistics, as well
as the transition to a new period with different aims and, partially
at any rate, a new method. His intimate knowledge of many
languages, his great power of combination, his clear-cut and always
lucid exposition—all this made him a natural leader, and made
his books for many years the standard handbooks of linguistic
science. Unlike Bopp and Grimm, he was exclusively a linguist,
or, as he called it himself, ' glottiker,' and never tired of claiming
for the science of linguistics (' glottik '), as opposed to philology,
the rank of a separate natural science. Schleicher specialized in
Slavonic and Lithuanian ; he studied the latter language in its
own home and took down a great many songs and tales from the
mouths of the peasants ; he was for some years a professor in the
University of Prague, and there acquired a conversational knowledge of Czech ; he spoke Russian, too, and thus in contradistinction to Bopp and Grimm had a first-hand knowledge of more
than one foreign language ; his interest in living speech is also
manifested in his specimens of the dialect of his native town,
Volkstümliches aus Sonneberg. When he was a child his father
very severely insisted on the constant and correct use of the educated language at home ; but the boy, perhaps all the more on
account of the paternal prohibition, was deeply attracted to the

---

[1] A young German linguist, to whom I sent the pamphlet early in 1886,
wrote to me : "Wenn man sich den spass machte und das ding übersetzte
mit der bemerkung, es sei vor vier jahren erschienen, wer würde einem
nicht trauen ? Merkwürdig, dass solche sachen so unbemerkt, ' dem kleinen
veilchen gleich,' dahinschwinden können." A short time afterwards the
pamphlet was reprinted with a short preface by Vilh. Thomsen (Copenhagen,
1886).

popular dialect he heard from his playfellows and to the fascinating folklore of the old townspeople, which he was later to take down and put into print. In the preface he says that the acquisition of foreign tongues is rendered considerably easier through the habit of speaking two dialects from childhood.

What makes Schleicher particularly important for the purposes of this volume is the fact that in a long series of publications he put forth not only details of his science, but original and comprehensive views on the fundamental questions of linguistic theory, and that these had great influence on the linguistic philosophy of the following decades. He was, perhaps, the most consistent as well as one of the clearest of linguistic thinkers, and his views therefore deserve to be examined in detail and with the greatest care.

Apart from languages, Schleicher was deeply interested both in philosophy and in natural science, especially botany. From these he fetched many of the weapons of his armoury, and they coloured the whole of his theory of language. In his student days at Tübingen he became an enthusiastic adherent of the philosophy of Hegel, and not even the Darwinian sympathies and views of which he became a champion towards the end of his career made him abandon the doctrines of his youth. As for science, he says that naturalists make us understand that in science nothing is of value except facts established through strictly objective observation and the conclusions based on such facts—this is a lesson that he thinks many of his colleagues would do well to take to heart. There can be no doubt that Schleicher in his practice followed a much more rigorous and sober method than his predecessors, and that his *Compendium* in that respect stands far above Bopp's *Grammar*. In his general reasonings on the nature of language, on the other hand, Schleicher did not always follow the strict principles of sober criticism, being, as we shall now see, too dependent on Hegelian philosophy, and also on certain dogmatic views that he had inherited from previous German linguists, from Schlegel downwards.

The Introductions to Schleicher's two first volumes are entirely Hegelian, though with a characteristic difference, for in the first he says that the changes to be seen in the realm of languages are decidedly historical and in no way resemble the changes that we may observe in nature, for " however manifold these may be, they never show anything but a circular course that repeats itself continually " (Hegel), while in language, as in everything mental, we may see new things that have never existed before. One generation of animals or plants is like another; the skill of animals has no history, as human art has; language is specifically human and mental: its development is therefore analogous to history, for in both we see a continual progress to new phases. In Schleicher's second volume, however, this view is expressly rejected in its main part, because Schleicher now wants to emphasize the natural character of language : it is true, he now says, that language shows a 'werden' which may be termed history in the wider sense of this word, but which is found in its purest form in nature ; for instance, in the growing of a plant. Language belongs to the natural sphere, not to the sphere of free mental activity, and this must be our starting-point if we would discover the method of linguistic science (ii. 21).

It would, of course, be possible to say that the method of linguistic science is that of natural science, and yet to maintain that the object of linguistics is different from that of natural science, but Schleicher more and more tends to identify the two, and when he was attacked for saying, in his pamphlet on the Darwinian theory, that languages were material things, real natural objects, he wrote in defence *Ueber die bedeutung der sprache für die naturgeschichte des menschen*, which is highly characteristic as the culminating point of the materialistic way of looking at languages. The activity, he says, of any organ, e.g. one of the organs of digestion, or the brain or muscles, is dependent on the constitution of that organ. The different ways in which different species, nay even different individuals, walk are evidently conditioned by the structure of the limbs ; the activity or function of the organ is, as it were, nothing but an aspect of the organ itself, even if it is not always possible by means of the knife or microscope of the scientist to demonstrate the material cause of the phenomenon. What is true of the manner of walking is true of language as well ; for language is nothing but the result, perceptible through the ear, of the action of a complex of material substances in the structure of the brain and of the organs of speech, with their nerves, bones, muscles, etc. Anatomists, however, have not yet been able to demonstrate differences in the structures of these organs corresponding to differences of nationality—to discriminate, that is, the organs of a Frenchman (*quâ* Frenchman) from those of a German (*quâ* German). Accordingly, as the chemist can only arrive at the elements which compose the sun by examining the light which it emits, while the source of that light remains inaccessible to him, so must we be content to study the nature of languages, not in their material antecedents but in their audible manifestations. It makes no great difference, however, for " the two things stand to each other as cause and effect, as substance and phenomenon : a philosopher [i.e. a Hegelian] would say that they are identical."

Now I, for one, fail to understand how this can be what Schleicher believes it to be, " a refutation of the objection that language is nothing but a consequence of the activity of these organs." The sun exists independently of the human observer ; but there could be no such thing as language if there was not besides the speaker a listener who might become a speaker in his turn. Schleicher speaks continually in his pamphlet as if structural differences in the brain and organs of speech were the real language, and as if it were only for want of an adequate method of examining this hidden structure that we had to content ourselves with studying language in its outward manifestation as audible speech. But this is certainly on the face of it preposterous, and scarcely needs any serious refutation. If the proof of the pudding is in the eating, the proof of a language must be in the hearing and under-standing ; but in order to be heard words must first be spoken, and in these two activities (that of producing and that of per-ceiving sounds) the real essence of language must consist, and these two activities are the primary (or why not the exclusive ?) object of the science of language.

Schleicher goes on to meet another objection that may be made to his view of the ' substantiality of language,' namely, that drawn from the power of learning other languages. Schleicher doubts the possibility of learning another language to perfection ; he would admit this only in the case of a man who exchanged his mother-tongue for another in his earliest youth ; " but then he becomes by that very fact a different being from what he was : brain and organs of speech develop in another direction." If Mr. So-and-So is said to speak and write German, English and French equally well, Schleicher first inclines to doubt the fact ; and then, granting that the same individual may " be at the same time a German, a Frenchman and an Englishman," he asks us to remember that all these three languages belong to the same family and may, from a broader point of view, be termed species of the same language ; but he denies the possibility of anyone's being equally at home in Chinese and German, or in Arabic and Hottentot, etc., because these languages are totally different in their innermost essence. (But what of bilingual children in Finland, speaking Swedish and Finnish, or in Greenland, speaking Danish and Eskimo, or in Java, speaking Dutch and Malay ?) Schleicher has to admit that our organs are to some extent flexible and capable of acquiring activities that they had not at first ; but one definite function is and remains nevertheless the only natural one, and thus " the possibility of a man's acquiring foreign languages more or less perfectly is no objection to our seeing the material basis of lan-guage in the structure of the brain and organs of speech."

Even if we admit that Schleicher is so far right that in nearly all (or all ?) cases of bilingualism one language comes more naturally than the other, he certainly exaggerates the difference, which is always one of degree ; and at any rate his final conclusion is wrong, for we might with the same amount of justice say that a man who has first learned to play the piano has acquired the structure of brain and fingers peculiar to a pianist, and that it is then unnatural for him also to learn to play the violin, because that would imply a different structure of these organs. In all these cases we have to do with a definite proficiency or skill, which can only be obtained by constant practice, though of course one man may be better predisposed by nature for it than another ; but then it is also the fact that people who speak no foreign language attain to very different degrees of proficiency in the use of their mother-tongue. It cannot be said too emphatically that we have here a fundamental question, and that Schleicher's view can never lead to a true conception of what language is, or to a real insight into its changes and historical development.

Schleicher goes on to say that the classification of mankind into races should not be based on the formation of the skull or on the character of the hair, or any such external criteria, as they are by no means constant, but rather on language, because this is a thoroughly constant criterion. This alone would give a perfectly natural system, one, for instance, in which all Turks would be classed together, while otherwise the Osmanli Turk belongs to the ' Caucasian ' race and the so-called Tataric Turks to the ' Mongolian ' race ; on the other hand, the Magyar and the Basque are not physically to be distinguished from the Indo-European, though their languages are widely dissimilar. According to Schleicher, therefore, the natural system of languages is also the natural system of mankind, for language is closely connected with the whole higher life of men, which is therefore taken into consideration in and with their language. In this book I am not concerned with the ethnographical division of mankind into races, and I therefore must content myself with saying that the very examples adduced by Schleicher seem to me to militate against his theory that a division of mankind based on language is the natural one : are we to reckon the Basque's son, who speaks nothing but French (or Spanish) as belonging to a different race from his father ? And does not Schleicher contradict himself when on p. 16 he writes that language is " ein völlig constantes merkmal," and p. 20 that it is " in fortwährender veränderung begriffen " ? So far as I see, Schleicher never expressly says that he thinks that the physical structure conditioning the structure of a man's language is hereditary, though some of his expressions point that way, and that may be what he means by the expression ' constant.' In other places (Darw. 25, Bed. 24) he allows external conditions of life to exercise some influence on the character of a language, as when languages of neighbouring peoples are similar (Aryans and Semites, for example, are the only nations possessing flexional languages). On such points, however, he gives only a few hints and suggestions.

III.—§ 5. Classification of Languages.

In the question of the classification of languages Schleicher introduces a deductive element from his strong preoccupation with Hegelian ideas. Hegel everywhere moves in trilogies ; Schleicher therefore must have three classes, and consequently has to tack together two of Pott's four classes (agglutinating and incorporating) ; then he is able philosophically to deduce the tripartition. For language consists in *meaning* (bedeutung ; matter, contents, root) and *relation* (beziehung ; form), tertium non datur. As it would be a sheer impossibility for a language to express form only, we obtain three classes :

I. Here meaning is the only thing indicated by sound ; relation is merely suggested by word-position : isolating languages.

II. Both meaning and relation are expressed by sound, but the formal elements are visibly tacked on to the root, which is itself invariable : agglutinating languages.

III. The elements of meaning and of relation are fused together or absorbed into a higher unity, the root being susceptible of inward modification as well as of affixes to denote form : flexional languages.

Schleicher employs quasi-mathematical formulas to illustrate these three classes : if we denote a root by R, a prefix by p and a suffix by s, and finally use a raised x to denote an inner modification, we see that in the isolated languages we have nothing but R (a sentence may be represented by $R\,R\,R\,R\ldots$), a word in the second class has the formula $R\,s$ or $p\,R$ or $p\,R\,s$, but in the third class we may have $p\,R^x\,s$ (or $R^x\,s$).

Now, according to Schleicher the three classes of languages are not only found simultaneously in the tongues of our own day, but they represent three stages of linguistic development ; " to the *nebeneinander* of the system corresponds the *nacheinander* of history." Beyond the flexional stage no language can attain ; the symbolic denotation of relation by flexion is the highest accomplishment of language ; speech has here effectually realized its object, which is to give a faithful phonetic image of thought. But before a language can become flexional it must have passed through an isolating and an agglutinating period. Is this theory borne out by historical facts ? Can we trace back any of the existing flexional languages to agglutination and isolation ? Schleicher himself answers this question in the negative : the earliest Latin was of as good a flexional type as are the modern Romanic languages. This would seem a sort of contradiction in terms ; but the orthodox Hegelian is ready with an answer to any objection ; he has the word of his master that History cannot begin till the human spirit becomes "conscious of its own freedom," and this consciousness is only possible after the complete development of language. The formation of Language and History are accordingly successive stages of human activity. Moreover, as history and historiography, i.e. literature, come into existence simultaneously, Schleicher is enabled to express the same idea in a way that "is only seemingly paradoxical," namely, that the development of language is brought to a conclusion as soon as literature makes its appearance ; this is a crisis after which language remains fixed ; language has now become a means, instead of being the aim, of intellectual activity. We never meet with any language that is developing or that has become more perfect ; in historical times all languages move only downhill ; linguistic history means decay of languages as such, subjugated as they are through the gradual evolution of the mind to greater freedom.

The reader of the above survey of previous classifications will easily see that in the matter itself Schleicher adds very little of his own. Even the expressions, which are here given throughout in Schleicher's own words, are in some cases recognizable as identical with, or closely similar to, those of earlier scholars.

He made one coherent system out of ideas of classification and development already found in others. What is new is the philosophical substructure of Hegelian origin, and there can be no doubt that Schleicher imagined that by this addition he contributed very much towards giving stability and durability to the whole system. And yet this proved to be the least stable and durable part of the structure, and as a matter of fact the Hegelian reasoning is not repeated by a single one of those who give their adherence to the classification. Nor can it be said to carry conviction, and undoubtedly it has seemed to most linguists at the same time too rigid and too unreal to have any importance.

But apart from the philosophical argument the classification proved very successful in the particular shape it had found in Schleicher. Its adoption into two such widely read works as Max Müller's and Whitney's Lectures on the Science of Language contributed very much. to the popularity of the system, though the former's attempt at ascribing to the tripartition a sociological importance by saying that juxtaposition (isolation) is characteristic of the 'family stage,' agglutination of 'the nomadic stage' and amalgamation (flexion) of the 'political stage' of human society was hardly taken seriously by anybody.

The chief reasons for the popularity of this classification are not far to seek. It is easy of handling and appeals to the natural fondness for clear-cut formulas through its specious appearance of regularity and rationality. Besides, it flatters widespread prejudices in so far as it places the two groups of languages highest that are spoken by those nations which have culturally and religiously exercised the deepest influence on the civilization of the world, Aryans and Semites. Therefore also Pott's view, according to which the incorporating or 'polysynthetic' American languages possess the same characteristics that distinguish flexion as against agglutination, only in a still higher degree, is generally tacitly discarded, for obviously it would not do to place some languages of American Indians higher than Sanskrit or Greek. But when these are looked upon as the very flower of linguistic development it is quite natural to regard the modern languages of Western Europe as degenerate corruptions of the ancient more highly flexional languages ; this is in perfect keeping with the prevalent admiration for classical antiquity and with the belief in a far past golden age. Arguments such as these may not have been consciously in the minds of the framers of the ordinary classification, but there can be no doubt that they have been unconsciously working in favour of the system, though very little thought seems to be required to show the fallacy of the assumption that high civilization has any intrinsic and necessary connexion with the *grammatical* construction of the language spoken by the race or nation concerned. No language of modern Europe presents the flexional type in a purer shape than Lithuanian, where we find preserved nearly the same grammatical system as in old Sanskrit, yet no one would assert that the culture of Lithuanian peasants is higher than that of Shakespeare, whose language has lost an enormous amount of the old flexions. Culture and language must be appraised separately, each on its own merits and independently of the other.

From a purely linguistic point of view there are many objections to the usual classification, and it will be well here to bring them together, though this will mean an interruption of the historical survey which is the main object of these chapters.

First let us look upon the tripartition as purporting a comprehensive classification of languages as existing side by side without any regard to historic development (the *nebeneinander*

of Schleicher). Here it does not seem to be an ideal manner of
classifying a great many objects to establish three classes of such
different dimensions that the first comprises only Chinese and
some other related languages of the Far East, and the third only
two families of languages, while the second includes hundreds
of unrelated languages of the most heterogeneous character.
It seems certain that the languages of Class I represent one definite
type of linguistic structure, and it may be that Aryan and Semitic
should be classed together on account of the similarity of their
structure, though this is by no means quite certain and has been
denied (by Bopp, and in recent times by Porzezinski); but what
is indubitable is that the ' agglutinating ' class is made to comprehend languages of the most diverse type, even if we follow Pott
and exclude from this class all incorporating languages.   Finnish
is always mentioned as a typically agglutinative language, yet
there we meet with such declensional forms as nominative *vesi*
' water,' *toinen* ' second,' partitive *vettä*, *toista*, genitive *veden*,
toisen, and such verbal forms as *sido-n* ' I bind,' *sido-t* ' thou
bindest,' *sito-o* ' he binds,' and the three corresponding persons
in the plural, *sido-mme*, *sido-tte*, *sito-vat*.   Here we are far from
having one unchangeable root to which endings have been glued,
for the root itself undergoes changes before the endings.   In
Kiyombe (Congo) the perfect of verbs is in many cases formed
by means of a vowel change that is a complete parallel to the
apophony in English *drink*, *drank*, thus *vanga* ' do,' perfect *venge*,
twala ' bring,' perfect *twele* or *twede*, etc. (*Anthropos*, ii. p. 761).
Examples like these show that flexion, in whatever way we may
define this term, is not the prerogative of the Aryans and Semites,
but may be found in other nations as well.   ' Agglutination ' is
either too vague a term to be used in classification, or else, if it
is taken strictly according to the usual definition, it is too definite
to comprise many of the languages which are ordinarily reckoned
to belong to the second class.

It will be seen, also, that those writers who aim at giving descriptions of a variety of human tongues, or of them all, do not content
themselves with the usual three classes, but have a greater number.
This began with Steinthal, who in various works tried to classify
languages partly from geographical, partly from structural points
of view, without, however, arriving at any definite or consistent
system. Friedrich Müller, in his great *Grundriss der Sprachwissenschaft*, really gives up the psychological or structural division of
languages, distributing the more than hundred different languages
that he describes among twelve races of mankind, characterized
chiefly by external criteria that have nothing to do with language.
Misteli establishes six main types : I. Incorporating. II. Root-

isolating. III. Stem-isolating. IV. Affixing (Anreihende). V. Agglutinating. VI. Flexional. These he also distributes so as to form four classes : (1) languages with sentence-words : I ; (2) languages with no words : II, III and IV ; (3) languages with apparent words : V ; and (4) languages with real words : VI. But the latter division had better be left alone ; it turns on the intricate question "What constitutes a word ?" and ultimately depends on the usual depreciation of 'inferior races' and corresponding exaltation of our own race, which is alone reputed capable of possessing 'real words.' I do not see why we should not recognize that the vocables of Greenlandic, Malay, Kafir or Finnish are just as 'real' words as any in Hebrew or Latin.

Our final result, then, is that the tripartition is insufficient and inadequate to serve as a comprehensive classification of languages actually existing. Nor shall we wonder at this if we see the way in which the theory began historically in an *obiter dictum* of Fr. v. Schlegel at a time when the inner structure of only a few languages had been properly studied, and if we consider the lack of clearness and definiteness inherent in such notions as agglutination and flexion, which are nevertheless made the corner-stones of the whole system. We therefore must go back to the wise saying of Humboldt quoted on p. 59, that the structural diversities of languages are too great for us to classify them comprehensively.

In a subsequent part of this work I shall deal with the tripartition as representing three successive stages in the development of such languages as our own (the *nacheinander* of Schleicher), and try to show that Schleicher's view is not borne out by the facts of linguistic history, which give us a totally different picture of development.

From both points of view, then, I think that the classification here considered deserves to be shelved among the hasty generalizations in which the history of every branch of science is unfortunately so rich.

III.—§ 6. Reconstruction.

Probably Schleicher's most original and important contribution to linguistics was his reconstruction of the Proto-Aryan language, *die indogermanische ursprache.* The possibility of inferentially constructing this parent language, which to Sanskrit, Greek, Latin, Gothic, etc., was what Latin was to Italian, Spanish, French, etc., was early in his thoughts (see quotations illustrating the gradual growth of the idea in Oertel, p. 39 f.), but it was not till the first edition of his *Compendium* that he carried it out in detail, giving there for each separate chapter (vowels, consonants, roots, stem-formation. declension, conjugation) first the Proto-Aryan forms and then those actually found in the different languages, from which the former were inferred. This arrangement has the advantage that the reader everywhere sees the historical evolution in the natural order, beginning with the oldest and then proceeding to the later stages, just as the Romanic scholar begins with Latin and then takes in successive stages Old French, Modern French, etc. But in the case of Proto-Aryan this procedure is apt to deceive the student and make him take these primitive forms as something certain, whose existence reposes on just as good evidence as the forms found in Sanskrit literature or in German or English as spoken in our own days. When he finds some forms given first and used to *explain* some others, there is some danger of his forgetting that the forms given first have a quite different status to the others, and that their only *raison d'être* is the desire of a modern linguist to explain existing forms in related languages which present certain similarities as originating from a common original form, which he does not find in his texts and has, therefore, to reconstruct. But apart from this there can be no doubt that the reconstruction of older forms (and the ingenious device, due to Schleicher, of denoting such forms by means of a preposed asterisk to distinguish them from forms actually found) has been in many ways beneficial to historical grammar. Only it may be questioned whether Schleicher did not go too far when he wished to base the whole grammar of all the Aryan languages on such reconstructions, instead of using them now and then to explain single facts.

Schleicher even ventured (and in this he seems to have had no follower) to construct an entire little fable in primitive Aryan: see " Eine fabel in indogermanischer ursprache," *Beiträge zur vergl. sprachforschung*, 5. 206 (1868). In the introductory remarks he complains of the difficulty of such attempts, chiefly because of the almost complete lack of particles capable of being inferred from the existing languages, but he seems to have entertained no doubt about the phonetic and grammatical forms of the words he employed. As the fable is not now commonly known, I give it here, with Schleicher's translation, as a document of this period of comparative linguistics.

AVIS AKVASAS KA

Avis, jasmin varna na ā ast, dadarka akvams, tam, vāgham garum vaghantam, tam, bhāram magham, tam, manum āku bharantam. Avis akvabhjams ā vavakat : kard aghnutai mai vidanti manum akvams agantam.

Akvāsas ā vavakant: krudhi avai, kard aghnutai vividvant-
svas: manus patis varnām avisāms karnanti svabhjam gharmam
vastram avibhjams ka varnā na asti.

Tat kukruvants avis agram ā bhugat.

[DAS] SCHAF UND [DIE] ROSSE

[Ein] schaf, [auf] welchem wolle nicht war (ein geschorenes
schaf) sah rosse, das [einen] schweren wagen fahrend, das [eine]
grosse last, das [einen] menschen schnell tragend. [Das] schaf
sprach [zu den] rossen: [Das] herz wird beengt [in] mir (es thut
mir herzlich leid), sehend [den] menschen [die] rosse treibend.

[Die] rosse sprachen: Höre schaf, [das] herz wird beengt [in
den] gesehend-habenden (es thut uns herzlich leid, da wir wissen):
[der] mensch, [der] herr macht [die] wolle [der] schafe [zu einem]
warmen kleide [für] sich und [den] schafen ist nicht wolle (die
schafe aber haben keine wolle mehr, sie werden geschoren; es
geht ihnen noch schlechter als den rossen).

Dies gehört habend bog (entwich) [das] schaf [auf das] feld
(es machte sich aus dem staube).

The question here naturally arises: Is it possible in the way
initiated by Schleicher to reconstruct extinct linguistic stages,
and what degree of probability can be attached to the forms thus
created by linguists? The answer certainly must be that in some
instances the reconstruction may have a very strong degree of
probability, namely, if the data on which it is based are unambiguous and the form to be reconstructed is not far removed
from that or those actually found; but that otherwise any reconstruction becomes doubtful, and naturally the more so according
to the extent of the reconstruction (as when a whole text is constructed) and to the distance in time that intervenes between the
known and the unknown stage. If we look at the genitives of
Lat. *genus* and Gr. *génos*, which are found as *generis* and *génous*,
it is easy to see that both presuppose a form with *s* between two
vowels, as we see a great many intervocalic *s*'s becoming *r* in Latin
and disappearing in Greek; but when Schleicher gives as the
prototype of both (and of corresponding forms in the other languages) Aryan *ganasas*, he oversteps the limits of the permissible
in so far as he ascribes to the vowels definite sounds not really
warranted by the known forms. If we knew the modern Scandinavian languages and English only, we should not hesitate to
give to the Proto-Gothonic genitive of the word for ' mother '
the ending -*s*, cf. Dan. *moders*, E. *mother's*; but G. *der mutter*
suffices to show that the conclusion is not safe, and as a matter
of fact, both in Old Norse and in Old English the genitive of this

word is without an *s*.   An analogous case is presented when
Schleicher   reconstructs the nom. of the word for 'father' as
patars, because he presupposes *-s* as the invariable sign of every
nom. sg. masc., although in this particular word not a single one
of the old languages has *-s* in the nominative.   All Schleicher's
reconstructions are based on the assumption that Primitive Aryan
had a very simple structure, only few consonant and fewer vowel
sounds, and great regularity in morphology ; but, as we shall see,
this assumption is completely gratuitous and was exploded only
a few years after his death.   Gabelentz (Spr 182), therefore, was
right when he said, with a certain irony, that the Aryan *ursprache*
had changed beyond recognition in the short time between
Schleicher and Brugmann.   The moral to be drawn from all
this seems to be that hypothetical and starred forms should be
used sparingly and with the extremest caution.

   With regard to inferential forms denoted by a star, the following note may not be out of place here.   Their purely theoretical
character is not always realized.   An example will illustrate what
I mean.   If etymological dictionaries give as the origin of F.
ménage (OF. *maisnage*) a Latin form *mansionaticum*, the etymology
may be correct although such a Latin word may never at any
time have been uttered.   The word was framed at some date,
no one knows exactly when, from the word which at various
times had the forms (acc.) *mansionem*, *masione*, *maison*, by
means of the ending which at first had the form *-aticum* (as
in *viaticum*), and finally (through several intermediate stages)
became *-age*; but at what stage of each the two elements met to
make the word which eventually became *ménage*, no one can tell,
so that the only thing really asserted is that *if* the word had been
formed at a very early date (which is far from probable) it would
have been *mansionaticum*.   It would, therefore, perhaps be more
correct to say that the word is from *mansione* + *-aticum*.

III.—§ 7. Curtius, Madvig, and Specialists.

   Second only to Schleicher among the linguists of those days
was Georg Curtius (1820–85), at one time his colleague in the
University of Prague.   Curtius's special study was Greek, and his
books on the Greek verb and on Greek etymology cleared up a
great many doubtful points ; he also contributed very much to
bridge the gulf between classical philology and Aryan linguistics.
His views on general questions were embodied in the book *Zur
Chronologie der indogermanischen Sprachforschung* (1873).   While
Schleicher died when his fame was at its highest and his theories
were seemingly victorious in all the leading circles, Curtius had

the misfortune to see a generation of younger men, including some of his own best disciples, such as Brugmann, advance theories that seemed to him to be in conflict with the most essential principles of his cherished science ; and though he himself, like Schleicher, had always been in favour of a stricter observance of sound-laws than his predecessors, his last book was a polemic against those younger scholars who carried the same point to the excess of admitting no exceptions at all, who believed in innumerable analogical formations even in the old languages, and whose reconstructions of primitive forms appeared to the old man as deprived of that classical beauty of the *ursprache* which was represented in his own and Schleicher's works (*Zur Kritik der neuesten Sprachforschung*, 1885). But this is anticipating.

If Curtius was a comparativist with a sound knowledge of classical philology, Johan Nikolai Madvig was pre-eminently a classical philologist who took a great interest in general linguistics and brought his critical acumen and sober common sense to bear on many of the problems that exercised the minds of his contemporaries. He was opposed to everything of a vague and mystical nature in the current theories of language and disliked the tendency of some scholars to find deep-lying mysterious powers at the root of linguistic phenomena. But he probably went too far in his rationalism, for example, when he entirely denied the existence of the sound-symbolism on which Humboldt had expatiated. He laid much stress on the identity of the linguistic faculty in all ages : the first speakers had no more intention than people to-day of creating anything systematic or that would be good for all times and all occasions—they could have no other object in view than that of making themselves understood at the moment ; hence the want of system which we find everywhere in languages : a different number of cases in singular and plural, different endings, etc. Madvig did not escape some inconsistencies, as when he himself would explain the use of the soft vowel *a* to denote the feminine gender by a kind of sound-symbolism, or when he thought it possible to determine in what order the different grammatical ideas presented themselves to primitive man (tense relation first in the verb, number before case in the noun). He attached too little value to phonological and etymological research, but on the whole his views were sounder than many which were set forth on the same subjects at the time ; his papers, however, were very little known, partly because they were written in Danish, partly because his style was extremely heavy and difficult, and when he finally brought out his *Kleine philologische schriften* in German (1875), he expressed his regret in the preface at finding that many of the theories he had put forward years before in Danish had in the meantime been independently arrived at by Whitney, who had had the advantage of expressing them in a world-language.

One of the most important features of the period with which we are here dealing is the development of a number of special branches of historical linguistics on a comparative basis. Curtius's work on Greek might be cited as one example ; in the same way there were specialists in Sanskrit (Westergaard and Benfey among others), in Slavonic (Miklosich and Schleicher), in Keltic (Zeuss), etc. Grimm had numerous followers in the Gothonic or Germanic field, while in Romanic philology there was an active and flourishing school, headed by Friedrich Diez, whose *Grammatik der romanischen Sprachen* and *Etymologisches Wörterbuch der romanischen Sprachen* were perhaps the best introduction to the methodical study of linguistics that anyone could desire ; the writer of these lines looks back with the greatest gratitude to that period of his youth when he had the good fortune to make the acquaintance of these truly classical works. Everything was so well arranged, so carefully thought out and so lucidly explained, that one had everywhere the pleasant feeling that one was treading on firm ground, the more so as the basis of the whole was not an artificially constructed nebulous *ursprache*, but the familiar forms and words of an historical language. Here one witnessed the gradual differentiation of Latin into seven or eight distinct languages, whose development it was possible to follow century by century in well-authenticated texts. The picture thus displayed before one's eyes of actual linguistic growth in all domains—sounds, forms, word-formation, syntax—and (a very important corollary) of the interdependence of these domains, could not but leave a very strong impression—not merely enthusiasm for what had been achieved here, but also a salutary skepticism of theories in other fields which had not a similarly solid basis.

III.—§ 8. Max Müller and Whitney.

Working, as we have seen, in many fields, linguists had now brought to light a shoal of interesting facts affecting a great many languages and had put forth valuable theories to explain these facts ; but most of their work remained difficult of access except to the specialist, and very little was done by the experts to impart to educated people in general those results of the new science which might be enjoyed without deeper study. But in 1861 Max Müller gave the first series of those *Lectures on the Science of Language* which, in numerous editions, did more than anything else to popularize linguistics and served to initiate a great many students into our science. In many ways these lectures were excellently adapted for this purpose, for the author had a certain knack of selecting interesting illustrations and of presenting his subject in a way that tended to create the same enthusiasm for it that he felt himself. But his arguments do not bear a close inspection. Too often, after stating a problem, he is found to fly off at a tangent and to forget what he has set out to prove for the sake of an interesting etymology or a clever paradox. He gives an uncritical acceptance to many of Schleicher's leading ideas ; thus, the science of linguistics is to him a physical science and has nothing to do with philology, which is an historical science. If, however, we look at the book itself, we shall find that everything that he counts on to secure the interest of his reader, everything that made his lectures so popular, is really non-naturalistic : all those brilliant exposés of word-history are really like historical anecdotes in a book on social evolution ; they may have some bearing on the fundamental problems, but these are rarely or never treated as real problems of natural science. Nor does he, when taken to task, maintain his view very seriously, but partly retracts it and half-heartedly ensconces himself behind the dictum that everything depends on the definition you give of " physical science " (see especially Ch 234, 442, 497)—thus calling forth Whitney's retort that " the implication here is that our author has a right at his own good pleasure to lay down such a definition of a physical science as should make the name properly applicable to the study of this particular one among the products of human capacities. . . . So he may prove that a whale is a fish, if you only allow him to define what a fish is " (M 23 f.).

Though Schleicher and Max Müller in their own day had few followers in defining linguistics as a natural or physical science— the opposite view was taken, for instance, by Curtius (K 154), Madvig and Whitney—there can be no doubt that the naturalistic point of view practically, though perhaps chiefly unconsciously, had wide-reaching effects on the history of linguistic science. It was intimately connected with the problems chiefly investigated and with the way in which they were treated. From Grimm through Pott to Schleicher and his contemporaries we see a growing interest in phonological comparisons ; more and more " sound-laws " were discovered, and those found were more and more rigorously applied, with the result that etymological investigation was attended with a degree of exactness of which former generations had no idea. But as these phonological studies were not, as a rule, based on a real, penetrating insight into the nature of speech-sounds, the work of the etymologist tended more and more to be purely mechanical, and the science of language was to a great extent deprived of those elements which are more intimately connected with the human 'soul.' Isolated vowels and consonants were compared, isolated flexional forms and isolated words were treated more and more in detail and explained by other isolated forms and words in other languages, all of them being like dead leaves shaken off a tree rather than parts of a living and moving whole. The speaking individual and the speaking community were too much lost sight of. Too often comparativists gained a considerable acquaintance with the sound-laws and the grammatical forms of various languages without knowing much about those languages themselves, or at any rate without possessing any degree of familiarity with them. Schleicher was not blind to the danger of this. A short time before his death he brought out an *Indogermanische Chrestomathie* (Weimar, 1869), and in the preface he justifies his book by saying that "it is of great value, besides learning the grammar, to be acquainted, however slightly, with the languages themselves. For a comparative grammar of related languages lays stress on what is common to a language and its sisters ; consequently, the languages may appear more alike than they are in reality, and their idiosyncrasies may be thrown into the shade. Linguistic specimens form, therefore, an indispensable supplement to comparative grammar." Other and even more weighty reasons might have been adduced, for grammar is after all only one side of a language, and it is certainly the best plan, if one wants to understand and appreciate the position of any language, to start with some connected texts of tolerable length, and only afterwards to see how its forms are related to and may be explained by those of other languages.

Though the mechanical school of linguists, with whom historical and comparative phonology was more and more an end in itself, prevailed to a great extent, the trend of a few linguists was different. Among these one must especially mention Heymann Steinthal, who drew his inspiration from Humboldt and devoted numerous works to the psychology of language. Unfortunately, Steinthal was greatly inferior to Schleicher in clearness and consistency of thought : "When I read a work of Steinthal's, and even many parts of Humboldt, I feel as if walking through shifting clouds," Max Müller remarks, with good reason, in a letter (*Life*, i. 256). This obscurity, in connexion with the remoteness of Steinthal's studies, which ranged from Chinese to the language of the Mande negroes, but paid little regard to European languages, prevented him from exerting any powerful influence on the linguistic thought of his generation, except perhaps through his emphatic assertion of the truth that language can only be understood and explained by means of psychology : his explanation of syntactic attraction paved the way for much in Paul's *Prinzipien*.

The leading exponent of general linguistics after the death of Schleicher was the American William Dwight Whitney, whose books, *Language and the Study of Language* (first ed. 1867) and its replica, *The Life and Growth of Language* (1875), were translated into several languages and were hardly less popular than those of his antagonist, Max Müller. Whitney's style is less brilliant than Max Müller's, and he scorns the cheap triumphs which the latter gains by the multiplication of interesting illustrations; he never wearies of running down Müller's paradoxes and inconsistencies,[1] from which he himself was spared by his greater general solidity and sobriety of thought. The chief point of divergence between them was, as already indicated, that Whitney looked upon language as a human institution that has grown slowly out of the necessity for mutual understanding; he was opposed to all kinds of mysticism, and words to him were conventional signs—not, of course, that he held that there ever was a gathering of people that settled the meaning of each word, but in the sense of " resting on a mutual understanding or a community of habit," no matter how brought about. But in spite of all differences between the two they are in many respects alike, when viewed from the coign of vantage of the twentieth century : both give expression to the best that had been attained by fifty or sixty years of painstaking activity to elucidate the mysteries of speech, and especially of Aryan words and forms, and neither of them was deeply original enough to see through many of the fallacies of the young science. Consequently, their views on the structure of Proto-Aryan, on roots and their rôle, on the building-up and decay of the form-system, are essentially the same as those of their contemporaries, and many of their theories have now crumbled away, including much of what they probably thought firmly rooted for all time.

[1] In numerous papers in *North Am. Review* and elsewhere, and finally in the pamphlet *Max Müller and the Science of Language, a Criticism* (New York, 1892). Müller's reply to the earlier attacks is found in *Chips from a German Workshop*, vol. iv.

CHAPTER IV

END OF NINETEENTH CENTURY

§ 1. Achievements about 1870. § 2. New Discoveries. § 3. Phonetic Laws and Analogy. § 4. General Tendencies.

IV.—§ 1. Achievements about 1870.

IN works of this period one frequently meets with expressions of pride and joy in the wonderful results that had been achieved in comparative linguistics in the course of a few decades. Thus Max Müller writes : "All this becomes clear and intelligible by the light of Comparative Grammar ; anomalies vanish, exceptions prove the rule, and we perceive more plainly every day how in language, as elsewhere, the conflict between the freedom claimed by each individual and the resistance offered by the community at large establishes in the end a reign of law most wonderful, yet perfectly rational and intelligible"; and again : "There is nothing accidental, nothing irregular, nothing without a purpose and meaning in any part of Greek or Latin grammar. No one who has once discovered this hidden life of language, no one who has once found out that what seemed to be merely anomalous and whimsical in language is but, as it were, a petrification of thought, of deep, curious, poetical, philosophical thought, will ever rest again till he has descended as far as he can descend into the ancient shafts of human speech," etc. (Ch 41 f.). Whitney says : "The difference between the old haphazard style of etymologizing and the modern scientific method lies in this : that the latter, while allowing everything to be theoretically possible, accepts nothing as actual which is not proved by sufficient evidence ; it brings to bear upon each individual case a wide circle of related facts ; it imposes upon the student the necessity of extended comparison and cautious deduction ; it makes him careful to inform himself as thoroughly as circumstances allow respecting the history of every word he deals with " (L 386). And Benfey, in his *Geschichte der Sprachwissenschaft* (1869, see pp. 562 f. and 596), arrives at the conclusion that the investigation of Aryan languages has already attained a very great degree of certainty, and that the reconstruction of Primitive Aryan, both in grammar and vocabulary, must be considered as in the main settled in such a way that only some details are still doubtful ; thus, it is certain that the first person singular ended in -*mi*, and that this is a phonetic reduction of the pronoun *ma*, and that the word for ' horse ' was *akva*. This feeling of pride is certainly in a great measure justified if we compare the achievements of linguistic science at that date with the etymologies of the eighteenth century ; it must also be acknowledged that 90 per cent. of the etymologies in the best-known Aryan languages which must be recognized as established beyond any reasonable doubt had already been discovered before 1870, while later investigations have only added a small number that may be considered firmly established, together with a great many more or less doubtful collocations. But, on the other hand, in the light of later research, we can now see that much of what was then considered firm as a rock did not deserve the implicit trust then placed in it.

IV.—§ 2. New Discoveries.

This is true in the first place with regard to the phonetic structure ascribed to Proto-Aryan. A series of brilliant discoveries made about the year 1880 profoundly modified the views of scholars about the consonantal and still more about the vocalic system of our family of languages. This is particularly true of the so-called palatal law.[1] So long as it was taken for granted that Sanskrit had in all essential points preserved the ancient sound system, while Greek and the other languages represented younger stages, no one could explain why Sanskrit in some cases had the palatals *c* and *j* (sounds approximately like the initial sounds of E. *chicken* and *joy*) where the other languages have the velar sounds *k* and *g*. It was now recognized that so far from the distribution of the two classes of sounds in Sanskrit being arbitrary, it followed strict rules,

---

[1] Who was the discoverer of the palatal law ? This has been hotly discussed, and as the law was in so far anticipated by other discoveries of the 'seventies as to be " in the air," it is perhaps futile to try to fix the paternity on any single man. However, it seems now perfectly clear that Vilhelm Thomsen was the first to mention it in his lectures (1875), but unfortunately the full and able paper in which he intended to lay it before the world was delayed for a couple of years and then kept in his drawers when he heard that Johannes Schmidt was preparing a paper on the same subject : it was printed in 1920 in the second volume of his *Samlede Afhandlinger* (from the original manuscript). Esaias Tegnér had found the law independently and had printed five sheets of a book *De ariska språkens palataler*, which he withdrew when he found that Collitz and de Saussure had expressed similar views. Karl Verner, too, had independently arrived at the same results ; see his *Afhandlinger og Breve*, 109 ff., 305.

though these were not to be seen from Sanskrit itself. Where
Sanskrit *a* following the consonant corresponded to Greek or
Latin *o*, Sanskrit had velar *k* or *g*; where, on the other hand,
it corresponded to Greek or Latin *e*, Sanskrit had palatal *c* or *j*.
Thus we have, for instance, *c* in Sansk. *ca*, ' and ' = Greek *te*,
Lat. *que*, but *k* in *kakša* = Lat. *coxa*; the difference between
the two consonants in a perfect like *cakara*, ' have done,' is
dependent on the same vowel alternation as that of Greek
léloipa; *c* in the verb *pacati*, ' cooks,' as against *k* in the substantive *pakas*, ' cooking,' corresponds to the vowels in Greek
légei as against *lógos*, etc. All this shows that Sanskrit itself
must once have had the vowels *e* and *o* instead of *a*; before the
front vowel *e* the consonant has then been fronted or palatalized,
as *ch* in E. *chicken* is due to the following front vowel, while
k has been preserved before *o* in *cock*. Sanskrit is thus shown
to be in some important respects less conservative than Greek,
a truth which was destined profoundly to modify many theories
concerning the whole family of languages. As Curtius said,
with some resentment of the change in view then taking place,
" Sanskrit, once the oracle of the rising science and trusted
blindly, is now put on one side; instead of the traditional *ex
oriente lux* the saying is now *in oriente tenebræ* " (K 97).

The new views held in regard to Aryan vowels also resulted
in a thorough revision of the theory of apophony (ablaut). The
great mass of Aryan vowel alternations were shown to form a
vast and singularly consistent system, the main features of which
may be gathered from the following tabulation of a few select
Greek examples, arranged into three columns, each representing
one ' grade ':

	I	II	III
(1)	pétomai	pótē	eptómai
	(s)ékhō	(s)ókhos	éskhon
(2)	leípō	léloipa	élipon
(3)	peúthomai	—	eputhómēn
(4)	dérkomai	dédorka	édrakon
(5)	teínō (*tenjo)	tónos	tatós

It is outside our scope to show how this scheme gives us a
natural clue to the vowels in such verbs as E. I *ride*, II *rode*, III
ridden (2), G. I *werde*, II *ward*, III *geworden* (4), or I *binde*, II *band*,
III *gebunden* (5). It will be seen from the Greek examples that
grade I is throughout characterized by the vowel *e* and grade
II by the vowel *o*; as for grade III, the vowel of I and II has
entirely disappeared in (1), where there is no vowel between the

two consonants, and in (2) and (3), where the element found after *e* and *o* and forming a diphthong with these has now become a full (syllabic) vowel *i* and *u* by itself. In (4) Sanskrit has in grade III a syllabic *r* (*adrçam* = Gr. *édrakon*), while Greek has *ra*, or in some instances *ar*, and Gothonic has *ur* or *or* according to the vowel of the following syllable. It was this fact that suggested to Brugmann his theory that in (5) Greek *a*, Lat. *in*, Goth. *un* in the third grade originated in syllabic *n̥*, and that *tatós* thus stood for **tn̥tós*; he similarly explained Gr. *déka*, Lat. *decem*, Gothic *taihun*, E. *ten* from **dekm̥* with syllabic *m*. I do not believe that his theory is entirely correct; but so much is certain, that in all instances grade III is characterized by a reduction of the vowel that appears in the two other grades as *e* and *o*, and there can be no doubt that this reduction is due to want of stress. This being so, it becomes impossible to consider *lip* the original root-form, which in *leip* and *loip* has been extended, and the new theory of apophony thus disposes of the old theory, based on the Indian grammarians' view that the shortest form was the root-form, which was then raised through ' guna ' and ' vrddhi.' This now is reversed, and the fuller form is shown to be the oldest, which in some cases was shortened according to a process paralleled in many living languages. Bopp was right in his rejection of Grimm's theory of an inner, significatory reason for apophony, as apophony is now shown to have been due to a mechanical cause, though a different one from that suggested by Bopp (see above, p. 53); and Grimm was also wrong in another respect, because apophony is found from the first in noun-formations as well as in verbs, where Grimm believed it to have been instituted to indicate tense differences, with which it had originally nothing to do. Apophony even appears in other syllables than the root syllable ; the new view thus quite naturally paved the way for skepticism with regard to the old doctrine that Aryan roots were necessarily monosyllabic ; and scholars soon began to admit dissyllabic ' bases ' in place of the old roots ; instead of *lip*, the earliest accessible form thus came to be something like *leipo* or *leipe*. In this way the new vowel system had far-reaching consequences and made linguists look upon many problems in a new light. It should be noted, however, that the mechanical explanation of apophony from difference in accent applies only to grade III, in contradistinction to grades I and II ; the reason of the alternation between the *e* of I and the *o* of II is by no means clear.

The investigations leading to the discovery of the palatal law and the new theory of apophony were only a part of the immense labour of a number of able linguists in the 'seventies and 'eighties, which cleared up many obscure points in Aryan phonology and morphology. One of the most famous discoveries was that of the Dane Karl Verner, that a whole series of consonant alternations in the old Gothonic languages was dependent on accent, and (more remarkable still) on the primeval accent, preserved in its oldest form in Sanskrit only, and differing from that of modern Gothonic languages in resting in some instances on the ending and in others on the root. When it was realized that the fact that German has *t* in *vater*, but *d* in *bruder*, was due to a different accentuation of the two words three or four thousand years ago, or that the difference between *s* and *r* in E. *was* and *were* was connected with the fact that perfect singulars in Sanskrit are stressed on the root, but plurals on the ending, this served not only to heighten respect for the linguistic science that was able to demonstrate such truths, but also to increase the feeling that the world of sounds was subject to strict laws comparable to those of natural science.

IV.—§ 3. Phonetic Laws and Analogy.

The 'blind' operation of phonetic laws became the chief tenet of a new school of 'young-grammarians' or 'junggrammatiker' (Brugmann, Delbrück, Osthoff, Paul and others), who somewhat noisily flourished their advance upon earlier linguists and justly roused the anger not only of their own teachers, including Curtius, but also of fellow-students like Johannes Schmidt and Collitz. For some years a fierce discussion took place on the principles of linguistic science, in which young-grammarians tried to prove deductively the truth of their favourite thesis that " Sound-laws admit of no exceptions " (first, it seems, enounced by Leskien). Osthoff wrongly maintained that sound changes belonged to physiology and analogical change to psychology; but though that distribution of the two kinds of change to two different domains was untenable, the distinction in itself was important and proved a valuable, though perhaps sometimes too easy instrument in the hands of the historical grammarian. It was quite natural that those who insisted on undeviating phonetic laws should turn their attention to those cases in which forms appeared that did not conform to these laws, and try to explain them; and thus they inevitably were led to recognize the immense importance of analogical formations in the economy of all languages. Such formations had long been known, but little attention had been paid to them, and they were generally termed 'false analogies' and looked upon as corruptions or inorganic formations found only or chiefly in a degenerate age, in which the true meaning and composition of the old forms was no longer understood. Men like Curtius were scandalized at the younger school explaining so many even of the noble forms of ancient Greek as due to this upstart force of analogy. His opponents contended that the name of ' false analogy ' was wrong and misleading : the analogy in itself was perfect and was handled with unerring instinct in each case. They likewise pointed out that analogical formations, so far from being perversions of a late age, really represented one of the vital principles of language, without which it could never have come into existence.

One of the first to take the new point of view and to explain it clearly was Hermann Paul. I quote from an early article (as translated by Sweet, CP 112) the following passages, which really struck a new note in linguistic theory :

"There is one simple fact which should never be left out of sight, namely, that even in the parent Indogermanic language, long before its split-up, there were no longer any roots, stems, and suffixes, but only ready-made *words*, which were employed without the slightest thought of their composite nature. And it is only of such ready-made words that the store is composed from which everyone draws when he speaks. He has no stock of stems and terminations at his disposal from which he could construct the form required for each separate occasion. Not that he must necessarily have heard and learnt by heart every form he uses. This would, in fact, be impossible. He is, on the contrary, able of himself to form cases of nouns, tenses of verbs, etc., which he has either never heard or else not noticed specially ; but, as there is no combining of stem and suffix, this can only be done on the pattern of the other ready-made combinations which he has learnt from his fellows. These latter are first learnt one by one, and then gradually associated into groups which correspond to the grammatical categories, but are never clearly conceived as such without special training. This grouping not only greatly aids the memory, but also makes it possible to produce other combinations. And this is what we call *analogy*."

"It is, therefore, clear that, while speaking, everyone is incessantly producing analogical forms. *Reproduction by memory* and *new-formation by means of association* are its two indispensable factors. It is a mistake to assume a language as given in grammar and dictionary, that is, the whole body of possible words and forms, as something concrete, and to forget that it is nothing but an abstraction devoid of reality, and that *the actual language exists only in the individual*, from whom it cannot be separated even in scientific investigation, if we will understand its nature and development. To comprehend the existence of each separate spoken form, we must not ask 'Is it current in the language?' or 'Is it conformable to the laws of the language as deduced by the grammarians?' but 'Has he who has just employed it previously had it in his memory, or has he formed it himself for the first time, and, if so, according to what analogy?' When, for instance, anyone employs the plural *milben* in German, it may be that he has learnt it from others, or else that he has only heard the singular *milbe*, but knows that such words as *lerche, schwalbe*, etc., form their plural *lerchen*, etc., so that the association *milbe-milben* is unconsciously suggested to him. He may also have heard the plural *milben*, but remembers it so imperfectly that he would forget it entirely were it not associated in his mind with a series of similar forms which help him to recall it. It is, therefore, often difficult to determine the share memory and creative fancy have had in each separate case."

Linguists thus set about it seriously to think of language in terms of speaking individuals, who have learnt their mother-tongue in the ordinary way, and who now employ it in their daily intercourse with other men and women, without in each separate case knowing what they owe to others and what they have to create on the spur of the moment. Just as Sokrates fetched philosophy down from the skies, so also now linguists fetched words and forms down from vocabularies and grammars and placed them where their natural home is, in the minds and on the lips of ordinary men who are neither lexicographers nor grammarians, but who nevertheless master their language with sufficient ease and correctness for all ordinary purposes. Linguists now were confronted with some general problems which had not greatly troubled their predecessors (with the solitary exception of Bredsdorff, whose work was entirely overlooked), namely, What are the causes of changes in language? How are they brought about, and how should they be classified? Many articles on these questions appeared in linguistic periodicals about the year 1880, but the profoundest and fullest treatment was found in a masterly book by H. Paul, *Prinzipien der Sprachgeschichte*, the first edition of which (1880) exercised a very considerable influence on linguistic thought, while the subsequent editions were constantly enlarged and improved so as to contain a wealth of carefully sifted material to illustrate the various processes of linguistic change. It should also be noted that Paul paid more and more attention to syntax, and that this part of grammar, which had been neglected by Bopp and Schleicher and their contemporaries, was about this time taken up by some of the leading linguists, who showed that the comparative and historical method was capable of throwing a flood of light on syntax no less than on morphology (Delbrück, Ziemer).

IV.—§ 4. General Tendencies.

While linguists in the 'eighties were taking up, as we have seen, a great many questions of vast general importance that had not been treated by the older generation, on the other hand they were losing interest in some of the problems that had occupied their predecessors. This was the case with the question of the ultimate origin of grammatical endings. So late as 1869 Benfey included among Bopp's 'brilliant discoveries' his theory that the s of the aorist and of the future was derived from the verb as, 'to be,' and that the endings of the Latin imperfect -*bam* and future -*bo* were from the synonymous verb $fu =$ Sanskrit *bhu* (Gesch 377), and the next year Raumer reckons the same theories among Bopp's 'most important discoveries.' But soon after this we see that speculations of this kind somehow go out of fashion. One of the last books to indulge in them to any extent is Scherer's once famous *Zur Geschichte der deutschen Sprache* (2nd ed., 1878), in the eighth chapter of which the writer disports himself among primitive roots, endings, prepositions and pronouns, which he identifies and differentiates with such extreme boldness and confidence in his own wild fancies that a sober-minded man of the twentieth century cannot but feel dazed and giddy. The ablest linguists of the new school simply left these theories aside: no new explanations of the same description were advanced, and the old ones were not substantiated by the ascertained phenomena of living languages. So much was found in these of the most absorbing interest that scholars ceased to care for what might lie behind Proto-Aryan; some even went so far as to deprecate in strong expressions any attempts at what they termed 'glottogonic' theories. To these matter-of-fact linguists all speculations as to the ultimate origin of language were futile and nebulous, a verdict which might be in no small degree justified by much of what had been written on the subject by quasi-philosophers and quasi-linguists. The aversion to these questions was shown as early as 1866, when La Société de Linguistique was founded in Paris. Section 2 of the statutes of the Society expressly states that "La Société n'admet aucune communication concernant, soit l'origine du langage, soit la création d'une langue universelle"—both of them questions which, as they *can* be treated in a scientific spirit, should not be left exclusively to dilettanti.

The last forty years have witnessed an extraordinary activity on the part of scholars in investigating all domains of the Aryan languages in the light of the new general views and by the aid of the methods that have now become common property. Phonological investigations have no doubt had the lion's share and have to a great extent been signalized by that real insight into physiological phonetics which had been wanting in earlier linguists ; but very much excellent work has also been done in morphology, syntax and semantics ; and in all these domains much has been gained by considering words not as mere isolated units, but as parts of sentences, or, better, of connected speech. In phonetics more and more attention has been paid to sentence phonetics and 'sandhi phenomena' ; the heightened interest in everything concerning 'accent' (stress and pitch) has also led to investigations of sentence-stress and sentence-melody ; the intimate connexion between forms and their use or function in the sentence, in other words their syntax, has been more and more recognized ; and finally, if semantics (the study of the significations of words) has become a real science instead of being a curiosity shop of isolated specimens, this has only been rendered possible through seeing words as connected with other words to form complete utterances. But this change of attitude could not have been brought about unless linguists had studied texts in the different languages to a far greater extent than had been done in previous periods ; thus, naturally, the antagonism formerly often felt between the linguistic and the purely philological study of the same language has tended to disappear, and many scholars have produced work both in their particular branch of linguistics and in the corresponding philology. There can be no doubt that this development has been profitable to both domains of scientific activity.

Another beneficial change is the new attitude taken with regard to the study of living speech. The science of linguistics had long stood in the sign of Cancer and had been constantly looking backwards—to its own great loss. Now, with the greater stress laid on phonetics and on the psychology of language, the necessity of observing the phenomena of actual everyday speech was more clearly perceived. Among pioneers in this respect I must specially mention Henry Sweet ; now there is a steadily growing interest in living speech as the necessary foundation of all general theorizing. And with interest comes knowledge.

It is outside the purpose of this volume to give the history of linguistic study during the last forty years in the same way as I have attempted to give it for the period before 1880, and I must therefore content myself with a few brief remarks on general tendencies. I even withstand the temptation to try and characterize the two greatest works on general linguistics that have appeared during this period, those by Georg v. d. Gabelentz and Wilhelm Wundt : important and in many ways excellent as they are, they have not exercised the same influence on contemporary linguistic research as some of their predecessors. Personally I owe incomparably much more to the former than to the latter, who is much less of a linguist than of a psychologist and whose pages seem to me often richer in words than in fertilizing ideas. As for the rest, I can give only a bare alphabetical list of some of the writers who during this period have dealt with the more general problems of linguistic change or linguistic theory, and must not attempt any appreciation of their works : Bally, Baudouin de Courtenay, Bloomfield, Bréal Delbrück, van Ginneken, Hale, Henry, Hirt, Axel Kock, Meillet Meringer, Noreen, Oertel, Pedersen, Sandfeld (Jensen), de Saussure, Schuchardt, Sechehaye, Streitberg, Sturtevant, Sütterlin, Sweet, Uhlenbeck, Vossler, Wechssler. In the following parts of my work there will be many opportunities of mentioning their views, especially when I disagree with them, for I am afraid it will be impossible always to indicate what I owe to their suggestions.

In the history of linguistic science we have seen in one period a tendency to certain large syntheses (the classification of languages into isolating, agglutinative and flexional, and the corresponding theory of three periods with its corollary touching the origin of flexional endings), and we have seen how these syntheses were later discredited, though never actually disproved, linguists contenting themselves with detailed comparisons and explanations of single words, forms or sounds without troubling about their ultimate origin or about the evolutionary tendencies of the whole system or structure of language. The question may therefore be raised, were Bopp and Schleicher wrong in attempting these large syntheses ? It would appear from the expressions of some modern linguists that they thought that any such comprehensive generalization or any glottogonic theory were in itself of evil. But this can never be admitted. Science, of its very nature, aims at larger and larger generalizations, more and more comprehensive formulas, so as finally to bring about that " unification of knowledge " of which Herbert Spencer speaks. It was therefore quite right of the early linguists to propound those great questions ; and their failure to solve them in a way that could satisfy the stricter demands of a later generation should not be charged too heavily against them. It was also quite right of the moderns to reject their premature solutions (though this was often done without any adequate examination), but

it was decidedly wrong to put the questions out of court altogether.[1] These great questions have to be put over and over
again, till a complete solution is found ; and the refusal to face
these difficulties has produced a certain barrenness in modern
linguistics, which must strike any impartial observer, however
much he admits the fertility of the science in detailed investigations. Breadth of vision is not conspicuous in modern
linguistics, and to my mind this lack is chiefly due to the fact
that linguists have neglected all problems connected with a
valuation of language. What is the criterion by which one word
or one form should be preferred to another ? (most linguists
refuse to deal with such questions of preference or of correctness
of speech). Are the changes that we see gradually taking place
in languages to be considered as on the whole beneficial or the
opposite ? (most linguists pooh-pooh such questions). Would it
be possible to construct an international language by which
persons in different countries could easily communicate with
one another ? (most linguists down to the present day have
looked upon all who favour such ideas as visionaries and Uto-
pians). It is my firm conviction that such questions as these
admit of really scientific treatment and should be submitted to
serious discussion. But before tackling those of them which
fall within the plan of this work, it will be well to deal with some
fundamental facts of what is popularly called the ' life ' of language,
and first of all with the manner in which a child acquires its
mother-tongue. For as language exists only in individuals and
means some specific activities of human beings which are not
inborn, but have to be learnt by each of them separately from
his fellow-beings, it is important to examine somewhat in detail
how this interaction of the individual and of the surrounding
society is brought about. This, then, will occupy us in Book II.

[1] " Es ist besser, bei solchen versuchen zu irren als gar nicht darüber
nachzudenken," Curtius, K 145.

BOOK II

THE CHILD

CHAPTER V

SOUNDS

§ 1. From Screaming to Talking. § 2. First Sounds. § 3. Sound-laws of the Next Stage. § 4. Groups of Sounds. § 5. Mutilations and Reduplications. § 6. Correction. § 7. Tone.

V.—§ 1. From Screaming to Talking.

A DANISH philosopher has said : " In his whole life man achieves nothing so great and so wonderful as what he achieved when he learnt to talk." When Darwin was asked in which three years of his life a man learnt most, he said : " The first three."

A child's linguistic development covers three periods—the screaming time, the crowing or babbling time, and the talking time. But the last is a long one, and must again be divided into two periods—that of the " little language," the child's own language, and that of the common language or language of the community. In the former the child is linguistically an individualist, in the latter he is more and more socialized.

Of the screaming time little need be said. A child's scream is not uttered primarily as a means of conveying anything to others, and so far is not properly to be called speech. But if from the child's side a scream is not a way of telling anything, its elders may still read something in it and hurry to relieve the trouble. And if the child comes to remark—as it soon will—that whenever it cries someone comes and brings it something pleasant, if only company, it will not be long till it makes use of this instrument whenever it is uneasy or wants something. The scream, which was at first a reflex action, is now a voluntary action. And many parents have discovered that the child has learnt to use its power of screaming to exercise a tyrannical power over them—so that they have had to walk up and down all night with a screaming child that prefers this way of spending the night to lying quietly in its cradle. The only course is brutally to let the baby scream till it is tired, and persist in never letting it get its desire *because* it screams for it, but only because what it desires is good for it. The child learns its lesson, and a scream is once more what it was at first, an involuntary, irresistible result of the fact that something is wrong.

Screaming has, however, another side. It is of physiological value as an exercise of all the muscles and appliances which are afterwards to be called into play for speech and song. Nurses say—and there may be something in it—that the child who screams loudest as a baby becomes the best singer later.

Babbling time produces pleasanter sounds which are more adapted for the purposes of speech. Cooing, crowing, babbling— i.e. uttering meaningless sounds and series of sounds—is a delightful exercise like sprawling with outstretched arms and legs or trying to move the tiny fingers. It has been well said that for a long time a child's dearest toy is its tongue—that is, of course, not the tongue only, but the other organs of speech as well, especially the lips and vocal chords. At first the movements of these organs are as uncontrolled as those of the arms, but gradually they become more systematic, and the boy knows what sound he wishes to utter and is in a position to produce it exactly.

First, then, come single vowels or vowels with a single consonant preceding them, as *la, ra, lö*, etc., though a baby's sounds cannot be identified with any of ours or written down with our letters. For, though the head and consequently the mouth capacity is disproportionally great in an infant and grows more rapidly than its limbs, there is still a great difference between its mouth capacity and that required to utter normal speech-sounds. I have else- where (PhG, p. 81 ff.) given the results of a series of measurings of the jaw in children and adults and discussed the importance of these figures for phonetic theory : while there is no growth of any importance during the talking period (for a child of five may have the same jaw-length as a man of thirty-seven), the growth is enormous during the first months of a child's life : in the case of my own child, from 45 mm. a few days after birth to 60 mm. at three months old and 75 mm. at eleven months, while the average of grown-up men is 99 mm. and of women 93 mm. The consequence is that the sounds of the baby are different from ours, and that even when they resemble ours the mechanism of production may be different from the normal one ; when my son during the first weeks said something like *la*, I was able to see distinctly that the tip of the tongue was not at all in the position required for our *l*. This want of congruence between the acoustic manners of operation in the infant and the adult no doubt gives us the key to many of the difficulties that have puzzled previous observers of small children.

Babbling or crowing begins not earlier than the third week ; it may be, not till the seventh or eighth week. The first sound exercises are to be regarded as muscular exercises pure and simple, as is clear from the fact that deaf-mutes amuse themselves with them, although they cannot themselves hear them. But the moment comes when the hearing child finds a pleasure in hearing its own sounds, and a most important step is taken when the little one begins to hear a resemblance between the sounds uttered by its mother or nurse and its own. The mother will naturally answer the baby's syllables by repeating the same, and when the baby recognizes the likeness, it secures an inexhaustible source of pleasure, and after some time reaches the next stage, when it tries itself to imitate what is said to it (generally towards the close of the first year). The value of this exercise cannot be over-estimated : the more that parents understand how to play this game with the baby—of saying something and letting the baby say it after, however meaningless the syllable-sequences that they make—the better will be the foundation for the child's later acquisition and command of language.

V.—§ 2. First Sounds.

It is generally said that the order in which the child learns to utter the different sounds depends on their difficulty : the easiest sounds are produced first. That is no doubt true in the main ; but when we go into details we find that different writers bring forward lists of sounds in different order. All are agreed, however, that among the consonants the labials, *p, b* and *m*, are early sounds, if not the earliest. The explanation has been given that the child can see the working of his mother's lips in these sounds and therefore imitates her movements. This implies far too much conscious thought on the part of the baby, who utters his ' ma ' or ' mo ' before he begins to imitate anything said to him by his surroundings. Moreover, it has been pointed out that the child's attention is hardly ever given to its mother's mouth, but is steadily fixed on her eyes. The real reason is probably that the labial muscles used to produce *b* or *m* are the same that the baby has exercised in sucking the breast or the bottle. It would be interesting to learn if blind children also produce the labial sounds first.

Along with the labial sounds the baby produces many other sounds—vowel and consonant—and in these cases one is certain that it has not been able to see how these sounds are produced by its mother. Even in the case of the labials we know that what distinguishes *m* from *b*, the lowering of the soft palate, and *b* from *p*, the vibrations of the vocal chords, is invisible. Some of the sounds produced by means of the tongue may be too hard to pronounce till the muscles of the tongue have been exercised in consequence of the child having begun to eat more solid things than milk.

By the end of the first year the number of sounds which the
little babbler has mastered is already considerable, and he loves
to combine long series of the same syllables, dadadada . . .,
nenenene . . . , bygnbygnbygn . . . , etc. That is a game which
need not even cease when the child is able to talk actual language.
It is strange that among an infant's sounds one can often detect
sounds—for instance *k, g, h*, and uvular *r*—which the child will find
difficulty in producing afterwards when they occur in real words,
or which may be unknown to the language which it will some day
speak. The explanation lies probably in the difference between
doing a thing in play or without a plan—when it is immaterial
which movement (sound) is made—and doing the same thing of
fixed intention when this sound, and this sound only, is required,
at a definite point in the syllable, and with this or that particular
sound before and after. Accordingly, great difficulties come to
be encountered when the child begins more consciously and systematically to imitate his elders. Some sounds come without effort
and may be used incessantly, to the detriment of others which
the child may have been able previously to produce in play ; and
a time even comes when the stock of sounds actually diminishes,
while particular sounds acquire greater precision. Dancing masters,
singing masters and gymnastic teachers have similar experiences.
After some lessons the child may seem more awkward than it was
before the lessons began.

The ' little language ' which the child makes for itself by
imperfect imitation of the sounds of its elders seems so arbitrary
that it may well be compared to the child's first rude drawings
of men and animals. A Danish boy named *Gustav* (1.6)[1] called
himself [dodado] and turned the name *Karoline* into [nnn]. Other
Danish children made *skammel* into [gramn] or [gap], *elefant* into
[vat], *Karen* into [gaja], etc. A few examples from English
children : Hilary M. (1.6) called *Ireland* (her sister) [a·ni],
Gordon M. (1.10) called *Millicent* (his sister) [dadu·]. Tony E.
(1.11) called his playmate *Sheila* [dubabud].

V.—§ 3. Sound-laws of the Next Stage.

As the child gets away from the peculiarities of his individual
' little language,' his speech becomes more regular, and a linguist
can in many cases see reasons for his distortions of normal words.
When he replaces one sound by another there is always some
common element in the formation of the two sounds, which causes

[1] In this book the age of a child is indicated by stating the number of
years and months completed : 1.6 thus means " in the seventh month of
the second year," etc.

a kindred impression on the ear, though *we* may have difficulty in detecting it because we are so accustomed to noticing the difference. There is generally a certain system in the sound substitutions of children, and in many instances we are justified in speaking of 'strictly observed sound-laws.' Let us now look at some of these.

Children in all countries tend to substitute [t] for [k] : both sounds are produced by a complete stoppage of the breath for the moment by the tongue, the only difference being that it is the back of the tongue which acts in one case, and the tip of the tongue in the other. A child who substitutes *t* for *k* will also substitute *d* for *g ;* if he says 'tat' for 'cat' he will say 'do' for 'go.'

R is a difficult sound. Hilary M. (2.0) has no *r*'s in her speech. Initially they become *w*, as in [wʌn] for 'run,' medially between vowels they become *l*, as in [veli, beli] for 'very, berry,' in consonantal combinations they are lost, as in [kaɨ, bʌʃ] for 'cry, brush.' Tony E. (1.10 to 3.0) for medial *r* between vowels first substituted *d*, as in [vedi] for 'very,' and later *g* [vegi] ; similarly in [muˑgi] for 'Muriel,' [tægi] for 'carry' ; he often dropped initial *r*, e.g. *oom* for 'room.' It is not unusual for children who use *w* for *r* in most combinations to say [tʃ] for *tr* and [dʒ] for *dr*, as in 'chee,' 'jawer' for 'tree,' 'drawer.' This illustrates the fact that what to us is *one* sound, and therefore represented in writing by *one* letter, appears to the child's ear as different sounds —and generally the phonetician will agree with the child that there are really differences in the articulation of the sound according to position in the syllable and to surroundings, only the child exaggerates the dissimilarities, just as we in writing one and the same letter exaggerate the similarity.

The two *th* sounds offer some difficulties and are often imitated as *f* and *v* respectively, as in 'frow' and 'muvver' for 'throw' and 'mother'; others say 'ze' or 'de' for 'the.' Hilary M. (2.0) has great difficulty with *th* and *s* ; *th* usually becomes [ʃ], [beʃ, tiˑʃ, ʃriˑ] for 'Beth,' 'teeth,' 'three' ; *s* becomes [ʃ], e.g. [franʃiʃ, ʃtiˑm] for 'Francis,' 'steam' ; in the same way *z* becomes [ʒ] as in [lʌbʒ, bouʒ] for 'loves,' 'Bowes' ; *sw* becomes [fw] as in [fwiŋ, fwiˑt] for 'swing,' 'sweet.' She drops *l* in consonantal combinations, e.g. [kiˑn, kaim, kɔk, ʃiˑp] for 'clean,' 'climb,' 'clock,' 'sleep.'

Sometimes it requires a phonetician's knowledge to understand the individual sound-laws of a child. Thus I pick out from some specimens given by O'Shea, p. 135 f. (girl, 2.9), the following words : *pell* (smell), *teeze* (sneeze), *poke* (smoke), *tow* (snow), and formulate the rule : *s* + a nasal became the voiceless stop corresponding to the nasal, a kind of assimilation, in which the place of articulation and the mouth-closure of the nasals were preserved, and the sound was made unvoiced and non-nasal as the *s*. In other combinations *m* and *n* were intact.

Some further faults are illustrated in Tony E.'s [tʃouz, pʌg, pus, tæm, pʌm, bæk, piˑz, nouʒ, ɔk, es, uˑ] for *clothes, plug, push, tram, plum, black, please, nose, clock, yes, you.*

V.—§ 4. Groups of Sounds.

Even when a sound by itself can be pronounced, the child often finds it hard to pronounce it when it forms part of a group of sounds. *S* is often dropped before another consonant, as in ' tummy ' for ' stomach.' Other examples have already been given above. Hilary M. (2.0) had difficulty with *lp* and said [hæpl] for ' help.' She also said [ointən] for ' ointment ' ; C. M. L. (2.3) said ' sikkums ' for ' sixpence.' Tony E. (2.0) turns *grannie* into [nægi]. When initial consonant groups are simplified, it is generally, though not always, the stop that remains : *b* instead of *bl-, br-, k* instead of *kr-, sk-, skr-, p* instead of *pl-, pr-, spr-*, etc. For the groups occurring medially and finally no general rule seems possible.

V.—§ 5. Mutilations and Reduplications.

To begin with, the child is unable to master long sequences of syllables ; he prefers monosyllables and often emits them singly and separated by pauses. Even in words that to us are inseparable wholes some children will make breaks between syllables, e.g. Shef-field, Ing-land. But more often they will give only part of the word, generally the last syllable or syllables ; hence we get pet-names like *Bet* or *Beth* for Elizabeth and forms like ' tatoes ' for potatoes, ' chine ' for machine, ' tina ' for concertina, ' tash ' for moustache, etc. Hilary M. (1.10) called an express-cart a *press-cart*, bananas and pyjamas *nanas* and *jamas*.

It is not, however, the production of long sequences of syllables in itself that is difficult to the child, for in its meaningless babbling it may begin very early to pronounce long strings of sounds without any break ; but the difficulty is to remember what sounds have to be put together to bring about exactly this or that word. We grown-up people may experience just the same sort of difficulty if after hearing once the long name of a Bulgarian minister or a Sanskrit book we are required to repeat it at once. Hence we should not wonder at such pronunciations as [pekəlout] for *petticoat* or [efelənt] for *elephant* (Beth M., 2.6) ; Hilary M. called a *caterpillar* a *pillarcat*. Other transpositions are *serreval* for *several* and *ocken* for *uncle*; cf. also *wops* for *wasp*.

To explain the frequent reduplications found in children's language it is not necessary, as some learned authors have done, to refer to the great number of reduplicated words in the languages of primitive tribes and to see in the same phenomenon in our own children an atavistic return to primitive conditions, on the Häckelian assumption that the development of each individual has to pass rapidly through the same ('phylogenetic') stages as the whole lineage of his ancestors. It is simpler and more natural to refer these reduplications to the pleasure always felt in repeating the same muscular action until one is tired. The child will repeat over and over again the same movements of legs and arms, and we do the same when we wave our hand or a handkerchief or when we nod our head several times to signify assent, etc. When we laugh we repeat the same syllable consisting of *h* and a more or less indistinct vowel, and when we sing a melody without words we are apt to 'reduplicate' indefinitely. Thus also with the little ones. Apart from such words as *papa* and *mamma*, to which we shall have to revert in another chapter (VIII, § 9), children will often form words from those of their elders by repeating one syllable; cf. *puff-puff*, *gee-gee*. Tracy (p. 132) records *pepe* for 'pencil,' *kaka* for 'Carrie.' For a few weeks (1.11) Hilary M. reduplicated whole words, e.g. *king-king*, *ring-ring* (i.e. bell), *water-water*. Tony F. (1.10) uses [touto] for his own name. Hence pet-names like *Dodo ;* they are extremely frequent in French —for instance, *Fifine, Lolotte, Lolo, Mimi ;* the name *Daudet* has arisen in a similar way from *Claudet*, a diminutive of Claude.

It is a similar phenomenon (a kind of partial reduplication) when sounds at a distance affect one another, as when Hilary M. (2.0) said [gɔgi] for *doggie*, [bɔbin] for *Dobbin*, [dezmən di·n] for *Jesmond Dene*, [baikikl] for *bicycle*, [kekl] for *kettle*. Tracy (p. 133) mentions *bopoo* for 'bottle,' in which *oo* stands for the hollow sound of syllabic *l*. One correspondent mentions *whoofing-cough* for 'whooping-cough' (where the final sound has crept into the first word) and *chicken-pops* for 'chicken-pox.' Some children say 'aneneme' for *anemone ;* and in S. L. (4.9) this caused a curious confusion during the recent war: "Mother, there must be two sorts of anenemies, flowers and Germans."

Dr. Henry Bradley once told me that his youngest child had a difficulty with the name *Connie*, which was made alternatingly [tɔni] and [kɔŋi], in both cases with two consonants articulated at the same point. Similar instances are mentioned in German books on children's language, thus *gigarr* for 'zigarre,' *baibift* for ' bleistift,' *autobobil* (Meringer),[1] *fotofafieren* (Stern), *ambam* for ' armband,' *dan* for ' dame,' *pap* for ' patte ' (Ronjat). I have given many Danish examples in my Danish book. Grammont's child (see *Mélanges linguistiques offerts à A. Meillet*, 1902) carried through these changes in a most systematic way.

V.—§ 6. Correction.

The time comes when the child corrects his mistakes—where it said ' tat ' it now says ' cat.' Here there are two possibilities which both seem to occur in actual life. One is that the child hears the correct sound some time before he is able to imitate it correctly ; he will thus still say *t* for *k*, though he may in some way object to other people saying ' tum ' for ' come.' Passy relates how a little French girl would say *tosson* both for *garçon* and *cochon* ; but she protested when anybody else said " C'est un petit cochon " in speaking about a boy, or vice versa. Such a child, as soon as it can produce the new sound, puts it correctly into all the places where it is required. This, I take it, is the ordinary procedure. Frans (my own boy) could not pronounce *h* and said *an, on* for the Danish pronouns *han, hun* ; but when he began to pronounce this sound, he never misplaced it (2.4).

The other possibility is that the child learns how to pronounce the new sound at a time when its own acoustic impression is not yet quite settled ; in that case there will be a period during which his use of the new sound is uncertain and fluctuating. When parents are in too great a hurry to get a child out of some false pronunciation, they may succeed in giving it a new sound, but the child will tend to introduce it in places where it does not belong. On the whole, it seems therefore the safest plan to leave it to the child itself to discover that its sound is not the correct one.

Sometimes a child will acquire a sound or a sound combination correctly and then lose it till it reappears a few months later. In an English family where there was no question of the influence of *h*-less servants, each child in succession passed through an *h*-less period, and one of the children, after pronouncing *h* correctly, lost the use of it altogether for two or three months. I have had similar experiences with Danish children. S. L. (ab. 2) said ' bontin ' for *bonnet ;* but five months earlier she had said *bonnet* correctly.

The path to perfection is not always a straight one. Tony E. in order to arrive at the correct pronunciation of *please* passed through the following stages : (1) [bi·], (2) [bli·], (3) [pi·z],

---

[1] An American child said *autonobile* [ɔtənobi·l] with partial assimilation of *m* to the point-stop *t*.

(4) [pwiˑʒ], (5) [beisk, meis, mais] and several other impossible forms. Tracy (p. 139) gives the following forms through which the boy A. (1.5) had to pass before being able to say *pussy : pooheh, poofie, poopoohie, poofee*. A French child had four forms [mèni, pèti, mèti, mèsi] before being able to say *merci* correctly (Grammont). A Danish child passed through *bejab* and *vamb* before pronouncing *svamp* ('sponge'), etc.

It is certain that all this while the little brain is working, and even consciously working, though at first it has not sufficient command of speech to say anything about it. Meringer says that children do not practise, but that their new acquisitions of sounds happen at once without any visible preparation. He may be right in the main with regard to the learning of single sounds, though even there I incline to doubt the possibility of a universal rule ; but Ronjat (p. 55) is certainly right as against Meringer with regard to the way in which children learn new and difficult combinations. Here they certainly do practise, and are proudly conscious of the happy results of their efforts. When Frans (2.11) mastered the combination *fl*, he was very proud, and asked his mother : " Mother, can you say *flyve* ? " ; then he came to me and told me that he could say *bluse* and *flue*, and when asked whether he could say *blad*, he answered : " No, not yet ; Frans cannot say *b-lad* " (with a little interval between the *b* and the *l*). Five weeks later he said : " Mother, won't you play upon the *klaver* (piano) ? " and after a little while, " Frans can say *kla* so well." About the same time he first mispronounced the word *manchetter*, and then (when I asked what he was saying, without telling him that anything was wrong) he gave it the correct sound, and I heard him afterwards in the adjoining room repeat the word to himself in a whisper.

How well children observe sounds is again seen by the way in which they will correct their elders if they give a pronunciation to which they are not accustomed—for instance, in a verse they have learnt by heart. Beth M (2.6) was never satisfied with her parents' pronunciation of " What will you buy me when you get there ? " She always insisted on their gabbling the first words as quickly as they could and then coming out with an emphatic *there*.

V.—§ 7. Tone.

As to the differences in the tone of a voice, even a baby shows by his expression that he can distinguish clearly between what is said to him lovingly and what sharply, a long time before he understands a single word of what is said. Many children are

able at a very early age to hit off the exact note in which something is said or sung.   Here is a story of a boy of more advanced
age.   In Copenhagen he had had his hair cut by a Swedish lady
and did not like it.   When he travelled with his mother to Norway,
as soon as he entered the house, he broke out with a scream :
" Mother, I hope I'm not going to have my hair cut ? "   He had
noticed the Norwegian intonation, which is very like the Swedish,
and it brought an unpleasant association of ideas.

CHAPTER VI

WORDS

VI.—§ 1. Introductory.

In the preceding chapter, in order to simplify matters, we have dealt with sounds only, as if they were learnt by themselves and independently of the meanings attached to them. But that, of course, is only an abstraction : to the child, as well as to the grown-up, the two elements, the outer, phonetic element, and the inner element, the meaning, of a word are indissolubly connected, and the child has no interest, or very little interest, in trying to imitate the sounds of its parents except just in so far as these mean something. That words have a meaning, the child will begin to perceive at a very early age. Parents may of course deceive themselves and attribute to the child a more complete and exact understanding of speech than the child is capable of. That the child looks at its father when it hears the word 'father,' may mean at first nothing more than that it follows its mother's glance ; but naturally in this way it is prepared for actually associating the idea of 'father' with the sound. If the child learns the feat of lifting its arms when it is asked " How big is the boy ? " it is not to be supposed that the single words of the sentence are understood, or that the child has any conception of size ; he only knows that when this series of sounds is said he is admired if he lifts his arms up : and so the sentence as a whole has the effect of a word of command. A dog has the same degree of understanding. Hilary M. (1.0), when you said to her at any time the refrain " He greeted me so," from " Here come three knights from Spain," would bow and salute with her hand, as she had seen some children doing it when practising the song.

The understanding of what is said always precedes the power of saying the same thing oneself—often precedes it for an extra-ordinarily long time. One father notes that his little daughter of a year and seven months brings what is wanted and understands questions while she cannot say a word. It often happens that parents some fine day come to regret what they have said in the presence of a child without suspecting how much it understands. " Little pitchers have long ears."

One can, however, easily err in regard to the range and certainty of a child's understanding. The Swiss philologist Tappolet noticed that his child of six months, when he said " Where is the window ? " made vague movements towards the window. He made the experiment of repeating his question in French—with the same intonation as in German, and the child acted just as it had done before. It is, properly speaking, only when the child begins to talk that we can be at all sure what it has really understood, and even then it may at times be difficult to sound the depths of the child's conception.

The child's acquisition of the meaning of words is truly a highly complicated affair. How many things are comprehended under one word ? The answer is not easy in all cases. The single Danish word *tæppe* covers all that is expressed in English by carpet, rug, blanket, counterpane, curtain (theatrical). And there is still more complication when we come to abstract ideas. The child has somehow to find out for himself with regard to his own language what ideas are considered to hang together and so come under the same word. He hears the word ' chair ' applied to a particular chair, then to another chair that perhaps looks to him totally different, and again to a third : and it becomes his business to group these together.

What Stern tells about his own boy is certainly exceptional, perhaps unique. The boy ran to a door and said *das ?* (' That ? ' —his way of asking the name of a thing). They told him ' tür.' He then went to two other doors in the room, and each time the performance was repeated. He then did the same with the seven chairs in the room. Stern says, " As he thus makes sure that the objects that are alike to his eye and to his sense of touch have also the same name, he is on his way to general conceptions." We should, however, be wary of attributing general ideas to little children.

VI.—§ 2. First Period.

In the first period we meet the same phenomena in the child's acquisition of word-meanings that we found in his acquisition of sounds. A child develops conceptions of his own which are as unintelligible and strange to the uninitiated as his sounds.

Among the child's first passions are animals and pictures of animals, but for a certain time it is quite arbitrary what animals are classed together under a particular name. A child of nine months noticed that his grandfather's dog said ' bow-wow ' and fancied that anything not human could say (and therefore should be called) *bow-wow*—pigs and horses included. A little girl of two called a horse *he* (Danish *hest*) and divided the animal kingdom into two groups, (1) horses, including all four-footed things, even a tortoise, and (2) fishes (pronounced *iz*), including all that moved without use of feet, for example, birds and flies. A boy of 1.8 saw a picture of a Danish priest in a ruff and was told that it was a *præst*, which he rendered as *bæp*. Afterwards seeing a picture of an aunt with a white collar which recalled the priest's ruff, he said again *bæp*, and this remained the name of the aunt, and even of another aunt, who was called ' other bæp.' These transferences are sometimes extraordinary. A boy who had had a pig drawn for him, the pig being called *öf*, at the age of 1.6 used *öf* (1) for a pig, (2) for drawing a pig, (3) for writing in general.

Such transferences may seem very absurd, but are not more so than some transferences occurring in the language of grown-up persons. The word *Tripos* passed from the sense of a three-legged stool to the man who sat on a three-legged stool to dispute with candidates for degrees at Cambridge. Then, as it was the duty of Mr. Tripos also to provide comic verses, these were called tripos verses, such verses being printed under that name till very near the end of the nineteenth century, though Mr. Tripos himself had disappeared long ago. And as the examination list was printed on the back of these verses, it was called the Tripos list, and it was no far cry to saying of a successful candidate, " he stands high on the Tripos," which now came to mean the examination itself.

But to return to the classifications in the minds of the children. Hilary M. (1.6 to 2.0) used the word *daisy* (1) of the flower itself, (2) of any flower, (3) of any conventional flower in a pattern, (4) of any pattern. One of the first words she said was *colour* (1.4), and she got into a way of saying it when anything striking attracted her attention. Originally she heard the word of a bright patch of colour in a picture. The word was still in use at the age of two. For some months anything that moved was a *fly*, every man was a *soldier*, everybody that was not a man was a *baby*. S. L. (1.8) used *bing* (1) for a door, (2) for bricks or building with bricks. The connexion is through the bang of a door or a tumbling castle of bricks, but the name was transferred to the objects. It is curious that at 1.3 she had the word *bang* for anything dropped, but not *bing* ; at 1.8 she had both, *bing* being specialized as above. From books about children's language I quote two illustrations. Ronjat's son used the word *papement*, which stands for ' kaffemensch,' in speaking about the grocer's boy who brought coffee ; but as he had a kind of uniform with a flat cap, *papement* was also used of German and Russian officers in the illustrated papers. Hilde Stern (1.9) used *bichu* for drawer or chest of drawers ; it originated in the word *bücher* (books), which was said when her picture-books were taken out of the drawer.

A warning is, however, necessary. When a grown-up person says that a child uses the same word to denote various things, he is apt to assume that the child gives a word two or three definite meanings, as *he* does. The process is rather in this way. A child has got a new toy, a horse, and at the same time has heard its elders use the word ' horse,' which it has imitated as well as it can. It now associates the word with the delight of playing with its toy. If the next day it says the same sound, and its friends give it the horse, the child gains the experience that the sound brings the fulfilment of its wish : but if it sets its eye on a china cow and utters the same sound, the father takes note that the sound also denotes a cow, while for the child it is perhaps a mere experiment—" Could not I get my wish for that nice thing fulfilled in the same way ? " If it succeeds, the experiment may very well be repeated, and the more or less faulty imitation of the word ' horse ' thus by the co-operation of those around it may become also firmly attached to ' cow.'

When Elsa B. (1.10), on seeing the stopper of a bottle in the garden, came out with the word ' beer,' it would be rash to conclude (as her father did) that the word ' beer ' to her meant a ' stopper ' : all we know is that her thoughts had taken that direction, and that some time before, on seeing a stopper, she had heard the word ' beer.'

Parents sometimes unconsciously lead a child into error about the use of words. A little nephew of mine asked to taste his father's beer, and when refused made so much to-do that the father said, " Come, let us have peace in the house." Next day, under the same circumstances, the boy asked for ' peace in the house,' and this became the family name for beer. Not infrequently what is said on certain occasions is taken by the child to be the *name* of some object concerned ; thus a sniff or some sound imitating it may come to mean a flower, and ' hurrah ' a flag. S. L. from an early age was fond of flowers, and at 1.8 used ' pretty ' or ' pretty-pretty ' as a substantive instead of the word ' flower,' which she learnt at 1.10.

I may mention here that analogous mistakes may occur when missionaries or others write down words from foreign languages with which they are not familiar. In the oldest list of Greenlandic words (of 1587) there is thus a word *panygmah* given with the signification ' needle ' ; as a matter of fact it means ' my daughter's ' : the Englishman pointed at the needle, but the Eskimo thought he wanted to know whom it belonged to. In an old list of words in the now extinct Polabian language we find " *scumbe*, yesterday, *subuda*, to-day, *janidiglia*, to-morrow " : the questions were put on a Saturday, and the Slav answered accordingly, for *subuta* (the same word as Sabbath) means Saturday, *skumpe* ' fasting-day,' and *ja nedila* ' it is Sunday.'

According to O'Shea (p. 131) " a child was greatly impressed with the horns of a buck the first time he saw him. The father used the term ' sheep ' several times while the creature was being inspected, and it was discovered afterwards that the child had made the association between the word and the animal's horns, so now *sheep* signifies primarily horns, whether seen in pictures or in real life." It is clear that mistakes of that kind will happen more readily if the word is said singly than when it is embodied in whole connected sentences : the latter method is on the whole preferable for many reasons.

VI.—§ 3. Father and Mother.

A child is often faced by some linguistic usage which obliges him again and again to change his notions, widen them, narrow them, till he succeeds in giving words the same range of meaning that his elders give them.

Frequently, perhaps most frequently, a word is at first for the child a proper name. ' Wood ' means not a wood in general, but the particular picture which has been pointed out to the child in the dining-room. The little girl who calls her mother's black muff ' muff,' but refuses to transfer the word to her own white one, is at the same stage. Naturally, then, the word *father* when first heard is a proper name, the name of the child's own father. But soon it must be extended to other individuals who have something or other in common with the child's father. One child will use it of all *men*, another perhaps of all men with beards, while ' lady ' is applied to all pictures of faces without beards ; a third will apply the word to father, mother and grandfather. When the child itself applies the word to another man it is soon corrected, but at the same time it cannot avoid hearing another child call a strange man ' father ' or getting to know that the gardener is Jack's ' father,' etc. The word then comes to mean to the child ' a grown-up person who goes with or belongs to a little one,' and he will say, " See, there goes a dog with his father." Or, he comes to know that the cat is the kittens' father, and the dog the puppies' father, and next day asks, " Wasps, are they the flies' father, or are they perhaps their mother ? " (as Frans did, 4.10). Finally, by such guessing and drawing conclusions he gains full understanding of the word, and is ready to make acquaintance later with its more remote applications, as 'The King is the father of his people ; Father O'Flynn ; Boyle was the father of chemistry,' etc.

Difficulties are caused to the child when its father puts himself on the child's plane and calls his wife 'mother' just as he calls his own mother 'mother,' though at other moments the child hears him call her 'grandmother' or 'grannie.' Professor Sturtevant writes to me that a neighbour child, a girl of about five years, called out to him, "I saw your girl and your mother," meaning 'your daughter and your wife.' In many families the words 'sister' ('Sissie') or 'brother' are used constantly instead of his or her real name. Here we see the reason why so often such names of relations change their meaning in the history of languages ; G. *vetter* probably at first meant 'father's brother,' as it corresponds to Latin *patruus* ; G. *base*, from 'father's sister,' came to mean also 'mother's sister,' 'niece' and 'cousin.' The word that corresponds etymologically to our *mother* has come to mean 'wife' or 'woman' in Lithuanian and 'sister' in Albanian.

The same extension that we saw in the case of 'father' now may take place with real proper names. Tony E. (3.5), when a fresh charwoman came, told his mother not to have *this Mary* : the last charwoman's name was Mary.[1] In exactly the same way a Danish child applied the name of their servant, Ingeborg, as a general word for servant: "Auntie's Ingeborg is called Ann," etc., and a German girl said *viele Augusten* for 'many girls.' This, of course, is the way in which *doll* has come to mean a 'toy baby,' and we use the same extension when we say of a statesman that he is no *Bismarck*, etc.

VI.—§ 4. The Delimitation of Meaning.

The association of a word with its meaning is accomplished for the child by a series of single incidents, and as many words are understood only by the help of the situation, it is natural that the exact force of many of them is not seized at once. A boy of 4.10, hearing that his father had seen the King, inquired, "Has he a head at both ends ? "—his conception of a king being derived from playing-cards. Another child was born on what the Danes call Constitution Day, the consequence being that he confused birthday and Constitution Day, and would speak of "my Consti-

[1] Cf. Beach-la-Mar, below, Ch. XII § 1.

tution Day," and then his brother and sister also began to talk of their Constitution Day.

Hilary M. (2.0) and Murdoch D. (2.6) used *dinner, breakfast* and *tea* interchangeably—the words might be translated ' meal.' Other more or less similar confusions may be mentioned here. Tony F. (2.8) used the term *sing* for (1) reading, (2) singing, (3) any game in which his elders amused him. Hilary said indifferently, ' Daddy, *sing* a story three bears,' and ' Daddy, *tell* a story three bears.' She cannot remember which is *knife* and which is *fork*. Beth M. (2.6) always used *can't* when she meant *won't*. It meant simply refusal to do what she did not want to.

VI.—§ 5. Numerals. Time.

It is interesting to watch the way in which arithmetical notions grow in extent and clearness. Many children learn very early to say *one, two*, which is often said to them when they learn how to walk ; but no ideas are associated with these syllables. In the same way many children are drilled to say *three* when the parents begin with *one, two*, etc. The idea of plurality is gradually developed, but a child may very well answer *two* when asked how many fingers papa has ; Frans used the combinations *some-two* and *some-three* to express ' more than one ' (2.4). At the age of 2.11 he was very fond of counting, but while he always got the first four numbers right, he would skip over 5 and 7 ; and when asked to count the apples in a bowl, he would say rapidly 1–2–3–4, even if there were only three, or stop at 3, even if there were five or more. At 3.4 he counted objects as far as 10 correctly, but might easily pass from 11 to 13, and if the things to be counted were not placed in a row he was apt to bungle by moving his fingers irregularly from one to another. When he was 3.8 he answered the question " What do 2 and 2 make ? " quite correctly, but next day to the same question he answered " Three," though in a doubtful tone of voice. This was in the spring, and next month I noted : " His sense of number is evidently weaker than it was : the open-air life makes him forget this as well as all the verses he knew by heart in the winter." When the next winter came his counting exercises again amused him, but at first he was in a fix as before about any numbers after 6, although he could repeat the numbers till 10 without a mistake. He was fond of doing sums, and had initiated this game himself by asking : " Mother, if I have two apples and get one more, haven't I then three ?" His sense of numbers was so abstract that he was caught by a tricky question : " If you have two eyes and one nose, how many ears have you ? " He answered at once, " Three ! " A child thus seems to think in

abstract numbers, and as he learns his numbers as 1, 2, 3, 4, etc.,
not as one pear, two pears, three pears, one may well be skeptical
about the justification for the recommendation made by many
pedagogues that at an early stage of the school-life a child should
learn to reckon with concrete things rather than with abstract
numbers.

A child will usually be familiar with the sound of higher
numerals long before it has any clear notion of what they mean.
Frans (3.6) said, "They are coming by a train that is called four
thirty-four," and (4.4) he asked, "How much is twice hundred?
Is that a thousand?"

A child's ideas of time are necessarily extremely vague to
begin with; it cannot connect very clear or very definite notions
with the expressions it constantly hears others employ, such as
'last Sunday,' 'a week ago,' or 'next year.' The other day I
heard a little girl say: "This is where we sat *next time*," evidently
meaning 'last time.' All observers of children mention the
frequent confusion of words like *to-morrow* and *yesterday*, and the
linguist remembers that Gothic *gistradagis* means 'to-morrow,'
though it corresponds formally with E. *yesterday* and G. *gestern*.

VI.—§ 6. Various Difficulties.

Very small children will often say *up* both when they want
to be taken up and when they want to be put down on the floor.
This generally means nothing else than that they have not yet
learnt the word *down*, and *up* to them simply is a means to obtain
a change of position. In the same way a German child used *hut
auf* for having the hat taken off as well as put on, but Meumann
rightly interprets this as an undifferentiated desire to have something happen with the hat. But even with somewhat more
advanced children there are curious confusions.

Hilary M. (2.0) is completely baffled by words of opposite meaning. She will say, "Daddy, my pinny is too *hot*; I must warm it
at the fire." She goes to the fire and comes back, saying, "That's
better; it's quite *cool* now." (The same confusion of *hot* and *cold*
was also reported in the case of one Danish and one German child;
cf. also Tracy, p. 134.) One morning while dressing she said,
"What a *nice* windy day," and an hour or two later, before
she had been out, "What a *nasty* windy day." She confuses
good and *naughty* completely. Tony F. (2.5) says, "Turn the
dark out."

Sometimes a mere accidental likeness may prove too much
for the child. When Hilary M. had a new doll (2.0) her mother
said to her: "And is that your *son*?" Hilary was puzzled, and

looking out of the window at the sun, said : " No, that's my sun."
It was very difficult to set her out of this confusion.[1]　Her sister
Beth (3.8), looking at a sunset, said : " That's what you call a *sun-
set* ; where Ireland (her sister) is (at school) it's a *summerset*."
About the same time, when staying at *Longwood Farm*, she said :
" I suppose if the trees were cut down it would be *Shortwood
Farm* ? "

An English friend writes to me : " I misunderstood the text,
' And there fell from his eyes as it were scales,' as I knew the word
scales only in the sense ' balances.'　The phenomenon seemed to
me a strange one, but I did not question that it occurred, any
more than I questioned other strange phenomena recounted in
the Bible.　In the lines of the hymn—

> Teach me to live that I may dread
> The grave as little as my bed—

I supposed that the words ' as little as my bed ' were descriptive
of my future grave, and that it was my duty according to the
hymn to fear the grave."

Words with several meanings may cause children much difficulty.　A Somerset child said, " Moses was not a good boy, and
his mother smacked 'un and smacked 'un and smacked 'un till
she couldn't do it no more, and then she put 'un in the ark of
bulrushes."　This puzzled the teacher till he looked at the passage
in Exodus : " And when she could *hide* him no longer, she laid
him in an ark of bulrushes."　Here, of course, we have technically
two different words *hide* ; but to the child the difficulty is
practically as great where we have what is called one and the
same word with two distinct meanings, or when a word is used
figuratively.

The word ' child ' means two different things, which in some
languages are expressed by two distinct words.　I remember my
own astonishment at the age of nine when I heard my godmother
talk of her children.　" But you have no children."　" Yes, Clara
and Eliza."　I knew them, of course, but they were grown up.

Take again the word *old*.　A boy knew that he was three years,
but could not be induced to say ' three years old '; no, he is three
years new, and his father too is new, as distinct from his grandmother, who he knows is old.　A child asked, " Why have
grand dukes and *grand* pianos got the same name ? " (Glenconner, p. 21).

When Frans was told (4.4) " Your eyes are running," he was
much astonished, and asked, " Are they running away ? "

---

[1] Cf. below on the disappearance of the word *son* because it sounds like
sun (Ch. XV. § 7).

Sometimes a child knows a word first in some secondary sense. When a country child first came to Copenhagen and saw a soldier, he said, " There is a tin-soldier " (2.0). Stern has a story about his daughter who was taken to the country and wished to pat the backs of the pigs, but was checked with the words, " Pigs always lie in dirt," when she was suddenly struck with a new idea ; " Ah, that is why they are called pigs, because they are so dirty : but what would people call them if they didn't lie in the dirt ? " History repeats itself : only the other day a teacher wrote to me that one of his pupils had begun his essay with the words : " Pigs are rightly called thus, for they are such swine."

Words of similar sound are apt to be confused. Some children have had trouble till mature years with *soldier* and *shoulder*, *hassock* and *cassock*, *diary* and *dairy*. Lady Glenconner writes : " They almost invariably say ' lemon ' [for melon], and if they make an effort to be more correct they still mispronounce it. ' Don't say melling.' ' Very well, then, mellum.' " Among other confusions mentioned in her book I may quote *Portugal* for ' purgatory,' King Solomon's three hundred *Columbines*, David and his great friend *Johnson*, Cain and *Mabel*—all of them showing how words from spheres beyond the ordinary ken of children are assimilated to more familiar ones.

Schuchardt has a story of a little coloured boy in the West Indies who said, " It's *three* hot in this room " : he had heard *too*= *two* and literally wanted to ' go one better.' According to Mr. James Payne, a boy for years substituted for the words ' *Hallowed* be Thy name ' ' *Harold* be Thy name.' Many children imagine that there is a *pole* to mark where the North Pole is, and even (like Helen Keller) that polar bears climb the Pole.

This leads us naturally to what linguists call ' popular etymology '—which is very frequent with children in all countries. I give a few examples from books. A four-year-old boy had heard several times about his nurse's *neuralgia*, and finally said : " I don't think it's *new* ralgia, I call it old ralgia." In this way *anchovies* are made into *hamchovies*, *whirlwind* into *worldwind*, and *holiday* into *hollorday*, a day to holloa. Professor Sturtevant writes : A boy of six or seven had frequently had his ear irrigated ; when similar treatment was applied to his nose, he said that he had been ' nosigated '— he had evidently given his own interpretation to the first syllable of *irrigate*.

There is an element of ' popular etymology ' in the following joke which was made by one of the Glenconner children when four years old : " I suppose you wag along in the *wagonette*, the *landau* lands you at the door, and you sweep off in the *brougham* " (pronounced broom).

VI.—§ 7. Shifters.

A class of words which presents grave difficulty to children are those whose meaning differs according to the situation, so that the child hears them now applied to one thing and now to another. That was the case with words like 'father,' and 'mother.' Another such word is 'enemy.' When Frans (4.5) played a war-game with Eggert, he could not get it into his head that he was Eggert's enemy : no, it was only Eggert who was the enemy. A stronger case still is 'home.' When a child was asked if his grandmother had been at home, and answered : " No, grandmother was at grandfather's," it is clear that for him ' at home ' meant merely ' at my home.' Such words may be called shifters. When Frans (3.6) heard it said that ' the one ' (glove) was as good as ' the other,' he asked, "Which is the one, and which is the other ? "—a question not easy to answer.

The most important class of shifters are the personal pronouns. The child hears the word ' I ' meaning ' Father,' then again meaning ' Mother,' then again ' Uncle Peter,' and so on unendingly in the most confusing manner. Many people realize the difficulty thus presented to the child, and to obviate it will speak of themselves in the third person as ' Father ' or ' Grannie ' or ' Mary,' and instead of saying ' you ' to the child, speak of it by its name. The child's understanding of what is said is thus facilitated for the moment : but on the other hand the child in this way hears these little words less frequently and is slower in mastering them.

If some children soon learn to say ' I ' while others speak of themselves by their name, the difference is not entirely due to the different mental powers of the children, but must be largely attributed to their elders' habit of addressing them by their name or by the pronouns. But Germans would not be Germans, and philosophers would not be philosophers, if they did not make the most of the child's use of ' I,' in which they see the first sign of self-consciousness. The elder Fichte, we are told, used to celebrate not his son's birthday, but the day on which he first spoke of himself as ' I.' The sober truth is, I take it, that a boy who speaks of himself as ' Jack ' can have just as full and strong a perception of himself as opposed to the rest of the world as one who has learnt the little linguistic trick of saying ' I.' But this does not suit some of the great psychologists, as seen from the following quotation : " The child uses no pronouns ; it speaks of itself in the third person, because it has no idea of its ' I ' (Ego) nor of its ' Not-I,' because it knows nothing of itself nor of others."

It is not an uncommon case of confusion for a child to use 'you' and 'your' instead of 'I,' 'me,' and 'mine.' The child has noticed that 'will you have ?' means 'will Jack have ?' so that he looks on 'you' as synonymous with his own name. In some children this confusion may last for some months. It is in some cases connected with an inverted word-order, 'do you' meaning 'I do'—an instance of 'echoism' (see below). Sometimes he will introduce a further complication by using the personal pronoun of the third person, as though he had started the sentence with 'Jack'—then 'you have his coat' means 'I have my coat.' He may even speak of the person addressed as 'I.' 'Will I tell a story ?' = 'Will you tell a story ?' Frans was liable to use these confused forms between the ages of two and two and a-half, and I had to quicken his acquaintance with the right usage by refusing to understand him when he used the wrong. Beth M. (2.6) was very jealous about her elder sister touching any of her property, and if the latter sat on her chair, she would shriek out : "That's *your* chair ; that's *your* chair."

The forms *I* and *me* are a common source of difficulty to English children. Both Tony E. (2.7 to 3.0) and Hilary M. (2.0) use *my* for *me* ; it is apparently a kind of blending of *me* and *I* ; e.g. "Give Hilary medicine, make *my* better," "Maggy is looking at *my*," "Give it *my*." See also O'Shea, p. 81 : '*my* want to do this or that ; *my* feel bad ; that is *my* pencil ; take *my* to bed.'

His and *her* are difficult to distinguish : "An ill lady, *his* legs were bad " (Tony E., 3.3).

C. M. L. (about the end of her second year) constantly used *wour* and *wours* for *our* and *ours*, the connexion being with *we*, as 'your' with *you*. In exactly the same way many Danish children say *vos* for *os* on account of *vi*. But all this really falls under our next chapter.

VI.—§ 8. Extent of Vocabulary.

The number of words which the child has at command is constantly increasing, but not uniformly, as the increase is affected by the child's health and the new experiences which life presents to him. In the beginning it is tolerably easy to count the words the child uses ; later it becomes more difficult, as there are times when his command of speech grows with astonishing rapidity. There is great difference between individual children. Statistics have often been given of the extent of a child's vocabulary at different ages, or of the results of comparing the vocabularies of a number of children.

An American child who was closely observed by his mother, Mrs. Winfield S. Hall, had in the tenth month 3 words, in the eleventh 12, in the twelfth 24, in the thirteenth 38, in the fourteenth 48, in the fifteenth 106, in the sixteenth 199, and in the seventeenth 232 words (*Child Study Monthly*, March 1897). During the first month after the same boy was six years old, slips of paper and pencils were distributed over the house and practically everything which the child said was written down. After two or three days these were collected and the words were put under their respective letters in a book kept for that purpose. New sets of papers were put in their places and other lists made. In addition to this, the record of his life during the past year was examined and all of his words not already listed were added. In this way his summer vocabulary was obtained; conversations on certain topics were also introduced to give him an opportunity to use words relating to such topics. The list is printed in the *Journal of Childhood and Adolescence*, January 1902, and is well worth looking through. It contains 2,688 words, apart from proper names and numerals. No doubt the child was really in command of words beyond that total.

This list perhaps is exceptional on account of the care with which it was compiled, but as a rule I am afraid that it is not wise to attach much importance to these tables of statistics. One is generally left in the dark whether the words counted are those that the child has understood, or those that it has actually used —two entirely different things. The passive or receptive knowledge of a language always goes far beyond the active or productive.

One also gets the impression that the observers have often counted up words without realizing the difficulties involved. What is to be counted as a word ? Are *I*, *me*, *we*, *us* one word or four ? Is *teacup* a new word for a child who already knows *tea* and *cup* ? And so for all compounds. Is *box* (= a place at a theatre) the same word as *box* (= workbox) ? Are the two *thats* in ' that man that you see ' two words or one ? It is clear that the process of counting involves so much that is arbitrary and uncertain that very little can be built on the statistics arrived at.

It is more interesting perhaps to determine what words at a given age a child does *not* know, or rather does not understand when he hears them or when they occur in his reading. I have myself collected such lists, and others have been given me by teachers, who have been astonished at words which their classes did not understand. A teacher can never be too cautious about assuming linguistic knowledge in his pupils—and this applies not only to foreign words, about which all teachers are on the alert, but also to what seem to be quite everyday words of the language of the country.

In connexion with the growth of vocabulary one may ask how many words are possessed by the average grown-up man ? Max Müller in his *Lectures* stated on the authority of an English clergyman that an English farm labourer has only about three hundred words at command. This is the most utter balderdash, but nevertheless it has often been repeated, even by such an authority on psychology as Wundt. A Danish boy can easily learn seven hundred English words in the first year of his study of the language—and are we to believe that a grown Englishman, even of the lowest class, has no greater stock than such a beginner ? If you go through the list of 2,000 to 3,000 words used by the American boy of six referred to above, you will easily convince yourself that they would far from suffice for the rudest labourer. A Swedish dialectologist, after a minute investigation, found that the vocabulary of Swedish peasants amounted to at least 26,000 words, and his view has been confirmed by other investigators. This conclusion is not invalidated by the fact that Shakespeare in his works uses only about 20,000 words and Milton in his poems only about 8,000. It is easy to see what a vast number of words of daily life are seldom or never required by a poet, especially a poet like Milton, whose works are on elevated subjects. The words used by Zola or Kipling or Jack London would no doubt far exceed those used by Shakespeare and Milton.[1]

VI.—§ 9. Summary.

To sum up, then. There are only very few words that are explained to the child, and so long as it is quite small it will not even understand the explanations that might be given. Some it learns because, when the word is used, the object is at the same time pointed at, but most words it can only learn by drawing conclusions about their meaning from the situation in which they arise or from the context in which they are used. These conclusions, however, are very uncertain, or they may be correct for the particular occasion and not hold good on some other, to the child's mind quite similar, occasion. Grown-up people are in the same position with regard to words they do not know, but which they come across in a book or newspaper, e.g. *demise*. The meanings of many words are at the same time extraordinarily vague and yet so strictly limited (at least in some respects) that the least deviation is felt as a mistake. Moreover, the child often learns a secondary or figurative meaning of a word before its simple

[1] Cf. the fuller treatment of this question in GS ch. ix.

meaning. But gradually a high degree of accuracy is obtained, the fittest meanings surviving—that is (in this connexion) those that agree best with those of the surrounding society. And thus the individual is merged in society, and the social character of language asserts itself through the elimination of everything that is the exclusive property of one person only.

GRAMMAR

VII.—§ 1. Introductory.

To learn a language it is not enough to know so many words. They must be connected according to the particular laws of the particular language. No one tells the child that the plural of 'hand' is *hands*, of 'foot' *feet*, of 'man' *men*, or that the past of 'am' is *was*, of 'love' *loved*; it is not informed when to say *he* and when *him*, or in what order words must stand. How can the little fellow learn all this, which when set forth in a grammar fills many pages and can only be explained by help of many learned words?

Many people will say it comes by 'instinct,' as if 'instinct' were not one of those fine words which are chiefly used to cover over what is not understood, because it says so precious little and seems to say so precious much. But when other people, using a more everyday expression, say that it all 'comes quite of itself,' I must strongly demur: so far is it from 'coming of itself' that it demands extraordinary labour on the child's part. The countless grammatical mistakes made by a child in its early years are a tell-tale proof of the difficulty which this side of language presents to him—especially, of course, on account of the unsystematic character of our flexions and the irregularity of its so-called 'rules' of syntax.

At first each word has only one form for the child, but he soon discovers that grown-up people use many forms which resemble one another in different connexions, and he gets a sense of the purport of these forms, so as to be able to imitate them himself or even develop similar forms of his own. These latter forms are what linguists call analogy-formations: by analogy with 'Jack's hat' and 'father's hat' the child invents such as 'uncle's hat' and 'Charlie's hat'—and inasmuch as these forms are 'correct,' no one can say on hearing them whether the child has really invented them or has first heard them used by others. It is just on account of the fact that the forms developed on the spur of the moment by each individual are in the vast majority of instances perfectly identical with those used already by other people, that the principle of analogy comes to have such paramount importance in the life of language, for we are all thereby driven to apply it unhesitatingly to all those instances in which we have no ready-made form handy : without being conscious of it, each of us thus now and then really creates something never heard before by us or anybody else.

VII.—§ 2. Substantives and Adjectives.

The -*s* of the possessive is so regular in English that it is not difficult for the child to attach it to all words as soon as the character of the termination has dawned upon him. But at first there is a time with many children in which words are put together without change, so that ' Mother hat ' stands for ' Mother's hat ' ; cf. also sentences like " Baby want baby milk."

After the *s*-form has been learnt, it is occasionally attached to pronouns, as *you's* for ' your,' or more rarely *I's* or *me's* for ' my.'

The -*s* is now in English added freely to whole groups of words, as in *the King of England's power*, where the old construction was *the King's power of England*, and in *Beaumont and Fletcher's plays* (see on the historical development of this group genitive my ChE iii.). In Danish we have exactly the same construction, and Danish children will very frequently extend it, placing the -*s* at the end of a whole interrogative sentence, e.g., ' Hvem er det da's ? ' (as if in English, ' Who is it then's,' instead of ' Whose is it then ? '). Dr. H. Bradley once wrote to me : " One of your samples of children's Danish is an exact parallel to a bit of child's English that I noted long ago. My son, when a little boy, used to say ' Who is that-'s ' (with a pause before the *s*) for ' Whom does that belong to ? ' "

Irregular plurals are often regularized, *gooses* for ' geese,' *tooths*, *knifes*, etc O'Shea mentions one child who inversely formed the plural *chieves* for *chiefs* on the analogy of *thieves*.

Sometimes the child becomes acquainted with the plural form first, and from it forms a singular. I have noticed this several times with Danish children, who had heard the irregular plural *kœr*, ' cows,' and then would say *en kø* instead of *en ko* (while others from the singular *ko* form a regular plural *koer*). French children will say *un chevau* instead of *un cheval*.

In the comparison of adjectives analogy-formations are frequent with all children, e.g. *the littlest, littler, goodest, baddest, splendider,* etc. One child is reported as saying *quicklier,* another as saying *quickerly,* instead of the received *more quickly.* A curious formation is " P'raps it was John, but *p'rapser* it was Mary."

O'Shea (p. 108) notices a period of transition when the child may use the analogical form at one moment and the traditional one the next. Thus S. (4.0) will say *better* perhaps five times where he says *gooder* once, but in times of excitement he will revert to the latter form.

VII.—§ 3. Verbs.

The child at first tends to treat all verbs on the analogy of *love, loved, loved,* or *kiss, kissed, kissed,* thus *catched, buyed, frowed* for ' caught, bought, threw or thrown,' etc., but gradually it learns the irregular forms, though in the beginning with a good deal of hesitation and confusion, as *done* for ' did,' *hunged* for ' hung,' etc. O'Shea gives among other sentences (p. 94): " I *drunked* my milk." " Budd *swunged* on the rings." " Grandpa *boughted* me a ring." " I *caughted* him." " Aunt Net *camed* to-day." " He *gaved* it to me "—in all of which the irregular form has been supplemented with the regular ending.

A little Danish incident may be thus rendered in English. The child (4.6): " I have seed a chestnut." " Where have you seen it ? " He : " I seen it in the garden." This shows the influence of the form last heard.

I once heard a French child say " Il a pleuvy " for ' plu ' from ' pleuvoir.' Other analogical forms are *prendu* for ' pris '; *assire* for ' asseoir ' (from the participle *assis*), *se taiser* for ' se taire ' (from the frequent injunction *taisez-vous*). Similar formations are frequent in all countries.

VII.—§ 4. Degrees of Consciousness.

Do the little brains *think* about these different forms and their uses ? Or is the learning of language performed as unconsciously as the circulation of the blood or the process of digestion ? Clearly they do not think about grammatical forms in the way pursued in grammar-lessons, with all the forms of the same word arranged side by side of one another, with rules and exceptions. Still there is much to lead us to believe that the thing does not go of itself without some thinking over. The fact that in later years we speak our language without knowing how we do it, the right words and phrases coming to us no one knows how or whence, is no proof that it was always so. We ride a bicycle without giving a thought to the machine, look around us, talk with a friend, etc., and yet there was a time when every movement had to be mastered by slow and painful efforts. There would be nothing strange in supposing that it is the same with the acquisition of language.

Of course, it would be idle to ask children straight out if they think about these things, and what they think. But now and then one notices something which shows that at an early age they think about points of grammar a good deal. When Frans was 2.9, he lay in bed not knowing that anyone was in the next room, and he was heard to say quite plainly: "Små hænder hedder det—lille hånd—små hænder—lille hænder, næ små hænder." ("They are called small hands—little hand—small hands—little hands, no, small hands " : in Danish *lille* is not used with a plural noun.) Similar things have been related to me by other parents, one child, for instance, practising plural forms while turning over the leaves of a picture-book, and another one, who was corrected for saying *nak* instead of *nikkede* ('nodded '), immediately retorted " *Stikker stak, nikker nak,*" thus showing on what analogy he had formed the new preterit. Frequently children, after giving a form which their own ears tell them is wrong, at once correct it : ' I sticked it in—I stuck it in.'

A German child, not yet two, said : "Papa, hast du mir was mitgebringt —gebrungen—gebracht ? " almost at a breath (Gabelentz), and another (2.5) said *hausin*, but then hesitated and added : "Man kann auch häuser sagen " (Meringer).

VII.—§ 5. Word-formation.

In the forming of words the child's brain is just as active. In many cases, again, it will be impossible to distinguish between what the child has heard and merely copied and what it has itself fashioned to a given pattern. If a child, for example, uses the word ' kindness,' it is probable that he has heard it before, but it is not certain, because he might equally well have formed the word himself. If, however, we hear him say ' kindhood,' or ' kindship,' or ' wideness,' ' broadness,' ' stupidness,' we know for certain that he has made the word up himself, because the resultant differs from the form used in the language he hears around him. A child who does not know the word ' spade ' may call the tool a *digger* ; he may speak of a lamp as a *shine*. He may say *it suns* when the sun is shining (cf. it rains), or ask his mother to *sauce* his pudding. It is quite natural that the enormous number of nouns and verbs of exactly the same form in English (*blossom, care, drink, end, fight, fish, ape, hand, dress,* etc.) should induce children to make new verbs according to the same pattern ;

I quote a few of the examples given by O'Shea: "I am going to *basket* these apples." "I *pailed* him out" (took a turtle out of a washtub with a pail). "I *needled* him" (put a needle through a fly).

Other words are formed by means of derivative endings, as *sorrified, lessoner* (O'Shea 32), *flyable* (able to fly, Glenconner 3); "This tooth ought to come out, because it is *crookening* the others" (a ten-year-old, told me by Professor Ayres). Compound nouns, too, may be freely formed, such as *wind-ship, eye-curtain* (O'Shea), a *fun-copy* of Romeo and Juliet (travesty, Glenconner 19). Bryan L. (ab. 5) said *springklers* for chrysalises ('because they wake up in the spring').

Sometimes a child will make up a new word through 'blending' two, as when Hilary M. (1.8 to 2) spoke of *rubbish* = the *rub*ber to pol*ish* the boots, or of the *backet*, from *bat* and *racquet*. Beth M. (2.0) used *breakolate*, from *break*fast and cho*colate*, and *Chally* as a child's name, a compound of two sisters, *Cha*rity and *Sa*lly.

VII.—§ 6. Word-division.

We are so accustomed to see sentences in writing or print with a little space left after each word, that we have got altogether wrong conceptions of language as it is spoken. Here words follow one another without the least pause till the speaker hesitates for a word or has come to the end of what he has to say. 'Not at all' sounds like 'not a tall.' It therefore requires in many cases a great deal of comparison and analysis on the part of the child to find out what is one and what two or three words. We have seen before that the question 'How big is the boy?' is to the child a single expression, beyond his powers of analysis, and to a much later age it is the same with other phrases. The child, then, may make false divisions, and either treat a group of words as one word or one word as a group of words. A girl (2.6) used the term 'Tanobijeu' whenever she wished her younger brother to get out of her way. Her parents finally discovered that she had caught up and shortened a phrase that some older children had used—''Tend to your own business' (O'Shea).

A child, addressing her cousin as 'Aunt Katie,' was told "I am not Aunt Katie, I am merely Katie." Next day she said: "Good-morning, Aunt merely-Katie" (translated). A child who had been praised with the words, 'You are a good boy,' said to his mother, "You're a good boy, mother" (2.8).

Cecil H. (4.0) came back from a party and said that she had been given something very nice to eat. "What was it?"

"Rats." "No, no." "Well, it was mice then." She had been asked if she would have 'some-ice,' and had taken it to be 'some mice.' S. L. (2.6) constantly used '*ababana*' for 'banana'; the form seems to have come from the question "Will you have a banana?" but was used in such a sentence as "May I have an ababana?" Children will often say *napple* for *apple* through a misdivision of *an-apple*, and *normous* for *enormous*; cf. Ch. X § 2.

A few examples may be added from children's speech in other countries. Ronjat's child said *nésey* for 'échelle,' starting from u'ne échelle; Grammont's child said *un tarbre*, starting from *cet arbre*, and *ce nos* for 'cet os,' from *un os*; a German child said *motel* for 'hotel,' starting from the combination 'im (h) otel' (Stern). Many German children say *arrhöe*, because they take the first syllable of 'diarrhöe' as the feminine article. A Dutch child heard the phrase ''k weet 't niet' ('I don't know'), and said "Papa, hij kweet 't niet" (Van Ginneken). A Danish child heard his father say, "Jeg skal op i *ministeriet*" ("I'm going to the Government office"), and took the first syllable as *min* (my); consequently he asked, "Skal du i dinisteriet?" A French child was told that they expected Munkácsy (the celebrated painter, in French pronounced as Mon-), and asked his aunt: "Est-ce que *ton Kácsy* ne viendra pas?" Antoinette K. (7.), in reply to "C'est bien, je te félicite," said, "Eh bien, moi je ne te *fais* pas *licite*."

The German 'Ich habe *antʒewortet*' is obviously on the analogy of *angenommen*, etc. (Meringer). Danish children not unfrequently take the verb *telefonere* as two words, and in the interrogative form will place the personal pronoun in the middle of it, 'Tele hun fonerer?' ('Does she telephone?') A girl asked to see *ele mer fant* (as if in English she had said 'ele more phant'). Cf. 'Give me *more handier-cap*' for 'Give me a greater handicap' —in a foot-race (O'Shea 108).

VII.—§ 7. Sentences.

In the first period the child knows nothing of grammar: it does not connect words together, far less form sentences, but each word stands by itself. 'Up' means what we should express by a whole sentence, 'I want to get up,' or 'Lift me up'; 'Hat' means 'Put on my hat,' or 'I want to put my hat on,' or 'I have my hat on,' or 'Mamma has a new hat on'; 'Father' can be either 'Here comes Father,' or 'This is Father,' or 'He is called Father,' or 'I want Father to come to me,' or 'I want this or that from Father.' This particular group of sounds is vaguely associated with the mental picture of the person in question, and is uttered at the sight of him or at the mere wish to see him or something else in connexion with him.

When we say that such a word means what we should express by a whole sentence, this does not amount to saying that the child's ' Up ' *is* a sentence, or a sentence-word, as many of those who have written about these questions have said. We might just as well assert that clapping our hands is a sentence, because it expresses the same idea (or the same frame of mind) that is otherwise expressed by the whole sentence ' This is splendid.' The word ' sentence ' presupposes a certain grammatical structure, which is wanting in the child's utterance.

Many investigators have asserted that the child's first utterances are not means of imparting information, but always an expression of the child's wishes and requirements. This is certainly somewhat of an exaggeration, since the child quite clearly can make known its joy at seeing a hat or a plaything, or at merely being able to recognize it and remember the word for it ; but the statement still contains a great deal of truth, for without strong feelings a child would not say much, and it is a great stimulus to talk that he very soon discovers that he gets his wishes fulfilled more easily when he makes them known by means of certain sounds.

Frans (1.7) was accustomed to express his longings in general by help of a long *m* with rising tone, while at the same time stretching out his hand towards the particular thing that he longed for. This he did, for example, at dinner, when he wanted water. One day his mother said, " Now see if you can say *vand* (water)," and at once he said what was an approach to the word, and was delighted at getting something to drink by that means. A moment later he repeated what he had said, and was inexpressibly delighted to have found the password which at once brought him something to drink. This was repeated several times. Next day, when his father was pouring out water for himself, the boy again said ' van,' ' van,' and was duly rewarded. He had not heard the word during the intervening twenty-four hours, and nothing had been done to remind him of it. After some repetitions (for he only got a few drops at a time) he pronounced the word for the first time quite correctly. The day after, the same thing occurred ; the word was never heard but at dinner. When he became rather a nuisance with his constant cries for water, his mother said : " Say please "—and immediately came his " Bebe vand " (" Water, please ")—his first attempt to put two words together.

Later—in this formless period—the child puts more and more words together, often in quite haphazard order : ' My go snow '

('I want to go out into the snow'), etc. A Danish child of 2.1 said the Danish words (imperfectly pronounced, of course) corresponding to "Oh papa lamp mother boom," when his mother had struck his father's lamp with a bang. Another child said "Papa hen corn cap" when he saw his father give corn to the hens out of his cap.

When Frans was 1.10, passing a post-office (which Danes call 'posthouse'), he said of his own accord the Danish words for 'post, house, bring, letter' (a pause between the successive words) —I suppose that the day before he had heard a sentence in which these words occurred. In the same month, when he had thrown a ball a long way, he said what would be in English 'dat was good.' This was not a sentence which he had put together for himself, but a mere repetition of what had been said to him, clearly conceived as a whole, and equivalent to 'bravo.' Sentences of this kind, however, though taken as units, prepare the way for the understanding of the words 'that' and 'was' when they turn up in other connexions.

One thing which plays a great rôle in children's acquisition of language, and especially in their early attempts to form sentences, is Echoism : the fact that children echo what is said to them. When one is learning a foreign language, it is an excellent method to try to imitate to oneself in silence every sentence which one hears spoken by a native. By that means the turns of phrases, the order of words, the intonation of the sentence are firmly fixed in the memory—so that they can be recalled when required, or rather recur to one quite spontaneously without an effort. What the grown man does of conscious purpose our children to a large extent do without a thought—that is, they repeat aloud what they have just heard, either the whole, if it is a very short sentence, or more commonly the conclusion, as much of it as they can retain in their short memories. The result is a matter of chance—it need not always have a meaning or consist of entire words. Much, clearly, is repeated without being understood, much, again, without being more than half understood. Take, for example (translated) :

Shall I carry you ?—Frans (1.9) : Carry you.
Shall Mother carry Frans ?—Carry Frans.
The sky is so blue.—So boo.
I shall take an umbrella.—Take rella.

Though this feature in a child's mental history has been often noticed, no one seems to have seen its full significance. One of the acutest observers (Meumann, p. 28) even says that it has no importance in the development of the child's speech. On the contrary, I think that Echoism explains very much indeed. First let us bear in mind the mutilated forms of words which a child

uses : *'chine* for machine, *'gar* for cigar, *Trix* for Beatrix, etc.
Then a child's frequent use of an indirect form of question rather
than direct, 'Why you smoke, Father ? ' which can hardly be
explained except as an echo of sentences like 'Tell me why you
smoke.' This plays a greater rôle in Danish than in English,
and the corresponding form of the sentence has been frequently
remarked by Danish parents. Another feature which is nearly
constant with Danish children at the age when echoing is habitual
is the inverted word order : this is used after an initial adverb
(*nu kommer hun*, etc.), but the child will use it in all cases (*kommer
hun*, etc.). Further, the extremely frequent use of the infinitive,
because the child hears it towards the end of a sentence, where
it is dependent on a preceding *can*, or *may*, or *must*. 'Not eat
that ' is a child's echo of 'You mustn't eat that.' In German
this has become the ordinary form of official order : " Nicht
hinauslehnen " (" Do not lean out of the window ").

VII.—§ 8. Negation and Question.

Most children learn to say 'no' before they can say 'yes'
—simply because negation is a stronger expression of feeling than
affirmation. Many little children use *nenenene* (short *ĕ*) as a
natural expression of fretfulness and discomfort. It is perhaps
so natural that it need not be learnt : there is good reason for
the fact that in so many languages words of negation begin with
n (or *m*). Sometimes the *n* is heard without a vowel : it is only
the gesture of 'turning up one's nose '. made audible.

At first the child does not express what it is that it does
not want—it merely puts it away with its hand, pushes away,
for example, what is too hot for it. But when it begins to express
in words what it is that it will not have, it does so often in the
form 'Bread no,' often with a pause between the words, as two
separate utterances, as when we might say, in our fuller forms of
expression : 'Do you offer me bread ? I won't hear of it.' So
with verbs : 'I sleep no.' Thus with many Danish children,
and I find the same phenomenon mentioned with regard to children
of different nations. Tracy says (p. 136): "Negation was expressed
by an affirmative sentence, with an emphatic *no* tacked on at
the end, exactly as the deaf-mutes do." The blind-deaf Helen
Keller, when she felt her little sister's mouth and her mother
spelt 'teeth ' to her, answered : " Baby teeth—no, baby eat—
no," i.e., baby cannot eat because she has no teeth. In the same
way, in German, 'Stul nei nei—schossel,' i.e., I won't sit on the
chair, but in your lap, and in French, 'Papa abeié ato non, iaian
abeié non,' i.e., Papa n'est pas encore habillé, Suzanne n'est pas

habillée (Stern, 189, 203). It seems thus that this mode of expression will crop up everywhere as an emphatic negation.

Interrogative sentences come generally rather early—it would be better to say questions, because at first they do not take the form of interrogative sentences, the interrogation being expressed by bearing, look or gesture : when it begins to be expressed by intonation we are on the way to question expressed in speech. Some of the earliest questions have to do with place : ' Where is . . . ? ' The child very often hears such sentences as ' Where is its little nose ? ' which are not really meant as questions ; we may also remark that questions of this type are of great practical importance for the little thing, who soon uses them to beg for something which has been taken away from him or is out of his reach. Other early questions are ' What's that ? ' and ' Who ? '

Later—generally, it would seem, at the close of the third year —questions with ' why ' crop up : these are of the utmost importance for the child's understanding of the whole world and its manifold occurrences, and, however tiresome they may be when they come in long strings, no one who wishes well to his child will venture to discourage them. Questions about time, such as ' When ? How long ? ' appear much later, owing to the child's difficulty in acquiring exact ideas about time.

Children often find a difficulty in double questions, and when asked ' Will you have brown bread or white ? ' merely answer the last word with ' Yes.' So in reply to ' Is that red or yellow ? ' ' Yes ' means ' yellow ' (taken from a child of 4.11). I think this is an instance of the short memories of children, who have already at the end of the question forgotten the beginning, but Professor Mawer thinks that the real difficulty here is in making a choice : they cannot decide between alternatives : usually they are silent, and if they say ' Yes ' it only means that they do not want to go without both or feel that they must say something.

VII.—§ 9. Prepositions and Idioms.

Prepositions are of very late growth in a child's language. Much attention has been given to the point, and Stern has collected statistics of the ages at which various children have first used prepositions : the earliest age is 1.10, the average age is 2.3. It does not, however, seem to me to be a matter of much interest how early an individual word of some particular grammatical class is first used ; it is much more interesting to follow up the gradual growth of the child's command of this class and to see how the first inevitable mistakes and confusions arise in the little brain. Stern makes the interesting remark that when the tendency to use prepositions first appears, it grows far more rapidly than the power to discriminate one preposition from another ; with his own children there came a time when they employed the same word as a sort of universal preposition in all relations. Hilda used *von*, Eva *auf*. I have never observed anything corresponding to this among Danish children.

All children start by putting the words for the most important concepts together without connective words, so ' Leave go bedroom ' (' May I have leave to go into the bedroom ? '), ' Out road ' (' I am going out on the road '). The first use of prepositions is always in set phrases learnt as wholes, like ' go to school,' ' go to pieces,' ' lie in bed,' ' at dinner.' Not till later comes the power of using prepositions in free combinations, and it is then that mistakes appear. Nor is this surprising, since in all languages prepositional usage contains much that is peculiar and arbitrary, chiefly because when we once pass beyond a few quite clear applications of time and place, the relations to be expressed become so vague and indefinite, that logically one preposition might often seem just as right as another, although usage has laid down a fast law that this preposition must be used in this case and that in another. I noted down a great number of mistakes my own boy made in these words, but in all cases I was able to find some synonymous or antonymous expression in which the preposition used would have been the correct one, and which may have been vaguely before his mind.

The multiple meanings of prepositions sometimes have strange results. A little girl was in her bath, and hearing her mother say : " I will wash you in a moment," answered : " No, you must wash me in the bath " ! She was led astray by the two uses of *in*. We know of the child at school who was asked " What is an average ? " and said : " What the hen lays eggs on." Even men of science are similarly led astray by prepositions. It is perfectly natural to say that something has passed over the threshold of consciousness : the metaphor is from the way in which you enter a house by stepping over the threshold. If the metaphor were kept, the opposite situation would be expressed by the statement that such and such a thing is outside the threshold of consciousness. But psychologists, in the thoughtless way of little children, take *under* to be always the opposite of *over*, and so speak of things ' lying under (or below) the threshold of our consciousness,' and have even invented a Latin word for the unconscious, viz. *subliminal*.[1]

---

[1] H. G. Wells writes (*Soul of a Bishop*, 94) : " He was lugging things now into speech that so far had been *scarcely above the threshold* of his conscious thought." Here we see the wrong interpretation of the preposition *over* dragging with it the synonym *above*.

Children may use verbs with an object which require a preposition (' Will you *wait* me ? '), or which are only used intransitively (' Will you *jump* me ? '), or they may mix up an infinitival with a direct construction (' Could you hear me sneezed ? '). But it is surely needless to multiply examples.

When many years ago, in my *Progress in Language,* I spoke of the advantages, even to natives, of simplicity in linguistic structure, Professor Herman Möller, in a learned review, objected to me that to the adult learning a foreign tongue the chief difficulty consists in " the countless chicaneries due to the tyrannical and capricious usage, whose tricks there is no calculating ; but these offer to the native child no such difficulty as morphology may," and again, in speaking of the choice of various prepositions, which is far from easy to the foreigner, he says : " But any considerable mental exertion on the part of the native child learning its mother-tongue is here, of course, out of the question." Such assertions as these cannot be founded on actual observation ; at any rate, it is my experience in listening to children's talk that long after they have reached the point where they make hardly any mistake in pronunciation and verbal forms, etc., they are still capable of using many turns of speech which are utterly opposed to the spirit of the language, and which are in the main of the same kind as those which foreigners are apt to fall into. Many of the child's mistakes are due to mixtures or blendings of two turns of expression, and not a few of them may be logically justified. But learning a language implies among other things learning what you may *not* say in the language, even though no reasonable ground can be given for the prohibition.

CHAPTER VIII

SOME FUNDAMENTAL PROBLEMS

§ 1. Why is the Native Language learnt so well ?   § 2. Natural Ability and Sex.   § 3. Mother-tongue and Other Tongue.   § 4. Playing at Language.   § 5. Secret Languages.   § 6. Onomatopœia.   § 7. Word-inventions.   § 8. 'Mamma' and 'Papa.'

VIII.—§ 1. Why is the Native Language learnt so well ?

How does it happen that children in general learn their mother-tongue so well ?   That this is a problem becomes clear when we contrast a child's first acquisition of its mother-tongue with the later acquisition of any foreign tongue.   The contrast is indeed striking and manifold : *here* we have a quite little child, without experience or prepossessions ; *there* a bigger child, or it may be a grown-up person with all sorts of knowledge and powers : *here* a haphazard method of procedure ; *there* the whole task laid out in a system (for even in the schoolbooks that do not follow the old grammatical system there is a certain definite order of progress from more elementary to more difficult matters) : *here* no professional teachers, but chance parents, brothers and sisters, nursery-maids and playmates ; *there* teachers trained for many years specially to teach languages : *here* only oral instruction ; *there* not only that, but reading-books, dictionaries and other assistance. And yet this is the result : *here* complete and exact command of the language as a native speaks it, however stupid the children ; *there*, in most cases, even with people otherwise highly gifted, a defective and inexact command of the language.   On what does this difference depend ?

The problem has never been elucidated or canvassed from all sides, but here and there one finds a partial answer, often given out to be a complete answer.   Often one side of the question only is considered, that which relates to sounds, as if the whole problem had been solved when one had found a reason for children acquiring a better pronunciation of their mother-tongue than one generally gets in later life of a foreign speech.

Many people accordingly tell us that children's organs of speech are especially flexible, but that this suppleness of the tongue and lips is lost in later life.   This explanation, however, does not hold water, as is shown sufficiently by the countless mistakes in sound made by children. If their organs were as flexible as is pretended, they could learn sounds correctly at once, while as a matter of fact it takes a long time before all the sounds and groups of sounds are imitated with tolerable accuracy. Suppleness is not something which is original, but something acquired later, and acquired with no small difficulty, and then only with regard to the sounds of one's own language, and not universally.

The same applies to the second answer (given by Bremer, *Deutsche Phonetik*, 2), namely, that the child's ear is especially sensitive to impressions. The ear also requires development, since at first it can scarcely detect a number of *nuances* which we grown-up people hear most distinctly.

Some people say that the reason why a child learns its native language so well is that it has no established habits to contend against. But that is not right either : as any good observer can see, the process by which the child acquires sounds is pursued through a continuous struggle against bad habits which it has acquired at an earlier stage and which may often have rooted themselves remarkably firmly.

Sweet (H 19) says among other things that the conditions of learning vernacular sounds are so favourable because the child has nothing else to do at the time. On the contrary, one may say that the child has an enormous deal to do while it is learning the language ; it is at that time active beyond all belief : in a short time it subdues wider tracts than it ever does later in a much longer time. The more wonderful is it that along with those tasks it finds strength to learn its mother-tongue and its many refinements and crooked turns.

Some point to heredity and say that a child learns that language most easily which it is disposed beforehand to learn by its ancestry, or in other words that there are inherited convolutions of the brain which take in this language better than any other. Perhaps there is something in this, but we have no definite, carefully ascertained facts. Against the theory stands the fact that the children of immigrants acquire the language of their foster-country to all appearance just as surely and quickly as children of the same age whose forefathers have been in the country for ages. This may be observed in England, in Denmark, and still more in North America. Environment clearly has greater influence than descent.

The real answer in my opinion (which is not claimed to be absolutely new in every respect) lies partly in the child itself, partly in the behaviour towards it of the people around it. In the first place, the time of learning the mother-tongue is the most favourable of all, namely, the first years of life. If one assumes that mental endowment means the capacity for development, without doubt all children are best endowed in their first years : from birth onwards there is a steady decline in the power of grasping what is new and of accommodating oneself to it. With some this decline is a very rapid one—they quickly become fossilized and unable to make a change in their habits ; with others one can notice a happy power of development even in old age ; but no one keeps very long in its full range the adaptability of his first years.

Further, we must remember that the child has far more abundant opportunities of hearing his mother-tongue than one gets, as a rule, with any language one learns later. He hears it from morning to night, and, be it noted, in its genuine shape, with the right pronunciation, right intonation, right use of words and right syntax : the language comes to him as a fresh, ever-bubbling spring. Even before he begins to say anything himself, his first understanding of the language is made easier by the habit that mothers and nurses have of repeating the same phrases with slight alterations, and at the same time doing the thing which they are talking about. " Now we must wash the little face, now we must wash the little forehead, now we must wash the little nose, now we must wash the little chin, now we must wash the little ear," etc. If *men* had to attend to their children, they would never use so many words—but in that case the child would scarcely learn to understand and talk as soon as it does when it is cared for by women.[1]

Then the child has, as it were, private lessons in its mother-tongue all the year round. There is nothing of the kind in the learning of a language later, when at most one has six hours a week and generally shares them with others. The child has another priceless advantage : he hears the language in all possible situations and under such conditions that language and situation ever correspond exactly to one another and mutually illustrate one another. Gesture and facial expression harmonize with the words

---

[1] Women know
The way to rear up children, (to be just)
They know a simple, merry, tender knack
Of stringing pretty words that make no sense,
And kissing full sense into empty words,
Which things are corals to cut life upon,
Although such trifles : children learn by such
Love's holy earnest in a pretty play
And get not over-early solemnized . . .
Such good do mothers. Fathers love as well
—Mine did, I know—but still with heavier brains,
And wills more consciously responsible,
And not as wisely, since less foolishly.
ELIZABETH BROWNING : *Aurora Leigh*, 10.

uttered and keep the child to a right understanding. Here there
is nothing unnatural, such as is often the case in a language-lesson
in later years, when one talks about ice and snow in June or
excessive heat in January. And what the child hears is just what
immediately concerns him and interests him, and again and again
his own attempts at speech lead to the fulfilment of his dearest
wishes, so that his command of language has great practical
advantages for him.

Along with what he himself sees the use of, he hears a great
deal which does not directly concern him, but goes into the little
brain and is stored up there to turn up again later. Nothing is
heard but leaves its traces, and at times one is astonished to
discover what has been preserved, and with what exactness. One
day, when Frans was 4.11 old, he suddenly said : " Yesterday—
isn't there some who say yesterday ? " (giving *yesterday* with the
correct English pronunciation), and when I said that it was an
English word, he went on : " Yes, it is Mrs. B. : she often says
like that, yesterday." Now, it was three weeks since that lady
had called at the house and talked English. It is a well-known
fact that hypnotized persons can sometimes say whole sentences
in a language which they do not know, but have merely heard in
childhood. In books about children's language there are many
remarkable accounts of such linguistic memories which had lain
buried for long stretches of time. A child who had spent the
first eighteen months of its life in Silesia and then came to Berlin,
where it had no opportunity of hearing the Silesian pronunciation,
at the age of five suddenly came out with a number of Silesian
expressions, which could not after the most careful investigation
be traced to any other source than to the time before it could talk
(Stern, 257 ff.). Grammont has a story of a little French girl,
whose nurse had talked French with a strong Italian accent ; the
child did not begin to speak till a month after this nurse had left,
but pronounced many words with Italian sounds, and some of
these peculiarities stuck to the child till the age of three.

We may also remark that the baby's teachers, though, regarded
as teachers of language, they may not be absolutely ideal, still
have some advantages over those one encounters as a rule later in
life. The relation between them and the child is far more cordial
and personal, just because they are not teachers first and foremost.
They are immensely interested in every little advance the child
makes. The most awkward attempt meets with sympathy, often
with admiration, while its defects and imperfections never expose
it to a breath of unkind criticism. There is a Slavonic proverb,
" If you wish to talk well, you must murder the language first."
But this is very often overlooked by teachers of language, who

demand faultless accuracy from the beginning, and often keep their pupils grinding so long at some little part of the subject that their desire to learn the language is weakened or gone for good. There is nothing of this sort in the child's first learning of his language.

It is here that our distinction between the two periods comes in, that of the child's own separate 'little language' and that of the common or social language. In the first period the little one is the centre of a narrow circle of his own, which waits for each little syllable that falls from his lips as though it were a grain of gold. What teachers of languages in later years would rejoice at hearing such forms as we saw before used in the time of the child's 'little language,' *fant* or *vat* or *ham* for 'elephant'? But the mother really does rejoice: she laughs and exults when he can use these syllables about his toy-elephant, she throws the cloak of her love over the defects and mistakes in the little one's imitations of words, she remembers again and again what his strange sounds stand for, and her eager sympathy transforms the first and most difficult steps on the path of language to the merriest game.

It would not do, however, for the child's 'little language' and its dreadful mistakes to become fixed. This might easily happen, if the child were never out of the narrow circle of its own family, which knows and recognizes its 'little language.' But this is stopped because it comes more and more into contact with others—uncles and aunts, and especially little cousins and playmates: more and more often it happens that the mutilated words are not understood, and are corrected and made fun of, and the child is incited in this way to steady improvement: the 'little language' gradually gives place to the 'common language,' as the child becomes a member of a social group larger than that of his own little home.

We have now probably found the chief reasons why a child learns his mother-tongue better than even a grown-up person who has been for a long time in a foreign country learns the language of his environment. But it is also a contributory reason that the child's linguistic needs, to begin with, are far more limited than those of the man who wishes to be able to talk about anything, or at any rate about something. Much more is also linguistically required of the latter, and he must have recourse to language to get all his needs satisfied, while the baby is well looked after even if it says nothing but *wawawawa*. So the baby has longer time to store up his impressions and continue his experiments, until by trying again and again he at length gets his lesson learnt in all its tiny details, while the man in the foreign country, who *must* make himself understood, as a rule goes on trying only till he has acquired a form of speech which he finds natives understand : at this point he will generally stop, at any rate as far as pronunciation and the construction of sentences are concerned (while his vocabulary may be largely increased). But this 'just recognizable' language is incorrect in thousands of small details, and, inasmuch as bad little habits quickly become fixed, the kind of language is produced which we know so well in the case of resident foreigners—who need hardly open their lips before everyone knows they are not natives, and before a practised ear can detect the country they hail from.[1]

VIII.—§ 2. Natural Ability and Sex.

An important factor in the acquisition of language which we have not considered is naturally the individuality of the child. Parents are apt to draw conclusions as to the abilities of their young hopeful from the rapidity with which he learns to talk ; but those who are in despair because their Tommy cannot say a single word when their neighbours' Harry can say a great deal may take comfort. Slowness in talking *may* of course mean deficiency of ability, or even idiocy, but not necessarily. A child who chatters early may remain a chatterer all his life, and children whose motto is 'Slow and sure' may turn out the deepest, most independent and most trustworthy characters in the end. There are some children who cannot be made to say a single word for a long time, and then suddenly come out with a whole sentence, which shows how much has been quietly fructifying in their brain. Carlyle was one of these : after eleven months of taciturnity he heard a child cry, and astonished all by saying, " What ails wee Jock ? " Edmund Gosse has a similar story of his own childhood, and other examples have been recorded elsewhere (Meringer, 194 ; Stern, 257).

[1] This is not the place to speak of the way in which prevalent methods of teaching foreign languages can be improved. A slavish copying of the manner in which English children learn English is impracticable, and if it were practicable it would demand more time than anyone can devote to the purpose. One has to make the most of the advantages which the pupils possess over babies, thus, their being able to read, their power of more sustained attention, etc. Phonetic explanation of the new sounds and phonetic transcription have done wonders to overcome difficulties of pronunciation. But in other respects it is possible to some extent to assimilate the teaching of a foreign language to the method pursued by the child in its first years : one should not merely sprinkle the pupil, but plunge him right down into the sea of language and enable him to swim by himself as soon as possible, relying on the fact that a great deal will arrange itself in the brain without the inculcation of too many special rules and explanations. For details I may refer to my book, *How to Teach a Foreign Language* (London, George Allen and Unwin).

The linguistic development of an individual child is not always in a steady rising line, but in a series of waves. A child who seems to have a boundless power of acquiring language suddenly stands still or even goes back for a short time. The cause may be sickness, cutting teeth, learning to walk, or often a removal to new surroundings or an open-air life in summer. Under such circumstances even the word ' I ' may be lost for a time.

Some children develop very rapidly for some years until they have reached a certain point, where they stop altogether, while others retain the power to develop steadily to a much later age. It is the same with some races : negro children in American schools may, while they are little, be up to the standard of their white schoolfellows, whom they cannot cope with in later life.

The two sexes differ very greatly in regard to speech—as in regard to most other things. Little girls, on the average, learn to talk earlier and more quickly than boys ; they outstrip them in talking correctly ; their pronunciation is not spoilt by the many bad habits and awkwardnesses so often found in boys. It has been proved by statistics in many countries that there are far more stammerers and bad speakers among boys and men than among girls and women. The general receptivity of women, their great power of, and pleasure in, imitation, their histrionic talent, if one may so say—all this is a help to them at an early age, so that they can get into other people's way of talking with greater agility than boys of the same age.

Everything that is conventional in language, everything in which the only thing of importance is to be in agreement with those around you, is the girls' strong point. Boys may often show a certain reluctance to do exactly as others do : the peculiarities of their ' little language ' are retained by them longer than by girls, and they will sometimes steadily refuse to correct their own abnormalities, which is very seldom the case with girls. Gaucherie and originality thus are two points between which the speech of boys is constantly oscillating. Cf. below, Ch. XIII.

VIII.—§ 3. Mother-tongue and Other Tongue.

The expression " mother-tongue " should not be understood too literally : the language which the child acquires naturally is not, or not always, his mother's language. When a mother speaks with a foreign accent or in a pronounced dialect, her children as a rule speak their language as correctly as other children, or keep only the slightest tinge of their mother's peculiarities. I have seen this very distinctly in many Danish families, in which the mother has kept up her Norwegian language all her life, and in which the children have spoken pure Danish. Thus also in two families I know, in which a strong Swedish accent in one mother, and an unmistakable American pronunciation in the other, have not prevented the children from speaking Danish exactly as if their mothers had been born and bred in Denmark. I cannot, therefore, agree with Passy, who says that the child learns his mother's sound system (Ch § 32), or with Dauzat's dictum to the same effect (V 20). The father, as a rule, has still less influence ; but what is decisive is the speech of those with whom the child comes in closest contact from the age of three or so, thus frequently servants, but even more effectually playfellows of his own age or rather slightly older than himself, with whom he is constantly thrown together for hours at a time and whose prattle is constantly in his ears at the most impressionable age, while he may not see and hear his father and mother except for a short time every day, at meals and on such occasions. It is also a well-known fact that the children of Danish parents in Greenland often learn the Eskimo language before Danish ; and Meinhof says that German children in the African colonies will often learn the language of the natives earlier than German (MSA 139).

This is by no means depreciating the mother's influence, which is strong indeed, but chiefly in the first period, that of the child's ' little language.' But that is the time when the child's imitative power is weakest. His exact attention to the minutiæ of language dates from the time when he is thrown into a wider circle and has to make himself understood by many, so that his language becomes really identical with that of the community, where formerly he and his mother would rest contented with what *they*, but hardly anyone else, could understand.

The influence of children on children cannot be overestimated.[1] Boys at school make fun of any peculiarities of speech noticed in schoolfellows who come from some other part of the country. Kipling tells us in *Stalky and Co.* how Stalky and Beetle carefully *kicked* McTurk out of his Irish dialect. When I read this, I was vividly reminded of the identical method my new friends applied to me when at the age of ten I was transplanted from Jutland to a school in Seeland and excited their merriment through some Jutlandish expressions and intonations. And so we may say that the most important factor in spreading the common or standard language is children themselves.

It often happens that children who are compelled at home to talk without any admixture of dialect talk pure dialect when playing with their schoolfellows out of doors. They can keep the

[1] Hence, also, the second or third child in a family will, as a rule, learn to speak more rapidly than the eldest.

two forms of speech distinct. In the same way they can learn two languages less closely connected. At times this results in very strange blendings, at least for a time ; but many children will easily pass from one language to the other without mixing them up, especially if they come in contact with the two languages in different surroundings or on the lips of different people.

It is, of course, an advantage for a child to be familiar with two languages : but without doubt the advantage may be, and generally is, purchased too dear. First of all the child in question hardly learns either of the two languages as perfectly as he would have done if he had limited himself to one. It may seem, on the surface, as if he talked just like a native, but he does not really command the fine points of the language. Has any bilingual child ever developed into a great artist in speech, a poet or orator ?

Secondly, the brain effort required to master two languages instead of one certainly diminishes the child's power of learning other things which might and ought to be learnt. Schuchardt rightly remarks that if a bilingual man has two strings to his bow, both are rather slack, and that the three souls which the ancient Roman said he possessed, owing to his being able to talk three different languages, were probably very indifferent souls after all. A native of Luxemburg, where it is usual for children to talk both French and German, says that few Luxemburgers talk both languages perfectly. " Germans often say to us : ' You speak German remarkably well for a Frenchman,' and French people will say, ' They are Germans who speak our language excellently.' Nevertheless, we never speak either language as fluently as the natives. The worst of the system is, that instead of learning things necessary to us we must spend our time and energy in learning to express the same thought in two or three languages at the same time." [1]

VIII.—§ 4. Playing at Language.

The child takes delight in making meaningless sounds long after it has learnt to talk the language of its elders. At 2.2 Frans amused himself with long series of such sounds, uttered with the most confiding look and proper intonation, and it was a joy to him when I replied with similar sounds. He kept up this game for years. Once (4.11) after such a performance he asked me : " Is that English ? "—" No."—" Why not ? "—" Because I under-stand English, but I do not understand what you say." An hour later he came back and asked : " Father, do you know all languages ? "—" No, there are many I don't know."—" Do you

[1] I translate this from Ido, see *The International Language*, May 1912.

know German ? "—" Yes." (Frans looked rather crestfallen : the servants had often said of his invented language that he was talking German. So he went on) " Do you know Japanese ? "—" No."—(Delighted) "So remember when I say something you don't understand, it's Japanese."

It is the same everywhere. Hawthorne writes : " Pearl mumbled something into his ear, that sounded, indeed, like human language, but was only such gibberish as children may be heard amusing themselves with, by the hour together " (*The Scarlet Letter*, 173). And R. L. Stevenson : " Children prefer the shadow to the substance. When they might be speaking intelligibly together, they chatter senseless gibberish by the hour, and are quite happy because they are making believe to speak French " (*Virginibus P.*, 236 ; cf. Glenconner, p. 40 ; Stern, pp. 76, 91, 103). Meringer's boy (2.1) took the music-book and sang a tune of his own making with incomprehensible words.

Children also take delight in varying the sounds of real words, introducing, for instance, alliterations, as " Sing a song of sixpence, A socket full of sye," etc. Frans at 2.3 amused himself by rounding all his vowels (o for a, y for i), and at 3.1 by making all words of a verse line he had learnt begin with d, then the same words begin with t. O'Shea (p. 32) says that "most children find pleasure in the production of variations upon some of their familiar words. Their purpose seems to be to test their ability to be original. The performance of an unusual act affords pleasure in linguistics as in other matters. H., learning the word *dessert*, to illustrate, plays with it for a time and exhibits it in a dozen or more variations— *dissert, dishert, děsot, des¹sert*, and so on."

Rhythm and rime appeal strongly to the children's minds. One English observer says that " a child in its third year will copy the rhythm of songs and verses it has heard in nonsense words." The same thing is noted by Meringer (p. 116) and Stern (p. 103). Tony E. (2.10) suddenly made up the rime " My mover, I lov-er," and Gordon M. (2.6) never tired of repeating a phrase of his own composition, " Custard over mustard." A Danish girl of 3.1 is reported as having a " curious knack of twisting all words into rimes : bestemor hestemor prestemor, Gudrun sludrun pludrun, etc."

VIII.—§ 5. Secret Languages.

Children, as we have seen, at first employ play-language for its own sake, with no *arrière-pensée*, but as they get older they may see that such language has the advantage of not being understood by their elders, and so they may develop a ' secret language ' consciously. Some such languages are confined to one school, others may be in common use among children of a certain age all over a country. 'M-gibberish' and 'S-gibberish' consist in inserting *m* and *s*, as in *goming mout tomdaym* or *gosings outs tosdays* for 'going out to-day'; 'Marrowskying' or 'Hospital Greek' transfers the initial letters of words, as *renty of plain* for 'plenty of rain,' *flutterby* for 'butterfly'; 'Ziph' or 'Hypernese' (at Winchester) substitutes *wa* for the first of two initial consonants and inserts *p* or *g*, making 'breeches' into *wareechepes* and 'penny' into *pegennepy*. From my own boyhood in Denmark I remember two languages of this sort, in which a sentence like 'du er et lille asen' became *dupu erper etpet lilpillepe apasenpen* and *durbe erbe erbe lirbelerbe arbeserbe* respectively. Closely corresponding languages, with insertion of *p* and addition of *-erbse*, are found in Germany; in Holland we find 'de schoone Mei' made into *depé schoopóonepé Meipéi*, besides an *-erwi-taal* with a variation in which the ending is *-erf*. In France such a language is called *javanais;* 'je vais bien' is made into *je-de-que vais-dai-qai bien-den-qen*. In Savoy the cowherds put *deg* after each syllable and thus make 'a-te kogneu se vaçhi' ('as-tu connu ce vacher?' in the local dialect) into *a-degá tc-dege ko-dego gnu-degu sé-degé va-dega chi-degi?* Nay, even among the Maoris of New Zealand there is a similar secret language, in which instead of 'kei te, haere au ki reira' is said *te-kei te-i-te te-haere-te-re te-a te-u te-ki te-re-te-i-te-ra*. Human nature is pretty much the same everywhere.[1]

VIII.—§ 6. Onomatopœia.

Do children really create new words? This question has been much discussed, but even those who are most skeptical in that respect incline to allow them this power in the case of words which imitate sounds. Nevertheless, it should be remembered that the majority of onomatopœic words heard from children are not their own invention, but are acquired by them in the same way as other words. Hence it is that such words have different forms in different languages. Thus to English *cockadoodledoo* corresponds French *coquerico*, German *kikeriki* and Danish *kykeliky*, to E. *quack-quack*, F. *cancan*, Dan. *raprap*, etc. These words are an imperfect representation of the birds' natural cry, but from their likeness to it they are easier for the child to seize than an entirely arbitrary name such as *duck*.

But, side by side with these, children do invent forms of their own, though the latter generally disappear quickly in favour of the

[1] I have collected a bibliographical list of such 'secret languages' in *Nord. Tidsskrift f. Filologi*, 4r. vol. 5.

traditional forms. Thus Frans (2.3) had coined the word *vakvak*, which his mother had heard sometimes without understanding what he meant, when one day he pointed at some crows while repeating the same word ; but when his mother told him that these birds were called *krager*, he took hold of this word with eagerness and repeated it several times, evidently recognizing it as a better name than his own. A little boy of 2.1 called soda-water *ft*, another boy said *ging* or *gingging* for a clock, also for the railway train, while his brother said *dann* for a bell or clock ; a little girl (1.9) said *pooh* (whispered) for ' match, cigar, pipe,' and *gagag* for ' hen,' etc.

When once formed, such words may be transferred to other things, where the sound plays no longer any rôle. This may be illustrated through two extensions of the same word *böom* or *bom*, used by two children first to express the sound of something falling on the floor ; then Ellen K. (1.9) used it for a ' blow,' and finally for anything disagreeable, e.g. soap in the eyes, while Kaare G. (1.8), after seeing a plate smashed, used the word for a broken plate and afterwards for anything broken, a hole in a dress, etc., also when a button had come off or when anything else was defective in any way.

VIII.—§ 7. Word-inventions.

Do children themselves create words—apart from onomatopœic words ? To me there is no doubt that they do. Frans invented many words at his games that had no connexion, or very little connexion, with existing words. He was playing with a little twig when I suddenly heard him exclaim : " This is called *lampetine*," but a little while afterwards he said *lanketine*, and then again *lampetine*, and then he said, varying the play, " Now it is *kluatine* and *traniklualalilua*" (3.6). A month later I write : " He is never at a loss for a self-invented word ; for instance, when he has made a figure with his bricks which resembles nothing whatever, he will say, ' That shall be *lindam*.' " When he played at trains in the garden, there were many stations with fanciful names, and at one time he and two cousins had a word *kukukounen* which they repeated constantly and thought great fun, but whose inner meaning I never succeeded in discovering. An English friend writes about his daughter : " When she was about two and a quarter she would often use some nonsense word in the middle of a perfectly intelligible sentence. When you asked her its meaning she would explain it by another equally unintelligible, and so on through a series as long as you cared to make it." At 2.10 she pretended she had lost her bricks, and when you showed her that they were just by her, she insisted that they were not ' bricks ' at all, but *mums*.

In all accounts of children's talk you find words which cannot be referred back to the normal language, but which have cropped up from some unsounded depth of the child's soul. I give a few from notes sent to me by Danish friends : *goi* ' comb,' *putput* ' stocking, or any other piece of garment,' *i-a-a* ' chocolate,' *gön* ' water to drink, milk ' (kept apart from the usual word *vand* for water, which she used only for water to wash in), *hesh* ' newspaper, book.' Some such words have become famous in psychological literature because they were observed by Darwin and Taine. Among less famous instances from other books I may mention *tibu* ' bird ' (Strümpel), *adi* ' cake ' (Ament), *be'lum-be'lum* ' toy with two men turning about,' *wakaka* ' soldier,' *nda* ' jar,' *pamma* ' pencil,' *bium* ' stocking ' (Meringer).

An American correspondent writes that his boy was fond of pushing a stick over the carpet after the manner of a carpet-sweeper and called the operation *jazing*. He coined the word *borkens* as a name for a particular sort of blocks with which he was accustomed to play. He was a nervous child and his imagination created objects of terror that haunted him in the dark, and to these he gave the name of *Boons*. This name may, however, be derived from *baboons*. Mr. Harold Palmer tells me that his daughter (whose native language was French) at an early age used ['fu'wɛ] for ' soap ' and [dɛ'dɛtʃ] for ' horse, wooden horse, merry-go-round.'

Dr. F. Poulsen, in his book *Rejser og rids* (Copenhagen, 1920), says about his two-year-old daughter that when she gets hold of her mother's fur-collar she will pet it and lavish on it all kinds of tender self-invented names, such as *apu* or *a-fo-me-me*. The latter word, " which has all the melodious euphony and vague signification of primitive language," is applied to anything that is rare and funny and worth rejoicing at. On a summer day's excursion there was one new *a-fo-me-me* after the other.

In spite of all this, a point on which all the most distinguished investigators of children's language of late years are agreed is that children never invent words. Wundt goes so far as to say that " the child's language is the result of the child's environment, the child being essentially a passive instrument in the matter " (S 1. 196)—one of the most wrong-headed sentences I have ever read in the works of a great scientist. Meumann says : " Preyer and after him almost every careful observer among child-psychologists have strongly held the view that it is impossible to speak of a child inventing a word." Similarly Meringer, L 220, Stern, 126, 273, 337 ff., Bloomfield, SL 12.

These investigators seem to have been led astray by expressions such as ' shape out of nothing,' ' invent,' ' original creation '

(Urschöpfung), and to have taken this doctrinaire attitude in partial defiance of the facts they have themselves advanced. Expressions like those adduced occur over and over again in their discussions, and Meumann says openly : "Invention demands a methodical proceeding with intention, a conception of an end to be realized." Of course, if that is necessary it is clear that we can speak of invention of words in the case of a chemist seeking a word for a new substance, and not in the case of a tiny child. But are there not many inventions in the technical world, which we do not hesitate to call inventions, which have come about more or less by chance ? Wasn't it so probably with gunpowder ? According to the story it certainly was so with blotting-paper : the foreman who had forgotten to add size to a portion of writing-paper was dismissed, but the manufacturer who saw that the paper thus spoilt could be turned to account instead of the sand hitherto used made a fortune. So according to Meumann blotting-paper has never been 'invented.' If in order to acknowledge a child's creation of a word we are to postulate that it has been produced out of nothing, what about bicycles, fountain-pens, typewriters— each of which was something existing before, carried just a little further ? Are they on that account not inventions ? One would think not, when one reads these writers on children's language, for as soon as the least approximation to a word in the normal language is discovered, the child is denied both 'invention' and 'the speech-forming faculty'! Thus Stern (p. 338) says that his daughter in her second year used some words which might be taken as proof of the power to create words, but for the fact that it was here possible to show how these 'new' words had grown out of normal words. *Eischei*, for instance, was used as a verb meaning 'go, walk,' but it originated in the words *eins, zwei* (one, two) which were said when the child was taught to walk. Other examples are given comparable to those mentioned above (106, 115) as mutilations of the first period. Now, even if all those words given by myself and others as original inventions of children could be proved to be similar perversions of 'real' words (which is not likely), I should not hesitate to speak of a word-creating faculty, for *eischei*, 'to walk,' is both in form and still more in meaning far enough from *eins, zwei* to be reckoned a totally new word.

We can divide words 'invented' by children into three classes :

    A. The child gives both sound and meaning.

    B. The grown-up people give the sound, and the child the meaning.

    C. The child gives the sound, grown-up people the meaning.

But the three classes cannot always be kept apart, especially when the child imitates the grown-up person's sound so badly or seizes the meaning so imperfectly that very little is left of what the grown-up person gives. As a rule, the self-created words will be very short-lived ; still, there are exceptions.

O'Shea's account of one of these words is very instructive. " She had also a few words of her own coining which were attached spontaneously to objects, and these her elders took up, and they became fixed in her vocabulary for a considerable period. A word resembling *Ndobbin* was employed for every sort of thing which she used for food. The word came originally from an accidental combination of sounds made while she was eating. By the aid of the people about her in responding to this term and repeating it, she 'selected' it and for a time used it purposefully. She employed it at the outset for a specific article of food ; then her elders extended it to other articles, and this aided her in making the extension herself. Once started in this process, she extended the term to many objects associated with her food, even objects as remote from her original experience as dining-room, high-chair, kitchen, and even apple and plum trees " (O'Shea, 27).

To Class A I assign most of the words already given as the child's creations, whether the child be great or small.

Class B is that which is most sparsely represented. A child in Finland often heard the well-known line about King Karl (Charles XII), " Han stod i rök och damm " (" He stood in smoke and dust "), and taking *rö* to be the adjective meaning ' red,' imagined the remaining syllables, which he heard as *kordamm*, to be the name of some piece of garment. This amused his parents so much that *kordamm* became the name of a dressing-gown in that family.

To Class C, where the child contributes only the sound and the older people give a meaning to what on the child's side was meaningless—a process that reminds one of the invention of blotting-paper—belong some of the best-known words, which require a separate section.

VIII.—§ 8. 'Mamma' and 'Papa.'

In the nurseries of all countries a little comedy has in all ages been played—the baby lies and babbles his ' mamama ' or ' amama ' or ' papapa ' or ' apapa ' or ' bababa ' or ' ababab ' without associating the slightest meaning with his mouth-games, and his grown-up friends, in their joy over the precocious child, assign to these syllables a rational sense, accustomed as they are themselves to the fact of an uttered sound having a content, a thought, an idea, corresponding to it. So we get a whole class

of words, distinguished by a simplicity of sound-formation—never
two consonants together, generally the same consonant repeated
with an *a* between, frequently also with an *a* at the end—words
found in many languages, often in different forms, but with
essentially the same meaning.

First we have words for 'mother.' It is very natural that
the mother who is greeted by her happy child with the sound
'mama' should take it as though the child were *calling* her 'mama,'
and since she frequently comes to the cradle when she hears the
sound, the child himself does learn to use these syllables when
he wants to call her. In this way they become a recognized word
for the idea 'mother'—now with the stress on the first syllable,
now on the second. In French we get a nasal vowel either in
the last syllable only or in both syllables. At times we have only
one syllable, *ma*. When once these syllables have become a regular
word they follow the speech laws which govern other words ; thus
among other forms we get the German *muhme*, the meaning of which
('aunt') is explained as in the words mentioned, p. 118. In very early
times *ma* in our group of languages was supplied with a termination,
so that we get the form underlying Greek *mētēr*, Lat. *mater* (whence
Fr. *mère*, etc.), our own *mother*, G. *mutter*, etc. These words
became the recognized grown-up words, while *mama* itself was
only used in the intimacy of the family. It depends on fashion,
however, how 'high up' *mama* can be used : in some countries
and in some periods children are allowed to use it longer than
in others.

The forms *mama* and *ma* are not the only ones for 'mother.'
The child's *am* has also been seized and maintained by the grown-
ups. The Albanian word for 'mother' is *ama*, the Old Norse
word for 'grandmother' is *amma*. The Latin *am-ita*, formed from
am with a termination added, came to mean 'aunt' and became
in OFr. *ante*, whence E. *aunt* and Modern Fr. *tante*. In Semitic
languages the words for 'mother' also have a vowel before *m* :
Assyrian *ummu*, Hebrew *'êm*, etc.

Baba, too, is found in the sense 'mother,' especially in Slavonic
languages, though it has here developed various derivative meanings, 'old woman,' 'grandmother,' or 'midwife.' In Tonga we
have *bama* 'mother.'

Forms with *n* are also found for 'mother'; so Sanskrit *naná*,
Albanian *nane*. Here we have also Gr. *nannē* 'aunt' and Lat.
nonna; the latter ceased in the early Middle Ages to mean 'grandmother' and became a respectful way of addressing women of a
certain age, whence we know it as *nun*, the feminine counterpart
of 'monk.' From less known languages I may mention Greenlandic *a'na·na* 'mother,' *'a·na* 'grandmother.'

Now we come to words meaning 'father,' and quite naturally, where the sound-groups containing *m* have already been interpreted in the sense 'mother,' a word for 'father' will be sought in the syllables with *p*. It is no doubt frequently noticed in the nursery that the baby says *mama* where one expected *papa*, and vice versa; but at last he learns to deal out the syllables 'rightly,' as we say. The history of the forms *papa*, *pappa* and *pa* is analogous to the history of the *m* syllables already traced. We have the same extension of the sound by *tr* in the word *pater*, which according to recognized laws of sound-change is found in the French *père*, the English *father*, the Danish *fader*, the German *vater*, etc. Philologists no longer, fortunately, derive these words from a root *pa* 'to protect,' and see therein a proof of the 'highly moral spirit' of our aboriginal ancestors, as Fick and others did. *Papa*, as we know, also became an honourable title for a reverend ecclesiastic, and hence comes the name which we have in the form *Pope*.

Side by side with the *p* forms we have forms in *b*—Italian *babbo*, Bulgarian *babá*, Serbian *bába*, Turkish *baba*. Beginning with the vowel we have the Semitic forms *ab*, *abu* and finally *abba*, which is well known, since through Greek *abbas* it has become the name for a spiritual father in all European languages, our form being *Abbot*.

Again, we have some names for 'father' with dental sounds: Sanskrit *tatá*, Russian *tata*, *tyatya*, Welsh *tat*, etc. The English *dad*, now so universal, is sometimes considered to have been borrowed from this Welsh word, which in certain connexions has an initial *d*, but no doubt it had an independent origin. In Slavonic languages *déd* is extensively used for 'grandfather' or 'old man.' Thus also *deite*, *teite* in German dialects. *Tata* 'father' is found in Congo and other African languages, also (*tatta*) in Negro-English (Surinam). And just as words for 'mother' change their meaning from 'mother' to 'aunt,' so these forms in some languages come to mean 'uncle': Gr. *theios* (whence Italian *zio*), Lithuanian *dede*, Russian *dyadya*.

With an initial vowel we get the form *atta*, in Greek used in addressing old people, in Gothic the ordinary word for 'father,' which with a termination added gives the proper name *Attila*, originally 'little father'; with another ending we have Russian *otec*. Outside our own family of languages we find, for instance, Magyar *atya*, Turkish *ata*, Basque *aita*, Greenlandic *a'ta·ta* 'father,' while in the last-mentioned language *a·ta* means 'grandfather.' [1]

---

[1] I subjoin a few additional examples. Basque *aita* 'father,' *ama* 'mother,' *anaya* 'brother' (*Zeitsch. f. rom. Phil.* 17, 146). Manchu *ama* 'father,' *eme* 'mother' (the vowel relation as in *haha* 'man,' *hehe* 'woman,'

The nurse, too, comes in for her share in these names, as she too is greeted by the child's babbling and is tempted to take it as the child's name for her ; thus we get the German and Scandinavian *amme*, Polish *niania*, Russian *nyanya*, cf. our *Nanny*. These words cannot be kept distinct from names for ' aunt,' cf. *amita* above, and in Sanskrit we find *mama* for ' uncle.'

It is perhaps more doubtful if we can find a name for the child itself which has arisen in the same way ; the nearest example is the Engl. *babe, baby*, German *bube* (with *u* as in *muhme* above) ; but *babe* has also been explained as a word derived normally from OFr. *baube*, from Lat. *balbus* ' stammering.' When the name *Bab* or *Babs* (*Babbe* in a Danish family) becomes the pet-name for a little girl, this has no doubt come from an interpretation put on her own meaningless sounds. Ital. *bambo* (*bambino*) certainly belongs here. We may here mention also some terms for ' doll,' Lat. *pupa* or *puppa*, G. *puppe* ; with a derivative ending we have Fr. *poupée*, E. *puppet* (Chaucer, A 3254, *popelote*). These words have a rich semantic development, cf. *pupa* (Dan. *puppe*, etc.) ' chrysalis,' and the diminutive Lat. *pupillus, pupilla*, which was used for ' a little child, minor,' whence E. *pupil* ' disciple,' but also for the little child seen in the eye, whence E. (and other languages) *pupil*, ' central opening of the eye.'

A child has another main interest—that is, in its food, the breast, the bottle, etc. In many countries it has been observed that very early a child uses a long *m* (without a vowel) as a sign that it wants something, but we can hardly be right in supposing that the sound is originally meant by children in this sense. They do not use it consciously till they see that grown-up people on hearing the sound come up and find out what the child wants. And it is the same with the developed forms which are uttered by the child in its joy at getting something to eat, and which are therefore interpreted as the child's expression for food : *am, mam, mammam*, or the same words with a final *a*—that is, really the same groups of sounds which came to stand for ' mother.' The determination of a particular form to a particular meaning is always due to the adults, who, however, can subsequently *teach* it to the child. Under this heading comes the sound *ham*, which Taine observed to be one child's expression for hunger or thirst (*h* mute ?), and similarly the word *mum*, meaning ' something to eat,' invented,

Gabelentz, S 389).   Kutenai *pa·* ' brother's daughter,' *papa* ' grandmother (said by male), grandfather, grandson,' *pat!* ' nephew,' *ma* ' mother,' *nana* ' younger sister ' (of girl), *alnana* ' sisters,' *tite* ' mother-in-law,' *titu* ' father' (of male)—(Boas, *Kutenai Tales*, Bureau of Am. Ethnol. 59, 1918).   Cf. also Sapir, "Kinship Terms of the Kootenay Indians " (*Amer. Anthropologist*, vol. 20).   In the same writer's *Yana Terms of Relationship* (Univ. of California, 1918) there seems to be very little from this source.

as we are told, by Darwin's son and often uttered with a rising intonation, as in a question, ' Will you give me something to eat ? ' Lindner's child (1.5) is said to have used *papp* for everything eatable and *mem* or *möm* for anything drinkable. In normal language we have forms like Sanskrit *māmsa* (Gothic *mimz*) and *mās* ' flesh,' our own *meat* (which formerly, like Dan. *mad*, meant any kind of food), German *mus* ' jam ' (whence also *gemüse*), and finally Lat. *mandere* and *manducare* ' to chew ' (whence Fr. *manger*) —all developments of this childish *ma*(*m*).

As the child's first nourishment is its mother's breast, its joyous *mamama* can also be taken to mean the breast. So we have the Latin *mamma* (with a diminutive ending *mammilla*, whence Fr. *mamelle*), and with the other labial sound Engl. *pap*, Norwegian and Swed. dial. *pappe*, Lat. *papilla*; with a different vowel, It. *poppa*, Fr. *poupe*, ' teat of an animal, formerly also of a woman '; with *b*, G. *bübbi*, obsolete E. *bubby*; with a dental, E. *teat* (G. *zitze*), Ital. *tetta*, Dan. *titte*, Swed. dial. *tatte*. Further we have words like E. *pap* ' soft food,' Latin *papare* ' to eat,' orig. ' to suck,' and some G. forms for the same, *pappen*, *pampen*, *pampfen*. Perhaps the beginning of the word *milk* goes back to the baby's *ma* applied to the mother's breast or milk ; the latter half may then be connected with Lat. *lac*. In Greenlandic we have *ama·ma* ' suckle.'

Inseparable from these words is the sound, a long *m* or *am*, which expresses the child's delight over something that tastes good ; it has by-forms in the Scotch *nyam* or *nyamnyam*, the English seaman's term *yam* ' to eat,' and with two dentals the French *nanan* ' sweetmeats.' Some linguists will have it that the Latin *amo* ' I love ' is derived from this *am*, which expresses pleasurable satisfaction. When a father tells me that his son (1.10) uses the wonderful words *nananœi* for ' chocolate ' and *jajajaja* for picture-book, we have no doubt here also a case of a grown person's interpretation of the originally meaningless sounds of a child.

Another meaning that grown-up people may attach to syllables uttered by the child is that of ' good-bye,' as in English *tata*, which has now been incorporated in the ordinary language.[1] Stern probably is right when he thinks that the French *adieu* would not have been accepted so commonly in Germany and other countries if it had not accommodated itself so easily, especially in the form commonly used in German, *ade*, to the child's natural word.

[1] *Tata* is also used for ' a walk ' (to go out for a ta-ta, or to go out ta-tas) and for ' a hat '—meanings that may very well have developed from the child's saying these syllables when going out or preparing to go out.

There are some words for 'bed, sleep' which clearly belong to this class : Tuscan *nanna* 'cradle,' Sp. *hacer la nana* 'go to sleep,' E. *bye-bye* (possibly associated with *good-bye*, instead of which is also said *byebye*) ; Stern mentions *baba* (Berlin), *beibei* (Russian), *bobo* (Malay), but *bischbisch*, which he also gives here, is evidently (like the Danish *visse*) imitative of the sound used for hushing.

Words of this class stand in a way outside the common words of a language, owing to their origin and their being continually new-created. One cannot therefore deduce laws of sound-change from them in their original shape ; and it is equally wrong to use them as evidence for an original kinship between different families of language and to count them as loan-words, as is frequently done (for example, when the Slavonic *baba* is said to be borrowed from Turkish). The English *papa* and *mam(m)a*, and the same words in German and Danish, Italian, etc., are almost always regarded as borrowed from French ; but Cauer rightly points out that Nausikaa (*Odyssey* 6. 57) addresses her father as *pappa fil*, and Homer cannot be suspected of borrowing from French. Still, it is true that fashion may play a part in deciding how long children may be permitted to say *papa* and *mamma*, and a French fashion may in this respect have spread to other European countries, especially in the seventeenth century. We may not find these words in early use in the *literatures* of the different countries, but this is no proof that the words were not used in the nursery. As soon as a word of this class has somewhere got a special application, this can very well pass as a loan-word from land to land—as we saw in the case of the words *abbot* and *pope*. And it may be granted with respect to the primary use of the words that there are certain national or quasi-national customs which determine what grown people expect to hear from babies, so that one nation expects and recognizes *papa*, another *dad*, a third *atta*, for the meaning 'father.'

When the child hands something to somebody or reaches out for something he will generally say something, and if, as often happens, this is *ta* or *da*, it will be taken by its parents and others as a real word, different according to the language they speak ; in England as *there* or *thanks*, in Denmark as *tak* 'thanks' [1] or *tag* 'take,' in Germany as *da* 'there,' in France as *tiens* 'hold,' in Russia as *day* 'give,' in Italy as *to*, (= *togli*) 'take.' The form *tê* in Homer is interpreted by some as an imperative of *teinō* 'stretch.' These instances, however, are slightly different

---

[1] The Swede Bolin says that his child said *tatt-tatt*, which he interprets as *tack*, even when handing something to others.

in character from those discussed in the main part of this chapter.[1]

---

[1] The views advanced in § 8 have some points in contact with the remarks found in Stern's ch. xix, p. 300, only that I lay more stress on the arbitrary interpretation of the child's meaningless syllables on the part of the grown-ups, and that I cannot approve his theory of the *m* syllables as 'centripetal' and the *p* syllables as 'centrifugal affective-volitional natural sounds.' Paul (P § 127) says that the nursery-language with its *bowwow, papa, mama*, etc., "is not the invention of the children; it is handed over to them just as any other language"; he overlooks the share children have themselves in these words, or in some of them; nor are they, as he says, formed by the grown-ups with a purely pedagogical purpose. Nor can I find that Wundt's chapter "Angebliche worterfindung des kindes" (S 1. 273–287) contains decisive arguments. Curtius (K 88) thinks that Gr. *patēr* was first shortened into *på* and this then extended into *páppa*—but certainly it is rather the other way round.

CHAPTER IX

THE INFLUENCE OF THE CHILD ON LINGUISTIC DEVELOPMENT

§ 1. Conflicting Views.   § 2. Meringer.   Analogy.   § 3. Herzog's Theory of Sound Changes.   § 4. Gradual Shiftings.   § 5. Leaps.   § 6. Assimilations, etc.   § 7. Stump-words.

IX.—§ 1. Conflicting Views.

WE all know that in historical times languages have been constantly changing, and we have much indirect evidence that in prehistoric times they did the same thing.   But when it is asked if these changes, unavoidable as they seem to be, are to be ascribed primarily to children and their defective imitation of the speech of their elders, or if children's language in general plays no part at all in the history of language, we find linguists expressing quite contrary views, without the question having ever been really thoroughly investigated.

Some hold that the child acquires its language with such perfection that it cannot be held responsible for the changes recorded in the history of languages : others, on the contrary, hold that the most important source of these changes is to be found in the transmission of the language to new generations.   How undecided the attitude even of the foremost linguists may be towards the question is perhaps best seen in the views expressed at different times by Sweet.   In 1882 he reproaches Paul with paying attention only to the shiftings going on in the pronunciation of the same individual, and not acknowledging " the much more potent cause of change which exists in the fact that one generation can learn the sounds of the preceding one by imitation only.   It is an open question whether the modifications made by the individual in a sound he has once learnt, independently of imitation of those around him, are not too infinitesimal to have any appreciable effect " (CP 153).   In the same spirit he asserted in 1899 that the process of learning our own language in childhood is a very slow one, " and the results are always imperfect. . . . If languages were learnt perfectly by the children of each generation, then languages would not change : English children would still speak a language as old at least as ' Anglo-Saxon,' and there would be no such languages as French and Italian. The changes in languages are simply slight mistakes, which in the course of generations completely alter the character of the language " (PS 75). But only one year later, in 1900, he maintains that the child's imitation " is in most cases practically perfect "—" the main cause of sound-change must therefore be sought elsewhere. The real cause of sound-change seems to be organic shifting—failure to hit the mark, the result either of carelessness or sloth . . . a slight deviation from the pronunciation learnt in infancy may easily pass unheeded, especially by those who make the same change in their own pronunciation" (H 19 f.). By the term "organic shifting " Sweet evidently, as seen from his preface, meant shifting in the pronunciation of the adult, thus a modification of the sound learnt ' perfectly ' in childhood. Paul, who in the first edition (1880) of his *Prinzipien der Sprachgeschichte* did not mention the influence of children, in all the following editions (2nd, 1886, p. 58 ; 3rd, 1898, p. 58 ; 4th, 1909, p. 63) expressly says that " die hauptveranlassung zum lautwandel in der übertragung der laute auf neue individuen liegt," while the shiftings within the same generation are very slight. Paul thus modified his view in the opposite direction of Sweet [1]—and did so under the influence of Sweet's criticism of his own first view !

When one finds scholars expressing themselves in this manner and giving hardly any reasons for their views, one is tempted to believe that the question is perhaps insoluble, that it is a mere toss-up, or that in the sentence " children's imitation is nearly perfect " the stress may be laid, according to taste, now on the word *nearly*, and now on the word *perfect*. I am, however, convinced that we can get a little farther, though only by breaking up the question, instead of treating it as one vague and indeterminate whole.

IX.—§ 2. Meringer. Analogy.

Among recent writers Meringer has gone furthest into the question, adhering in the main to the general view that, just as in other fields, social, economic, etc., it is grown-up men who take the lead in new developments, so it is grown-up men, and not women or children, who carry things forward in the field of

[1] The same inconsistency is found in Dauzat, who in 1910 thought that nothing, and in 1912 that nearly everything, was due to imperfect imitation by the child (V 22 ff., Ph 53, cf. 3). Wechssler (L p. 86) quotes passages from Bremer, Passy, Rousselot and Wallensköld, in which the chief cause of sound changes is attributed to the child ; to these might be added Storm (*Phonetische Studien*, 5. 200) and A. Thomson (IF 24, 1909, p. 9), probably also Grammont (*Mél. linguist.* 61). Many writers seem to imagine that the question is settled when they are able to adduce a certain number of *parallel* changes in the pronunciation of some child and in the historical evolution of languages.

language. In one place he justifies his standpoint by a reference
to a special case, and I will take this as the starting-point of my
own consideration of the question. He says : "It can be shown
by various examples that they [changes in language] are decidedly
not due to children. In Ionic, Attic and Lesbian Greek the
words for ' hundreds ' are formed in -kosioi (diakósioi, etc.), while
elsewhere (in Doric and Bœotian) they appear as -kátioi. How
does the o arise in -kósioi ? It is generally said that it comes
from o in the ' tens ' in the termination -konta. Can it be children
who have formed the words for hundreds on the model of the
words for tens, children under six years old, who are just learning
to talk ? Such children generally have other things to attend
to than to practise themselves in numerals above a hundred."
Similar formations are adduced from Latin, and it is stated that
the personal pronouns are especially subject to change, but children
do not use the personal pronouns till an age when they are already
in firm possession of the language. Meringer then draws the
conclusion that the share which children take in bringing about
linguistic change is a very small one.

Now, I should like first to remark that even if it is possible to
point to certain changes in language which cannot be ascribed
to little children, this proves nothing with regard to the very
numerous changes which lie outside these limits. And next,
that all the cases here mentioned are examples of formation by
analogy. But from the very nature of the case, the conditions
requisite for the occurrence of such formations are exactly the
same in the case of adults and in that of the children. For what
are the conditions ? Some one feels an impulse to express something, and at the moment has not got the traditional form at
command, and so is driven to evolve a form of his own from the
rest of the linguistic material. It makes no difference whether
he has never heard a form used by other people which expresses
what he wants, or whether he has heard the traditional form,
but has not got it ready at hand at the moment. The method of
procedure is exactly the same whether it takes place in a three-
year-old or in an eighty-three-year-old brain : it is therefore
senseless to put the question whether formations by analogy are
or are not due to children. A formation by analogy is by
definition a non-traditional form. It is therefore idle to ask if
it is due to the fact that the language is transmitted from generation
to generation and to the child's imperfect repetition of what has
been transmitted to it, and Meringer's argument thus breaks
down in every respect.

It must not, of course, be overlooked that children naturally
come to invent more formations by analogy than grown-up people,

because the latter in many cases have heard the older forms so
often that they find a place in their speech without any effort
being required to recall them. But that does not touch the
problem under discussion ; besides, formations by analogy are
unavoidable and indispensable, in the talk of all, even of the
most 'grown-up': one cannot, indeed, move in language without
having recourse to forms and constructions that are not directly
and fully transmitted to us : speech is not alone reproduction,
but just as much new-production, because no situation and no
impulse to communication is in every detail exactly the same
as what has occurred on earlier occasions.

IX.—§ 3. Herzog's Theory of Sound Changes.

If, leaving the field of analogical changes, we begin to inquire
whether the purely phonetic changes can or must be ascribed to
the fact that a new generation has to learn the mother-tongue
by imitation, we shall first have to examine an interesting theory
in which the question is answered in the affirmative, at least with
regard to those phonetic changes which are gradual and not
brought about all at once ; thus, when in one particular language
one vowel, say [e·], is pronounced more and more closely till
finally it becomes [i·], as has happened in E. *see*, formerly pronounced [se·] with the same vowel as in G. *see*, now [si·]. E.
Herzog maintains that such changes happen through transference
to new generations, even granted that the children imitate the
sound of the grown-up people perfectly. For, it is said, children
with their little mouths cannot produce acoustically the same
sound as adults, except by a different position of the speech-
organs ; this position they keep for the rest of their lives, so that
when they are grown-up and their mouth is of full size they produce
a rather different sound from that previously heard—which altered
sound is again imitated by the next generation with yet another
position of the organs, and so on. This continuous play of
generation *v.* generation may be illustrated in this way :

ARTICULATION *corresponding to* SOUND.

1st generation	{ young	A1	..	..	..	.. S1
	old	A1	..	..	..	.. S2
2nd generation	{ young	A2	..	..	..	.. S2
	old	A2	..	..	..	.. S3
3rd generation	{ young	A3	..	..	..	.. S3
	old	A3	..	..	..	.. S4, etc.[1]

[1] See E. Herzog, *Streitfragen der roman. philologie*, i. (1904), p. 57—I
modify his symbols a little.

It is, however, easy to prove that this theory cannot be correct. (1) It is quite certain that the increase in size of the mouth is far less important than is generally supposed (see my *Fonetik*, p. 379 ff., PhG, p. 80 ff. ; cf. above, V § 1).   (2) It cannot be proved that people, after once learning one definite way of producing a sound, go on producing it in exactly the same way, even if the acoustic result is a different one.   It is much more probable that each individual is constantly adapting himself to the sounds heard from those around him, even if this adaptation is neither as quick nor perhaps as perfect as that of children, who can very rapidly accommodate their speech to the dialect of new surroundings : if very far-reaching changes are rare in the case of grown-up people, this proves nothing against such small adaptations as are here presupposed. In favour of the continual regulation of the sound through the ear may be adduced the fact that adults who become perfectly deaf and thus lose the control of sounds through hearing may come to speak in such a way that their words can hardly be understood by others.   (3) The theory in question also views the relations between successive generations in a way that is far removed from the realities of life : from the wording one might easily imagine that there were living together at any given time only individuals of ages separated by, say, thirty years' distance, while the truth of the matter is that a child is normally surrounded by people of all ages and learns its language more or less from all of them, from Grannie down to little Dick from over the way, and that (as has already been remarked) its chief teachers are its own brothers and sisters and other playmates of about the same age as itself. If the theory were correct, there would at any rate be a marked difference in vowel-sounds between anyone and his grandfather, or, still more, great-grandfather : but nothing of the kind has ever been described.   (4) The chief argument, however, against the theory is this, that were it true, then all shiftings of sounds at all times and in all languages would proceed in exactly the same direction. But this is emphatically contradicted by the history of language. The long *a* in English in one period was rounded and raised into *o*, as in OE. *stan, na, ham*, which have become *stone, no, home ;* but when a few centuries later new long *a*'s had entered the language, they followed the opposite direction towards *e*, now [ei], as in *name, male, take*. Similarly in Danish, where an old stratum of long *a*'s have become *å*, as in *ål, gås*, while a later stratum tends rather towards [æ], as in the present pronunciation of *gade, hale*, etc. At the same time the long *a* in Swedish tends towards the rounded pronunciation (cf. Fr. *âme, pas*) : in one sister language we thus witness a repetition of the old shifting, in the other a tendency in the opposite direction. And it is the same with all those languages which we can pursue far enough back : they all present the same picture of varying vowel shiftings in different directions, which is totally incompatible with Herzog's view.

IX.—§ 4. Gradual Shiftings.

We shall do well to put aside such artificial theories and look soberly at the facts. When some sounds in one century go one way, and in another, another, while at times they remain long unchanged, it all rests on this, that for human habits of this sort there is no standard measure. Set a man to saw a hundred logs, measuring No. 2 by No. 1, No. 3 by No. 2, and so on, and you will see considerable deviations from the original measure—perhaps all going in the same direction, so that No. 100 is very much longer than No. 1 as the result of the sum of a great many small deviations—perhaps all going in the opposite direction ; but it is also possible that in a certain series he was inclined to make the logs too long, and in the next series too short, the two sets of deviations about balancing one another.

It is much the same with the formation of speech sounds : at one moment, for some reason or other, in a particular mood, in order to lend authority or distinction to our words, we may happen to lower the jaw a little more, or to thrust the tongue a little more forward than usual, or inversely, under the influence of fatigue or laziness, or to sneer at someone else, or because we have a cigar or potato in our mouth, the movements of the jaw or of the tongue may fall short of what they usually are. We have all the while a sort of conception of an average pronunciation, of a normal degree of opening or of protrusion, which we aim at, but it is nothing very fixed, and the only measure at our disposal is that we are or are not understood. What is understood is all right : what does not meet this requirement must be repeated with greater correctness as an answer to ' I beg your pardon ? '

Everyone thinks that he talks to-day just as he did yesterday, and, of course, he does so in nearly every point. But no one knows if he pronounces his mother-tongue in every respect in the same manner as he did twenty years ago. May we not suppose that what happens with faces happens here also ? One lives with a friend day in and day out, and he appears to be just what he was years ago, but someone who returns home after a long absence is at once struck by the changes which have gradually accumulated in the interval.

Changes in the sounds of a language are not, indeed, so rapid as those in the appearance of an individual, for the simple reason that it is not enough for one man to alter his pronunciation,

many must co-operate : the social nature and social aim of language has the natural consequence that all must combine in the
same movement, or else one neutralizes the changes introduced
by the other ; each individual also is continually under the influence of his fellows, and involuntarily fashions his pronunciation
according to the impression he is constantly receiving of other
people's sounds.   But as regards those little gradual shiftings of
sounds which take place in spite of all this control and its conservative influence, changes in which the sound and the articulation
alter simultaneously, I cannot see that the transmission of the
language to a new generation need exert any essential influence :
we may imagine them being brought about equally well in a society
which for hundreds of years consisted of the same adults who
never died and had no issue.

IX.—§ 5. Leaps.

While in the shiftings mentioned in the last paragraphs
articulation and acoustic impression went side by side, it is
different with some shiftings in which the old sound and the new
resemble one another to the ear, but differ in the position of the
organs and the articulations. For instance, when [þ] as in E.
thick becomes [f] and [ð] as in E. *mother* becomes [v], one can
hardly conceive the change taking place in the pronunciation of
people who have learnt the right sound as children. It is very
natural, on the other hand, that children should imitate the
harder sound by giving the easier, which is very like it, and which
they have to use in many other words : forms like *fru* for *through*,
wiv, *muvver* for *with*, *mother*, are frequent in the mouths of children
long before they begin to make their appearance in the speech
of adults, where they are now beginning to be very frequent in
the Cockney dialect. (Cf. MEG i. 13. 9.) The same transition is
met with in Old Fr., where we have *muef* from *modu*, *nif* from
nidu, *fief* from *feodu*, *seif*, now *soif*, from *site*, *estrif* (E. *strife*) from
stridh, *glaive* from *gladiu*, *parvis* from *paradis*, and possibly *avoutre*
from *adulteru*, *poveir*, now *pouvoir*, from *potere*. In Old Gothonic
we have the transition from þ to *f* before *l*, as in Goth. *þlaqus*=
MHG. *vlach*, Goth. *þlaihan*=OHG. *flêhan*, *þliuhan*=OHG. *fliohan* ;
cf. also E. *file*, G. *feile*=ON. *þēl*, OE. *þengel* and *fengel* ' prince,'
and probably G. *finster*, cf. OHG. *dinstar* (with *d* from þ), OE. *þeostre*.
In Latin we have the same transition, e.g. in *fumus*, corresponding
to Sansk. *dhumás*, Gr. *thumós*.[1]

---

[1] In Russian *Marfa*, *Fyodor*, etc., we also have *f* corresponding to original
þ, but in this case it is not a transition within one and the same language,
but an imperfect imitation on the part of the (adult !) Russians of a sound
in a foreign language (Greek *th*) which was not found in their own language.

The change from the back-open consonant [x]—the sound in
G. *buch* and Scotch *loch*—to *f*, which has taken place in *enough*,
cough, etc., is of the same kind. Here clearly we have no gradual
passage, but a jump, which could hardly take place in the case
of those who had already learnt how to pronounce the back
sound, but is easily conceivable as a case of defective imitation
on the part of a new generation. I suppose that the same remark
holds good with regard to the change from *kw* to *p*, which is found
in some languages, for instance, Gr. *hippos*, corresponding to Lat.
equus, Gr. *hepomai*=Lat. *sequor*, *hêpar*=Lat. *jecur*; Rumanian
apa from Lat. *aqua*, Welsh *map*, ' son '=Gaelic *mac*, *pedwar*=Ir.
cathir, ' four,' etc. In France I have heard children say [pizin]
and [pidin] for *cuisine*.

IX.—§ 6. Assimilations, etc.

There is an important class of sound changes which have
this in common with the class just treated, that the changes take
place suddenly, without an intermediate stage being possible, as
in the changes considered in IX § 4. I refer to those cases
of assimilation, loss of consonants in heavy groups and transposition (metathesis), with which students of language are familiar
in all languages. Instances abound in the speech of all children ;
see above, V § 4.

If now we dared to assert that such pronunciations are never
heard from people who have passed their babyhood, we should
here have found a field in which children have exercised a great
influence on the development of language : but of course we
cannot say anything of the sort. Any attentive observer can
testify to the frequency of such mispronunciations in the speech
of grown-up people. In many cases they are noticed neither by
the speaker nor by the hearer, in many they may be noticed, but
are considered too unimportant to be corrected, and finally, in
some cases the speaker stops to repeat what he wanted to say in
a corrected form. Now it would not obviously do, from their
frequency in adult speech, to draw the inference : " These changes
are not to be ascribed to children," because from their frequent
appearance on the lips of the children one could equally well infer :
" They are not to be ascribed to grown-up people." When we
find in Latin *impotens* and *immeritus* with *m* side by side with
indignus and *insolitus* with *n*, or when English *handkerchief* is
pronounced with [ŋk] instead of the original [ndk], the change
is not to be charged against children or grown-up people exclusively, but against both parties together : and so when *t* is lost
in *waistcoat* [weskət], or *postman* or *castle*, or *k* in *asked*. There

is certainly this difference, that when the change is made by older people, we get in the speech of the same individual first the heavier and then the easier form, while the child may take up the easier pronunciation first, because it hears the [n] before a lip consonant as [m], and before a back consonant as [ŋ], or because it fails altogether to hear the middle consonant in *waistcoat*, *postman*, *castle* and *asked*. But all this is clearly of purely theoretical interest, and the result remains that the influence of the two classes, adults and children, cannot possibly be separated in this domain.[1]

IX.—§ 7. Stump-words.

Next we come to those changes which result in what one may call 'stump-words.' There is no doubt that words may undergo violent shortenings both by children and adults, but here I believe we can more or less definitely distinguish between their respective contributions to the development of language. If it is the end of the word that is kept, while the beginning is dropped, it is probable that the mutilation is due to children, who, as we have seen (VII § 7), echo the conclusion of what is said to them and forget the beginning or fail altogether to apprehend it. So we get a number of mutilated Christian names, which can then be used by grown-up people as pet-names. Examples are *Bert* for Herbert or Albert, *Bella* for Arabella, *Sander* for Alexander, *Lottie* for Charlotte, *Trix* for Beatrix, and with childlike sound-substitution *Bess* (and *Bet*, *Betty*) for Elizabeth. Similarly in other languages, from Danish I may mention *Bine* for Jakobine, *Line* for Karoline, *Stine* for Kristine, *Dres* for Andres : there are many others.

If this way of shortening a word is natural to a child who hears the word for the first time and is not able to remember the beginning when he comes to the end of it, it is quite different when others clip words which they know perfectly well : they will naturally keep the beginning and stop before they are half through the word, as soon as they are sure that their hearers understand what is alluded to. Dr. Johnson was not the only one who " had a way of contracting the names of his friends, as Beauclerc, *Beau* ; Boswell, *Bozzy* ; Langton, *Lanky* ; Murphy, *Mur* ; Sheridan, *Sherry* ; and Goldsmith, *Goldy*, which Gold-

---

[1] Reduplications and assimilations at a distance, as in Fr. *tante* from the older *ante* (whence E. *aunt*, from Lat. *amita*) and *porpentine* (frequent in this and analogous forms in Elizabethan writers) for porcupine (*porkepine*, *porkespine*) are different from the ordinary assimilations of neighbouring sounds in occurring much less frequently in the speech of adults than in children ; cf., however, below, Ch. XV 4.

smith resented " (Boswell, *Life*, ed. P. Fitzgerald, 1900, i. 486). Thackeray constantly says *Pen* for Arthur Pendennis, *Cos* for Costigan, *Fo* for Foker, *Pop* for Popjoy, *old Col* for Colchicum. In the beginning of the last century Napoleon Bonaparte was generally called *Nap* or *Boney* ; later we have such shortened names of public characters as *Dizzy* for Disraeli, *Pam* for Palmerston, *Labby* for Labouchere, etc. These evidently are due to adults, and so are a great many other clippings, some of which have completely ousted the original long words, such as *mob* for mobile, *brig* for brigantine, *fad* for fadaise, *cab* for cabriolet, *navvy* for navigator, while others are still felt as abbreviations, such as *photo* for photograph, *pub* for public-house, *caps* for capital letters, *spec* for speculation, *sov* for sovereign, *zep* for Zeppelin, *divvy* for dividend, *hip* for hypochondria, *the Cri* and *the Pavvy* for the Criterion and the Pavilion, and many other clippings of words which are evidently far above the level of very small children. The same is true of the abbreviations in which school and college slang abounds, words like *Gym*(nastics), *undergrad*(uate), *trig*-(onometry), *lab*(oratory), *matric*(ulation), *prep*(aration), *the Guv* for the governor, etc. The same remark is true of similar clippings in other languages, such as *kilo* for kilogram, G. *ober* for oberkellner, French *aristo*(crate), *réac*(tionnaire), college terms like *desse* for descriptive (géométrie d.), *philo* for philosophie, *preu* for premier, *seu* for second ; Danish numerals like *tres* for tresindstyve (60), *halvfjerds*(indstyve), *firs*(indstyve). We are certainly justified in extending the principle that abbreviation through throwing away the end of the word is due to those who have previously mastered the full form, to the numerous instances of shortened Christian names like *Fred* for Frederick, *Em* for Emily, *Alec* for Alexander, *Di* for Diana, *Vic* for Victoria, etc. In other languages we find similar clippings of names more or less carried through systematically, e.g. Greek *Zeuxis* for Zeuxippos, Old High German *Wolfo* for Wolfbrand, Wolfgang, etc., Icelandic *Sigga* for Sigríðr, *Siggi* for Sigurðr, etc.

I see a corroboration of my theory in the fact that there are hardly any *family* names shortened by throwing away the begin-ning : children as a rule have no use for family names.[1] The rule, however, is not laid down as absolute, but only as holding in the main. Some of the exceptions are easily accounted for. *'Cello* for violoncello undoubtedly is an adults' word, originating

[1] Karl Sundén, in his diligent and painstaking book on *Elliptical Words in Modern English* (Upsala, 1904) [i.e. clipped proper names, for common names are not treated in the long lists given], mentions only two examples of surnames in which the final part is kept (*Bart* for Islebart, *Piggy* for Guineapig, from obscure novels), though he has scores of examples in which the beginning is preserved.

in France or Italy : but here evidently it would not do to take the beginning, for then there would be confusion with violin (violon). *Phone* for telephone : the beginning might just as well stand for telegraph. *Van* for caravan : here the beginning would be identical with *car*. *Bus*, which made its appearance immediately after the first omnibus was started in the streets of London (1829), probably was thought expressive of the sound of these vehicles and suggested *bustle*. But *bacco* (*baccer, baccy*) for tobacco and *taters* for potatoes belong to a different sphere altogether : they are not clippings of the usual sort, but purely phonetic developments, in which the first vowel has been dropped in rapid pronunciation (as in *I s'pose*), and the initial voiceless stop has then become inaudible ; Dickens similarly writes *'tickerlerly* as a vulgar pronunciation of particularly.[1]

---

[1] It is often said that stress is decisive of what part is left out in word-clippings, and from an a priori point of view this is what we should expect. But as a matter of fact we find in many instances that syllables with weak stress are preserved, e.g. in *Mac*(donald), *Pen*(dennis), the *Cri*, *Vic*, *Nap*, *Nat* for Nathaniel (orig. pronounced with [t], not [þ]), *Val* for Percival, *Trix*, etc. The middle is never kept as such with omission of the beginning and the ending ; *Liz* (whence *Lizzy*) has not arisen at one stroke from Elizabeth, but mediately through *Eliz*. Some of the adults' clippings originate through abbreviations in *writing*, thus probably most of the college terms (*exam, trig*, etc.), thus also journalists' clippings like *ad* for advertisement, *par* for paragraph ; cf. also *caps* for capitals. On stump-words see also below, Ch. XIV, §§ 8 and 9.

CHAPTER X

THE INFLUENCE OF THE CHILD—*continued*

§ 1. Confusion of Words. § 2. Metanalysis. § 3. Shiftings of Meanings.
  § 4. Differentiations. § 5. Summary. § 6. Indirect Influence. § 7.
New Languages.

X.—§ 1. Confusion of Words.

SOME of the most typical childish sound-substitutions can hardly
be supposed to leave any traces in language as permanently
spoken, because they are always thoroughly corrected by the
children themselves at an early age; among these I reckon the almost
universal pronunciation of *t* instead of *k*. When, therefore, we
do find that in some words a *t* has taken the place of an earlier
k, we must look for some more specific cause of the change : but
this may, in some cases at any rate, be found in a tendency of
children's speech which is totally independent of the inability
to pronounce the sound of *k* at an early age, and is, indeed, in
no way to be reckoned among phonetic tendencies, namely, the
confusion resulting from an association of two words of similar
sound (cf. above, p. 122). This, I take it, is the explanation of
the word *mate* in the sense ' husband or wife,' which has replaced
the earlier *make* : a confusion was here natural, because the word
mate, ' companion,' was similar not only in sound, but also in
signification. The older name for the ' soft roe ' of fishes was
milk (as Dan. *mœlk*, G. *milch*), but from the fifteenth century
milt has been substituted for it, as if it were the same organ as
the *milt*, ' the spleen.' Children will associate words of similar
sound even in cases where there is no connecting link in their
significations ; thus we have *bat* for earlier *bak*, *bakke* (the animal,
vespertilio), though the other word *bat*, ' a stick,' is far removed
in sense.

I think we must explain the following cases of isolated sound-
substitution as due to the same confusion with unconnected words
in the minds of children hearing the new words for the first time :
trunk in the sense of ' proboscis of an elephant,' formerly *trump*,
from Fr. *trompe*, confused with *trunk*, ' stem of a tree ' ; *stark-
naked*, formerly *start-naked*, from *start*, ' tail,' confused with *stark*,
' stiff ' ; *vent*, ' air-hole,' from Fr. *fente*, confused with *vent*,

'breath' (for this *v* cannot be due to the Southern dialectal transition from *f*, as in *vat* from *fat*, for that transition does not, as a rule, take place in French loans) ; *cocoa* for *cacao*, confused with *coconut*; *match*, from Fr. *mèche*, by confusion with the other *match* ; *chine*, ' rim of cask,' from *chime*, cf. G. *kimme*, ' border,' confused with *chine*, ' backbone.' I give some of these examples with a little diffidence, though I have no doubt of the general principle of childish confusion of unrelated words as one of the sources of irregularities in the development of sounds.

These substitutions cannot of course be separated from instances of ' popular etymology,' as when the phrase *to curry favour* was substituted for the former *to curry favel*, where *favel* means ' a fallow horse,' as the type of fraud or duplicity (cf. G. *den fahlen hengst reiten*, ' to act deceitfully,' *einen auf einem fahlen pferde ertappen*, ' to catch someone lying ').

X.—§ 2. Metanalysis.

We now come to the phenomenon for which I have ventured to coin the term ' metanalysis,' by which I mean that words or word-groups are by a new generation analyzed differently from the analysis of a former age. Each child has to find out for himself, in hearing the connected speech of other people, where one word ends and the next one begins, or what belongs to the kernel and what to the ending of a word, etc. (VII § 6). In most cases he will arrive at the same analysis as the former generation, but now and then he will put the boundaries in another place than formerly, and the new analysis may become general. *A naddre* (the ME. form for OE. *an nædre*) thus became *an adder*, *a napron* became *an apron*, *an nauger* : *an auger*, *a numpire* : *an umpire* ; and in psychologically the same way *an ewte* (older form *evete*, OE. *efete*) became *a newt* : metanalysis accordingly sometimes shortens and sometimes lengthens a word. *Riding* as a name of one of the three districts of Yorkshire is due to a metanalysis of *North Thriding* (ON. *þriðjungr*, ' third part '), as well as of *East Thriding, West Thriding*, after the sound of *th* had been assimilated to the preceding *t*.

One of the most frequent forms of metanalysis consists in the subtraction of an *s*, which originally belonged to the kernel of a word, but is mistaken for the plural ending ; in this way we have *pea* instead of the earlier *peas*, *pease*, *cherry* for ME. *cherris*, Fr. *cerise*, *asset* from *assets*, Fr. *assez*, etc. Cf. also the vulgar *Chinee*, *Portuguee*, etc.[1]

[1] See my MEG ii. 5. 6, and my paper on ' Subtraktionsdannelser," in *Festskrift til Vilh. Thomsen*, 1894, p. 1 ff.

The influence of a new generation is also seen in those cases in which formerly separate words coalesce into one, as when *he breakfasts, he breakfasted,* is said instead of *he breaks fast, he broke fast* ; cf. *vouchsafe, don* (third person, *vouchsafes, dons*), instead of *vouch safe, do on* (third person, *vouches safe, does on*). Here, too, it is not probable that a person who has once learnt the real form of a word, and thus knows where it begins and where it ends, should have subsequently changed it : it is much more likely that all such changes originate with children who have once made a wrong analysis of what they have heard and then go on repeating the new forms all their lives.

X.—§ 3. Shiftings of Meanings.

Changes in the meaning of words are often so gradual that one cannot detect the different steps of the process, and changes of this sort, like the corresponding changes in the sounds of words, are to be ascribed quite as much to people already acquainted with the language as to the new generation. As examples we may mention the laxity that has changed the meaning of *soon*, which in OE. meant ' at once,' and in the same way of *presently*, originally ' at present, now,' and of the old *anon*. *Dinner* comes from OF. *disner*, which is the infinitive of the verb which in other forms was *desjeun*, whence modern French *déjeune* (Lat. **desjejunare*) ; it thus meant ' breakfast,' but the hour of the meal thus termed was gradually shifted in the course of centuries, so that now we may have dinner twelve hours after breakfast. When *picture*, which originally meant ' painting,' came to be applied to drawings, photographs and other images ; when *hard* came to be used as an epithet not only of nuts and stones, etc., but of words and labour ; when *fair*, besides the old sense of ' beautiful,' acquired those of ' blond ' and ' morally just ' ; when *meat*, from meaning all kinds of food (as in *sweetmeats, meat and drink*), came to be restricted practically to one kind of food (butcher's meat) ; when the verb *grow*, which at first was used only of plants, came to be used of animals, hairs, nails, feelings, etc., and, instead of implying always increase, might even be combined with such a predicative as *smaller and smaller* ; when *pretty*, from the meaning ' skilful, ingenious,' came to be a general epithet of approval (cf. the modern American, *a cunning child*=' sweet '), and, besides meaning good-looking, became an adverb of degree, as in *pretty bad* : neither these nor countless similar shiftings need be ascribed to any influence on the part of the learners of English ; they can easily be accounted for as the product of innumerable small extensions and restrictions on the part of the users of the language after they have once acquired it.

But along with changes of this sort we have others that have come about with a leap, and in which it is impossible to find intermediate stages between two seemingly heterogeneous meanings, as when *bead*, from meaning a ' prayer,' comes to mean ' a perforated ball of glass or amber.' In these cases the change is occasioned by certain connexions, where the whole sense can only be taken in one way, but the syntactical construction admits of various interpretations, so that an ambiguity at one point gives occasion for a new conception of the meaning of the word. The phrase *to count your beads* originally meant ' to count your prayers,' but because the prayers were reckoned by little balls, the word *beads* came to be transferred to these objects, and lost its original sense.[1] It seems clear that this misapprehension could not take place in the brains of those who had already associated the word with the original signification, while it was quite natural on the part of children who heard and understood the phrase as a whole, but unconsciously analyzed it differently from the previous generation.

There is another word which also meant ' prayer ' originally, but has lost that meaning, viz. *boon*; through such phrases as ' ask a boon ' and ' grant a boon ' it came to be taken as meaning ' a favour ' or ' a good thing received.'

Orient was frequently used in such connexions as ' orient pearl ' and ' orient gem,' and as these were lustrous, *orient* became an adjective meaning ' shining,' without any connexion with the geographical orient, as in Shakespeare, *Venus* 981, " an orient drop " (a tear), and Milton, PL i. 546, " Ten thousand banners rise into the air, With orient colours waving."

There are no connecting links between the meanings of ' glad ' and ' obliged,' ' forced,' but when *fain* came to be chiefly used in combinations like ' he was fain to leave the country,' it was natural for the younger generation to interpret the whole phrase as implying necessity instead of gladness.

We have similar phenomena in certain syntactical changes. When *me thinks* and *me likes* gave place to *I think* and *I like*, the chief cause of the change was that the child heard combinations like *Mother thinks* or *Father likes*, where *mother* and *father* can be either nominative or accusative-dative, and the construction is thus syntactically ambiguous. This leads to a ' shunting ' of the meaning as well as of the construction of the verbs, which must

---

[1] Semantic changes through ambiguous syntactic combinations have recently been studied especially by Carl Collin ; see his *Semasiologiska studier*, 1906, and *Le Développement de Sens du Suffixe -ATA*, Lund, 1918, ch. iii and iv. Collin there treats especially of the transition from abstract to concrete nouns ; he does not, as I have done above, speak of the rôle of the younger generation in such changes.

have come about in a new brain which was not originally acquainted with the old construction.

As one of the factors bringing about changes in meaning many scholars mention forgetfulness ; but it is important to keep in view that what happens is not real forgetting, that is, snapping of threads of thought that had already existed within the same consciousness, but the fact that the new individual never develops the threads of thought which in the elder generation bound one word to another. Sometimes there is no connexion of ideas in the child's brain : a word is viewed quite singly as a whole and isolated, till later perhaps it is seen in its etymological relation. A little girl of six asked when she was born. " You were born on the 2nd of October." "Why, then, I was born on my birthday ! " she cried, her eyes beaming with joy at this wonderfully happy coincidence. Originally *Fare well* was only said to some one going away. If now the departing guest says *Farewell* to his friend who is staying at home, it can only be because the word *Farewell* has been conceived as a fixed formula, without any consciousness of the meaning of its parts.

Sometimes, on the other hand, new connexions of thought arise, as when we associate the word *bound* with *bind* in the phrase ' he is bound for America.' Our ancestors meant ' he is ready to go ' (ON. *búinn*, ' ready '), not ' he is under an obligation to go.' The establishment of new associations of this kind seems naturally to take place at the moment when the young mind makes acquaintance with the word : the phenomenon is, of course, closely related to " popular etymology " (see Ch. VI § 6).

X.—§ 4. Differentiations.

Linguistic ' splittings ' or differentiations, whereby one word becomes two, may also be largely due to the transmission of the language to a new generation. The child may hear two pronunciations of the same word from different people, and then associate these with different ideas. Thus Paul Passy learnt the word *meule* in the sense of ' grindstone ' from his father, and in the sense of ' haycock ' from his mother ; now the former in both senses pronounced [mœl], and the latter in both [mø·l], and the child thus came to distinguish [mœl] ' grindstone ' and [mø·l] ' haycock ' (Ch 23).

Or the child may have learnt the word at two different periods of its life, associated with different spheres. This, I take it, may be the reason why some speakers make a distinction between two pronunciations of the word *medicine*, in two and in three syllables : they take [medsin], but study [medisin].

Finally, the child can itself split words. A friend writes : " I remember that when a schoolboy said that it was a good thing that the new Headmaster was Dr. Wood, because he would then know when boys were 'shamming,' a schoolfellow remarked, 'Wasn't it funny ? He did not know the difference between Doct*or* and Doct*er*.'" In Danish the Japanese are indiscriminately called either *Japanerne* or *Japaneserne* ; now, I once overheard my boy (6.10) lecturing his playfellows : "*Japaneserne*, that is the soldiers of Japan, but *Japanerne*, that is students and children and such-like.'" It is, of course, possible that he may have heard one form originally when shown some pictures of Japanese soldiers, and the other on another occasion, and that this may have been the reason for his distinction. However this may be, I do not doubt that a number of differentiations of words are to be ascribed to the transmission of the language to a new generation. Others may have arisen in the speech of adults, such as the distinction between *off* and *of* (at first the stressed and unstressed form of the same preposition), or between *thorough* and *through* (the former is still used as a preposition in Shakespeare : "thorough bush, thorough brier "). But complete differentiation is not established till some individuals from the very first conceive the forms as two independent words.

X.—§ 5. Summary.

Instead of saying, as previous writers on these questions have done, either that children have no influence or that they have the chief influence on the development of language, it will be seen that I have divided the question into many, going through various fields of linguistic change and asking in each what may have been the influence of the child. The result of this investigation has been that there are certain fields in which it is both impossible and really also irrelevant to separate the share of the child and of the adult, because both will be apt to introduce changes of that kind ; such are assimilations of neighbouring sounds and droppings of consonants in groups. Also, with regard to those very gradual shiftings either of sound or of meaning in which it is natural to assume many intermediate stages through which the sound or signification must have passed before arriving at the final result, children and adults must share the responsibility for the change. Clippings of words occur in the speech of both classes, but as a rule adults will keep the beginning of a word, while very small children will perceive or remember only the end of a word and use that for the whole. But finally there are some kinds of changes which must wholly or chiefly be charged to the account of children : such are those leaps in sound or signification in which intermediate stages are out of the question, as well as confusions of similar words and misdivisions of words, and the most violent differentiations of words.

I wish, however, here to insist on one point which has, I think, become more and more clear in the course of our disquisition, namely, that we ought not really to put the question like this : Are linguistic changes due to children or to grown-up people ? The important distinction is not really one of age, which is evidently one of degree only, but that between the first learners of the sound or word in question and those who use it after having once learnt it. In the latter case we have mainly to do with infinitesimal glidings, the results of which, when summed up in the course of long periods of time, may be very considerable indeed, but in which it will always be possible to detect intermediate links connecting the extreme points. In contrast to these changes occurring *after* the correct (or original) form has been acquired by the individual, we have changes occurring *simultaneously* with the first acquisition of the word or form in question, and thus due to the fact of its transmission to a new generation, or, to speak more generally, and, indeed, more correctly, to new individuals. The exact age of the learner here is of little avail, as will be seen if we take some examples of metanalysis. It is highly probable that the first users of forms like *a pea* or *a cherry*, instead of *a pease* and *a cherries*, were little children ; but *a Chinee* and *a Portuguee* are not necessarily, or not pre-eminently, children's words : on the other hand, it is to me indubitable that these forms do not spring into existence in the mind of someone who has previously used the forms *Chinese* and *Portuguese* in the singular number, but must be due to the fact that the forms *the Chinese* and *the Portuguese* (used as plurals) have been at once apprehended as made up of *Chinee*, *Portuguee* + the plural ending -*s* by a person hearing them for the first time ; similarly in all the other cases. We shall see in a later chapter that the adoption (on the part of children and adults alike) of sounds and words from a foreign tongue presents certain interesting points of resemblance with these instances of change : in both cases the innovation begins when some individual is first made acquainted with linguistic elements that are new to him.

X.—§ 6. Indirect Influence.

We have hitherto considered what elements of the language may be referred to a child's first acquisition of language. But we have not yet done with the part which children play in linguistic development. There are two things which must be sharply distinguished from the phenomena discussed in the preceding chapter—the first, that grown-up people in many cases catch up the words and forms used by children and thereby give them a power of survival which they would not have otherwise ; the second, that grown-up people alter their own language so as to meet children half-way.

As for the first point, we have already seen examples in which mothers and nurses have found the baby's forms so pretty that they have adopted them themselves. Generally these forms are confined to the family circle, but they may under favourable circumstances be propagated further. A special case of the highest interest has been fully discussed in the section about words of the *mamma*-class.

As for the second point, grown-up people often adapt their speech to the more or less imaginary needs of their children by pronouncing words as they do, saying *dood* and *tum* for ' good ' and ' come,' etc. This notion clearly depends on a misunderstanding, and can only retard the acquisition of the right pronunciation ; the child understands *good* and *come* at least as well, if not better, and the consequence may be that when he is able himself to pronounce [g] and [k] he may consider it immaterial, because one can just as well say [d] and [t] as [g] and [k], or may be bewildered as to which words have the one sound and which the other. It can only be a benefit to the child if all who come in contact with it speak from the first as correctly, elegantly and clearly as possible—not, of course, in long, stilted sentences and with many learned book-words, but naturally and easily. When the child makes a mistake, the most effectual way of correcting it is certainly the indirect one of seeing that the child, soon after it has made the mistake, hears the correct form. If he says ' A waps stinged me ': answer, ' It stung you : did it hurt much when the wasp stung you ? ' etc. No special emphasis even is needed ; next time he will probably use the correct form.

But many parents are not so wise ; they will say *stinged* themselves when once they have heard the child say so. And nurses and others have even developed a kind of artificial nursery language which they imagine makes matters easier for the little ones, but which is in many respects due to erroneous ideas of how children ought to talk rather than to real observation of the way children do talk. Many forms are handed over traditionally from one nurse to another, such as *totties*, *tootems* or *tootsies* for ' feet ' (from *trotters ?*), *toothy-peg* for ' tooth,' *tummy* or *tumtum* for ' stomach,' *tootleums* for ' babies,' *shooshoo* for ' a fly.' I give a connected specimen of this nursery language (from Egerton,

Keynotes, 85) : " Didsum was denn ? Oo did ! Was ums de prettiest itta sweetums denn ? Oo was. An' did um put 'em in a nasty shawl an' joggle 'em in an ole puff-puff, um did, was a shame ! Hitchy cum, hitchy cum, hitchy cum hi, Chinaman no likey me." This reminds one of pidgin-English, and in a later chapter we shall see that that and similar bastard languages are partly due to the same mistaken notion that it is necessary to corrupt one's language to be easily understood by children and inferior races.

Very frequently mothers and nurses talk to children in diminutives. When many of these have become established in ordinary speech, losing their force as diminutives and displacing the proper words, this is another result of nursery language. The phenomenon is widely seen in Romance languages, where *auricula*, Fr. *oreille*, It. *orecchio*, displaces *auris*, and *avicellus*, Fr. *oiseau*, It. *uccello*, displaces *avis* ; we may remember that classical Latin had already *oculus*, for ' eye.'[1] It is the same in Modern Greek. An example of the same tendency, though not of the same formal means of a diminutive ending, is seen in the English *bird* (originally = ' young bird ') and *rabbit* (originally = ' young rabbit '), which have displaced *fowl* and *coney*.

A very remarkable case of the influence of nursery language on normal speech is seen in many countries, viz. in the displacing of the old word for ' right ' (as opposed to left). The distinction of right and left is not easy for small children : some children in the upper classes at school only know which is which by looking at some wart, or something of the sort, on one of their hands, and have to think every time. Meanwhile mothers and nurses will frequently insist on the use of the right (dextera) hand, and when they are not understood, will think they make it easier for the child by saying ' No, the *right* hand,' and so it comes about that in many languages the word that originally means ' correct ' is used with the meaning ' dexter.' So we have in English *right*, in German *recht*, which displaces *zeso*, Fr. *droit*, which displaces *destre* ; in Spanish also *la derecha* has begun to be used instead of *la diestra* ; similarly, in Swedish *den vackra handen* instead of *högra*, and in Jutlandish dialects *den kjön hånd* instead of *höjre*.

X.—§ 7. New Languages.

In a subsequent chapter (XIV § 5) we shall consider the theory that epochs in which the changes of some language proceed at a

---

[1] I know perfectly well that in these and in other similar words there were reasons for the original word disappearing as unfit (shortness, possibility of mistakes through similarity with other words, etc.). What interests me here is the fact that the substitute is a word of the nursery.

more rapid pace than at others are due to the fact that in times of fierce, widely extended wars many men leave home and remain abroad, either as settlers or as corpses, while the women left behind have to do the field-work, etc., and neglect their homes, the consequence being that the children are left more to themselves, and therefore do not get their mistakes in speech corrected as much as usual.

A somewhat related idea is at the bottom of a theory advanced as early as 1886 by the American ethnologist Horatio Hale (see "The Origin of Languages," in the American Association for the Advancement of Science, XXXV, 1886, and "The Development of Language," the Canadian Institute, Toronto, 1888). As these papers seem to have been entirely unnoticed by leading philologists, I shall give a short abstract of them, leaving out what appears to me to be erroneous in the light of recent linguistic thought and research, namely, his application of the theory to explain the supposed three stages of linguistic development, the monosyllabic, the agglutinative and the flexional.

Hale was struck with the fact that in Oregon, in a region not much larger than France, we find at least thirty different families of languages living together. It is impossible to believe that thirty separate communities of speechless precursors of man should have begun to talk independently of one another in thirty distinct languages in this district. Hale therefore concludes that the origin of linguistic stocks is to be found in the language-making instinct of very young children. When two children who are just beginning to speak are thrown much together, they sometimes invent a complete language, sufficient for all purposes of mutual intercourse, and yet totally unintelligible to their parents. In an ordinary household, the conditions under which such a language would be formed are most likely to occur in the case of twins, and Hale now proceeds to mention those instances—five in all— that he has come across of languages framed in this manner by young children. He concludes : "It becomes evident that, to ensure the creation of a speech which shall be a parent of a new language stock, all that is needed is that two or more young children should be placed by themselves in a condition where they will be entirely, or in a large degree, free from the presence and influence of their elders. They must, of course, continue in this condition long enough to grow up, to form a household, and to have descendants to whom they can communicate their new speech."

These conditions he finds among the hunting tribes of America, in which it is common for single families to wander off from the main band. "In modern times, when the whole country is occupied, their flight would merely carry them into the territory of another tribe, among whom, if well received, they would quickly be absorbed. But in the primitive period, when a vast uninhabited region stretched before them, it would be easy for them to find some sheltered nook or fruitful valley. . . . If under such circumstances disease or the casualties of a hunter's life should carry off the parents, the survival of the children would, it is evident, depend mainly upon the nature of the climate and the ease with which food could be procured at all seasons of the year. In ancient Europe, after the present climatal conditions were established, it is doubtful if a family of children under ten years of age could have lived through a single winter. We are not, therefore, surprised to find that no more than four or five language stocks are represented in Europe. . . . Of Northern America, east of the Rocky Mountains and north of the tropics, the same may be said. . . . But there is one region where Nature seems to offer herself as the willing nurse and bountiful stepmother of the feeble and unprotected . . . California. Its wonderful climate (follows a long description). . . . Need we wonder that, in such a mild and fruitful region, a great number of separate tribes were found, speaking languages which a careful investigation has classed in nineteen distinct linguistic stocks ? " In Oregon, and in the interior of Brazil, Hale finds similar climatic conditions with the same result, a great number of totally dissimilar languages, while in Australia, whose climate is as mild as that of any of these regions, we find hundreds, perhaps thousands, of petty tribes, as completely isolated as those of South America, but all speaking languages of the same stock—because "the other conditions are such as would make it impossible for an isolated group of young children to survive. The whole of Australia is subject to severe droughts, and is so scantily provided with edible products that the aborigines are often reduced to the greatest straits."

This, then, is Hale's theory. Let us now look a little closer into the proofs adduced. They are, as it will be seen, of a twofold order. He invokes the language-creating tendencies of young children on the one hand, and on the other the geographical distribution of linguistic stocks or genera.

As to the first, it is true that so competent a psychologist as Wundt denies the possibility in very strong terms.[1] But facts certainly do not justify this foregone conclusion. I must first refer the reader to Hale's own report of the five instances known

[1] " Einige namentlich in der ältern litteratur vorkommende angaben über kinder, die sich zusammen aufwachsend eine eigene sprache gebildet haben sollen, sind wohl ein für allemal in das gebiet der fabel zu verweisen " (S 1. 286).

to him. Unfortunately, the linguistic material collected by him is so scanty that we can form only a very imperfect idea of the languages which he says children have developed and of the relation between them and the language of the parents. But otherwise his report is very instructive, and I shall call special attention to the fact that in most cases the children seem to have been ' spoilt ' by their parents ; this is also the case with regard to one of the families, though it does not appear from Hale's own extracts from the book in which he found his facts (G. Watson, *Universe of Language*, N.Y., 1878).

The only word recorded in this case is *nī-si-boo-a* for ' carriage ' ; how that came into existence, I dare not conjecture ; but when it is said that the syllables of it were sometimes so repeated that they made a much longer word, this agrees very well with what I have myself observed with regard to ordinary children's playful word-coinages. In the next case, described by E. R. Hun, M.D., of Albany, more words are given. Some of these bear a strong resemblance to French, although neither the parents nor servants spoke that language ; and Hale thinks that some person may have " amused herself, innocently enough, by teaching the child a few words of that tongue." This, however, does not seem necessary to explain the words recorded. *Feu*, pronounced, we are told, like the French word, signified ' fire, light, cigar, sun ' : it may be either E. *fire* or else an imitation of the sound *fff* without a vowel, or [fə·] used in blowing out a candle or a match or in smoking, so as to amuse the child, exactly as in the case of one of my little Danish friends, who used *fff* as the name for ' smoke, steam,' and later for ' funnel, chimney,' and finally anything standing upright against the sky, for instance, a flagstaff. *Petee-petee*, the name which the Albany girl gave to her brother, and which Dr. Hun derived from F. *petit*, may be just as well from E. *pet* or *petty* ; and to explain her word for ' I,' *ma*, we need not go to F. *moi*, as E. *me* or *my* may obviously be thus distorted by any child. Her word for ' not ' is said to have been *ne-pas*, though the exact pronunciation is not given. This cannot have been taken from the French, at any rate not from real French, as *ne* and *pas* are here separated, and *ne* is more often than not pronounced without the vowel or omitted altogether ; the girl's word, if pronounced something like ['nepa·] may be nothing else than an imperfect childish pronunciation of *never*, cf. the negroes' form *nebber*. *Too*, ' all, everything,' of course resembles Fr. *tout*, but how should anyone have been able to teach this girl, who did not speak any intelligible language, a French word of this abstract character ? Some of the other words admit of a natural explanation from English : *go-go*, ' delicacy, as sugar,

candy or dessert,' is probably *goody-goody*, or a reduplicated form
of *good*; *deer*, 'money,' may be from *dear*, 'expensive'; *odo*,
'to send for, to go out, to take away,' is evidently *out*, as in *ma
odo*, 'I want to go out'; *gaän*, 'God,' must be the English word,
in spite of the difference in pronunication, for the child would never
think of inventing this idea on its own accord; *pa-ma*, 'to go to
sleep, pillow, bed,' is from *by-bye* or an independent word of the
mamma-class; *mea*, 'cat, fur,' of course is imitative of the sound
of the cat. For the rest of the words I have no conjectures to
offer. Some of the derived meanings are curious, though perhaps
not more startling than many found in the speech of ordinary
children; *papa* and *mamma* separately had their usual signification,
but *papa-mamma* meant 'church, prayer-book, cross, priest':
the parents were punctual in church observances; *gar odo*,
'horse out, to send for the horse,' came to mean 'pencil and
paper, as the father used, when the carriage was wanted, to write
an order and send it to the stable. In the remaining three cases
of 'invented' languages no specimens are given, except *shindikik*,
'cat.' In all cases the children seem to have talked together
fluently when by themselves in their own gibberish.

But there exists on record a case better elucidated than Hale's
five cases, namely that of the Icelandic girl Sæunn. (See Jonasson
and Eschricht in *Dansk Maanedsskrift*, Copenhagen, 1858.) She
was born in the beginning of the last century on a farm in
Húnavatns-syssel in the northern part of Iceland, and began early
to converse with her twin brother in a language that was entirely
unintelligible to their surroundings. Her parents were disquieted,
and therefore resolved to send away the brother, who died soon
afterwards. They now tried to teach the girl Icelandic, but
soon (too soon, evidently!) came to the conclusion that she could
not learn it, and then they were foolish enough to learn *her*
language, as did also her brothers and sisters and even some of
their friends. In order that she might be confirmed, her elder
brother translated the catechism and acted as interpreter between
the parson and the girl. She is described as intelligent—she
even composed poetry in her own language—but shy and dis-
trustful. Jonasson gives a few specimens of her language, some
of which Eschricht succeeds in interpreting as based on Icelandic
words, though strangely disfigured. The language to Jonasson,
who had heard it, seemed totally dissimilar to Icelandic in sounds
and construction; it had no flexions, and lacked pronouns.
The vocabulary was so limited that she very often had to supplement a phrase by means of nods or gestures; and it was difficult
to carry on a conversation with her in the dark. The ingenuity
of some of the compounds and metaphors is greatly admired by

Jonasson, though to the more sober mind of Eschricht they appear rather childish or primitive, as when a ' wether ' is called *mepok-ill* from *me* (imitation of the sound) + *pok*, ' a little bag ' (Icel. *poki*) + *ill*, ' to cut.' The only complete sentence recorded is ' Dirfa offo nonona uhuh,' which means : ' Sigurdur gets up extremely late.' In his analysis of the whole case Eschricht succeeds in stripping it of the mystical glamour in which it evidently appeared to Jonasson as well as to the girl's relatives ; he is undoubtedly right in maintaining that if the parents had persisted in only talking Icelandic to her, she would soon have forgotten her own language ; he compares her words with some strange disfigurements of Danish which he had observed among children in his own family and acquaintanceship.

I read this report a good many years ago, and afterwards I tried on two occasions to obtain precise information about similar cases I had seen mentioned, one in Halland (Sweden) and the other in Finland, but without success. But in 1903, when I was lecturing on the language of children in the University of Copenhagen, I had the good fortune to hear of a case not far from Copenhagen of two children speaking a language of their own. I investigated the case as well as I could, by seeing and hearing them several times and thus checking the words and sentences which their teacher, who was constantly with them, kindly took down in accordance with my directions. I am thus enabled to give a fairly full account of their language, though unfortunately my investigation was interrupted by a long voyage in 1904.

The boys were twins, about five and a half years old when I saw them, and so alike that even the people who were about them every day had difficulty in distinguishing them from each other. Their mother (a single woman) neglected them shamefully when they were quite small, and they were left very much to shift for themselves. For a long time, while their mother was ill in a hospital, they lived in an out-of-the-way place with an old woman, who is said to have been very deaf, and who at any rate troubled herself very little about them. When they were four years old, the parish authorities discovered how sadly neglected they were and that they spoke quite unintelligibly, and therefore sent them to a ' children's home ' in Seeland, where they were properly taken care of. At first they were extremely shy and reticent, and it was a long time before they felt at home with the other children. When I first saw them, they had in so far learnt the ordinary language that they were able to understand many everyday sentences spoken to them, and could do what they were told (e.g. ' Take the footstool and put it in my room near the stove '), but they could not speak Danish and said very little in the presence of anybody else. When they were by themselves they conversed pretty freely and in a completely unintelligible gibberish, as I had the opportunity to convince myself when standing behind a door one day when they thought they were not observed. Afterwards I got to be in a way good friends with them—they called me *py-ma*, *py* being their word for 'smoke, smoking, pipe, cigar,' so that I got my name from the chocolate cigars which I used to ingratiate myself with them—and then I got them to repeat words and phrases which their teacher had written out for me, and thus was enabled to write down everything phonetically.

An analysis of the sounds occurring in their words showed me that their vocal organs were perfectly normal. Most of the words were evidently Danish words, however much distorted and shortened ; a voiceless *l*, which does not occur in Danish, and which I write here *lh*, was a very frequent sound. This, combined with an inclination to make many words end in *-p*, was enough to disguise words very effectually, as when *sort* (black) was made *lhop*. I shall give the children's pronunciations of the names of some of their new playfellows, adding in brackets the Danish substratum : *lhep* (Svend), *lhip* (Vilhelm), *lip* (Elisabeth), *lop* (Charlotte), *bap* (Mandse) ; similarly the doctor was called *dop*. In many cases there was phonetic assimilation at a distance, as when milk (mælk) was called *bep*, flower (blomst) *bop*, light (lys) *lhylh*, sugar (sukker) *lholh*, cold (kulde) *lhulh*, sometimes also *ulh*, bed (seng) *sœjs*, fish (fisk) *se-is*.

I subjoin a few complete sentences : *nina enaj una enaj hœna mad enaj*, ' we shall not fetch food for the young rabbits ' : *nina* rabbit (kanin), *enaj* negation (nej, no), repeated several times in each negative sentence, as in Old English and in Bantu languages, *una* young (unge). *Bap ep dop*, 'Mandse has broken the hobby-horse,' literally ' Mandse horse piece.' *Hos ia bov lhalh*, ' brother's trousers are wet, Maria,' literally ' trousers Maria brother water.' The words are put together without any flexions, and the word order is totally different from that of Danish.

Only in one case was I unable to identify words that I understood either as ' little language ' forms of Danish words or else as sound-imitations ; but then it must be remembered that they spoke a good deal that neither I nor any of the people about them could make anything of. And then, unfortunately, when I began to study it, their language was already to a great extent ' humanized ' in comparison to what it was when they first came to the children's home. In fact, I noticed a constant progress during the short time I observed the boys, and in some of the last sentences I have noted, I even find the genitive case employed.

The idiom of these twins cannot, of course, be called an independent, still less a complete or fully developed language; but if they were able to produce something so different from the language spoken around them at the beginning of the twentieth century and in a civilized country, there can to my mind be no doubt that Hale is right in his contention that children left to themselves even more than these were, in an uninhabited region where they were still not liable to die from hunger or cold, would be able to develop a language for their mutual understanding that might become so different from that of their parents as really to constitute a new stock of language. So that we can now pass to the other—geographical—side of what Hale advances in favour of his theory.

So far as I can see, the facts here tally very well with the theory. Take, on the one hand, the Eskimo languages, spoken with astonishingly little variation from the east coast of Greenland to Alaska, an immense stretch of territory in which small children if left to themselves would be sure to die very soon indeed. Or take the Finnish-Ugrian languages in the other hemisphere, exhibiting a similar close relationship, though spread over wide areas. And then, on the other hand, the American languages already adduced by Hale. I do not pretend to any deeper knowledge of these languages; but from the most recent works of very able specialists I gather an impression of the utmost variety in phonetics, in grammatical structure and in vocabulary; see especially Roland B. Dixon and Alfred L. Kroeber, "The Native Languages of California," in the *American Anthropologist*, 1903. Even where recent research seems to establish some kind of kinship between families hitherto considered as distinguished stocks (as in Dixon's interesting paper, "Linguistic Relationships within the Shasta-Achomawi Stock," XV Congrès des Américanistes, 1906) the similarities are still so incomplete, so capricious and generally so remote that they seem to support Hale's explanation rather than a gradual splitting of the usual kind.

As for Brazil, I shall quote some interesting remarks from C. F. P. v. Martius, *Beiträge zur Ethnographie u. Sprachenkunde Amerika's*, 1867, i. p. 46 : "In Brazil we see a scant and unevenly distributed native population, uniform in bodily structure, temperament, customs and manner of living generally, but presenting a really astonishing diversity in language. A language is often confined to a few mutually related individuals; it is in truth a family heirloom and isolates its speakers from all other people so as to render any attempt at understanding impossible. On the vessel in which we travelled up the rivers in the interior of Brazil, we often, among twenty Indian rowers, could count only

three or four that were at all able to speak together . . . they
sat there side by side dumb and stupid."

Hale's theory is worthy, then, of consideration, and now, at
the close of our voyage round the world of children's language,
we have gained a post of vantage from which we can overlook
the whole globe and see that the peculiar word-forms which children
use in their 'little language' period can actually throw light
on the distribution of languages and groups of languages over
the great continents. Yes,

> Scorn not the little ones ! You oft will find
> They reach the goal, when great ones lag behind.

BOOK III

THE INDIVIDUAL AND THE WORLD

CHAPTER XI

THE FOREIGNER

XI.—§ 1. The Substratum Theory.

IT seems evident that if we wish to find out the causes of linguistic change, a fundamental division must be into—

(1) Changes that are due to the transference of the language to new individuals, and

(2) Changes that are independent of such transference.

It may not be easy in practice to distinguish the two classes, as the very essence of the linguistic life of each individual is a continual give-and-take between him and those around him ; still, the division is in the main clear, and will consequently be followed in the present work.

The first class falls again naturally into two heads, according as the new individual does not, or does already, possess a language. With the former, i.e. with the native child learning his ' mother-tongue,' we have dealt at length in Book II, and we now proceed to an examination of the influence exercised on a language through its transference to individuals who are already in possession of another language—let us, for the sake of shortness, call them foreigners.

While some earlier scholars denied categorically the existence of mixed languages, recent investigators have attached a very great importance to mixtures of languages, and have studied actually occurring mixtures of various degrees and characters with the greatest accuracy : I mention here only one name, that of Hugo Schuchardt, who combines profundity and width of knowledge with a truly philosophical spirit, though the form of his numerous scattered writings makes it difficult to gather a just idea of his views on many questions.

Many scholars have recently attached great importance to the subtler and more hidden influence exerted by one language on another in those cases in which a population abandons its original language and adopts that of another race, generally in consequence of military conquest. In these cases the theory is that people keep many of their speech-habits, especially with regard to articulation and accent, even while using the vocabulary, etc., of the new language, which thus to a large extent is tinged by the old language. There is thus created what is now generally termed a *substratum* underlying the new language. As the original substratum modifying a language which gradually spreads over a large area varies according to the character of the tribes subjugated in different districts, this would account for many of those splittings-up of languages which we witness everywhere.

Hirt goes so far as to think it possible by the help of existing dialect boundaries to determine the extensions of aboriginal languages (Idg 19).

There is certainly something very plausible in this manner of viewing linguistic changes, for we all know from practical everyday experience that the average foreigner is apt to betray his nationality as soon as he opens his mouth : the Italian's or the German's English is just as different from the 'real thing' as, inversely, the Englishman's Italian or German is different from the Italian or German of a native : the place of articulation, especially that of the tongue-tip consonants, the aspiration or want of aspiration of p, t, k, the voicing or non-voicing of b, d, g, the diphthongization or monophthongization of long vowels, the syllabification, various peculiarities in quantity and in tone-movements—all such things are apt to colour the whole acoustic impression of a foreigner's speech in an acquired language, and it is, of course, a natural supposition that the aboriginal inhabitants of Europe and Asia were just as liable to transfer their speech habits to new languages as their descendants are nowadays. There is thus a priori a strong probability that linguistic substrata have exercised some influence on the development of conquering languages. But when we proceed to apply this natural inference to concrete examples of linguistic history, we shall see that the theory does not perhaps suffice to explain everything that its advocates would have it explain, and that there are certain difficulties which have not always been faced or appraised according to their real value. A consideration of these concrete examples will naturally lead up to a discussion of the general principles involved in the substratum theory.

XI.—§ 2. French *u* and Spanish *h*.

First I shall mention Ascoli's famous theory that French [y˙] for Latin *u*, as in *dur*, etc., is due to Gallic influence, cf. Welsh *i* in *din* from *dun*, which presupposes a transition from *u* to [y].

Ascoli found a proof in the fact that Dutch also has the pronunciation [y·], e.g. in *duur*, on the old Keltic soil of the Belgæ, to which
Schuchardt (SlD 126) added his observation of [y] in dialectal
South German (Breisgau), in a district in which there had formerly
been a strong Keltic element. This looks very convincing at
first blush. On closer inspection, doubts arise on many points.
The French transition cannot with certainty be dated very early,
for then *c* in *cure* would have been palatalized and changed as
c before *i* (Lenz, KZ 39. 46); also the treatment of the vowel
in French words taken over into English, where it is not identified
with the native [y], but becomes [iu], is best explained on the assumption that about 1200 A.D. the sound had not advanced farther
on its march towards the front position than, say, the Swedish
' mixed-round ' sound in *hus*. The district in which [y] is found
for *u* is not coextensive with the Keltic possessions; there were
very few Kelts in what is now Holland, and inversely South German
[y] for *u* does not cover the whole Keltic domain; [y] is found
outside the French territory proper, namely, in Franco-Provençal
(where the substratum was Ligurian) and in Provençal (where there
were very few Galli; cf. Wechssler, L 113). Thus the province
of [y] is here too small and there too large to make the argument
conclusive. Even more fatal is the objection that the Gallic
transition from *u* to *y* is very uncertain (Pedersen, GKS 1. § 353).
So much is certain, that the fronting of *u* was not a *common* Keltic
transition, for it is not found in the Gaelic (Goidelic) branch.[1]
On the other hand, the transition from [u] to [y] occurs elsewhere,
independent of Keltic influence, as in Old Greek (cf. also the Swedish
sound in *hus*): why cannot it, then, be independent in French ?

Another case adduced by Ascoli is initial *h* instead of Latin
f in the country anciently occupied by the Iberians. Now, Basque
has no *f* sound at all in any connexion ; if the same aversion to
f had been the cause of the Spanish substitution of *h* for *f*, we should
expect the substitution to have been made from the moment when
Latin was first spoken in Hispania, and we should expect it to be
found in all positions and connexions. But what do we find
instead ?   First, that Old Spanish had *f* in many cases where modern
Spanish has *h* (i.e. really no sound at all), and this cannot be

---

[1] Cf. against the assumption of Keltic influence in this instance Meyer-
Lübke, *Die Romanischen Sprachen, Kultur der Gegenwart*, p. 457, and Ett-
mayer in Streitberg's *Gesch.* 2. 265.   H. Mutschmann, *Phonology of the North-
Eastern Scotch Dialect*, 1909, p. 53, thinks that the fronting of *u* in Scotch
is similar to that of Latin *ū* on Gallic territory, and like it is ascribable to
the Keltic inhabitants : he forgets, however, that the corresponding fronting
is not found in the Keltic spoken in Scotland.   Moreover, the complicated
Scotch phenomena cannot be compared with the French transition, for
the sound of [u] remains in many cases, and [i] generally corresponds to
earlier [o], whatever the explanation may be.

altogether ascribed to 'Latinizing scribes.' On the contrary, the transition $f > h$ seems to have taken place many centuries after the Roman invasion, since the Spanish-speaking Jews of Salonika, who emigrated from Spain about 1500, have to this day preserved the f sound among other archaic traits (see F. Hanssen, *Span. Gramm.* 45; Wiener, *Modern Philology*, June 1903, p. 205). And secondly, that f has been kept in certain connexions; thus, before [w], as in *fui, fuiste, fué*, etc., before r and l, as in *fruto, flor*, etc. This certainly is inexplicable if the cause of $f > h$ had been the want of power on the part of the aborigines to produce the f sound at all, while it is simple enough if we assume a later transition, taking place possibly at first between two vowels, with a subsequent generalization of the f-less forms. Diez is here, as not infrequently, more sensible than some of his successors (see *Gramm. d. roman. spr.*, 4th ed., 1. 283 f., 373 f.).

XI.—§ 3. Gothonic and Keltic.

Feist (KI 480 ff.; cf. PBB 36. 307 ff., 37. 112 ff.) applies the substratum theory to the Gothonic (Germanic) languages. The Gothons are autochthonous in northern Europe, and very little mixed with other races; they must have immigrated just after the close of the glacial period. But the arrival of Aryan (Indogermanic) tribes cannot be placed earlier than about 2000 B.C.; they made the original inhabitants give up their own language. The nation that thus Aryanized the Gothons cannot have been other than the Kelts; their supremacy over the Gothons is proved by several loan-words for cultural ideas or state offices, such as Gothic *reiks* 'king,' *andbahts* 'servant.' The Aryan language which the Kelts taught the Gothons was subjected in the process to considerable changes, the old North Europeans pronouncing the new language in accordance with their previous speech habits; instead of taking over the free Aryan accent, they invariably stressed the initial syllable, and they made sad havoc of the Aryan flexion.

The theory does not bear close inspection. The number of Keltic loan-words is not great enough for us to infer such an overpowering ascendancy on the part of the Kelts as would force the subjected population to make a complete surrender of their own tongue. Neither in number nor in intrinsic significance can these loans be compared with the French loans in English: and yet the Normans did not succeed in substituting their own language for English. Besides, if the theory were true, we should not merely see a certain number of Keltic loan-words, but the whole speech, the complete vocabulary as well as the entire grammar, would be Keltic; yet as a matter of fact there is a wide gulf between Keltic and Gothonic, and many details, lexical and grammatical, in the latter group resemble other Aryan languages rather than Keltic. The stressing of the first syllable is said to be due to the aboriginal language. If that were so, it would mean that this population, in adopting the new speech, had at once transferred its own habit of stressing the first syllable to all the new words, very much as Icelanders are apt to do nowadays. But this is not in accordance with well established facts in the Gothonic languages: we know that when the consonant shift took place, it found the stress on the same syllables as in Sanskrit, and that it was this stress on many middle or final syllables that afterwards changed many of the shifted consonants from voiceless to voiced (Verner's law).[1] This fact in itself suffices to prove that the consonant shift and the stress shift cannot have taken place simultaneously, and thus cannot be due to one and the same cause, as supposed by Feist. Nor can the havoc wrought in the old flexions be due to the inability of a new people to grasp the minute *nuances* and intricate system of another language than its own; for in that case too we should have something like the formless 'Pidgin English' from the very beginning, whereas the oldest Gothonic languages still preserve a great many old flexions and subtle syntactical rules which have since disappeared. As a matter of fact, many of the flexions of primitive Aryan were much better preserved in Gothonic languages than in Keltic.

XI.—§ 4. Etruscan and Indian Consonants.

In another place in the same work (KI 373) Feist speaks of the Etruscan language, and says that this had only one kind of stop consonants, represented by the letters *k* (*c*), *t*, *p*, besides the aspirated stops *kh*, *th*, *ph*, which in some instances correspond to Latin and Greek tenues. This, he says, reminds one very strongly of the sound system of High German (oberdeutschen) dialects, and more particularly of those spoken in the Alps. Feist here (and in PBB 36. 340 ff.) maintains that these sounds go back to a Pre-Gothonic Alpine population, which he identifies with the ancient Rhætians; and he sees in this a strong support of a linguistic connexion between the Rhætians and Etruscans. He finds further striking analogies between the Gothonic and the Armenian sound systems; the predilection for voiceless stops and aspirated sounds in Etruscan, in the domain of the ancient Rhætians and in Asia Minor is accordingly ascribed to the speech habits of one and the same aboriginal race.

---

[1] Curiously enough, Feist uses this argument himself against Hirt in his earlier paper, PBB 37. 121.

Here, too, there are many points to which I must take exception. It is not quite certain that the usual interpretation of Etruscan letters is correct; in fact, much may be said in favour of the hypothesis that the letters rendered *p, t, k* stand really for the sounds of *b, d, g,* and that those transcribed *ph, th, kh* (or Greek ϕ, ϑ, χ) represent ordinary *p, t, k.* However this may be, Feist seems to be speaking here almost in the same breath of the first (or common Gothonic) shift and of the second (or specially High German) shift, although they are separated from each other by several centuries and neither cover the same geographical ground nor lead to the same phonetic result. Neither Armenian nor primitive Gothonic can be said to be averse to voiced stops, for in both we find voiced *b, d, g* for the old 'mediæ aspiratæ.' And in both languages the old voiceless stops became at first probably not aspirates, but simply voiceless spirants, as in English *f*ather, *th*ing, and Scotch lo*ch*. Further, it should be noted that we do not find the tendency to unvoice stops and to pronounce affricates either in Rhæto-Romanic (Ladin) or in Tuscan Italian; both languages have unaspirated *p, t, k* and voiced *b, d, g,* and the Tuscan pronunciation of *c* between two vowels as [x], thus in *la casa* [la xa·sa], but not in *a casa* = [akka·sa], could not be termed 'aspiration' except by a non-phonetician; this pronunciation can hardly have anything to do with the old Etruscan language.

According to a theory which is very widely accepted, the Dravidian languages exerted a different influence on the Aryan languages when the Aryans first set foot on Indian soil, in making them adopt the 'cacuminal' (or 'inverted') sounds *ḍ, ṭ, ṇ* with *ḍh* and *ṭh,* which were not found in primitive Aryan. But even this theory does not seem to be quite proof against objections. It is easy to admit that natives accustomed to one place of articulation of their *d, t, n* will unconsciously produce the *d, t, n* of a new language they are learning in the same place; but then they will do it everywhere. Here, however, both Dravidian and Sanskrit possess pure dental *d, t, n,* pronounced with the tip of the tongue touching the upper teeth, besides cacuminal *ḍ, ṭ, ṇ,* in which it touches the gum or front part of the hard palate. In Sanskrit we find that the cacuminal articulation occurs only under very definite conditions, chiefly under the influence of *r.* Now, a trilled tongue-point *r* in most languages, for purely physiological reasons which are easily accounted for, tends to be pronounced further back than ordinary dentals; and it is therefore quite natural that it should spontaneously exercise an influence on neighbouring dentals by drawing them back to its own point of articulation. This may have happened in India quite independently of the occurrence of the same sounds in other vernaculars, just as we find the same influence very pronouncedly in Swedish and in East Norwegian, where *d*, *t*, *n*, *s* are cacuminal (supradental) in such words as *bord*, *kort*, *barn*, *först*, etc. According to Grandgent (*Neuere Sprachen*, 2. 447), *d* in his own American English is pronounced further back than elsewhere before and after *r*, as in *dry*, *hard*; but in none of these cases need we conjure up an extinct native population to account for a perfectly natural development.

XI.—§ 5. Gothonic Sound-shift.

Since the time of Grimm the Gothonic consonant changes have harassed the minds of linguists; they became *the* sound-shift and were considered as something *sui generis*, something out of the common, which required a different explanation from all other sound-shifts. Several explanations have been offered, to some of which we shall have to revert later; none, however, has been so popular as that which attributes the shift to an ethnic substratum. This explanation is accepted by Hirt, Feist, Meillet and others, though their agreement ceases when the question is asked: What nationality and what language can have been the cause of the change? While some cautiously content themselves with saying that there must have been an original population, others guess at Kelts, Finns, Rhætians or Etrurians—all fascinating names to minds of a speculative turn.

The latest treatment of the question that I have seen is by K. Wessely (in *Anthropos*, XII–XIII 540 ff., 1917). He assumes the following different substrata, beginning with the most recent: a Rhæto-Romanic for the Upper-German shift, a Keltic for the common High-German shift, and a Finnic for the first Germanic shift with the Vernerian law. This certainly has the merit of neatly separating sound-shifts that are chronologically apart, except with regard to the last-mentioned shift, for here the Finns are made responsible for two changes that were probably separated by centuries and had really no traits in common. It is curious to see the transition from *p* to *f* and from *t* to *þ*—both important elements of the first shift—here ascribed to Finnic, for as a matter of fact the two sounds *f* and *þ* are not found in present-day Finnish, and were not found in primitive Ugro-Finnic.[1]

---

[1] Feist, on the other hand (PBB 36. 329), makes the Kelts responsible for the shift from *p* to *f*, because initial *p* disappears in Keltic: but disappearance is not the same thing as being changed into a spirant, and there is no necessity for assuming that the sound before disappearing had been changed into *f*. Besides, it is characteristic of the Gothonic shift that it affects all stops equally, without regard to the place of articulation, while the Keltic change affects only the one sound *p*.

When Wessely thinks that the change discovered by Verner is also due to Finnic influence, his reasons are two : an alleged parallelism with the Finnic consonant change which he terms 'Setälä's law,' and then the assumption that such a shift, conditioned by the place of the accent, is foreign to the Aryan race (p. 543). When, however, we find a closely analogous case only four hundred years ago in English, where a number of consonants were voiced according to the place of the stress,[1] are we also to say that it is foreign to the Anglo-Saxon race and therefore presupposes some non-Aryan substratum ? As a matter of fact, the parallelism between the English and the old Gothonic shift is much closer than that between the latter and the Finnic consonant-gradation : in English and in old Gothonic the stress place is decisive, while in the Finnic shift it is very doubtful whether stress goes for anything ; in both English and old Gothonic the same consonants are affected (spirants, in English also the combinations [tʃ, ks], but otherwise no stops), while in Finnic it is the stops that are primarily affected. In old Gothonic, as in English, the change is simply voicing, and we have nothing corresponding to the reduction of double consonants and of consonant groups in Finnic *pappi / papin*, *otta / otat*, *kukka / kukan*, *parempi / paremman*, *jalka / jalan*, etc. On the whole, Wessely's paper shows how much easier it is to advance hypotheses than to find truths.

XI.—§ 6. Natural and Specific Changes.

Meillet (MSL 19. 164 and 172 ; cf. *Bulletin* 19. 50 and *Germ.* 18) thinks that we must distinguish between such phonetic changes as are natural, i.e. due to universal tendencies, and such as are peculiar to certain languages. In the former class he includes the opening and the voicing of intervocalic consonants ; there is also a natural and universal tendency to shorten long words and to slur the pronunciation towards the end of a word. In the latter class (changes which are peculiar to and characteristic of a particular language) he reckons the consonant shifts in Gothonic and Armenian, the weakening of consonants in Greek and in Iranian, the tendency to unround back vowels in English and Slav. Such changes can only be accounted for on the supposition of a change of language : they must be due to people whose own language had habits foreign to Aryan. Unfortunately, Meillet cannot tell us how to measure the difference between natural and

[1] ME. *knowleche*, *stonĕs* [stɔ·nes], *off*, *with* [wiþ] become MnE. *knowledge*, *stones* [stounz], *of* [ɔv, əv], *with* [wið], etc. ; cf. also *possess*, *discern* with [z], *exert* with [gz], but *exercise* with [ks]. See my *Studier over eng. kasus*, 1891, 178 ff., now MEG i. 6. 5 ff., and (for the phonetic explanation) LPh p. 121.

peculiar shifts ; he admits that they cannot always be clearly separated ; and when he says that there are some extreme cases ' relativement nets,' such as those named above, I must confess that I do not see why the change from the sharp tenuis, as in Fr. *p, t, k,* to a slightly aspirated sound, as in English (*Bulletin* 19. 50),[1] or the relaxing of the closure which finally led to the sounds of [f, ꝥ, x], should be less ' natural ' than a hundred other changes and should require the calling in of a *deus ex machina* in the shape of an aboriginal population.   The unrounding of E. *u* in *hut*, etc., to which he alludes, began about 1600—what ethnic substratum does that postulate, and is any such required, more than for, say, the diphthongizing of long *a* and *o* ?

Meillet (MSL 19. 172) also says that there are certain speech sounds which are, as it were, natural and are found in nearly all languages, thus *p, t, k, n, m,* and among the vowels *a, i, u,* while other sounds are found only in some languages, such as the two English *th* sounds or, among the vowels, Fr. *u* and Russian *y*.   But when he infers that sounds of the former class are stable and remain unchanged for many centuries, whereas those of the latter are apt to change and disappear, the conclusion is not borne out by actual facts.   The consonants *p, t, k, n, m* are said to have remained unchanged in many Aryan languages from the oldest times till the present day—that is, only initially before vowels, which is a very important reservation and really amounts to an admission that in the vast majority of cases these sounds are just as unstable as most other things on this planet, especially if we remember that nothing could well be more unstable than *k* before front vowels, as seen in It. [tʃ] and Sp. [ꝥ] in *cielo*, Fr. [s] in *ciel*, and [ʃ] in *chien*, Eng. and Swedish [tʃ] in *chin, kind*, Norwegian [c] in *kind*, Russian [tʃ] in *četyre* ' four ' and [s] in *sto* ' hundred,' etc.   As an example of a typically unstable sound Meillet gives bilabial *f*, and it is true that this sound is so rare that it is difficult to find it represented in any language ; the reason is simply that the upper teeth normally protrude above the lower jaw, and that consequently the lower lip articulates easily against the upper teeth, with the natural result that where we should theoretically expect the bilabial *f* the labiodental *f* takes its place.   And *s*, which is found almost universally, and should therefore on Meillet's theory be very stable, is often seen to change into *h* or [x] or to disappear.   On the whole, then, we see that it is not the ' naturalness ' or universality of a

---

[1] Sharp tenues and aspirated tenues may alternate even in the life of one individual, as I have observed in the case of my own son, who at the age of 1.9 used the sharp French sounds, but five months later substituted strongly aspirated *p, t, k,* with even stronger aspiration than the usual Danish sounds, which it took him ten or eleven months to learn with perfect certainty.

consonant so much as its position in the syllable and word that
decides the question ' change or no change.' The relation between
stability and naturalness is seen, perhaps, most clearly in such an
instance as long [a·] : this sound is so natural that English, from
the oldest Aryan to present-day speech, has never been without
it ; yet at no time has it been stable, but as soon as one class of
words with long [a·] is changed, a new class steps into its shoes :
(1) Aryan *māter*, now *mother* ; (2) lengthening of a short *a* before
n : *gās*, *brāhta*, now *goose*, *brought* ; (3) levelling of *ai* : *stān*, now
stone ; (4) lengthening of short *a* : *cāld*, now *cold* ; (5) later lengthening of *a* in open syllable : *nāme*, now [neim] ; (6) mod. *carve*, *calm*,
path and others from various sources ; and (7) vulgar speech is now
developing new levellings of diphthongs in [ma·l, pa·(ə)] for *mile*,
power.

XI.—§ 7. Power of Substratum.

V. Bröndal has made the attempt to infuse new blood into
the substratum theory through his book, *Substrater og Laan i
Romansk og Germansk* (Copenhagen, 1917). The effect of a substratum, according to him, is the establishment of a ' constant
idiom,' working " without regard to place and time " (p. 76) and
changing, for instance, Latin into Old French, Old French into
Classical French, and Classical French into Modern French. His
task, then, is to find out certain tendencies operating at these
various periods ; these are ascribed to the Keltic substratum,
and Bröndal then passes in review a great many languages spoken
in districts where Kelts are known to have lived in former times,
in order to find the same tendencies there. If he succeeds in this
to his own satisfaction, it is only because the ' tendencies ' established are partly so vague that they will fit into any language,
partly so ill-defined phonetically that it becomes possible to press
different, nay, in some cases even directly contrary movements
into the same class. But considerations of space forbid me to
enter on a detailed criticism here. I must content myself with
taking exception to the principle that the effect of the ethnic
substratum may show itself several generations after the speech
substitution took place. If Keltic ever had ' a finger in the pie,'
it must have been immediately on the taking over of the new
language. An influence exerted in such a time of transition may
have far-reaching after-effects, like anything else in history, but
this is not the same thing as asserting that a similar modification
of the language may take place after the lapse of some centuries
as an effect of the same cause. Suppose we have a series of manuscripts, A, B, C, D, etc., of which B is copied from A, C from B,

etc., and that B has an error which is repeated in all the following copies ; now, if M suddenly agrees with A (which the copyist has never seen), we infer that this reading is independent of A. In the same way with a language : each individual learns it from his contemporaries, but has no opportunity of hearing those who have died before his own time. It is possible that the transition from *a* to *œ* in Old English (as in *fœder*) is due to Keltic influence, but when we find, many centuries later, that *a* is changed into [æ] (the present sound) in words which had not *œ* in OE., e.g. *crab, hallow, act,* it is impossible to ascribe this, as Bröndal does, to a ' constant Keltic idiom ' working through many generations who had never spoken or heard any Keltic. ' Atavism,' which skips over one or more generations, is unthinkable here, for words and sounds are nothing but habits acquired by imitation.

So far, then, our discussion of the substratum theory has brought us no very positive results. One of the reasons why the theories put forward of late years have been on the whole so unsatisfactory is that they deal with speech substitutions that have taken place so far back that absolutely nothing, or practically nothing, is known of those displaced languages which are supposed to have coloured languages now existing. What do we know beyond the mere name of Ligurians or Veneti or Iberians ? Of the Pre-Germanic and Pre-Keltic peoples we know not even the names. As to the old Kelts who play such an eminent rôle in all these speculations, we know extremely little about their language at this distant date, and it is possible that in some cases, at any rate, the Kelts may have been only comparatively small armies conquering this or that country for a time, but leaving as few linguistic traces behind them as, say, the armies of Napoleon in Russia or the Cimbri and Teutoni in Italy. Linguists have turned from the ' glottogonic ' speculations of Bopp and his disciples, only to indulge in dialectogonic speculations of exactly the same visionary type.

XI.—§ 8. Types of Race-mixture.

It would be a great mistake to suppose that the conditions, and consequently the linguistic results, are always the same, whenever two different races meet and assimilate. The chief classes of race-mixture have been thus described in a valuable paper by George Hempl (*Transactions of the American Philological Association*, XXIX, p. 31 ff., 1898).

(1) The conquerors are a comparatively small body, who become the ruling class, but are not numerous enough to impose their language on the country. They are forced to learn the language of their subjects, and their grandchildren may come to know that

language better than they know the language of their ancestors. The language of the conquerors dies out, but bequeaths to the native language its terms pertaining to government, the army, and those other spheres of life that the conquerors had specially under their control. Historic examples are the cases of the Goths in Italy and Spain, the Franks in Gaul, the Normans in France and the Norman-French in England. Of course, the greater the number of the conquerors and the longer they had been close neighbours of the people they conquered, or maintained the bonds that united them to their mother-country, the greater was their influence. Thus the influence of the Franks on the language of France was greater than that of the Goths on the language of Spain, and the influence of the Norman-French in England was greater still. Yet in each case the minority ultimately succumbed.

(2a) The conquest is made by many bodies of invaders, who bring with them their whole households and are followed for a long period of time by similar hordes of their kinsmen. The conquerors constitute the upper and middle classes and a part of the lower classes of the new community. The natives recede before the conquerors or become their slaves : their speech is regarded as servile and is soon laid aside, except for a few terms pertaining to the humbler callings, the names of things peculiar to the country and place-names. Examples : Angles and Saxons in Britain and Europeans in America and Australia, though in the last case we can hardly speak of race-mixture between the natives and the immigrants.

(2b) A more powerful nation conquers the people and annexes its territory, which is made a province, to which not only governors and soldiers, but also merchants and even colonists are sent. These become the upper class and the influential part of the middle class. If centuries pass and the province is still subjected to the direct influence of the ruling country, it will more and more imitate the speech and the habits and customs of that country. Such was the history of Italy, Spain and Gaul under the Romans ; similar, also, is the story of the Slavs of Eastern Germany and of the Dutch in New York State ; such is the process going on to-day among the French in Louisiana and among the Germans in their original settlements in Pennsylvania.

(3) Immigrants come in scattered bands and at different times ; they become servants or follow other humble callings. It is usually not to their advantage to associate with their fellow-countrymen, but rather to mingle with the native population. The better they learn to speak the native tongue, the faster they get on in the world. If their children in their dress or speech betray their foreign origin, they are ridiculed as 'Dutch' or Irish,

or whatever it may be. They therefore take pains to rid themselves of all traces of their alien origin and avoid using the speech of their parents. In this way vast numbers of newcomers may be assimilated year by year till they constitute a large part of the new race, while their language makes practically no impression on the language of the country. This is the story of what is going on in all parts of the United States to-day.

It will be seen that in classes 1 and 3 the speech of the natives prevails, while in the two classes comprised under 2 it is that of the conqueror which eventually triumphs. Further, that, in all cases except type 2b, that language prevails which is spoken by what is at the time the majority.

Sound substitution is found in class 3 in the case of foreigners who come to America after they have learnt to speak, and of the children of foreigners who keep up their original language at home. If, however, while they are still young, they are chiefly thrown with English-speaking people, they usually gain a thorough mastery of the English language ; thus most of the children, and practically all of the grandchildren, of immigrants, by the time they are grown-up, speak English without foreign taint. Their origin has thus no permanent influence on their adopted language. The same thing is true when a small ruling minority drops its foreign speech and learns that of the majority (class 1), and practically also (class 2a) when a native minority succumbs to a foreign majority, though here the ultimate language may be slightly influenced by the native dialect.

It is different with class 2b : when a whole population comes in the course of centuries to surrender its natural speech for that of a ruling minority, sound substitution plays an important part, and to a great extent determines the character and future of the language. Hempl here agrees with Hirt in seeing in this fact the explanation of much (N.B. not all !) of the difference between the Romanic languages and of the difference between natural High German and High German spoken in Low German territory, and he is therefore not surprised when he is told by Nissen that the dialects of modern Italy correspond geographically pretty closely to the non-Latin languages once spoken in the Peninsula. But he severely criticizes Hirt for going so far as to explain the differentiation of Aryan speech by the theory of sound substitution. Hirt assumes conditions like those in class 1, and yet thinks that the results would be like those of class 2a. " It is essential to Hirt's theory that the conquering bodies of Indo-Europeans should be small compared with the number of the people they conquered. . . . If we wish to prove that the differentiation of Indo-European speech was like the differentiation of Romance speech, we must be able to show that the conditions under which the differentiations took place were alike or equivalent. But even a cursory examination of the manner in which the Romance countries were Romanized . . . will make it clear that no parallel could possibly be drawn between the conditions under which the Romance languages arose and those that we can suppose to have existed while the Indo-European languages took shape." Hempl also criticizes the way in which the Germanic consonant-shift is supposed by Hirt to be due to sound-substitution : when instead of the original

Germanic has

t	th	d	dh
þ	þ	t	ð,

these latter sounds, on Hirt's theory, must be either the native sounds that the conquered people substituted for the original sounds, or else they have developed out of such sounds as the natives substituted. If the first be true, we ask ourselves why the conquered people did not use their *t* for the Indo-European *t*, instead of substituting it for *d*, and then substituting þ for the Indo-European *t*. If the second supposition be true, the native population introduced into the language sounds very similar to the original *t*, *th*, *d*, *dh*, and all the change from that slightly variant form to the one that we find in Germanic was of subsequent development —and must be explained by the usual methods after all.

I have dwelt so long on Hempl's paper because, in spite of its (to my mind) fundamental importance, it has been generally overlooked by supporters of the substratum theory. To construct a true theory, it will be necessary to examine the largest possible number of facts with regard to race-mixture capable of being tested by scientific methods. In this connexion the observations of Lenz in South America and of Puşcariu in Rumania are especially valuable. The former found that the Spanish spoken in Chile was greatly influenced in its sounds by the speech of the native Araucanians (see *Zeitschr. f. roman. Philologie*, 17. 188 ff., 1893). Now, what were the facts in regard to the population speaking this language ? The immigrants were chiefly men, who in many cases necessarily married native women and left the care of their children to a great extent in the hands of Indian servants. As the natives were more warlike than in many other parts of South America, there was for a very long time a continuous influx of Spanish soldiers, many of whom, after a short time, settled down peacefully in the country. More Spanish soldiers, indeed, arrived in Chile in the course of the sixteenth and seventeenth centuries than in the whole of the rest of

South America. Accordingly, by the beginning of the eighteenth century the Indians had been either driven back or else assimilated, and at the beginning of the War of Liberation early in the nineteenth century Chile was the only State in which there was a uniform Spanish-speaking population. In the greater part of Chile the population is denser than anywhere else in South America, and this population speaks nothing but Spanish, while in Peru and Bolivia nearly the whole rural population still speaks more or less exclusively Keshua or Aimará, and these languages are also used occasionally, or at any rate understood, by the whites. Chile is thus the only country in which a real Spanish people's dialect could develop. (In Hempl's classification this would be a typical case of class 2a.) In the other Spanish-American countries the Spanish-speakers are confined to the upper ruling class, there being practically no lower class with Spanish as its mother-tongue, except in a couple of big cities. Thus we understand that the Peruvian who has learnt his Spanish at school has a purer Castilian pronunciation than the Chilean ; yet, apart from pronunciation, the educated Chilean's Spanish is much more correct and fluent than that of the other South Americans, whose language is stiff and vocabulary scanty, because they have first learnt some Indian language in childhood. Lenz's Chileans, who have often been invoked by the adherents of the unlimited substratum theory, thus really serve to show that sound substitution takes place only under certain well-defined conditions.

Puşcariu (in *Prinzipienfragen der romanischen Sprachwissenschaft, Beihefte zur Zschr. f. rom. Phil.*, 1910) says that in a Saxon village which had been almost completely Rumanianized he had once talked for hours with a peasant without noticing that he was not a native Rumanian : he was, however, a Saxon, who spoke Saxon with his wife, but Rumanian with his son, because the latter language was easier to him, as he had acquired the Rumanian basis of articulation. Here, then, there was no sound substitution, and in general we may say that the less related two languages are, the fewer will be the traces of the original language left on the new language (p. 49). The reason must be that people who naturally speak a closely related language are easily understood even when their acquired speech has a tinge of dialect : there is thus no inducement for them to give up their pronunciation. Puşcariu also found that it was much more difficult for him to rid himself of his dialectal traits in Rumanian than to acquire a correct pronunciation of German or French. He therefore disbelieves in a direct influence exerted by the indigenous languages on the formation of the Romanic languages (and thus goes much further than Hempl). All these languages, and particularly Rumanian, during

the first centuries of the Middle Ages underwent radical trans-
formations not paralleled in the thousand years ensuing. This
may have been partly due to an influence exerted by ethnic mixture
on the whole character of the young nations and through that also
on their language. But other factors have certainly also played
an important rôle, especially the grouping round new centres
with other political aims than those of ancient Rome, and consequent isolation from the rest of the Romanic peoples. Add to this
the very important emancipation of the ordinary conversational
language from the yoke of Latin. In the first Christian centuries
the influence of Latin was so overpowering in official life and in
the schools that it obstructed a natural development. But soon
after the third century the educational level rapidly sank, and
political events broke the power not only of Rome, but also of its
language. The speech of the masses, which had been held in fetters
for so long, now asserted itself in full freedom and with elemental
violence, the result being those far-reaching changes by which
the Romanic languages are marked off from Latin. Language
and nation or race must not be confounded : witness Rumania,
whose language shows very few dialectal variations, though the
populations of its different provinces are ethnically quite distinct
(ib. p. 51).

XI.—§ 9. Summary.

The general impression gathered from the preceding investigation must be that it is impossible to ascribe to an ethnic substratum
all the changes and dialectal differentiations which some linguists
explain as due to this sole cause. Many other influences must
have been at work, among which an interruption of intercourse
created by natural obstacles or social conditions of various kinds
would be of prime importance. If we take ethnic substrata as
the main or sole source of dialectal differentiation, it will be hard
to account for the differences between Icelandic and Norwegian,
for Iceland was very sparsely inhabited when the ' land-taking '
took place, and still harder to account for the very great divergences that we witness between the dialects spoken in the Faroe
Islands. A mere turning over the leaves of Bennike and Kris-
tensen's maps of Danish dialects (or the corresponding maps of
France) will show the impossibility of explaining the crisscross of
boundaries of various phonetic phenomena as entirely due to
ethnical differences in the aborigines. On the other hand, the speech
of Russian peasants is said to be remarkably free from dialectal
divergences, in spite of the fact that it has spread in comparatively recent times over districts inhabited by populations with

languages of totally different types (Finnic, Turkish, Tataric). I
thus incline to think that sound substitution cannot have produced radical changes, but has only played a minor part in the
development of languages. There are, perhaps, also interesting
things to be learnt from conditions in Finland. Here Swedish
has for many centuries been the language of the ruling minority,
and it was only in the course of the nineteenth century that Finnish
attained to the dignity of a literary language. The sound systems
of Swedish and Finnish are extremely unlike : Finnish lacks many
of the Swedish sounds, such as *b*, *d* (what is written *d* is either
mute or else a kind of weak *r*), *g* and *f*. No word can begin with
more than one consonant, consequently Swedish *strand* and *skräd-
dare*, ' tailor,' are represented in the form of the loan-words *ranta*
and *räätäli*. Now, in spite of the fact that most Swedish-speaking
people have probably spoken Finnish as children and have had
Finnish servants and playfellows to teach them the language,
none of these peculiarities have influenced their Swedish : what
makes them recognizable as hailing from Finland (' finska
brytningen ') is not simplification of consonant groups or substitution of *p* for *b*, etc., but such small things as the omission of the
' compound tone,' the tendency to lengthen the second consonant
in groups like *ns*, and European (' back ') *u* instead of the Swedish
mixed vowel.

But if sound substitution as a result of race-mixture and of
conquest cannot have played any very considerable part in the
differentiation of languages as wholes, there is another domain
in which sound substitution is very important, that is, in the shape
which loan-words take in the languages into which they are introduced. However good the pronunciation of the first introducer
of a word may have been, it is clear that when a word is extensively
used by people with no intimate and first-hand knowledge of the
language from which it was taken, most of them will tend to pronounce it with the only sounds with which they are familiar, those
of their own language. Thus we see that the English and Russians, who have no [y] in their own speech, substitute for it the
combination [ju, iu] in recent loans from French. Scandinavians
have no voiced [z] and [ʒ] and therefore, in such loans from French
or English as *kusine*, *budget*, *jockey*, etc., substitute the voiceless
[s] and [ʃj], or [sj]. The English will make a diphthong of the
final vowels of such words as *bouquet*, *beau* [buˑkei, bou], and will
slur the *r* of such French words as *boulevard*, etc. The same transference of speech habits from one's native language also affects
such important things as quantity, stress and tone : the English
have no final short stressed vowels, such as are found in *bouquet*,
beau ; hence their tendency to lengthen as well as diphthongize

these sounds, while the French will stress the final syllable of recent loans, such as *jury, reporter*. These phenomena are so universal and so well known that they need no further illustration.

The more familiar such loan-words are, the more unnatural it would be to pronounce them with foreign sounds or according to foreign rules of quantity and stress; for this means in each case a shunting of the whole speech-apparatus on to a different track for one or two words and then shifting back to the original ' basis of articulation '—an effort that many speakers are quite incapable of and one that in any case interferes with the natural and easy flow of speech.

XI.—§ 10. General Theory of Loan-words.

In the last paragraphs we have already broached a very important subject, that of loan-words.[1] No language is entirely free from borrowed words, because no nation has ever been completely isolated. Contact with other nations inevitably leads to borrowings, though their number may vary very considerably. Here we meet with a fundamental principle, first formulated by E. Windisch (in his paper " Zur Theorie der Mischsprachen und Lehnwörter," *Verh. d. sächsischen Gesellsch. d. Wissensch.*, XLIX, 1897, p. 107 ff.): " It is not the foreign language a nation learns that turns into a mixed language, but its own native language becomes mixed under the influence of a foreign language." When we try to learn and talk a foreign tongue we do not introduce into it words taken from our own language ; our endeavour will always be to speak the other language as purely as possible, and generally we are painfully conscious of every native word that we intrude into phrases framed in the other tongue. But what we thus avoid in speaking a foreign language we very often do in our own. Frederick the Great prided himself on his good French, and in his French writings we do not find a single German word, but whenever he wrote German his sentences were full of French words and phrases. This being the general practice, we now understand why so few Keltic words were taken over into French and English. There was nothing to induce the ruling classes to learn

---

[1] I use the terms *loan-words* and *borrowed words* because they are convenient and firmly established, not because they are exact. There are two essential respects in which linguistic borrowing differs from the borrowing of, say, a knife or money : the lender does not deprive himself of the use of the word any more than if it had not been borrowed by the other party, and the borrower is under no obligation to return the word at any future time. Linguistic ' borrowing ' is really nothing but imitation, and the only way in which it differs from a child's imitation of its parents' speech is that here something is imitated which forms a part of a speech that is not imitated as a whole.

the language of the inferior natives : it could never be fashionable for them to show an acquaintance with a despised tongue by using now and then a Keltic word.   On the other hand, the Kelt would have to learn the language of his masters, and learn it well ; and he would even among his comrades like to show off his knowledge by interlarding his speech with words and turns from the language of his betters.   Loan-words always show a superiority of the nation from whose language they are borrowed, though this superiority may be of many different kinds.

In the first place, it need not be extensive : indeed, in some of the most typical cases it is of a very partial character and touches only on one very special point.   I refer to those instances in which a district or a people is in possession of some special thing or product wanted by some other nation and not produced in that country.   Here quite naturally the name used by the natives is taken over along with the thing.   Obvious examples are the names of various drinks : *wine* is a loan from Latin, *tea* from Chinese, *coffee* from Arabic, *chocolate* from Mexican, and *punch* from Hindustani.   A certain type of carriage was introduced about 1500 from Hungary and is known in most European languages by its Magyar name : E. *coach*, G. *kutsche*, etc.   *Moccasin* is from Algonquin, *bamboo* from Malay, *tulip* and *turban* (ultimately the same word) from Persian.   A slightly different case is when some previously unknown plant or animal is made known through some foreign nation, as when we have taken the name of *jasmine* from Persian, *chimpanzee* from some African, and *tapir* from some Brazilian language.   It is characteristic of all words of this kind that only a few of them are taken from each foreign language, and that they have nearly all of them gone the round of all civilized languages, so that they are now known practically all over the world.

Other loan-words form larger groups and bear witness to the cultural superiority of some nation in some one specified sphere of activity or branch of knowledge : such are the Arabic words relating to mathematics and astronomy (*algebra*, *zero*, *cipher*, *azimuth*, *zenith*, in related fields *tariff*, *alkali*, *alcohol*), the Italian words relating to music (*piano*, *allegro*, *andante*, *solo*, *soprano*, etc.) and commerce (*bank*, *bankrupt*, *balance*, *traffic*, *ducat*, *florin*) —one need not accumulate examples, as everybody interested in the subject of this book will be able to supply a great many from his own reading.   The most comprehensive groups of this kind are those French, Latin and Greek words that have flooded the whole world of Western civilization from the Middle Ages and the Renaissance and have given a family-character to all those parts of the vocabularies of otherwise different languages which are concerned with the highest intellectual and technical activities. See the detailed discussion of these strata of loan-words in English in GS ch. v and vi.

When one nation has imbibed for centuries the cultural influence of another, its language may have become so infiltrated with words from the other language that these are found in most sentences, at any rate in nearly every sentence dealing with things above the simplest material necessities. The best-known examples are English since the influx of French and classical words, and Turkish with its wholesale importations from Arabic. Another example is Basque, in which nearly all expressions for religious and spiritual ideas are Romanic. Basque is naturally very poor in words for general ideas; it has names for special kinds of trees, but 'tree' is *arbolia*, from Spanish *árbol*, 'animal' is *animale*, 'colour' *colore*, 'plant' *planta* or *landare*, 'flower' *lore* or *lili*, 'thing' *gauza*, 'time' *dembora*. Thus also many of its names for utensils and garments, weights and measures, arms, etc., are borrowed; 'king' is *errege*, 'law' *lege*, *lage*, 'master' *maisu*, etc. (See *Zs. f. roman. Phil.*, 17. 140 ff.)

In a great many cases linguistic borrowing must be considered a necessity, but this is not always so. When a nation has once got into the habit of borrowing words, people will very often use foreign words where it would have been perfectly possible to express their ideas by means of native speech-material, the reason for going out of one's own language being in some cases the desire to be thought fashionable or refined through interlarding one's speech with foreign words, in others simply laziness, as is very often the case when people are rendering thoughts they have heard or read in a foreign tongue. Translators are responsible for the great majority of these intrusive words, which might have been avoided by a resort to native composition or derivation, or very often by turning the sentence a little differently from the foreign text. The most thoroughgoing speech mixtures are due much less to real race-mixture than to continued cultural contact, especially of a literary character, as is seen very clearly in English, where the Romanic element is only to a very small extent referable to the Norman conquerors, and far more to the peaceful relations of the following centuries. That Greek and Latin words have come in through the medium of literature hardly needs saying. Many of these words are superfluous : " The native words *cold, cool, chilly, icy, frosty*, might have seemed sufficient for all purposes, without any necessity for importing *frigid, gelid* and *algid*, which, as a matter of fact, are found neither in Shakespeare nor in the Authorized Version of the Bible nor in the poetical works of Milton, Pope, Cowper and Shelley " (GS § 136). But on the other hand it cannot be denied that the imported words have in many instances enriched the language through enabling its users to obtain greater variety and to find expressions for many subtle shades of thought. The question of the value of loan-words cannot be dismissed offhand, as the ' purists ' in many countries are inclined to imagine, with the dictum that foreign words should be shunned like the plague, but requires for its solution a careful consideration of the merits and demerits of each separate foreign term viewed in connexion with the native resources for expressing that particular idea.

XI.—§ 11. Classes of Loan-words.

It is quite natural that there should be a much greater inclination everywhere to borrow ' full ' words (substantives, adjectives, notional verbs) than ' empty ' words (pronouns, prepositions, conjunctions, auxiliary verbs), to which class most of the ' grammatical ' words belong. But there is no hard-and-fast limit between the two classes. It is rare for a language to take such words as numerals from another language ; yet examples are found here and there—thus, in connexion with special games, etc. Until comparatively recently, dicers and backgammon-players counted in England by means of the French words *ace, deuce, tray, cater, cinque, size*, and with the English game of lawn tennis the English way of counting (fifteen love, etc.) has been lately adopted in Russia and to some extent also in Denmark. In some parts of England Welsh numerals were until comparatively recent times used in the counting of sheep. Cattle-drivers in Jutland used to count from 20 to 90 in Low German learnt in Hamburg and Holstein, where they sold their cattle. In this case the clumsiness and want of perspicuity of the Danish expressions (*halvtredsindstyve* for Low German *föfdix*, etc.) may have been one of the reasons for preferring the German words ; in the same way the clumsiness of the Eskimo way of counting ("third toe on the second foot of the fourth man," etc.) has favoured the introduction into Greenlandic of the Danish words for 100 and 1,000 : with an Eskimo ending, *untritigdlit* and *tusintigdlit*. Most Japanese numerals are Chinese. And of course *million* and *milliard* are used in most civilized countries.

Prepositions, too, are rarely borrowed by one language from another. Yet the Latin (Ital.) *per* is used in English, German and Danish, and the French *à* in the two latter languages, and both are extending their domain beyond the commercial language in which they were first used. The Greek *kata*, at first also commercial, has in Spanish found admission into the ordinary language and has become the pronoun *cada* ' each.'

Personal and demonstrative pronouns, articles and the like are
scarcely ever taken over from one language to another. They are
so definitely woven into the innermost texture of a language that
no one would think of giving them up, however much he might
like to adorn his speech with words from a foreign source. If,
therefore, in one instance we find a case of a language borrowing
words of this kind, we are justified in thinking that exceptional
causes must have been at work, and such really proves to be the
case in English, which has adopted the Scandinavian forms *they*,
them, their. It is usual to speak of English as being a mixture of
native Old English ('Anglo-Saxon') and French, but as a matter
of fact the French influence, powerful as it is in the vocabulary
and patent as it is to the eyes of everybody, is superficial in comparison with the influence exercised in a much subtler way by the
Scandinavian settlers in the North of England. The French
influence is different in extent, but not in kind, from the French
influence on German or the old Gothonic influence on Finnic ;
it is perhaps best compared with the German influence on Danish
in the Middle Ages. But the Scandinavian influence on English
is of a different kind. The number of Danish and Norwegian
settlers in England must have been very large, as is shown by
the number of Scandinavian place-names ; yet that does not
account for everything. A most important factor was the great
similarity of the two languages, in spite of numerous points of
difference. Accordingly, when their fighting was over, the invaders
and the original population would to some extent be able to make
themselves understood by one another, like people talking two
dialects of the same language, or like students from Copenhagen
and from Lund nowadays. Many of the most common words
were absolutely identical, and others differed only slightly. Hence
it comes that in the Middle English texts we find a great many
double forms of the same word, one English and the other Scandinavian, used side by side, some of these doublets even surviving
till the present day, though now differentiated in sense (e.g. *whole,
hale* ; *no, nay* ; *from, fro* ; *shirt, skirt*), while in other cases one
only of the two forms, either the native or the Scandinavian, has
survived ; thus the Scandinavian *sister* and *egg* have ousted the
English *sweostor* and *ey*. We find, therefore, a great many words
adopted of a kind not usually borrowed ; thus, everyday verbs and
adjectives like *take, call, hit, die, ill, ugly, wrong*, and among substantives such non-technical ones as *fellow, sky, skin, wing*, etc.
(For details see my GS ch. iv.) All this indicates an intimate fusion
of the two races and of the two languages, such as is not provided
for in any of the classes described by Hempl (above, § 8). In
most speech-mixtures the various elements remain distinct and can

be separated, just as after shuffling a pack of cards you can pick
out the hearts, spades, etc. ; but in the case of English and Scandinavian we have a subtler and more intimate fusion, very much
as when you put a lump of sugar into a cup of tea and a few minutes
afterwards are quite unable to say which is tea and which is sugar.

XI.—§ 12. Influence on Grammar.

The question has often been raised whether speech-mixture
affects the grammar of a language which has borrowed largely
from some other language. The older view is expressed pointedly
by Whitney (L 199) : " Such a thing as a language with a mixed
grammatical apparatus has never come under the cognizance of
linguistic students : it would be to them a monstrosity ; it seems
an impossibility." This is an exaggeration, and cannot be justified,
for the simple reason that the vocabulary of a language and its
' grammatical apparatus ' cannot be nicely separated in the way
presupposed : indeed, much of the borrowed material mentioned
in our last paragraphs does belong to the grammatical apparatus.
But there is, of course, some truth in Whitney's dictum. When
a word is borrowed it is not as a rule taken over with all the elaborate
flexion which may belong to it in its original home ; as a rule,
one form only is adopted, it may be the nominative or some other
case of a noun, the infinitive or the present or the naked stem of
a verb. This form is then either used unchanged or with the endings of the adopting language, generally those of the most ' regular '
declension or conjugation. It is an exceptional case when more
than one flexional form is taken over, and this case does not occur
in really popular loans. In learned usage we find in older Danish
such case-flexion as gen. *Christi*, dat. *Christo*, by the side of nom.
Christus, also, e.g., *i theatro*, and still sometimes in German we
have the same usage : e.g. *mit den pronominibus*. In a somewhat
greater number of instances the plural form is adopted as well as
the singular form, as in English *fungi*, *formulæ*, *phenomena*, *sera-
phim*, etc., but the natural tendency is always towards using the
native endings, *funguses*, *formulas*, etc., and this has prevailed in
all popular words, e.g. *ideas*, *circuses*, *museums*. As the formation
of cases, tenses, etc., in different languages is often very irregular,
and the distinctive marks are often so intimately connected with
the kernel of the word and so unsubstantial as not to be easily
distinguished, it is quite natural that no one should think of
borrowing such endings, etc., and applying them to native words.
Schuchardt once thought that the English genitive ending *s* had
been adopted into Indo-Portuguese (in the East Indies), where *gobernadors casa* stands for ' governor's house,' but he now explains the

form more correctly as originating in the possessive pronoun *su*: *gobernador su casa* (dem g. sein haus, *Sitzungsber. der preuss. Akademie*, 1917, 524).

It was at one time commonly held that the English plural ending *s*, which in Old English was restricted in its application, owes its extension to the influence of French. This theory, I believe, was finally disposed of by the six decisive arguments I brought forward against it in 1891 (reprinted in ChE § 39). But after what has been said above on the Scandinavian influence, I incline to think that E. Classen is right in thinking that the Danes count for something in bringing about the final victory of *-s* over its competitor *-n*, for the Danes had no plural in *-n*, and *-s* reminded them of their own *-r* (*Mod. Language Rev.* 14. 94 ; cf. also *-s* in the third person of verbs, Scand. *-r*). Apart from this particular point, it is quite natural that the Scandinavians should have exercised a general levelling influence on the English language, as many niceties of grammar would easily be sacrificed where mutual intelligibility was so largely brought about by the common vocabulary. Accordingly, we find that in the regions in which the Danish settlements were thickest the wearing away of grammatical forms was a couple of centuries in advance of the same process in the southern parts of the country.

Derivative endings certainly belong to the ' grammatical apparatus ' of a language ; yet many such endings have been taken over into another language as parts of borrowed words and have then been freely combined with native speech-material. The phenomenon is extremely frequent in English, where we have, for instance, the Romanic endings *-ess* (*shepherdess, seeress*), *-ment* (*endearment, bewilderment*), *-age* (*mileage, cleavage, shortage*), *-ance* (*hindrance, forbearance*) and many more. In Danish and German the number of similar instances is much more restricted, yet we have, for instance, recent words in *-isme, -ismus* and *-ianer* ; cf. also older words like *bageri, bäckerei*, etc. It is the same with prefixes : English has formed many words with *de-, co-, inter-, pre-, anti-* and other classical prefixes : *de-anglicize, co-godfather, intermarriage, at pre-war prices, anti-slavery*, etc. (quotations in my GS § 124 ; cf. MEG ii. 14. 66). *Ex-* has established itself in many languages : *ex-king, ex-roi, ex-konge, ex-könig*, etc. In Danish the prefix *be-*, borrowed from German, is used very extensively with native words : *bebrejde, bebo, bebygge*, and this is not the only German prefix that is productive in the Scandinavian languages.

With regard to syntax, very little can be said except in a general way : languages certainly do influence each other syntactically, and those who know a foreign language only imperfectly are apt to transfer to it methods of construction from their own tongue. Many instances of this have been collected by Schuchardt, SlD. But it is doubtful whether these syntactical influences have the same *permanent* effects on any language as those exerted on one's own language by the habit of translating foreign works into it : in this purely literary way a great many idioms and turns of phrases have been introduced into English, German and the Scandinavian languages from French and Latin, and into Danish and Swedish from German. The accusative and infinitive construction, which had only a very restricted use in Old English, has very considerably extended its domain through Latin influence, and the so-called ' absolute construction ' (in my own grammatical terminology called ' duplex subjunct ') seems to be entirely due to imitation of Latin syntax. In the Balkan tongues there are some interesting instances of syntactical agreement between various languages, which must be due to oral influence through the necessity imposed on border peoples of passing continually from one language to another : the infinitive has disappeared from Greek, Rumanian and Albanian, and the definite article is placed after the substantive in Rumanian, Albanian and Bulgarian.

XI.—§ 13. Translation-loans.

Besides direct borrowings we have also indirect borrowings or ' translation loan-words,' words modelled more or less closely on foreign ones, though consisting of native speech-material. I take some examples from the very full and able paper " Notes sur les Calques Linguistiques " contributed by Kr. Sandfeld to the *Festschrift Vilh. Thomsen*, 1912 : *œdificatio* : G. erbauung, Dan. opbyggelse ; *œquilibrium* : G. gleichgewicht, Dan. ligevægt ; *beneficium* : G. wohltat, Dan. velgerning ; *conscientia* : Goth. miþwissi, G. gewissen, Dan. samvittighed, Swed. samvete, Russ. soznanie ; *omnipotens* : E. almighty, G. allmächtig, Dan. almægtig ; *arrière-pensée* : hintergedanke, bagtanke ; *bien-être* : wohlsein, velvære ; *exposition* : austellung, udstilling ; etc. Sandfeld gives many more examples, and as he has in most instances been able to give also corresponding words from various Slavonic languages as well as from Magyar, Finnic, etc., he rightly concludes that his collections serve to throw light on that community in thought and expression which Bally has well termed " la mentalité européenne." (But it will be seen that English differs from most European languages in having a much greater propensity to swallowing foreign words raw, as it were, than to translating them.)

CHAPTER XII

PIDGIN AND CONGENERS

§ 1. Beach-la-Mar. § 2. Grammar. § 3. Sounds. § 4. Pidgin. § 5. Grammar, etc. § 6. General Theory. § 7. Mauritius Creole. § 8. Chinook Jargon. § 9. Chinook continued. § 10. Makeshift Languages. § 11. Romanic Languages.

XII.—§ 1. Beach-la-Mar.

As a first typical example of a whole class of languages now found in many parts of the world where people of European civilization have come into contact with men of other races, we may take the so-called *Beach-la-mar* (or Beche-le-mar, or Beche de mer English);[1] it is also sometimes called Sandalwood English. It is spoken and understood all over the Western Pacific, its spread being largely due to the fact that the practice of 'blackbirding' often brought together on the same plantation many natives from different islands with mutually incomprehensible languages, whose only means of communication was the broken English they had picked up from the whites. And now the natives learn this language from each other, while in many places the few Europeans have to learn it from the islanders. " Thus the native use of Pidgin-English lays down the rules by which the Europeans let themselves be guided when learning it. Even Englishmen do not find it quite easy at the beginning to understand Pidgin-English, and have to learn it before they are able to speak it properly " (Landtman).

[1] The etymology of this name is rather curious : Portuguese *bicho de mar*, from *bicho* 'worm,' the name of the sea slug or trepang, which is eaten as a luxury by the Chinese, was in French modified into *bêche de mer*, 'seaspade'; this by a second popular etymology was made into English *beach-la-mar* as if a compound of *beach*.

My sources are H. Schuchardt, KS v. (Wiener Academie, 1883) ; id. in ESt xiii. 158 ff., 1889 ; W. Churchill, *Beach-la-Mar, the Jargon or Trade Speech of the Western Pacific* (Carnegie Institution of Washington, 1911); Jack London, *The Cruise of the Snark* (Mills & Boon, London, 1911 ?), G. Landtman in *Neuphilologische Mitteilungen* (Helsingfors, 1918, p. 62 ff. Landtman calls it " the Pidgin-English of British New Guinea," where he learnt it, though it really differs from Pidgin-English proper ; see below) ; "The Jargon English of Torres Straits" in *Reports of the Cambridge Anthropological Expedition to Torres Straits*, vol. iii. p. 25 1 ff., Cambridge, 1907.

I shall now try to give some idea of the structure of this lingo.

The vocabulary is nearly all English. Even most of the words which ultimately go back to other languages have been admitted only because the English with whom the islanders were thrown into contact had previously adopted them into their own speech, so that the islanders were justified in believing that they were really English. This is true of the Spanish or Portuguese *savvy*, ' to know,' and *pickaninny*, ' child ' or ' little one ' (a favourite in many languages on account of its symbolic sound; see Ch. XX § 8), as well as the Amerindian *tomahawk*, which in the whole of Australia is the usual word for a small axe. And if we find in Beach-la-mar the two Maori words *tapu* or *taboo* and *kai*, or more often *kaikai*, ' to eat ' or ' food,' they have probably got into the language through English—we know that both are very extensively used in Australia, while the former is known all over the civilized world. *Likkilik* or *liklik*, ' small, almost,' is said to be from a Polynesian word *liki*, but may be really a perversion of Engl. *little*. Landtman gives a few words from unknown languages used by the Kiwais, though not derived from their own language. The rest of the words found in my sources are English, though not always pure English, in so far as their signification is often curiously distorted.

Nusipepa means ' a letter, any written or printed document,' *mary* is the general term for ' woman ' (cf. above, p. 118), *pisupo* (peasoup) for all foreign foods which are preserved in tins ; *squareface*, the sailor's name for a square gin-bottle, is extended to all forms of glassware, no matter what the shape. One of the earliest seafarers is said to have left a bull and a cow on one of the islands and to have mentioned these two words together ; the natives took them as one word, and now *bullamacow* or *pulu-makau* means ' cattle, beef, also tinned beef ' ; *pulomokau* is now given as a native word in a dictionary of the Fijian language.[1] *Bulopenn*, which means ' ornament,' is said to be nothing but the English *blue paint*. All this shows the purely accidental character of many of the linguistic acquisitions of the Polynesians.

As the vocabulary is extremely limited, composite expressions are sometimes resorted to in order to express ideas for which we have simple words, and not unfrequently the devices used appear to us very clumsy or even comical. A piano is called ' big fellow bokus (box) you fight him he cry,' and a

---

[1] Similarly the missionary G. Brown thought that *tobi* was a native word of the Duke of York Islands for ' wash,' till one day he accidentally discovered that it was their pronunciation of English *soap*.

concertina 'little fellow bokus you shove him he cry, you pull him he cry.' *Woman he got faminil* ('family') *inside* means 'she is with child.' *Inside* is also used extensively about mental states : *jump inside* 'be startled,' *inside tell himself* 'to consider,' *inside bad* 'grieved or sorry,' *feel inside* 'to know,' *feel another kind inside* 'to change one's mind.' *My throat he fast* 'I was dumb.' *He took daylight a long time* 'lay awake.' *Bring fellow belong make open bottle* 'bring me a corkscrew.' *Water belong stink* 'perfumery.' The idea of being bald is thus expressed : *grass belong head belong him all he die finish*, or with another variant, *coconut belong him grass no stop*, for *coconut* is taken from English slang in the sense 'head' (Schuchardt has the sentence : *You no savvy that fellow white man coconut belong him no grass ?*). For 'feather' the combination *grass belong pigeon* is used, *pigeon* being a general term for any bird.

A man who wanted to borrow a saw, the word for which he had forgotten, said : 'You give me brother belong tomahawk, he come he go.' A servant who had been to Queensland, where he saw a train, on his return called it 'steamer he walk about along bush.' Natives who watched Landtman when he enclosed letters in envelopes named the latter 'house belong letter.' Many of these expressions are thus picturesque descriptions made on the spur of the moment if the proper word is not known.

XII.—§ 2. Grammar.

These phrases have already illustrated some points of the very simple grammar of this lingo. Words have only one form, and what is in our language expressed by flexional forms is either left unexpressed or else indicated by auxiliary words. The plural of nouns is like the singular (though the form *men* is found in my texts alongside of *man*) ; when necessary, the plural is indicated by means of a prefixed *all : all he talk* 'they say' (also *him fellow all* 'they') ; *all man* 'everybody' ; a more indefinite plural is *plenty man* or *full up man*. For 'we' is said *me two fella* or *me three fellow*, as the case may be ; *me two fellow Lagia* means 'I and Lagia.' If there are more, *me altogether man* or *me plenty man* may be said, though *we* is also in use. *Fellow* (*fella*) is a much-vexed word ; it is required, or at any rate often used, after most pronouns, thus, *that fellow hat, this fellow knife, me fellow, you fellow, him fellow* (not *he fellow*) ; it is found very often after an adjective and seems to be required to prop up the adjective before the substantive : *big fellow name, big fellow tobacco, another fellow man*. In other cases no *fellow* is used, and it seems difficult to give definite rules ; after a numeral it is frequent : *two fellow men* (*man ?*), *three fellow bottle*. There is a curious employment in *ten fellow ten one fellow*, which means 101. It is used adverbially in *that man he cry big fellow* ' he cries loudly.'

The genitive is expressed by means of *belong* (or *belong-a, long, along*), which also serves for other prepositional relations. Examples : *tail belong him, pappa belong me, wife belong you, belly belong me walk about too much* (I was seasick), *me savvee talk along white man ; rope along bush* means liana. *Missis ! man belong bullamacow him stop* (the butcher has come). *What for you wipe hands belong-a you on clothes belong esseppoon ?* (spoon, i.e. napkin). Cf. above the expressions for ' bald.' *Piccaninny belong banana* ' a young b. plant.' *Belong* also naturally means ' to live in, be a native of ' ; *boy belong island, he belong Burriburrigan*. The preposition *along* is used about many local relations (in, at, on, into, on board). From such combinations as *laugh along* (1. at) and *he speak along this fella* the transition is easy to cases in which *along* serves to indicate the indirect object : *he give'm this fella Eve along Adam*, and also a kind of direct object, as in *fight alonga him, you gammon along me* (deceive, lie to me), and with the form *belong* : *he puss-puss belong this fellow* (*puss-puss* orig. a cat, then as a verb to caress, make love to).

There is no distinction of gender : *that woman he brother belong me* = ' she is my sister ' ; *he* (before the verb) and *him* (in all other positions) serve both for he, she and it. There is a curious use of *'m, um* or *em*, in our texts often written *him*, after a verb as a ' vocal sign of warning that an object of the verb is to follow,' no matter what that object is.

Churchill says that " in the adjective comparison is unknown ; the islanders do not know how to think comparatively— at least, they lack the form of words by which comparison may be indicated ; *this big, that small* is the nearest they can come to the expression of the idea that one thing is greater than another." But Landtman recognizes *more big* and also *more better* : ' no good make him that fashion, more better make him all same.' The same double comparative I find in another place, used as a kind of verb meaning ' ought to, had better ' : *more better you come out*. *Too* simply means ' much ' : *he savvy too much* ' he knows much ' (praise, no blame), *he too much talk*. A synonym is *plenty too much*. Schuchardt gives the explanation of this trait : " The white man was the teacher of the black man, who imitated his manner of speaking. But the former would constantly use the strongest expressions and exaggerate in a manner that he would only occasionally resort to in speaking to his own countrymen. He did not say, 'You are very lazy,' but 'You are too lazy,' and this will account for the fact that 'very' is called *too much* in Beach-la-mar as well as *tumussi* in the Negro-English of Surinam" (*Spr. der Saramakkaneger*, p. iv).

Verbs have no tense-forms ; when required, a future may be indicated by means of *by and by* : *brother belong-a-me by and by he dead* (my br. is dying), *bymby all men laugh along that boy* ; *he small now, bymbye he big*. It may be qualified by additions like *bymby one time, bymby little bit, bymby big bit*, and may be used also of the 'postpreterit' (of futurity relative to a past time) : *by and by boy belong island he speak*. Another way of expressing the future is seen in *that woman he close up born* (!) *him piccaninny* 'that woman will shortly give birth to a child.' The usual sign of the perfect is *been*, the only idiomatic form of the verb to be : *you been take me along three year ; I been look round before*. But *finish* may also be used : *me look him finish* (I have seen him), *he kaikai all finish* (he has eaten it all up).

Where we should expect forms of the verb 'to be,' there is either no verb or else *stop* is used : *no water stop* (there is no water), *rain he stop* (it rains), *two white men stop Matupi* (live in), *other day plenty money he stop* (. . . I had . . .). For 'have' they say *got*. *My belly no got kaikai* (I am hungry), *he got good hand* (is skilful).

XII.—§ 3. Sounds.

About the phonetic structure of Beach-la-mar I have very little information ; as a rule the words in my sources are spelt in the usual English way. Churchill speaks in rather vague terms about difficulties which the islanders experience in imitating the English sounds, and especially groups of consonants : " Any English word which on experiment proved impracticable to the islanders has undergone alteration to bring it within the scope of their familiar range of sounds or has been rejected for some facile synonym." Thus, according to him, the conjunction *if* could not be used on account of the *f*, and that is the reason for the constant use of *suppose* (*s'pose, pose, posum* = s'pose him)—but it may be allowable to doubt this, for as a matter of fact *f* occurs very frequently in the language—for instance, in the well-worn words *fellow* and *finish*. *Suppose* probably is preferred to *if* because it is fuller in form and less abstract, and therefore easier to handle, while the islanders have many occasions to hear it in other combinations than those in which it is an equivalent of the conjunction.

Landtman says that with the exception of a few sounds (*j*, *ch*, and *th* as in *nothing*) the Kiwai Papuans have little difficulty in pronouncing English words.

Schuchardt gives a little more information about pronunciation, and instances *esterrong* = *strong*, *esseppoon* = *spoon*, *essauce-pen* = *saucepan*, *pellate* = *plate*, *coverra* = *cover*, *millit* = *milk*, *bock-kiss* = *box* (in Churchill *bokus*, *bokkis*) as mutilations due to the native speech habits. He also gives the following letter from a native of the New Hebrides, communicated to him by R. H. Codrington ; it shows many sound substitutions :

Misi Kamesi Arelu Jou no kamu ruki mi Mi no ruki iou Jou ruku Mai Poti i ko Mae tete Vakaromala mi raiki i tiripi Ausi parogi iou i rukauti Mai Poti mi nomoa kaikai mi angikele nau Poti mani Mae i kivi iou Jamu Vari koti iou kivi tamu te pako paraogi mi i penesi nomoa te Pako.

Oloraiti Ta, MATASO.

This means as much as :

Mr. Comins, (How) are you ? You no come look me ; me no look you ; you look my boat he go Mae to-day. Vakaromala me like he sleep house belong you, he look out my boat, me no more kaikai, me hungry now, boat man Mae he give you yam very good, you give some tobacco belong (here = to) me, he finish, no more tobacco.

All right Ta, MATASO.

There are evidently many degrees of approximation to the true English sounds.

This letter also shows the characteristic tendency to add a vowel, generally a short *i*, to words ending in consonants. This is old, for I find in Defoe's *Farther Adventures of Robinson Crusoe* (1719, p. 211) : " All those natives, as also those of Africa, when they learn English, they always add two E's at the end of the words where we use one, and make the accent upon them, as *makee, takee* and the like." (Note the un-phonetic expressions !) Landtman, besides this addition, as in *belongey*, also mentions a more enigmatic one of *lo* to words ending in vowels, as *clylo* for ' cry ' (cf. below on Pidgin).

XII.—§ 4. Pidgin.

I now turn to Pidgin-English. As is well known, this is the name of the jargon which is very extensively used in China, and to some extent also in Japan and California, as a means of communication between English-speaking people and the yellow population. The name is derived from the Chinese distortion of the Engl. word *business*. Unfortunately, the sources available for Pidgin-English as actually spoken in the East nowadays are neither so full nor so exact as those for Beach-la-mar, and the following sketch, therefore, is not quite satisfactory.[1]

Pidgin-English must have developed pretty soon after the first beginning of commercial relations between the English and Chinese. In *Engl. Studien*, 44. 298, Prick van Wely has printed some passages of C. F. Noble's *Voyage to the East Indies in 1747 and 1748*, in which the Chinese are represented as talking to the writer in a " broken and mixed dialect of English and Portuguese," the specimens given corresponding pretty closely to the Pidgin of our own days. Thus, *he no cari Chinaman's Joss, hap oter Joss*, which is rendered, ' that man does not worship our god, but has another god '; the Chinese are said to be unable to pronounce *r* and to use the word *chin-chin* for compliments and *pickenini* for ' small.'

The latter word seems now extinct in Pidgin proper, though we have met it in Beach-la-mar, but *Joss* is still very frequent in Pidgin : it is from Portuguese *Deus*, *Deos* (or Span. *Dios*) : *Joss-house* is a temple or church, *Joss-pidgin* religion, *Joss-pidgin man* a clergyman, *topside Joss-pidgin man* a bishop. *Chin-chin*, according to the same source, is from Chinese *ts'ing-ts'ing*, Pekingese *ch'ing-ch'ing*, a term of salutation answering to ' thank you, adieu,' but the English have extended its sphere of application very considerably, using it as a noun meaning ' salutation, compliment,' and as a verb meaning " to worship (by bowing and striking the chin), to reverence, adore, implore, to deprecate anger, to wish one something, invite, ask " (Leland). The explanation given here within parentheses shows how the Chinese word has been interpreted by popular etymology, and no doubt it owes its extensive use partly to its sound, which has taken the popular fancy. *Chin-chin joss* means religious worship of any kind.

Simpson says : " Many of the words in use are of unknown origin. In a number of cases the English suppose them to be

[1] There are many specimens in Charles G. Leland, *Pidgin-English Sing-Song, or Songs and Stories in the China-English Dialect, with a Vocabulary* (5th ed., London, 1900), but they make the impression of being artificially made-up to amuse the readers, and contain a much larger proportion of Chinese words than the rest of my sources would warrant. Besides various articles in newspapers I have used W. Simpson, " China's Future Place in Philology " (*Macmillan's Magazine*, November 1873) and Dr. Legge's article " Pigeon English " in *Chambers's Encyclopædia*, 1901 (s.v. China). The chapters devoted to Pidgin in Karl Lentzner's *Dictionary of the Slang-English of Australia and of some Mixed Languages* (Halle, 1892) give little else but wholesale reprints of passages from some of the sources mentioned above.

Chinese, while the Chinese, on the other hand, take them to be English." Some of these, however, admit now of explanation, and not a few of them point to India, where the English have learnt them and brought them further East. Thus *chit*, *chitty*, 'a letter, an account,' is Hindustani *chitthī*; *godown* 'warehouse' is an English popular interpretation of Malay *gadong*, from Tamil *gidangi*. *Chowchow* seems to be real Chinese and to mean 'mixed preserves,' but in Pidgin it has acquired the wider signification of 'food, meal, to eat,' besides having various other applications : a chowchow cargo is an assorted cargo, a 'general shop' is a chowchow shop. *Cumshaw* 'a present' is Chinese. But *tiffin*, which is used all over the East for 'lunch,' is really an English word, properly *tiffing*, from the slang verb *to tiff*, to drink, esp. to drink out of meal-times. In India it was applied to the meal, and then reintroduced into England and believed to be a native Indian word.

XII.—§ 5. Grammar, etc.

Among points not found in Beach-la-mar I shall mention the extensive use of *piecee*, which in accordance with Chinese grammar is required between a numeral and the noun indicating what is counted; thus in a Chinaman's description of a three-masted screw steamer with two funnels : "Thlee piecee bamboo, two piecee puff-puff, walk-along inside, no can see " (walk-along = the engine). *Side* means any locality : *he belongey China-side now* (he is in China), *topside* above, or high, *bottom-side* below, *farside* beyond, *this-side* here, *allo-side* around. In a similar way *time* (pronounced *tim* or *teem*) is used in *that-tim* then, when, *what-tim* when ? *one-tim* once, only, *two-tim* twice, again, *nother-tim* again.

In one respect the Chinese sound system is accountable for a deviation from Beach-la-mar, namely in the substitution of *l* for *r*: *loom, all light* for 'room, all right,' etc., while the islanders often made the inverse change. But the tendency to add a vowel after a final consonant is the same : *makee, too muchee*, etc. The enigmatic termination *lo*, which Landtman found in some words in New Guinea, is also added to some words ending in vowel sounds in Pidgin, according to Leland, who instances *die-lo*, die; in his texts I find the additional examples *buy-lo*, *say-lo*, *pay-lo*, *hear-lo*, besides *wailo*, or *wylo*, which is probably from *away*; it means 'go away, away with you ! go, depart, gone.' Can it be the Chinese sign of the past tense *la, lao*, generalized ?

Among usual expressions must be mentioned *number one* (*numpa one*) 'first-class, excellent,' *catchee* 'get, possess, hold, bring,' etc., *ploper* (*plopa*) 'proper, good, nice, correct': *you belong ploper?* 'are you well?'

Another word which was not in use among the South Sea islanders, namely *have*, in the form *hab* or *hap* is often used in Pidgin, even to form the perfect. *Belong* (*belongy*) is nearly as frequent as in Beach-la-mar, but is used in a different way: 'My belongy Consoo boy,' 'I am the Consul's servant.' 'You belong clever inside,' 'you are intelligent.' The usual way of asking the price of something is 'how much belong?'

XII.—§ 6. General Theory.

Lingos of the same type as Beach-la-mar and Pidgin-English are found in other parts of the world where whites and natives meet and have to find some medium of communication. Thus a Danish doctor living in Belgian Congo sends me a few specimens of the 'Pidgin' spoken there: to indicate that his master has received many letters from home, the 'boy' will say, "Massa catch plenty mammy-book" (*mammy* meaning 'woman, wife'). *Breeze* stands for air in general; if the boy wants to say that he has pumped up the bicycle tyres, he will say, "Plenty breeze live for inside," *live* being here the general term for 'to be' (Beach-l. *stop*); 'is your master in?' becomes 'Massa live?' and the answer is 'he no live' or 'he live for hup' (i.e. he is upstairs). If a man has a stomach-ache he will say 'he hurt me for belly plenty too much'—*too much* is thus used exactly as in Beach-la-mar and Chinese Pidgin. The similarity of all these jargons, in spite of unavoidable smaller differences, is in fact very striking indeed.

It may be time now to draw the moral of all this. And first I want to point out that these languages are not 'mixed languages' in the proper sense of that term. Churchill is not right when he says that Beach-la-mar "gathered material from every source, it fused them all." As a matter of fact, it is English, and nothing but English, with very few admixtures, and all of these are such words as had previously been adopted into the English speech of those classes of the population, sailors, etc., with whom the natives came into contact: they were therefore justified in their belief that these words formed part of the English tongue and that what they learned themselves was real English. The natives really adhere to Windisch's rule about the adoption of loan-words (above, XI § 10). If there are more Chinese words in Pidgin than there are Polynesian ones in Beach-la-mar, this is a natural consequence of the fact that the Chinese civilization ranked incomparably

much higher than the Polynesian, and that therefore the
English living in China would adopt these words into their own
speech. Still, their number is not very large. And we have
seen that there are some words which the Easterners must
naturally suppose to be English, while the English think that
they belong to the vernacular, and in using them each party
is thus under the delusion that he is rendering a service to the
other.

This leads me to my second point : those deviations from
correct English, those corruptions of pronunciation and those
simplifications of grammar, which have formed the object of
this short sketch, are due just as much to the English as to the
Easterners, and in many points they began with the former
rather than with the latter (cf. Schuchardt, *Auf anlass des
Volapüks*, 1888, 8 ; KS 4. 35, SlD 36 ; ESt 15. 292). From
Schuchardt I take the following quotation : " The usual question
on reaching the portico of an Indian bungalow is, *Can missus see ?*
—it being a popular superstition amongst the Europeans that
to enable a native to understand English he must be addressed
as if he were deaf, and in the most infantile language." This
tendency to meet the ' inferior races ' half-way in order to facilitate matters for them is by Churchill called " the one supreme
axiom of international philology : the proper way to make a
foreigner understand what you would say is to use broken
English. He speaks it himself, therefore give him what he uses."
We recognize here the same mistaken notion that we have seen
above in the language of the nursery, where mothers and others
will talk a curious sort of mangled English which is believed to
represent real babytalk, though it has many traits which are
purely conventional. In both cases these more or less artificial
perversions are thought to be an aid to those who have not yet
mastered the intricacies of the language in question, though the
ultimate result is at best a retardation of the perfect acquisition
of correct speech.

My view, then, is that Beach-la-mar as well as Pidgin is
English, only English learnt imperfectly, in consequence partly
of the difficulties always inherent in learning a totally different
language, partly of the obstacles put in the way of learning by
the linguistic behaviour of the English-speaking people themselves. The analogy of its imperfections with those of a baby's
speech in the first period is striking, and includes errors of pronunciation, extreme simplification of grammar, scantiness of
vocabulary, even to such peculiarities as that the word *too* is
apprehended in the sense of ' very much,' and such phrases as
you better go, etc.

XII.—§ 7. Mauritius Creole.

The view here advanced on the character of these ' Pidgin '
languages is corroborated when we see that other languages under
similar circumstances have been treated in exactly the same way
as English. With regard to French in the island of Mauritius,
formerly Ile de France, we are fortunate in possessing an excellent treatment of the subject by M. C. Baissac (*Étude sur le
Patois Créole Mauricien*, Nancy, 1880 ; cf. the same writer's *Le
Folk-lore de l'Ile-Maurice*, Paris, 1888, Les littératures populaires,
tome xxvii). The island was uninhabited when the French
occupied it in 1715 ; a great many slaves were imported from
Madagascar, and as a means of intercourse between them and
their French masters a French Creole language sprang up, which
has survived the English conquest (1810) and the subsequent
wholesale introduction of coolies from India and elsewhere. The
paramount element in the vocabulary is French ; one may read
many pages in Baissac's texts without coming across any foreign
words, apart from the names of some indigenous animals and
plants. In the phonetic structure there are a few all-pervading
traits : the front-round vowels are replaced by the corresponding
unrounded vowels or in a few cases by [u], and instead of [ʃ, ʒ]
we find [s, z] ; thus *éré* heureux, *éne plime* une plume, *sakéne*
chacun(e), *zize* juge, *zunu* genou, *suval* cheval : I replace Baissac's
notation, which is modelled on the French spelling, by a more
phonetic one according to his own indications ; but I keep his
final *e muet*.

The grammar of this language is as simple as possible. Substantives have the same form for the two numbers : *dé suval*
deux chevaux. There is no definite article. The adjective is
invariable, thus also *sa* for ce, cet, cette, ces, ceci, cela, celui,
celle, ceux, celles. *Mo* before a verb is ' I,' before a substantive
it is possessive : *mo koné* I know, *mo lakaze* my house ; in the
same way *to* is you and your, but in the third person a distinction is made, for *li* is he or she, but his or her is *so*, and
here we have even a plural, *zaute* from ' les autres,' which form
is also used as a plural of the second person : *mo va alle av zaut*,
I shall go with you.

The genitive is expressed by word-order without any preposition : *lakase so papa* his father's house ; also with *so* before the
nominative : *so piti ppa Azor* old Azor's child.

The form in which the French words have been taken over
presents some curious features, and in some cases illustrates the
difficulty the blacks felt in separating the words which they
heard in the French utterance as one continuous stream of

sounds. There is evidently a disinclination to begin a word with a vowel, and sometimes an initial vowel is left out, as *bitation* habitation, *tranzé* étranger, but in other cases *z* is taken from the French plural article : *zozo* oiseau, *zistoire*, *zenfan*, *zimaze* image, *zalfan* éléphant, *zanimo* animal, or *n* from the French indefinite article : *name* ghost, *nabi* (or *zabi*) habit. In many cases the whole French article is taken as an integral part of the word, as *lérat* rat, *léroi*, *licien* chien, *latabe* table, *lére* heure (often as a conjunction 'when') ; thus also with the plural article *lizié* from *les yeux*, but without the plural signification : *éne lizié* an eye. Similarly *éne lazoie* a goose. Words that are often used in French with the so-called partitive article keep this ; thus *disel* salt, *divin* wine, *duri* rice, *éne dipin* a loaf ; here also we meet with one word from the French plural : *éne dizéf* an egg, from *des œufs*. The French mass-word with the partitive article *du monde* has become *dimunde* or *dumune*, and as it means 'people' and no distinction is made between plural and singular, it is used also for 'person' : *éne vié dimunde* an old man.

Verbs have only one form, generally from the French infinitive or past participle, which in most cases would fall together (*manzé* = manger, mangé ; *kuri* = courir, couru) ; this serves for all persons in both numbers and all moods. But tenses are indicated by means of auxiliary words : *va* for the future, *té* (from *été*) for the ordinary past, and *fine* for the perfect : *mo manzé* I eat, *mo va manzé* I shall eat, *mo té manzé* I ate, *mo fine manzé* I have eaten, *mo fine fini* I have finished. Further, there is a curious use of *aprè* to express what in English are called the progressive or expanded tenses : *mo aprè manzé* I am eating, *mo té aprè manzé* I was eating, and of *pour* to express the immediate future : *mo pour manzé* I am going to eat, and finally an immediate past may be expressed by *fék* : *mo fék manzé* I have just been eating (je ne fais que de manger). As these may be combined in various ways (*mo va fine manzé* I shall have eaten, even *mo té va fék manzé* I should have eaten a moment ago, etc.), the language has really succeeded in building up a very fine and rich verbal system with the simplest possible means and with perfect regularity.

The French separate negatives have been combined into one word each : *napa* not (there is not), *narien* nothing, and similarly *nék* only.

In many cases the same form is used for a substantive or adjective and for a verb : *mo soif, mo faim* I am thirsty and hungry ; *li content so madame* he is fond of his wife.

Côte (or *à côte*) is a preposition 'by the side of, near,' but also means 'where' : *la case àcote li resté* 'the house in which he lives' ; cf. Pidgin *side*.

In all this, as will easily be seen, there is very little French grammar ; this will be especially evident when we compare the French verbal system with its many intricacies : difference according to person, number, tense and mood with their endings, changes of root-vowels and stress-place, etc., with the unchanged verbal root and the invariable auxiliary syllables of the Creole. But there is really as little in the Creole dialect of Malagasy grammar, as I have ascertained by looking through G. W. Parker's *Grammar* (London, 1883) : both nations in forming this means of communication have, as it were, stripped themselves of all their previous grammatical habits and have spoken as if their minds were just as innocent of grammar as those of very small babies, whether French or Malagasy. Thus, and thus only, can it be explained that the grammar of this variety of French is for all practical purposes identical with the grammar of those two varieties of English which we have previously examined in this chapter

No one can read Baissac's collection of folk-tales from Mauritius without being often struck with the felicity and even force of this language, in spite of its inevitable *naïveté* and of the childlike simplicity of its constructions. If it were left to itself it might develop into a really fine idiom without abandoning any of its characteristic traits. But as it is, it seems to be constantly changing through the influence of real French, which is more and more taught to and imitated by the islanders, and the day may come when most of the features described in this rapid sketch will have given place to something which is less original, but will be more readily understood by Parisian globe-trotters who may happen to visit the distant island.

XII.—§ 8. Chinook Jargon.

The view here advanced may be further put to the test if we examine a totally different language developed in another part of the world, viz. in Oregon. I give its history in an abridged form from Hale.[1] When the first British and American trading ships appeared on the north-west coast of America, towards the end of the eighteenth century, they found a great number of distinct languages, the Nootka, Nisqually, Chinook, Chihailish and

---

[1] See *An International Idiom. A Manual of the Oregon Trade Language, or Chinook Jargon*, by Horatio Hale (London, 1890). Besides this I have used a *Vocabulary of the Jargon or Trade Language of Oregon* [by Lionnet] published by the Smithsonian Institution (1853), and George Gibbs, *A Dictionary of the Chinook Jargon* (Smithsonian Inst., 1863). Lionnet spells the words according to the French fashion, while Gibbs and Hale spell them in the English way. I have given them with the continental values of the vowels in accordance with the indications in Hale's glossary.

others, all of them harsh in pronunciation, complex in structure, and each spoken over a very limited space. The traders learnt a few Nootka words and the Indians a few English words. Afterwards the traders began to frequent the Columbia River, and naturally attempted to communicate with the natives there by means of the words which they had found intelligible at Nootka. The Chinooks soon acquired these words, both Nootka and English. When later the white traders made permanent establishments in Oregon, a real language was required ; and it was formed by drawing upon the Chinook for such words as were requisite, numerals, pronouns, and some adverbs and other words. Thus enriched, ' the Jargon,' as it now began to be styled, became of great service as a means of general intercourse. Now, French Canadians in the service of the fur companies were brought more closely into contact with the Indians, hunted with them, and lived with them on terms of familiarity. The consequence was that several French words were added to the slender stock of the Jargon, including the names of various articles of food and clothing, implements, several names of the parts of the body, and the verbs to run, sing and dance, also one conjunction, *puis*, reduced to *pi*.

"The origin of some of the words is rather whimsical. The Americans, British and French are distinguished by the terms *Boston*, *Kinchotsh* (King George), and *pasaiuks*, which is presumed to be the word *Français* (as neither *f*, *r* nor the nasal *n* can be pronounced by the Indians) with the Chinook plural termination *uks* added. . . . ' Foolish ' is expressed by *pelton* or *pilton*, derived from the name of a deranged person, one Archibald Pelton, whom the Indians saw at Astoria ; his strange appearance and actions made such an impression upon them, that thenceforward anyone behaving in an absurd or irrational manner " was termed *pelton*.

The phonetic structure is very simple, and contains no sound or combination that is not easy to Englishmen and Frenchmen as well as to Indians of at least a dozen tribes. The numerous harsh Indian velars either disappear entirely or are softened to *h* and *k*. On the other hand, the *d*, *f*, *r*, *v*, *z* of the English and French become in the mouth of a Chinook *t*, *p*, *l*, *w*, *s*. Examples :

Chinook :		
thliakso	*yakso*	hair
etsghot	*itshut*	black bear
tkalaitanam	*kalaitan*	arrow, shot, bullet
ntshaika	*nesaika*	we
mshaika	*mesaika*	we
thlaitshka	*klaska* (*tlaska*)	they
tkhlon	*klon* (*tlun*)	three

English :	handkerchief	hakatshum (kenkeshim)	handkerchief
	cry	klai, kalai (kai)	cry, mourn
	fire	paia	fire, cook, ripe
	dry	tlai, delai	dry
French :	courir	kuli	run
	la bouche	labus (labush)	mouth
	le mouton	lemuto	sheep

The forms in parentheses are those of the French glossary (1853).

It will be noticed that many of the French words have the definite article affixed (a trait noticed in many words in the French Creole dialect of Mauritius). More than half of the words in Hale's glossary beginning with *l* have this origin, thus *labutai* bottle, *lakloa* cross, *lamie* an old woman (la vieille), *lapushet* fork (la fourchette), *latlá* noise (faire du train), *lidú* finger, *lejaub* (or *diaub*, *yaub*) devil (le diable), *léma* hand, *liplét* missionary (le prêtre), *litá* tooth. The plural article is found in *lisáp* egg (les œufs)—the same word in which Mauritius French has also adopted the plural form.

Some of the meanings of English words are rather curious ; thus, *kol* besides ' cold ' means ' winter,' and as the years, as with the old Scandinavians, are reckoned by winters, also ' year.' *Sun* (*son*) besides ' sun ' also means ' day.' *Spos* (often pronounced *pos*), as in Beach-la-mar, is a common conjunction, ' if, when.'

The grammar is extremely simple. Nouns are invariable ; the plural generally is not distinguished from the singular ; sometimes *haiu* (*ayo*) ' much, many ' is added by way of emphasis. The genitive is shown by position only : *kahta nem maika papa ?* (lit., what name thou father) what is the name of your father ? The adjective precedes the noun, and comparison is indicated by periphrasis. ' I am stronger than thou ' would be *weke maika skukum kahkwa naika*, lit. ' not thou strong as I.' The superlative is indicated by the adverb *haiás* ' great, very ' : *haiás oliman okuk kanim*, that canoe is the oldest, lit., very old that canoe, or (according to Gibbs) by *elip* ' first, before ' : *elip klosh* ' best.'

The numerals and pronouns are from the Chinook, but the latter, at any rate, are very much simplified. Thus the pronoun for ' we ' is *nesaika*, from Chinook *ntshaika*, which is the exclusive form, meaning ' we here,' not including the person or persons addressed.

Like the nouns, the verbs have only one form, the tense being left to be inferred from the context, or, if strictly necessary,

being indicated by an adverb. The future in the sense of
'about to, ready to,' may be expressed by *tike*, which means
properly 'wish,' as *naika papa tike mimalus* (*mimelust*) my
father is about to die. The verb 'to be' is not expressed:
maika pelton, thou art foolish.

There is a much-used verb *mámuk*, which means 'make, do,
work' and forms causatives, as *mamuk chako* 'make to come,
bring,' *mamuk mimalus* 'kill.' With a noun : *mamuk lalam*
(Fr. la rame) 'make oar,' i.e. 'to row,' *mamuk pepe* (make paper)
'write,' *mamuk po* (make blow) 'fire a gun.'

There is only one true preposition, *kopa*, which is used in
various senses—to, for, at, in, among, about, etc. ; but even
this may generally be omitted and the sentence remain intelligible. The two conjunctions *spos* and *pi* have already been
mentioned.

XII.—§ 9. Chinook continued.

In this way something is formed that may be used as a
language in spite of the scantiness of its vocabulary. But a
good deal has to be expressed by the tone of the voice, the look
and the gesture of the speaker. "The Indians in general,"
says Hale (p. 18), "are very sparing of their gesticulations. No
languages, probably, require less assistance from this source than
theirs. . . . We frequently had occasion to observe the sudden
change produced when a party of the natives, who had been
conversing in their own tongue, were joined by a foreigner, with
whom it was necessary to speak in the Jargon. The coun-
tenances, which had before been grave, stolid and inexpressive,
were instantly lighted up with animation ; the low, monotonous
tone became lively and modulated ; every feature was active ;
the head, the arms and the whole body were in motion, and
every look and gesture became instinct with meaning."

In British Columbia and in parts of Alaska this language is
the prevailing medium of intercourse between the whites and
the natives, and there Hale thinks that it is likely to live "for
hundreds, and perhaps thousands, of years to come." The
language has already the beginning of a literature : songs,
mostly composed by women, who sing them to plaintive native
tunes. Hale gives some lyrics and a sermon preached by Mr.
Eells, who has been accustomed for many years to preach to
the Indians in the Jargon and who says that he sometimes even
thinks in this idiom.

Hale counted the words in this sermon, and found that to
express the whole of its "historic and descriptive details, its

arguments and its appeals," only 97 different words were required, and not a single grammatical inflexion. Of these words, 65 were from Amerindian languages (46 Chinook, 17 Nootka, 2 Salish), 23 English and 7 French.

It is very instructive to go through the texts given by Hale and to compare them with the real Chinook text analysed in Boas's *Handbook of American Indian Languages* (Washington, 1911, p. 666 ff.): the contrast could not be stronger between simplicity carried to the extreme point, on the one hand, and an infinite complexity and intricacy on the other. But though it must be admitted that astonishingly much can be expressed in the Jargon by its very simple and few means, a European mind, while bewildered in the entangled jumble of the Chinook language, cannot help missing a great many *nuances* in the Jargon, where thoughts are reduced to their simplest formula and where everything is left out that is not strictly necessary to the least exacting minds.

XII.—§ 10. Makeshift Languages.

To sum up, this Oregon trade language is to be classed together with Beach-la-mar and Pidgin-English, not perhaps as ' bastard ' or ' mongrel ' languages—such expressions taken from biology always convey the wrong impression that a language is an ' organism ' and had therefore better be avoided—but rather as makeshift languages or minimum languages, means of expression which do not serve all the purposes of ordinary languages, but may be used as substitutes where fuller and better ones are not available.

The analogy between this Jargon and the makeshift languages of the East is closer than might perhaps appear at first blush, only we must make it clear to ourselves that English is in the two cases placed in exactly the inverse position. Pidgin and Beach-la-mar are essentially English learnt imperfectly by the Easterners, the Oregon Jargon is essentially Chinook learnt imperfectly by the English. Just as in the East the English not only suffered but also abetted the yellows in their corruption of the English language, so also the Amerindians met the English half-way through simplifying their own speech. If in Polynesia and China the makeshift language came to contain some Polynesian and Chinese words, they were those which the English themselves had borrowed into their own language and which the yellows therefore must think formed a legitimate part of the language they wanted to speak; and in the same way the American Jargon contains such words from the European languages as had been previously adopted by the reds. If the Jargon embraces so many French terms for the various parts of the body, one concomitant reason probably is that these names in the original Chinook language presented special difficulties through being specialized and determined by possessive affixes (my foot, for instance, is *lekxeps*, thy foot *tămēps*, its foot *lelaps*, our (dual inclusive) feet *tetxaps*, your (dual) feet *temtaps*; I simplify the notation in Boas's *Handbook*, p. 586), so that it was incomparably easier to take the French *lepi* and use it unchanged in all cases, no matter what the number, and no matter who the possessor was. The natives, who had learnt such words from the French, evidently used them to other whites under the impression that thereby they could make themselves more readily understood, and the British and American traders probably imagined them to be real Chinook; anyhow, their use meant a substantial economy of mental exertion.

The chief point I want to make, however, is with regard to grammar. In all these languages, both in the makeshift English and French of the East and in the makeshift Amerindian of the North-West, the grammatical structure has been simplified very much beyond what we find in any of the languages involved in their making, and simplified to such an extent that it may be expressed in very few words, and those nearly the same in all these languages, the chief rule being common to them all, that substantives, adjectives and verbs remain always unchanged. The vocabularies are as the poles asunder—in the East English and French, in America Chinook, etc.—but the morphology of all these languages is practically identical, because in all of them it has reached the vanishing-point. This shows conclusively that the reason of this simplicity is not the Chinese substratum or the influence of Chinese grammar, as is so often believed. Pidgin-English cannot be described, as is often done, as English with Chinese pronunciation and Chinese grammar, because in that case we should expect Beach-la-mar to be quite different from it, as the substratum there would be Melanesian, which in many ways differs from Chinese, and further we should expect the Mauritius Creole to be French with Malagasy pronunciation and Malagasy grammar, and on the other hand the Oregon trade language to be Chinook with English pronunciation and English grammar—but in none of these cases would this description tally with the obvious facts. We might just as well say that the speech of a two-year-old child in England is English with Chinese grammar, and that of the two-year-old French child is French modelled on Chinese grammar: the truth on the contrary, is that in all these seemingly so different cases the same mental factor is at work, namely, imperfect mastery of a language, which in its initial stage, in the child with its first language and in the grown-up with a second language learnt by imperfect methods, leads to a superficial knowledge of the most indispensable words, with total disregard of grammar. Often, here and there, this is combined with a wish to express more than is possible with the means at hand, and thus generates the attempts to express the inexpressible by means of those more or less ingenious and more or less comical devices, with paraphrases and figurative or circuitous designations, which we have seen first in the chapters on children's language and now again in Beach-la-mar and its congeners.

Exactly the same characteristics are found again in the *lingua geral Brazilica*, which in large parts of Brazil serves as the means of communication between the whites and Indians or negroes and also between Indians of different tribes. It "possesses neither declension nor conjugation" and "places words after one another without grammatical flexion, with disregard of *nuances* in sentence structure, but in energetic brevity," it is "easy of pronunciation," with many vowels and no hard consonant groups—in all these respects it differs considerably from the original Tupí, from which it has been evolved by the Europeans.[1]

Finally, I would point the contrast between these makeshift languages and slang : the former are an outcome of linguistic poverty ; they are born of the necessity and the desire to make oneself understood where the ordinary idiom of the individual is of no use, while slang expressions are due to a linguistic exuberance : the individual creating them knows perfectly well the ordinary words for the idea he wants to express, but in youthful playfulness he is not content with what is everybody's property, and thus consciously steps outside the routine of everyday language to produce something that is calculated to excite merriment or even admiration on the part of his hearers. The results in both cases may sometimes show related features, for some of the figurative expressions of Beach-la-mar recall certain slang words by their bold metaphors, but the motive force in the two kinds is totally different, and where a comic effect is produced, in one case it is intentional and in the other unintentional.

XII.—§ 11. Romanic Languages.

When Schuchardt began his studies of the various Creole languages formed in many parts of the world where Europeans

---

[1] See Martius, *Beitr. zur Ethnogr. und Sprachenkunde Amerikas* (Leipzig, 1867), i. 364 ff. and ii 23 ff.

speaking various Romanic and other languages had come into contact with negroes, Polynesians and other races, it was with the avowed intention of throwing light on the origin of the Romanic languages from a contact between Latin and the languages previously spoken in the countries colonized by the Romans. We may now raise the question whether Beach-la-mar—to take that as a typical example of the kind of languages dealt with in this chapter—is likely to develop into a language which to the English of Great Britain will stand in the same relation as French or Portuguese to Latin. The answer cannot be doubtful if we adhere tenaciously to the points of view already advanced. Development into a separate language would be imaginable only on condition of a complete, or a nearly complete, isolation from the language of England (and America)—and how should that be effected nowadays, with our present means of transport and communication ? If such isolation were indeed possible, it would also result in the breaking off of communication between the various islands in which Beach-la-mar is now spoken, and that would probably entail the speedy extinction of the language itself in favour of the Polynesian language of each separate island. On the contrary, what will probably happen is a development in the opposite direction, by which the English of the islanders will go on constantly improving so as to approach correct usage more and more in every respect : better pronunciation and syntax, more flexional forms and a less scanty vocabulary—in short, the same development that has already to a large extent taken place in the English of the coloured population in the United States. But this means a gradual extinction of Beach-la-mar as a separate idiom through its complete absorption in ordinary English (cf. above, p. 228, on conditions at Mauritius).

Do these ' makeshift languages,' then, throw any light on the development of the Romanic languages ? They may be compared to the very first initial stage of the Latin language as spoken by the barbarians, many of whom may be supposed to have mutilated Latin in very much the same way as the Pacific islanders do English. But by and by they learnt Latin much better, and if now the Romanic languages have simplified the grammatical structure of Latin, this simplification is not to be placed on the same footing as the formlessness of Beach-la-mar, for that is complete and has been achieved at one blow : the islanders have never (i.e. have not yet) learnt the English form-system. But the inhabitants of France, Spain, etc., did learn the Latin form system as well as the syntactic use of the forms. This is seen by the fact that when French and the other languages

began to be written down, there remained in them a large quantity
of forms and syntactic applications that agree with Latin but
have since then become extinct : in its oldest written form,
therefore, French is very far from the amorphous condition of
Beach-la-mar : in its nouns it had many survivals of the Latin
case system (gen. pl. corresponding to -*orum* ; an oblique case
different from the nominative and formed in various ways according to the rules of Latin declensions), in the verbs we find an
intricate system of tenses, moods and persons, based on the
Latin flexions. It is true that these had been already to some
degree simplified, but this must have happened in the same
gradual way as the further simplification that goes on before
our very eyes in the written documents of the following centuries : the distance from the first to the tenth century must have
been bridged over in very much the same way as the distance
between the tenth and the twentieth century. No cataclysm
such as that through which English has become Beach-la-mar
need on any account be invoked to explain the perfectly natural
change from Latin to Old French and from Old French to
Modern French.

CHAPTER XIII

THE WOMAN

§ 1. Women's Languages. § 2. Tabu. § 3. Competing Languages. § 4. Sanskrit Drama. § 5. Conservatism. § 6. Phonetics and Grammar § 7. Choice of Words. § 8. Vocabulary. § 9. Adverbs. § 10. Periods. § 11. General Characteristics.

XIII.—§ 1. Women's Languages.

THERE are tribes in which men and women are said to speak totally different languages, or at any rate distinct dialects. It will be worth our while to look at the classical example of this, which is mentioned in a great many ethnographical and linguistic works, viz. the Caribs or Caribbeans of the Small Antilles. The first to mention their distinct sex dialects was the Dominican Breton, who, in his *Dictionnaire Caraïbe-français* (1664), says that the Caribbean chief had exterminated all the natives except the women, who had retained part of their ancient language. This is repeated in many subsequent accounts, the fullest and, as it seems, most reliable of which is that by Rochefort, who spent a long time among the Caribbeans in the middle of the seventeenth century: see his *Histoire naturelle et morale des Iles Antilles* (2e éd., Rotterdam, 1665, p. 449 ff.). Here he says that "the men have a great many expressions peculiar to them, which the women understand but never pronounce themselves. On the other hand, the women have words and phrases which the men never use, or they would be laughed to scorn. Thus it happens that in their conversations it often seems as if the women had another language than the men. . . . The savage natives of Dominica say that the reason for this is that when the Caribs came to occupy the islands these were inhabited by an Arawak tribe which they exterminated completely, with the exception of the women, whom they married in order to populate the country. Now, these women kept their own language and taught it to their daughters. . . . But though the boys understand the speech of their mothers and sisters, they nevertheless follow their fathers and brothers and conform to their speech from the age of five or six. . . . It is asserted that there is some similarity between the speech of the continental Arawaks and that of the Carib women. But the Carib men and women on the continent speak the same language, as they have never corrupted their natural speech by marriage with strange women."

This evidently is the account which forms the basis of everything that has since been written on the subject. But it will be noticed that Rochefort does not really speak of the speech of the two sexes as totally distinct languages or dialects, as has often been maintained, but only of certain differences within the same language. If we go through the comparatively full and evidently careful glossary attached to his book, in which he denotes the words peculiar to the men by the letter H and those of the women by F, we shall see that it is only for about one-tenth of the vocabulary that such special words have been indicated to him, though the matter evidently interested him very much, so that he would make all possible efforts to elicit them from the natives. In his lists, words special to one or the other sex are found most frequently in the names of the various degrees of kinship; thus, 'my father' in the speech of the men in *youmáan*, in that of the women *noukóuchili*, though both in addressing him say *bába*; 'my grandfather' is *itámoulou* and *nárgouti* respectively, and thus also for maternal uncle, son (elder son, younger son), brother-in-law, wife, mother, grandmother, daughter, cousin—all of these are different according as a man or a woman is speaking. It is the same with the names of some, though far from all, of the different parts of the body, and with some more or less isolated words, as friend, enemy, joy, work, war, house, garden, bed, poison, tree, sun, moon, sea, earth. This list comprises nearly every notion for which Rochefort indicates separate words, and it will be seen that there are innumerable ideas for which men and women use the same word. Further, we see that where there are differences these do not consist in small deviations, such as different prefixes or suffixes added to the same root, but in totally distinct roots. Another point is very important to my mind : judging by the instances in which plural forms are given in the lists, the words of the two sexes are inflected in exactly the same way ; thus the grammar is common to both, from which we may infer that we have not really to do with two distinct languages in the proper sense of the word.

Now, some light may probably be thrown on the problem of this women's language from a custom mentioned in some of the old books written by travellers who have visited these islands. Rochefort himself (p. 497) very briefly says that " the women do not eat till their husbands have finished their meal," and Lafitau (1724) says that women never eat in the company of their husbands and never mention them by name, but must wait upon them as their slaves ; with this Labat agrees.

XIII.—§ 2. Tabu.

The fact that a wife is not allowed to mention the name of her husband makes one think that we have here simply an instance of a custom found in various forms and in varying degrees throughout the world—what is called verbal tabu : under certain circumstances, at certain times, in certain places, the use of one or more definite words is interdicted, because it is superstitiously believed to entail certain evil consequences, such as exasperate demons and the like.   In place of the forbidden words it is therefore necessary to use some kind of figurative paraphrase, to dig up an otherwise obsolete term, or to disguise the real word so as to render it more innocent.

Now as a matter of fact we find that verbal tabu was a common practice with the old Caribs : when they were on the war-path they had a great number of mysterious words which women were never allowed to learn and which even the young men might not pronounce before passing certain tests of bravery and patriotism ; these war-words are described as extraordinarily difficult (" un baragoin fort difficile," Rochefort, p. 450).   It is easy to see that when once a tribe has acquired the habit of using a whole set of terms under certain frequently recurring circumstances, while others are at the same time strictly interdicted, this may naturally lead to so many words being reserved exclusively for one of the sexes that an observer may be tempted to speak of separate ' languages ' for the two sexes.   There is thus no occasion to believe in the story of a wholesale extermination of all male inhabitants by another tribe, though on the other hand it is easy to understand how such a myth may arise as an explanation of the linguistic difference between men and women, when it has become strong enough to attract attention and therefore has to be accounted for

In some parts of the world the connexion between a separate women's language and tabu is indubitable.   Thus among the Bantu people of Africa.   With the Zulus a wife is not allowed to mention the name of her father-in-law and of his brothers, and if a similar word or even a similar syllable occurs in the ordinary language, she must substitute something else of a similar meaning. In the royal family the difficulty of understanding the women's language is further increased by the woman's being forbidden to mention the names of her husband, his father and grandfather as well as his brothers.   If one of these names means something like " the son of the bull," each of these words has to be avoided, and all kinds of paraphrases have to be used.   According to Kranz the interdiction holds good not only for meaning elements of the name, but even for certain sounds entering into them ; thus, if

the name contains the sound *z*, *amanzi* ' water ' has to be altered
into *amandabi*. If a woman were to contravene this rule she
would be indicted for sorcery and put to death. The substitutes
thus introduced tend to be adopted by others and to constitute a
real women's language.

With the Chiquitos in Bolivia the difference between the grammars
of the two sexes is rather curious (see V. Henry, " Sur le parler
des hommes et le parler des femmes dans la langue chiquita," *Revue
de linguistique*, xii. 305, 1879). Some of Henry's examples may
be thus summarized : men indicate by the addition of *-tii* that a
male person is spoken about, while the women do not use this
suffix and thus make no distinction between ' he ' and ' she,' ' his '
and ' her.' Thus in the men's speech the following distinctions
would be made :

> He went to his house : *yebotii ti n-ipoostii*.
> He went to her house : *yebotii ti n-ipoos*.
> She went to his house : *yebo ti n-ipoostii*.

But to express all these different meanings the women would have
only one form, viz.

> *yebo ti n-ipoos*,

which in the men's speech would mean only ' She went to her
house.'

To many substantives the men prefix a vowel which the women
do not employ, thus *o-petas* ' turtle,' *u-tamokos* ' dog,' *i-pis* ' wood.'
For some very important notions the sexes use distinct words ; thus,
for the names of kinship, ' my father ' is *iyai* and *išupu*, ' my mother '
ipaki and *ipapa*, ' my brother ' *tsaruki* and *ičibausi* respectively.

Among the languages of California, Yana, according to Dixon
and Kroeber (*The American Anthropologist*, n.s. 5. 15), is the
only language that shows a difference in the words used by men
and women—apart from terms of relationship, where a distinction
according to the sex of the speaker is made among many Californian
tribes as well as in other parts of the world, evidently " because
the relationship itself is to them different, as the sex is different."
But in Yana the distinction is a linguistic one, and curiously enough,
the few specimens given all present a trait found already in the
Chiquito forms, namely, that the forms spoken by women are shorter
than those of the men, which appear as extensions, generally by
suffixed *-(n)a*, of the former.

It is surely needless to multiply instances of these customs, which
are found among many wild tribes ; the curious reader may be
referred to Lasch, S. pp. 7–13, and H. Ploss and M. Bartels, *Das Weib
in der Natur und Völkerkunde* (9th ed., Leipzig, 1908). The latter

says that the Suaheli system is not carried through so as to replace
the ordinary language, but the Suaheli have for every object which
they do not care to mention by its real name a symbolic word understood by everybody concerned. In especial such symbols are used
by women in their mysteries to denote obscene things. The words
chosen are either ordinary names for innocent things or else taken
from the old language or other Bantu languages, mostly Kiziguha,
for among the Waziguha secret rites play an enormous rôle. Bartels
finally says that with us, too, women have separate names for
everything connected with sexual life, and he thinks that it is the
same feeling of shame that underlies this custom and the interdiction of pronouncing the names of male relatives. This, however,
does not explain everything, and, as already indicated, superstition
certainly has a large share in this as in other forms of verbal tabu.
See on this the very full account in the third volume of Frazer's
The Golden Bough.

XIII.—§ 3. Competing Languages.

A difference between the language spoken by men and that
spoken by women is seen in many countries where two languages
are struggling for supremacy in a peaceful way—thus without any
question of one nation exterminating the other or the male part
of it. Among German and Scandinavian immigrants in America
the men mix much more with the English-speaking population,
and therefore have better opportunities, and also more occasion, to
learn English than their wives, who remain more within doors.
It is exactly the same among the Basques, where the school, the
military service and daily business relations contribute to the
extinction of Basque in favour of French, and where these factors
operate much more strongly on the male than on the female population : there are families in which the wife talks Basque, while
the husband does not even understand Basque and does not allow
his children to learn it (Bornecque et Mühlen, *Les Provinces fran-
çaises*, 53). Vilhelm Thomsen informs me that the old Livonian
language, which is now nearly extinct, is kept up with the
greatest fidelity by the women, while the men are abandoning it
for Lettish. Albanian women, too, generally know only Albanian,
while the men are more often bilingual.

XIII.—§ 4. Sanskrit Drama.

There are very few traces of real sex dialects in our Aryan languages, though we have the very curious rule in the old Indian
drama that women talk Prakrit (*prākrta*, the natural or vulgar
language) while men have the privilege of talking Sanskrit (*sam-

skrta, the adorned language). The distinction, however, is not
one of sex really, but of rank, for Sanskrit is the language of gods,
kings, princes, brahmans, ministers, chamberlains, dancing-masters
and other men in superior positions and of a very few women of
special religious importance, while Prakrit is spoken by men of an
inferior class, like shopkeepers, law officers, aldermen, bathmen,
fishermen and policemen, and by nearly all women.   The difference
between the two 'languages' is one of degree only : they are two
strata of the same language, one higher, more solemn, stiff and
archaic, and another lower, more natural and familiar, and this easy,
or perhaps we should say slipshod, style is the only one recognized
for ordinary women. The difference may not be greater than that
between the language of a judge and that of a costermonger in a
modern novel, or between Juliet's and her nurse's expressions
in Shakespeare, and if all women, even those we should call the
'heroines' of the plays, use only the lower stratum of speech, the
reason certainly is that the social position of women was so inferior
that they ranked only with men of the lower orders and had no
share in the higher culture which, with the refined language, was
the privilege of a small class of selected men.

XIII.—§ 5. Conservatism.

As Prakrit is a 'younger' and 'worn-out' form of Sanskrit,
the question here naturally arises : What is the general attitude
of the two sexes to those changes that are constantly going on
in languages ? Can they be ascribed exclusively or predominantly
to one of the sexes ? Or do both equally participate in them ?
An answer that is very often given is that as a rule women are more
conservative than men, and that they do nothing more than keep
to the traditional language which they have learnt from their
parents and hand on to their children, while innovations are due
to the initiative of men. Thus Cicero in an often-quoted passage
says that when he hears his mother-in-law Lælia, it is to him as
if he heard Plautus or Nævius, for it is more natural for women to
keep the old language uncorrupted, as they do not hear many
people's way of speaking and thus retain what they have first learnt
(*De oratore*, III. 45). This, however, does not hold good in every
respect and in every people. The French engineer, Victor Renault,
who lived for a long time among the Botocudos (in South America)
and compiled vocabularies for two of their tribes, speaks of the
ease with which he could make the savages who accompanied him
invent new words for anything. " One of them called out the
word in a loud voice, as if seized by a sudden idea, and the others
would repeat it amid laughter and excited shouts, and then it

was universally adopted. But the curious thing is that it was nearly always the women who busied themselves in inventing new words as well as in composing songs, dirges and rhetorical essays. The word-formations here alluded to are probably names of objects that the Botocudos had not known previously . . . as for horse, *krainejoune*, ' head-teeth '; for ox, *po-kekri*, ' foot-cloven '; for donkey, *mgo-jonne-orône*, ' beast with long ears.' But well-known objects which have already got a name have often similar new denominations invented for them, which are then soon accepted by the family and community and spread more and more " (*v.* Martius, *Beitr. zur Ethnogr. u. Sprachenkunde Amerikas*, 1867, i. 330).

I may also quote what E. R. Edwards says in his *Étude phonétique de la langue japonaise* (Leipzig, 1903, p. 79) : " In France and in England it might be said that women avoid neologisms and are careful not to go too far away from the written forms : in Southern England the sound written *wh* [ʍ] is scarcely ever pronounced except in girls' schools. In Japan, on the contrary, women are less conservative than men, whether in pronunciation or in the selection of words and expressions. One of the chief reasons is that women have not to the same degree as men undergone the influence of the written language. As an example of the liberties which the women take may be mentioned that there is in the actual pronunciation of Tokyo a strong tendency to get rid of the sound (*w*), but the women go further in the word *atashi*, which men pronounce *watashi* or *watakshi*, ' I.' Another tendency noticed in the language of Japanese women is pretty widely spread among French and English women, namely, the excessive use of intensive words and the exaggeration of stress and tone-accent to mark emphasis. Japanese women also make a much more frequent use than men of the prefixes of politeness *o-*, *go-* and *mi-*."

XIII.—§ 6. Phonetics and Grammar.

In connexion with some of the phonetic changes which have profoundly modified the English sound system we have express statements by old grammarians that women had a more advanced pronunciation than men, and characteristically enough these statements refer to the raising of the vowels in the direction of [i] ; thus in Sir Thomas Smith (1567), who uses expressions like " mulierculæ quædam delicatiores, et nonnulli qui volunt isto modo videri loqui urbanius," and in another place " fœminæ quædam delicatiores," further in Mulcaster (1582)[1] and in Milton's

---

[1] " *Ai* is the man's diphthong, and soundeth full : *ei*, the woman's, and soundeth finish [i.e. fineish] in the same both sense, and vse, *a woman is deintie, and feinteth soon, the man fainteth not bycause he is nothing daintie.*" Thus what is now distinctive of refined as opposed to vulgar pronunciation was then characteristic of the fair sex.

teacher, Alexander Gill (1621), who speaks about "nostræ Mopsæ, quæ quidem ita omnia attenuant."

In France, about 1700, women were inclined to pronounce *e* instead of *a*; thus Alemand (1688) mentions *Barnabé* as "façon de prononcer mâle" and *Bernabé* as the pronunciation of "les gens polis et délicats . . . les dames surtout"; and Grimarest (1712) speaks of "ces marchandes du Palais, qui au lieu de *madame, boulevart*, etc., prononcent *medeme, boulevert*" (Thurot i. 12 and 9).

There is one change characteristic of many languages in which it seems as if women have played an important part even if they are not solely responsible for it : I refer to the weakening of the old fully trilled tongue-point *r*. I have elsewhere (*Fonetik*, p. 417 ff.) tried to show that this weakening, which results in various sounds and sometimes in a complete omission of the sound in some positions, is in the main a consequence of, or at any rate favoured by, a change in social life : the old loud trilled point sound is natural and justified when life is chiefly carried on out-of-doors, but indoor life prefers, on the whole, less noisy speech habits, and the more refined this domestic life is, the more all kinds of noises and even speech sounds will be toned down. One of the results is that this original *r* sound, the rubadub in the orchestra of language, is no longer allowed to bombard the ears, but is softened down in various ways, as we see chiefly in the great cities and among the educated classes, while the rustic population in many countries keeps up the old sound with much greater conservatism. Now we find that women are not unfrequently mentioned in connexion with this reduction of the trilled *r*; thus in the sixteenth century in France there was a tendency to leave off the trilling and even to go further than to the present English untrilled point *r* by pronouncing [z] instead, but some of the old grammarians mention this pronunciation as characteristic of women and a few men who imitate women (Erasmus : mulierculæ Parisinæ ; Sylvius : mulierculæ . . . Parrhisinæ, et earum modo quidam parum viri ; Pillot : Parisinæ mulierculæ . . . adeo delicatulæ sunt, ut pro *pere* dicant *pese*). In the ordinary language there are a few remnants of this tendency; thus, when by the side of the original *chaire* we now have also the form *chaise*, and it is worthy of note that the latter form is reserved for the everyday signification (Engl. chair, seat) as belonging more naturally to the speech of women, while *chaire* has the more special signification of 'pulpit, professorial chair.' Now the same tendency to substitute [z]—or after a voiceless sound [s]—for *r* is found in our own days among the ladies of Christiania, who will say *gzuelig* for *gruelig* and *fsygtelig* for *frygtelig* (Brekke, *Bidrag til dansknorskens lydlære*, 1881, p. 17 ; I have often heard the sound myself). And even in far-off Siberia we find that the Chuckchi women will say

nídzak or *nízak* for the male *nirak* ' two,' *zërka* for *rërka* ' walrus,'
etc. (Nordqvist ; see fuller quotations in my *Fonetik*, p. 431).

In present-day English there are said to be a few differences
in pronunciation between the two sexes ; thus, according to Daniel
Jones, *soft* is pronounced with a long vowel [soˑft] by men and with
a short vowel [soft] by women ; similarly [gɛel] is said to be a
special ladies' pronunciation of *girl*, which men usually pronounce
[gəˑl] ; cf. also on *wh* above, p. 243.   So far as I have been able to
ascertain, the pronunciation [tʃuldrən] for [tʃildrən] *children* is
much more frequent in women than in men.   It may also be that
women are more inclined to give to the word *waistcoat* the full
long sound in both syllables, while men, who have occasion to
use the word more frequently, tend to give it the historical form
[weskət] (for the shortening compare *breakfast*).   But even if such
observations were multiplied—as probably they might easily be
by an attentive observer—they would be only more or less isolated
instances, without any deeper significance, and on the whole we
must say that from the phonetic point of view there is scarcely
any difference between the speech of men and that of women : the
two sexes speak for all intents and purposes the same language.

XIII.—§ 7. Choice of Words.

But when from the field of phonetics we come to that of vocabulary and style, we shall find a much greater number of differences,
though they have received very little attention in linguistic works.
A few have been mentioned by Greenough and Kittredge : " The
use of *common* in the sense of ' vulgar ' is distinctly a feminine
peculiarity.   It would sound effeminate in the speech of a man.   So,
in a less degree, with *person* for ' woman,' in contrast to ' lady.'
Nice for ' fine ' must have originated in the same way " (W, p. 54).

Others have told me that men will generally say ' It's very
good of you,' where women will say ' It's very *kind* of you.'
But such small details can hardly be said to be really characteristic
of the two sexes.   There is no doubt, however, that women in all
countries are shy of mentioning certain parts of the human body
and certain natural functions by the direct and often rude denominations which men, and especially young men, prefer when among
themselves.   Women will therefore invent innocent and euphemistic
words and paraphrases, which sometimes may in the long run come
to be looked upon as the plain or blunt names, and therefore in their
turn have to be avoided and replaced by more decent words.

In Pinero's *The Gay Lord Quex* (p. 116) a lady discovers some
French novels on the table of another lady, and says : " This is
a little—h'm—isn't it ? "—she does not even dare to say the word

'indecent,' and has to express the idea in inarticulate language. The word 'naked' is paraphrased in the following description by a woman of the work of girls in ammunition works : " They have to take off every stitch from their bodies in one room, and run *in their innocence and nothing else* to another room where the special clothing is " (Bennett, *The Pretty Lady*, 176).

On the other hand, the old-fashioned prudery which prevented ladies from using such words as *legs* and *trousers* (" those manly garments which are rarely mentioned by name," says Dickens, *Dombey*, 335) is now rightly looked upon as exaggerated and more or less comical (cf. my GS § 247).

There can be no doubt that women exercise a great and universal influence on linguistic development through their instinctive shrinking from coarse and gross expressions and their preference for refined and (in certain spheres) veiled and indirect expressions. In most cases that influence will be exercised privately and in the bosom of the family ; but there is one historical instance in which a group of women worked in that direction publicly and collectively ; I refer to those French ladies who in the seventeenth century gathered in the Hôtel de Rambouillet and are generally known under the name of *Précieuses*. They discussed questions of spelling and of purity of pronunciation and diction, and favoured all kinds of elegant paraphrases by which coarse and vulgar words might be avoided. In many ways this movement was the counterpart of the literary wave which about that time was inundating Europe under various names—Gongorism in Spain, Marinism in Italy, Euphuism in England ; but the Précieuses went further than their male confrères in desiring to influence everyday language. When, however, they used such expressions as, for ' nose,' ' the door of the brain,' for ' broom ' ' the instrument of cleanness,' and for ' shirt ' ' the constant companion of the dead and the living' (la compagne perpétuelle des morts et des vivants), and many others, their affectation called down on their heads a ripple of laughter, and their endeavours would now have been forgotten but for the immortal satire of Molière in *Les Précieuses ridicules* and *Les Femmes savantes*. But apart from such exaggerations the feminine point of view is unassailable, and there is reason to congratulate those nations, the English among them, in which the social position of women has been high enough to secure greater purity and freedom from coarseness in language than would have been the case if men had been the sole arbiters of speech.

Among the things women object to in language must be specially mentioned anything that smacks of swearing[1]; where a man will

---

[1] There are great differences with regard to swearing between different nations ; but I think that in those countries and in those circles in which

say " He told an infernal lie," a women will rather say, " He told a most dreadful fib." Such euphemistic substitutes for the simple word ' hell ' as ' the other place,' ' a very hot ' or ' a very uncomfortable place ' probably originated with women. They will also use *ever* to add emphasis to an interrogative pronoun, as in " Whoever told you that ? " or " Whatever do you mean ? " and avoid the stronger ' who the devil ' or ' what the dickens.' For surprise we have the feminine exclamations ' Good gracious,' ' Gracious me,' ' Goodness gracious,' ' Dear me ' by the side of the more masculine ' Good heavens,' ' Great Scott.' ' To be sure ' is said to be more frequent with women than with men. Such instances might be multiplied, but these may suffice here. It will easily be seen that we have here civilized counterparts of what was above mentioned as sexual tabu ; but it is worth noting that the interdiction in these cases is ordained by the women themselves, or perhaps rather by the older among them, while the young do not always willingly comply.

Men will certainly with great justice object that there is a danger of the language becoming languid and insipid if we are always to content ourselves with women's expressions, and that vigour and vividness count for something. Most boys and many men have a dislike to some words merely because they feel that they are used by everybody and on every occasion : they want to avoid what is commonplace and banal and to replace it by new and fresh expressions, whose very newness imparts to them a flavour of their own. Men thus become the chief renovators of language, and to them are due those changes by which we sometimes see one term replace an older one, to give way in turn to a still newer one, and so on. Thus we see in English that the old verb *weorpan*, corresponding to G. *werfen*, was felt as too weak and therefore supplanted by *cast*, which was taken from Scandinavian ; after some centuries *cast* was replaced by the stronger *throw*, and this now, in the parlance of boys especially, is giving way to stronger expressions like *chuck* and *fling*. The old verbs, or at any rate *cast*, may be retained in certain applications, more particularly in some fixed combinations and in figurative significations, but it is now hardly possible to say, as Shakespeare does, " They cast their caps up." Many such innovations on their first appearance are counted as slang, and some never make their way into received speech ; but I am not in this connexion concerned with the distinction between slang

swearing is common it is found much more extensively among men than among women : this at any rate is true of Denmark. There is, however, a general social movement against swearing, and now there are many men who never swear. A friend writes to me : "The best English men hardly swear at all. . . . I imagine some of our fashionable women now swear as much as the men they consort with."

and recognized language, except in so far as the inclination or
disinclination to invent and to use slang is undoubtedly one of the
"human secondary sexual characters." This is not invalidated
by the fact that quite recently, with the rise of the feminist movement, many young ladies have begun to imitate their brothers in
that as well as in other respects.

XIII.—§ 8. Vocabulary.

This trait is indissolubly connected with another : the vocabulary
of a woman as a rule is much less extensive than that of a man.
Women move preferably in the central field of language, avoiding
everything that is out of the way or bizarre, while men will often
either coin new words or expressions or take up old-fashioned ones,
if by that means they are enabled, or think they are enabled, to
find a more adequate or precise expression for their thoughts.
Woman as a rule follows the main road of language, where man is
often inclined to turn aside into a narrow footpath or even to strike
out a new path for himself. Most of those who are in the habit
of reading books in foreign languages will have experienced a much
greater average difficulty in books written by male than by female
authors, because they contain many more rare words, dialect words,
technical terms, etc. Those who want to learn a foreign language
will therefore always do well at the first stage to read many ladies'
novels, because they will there continually meet with just those
everyday words and combinations which the foreigner is above
all in need of, what may be termed the indispensable small-change
of a language.

This may be partly explicable from the education of women,
which has up to quite recent times been less comprehensive and
technical than that of men. But this does not account for everything, and certain experiments made by the American professor
Jastrow would tend to show that we have here a trait that is independent of education. He asked twenty-five university students
of each sex, belonging to the same class and thus in possession of
the same preliminary training, to write down as rapidly as possible a
hundred words, and to record the time. Words in sentences were
not allowed. There were thus obtained 5,000 words, and of these
many were of course the same. But the community of thought
was greater in the women ; while the men used 1,375 different
words, their female class-mates used only 1,123. Of 1,266 unique
words used, 29·8 per cent. were male, only 20·8 per cent. female.
The group into which the largest number of the men's words fell
was the animal kingdom ; the group into which the largest number
of the women's words fell was wearing apparel and fabrics ; while

the men used only 53 words belonging to the class of foods, the women used 179. "In general the feminine traits revealed by this study are an attention to the immediate surroundings, to the finished product, to the ornamental, the individual, and the concrete; while the masculine preference is for the more remote, the constructive, the useful, the general and the abstract." (See Havelock Ellis, *Man and Woman*, 4th ed., London, 1904, p. 189.)

Another point mentioned by Jastrow is the tendency to select words that rime and alliterative words; both these tendencies were decidedly more marked in men than in women. This shows what we may also notice in other ways, that men take greater interest in words as such and in their acoustic properties, while women pay less attention to that side of words and merely take them as they are, as something given once for all. Thus it comes that some men are confirmed punsters, while women are generally slow to see any point in a pun and scarcely ever perpetrate one themselves. Or, to get to something of greater value : the science of language has very few votaries among women, in spite of the fact that foreign languages, long before the reform of female education, belonged to those things which women learnt best in and out of schools, because, like music and embroidery, they were reckoned among the specially feminine ' accomplishments.'

Woman is linguistically quicker than man : quicker to learn, quicker to hear, and quicker to answer. A man is slower : he hesitates, he chews the cud to make sure of the taste of words, and thereby comes to discover similarities with and differences from other words, both in sound and in sense, thus preparing himself for the appropriate use of the fittest noun or adjective.

XIII.—§ 9. Adverbs.

While there are a few adjectives, such as *pretty* and *nice*, that might be mentioned as used more extensively by women than by men, there are greater differences with regard to adverbs. Lord Chesterfield wrote (*The World*, December 5, 1754) : "Not contented with enriching our language by words absolutely new, my fair countrywomen have gone still farther, and improved it by the application and extension of old ones to various and very different significations. They take a word and change it, like a guinea into shillings for pocket-money, to be employed in the several occasional purposes of the day. For instance, the adjective *vast* and its adverb *vastly* mean anything, and are the fashionable words of the most fashionable people. A fine woman . . . is *vastly* obliged, or *vastly* offended, *vastly* glad, or *vastly* sorry. Large objects are *vastly* great, small ones are *vastly* little ; and I had lately the pleasure to hear a fine woman pronounce, by a happy metonymy, a very small gold snuff-box, that was produced in company, to be *vastly* pretty, because it was so *vastly* little." Even if that particular adverb to which Lord Chesterfield objected has now to a great extent gone out of fashion, there is no doubt that he has here touched on a distinctive trait : the fondness of women for hyperbole will very often lead the fashion with regard to adverbs of intensity, and these are very often used with disregard of their proper meaning, as in German *riesig klein*, English *awfully pretty*, *terribly nice*, French *rudement joli*, *affreusement délicieux*, Danish *rœdsom morsom* (horribly amusing), Russian *strast' kakoy lovkiy* (terribly able), etc. *Quite*, also, in the sense of ' very,' as in ' she was quite charming ; it makes me quite angry,' is, according to Fitzedward Hall, due to the ladies. And I suspect that *just sweet* (as in Barrie : " Grizel thought it was just sweet of him ") is equally characteristic of the usage of the fair sex.

There is another intensive which has also something of the eternally feminine about it, namely *so*. I am indebted to Stoffel (Int. 101) for the following quotation from *Punch* (January 4, 1896) : " This little adverb is a great favourite with ladies, in conjunction with an adjective. For instance, they are very fond of using such expressions as ' He is *so* charming ! ' ' It is *so* lovely ! ' etc." Stoffel adds the following instances of strongly intensive *so* as highly characteristic of ladies' usage : ' Thank you *so* much ! ' ' It was *so* kind of you to think of it ! ' ' That's *so* like you ! ' ' I'm *so* glad you've come ! ' ' The bonnet is *so* lovely ! '

The explanation of this characteristic feminine usage is, I think, that women much more often than men break off without finishing their sentences, because they start talking without having thought out what they are going to say ; the sentence ' I'm so glad you've come ' really requires some complement in the shape of a clause with *that*, ' so glad that I really must kiss you,' or, ' so glad that I must treat you to something extra,' or whatever the consequence may be. But very often it is difficult in a hurry to hit upon something adequate to say, and ' so glad that I cannot express it ' frequently results in the inexpressible remaining unexpressed, and when that experiment has been repeated time after time, the linguistic-consequence is that a strongly stressed *so* acquires the force of ' very much indeed.' It is the same with *such*, as in the following two extracts from a modern novel (in both it is a lady who is speaking) : " Poor Kitty ! she has been in *such* a state of mind," and " Do you know that you look *such* a duck this afternoon. . . . This hat suits you *so*—you are *such* a *grande dame* in it." Exactly the same thing has happened with Danish *så* and *sådan*,

G. *so* and *solch* ; also with French *tellement,* though there perhaps
not to the same extent as in English.

We have the same phenomenon with *to a degree,* which properly
requires to be supplemented with something that tells us what
the degree is, but is frequently left by itself, as in ' His second
marriage was irregular to a degree.'

XIII.—§ 10. Periods.

The frequency with which women thus leave their exclamatory
sentences half-finished might be exemplified from many passages
in our novelists and dramatists. I select a few quotations.
The first is from the beginning of *Vanity Fair* : " This almost caused
Jemima to faint with terror. ' Well, I never,' said she. ' What
an audacious '—emotion prevented her from completing either
sentence." Next from one of Hankin's plays. " Mrs. Eversleigh :
I must say ! (but words fail her)." And finally from Compton
Mackenzie's *Poor Relations* : " ' The trouble you must have taken,'
Hilda exclaimed." These quotations illustrate types of sentences
which are becoming so frequent that they would seem soon to
deserve a separate chapter in modern grammars, ' Did you ever ? '
' Well, I never ! ' being perhaps the most important of these
' stop-short ' or ' pull-up ' sentences, as I think they might be
termed.

These sentences are the linguistic symptoms of a peculiarity
of feminine psychology which has not escaped observation. Mere-
dith says of one of his heroines : " She thought in blanks, as girls
do, and some women," and Hardy singularizes one of his by calling
her " that novelty among women—one who finished a thought
before beginning the sentence which was to convey it."

The same point is seen in the typical way in which the two
sexes build up their sentences and periods ; but here, as so often
in this chapter, we cannot establish absolute differences, but
only preferences that may be broken in a great many instances
and yet are characteristic of the sexes as such. If we compare
long periods as constructed by men and by women, we shall in the
former find many more instances of intricate or involute structures
with clause within clause, a relative clause in the middle of a con-
ditional clause or vice versa, with subordination and sub-subordina-
tion, while the typical form of long feminine periods is that of
co-ordination, one sentence or clause being added to another on the
same plane and the gradation between the respective ideas being
marked not grammatically, but emotionally, by stress and intonation, and in writing by underlining. In learned terminology we
may say that men are fond of hypotaxis and women of parataxis.

Or we may use the simile that a male period is often like a set of Chinese boxes, one within another, while a feminine period is like a set of pearls joined together on a string of *ands* and similar words. In a Danish comedy a young girl is relating what has happened to her at a ball, when she is suddenly interrupted by her brother, who has slyly taken out his watch and now exclaims : " I declare ! you have said *and then* fifteen times in less than two and a half minutes."

XIII.—§ 11. General Characteristics.

The greater rapidity of female thought is shown linguistically, among other things, by the frequency with which a woman will use a pronoun like *he* or *she*, not of the person last mentioned, but of somebody else to whom her thoughts have already wandered, while a man with his slower intellect will think that she is still moving on the same path. The difference in rapidity of perception has been tested experimentally by Romanes : the same paragraph was presented to various well-educated persons, who were asked to read it as rapidly as they could, ten seconds being allowed for twenty lines. As soon as the time was up the paragraph was removed, and the reader immediately wrote down all that he or she could remember of it. It was found that women were usually more successful than men in this test. Not only were they able to read more quickly than the men, but they were able to give a better account of the paragraph as a whole. One lady, for instance, could read exactly four times as fast as her husband, and even then give a better account than he of that small portion of the paragraph he had alone been able to read. But it was found that this rapidity was no proof of intellectual power, and some of the slowest readers were highly distinguished men. Ellis (*Man and W.* 195) explains this in this way : with the quick reader it is as though every statement were admitted immediately and without inspection to fill the vacant chambers of the mind, while with the slow reader every statement undergoes an instinctive process of cross-examination ; every new fact seems to stir up the accumulated stores of facts among which it intrudes, and so impedes rapidity of mental action.

This reminds me of one of Swift's " Thoughts on Various Subjects " : " The common fluency of speech in many men, and most women, is owing to the scarcity of matter, and scarcity of words ; for whoever is a master of language, and hath a mind full of ideas, will be apt in speaking to hesitate upon the choice of both : whereas common speakers have only one set of ideas, and one set of words to clothe them in ; and these are always ready at the mouth. So people come faster out of a church when it is almost empty, than when a crowd is at the door " (*Works*, Dublin, 1735, i. 305).

The volubility of women has been the subject of innumerable jests : it has given rise to popular proverbs in many countries,[1] as well as to Aurora Leigh's resigned " A woman's function plainly is—to talk " and Oscar Wilde's sneer, " Women are a decorative sex. They never have anything to say, but they say it charmingly." A woman's thought is no sooner formed than uttered. Says Rosalind, " Do you not know I am a woman ? when I think, I must speak " (*As You Like It*, III. 2. 264). And in a modern novel a young girl says : " I talk so as to find out what I think. Don't you ? Some things one can't judge of till one hears them spoken " (Housman, *John of Jingalo*, 346).

The superior readiness of speech of women is a concomitant of the fact that their vocabulary is smaller and more central than that of men. But this again is connected with another indubitable fact, that women do not reach the same extreme points as men, but are nearer the average in most respects. Havelock Ellis, who establishes this in various fields, rightly remarks that the statement that genius is undeniably of more frequent occurrence among men than among women has sometimes been regarded by women as a slur upon their sex, but that it does not appear that women have been equally anxious to find fallacies in the statement that idiocy is more common among men. Yet the two statements must be taken together. Genius is more common among men by virtue of the same general tendency by which idiocy is more common among men. The two facts are but two aspects of a larger zoological fact—the greater variability of the male (*Man and W.* 420).

In language we see this very clearly : the highest linguistic genius and the lowest degree of linguistic imbecility are very rarely found among women. The greatest orators, the most famous literary artists, have been men ; but it may serve as a sort of consolation to the other sex that there are a much greater number of men than of women who cannot put two words together intelligibly, who stutter and stammer and hesitate, and are unable to find suitable expressions for the simplest thought. Between these two extremes the woman moves with a sure and supple tongue which is ever ready to find words and to pronounce them in a clear and intelligible manner.

---

[1] " Où femme y a, silence n'y a." " Deux femmes font un plaid, trois un grand caquet, quatre un plein marché." " Due donne e un' oca fanno una fiera " (Venice). " The tongue is the sword of a woman, and she never lets it become rusty " (China). " The North Sea will sooner be found wanting in water than a woman at a loss for a word " (Jutland).

Nor are the reasons far to seek why such differences should have developed. They are mainly dependent on the division of labour enjoined in primitive tribes and to a great extent also among more civilized peoples   For thousands of years the work that especially fell to men was such as demanded an intense display of energy for a comparatively short period, mainly in war and in hunting. Here, however, there was not much occasion to talk, nay, in many circumstances talk might even be fraught with danger. And when that rough work was over, the man would either sleep or idle his time away, inert and torpid, more or less in silence. Woman, on the other hand, had a number of domestic occupations which did not claim such an enormous output of spasmodic energy. To her was at first left not only agriculture, and a great deal of other work which in more peaceful times was taken over by men ; but also much that has been till quite recently her almost exclusive concern—the care of the children, cooking, brewing, baking, sewing, washing, etc.,—things which for the most part demanded no deep thought, which were performed in company and could well be accompanied with a lively chatter. Lingering effects of this state of things are seen still, though great social changes are going on in our times which may eventually modify even the linguistic relations of the two sexes.

CHAPTER XIV

CAUSES OF CHANGE

XIV.—§ 1. Anatomy.

In accordance with the programme laid down in the opening paragraph of Book III, we shall now deal in detail with those linguistic changes which are not due to transference to new individuals. The chapter on woman's language has served as a kind of bridge between the two main divisions, in so far as the first sections treated of those women's dialects which were, or were supposed to be, due to the influence of foreigners.

Many theories have been advanced to explain the indubitable fact that languages change in course of time. Some scholars have thought that there ought to be one fundamental cause working in all instances, while others, more sensibly, have maintained that a variety of causes have been and are at work, and that it is not easy to determine which of them has been decisive in each observed case of change. The greatest attention has been given to phonetic change, and in reading some theorists one might almost fancy that sounds were the only thing changeable, or at any rate that phonetic changes were the only ones in language which had to be accounted for. Let us now examine some of the theories advanced.

Sometimes it is asserted that sound changes must have their cause in changes in the anatomical structure of the articulating organs. This theory, however, need not detain us long (see the able discussion in Oertel, p. 194 ff.), for no facts have been alleged to support it, and one does not see why small anatomical variations should cause changes so long as any teacher of languages on the phonetic method is able to teach his pupils practically every speech sound, even those that their own native language has been without for centuries. Besides, many phonetic changes do not at all lead to new sounds being developed or old ones lost, but simply to the old sounds being used in new places or disused in some of the places where they were formerly found. Some tribes have a custom of mutilating their lips or teeth, and that of course must have caused changes in their pronunciation, which are said to have persisted even after the custom was given up. Thus, according to Meinhof (MSA 60) the Yao women insert a big wooden disk within the upper lip, which makes it impossible for them to pronounce [f], and as it is the women that teach their children to speak, the sound of [f] has disappeared from the language, though now it is beginning to reappear in loan-words. It is clear, however, that such customs can have exercised only the very slightest influence on language in general.

XIV.—§ 2. Geography.

Some scholars have believed in an influence exercised by climatic or geographical conditions on the character of the sound system, instancing as evidence the harsh consonants found in the languages of the Caucasus as contrasted with the pleasanter sounds heard in regions more favoured by nature. But this influence cannot be established as a general rule. "The aboriginal inhabitants of the north-west coast of America found subsistence relatively easy in a country abounding in many forms of edible marine life ; nor can they be said to have been subjected to rigorous climatic conditions ; yet in phonetic harshness their languages rival those of the Caucasus. On the other hand, perhaps no people has ever been subjected to a more forbidding physical environment than the Eskimos, yet the Eskimo language not only impresses one as possessed of a relatively agreeable phonetic system when compared with the languages of the north-west coast, but may even be thought to compare favourably with American Indian languages generally " (Sapir, *American Anthropologist*, XIV (1912), 234). It would also on this theory be difficult to account for the very considerable linguistic changes which have taken place in historical times in many countries whose climate, etc., cannot during the same period have changed correspondingly.

A geographical theory of sound-shifting was advanced by Heinrich Meyer-Benfey in *Zeitschr. f. deutsches Altert.* 45 (1901), and has recently been taken up by H. Collitz in *Amer. Journal of Philol.* 39 (1918), p. 413. Consonant shifting is chiefly found in mountain regions ; this is most obvious in the High German shift, which started from the Alpine district of Southern Germany. After leaving the region of the high mountains it gradually decreases in strength ; yet it keeps on extending, with steadily diminishing energy, over part of the area of the Franconian dialects. But having reached the plains of Northern Germany, the movement stops. The same theory applies to languages in which a similar shifting is found, e.g. Old and Modern Armenian, the Soho language in South Africa, etc. "However strange it may appear at the first glance," says Collitz, "that certain consonant changes should depend on geographical surroundings, the connexion is easily understood. The change of media to tenuis and that of tenuis to affricate or aspirate are linked together by a common feature, viz. an increase in the intensity of expiration. As the common cause of both these shiftings we may therefore regard a change in the manner in which breath is used for pronunciation. The habitual use of a larger volume of breath means an increased activity of the lungs. Here we have reached the point where the connexion with geographical or climatic conditions is clear, because nobody will deny that residence in the mountains, especially in the high mountains, stimulates the lungs."

When this theory was first brought to my notice, I wrote a short footnote on it (PhG 176), in which I treated it with perhaps too little respect, merely mentioning the fact that my countrymen, the Danes, in their flat country were developing exactly the same shift as the High Germans (making p, t, k into strongly aspirated or affricated sounds and unvoicing b, d, g) ; I then asked ironically whether that might be a consequence of the indubitable fact that an increasing number of Danes every summer go to Switzerland and Norway for their holidays. And even now, after the theory has been endorsed by so able an advocate as Collitz, I fail to see how it can hold water. The induction seems faulty on both sides, for the shift is found among peoples living in plains, and on the other hand it is not shared by all mountain peoples—for example, not by the Italian and Ladin speaking neighbours of the High Germans in the Alps. Besides, the physiological explanation is not impeccable, for walking in the mountains affects the way in which we breathe, that is, it primarily affects the lungs, but the change in the consonants is primarily one not in the lungs, but in the glottis ; as the connexion between these two things is not necessary, the whole reasoning is far from being cogent. At any rate, the theory can only with great difficulty be applied to the first Gothonic shift, for how do we know that that started in mountainous regions ? and who knows whether the sounds actually found as f, $þ$ and h for original p, t, k, had first been aspirated and affricated stops ? It seems much more probable that the transition was a direct one, through slackening and opening of the stoppage, but in that case it has nothing to do with the lungs or way of breathing.

XIV.—§ 3. National Psychology.

We are much more likely to ' burn,' as the children say, when, instead of looking for the cause in such outward circumstances, we try to find it in the psychology of those who initiate the change. But this does not amount to endorsing all the explanations of this kind which have found favour with linguists. Thus, since the times of Grimm it has been usual to ascribe the well-known consonant shift to psychological traits believed to be characteristic of the Germans. Grimm says that the sound shift is a consequence of the progressive tendency and desire of liberty found in the Germans (GDS 292) ; it is due to their courage and pride in the period of the great migration of tribes (ib. 306) : "When quiet and morality returned, the sounds remained, and it may be reckoned as evidence of the superior gentleness and modera-tion of the Gothic, Saxon and Scandinavian tribes that they contented themselves with the first shift, while the wilder force of the High Germans was impelled to the second shift." (Thus also Westphal.) Curtius finds energy and juvenile vigour in the Germanic sound shift (KZ 2. 331, 1852). Müllenhof saw in the transition from p, t, k to f, $\flat$, h a sign of weakening, the Germans having apparently lost the power of pronouncing the hard stops ; while further, the giving up of the aspirated ph, th, kh, bh, dh, gh was due to enervation or indolence. But the succeeding transition from the old b, d, g to p, t, k showed that they had afterwards pulled themselves together to new exertions, and the regularity with which all these changes were carried through evidenced a great steadiness and persevering force (*Deutsche Altcr-tumsk.* 2. 197). His disciple Wilhelm Scherer saw in the whole history of the German language alternating periods of rise and decline in popular taste ; he looked upon sound changes from the æsthetic point of view and ascribed the (second) consonant shift to a feminine period in which consonants were neglected because the nation took pleasure in vocalic sounds.

XIV.—§ 4. Speed of Utterance.

Wundt gives a different though somewhat related explanation of the Germanic shift as due to a "revolution in culture, as the subjugation of a native population through warlike immi-grants, with resulting new organization of the State " (S 1. 424) : this increased the speed of utterance, and he tries in detail to show that increased speed leads naturally to just those changes in consonants which are found in the Gothonic shift (1. 420 ff.). But even if we admit that the average speed of talking (tempo der rede) is now probably greater than formerly, the whole theory is built up on so many doubtful or even manifestly incorrect details both in linguistic history and in general phonetic theory that it cannot be accepted. It does not account for the actual facts of the consonant shifts ; moreover, it is difficult to see why such phenomena as this shift, if they were dependent on the speed of utterance, should occur only at these particular historical times and within comparatively narrow geographical limits, for there is much to be said for the view that in all periods the speech of the Western nations has been constantly gaining in rapidity as life in general has become accelerated, and in no period probably more than during the last century, which has witnessed no radical consonant shift in any of the leading civilized nations.

XIV.—§ 5. Periods of Rapid Change.

All these theories, different though they are in detail, have this in common, that they endeavour to explain one particular change, or set of changes, from one particular psychological trait supposed to be prevalent at the time when the change took place, but they fail because we are not able scientifically to demonstrate any intimate connexion between the pronunciation of particular sounds and a certain state of mind, and also because our knowledge of the fluctuations of collective psychology is still so very imperfect. But it is interesting to contrast these theories with the explanation of the very same sound shifts mentioned in a previous chapter (XI), and there shown to be equally unsatisfactory, the explanation, namely, that the fundamental cause of the consonant shift is to be found in the peculiar pronunciation of an aboriginal population. In both cases the Gothonic shifts are singled out, because since the time of Grimm the attention of scholars has been focused on these changes more than on any others—they are looked upon as changes *sui generis*, and therefore requiring a special explanation, such as is not thought necessary in the case of the innumerable minor changes that fill most of the pages of the phonological section of any historical grammar. But the sober truth seems to be that these shifts are not different in kind from those that have made, say, Fr. *sève, frère, chien, ciel, faire, changer* out of Lat. *sapa, fratrem, canem, kœlum, fakere, cambiare*, etc., or those that have changed the English vowels in *fate, feet, fight, foot, out* from what they were when the letters which denote them still had their 'continental' values. Our main endeavour, therefore, must be to find out general reasons why sounds should not always remain unchanged. This seems more important, at any rate as a preliminary investigation, than attempting offhand to assign particular reasons why in such and such a century this or that sound was changed in some particular way.

If, however, we find a particular period especially fertile in linguistic changes (phonetic, morphological, semantic, or all at once), it is quite natural that we should turn our attention to the social state of the community at that time in order, if possible, to discover some specially favouring circumstances. I am thinking especially of two kinds of condition which may operate. In the first place, the influence of parents, and grown-up people generally, may be less than usual, because an unusual number of parents may be away from home, as in great wars of long duration, or may have been killed off, as in the great plagues ; cf. also what was said above of children left to shift for themselves in certain favoured regions of North America (Ch. X § 7). Secondly, there may be periods in which the ordinary restraints on linguistic change make themselves less felt than usual, because the whole community is animated by a strong feeling of independence and wants to break loose from social ties of many kinds, including those of a powerful school organization or literary tradition. This probably was the case with North America in the latter half of the eighteenth century, when the new nation wished to manifest its independence of old England and therefore, among other things, was inclined to throw overboard that respect for linguistic authority which under normal conditions makes for conservatism. If the divergence between American and British English is not greater than it actually is, this is probably due partly to the continual influx of immigrants from the old country, and partly to that increased facility of communication between the two countries in recent times which has made mutual linguistic influence possible to an extent formerly undreamt-of. But in the case of the Romanic languages both of the conditions mentioned were operating : during the centuries in which they were framed and underwent the strongest differentiation, wars with the intruding ' barbarians ' and a series of destructive plagues kept away or killed a great many grown-up people, and at the same time each country released itself from the centralizing influence of Rome, which in the first centuries of the Christian era had been very powerful in keeping up a fairly uniform and conservative pronunciation and phraseology throughout the whole Empire.[1] There were thus at that time various forces at work which, taken together, are quite sufficient to explain the wide

---

[1] The uniformity in the speech of the whole Roman Empire during the first centuries of our Christian era was kept up, among other things, through the habit of removing soldiers and officials from one country to the other. This ceased later, each district being left to shift more or less for itself.

divergence in linguistic structure that separated French, Provençal, Spanish, etc., from classical Latin (cf. above, XI § 8, p. 206).

In the history of English, one of the periods most fertile in change is the fourteenth and fifteenth centuries : the wars with France, the Black Death (which is said to have killed off about one-third of the population) and similar pestilences, insurrections like those of Wat Tyler and Jack Cade, civil wars like those of the Roses, decimated the men and made home-life difficult and unsettled. In the Scandinavian languages the Viking age is probably the period that witnessed the greatest linguistic changes —if I am right, not, as has sometimes been said, on account of the heroic character of the period and the violent rise in self-respect or self-assertion, but for the more prosaic reason that the men were absent and the women had other things to attend to than their children's linguistic education. I am also inclined to think that the unparalleled rapidity with which, during the last hundred years, the vulgar speech of English cities has been differentiated from the language of the educated classes (nearly all long vowels being shifted, etc.) finds its natural explanation in the unexampled misery of child-life among industrial workers in the first half of the last century—one of the most disgraceful blots on our overpraised civilization.

XIV.—§ 6. The Ease Theory.

If we now turn to the actuating principles that determine the general changeability of human speech habits, we shall find that the moving power everywhere is an impetus starting from the individual, and that there is a curbing power in the mere fact that language exists not for the individual alone, but for the whole community. The whole history of language is, as it were, a tug-of-war between these two principles, each of which gains victories in turn.

First of all we must make up our minds with regard to the disputed question whether the changes of language go in the direction of greater ease, in other words, whether they manifest a tendency towards economy of effort. The prevalent opinion among the older school was that the chief tendency was, in Whitney's words, " to make things easy to our organs of speech, to economize time and effort in the work of expression " (L 28). Curtius very emphatically states that " Bequemlichkeit ist und bleibt der hauptanlass des lautwandels unter allen umständen " (*Griech. etym.* 23 ; cf. C 7). But Leskien, Sievers, and since them other recent writers, hold the opposite view (see quotations and summaries in Oertel 204 f., Wechssler L 88 f.), and their view has prevailed to the extent that Sütterlin (WW 33) characterizes the old view as " empty talk," " a wrong scent," and " worthless subterfuges now rejected by our science."

Such strong words may, however, be out of place, for is it so very foolish to think that men in this, as in all other respects, tend to follow ' the line of least resistance ' and to get off with as little exertion as possible ?   The question is only whether this universal tendency can be shown to prevail in those phonetic changes which are dealt with in linguistic history.

Sütterlin thinks it enough to mention some sound changes in which the new sound is more difficult than the old ; these being admitted, he concludes (and others have said the same thing) that those other instances in which the new sound is evidently easier than the old one cannot be explained by the principle of ease. But it seems clear that this conclusion is not valid : the correct inference can only be that the tendency towards ease may be at work in some cases, though not in all, because there are other forces which may at times neutralize it or prove stronger than it.   We shall meet a similar all-or-nothing fallacy in the chapter on Sound Symbolism.

Now, it is sometimes said that natives do not feel any difficulty in the sounds of their own language, however difficult these may be to foreigners.   This is quite true if we speak of a *conscious* perception of this or that sound being difficult to produce ; but it is no less true that the act of speaking always requires some exertion, muscular as well as psychical, on the part of the speaker, and that he is therefore apt on many occasions to speak with as little effort as possible, often with the result that his voice is not loud enough, or that his words become indistinct if he does not move his tongue, lips, etc., with the required precision or force.   You may as well say that when once one has learnt the art of writing, it is no longer any effort to form one's letters properly ; and yet how many written communications do we not receive in which many of the letters are formed so badly that we can do little but guess from the context what each form is meant for ! There can be no doubt that the main direction of change in the development of our written alphabet has been towards forms requiring less and less exertion—and similar causes have led to analogous results in the development of spoken sounds.

It is not always easy to decide which of two articulations is the easier one, and opinions may in some instances differ—we may also find in two neighbouring nations opposite phonetic developments, each of which may perhaps be asserted by speakers of the language to be in the direction of greater ease.   " To judge of the difficulty of muscular activity, the muscular quantity at play cannot serve as an absolute measure. Is [d] absolutely more awkward to produce than [ð] ? When a man is running full tilt, it is under certain circumstances easier for him to rush against the wall than to stop suddenly at some distance from it : when the tongue is in motion, it may be easier for it to thrust itself against the roof of the mouth or the teeth, i.e. to form a stop (a plosive), than to halt at a millimetre's distance, i.e. to form a fricative " (Verner 78). In the same sense I wrote in 1904 : " Many an articulation which obviously requires greater muscular movements is yet easier of execution than another in which the movement is less, but has to be carried out with greater precision : it requires less effort to chip wood than to operate for cataract " (PhG 181).

In other cases, however, no such doubt is possible : [s], [f] or [x] require more muscular exertion than [h], and a replacement of one of them by [h] therefore necessarily means a lessening of effort. Now, I am firmly convinced that whenever a phonologist finds one of these oral fricatives standing regularly in one language against [h] in another, he will at once take the former sound to be the original and [h] to be the derived sound : an indisputable indication that the instinctive feeling of all linguists is still in favour of the view that a movement towards the easier sound is the rule, and not the exception.

In thus taking up the cudgels for the ease theory I am not afraid of hearing the objection that I ascribe too great power to human laziness, indolence, inertia, shirking, easygoingness, sloth, sluggishness, lack of energy, or whatever other beautiful synonyms have been invented for ' economy of effort ' or ' following the line of least resistance.' The fact remains that there *is* such a ' tendency ' in all human beings, and by taking it into account in explaining changes of sound we are doing nothing else than applying here the same principle that attributes many simplifications of form to ' analogy ' : we see the same psychological force at work in the two different domains of phonetics and morphology.

It is, of course, no serious objection to this view that if this had been always the direction of change, speaking must have been uncommonly troublesome to our earliest ancestors [1]—who says it wasn't ?—or that " if certain combinations were really irksome in themselves, why should they have been attempted at all ; why should they often have been maintained so long ? " (Oertel 204)—as if people at a remote age had been able to compare consciously two articulations and to choose the easier one !

---

[1] " Dass unsere ältesten vorfahren sich das sprechen erstaunlich unbequem gemacht haben," Delbrück, E 155.

Neither in language nor in any other activity has mankind at once hit upon the best or easiest expedients.

XIV.—§ 7. Sounds in Connected Speech.

In the great majority of linguistic changes we have to consider the ease or difficulty, not of the isolated sound, but of the sound in that particular conjunction with other sounds in which it occurs in words.[1] Thus in the numerous phenomena comprised under the name of assimilation. There is an interesting account in the *Proceedings of the Philological Society* (December 17, 1886) of a discussion of these problems, in which Sweet, while maintaining that " cases of saving of effort were very rare or non-existent " and that " all the ordinary sounds of language were about on a par as to difficulty of production," said that assimilation " sprang from the desire to save space in articulation and secure ease of transition. Thus *pn* became *pm*, or else *mn*." But in both these changes there is saving of effort, for in the former the movement of the tip of the tongue required for [n], and in the latter the movement of the soft palate required for [p], is done away with[2] : the term " saving of space " can have no other meaning than economy of muscular energy. And the same is true of what Sweet terms " saving of time," which he finds effected by dropping superfluous sounds, especially at the end of words, e.g. [g] after [ŋ] in E. *sing*. Here, of course, one articulation (of the velum) is saved—and this need not even be accompanied by the saving of any time, for in such cases the remaining sound is often lengthened so as to make up for the loss.[3]

If, then, all assimilations are to be counted as instances of saving of effort, it is worth noting that a great many phonetic

[1] Sometimes appearances may be deceptive : when [nr, mr] become [ndr, mbr], it looks on the paper as if something had been added and as if the transition therefore militated against the principle of ease : in reality, the old and the new combinations require exactly the same amount of muscular activity, and the change simply consists in want of precision in the movement of the velum palati, which comes a fraction of a second too soon. If anything, the new group is a trifle easier than the old. See LPh 5. 6 for explanation and examples (E. *thunder* from þunor sb., þunrian vb. ; *timber*, cf. Goth. *timrian*, G. *zimmer*, etc.).

[2] This is rendered most clear by my ' analphabetic ' notation (α means lips, β tip of tongue, δ soft palate, velum palati, and ε glottis ; 0 stands for closed position, 1 for approximation, 3 for open position) ; the three sound combinations are thus analysed (cf. my *Lehrbuch der Phonetik*) :

	p	n	p	m	m	n
α	0	3	0	0	0	3
β	3	0	3	3	3	0
δ	0	3	0	3	3	3
ε	3	1	3	1	1	1

[3] The only clear cases of saving of time are those in which long sounds are shortened, and even they must be looked upon as a saving of effort.

changes which are not always given under the heading of assimilation should really be looked upon as such.   If Lat. *saponem* yields
Fr. *savon*, this is the result of a whole series of assimilations : first
[p] becomes [b], because the vocal vibrations continue from the
vowel before to the vowel after the consonant, the opening of
the glottis being thus saved ; then the transition of [b] to [v]
between vowels may be considered a partial assimilation to the
open lip position of the vowels ; the vowel [o] is nasalized in consequence of an assimilation to the nasal [n] (anticipation of the low
position of the velum), and the subsequent dropping of the consonant [n] is a clear case of a different kind of assimilation (saving
of a tip movement) ; at an early stage the two final sounds of
saponem had disappeared, first [m] and later the indistinct vowel
resulting from *e* : whether we reckon these disappearances as
assimilations or not, at any rate they constitute a saving of effort.
All droppings of sounds, whether consonants (as *t* in E. *castle*, *postman*, etc.) or vowels (as in E. *p'rhaps*, *bus'ness*, etc.), are to be
viewed in the same light, and thus by their enormous number in
the history of all languages form a strong argument in favour of
the ease theory.

There is one more thing to be considered which is generally
overlooked.   In such assimilations as It. *otto*, *sette*, from *octo*,
septem, a greater ease is effected not only by the assimilation as
such, by which one of the consonants is dropped—for that would
have been obtained just as well if the result had been *occo*, *seppe*—
but also by the fact that it is the tip action which has been retained in both cases, for the tip of the tongue is much more flexible
and more easily moved than either the lips or the back of the tongue.
On the whole, many sound changes show how the tip is favoured
at the cost of other organs, thus in the frequent transition of
final -*m* to -*n*, found, for instance, in old Gothonic, in Middle
English, in ancient Greek, in Balto-Slavic, in Finnish and in
Chinese.

In the discussion referred to above Sweet was seconded by
Lecky, who said that " assimilations vastly multiplied the number
of elementary sounds in a language, and therefore could not be
described as facilitating pronunciation."   This is a great exaggeration, for in the vast majority of instances assimilation introduces
no new sounds at all (see, for instance, the lists in my LPh ch. xi.).
Lecky was probably thinking of such instances as when [k, g]
before front vowels become [tʃ, dʒ] or similar combinations, or
when mutation caused by [i] changes [u, o] into [y, ø], which sounds
were not previously found in the language.   Here we might perhaps
say that those individuals who for the sake of their own ease
introduced new sounds made things more difficult for coming

generations (though even that is not quite certain), and the case would then be analogous to that of a man who has learnt a foreign expression for a new idea and then introduces it into his own language, thus burdening his countrymen with a new word instead of thinking how the same idea might have been rendered by means of native speech-material—in both cases a momentary alleviation is obtained at the cost of a permanent disadvantage, but neither case can be alleged against the view that the prevalent tendency among human beings is to prefer the easiest and shortest cut.

XIV.—§ 8. Extreme Weakenings.

When this lazy tendency is indulged to the full, the result is an indistinct protracted vocal murmur, with here and there possibly one or other sound (most often an *s*) rising to the surface : think, for instance, of the way in which we often hear grace said, prayers mumbled and other similar formulas muttered inarticulately, with half-closed lips and the least possible movement of the rest of the vocal organs. This is tolerated more or less in cases in which the utterance is hardly meant as a communication to any human being ; otherwise it will generally be met with a request to repeat what has been said, the social curb being thus applied to the easygoing tendencies of the individual. Now, as a matter of fact, there are in every language a certain number of word-forms that can only be explained by this very laziness in pronouncing, which in extreme cases leads to complete unintelligibility.

Russian *sudar'* (*gosudar'*), 'sir,' is colloquially shortened into a mere *s*, which may in subservient speech be added to almost any word as a meaningless enclitic. And curiously enough the same sound is used in exactly the same way in conversational Spanish, as *buenos* for *bueno* ' good,' only here it is a weakening of *señor* (Hanssen, *Span. gramm.* 60) : thus two entirely different words, from identical psychological motives, yield the same result in two distant countries. Fr. *monsieur*, instead of [mõsjœ·r], a might be expected, sounds [mɔsjø] and extremely frequently [msjø] and even [psjø], with a transition not otherwise found in French. *Madame* before a name is very often shortened into [mam] ; in English the same word becomes a single sound in *yes'm*. The weakening of *mistress* into *miss* and the old-fashioned *mas* for *master* also belong here, as do It. forms for *signore, signora* : *gnor si, gnor no, gnora si, sor Luigi, la sora sposa*, and Sp. *usted* ' you ' for *vuestra merced*. Formulas of greeting and of politeness are liable to similar truncations, e.g. E. *how d(e) do*, Dan. [gda'] or even [da'] for *goddag*, G. [gmõin, gmõ] for *guten morgen*, [na·mt] for *guten abend* ; Fr. *s'il vous plaît* often becomes [siuplɛ, splɛ], and the synonymous Dan. *vær så god* is shortened into *værsgo*, of which often only [sgo'] remains. In Russian popular speech some small words are frequently inserted as a vague indication that the utterance or idea belongs to some one else : *griu, grit, grim, gril*, various mutilated forms of the verb *govorit'* ' say,' *mol* from *molvit'* ' speak,' *de* from *dejati* (Boyer et Speranski, *Manuel* 293 ff.) ; cp. the obsolete E. *co, quo*, for *quoth*. In all the Balkan languages a particle *vre* is extensively used, which Hatzidakis has explained from the vocative of OGr. *mōrós*. Modern Gr. *thà* is now a particle of futurity, but originates in *thená*, from *thélei*, ' he will ' + *nà* from *hína*, ' that.' These examples must suffice to show that we have here to do with a universal tendency in all languages.

XIV.—§ 9. The Principle of Value.

To explain such deviations from normal phonetic development some scholars have assumed that a word or form in frequent use is liable to suffer exceptional treatment. Thus Vilhelm Thomsen, in his brilliant paper (1879) on the Romanic verb *andare, andar, anar, aller*, which he explains convincingly from Lat. *ambulare*, says that this verb " belongs to a group of words which in all languages stand as it were without the pale of the laws, that is, words which from their frequent employment are exposed to far more violent changes than other words, and therefore to some extent follow paths of their own."[1] Schuchardt (*Ueber die lautgesetze*, 1885) turned upon the ' young grammarians,' Paul among the rest, who did not recognize this principle, and said that one word (or one sound) may need 10,000 repetitions in order to be changed into another one, and that consequently another word, which in the same time is used only 8,000 times, must be behindhand in its phonetic development. Quite apart from the fact that this number is evidently too small (for a moderately loquacious woman will easily pronounce such a word as *he* half a dozen times as often as these figures every year), it is obvious that the reasoning must be wrong, for were frequency the only decisive factor, G. *morgen* would have been treated in every other connexion exactly as it is in *guten morgen*, and that is just what has not happened. Frequency of repetition would in itself tend to render the habitude firmly rooted, thus really capable of resisting change, rather than the opposite ; and instead of the purely mechanical explanation from the number of times a word is repeated, we must look for

---

[1] In the reprint in *Samlede Afhandlinger*, ii. 417 (1920), a few lines are added in which Thomsen fully accepts the explanation which I gave as far back as 1886.

a more psychological explanation. This naturally must be found in the ease with which a word is understood in the given connexion or situation, and especially in its worthlessness for the purpose of communication. Worthlessness, however, is not the moving power, but merely the reason why less restraint than usual is imposed on the ever-present inclination of speakers to minimize effort. A parallel from another, though cognate, sphere of human activity may perhaps bring out my point of view more clearly. The taking off of one's hat, combined with a low bow, served from the first to mark a more or less servile submissiveness to a prince or conqueror ; then the gesture was gradually weakened, and a slight raising of the hat came to be a polite greeting even between equals ; this is reduced to a mere touching of the hat or cap, and among friends the slightest movement of the hand in the direction of the hat is thought a sufficient greeting. When, however, it is important to indicate deference, the full ceremonial gesture is still used (though not to the same extent by all nations) ; otherwise no value is attached to it, and the inclination to spare oneself all unnecessary exertion has caused it to dwindle down to the slightest muscular action possible.

The above instances of the truncation of everyday formulas, etc., illustrate the length to which the ease principle can be carried when a word has little significatory value and the intention of the speaker can therefore be vaguely, but sufficiently, understood if the proper sound is merely suggested or hinted at. But in most words, and even in the words mentioned above, when they are to bear their full meaning, the pronunciation cannot be slurred to the same extent, if the speaker is to make himself understood. It is consequently his interest to pronounce more carefully, and this means greater conservatism and slower phonetic development on the whole.

There are naturally many degrees of relative value or worthlessness, and words may vary accordingly. An illustration may be taken from my own mother-tongue : the two words *rigtig nok*, literally ' correct enough,' are pronounced ['recti 'nɔk] or ['regdi 'nɔk] when keeping their full signification, but when they are reduced to an adverb with the same import as the weakened English *certainly* or (*it is*) *true* (*that*), there are various shortened pronunciations in frequent use : ['rectnɔg, 'regdnɔg, 'regnɔg, 'renɔg, 'renəg]. The worthlessness may affect a whole phrase, a word, or merely one syllable or sound.

XIV.—§ 10. Application to Case System, etc.

Our principle is important in many domains of linguistic history. If it is asked why the elaborate Old English system of cases and genders has gradually disappeared, an answer that will meet with the approval of most linguists of the ordinary school is (in the words of J. A. H. Murray) : "The total loss of grammatical gender in English, and the almost complete disappearance of cases, are purely phonetic phenomena "—supplemented, of course, by the recognition of the action of analogy, to which is due, for instance, the levelling of the nom. and dative plural OE. *stanas* and *stanum* under the single form *stones*. The main explanation thus is the following : a phonetic law, operating without regard to the signification, caused the OE. unstressed vowels *-a*, *-e*, *-u* to become merged in an obscure *-e* in Middle English ; as these endings were very often distinctive of cases, the Old English cases were consequently lost. Another phonetic law was operating similarly by causing the loss of final *-n*, which also played an important rôle in the old case system. And in this way phonetic laws and analogy have between them made a clean sweep of it, and we need look nowhere else for an explanation of the decay of the old declensions.

Here I beg to differ : a 'phonetic law' is not an explanation, but something to be explained ; it is nothing else but a mere statement of facts, a formula of correspondence, which says nothing about the cause of change, and we are therefore justified if we try to dig deeper and penetrate to the real psychology of speech. Now, let us for a moment suppose that each of the terminations *-a*, *-e*, *-u* bore in Old English its own distinctive and sharply defined meaning, which was necessary to the right understanding of the sentences in which the terminations occurred (something like the endings found in artificial languages like Ido). Would there in that case be any probability that a phonetic law tending to their levelling could ever have succeeded in establishing itself ? Most certainly not ; the all-important regard for intelligibility would have been sure to counteract any inclination towards a slurred pronunciation of the endings. Nor would there have been any occasion for new formations by analogy, as the formations were already sufficiently analogous. But such a regularity was very far from prevailing in Old English, as will be particularly clear from the tabulation of the declensions as printed in my *Chapters on English*, p. 10 ff. : it makes the whole question of causality appear in a much clearer light than would be possible by any other arrangement of the grammatical facts : the cause of the decay of the Old English apparatus of declensions lay in its manifold incongruities. The same termination did not always denote the same thing : *-u* might be the nom. sg. masc. (*sunu*) or fem. (*duru*), or the acc. or the dat., or the nom. or acc. pl. neuter (*hofu*) ; *-a* might be the nom. sg. masc. (*guma*), or the dat. sg. masc. (*suna*),

or the gen. sg. fem. (*dura*), or the nom. pl. masc. or fem., or
finally the gen. pl. ; -*an* might be the acc. or dat. or gen. sg. or
the nom. or acc. pl., etc. If we look at it from the point of view
of function, we get the same picture ; the nom. pl., for instance,
might be denoted by the endings -*as*, -*an*, -*a*, -*e*, -*u*, or by mutation
without ending, or by the unchanged kernel ; the dat. sg. by
-*e*, -*an*, -*re*, -*um*, by mutation, or the unchanged kernel. The
whole is one jumble of inconsistency, for many relations plainly
distinguished from each other in one class of words were but
imperfectly, if at all, distinguishable in another class. Add to
this that the names used above, dative, accusative, etc., have
no clear and definite meaning in the case of Old English, any
more than in the case of kindred tongues ; sometimes it did not
matter which of two or more cases the speaker chose to employ :
some verbs took indifferently now one, now another case, and
the same is to some extent true with regard to prepositions. No
wonder, therefore, that speakers would often hesitate which of
two vowels to use in the ending, and would tend to indulge in the
universal inclination to pronounce weak syllables indistinctly
and thus confuse the formerly distinct vowels *a*, *i*, *e*, *u* into the
one neutral vowel [ə], which might even be left out without
detriment to the clear understanding of each sentence.[1] The
only endings that were capable of withstanding this general rout
were the two in *s*, -*as* for the plural and -*es* for the gen. sg. ;
here the consonant was in itself more solid, as it were, than the
other consonants used in case endings (*n*, *m*), and, which is more
decisive, each of these terminations was confined to a more
sharply limited sphere of use than the other endings, and the
functions for which they served, that of the plural and that of
the genitive, are among the most indispensable ones for clearness
of thought. Hence we see that these endings from the earliest
period of the English language tend to be applied to other
classes of nouns than those to which they were at first confined
(-*as* to masc. *o* stems . . .), so as to be at last used with practically
all nouns.

If explanations like Murray's of the simplification of the
English case system are widely accepted, while views like those
attempted here will strike most readers of linguistic works as
unfamiliar, the reason may, partly at any rate, be the usual
arrangement of historical and other grammars. Here we first
have chapters on phonology, in which the facts are tabulated,

---

[1] The above remarks are condensed from the argument in ChE 38 ff.
Note also what is said below (Ch. XIX § 13) on the loss of Lat. final -*s* in the
Romanic languages after it had ceased to be necessary for the grammatical
understanding of sentences.

each vowel being dealt with separately, no matter what its function is in the flexional system ; then, after all the sounds have been treated in this way, we come to morphology (accidence, formenlehre), in which it is natural to take the phonological facts as granted or already known : these therefore come to be looked upon as primary and morphology as secondary, and no attention is paid to the *value* of the sounds for the purposes of mutual understanding.

But everyday observations show that sounds have not always the same value. In ordinary conversation one may frequently notice how a proper name or technical term, when first introduced, is pronounced with particular care, while no such pains is taken when it recurs afterwards : the stress becomes weaker, the unstressed vowels more indistinct, and this or that consonant may be dropped. The same principle is shown in all the abbreviations of proper names and of long words in general which have been treated above (Ch IX § 7) : here the speaker has felt assured that his hearer has understood what or who he is talking about, as soon as he has pronounced the initial syllable or syllables, and therefore does not take the trouble to pronounce the rest of the word. It has often been pointed out (see, e.g., Curtius K 72) that stem or root syllables are generally better preserved than the rest of the word : the reason can only be that they have greater importance for the understanding of the idea as a whole than other syllables.[1] But it is especially when we come to examine stress phenomena that we discover the full extent of this principle of value.

XIV.—§ 11. Stress Phenomena.

Stress is generally believed to be dependent exclusively on the force with which the air-current is expelled from the lungs, hence the name of 'expiratory accent'; but various observations and considerations have led me to give another definition (LPh 7. 32, 1913) : stress is energy, intensive muscular activity not

---

[1] Against this it has been urged that Fr. *oncle* has not preserved the stem syllable of Lat. *avunculus* particularly well. But this objection is a little misleading. It is quite true that at the time when the word was first framed the syllable *av-* contained the main idea and *-unculus* was only added to impart an endearing modification to that idea (' dear little uncle ') ; but after some time the semantic relation was altered ; *avus* itself passed out of use, while *avunculus* was handed down from generation to generation as a ready-made whole, in which the ordinary speaker was totally unable to suspect that *av-* was the really significative stem. He consequently treated it exactly as any other polysyllable of the same structure, and *avun-* (phonetically [awuŋ, auuŋ]) was naturally made into one syllable. Nothing, of course, can be protected by a sense of its significance unless it is still felt as significant. That hardly needs saying.

of one organ, but of *all the speech organs at once*. To pronounce
a ' stressed ' syllable all organs are exerted to the utmost. The
muscles of the lungs are strongly innervated ; the movements
of the vocal chords are stronger, leading on the one hand in
voiced sounds to a greater approximation of the vocal chords,
with less air escaping, but greater amplitude of vibrations and
also greater risings or fallings of the tone. In voiceless sounds,
on the other hand, the vocal chords are kept at greater distance
(than in unstressed syllables) and accordingly allow more air to
escape. In the upper organs stress is characterized by marked
articulations of the velum palati, of the tongue and of the lips.
As a result of all this, stressed syllables are loud, i.e. can be heard
at great distance, and distinct, i.e. easy to perceive in all their
components. Unstressed syllables, on the contrary, are produced with less exertion in every way : in voiced sounds the
distance between the vocal chords is greater, which leads to the
peculiar ' voice of murmur ' ; but in voiceless sounds the glottis
is not opened very wide. In the upper organs we see corresponding
slack movements ; thus the velum does not shut off the nasal cavity
very closely, and the tongue tends towards a neutral position,
in which it moves very little either up and down or backwards
and forwards. The lips also are moved with less energy, and the
final result is dull and indistinct sounds. Now, all this is of the
greatest importance in the history of languages.

The psychological importance of various elements is the chief,
though not the only, factor that determines sentence stress (see, for
instance, the chapters on stress in my LPh xiv. and MEG v.). Now,
it is well known that sentence stress plays a most important rôle in
the historical development of any language ; it has determined
not only the difference in vowel between [wɔz] and [wəz], both
written *was*, or between the demonstrative [ðæt] and the relative
[ðət], both written *that*, but also that between *one* and *an* or *a*,
originally the same word, and between Fr. *moi* and *me*, *toi* and *te*
—one might give innumerable other instances. Value also plays
a not unimportant rôle in determining which syllable among
several in long words is stressed most, and in some languages
it has revolutionized the whole stress system. This happened with
old Gothonic, whence in modern German, Scandinavian, and in
the native elements of English we have the prevalent stressing of
the root syllable, i.e. of that syllable which has the greatest
psychological value, as in 'wishes, be'speak, etc.

Now, it is generally said that if double forms arise like *one* and
an, *moi* and *me*, the reason is that the sounds were found under
' different phonetic conditions ' and therefore developed differently,
exactly as the difference between *an* and *a* or between Fr. *fol*

and *fou* is due to the same word being placed in one instance before
a word beginning with a vowel and in the other before a consonant,
that is to say, in different external conditions. But it won't do
to identify the two things : in the latter case we really have something external or mechanical, and here we may rightly use
the expression ' phonetic condition,' but the difference between
a strongly and a weakly stressed form of the same word depends
on something internal, on the very soul of the word. Stress is
not what the usual way of marking it in writing and printing might
lead us to think—something that hangs outside or above the
word—but is at least as important an element of the word as
the ' speech sounds ' which go to make it up. Stress alternation
in a sentence cannot consequently be reckoned a ' phonetic
condition ' of the same order as the initial sound of the next word.
If we say that the different treatment of the vowel seen in *one*
and *an* or *moi* and *me* is occasioned by varying degrees of stress,
we have ' explained ' the secondary sound change only, but not
the primary change, which is that of stress itself, and that
change is due to the different significance of the word under varying
circumstances, i.e. to its varying value for the purposes of the
exchange of ideas. Over and above mechanical principles we
have here and elsewhere psychological principles, which no one
can disregard with impunity.

XIV.—§ 12. Non-phonetic Changes.

Considerations of ease play an important part in all departments of language development. It is impossible to draw a sharp
line between phonetic and syntactic phenomena. We have what
might be termed prosiopesis when the speaker begins, or thinks
he begins, to articulate, but produces no audible sound till one
or two syllables after the beginning of what he intended to say.
This phonetically is ' aphesis,' but in many cases leads to the
omission of whole words ; this may become a regular speech habit,
more particularly in the case of certain set phrases, e.g. (Good)
morning / (Do you) *see* ? / (Will) *that do* ? / (I shall) *see you
again this afternoon* ; Fr. (na)*turellement* / (Je ne me) *rappelle
plus,* etc.

On the other hand, we have aposiopesis if the speaker does
not finish his sentence, either because he hesitates which word
to employ or because he notices that the hearer has already caught
his meaning. Hence such syntactic shortenings as *at Brown's*
(house, or shop, or whatever it may be), which may then be
extended to other places in the sentence ; the *grocer's* was closed
St. Paul's is very grand, etc. Similar abbreviations due to

the natural disinclination to use more circumstantial expressions
than are necessary to convey one's meaning are seen when, instead
of *my straw hat*, one says simply *my straw*, if it is clear to one's
hearers that one is talking of a hat ; thus *clay* comes to be used
for *clay pipe*, *return* for *return ticket* ('We'd better take returns')
the Haymarket for *the Haymarket Theatre*, etc. Sometimes these
shortenings become so common as to be scarcely any longer felt
as such, e.g. *rifle*, *landau*, *bugle*, for *rifle gun*, *landau carriage*, *bugle
horn* (further examples MEG ii. 8. 9).   In Maupassant (*Bel Ami*
81) I find the following scrap of conversation which illustrates
the same principle in another domain : " Voilà six mois que je
suis *employé aux bureaux du chemin de fer du Nord*." " Mais
comment diable n'as-tu pas trouvé mieux qu'une place *d'employé
au Nord ?* " [1]

The tendency to economzie effort also manifests itself when
the general ending *-er* is used instead of a more specific expression :
sleeper for *sleeping-car* ; *bedder* at college for *bedmaker ; speecher*,
footer, *brekker* (Harrow) for *speech-day*, *football*, *breakfast*, etc.
Thus also when some noun or verb of a vague or general meaning
is used because one will not take the trouble to think of the exact
expression required, very often *thing* (sometimes extended *thingum-
bob*, cf. Dan. *tingest*, G. *dingsda*), Fr. *chose*, *machin* (even in place
of a personal name) ; further, the verb *do* or *fix* (this especially
in America).   In some cases this tendency may permanently
affect the meaning of a common noun which has to serve so
often instead of a specific name that at last it acquires a special
signification ; thus, *corn* in England = 'wheat,' in Ireland = ' oats,'
in America = ' maize,' *deer*, orig. ' animal,' Fr. *herbe*, now ' grass,'
etc.   As many people, either from ignorance or from carelessness,
are far from being precise in thought and expression—they " Mean
not, but blunder round about a meaning "—words come to be
applied in senses unknown to former generations, and some of
these senses may gradually become fixed and established.   In
some cases the final result of such want of precision may even be
beneficial ; thus English at first had no means of expressing
futurity in verbs.   Then it became more and more customary
to say ' he will come,' which at first meant ' he has the will
to come,' to express his future coming apart from his volition
—thus, also, ' it will rain,' etc.   Similarly ' I shall go,' which

---

[1] Compare also the results of the same principle seen in writing.   In
a letter a proper name or technical term when first introduced is probably
written in full and very distinctly, while afterwards it is either written
carelessly or indicated by a mere initial.   Any shorthand-writer knows
how to utilize this principle systematically.

originally meant 'I am obliged to go,' was used in a less accurate way, where no obligation was thought of, and thus the language acquired something which is at any rate a make-shift for a future tense of the verb. But considerations of space prevent me from diving too deeply into questions of semantic change.

CHAPTER XV

CAUSES OF CHANGE—*continued*

XV.—§ 1. Emotional Exaggerations.

In the preceding chapter we have dwelt at great length on those changes which tend to render articulations easier and more convenient. But, important as they are, these are not the only changes that speech sounds undergo : there are other moods than that of ordinary listless everyday conversation, and they may lead to modifications of pronunciation which are different from and may even be in direct opposition to those mentioned or hinted at above. Thus, anger or other violent emotions may cause emphatic utterance, in which, e.g., stops may be much more strongly aspirated than they are in usual quiet parlance ; even French, which has normally unaspirated ('sharp') [t] and [k], under such circumstances may aspirate them strongly—'*Mais taisez-vous donc !*' Military commands are characterized by peculiar emphasizings, even in some cases distortions of sounds and words. Pomposity and consequential airs are manifested in the treatment of speech sounds as well as in other gestures. Irony, scoffing, banter, amiable chaffing—each different mood or temper leaves its traces on enunciation. Actors and orators will often use stronger articulations than are strictly necessary to avoid those misunderstandings or that unintelligibility which may ensue from slipshod or indistinct pronunciation.[1] In short, anyone who will take careful note of the way in which people do really talk will find in the most everyday conversation as well as on more solemn occasions the greatest variety of such modifications and deviations from what might be termed 'normal' pronunciation ; these, however, pass

---

[1] " His pronunciation of some words is so distinct that an idea crossed me once that he might be an actor " (Shaw, *Cashel Byron's Profession*, 66).

unnoticed under ordinary circumstances, when the attention is directed exclusively to the contents and general purport of the spoken words. A vowel or a consonant will be made a trifle shorter or longer than usual, the lips will open a little too much, an [e] will approach [æ] or [i], the off-glide after a final [t] will sound nearly as [s], the closure of a [d] will be made so loosely that a little air will escape and the sound therefore will be approximately a [ð] or a weak fricative point [r], etc. Most of these modifications are so small that they cannot be represented by letters, even by those of a very exact phonetic alphabet, but they exist all the same, and are by no means insignificant to those who want to understand the real essence of speech and of linguistic change, for life is built up of such minutiæ. The great majority of such alterations are of course made quite unconsciously, but by the side of these we must recognize that there are some individuals who more or less consciously affect a certain mode of enunciation, either from artistic motives, because they think it beautiful, or simply to ' show off '—and sometimes such pronunciations may set the fashion and be widely imitated (cf. below, p. 292).

Tender emotions may lead to certain lengthenings of sounds. The intensifying effect of lengthening was noticed by A. Gill, Milton's teacher, in 1621, see Jiriczek's reprint, p. 48 : " Atque vt Hebræi, ad ampliorem vocis alicuius significationem, syllabas adaugent [cf. here below, Ch. XX § 9] ; sic nos syllabarum tempora : vt, *grēt* [the diæresis denotes vowel-length] magnus, *grēet* ingens ; *monstrus* prodigiosum, *mönstrus* valde prodigiosum, *möönstrus* prodigiosum adeo vt hominem stupidet." Cf. also the lengthening in the exclamation *God !*, by novelists sometimes written *Gawd* or *Gord*. But it is curious that the same emotional lengthening will sometimes affect a consonant (or first part of a diphthong) in a position in which otherwise we always have a short quantity ; thus, Danish clergymen, when speaking with unction, will lengthen the [l] of *glæde* ' joy,' which is ridiculed by comic writers through the unphonetic spelling *ge-lædè* ; and in the same way I find in Kipling (*Stalky* 119) : " We'll make it a *be-autiful* house," and in O. Henry (*Roads of Destiny* 133) : " A regular Paradise Lost for elegance of scenery and *be-yooty* of geography." I suppose that the spellings *ber-luddy* and *bee-luddy*, which I find in recent novels, are meant to indicate the pronunciation [blˑ-ʌdi], thus the exact counterpart of the Danish example. An unstressed vowel before the stressed syllable is similarly lengthened in " Dee-lightful couple ! " (Shaw, *Doctor's Dilemma* 41) ; American girl students will often say ['diˑliʃ] for *delicious*.

XV.—§ 2. Euphony.

It was not uncommon in the seventeenth and eighteenth centuries to ascribe phonetic changes to a desire for euphony, a view which is represented in Bopp's earliest works. But as early as 1821 Bredsdorff says that " people will always find that euphonious which they are accustomed to hear : considerations of euphony consequently will not cause changes in a language, but rather make for keeping it unchanged. Those changes which are generally supposed to be based on euphony are due chiefly to convenience, in some instances to care of distinctness." This is quite true, but scarcely the whole truth. Euphony depends not only on custom, but even more on ease of articulation and on ease of perception : what requires intricate or difficult movements of the organs of speech will always be felt as cacophonous, and so will anything that is indistinct or blurred. But nations, as well as individuals, have an artistic feeling for these things in different degrees, and that may influence the phonetic character of a language, though perhaps chiefly in its broad features, while it may be difficult to point out any particular details in phonological history which have been thus worked upon. There can be no doubt that the artistic feeling is much more developed in the French than in the English nation, and we find in French fewer obscure vowels and more clearly articulated consonants than in English (cf. also my remarks on French accent, GS § 28).

XV.—§ 3. Organic Influences.

Some modifications of speech sounds are due to the fact that the organs of speech are used for other purposes than that of speaking. We all know the effect of someone trying to speak with his mouth full of food, or with a cigar or a pipe hanging between his lips and to some extent impeding their action. Various emotions are expressed by facial movements which may interfere with the production of ordinary speech sounds. A child that is crying speaks differently from one that is smiling or laughing. A smile requires a retraction of the corners of the mouth and a partial opening of the lips, and thus impedes the formation of that lip-closure which is an essential part of the ordinary [m] ; hence most people when smiling will substitute the labiodental *m*, which to the ear greatly resembles the bilabial [m]. A smile will also often modify the front-round vowel [y] so as to make it approach [i]. Sweet may be right in supposing that " the habit of speaking with a constant smile or grin " is the reason for the Cockney unrounding of the vowel in [nau] for *no*. Schuchardt

(*Zs. f. rom. Phil.* 5. 314) says that in Andalusian *quia !* instead of *ca !* the lips, under the influence of a certain emotion, are drawn scoffingly aside. Inversely, the rounding in *Josu !* instead of *Jesu !* is due to wonder (ib.); and exactly in the same way we have the surprised or pitying exclamation *jøses !* from *Jesus* in Danish. Compare also the rounding in Dan. and G. [nø·] for [ne·, nɛ·] (*nej, nein*). Lundell mentions that in Swedish a caressing *lilla vän* often becomes *lylla vön*, and I have often observed the same rounding in Dan. *min lille ven*. Schuchardt also mentions an Italian [ʃ] instead of [s] under the influence of pain or anger (*mi duole la teſta* ; *ti do uno ſchiaffo*) ; a Danish parallel is the frequent [ʃluð'ər] for *sludder* ' nonsense.' We are here verging on the subject of the symbolic value of speech sounds, which will occupy us in a later chapter (XX).

Observe, too, how people will pronounce under the influence of alcohol : the tongue is not under control and is incapable of accurately forming the closure necessary for [t], which therefore becomes [r], and the thin rill necessary for [s], which therefore comes to resemble [ʃ] ; there is also a general tendency to run sounds and syllables together.[1]

XV.—§ 4. Lapses and Blendings.

All these deviations are due to influences from what is outside the sphere of language as such. But we now come to something of the greatest importance in the life of language, the fact, namely, that deviations from the usual or normal pronunciation are very often due to causes inside the language itself, either by lingering reminiscences of what has just been spoken or by anticipation of something that the speaker is just on the point of pronouncing. The process of speech is a very complicated one, and while one thing is being said, the mind is continually active in preparing what has to be said next, arranging the ideas and fashioning the linguistic expression in all its details. Each word is a succession of sounds, and for each of these a complicated set of orders has to be issued from the brain to the various speech organs. Sometimes these get mixed up, and a command is sent down to one organ a moment too early or too late. The inclination to make mistakes naturally increases with the number of identical or

---

[1] Dickens, *D. Cop.* 2. 149 neverbe*r*rer, 150 I'mafraid you'reno*r*well (ib. also *r* for *n* : Amigoa*r*awaysoo, Goo*r*i = Good night). | *Our Mut. Fr.* 602 le*r*rers. | Thackeray, *Newc.* 163 W*h*as that ? | Anstey, *Vice V.* 328 *sh*upper, I *sh*pose, wha*rr*iplease, say tha*rr*again. | Meredith, *R. Feverel* 272 Nor a bir of it. | Walpole, *Duch. of Wrex.* 323-4 non*sh*ens*h*, Wa*sh* the matter ? | Galsworthy, *In Chanc.* 17 cur*sh*, un*sh*tood'm. Cf. also Fijn van Draat, ESt 34. 363 ff.

similar sounds in close proximity. This is well known from those
'jaw-breaking' tongue-tests with which people amuse themselves in all countries and of which I need give only one typical
specimen :

> She sells seashells on the seashore ,
> The shells she sells are seashells, I'm sure,
> For if she sells seashells on the seashore,
> Then I'm sure she sells seashore shells.

If the mind is occupied with one sound while another is being
pronounced, and thus either runs in advance of or lags behind
what should be its immediate business, the linguistic result may
be of various kinds. The simplest case of influencing is assimilation of two contiguous sounds, which we have already considered
from a different point of view. Next we have assimilative influence on a sound at a distance, as when we lapse into *she shells*
instead of *sea shells* or *she sells* ; such is Fr. *chercher* for older
sercher (whence E. *search*) from Lat. *circare*, Dan. and G. vulgar
ſerſant for *sergeant* ; a curious mixed case is the pronunciation of
transition as [træn'siʒən] : the normal development is [træn'ziſən],
but the voice-articulation of the two hissing sounds is reversed
(possibly under accessory influence from the numerous words in
which we have [træns] with [s], and from words ending in [iʒən],
such as *vision, division*). Further examples of such assimilation
at a distance or consonant-harmonization (*malmsey* from *malvesie*,
etc.) may be found in my LPh 11. 7, where there are also examples
of the corresponding harmonizings of vowels : Fr. *camarade*, It.
uguale, Braganza, from *camerade, eguale, Brigantia*, etc. In Ugro-
Finnic and Turkish this harmony of vowels has been raised to
a principle pervading the whole structure of the language, as
seen, e.g., most clearly in the varying plural endings in Yakut
agalar, äsälär, ogolor, dörölör, ' fathers, bears, children, muzzles.'

What escapes at the wrong place and causes confusion may
be a part of the same word or of a following word · as examples
of the latter case may be given a few of the lapses recorded in
Meringer and Mayer's *Versprechen und Verlesen* (Stuttgart, 1895):
instead of saying *Lateinisches lehnwort* Meringer said *Laten-
isches . . .* and then corrected himself ; *paster noster* instead of
pater noster ; *wenn das wesser . . . wetter wieder besser ist*. This
phenomenon is termed in Danish *at bakke snagvendt* (for *snakke
bagvendt*) and in English *Spoonerism*, from an Oxford don, W. A.
Spooner, about whom many comic lapses are related (" Don't
you ever feel a half-warmed fish " instead of " half-formed
wish ").

The simplest and most frequently occurring cases in which
the order for a sound is issued too early or too late are those trans-

positions of two sounds which the linguists term 'metatheses.' They occur most frequently with *s* in connexion with a stop (*wasp, waps; ask, ax*) and with *r* (chiefly, perhaps exclusively, the trilled form of the sound) and a vowel (*third*, OE. *pridda*). A more complicated instance is seen in Fr. *trésor* for *tésor, thesaurum*. If the mind does not realize how far the vocal organs have got, the result may be the skipping of some sound or sounds; this is particularly likely to happen when the same sound has to be repeated at some little distance, and we then have the phenomenon termed 'haplology,' as in *eighteen*, OE. *eahtatiene*, and in the frequent pronunciation *probly* for *probably*, Fr. *contrôle, idolatrie* for *contrerôle, idololatrie*, Lat. *stipendium* for *stipipendium*, and numerous similar instances in every language (LPh 11. 9). Sometimes a sound may be skipped because the mind is confused through the fact that the same sound has to be pronounced a little later; thus the old Gothonic word for 'bird' (G. *vogel*, OE. *fugol*; E. *fowl* with a modified meaning) is derived from the verb *fly*, OE. *fleogan*, and originally had some form like **fluglo* (OE. had an adj. *flugol*); in recent times *flugelman* (G. flügelmann) has become *fugleman*. It. has *Federigo* for *Frederigo*—thus the exactly opposite result of what has been brought about in *trésor* from the same kind of mental confusion.

When words are often repeated in succession, sounds from one of them will often creep into another, as is seen very often in numerals: the nasal which was found in the old forms for 7, 9 and 10 and is still seen in E. *seven, nine, ten*, has no place in the word for 8, and accordingly we have in the ordinal ON. *sjaundi, átti, níundi, tíundi*, but already in ON. we find *áttandi* by the side of *átti*, and in Dan. the present-day forms are *syvende, ottende, niende, tiende*; in the same way OFr. had *sedme, uidme, noefme, disme* (which have all now disappeared with the exception of *dîme* as a substantive). In the names of the months we had the same formation of a series in OFr.: *septembre, octembre, novembre, decembre*, but learned influence has reinstated *octobre*. G. *elf* for older *eilf* owes its vowel to the following *zwelf*; and as now the latter has given way to *zwölf* (the vowel being rounded in consequence of the *w*) many dialects count *zehn, ölf, zwölf*. Similarly, it seems to be due to their frequent occurrence in close contact with the verbal forms in *-no* that the Italian plural pronouns *egli, elle* are extended with that ending: *eglino amano, elleno dicono*. Diez compares the curious Bavarian *wo-st bist, dem-st gehörst*, etc., in which the personal ending of the verb is transferred to some other word with which it has nothing to do (on this phenomenon see Herzog, *Streitfragen d. roman. phil.* 48, Buergel Goodwin, *Umgangsspr. in Südbayern* 99).

In speaking, the mind is occupied not only with the words one is already pronouncing or knows that one is going to pronounce, but also with the ideas which one has to express but for which one has not yet chosen the linguistic form. In many cases two synonyms will rise to the consciousness at the same time, and the hesitation between them will often result in a compromise which contains the head of one and the tail of another word. It is evident that this process of blending is intimately related to those we have just been considering; see the detailed treatment in Ch. XVI § 6.

Syntactical blends are very frequent. Hesitation between *different from* and *other than* will result in *different than* or *another from*, and similarly we occasionally find *another to*, *different to*, *contrary than*, *contrary from*, *opposite from*, *anywhere than*. After a clause introduced by *hardly* or *scarcely* the normal conjunction is *when*, but sometimes we find *than*, because that is regular after the synonymous *no sooner*.

XV.—§ 5. Latitude of Correctness.

It is a natural consequence of the essence of human speech and the way in which it is transmitted from generation to generation that we have everywhere to recognize a certain latitude of correctness, alike in the significations in which the words may be used, in syntax and in pronunciation. The nearer a speaker keeps to the centre of what is established or usual, the easier will it be to understand him. If he is 'eccentric' on one point or another, the result may not always be that he conveys no idea at all, or that he is misunderstood, but often merely that he is understood with some little difficulty, or that his hearers have a momentary feeling of something odd in his choice of words, or expressions or pronunciation. In many cases, when someone has overstepped the boundaries of what is established, his hearers do not at once catch his meaning and have to gather it from the whole context of what follows : not unfrequently the meaning of something you have heard as an incomprehensible string of syllables will suddenly flash upon you without your knowing how it has happened. Misunderstandings are, of course, most liable to occur if words of different meaning, which in themselves would give sense in the same collocation, are similar in sound : in that case a trifling alteration of one sound, which in other words would create no difficulty at all, may prove pernicious. Now, what is the bearing of these considerations on the question of sound changes ?

The latitude of correctness is very far from being the same in different languages. Some sounds in each language move within narrow boundaries, while others have a much larger field assigned to them ; each language is punctilious in some, but not in all points. Deviations which in one language would be considered trifling, in another would be intolerable perversions. In German, for instance, a wide margin is allowed for the (local and individual) pronunciation of the diphthong written *eu* or *äu* (in *eule*, *träume*) : it may begin with [ɔ] or [œ] or even [æ, aˑ], and it may end in [i], or the corresponding rounded vowel [y], or one of the mid front vowels, rounded or not, it does not matter much ; the diphthong is recognized or acknowledged in many shapes, while the similar diphthong in English, as in *toy*, *voice*, allows a far less range of variation (for other examples see LPh 16. 22).

Now, it is very important to keep in mind that there is an intimate connexion between phonetic latitude and the significations of words. If there are in a language a great many pairs of words which are identical in sound except for, say, the difference between [eˑ] and [iˑ] (or between long and short [i], or between voiced [b] and voiceless [p], or between a high and a low tone, etc.), then the speakers of that language necessarily will make that distinction with great precision, as otherwise too many misunderstandings would result. If, on the other hand, no mistakes worth speaking of would ensue, there is not the same inducement to be careful. In English, and to a somewhat lesser degree in French, it is easy to make up long lists of pairs of words where the sole difference is between voice and voicelessness in the final consonant (*cab cap*, *bad bat*, *frog frock*, etc.) ; hence final [b] and [p], [d] and [t], [g] and [k] are kept apart conscientiously, while German possesses very few such pairs of words ; in German, consequently, the natural tendency to make final consonants voiceless has not been checked, and all final stopped consonants have now become voiceless. In initial and medial position, too, there are very few examples in German of the same distinction (see the lists, LPh 6. 78), and this circumstance makes us understand why Germans are so apt to efface the difference between [b, d, g] and [p, t, k]. On the other hand, the distinction between a long and a short vowel is kept much more effectively in German than in French, because in German ten or twenty times as many words would be liable to confusion through pronouncing a long instead of a short vowel or vice versa. In French no two words are kept apart by means of stress, as in English or German ; so the rule laid down in grammars that the stress falls on the final syllable of the word is very frequently broken through for rhythmic and other reasons. Other similar instances might easily be advanced.

XV.—§ 6. Equidistant and Convergent Changes.

Phonetic shifts are of two kinds : the shifted sound may be identical with one already found in the language, or it may be a new sound. In the former, but not in the latter kind, fresh possibilities of confusions and misunderstandings may arise. Now, in some cases one sound (or series of sounds) marches into a position which has just been abandoned by another sound (or series of sounds), which has in its turn shifted into some other place. A notable instance is the old Gothonic consonant shift : Aryan *b*, *d*, *g* cannot have become Gothonic *p*, *t*, *k* till after primitive *p*, *t*, *k* had already become fricatives [f, þ, x (h)], for had the shift taken place before, intolerable confusion would have reigned in all parts of the vocabulary. Another instructive example is seen in the history of English long vowels. Not till OE. long *a* had been rounded into something like [ɔ·] (OE. *stan*, ME. *stoon, stone*) could a new long *a* develop, chiefly through lengthening of an old short *a* in certain positions. Somewhat later we witness the great vowel-raising through which the phonetic value of the long vowels (written all the time in essentially the same way) has been constantly on the move and yet the distance between them has been kept, so that no confusions worth speaking of have ever occurred. If we here leave out of account the rounded back vowels and speak only of front vowels, the shift may be thus represented through typical examples (the first and the last columns show the spelling, the others the sounds) :

	Middle English.		Elizabethan.	Present English.	
(1)	*bite*	bi·tə	beit	bait	*bite*
(2)	*bete*	be·tə	bi·t	bi·t	*beet*
(3)	*bete*	bɛ·tə	be·t	bi·t	*beat*
(4)	*abate*	a'ba·tə	ə'bæ·t	ə'beit	*abate*

When the sound of (2) was raised into [i·], the sound of (1) had already left that position and had been diphthongized, and when the sound of (3) was raised from an open into a close *e*, (2) had already become [i·] ; (4) could not become (æ·] or [ɛ·] till (3) had become a comparatively close *e* sound. The four vowels, as it were, climbed the ladder without ever reaching each other— a climbing which took centuries and in each case implied intermediate steps not indicated in our survey. No clashings could occur so long as each category kept its distance from the sounds above and below, and thus we find that the Elizabethans as scrupulously as Chaucer kept the four classes of words apart in their rimes. But in the seventeenth century class (3) was raised, and as no corresponding change had taken place with (2), the two classes have now fallen together with the single sound [i·]. This entails a certain number of homophones such as had not been created through the preceding equidistant changes.

XV.—§ 7. Homophones.

The reader here will naturally object that the fact of new homophones arising through this vowel change goes against the theory that the necessity of certain distinctions can keep in check the tendency to phonetic changes. But homophones do not always imply frequent misunderstandings : some homophones are more harmless than others. Now, if we look at the list of the homophones created by this raising of the close *e* (MEG i. 11. 74), we shall soon discover that very few mistakes of any consequence could arise through the obliteration of the distinction between this vowel and the previously existing [i·]. For substantives and verbal forms (like *bean* and *been, beet beat, flea flee, heel heal, leek leak, meat meet, reed read, sea see, seam seem, steel steal*), or substantives and adjectives (like *deer dear, leaf lief, shear sheer, week weak*) will generally be easily distinguished by their position in the sentence ; nor will a plural such as *feet* be often mistaken for the singular *feat*. Actual misunderstandings of any importance are only imaginable when the two words belong to the same ' part of speech,' but of such pairs we meet only few : *beach beech, breach breech, mead meed, peace piece, peal peel, quean queen, seal ceil, wean ween, wheal wheel*. I think the judicious reader will agree with me that confusions due to these words being pronounced in the same way will be few and far between, and one understands that they cannot have been powerful enough to prevent hundreds of other words from having their sound changed. An effective prevention can only be expected when the falling together in sound would seriously impair the understanding of many sentences.

It is, moreover, interesting to note how many of the words which were made identical with others through this change were already rare at the time or have at any rate become obsolete since : this is true of *breech, lief, meed, mete* (adj.), *quean, weal, wheal, ween* and perhaps a few others. Now, obsolescence of some words is always found in connexion with such convergent sound changes. In some cases the word had already become rare before the change in sound took place, and then it is obvious that it cannot have offered serious resistance to the change that was setting in. In other cases the dying out of a word must be looked upon as a consequence of the sound change which had actually taken place. Many scholars are now inclined to see in phonetic coalescence one of the chief reasons why words fall into disuse, see, e.g., Liebisch (PBB XXIII, 228, many German examples in O. Weise, *Unsere Mutterspr.*, 3d ed., 206) and Gilliéron, *La faillite de l'étymologie phonétique* (Neuveville, 1919—a book whose sensational title is hardly justified by its contents).

The drawbacks of homophones [1] are counteracted in various ways. Very often a synonym steps forward, as when *lad* or *boy* is used in nearly all English dialects to supplant *son*, which has become identical in sound with *sun* (cf. above p. 120, a childish instance). Very often it becomes usual to avoid misunderstandings through some addition, as when we say *the sole of her foot*, because *her sole* might be taken to mean *her soul*, or when the French say *un dé à coudre* or *un dé à jouer* (cf. E. *minister of religion* and *cabinet minister*, the *right-hand* corner, the *subject-matter*, where the same expedient is used to obviate ambiguities arisen from other causes). Chinese, of course, is the classical example of a language abounding in homophones caused by convergent sound changes, and it is highly interesting to study the various ways in which that language has remedied the resulting drawbacks, see, e.g., B. Karlgren, *Ordet och pennan i Mittens rike* (Stockholm, 1918), p. 49 ff. But on the whole we must say that the ways in which these phonetic inconveniences are counteracted are the same as those in which speakers react against misunderstandings arising from semantic or syntactic causes: as soon as they perceive that their meaning is not apprehended they turn their phrases in a different way, choosing some other expression for their thought, and by this means language is gradually freed from ambiguity.

[1] The inconveniences arising from having many homophones in a language are eloquently set forth by Robert Bridges, *On English Homophones* (S.P.E., Oxford, 1919)—but I would not subscribe to all the Laureate's views, least of all to his practical suggestions and to his unjustifiable attacks on some very meritorious English phoneticians. He seems also to exaggerate the dangers, e.g. of the two words *know* and *no* having the same sound, when he says (p. 22) that unless a vowel like that in *law* be restored to the negative *no*, " I should judge that the verb *to know* is doomed. The third person singular of its present tense is *nose*, and its past tense is *new*, and the whole inconvenience is too radical and perpetual to be received all over the world." But surely the rôle of these words in connected speech is so different, and is nearly always made so clear by the context, that it is very difficult to imagine real sentences in which there would be any serious change of mistaking *know* for *no*, or *knows* for *nose*, or *knew* for *new*. I repeat: it is not homophony as such—the phenomenon shown in the long lists lexicographers can draw up of words of the same sound—that is decisive, but the chances of mistakes in connected speech. It has been disputed whether the loss of Gr. *humeîs*, ' ye,' was due to its identity in sound with *hemeîs*, ' we '; Hatzidakis says that the new formation *eseîs* is earlier than the falling together of *e* and *u* [y] in the sound [i]. But according to Dieterich and C. D. Buck (*Classical Philology*, 9. 90, 1914) the confusion of *u* and *i* or *e* dates back to the second century. Anyhow, all confusion is now obviated, for both the first and the second persons pl. have new forms which are unambiguous : *emeîs* and *eseîs* or *seîs*.

XV.—§ 8. Significative Sounds preserved.

My contention that the significative side of language has in so far exercised an influence on phonetic development that the possibility of many misunderstandings may effectually check the coalescence of two hitherto distinct sounds should not be identified with one of the tenets of the older school (Curtius included) against which the 'young grammarians' raised an emphatic protest, namely, that a tendency to preserve significative sounds and syllables might produce exceptions to the normal course of phonetic change. Delbrück and his friends may be right in much of what they said against Curtius—for instance, when he explained the retention of *i* in some Greek optative forms through a consciousness of the *original* meaning of this suffix ; but their denial was in its way just as exaggerated as his affirmation. It cannot justly be urged against the influence of signification that a preservation of a sound on that account would only be imaginable on the supposition that the speaker was conscious of a threatened sound change and wanted to avoid it. One need not suppose a speaker to be on his guard against a 'sound law' : the only thing required is that he should feel, or be made to feel, that he is not understood when he speaks indistinctly ; if on that account he has to repeat his words he will naturally be careful to pronounce the sound he has skipped or slurred, and may even be tempted to exaggerate it a little.

There do not seem to be many quite unimpeachable examples of words which have received exceptional phonetic treatment to obviate misunderstandings arising from homophony ; other explanations (analogy from other forms of the same word, etc.) can generally be alleged more or less plausibly. But this does seem to be the easiest explanation of the fact that the E. preposition *on* has always the full vowel [ɔ], though in nine cases out of ten it is weakly stressed and though all the other analogous prepositions (*to, for, of, at*) in the corresponding weak positions in sentences are generally pronounced with the 'neutral' vowel [ə]. But if *on* were similarly pronounced, ambiguity would very often result from its phonetic identity with the weak forms of the extremely frequent little words *an* (the indefinite article) and *and* (possibly also *in*), not to mention the great number of [ən]s in words like *drunken, shaken, deepen,* etc., where the forms without -*en* also exist. With the preposition *upon* the same considerations do not hold good, hence the frequency of the pronunciation [əpən] in weak position. Considerations of clearness have also led to the disuse of the formerly frequent form *o* (*o'*) which was the 'natural' development of each of the two prepositions *on* and *of*. The form written *a* survives only in some fossilized combinations like *ashore*; in several others it has now disappeared (*set the clock going*, formerly *a-going*, etc.).

Sometimes, when all ordinary words are affected by a certain sound change, some words prove refractory because in their case the old sound is found to be more expressive than the new one. When the long E. [iˑ] was diphthongized into [ai], the words *pipe* and *whine* ceased to be good echoisms, but some dialects have *peep* 'complain,' which keeps the old sound of the former, and the Irish say *wheen* (Joyce, *English as we speak it in Ireland*, 103). In *squeeze* the [iˑ] sound has been retained as more expressive— the earlier form was *squize*; and the same is the case with some words meaning ' to look narrowly ' : *peer, peek, keek*, earlier *pire, pike, kike* (cf. Dan. *pippe, kikke, kige*, G. *kieken*).[1] In the same way, when the old [aˑ] was changed into [ɛˑ, ei], the word *gape* ceased to be expressive (as it is still in Dan. *gabe*), but in popular speech the tendency to raise the vowel was resisted, and the old sound [gaˑp] persisted, spelt *garp* as a London form in 1817 (Ellis, EEP v. 228) and still common in many dialects (see *gaup, garp* in EDD); Professor Hempl told me that [gaˑp] was also a common pronunciation in America. In the chapter on Sound Symbolism (XX) we shall see some other instances of exceptional phonetic treatment of symbolic words (especially *tiny, teeny, little, cuckoo*).

XV.—§ 9. Divergent Changes and Analogy.

Besides equidistant and convergent sound changes we have divergent changes, through which sounds at one time identical have separated themselves later. This is a mere consequence of the fact that it is rare for a sound to be changed equally in all positions in which it occurs. On the contrary, one must admit that the vast majority of sound changes are conditioned by some such circumstance as influence of neighbouring sounds, position as initial, medial or final (often with subdivisions, as position between vowels, etc.), place in a strongly or weakly stressed syllable, and so forth. One may take as examples some familiar instances from French : Latin *c* (pronounced [k]), is variously treated before *o* (*corpus* > *corps*), *a* (*canem* > *chien*), and *e* (*centum* > *cent*) ; in *amicum* > *ami* it has totally disappeared. Lat. *a*

---

[1] The NED has not arrived at this explanation; it says : "*Peer* is not a phonetic development of *pire*, and cannot, so far as is at present known, be formally identified with that word " ; "the verbs *keek, peek*, and *peep* are app. closely allied to each other. *Kike* and *pike*, as earlier forms of *keek* and *peek*, occur in Chaucer ; *pepe, peep* is of later appearance. . . . The phonetic relations between the forms *pike, peek, peak*, are as yet unexplained."

becomes *e* in a stressed open syllable (*natum* > *né*), except before a nasal (*amat* > *aime*) ; but after *c* we have a different treatment (*canem* > *chien*), and in a close syllable it is kept (*arborem* > *arbre*) ; in weak syllables it is kept initially (*amorem* > *amour*), but becomes [ə] (spelt *e*) finally (*bona* > *bonne*). This enumeration of the chief rules will serve to show the far-reaching differentiation which in this way may take place among words closely related as parts of the same paradigm or family of words ; thus, for Lat. *amo, amas, amat, amamus, amatis, amant* we get OFr. *aim, aimes, aime, amons, amez, aiment,* until the discrepancy is removed through analogy, and we get the regular modern forms *aime, aimes, aime, aimons, aimez, aiment.* The levelling tendency, however, is not strong enough to affect the initial *a* in *amour* and *amant,* which are felt as less closely connected with the verbal forms. What were at first only small differences may in course of time become greater through subsequent changes, as when the difference between *feel* and *felt, keep* and *kept,* etc., which was originally one of length only, became one of vowel quality as well, through the raising of long [eˑ] to [iˑ], while short [e] was not raised. And thus in many other cases. Different nations differ greatly in the degree in which they permit differentiation of cognate words ; most nations resent any differentiation in initial sounds, while the Kelts have no objection to ' the same word ' having as many as four different beginnings (for instance *t-, d-, n-, nh-*) according to circumstances. In Icelandic the word for ' other, second ' has for centuries in different cases assumed such different forms as *annarr, önnur, öðrum, aðrir,* forms which in the other Scandinavian languages have been levelled down.

It is a natural consequence of the manner in which phonology is usually investigated and represented in manuals of historical grammar—which start with some old stage and follow the various changes of each sound in later stages—that these divergent changes have attracted nearly the sole attention of scholars ; this has led to the prevalent idea that sound laws and analogy are the two opposed principles in the life of languages, the former tending always to destroy regularity and harmony, and the latter reconstructing what would without it be chaos and confusion.[1]

---

[1] See, for instance, the following strong expressions : " Une langue est sans cesse rongée et menacée de ruine par l'action des lois phonétiques, qui, livrées à elles-mêmes, opéreraient avec une régularité fatale et désagrégeraient le système grammatical. . . . Heureusement l'analogie (c'est ainsi qu'on désigne la tendance inconsciente à conserver ou recréer ce que les lois phonétiques menacent ou détruisent) a peu à peu effacé ces différences . . . il s'agit d'une perpétuelle dégradation due aux changements phonétiques aveugles, et qui est toujours ou prévenue ou réparée par une réorganisation parallèle du système " (Bally, LV 44 f.).

This view, however, is too rigorous and does not take into account the manysidedness of linguistic life. It is not every irregularity that is due to the operation of phonetic laws, as we have in all languages many survivals of the confused manner in which ideas were arranged and expressed in the mind of primitive man. On the other hand, there are many phonetic changes which do not increase the number of existing irregularities, but make for regularity and a simpler system through abolishing phonetic distinctions which had no semantic or functional value ; such are, for instance, those convergent changes of unstressed vowels which have simplified the English flexional system (Ch. XIV § 10 above). And if we were in the habit of looking at linguistic change from the other end, tracing present sounds back to former sounds instead of beginning with antiquity, we should see that convergent changes are just as frequent as divergent ones. Indeed, many changes may be counted under both heads ; an *a*, which is dissociated from other *a*'s through becoming *e*, is identified with and from henceforth shares the destiny of other *e*'s, etc.

XV.—§ 10. Extension of Sound Laws.

If a phonetic change has given to some words two forms without any difference in signification, the same alternation may be extended to other cases in which the sound in question has a different origin (' phonetic analogy '). An undoubted instance is the unhistoric *r* in recent English. When the consonantal [r] was dropped finally and before a consonant while it was retained before a vowel, and words like *better*, *here* thus came to have two forms [betə, hiə] and [betər (əf), hiər (ən ðɛ‘ə)] *better off*, *here and there*, the same alternation was transferred to words like *idea*, *drama* [ai'diə, dra·mə], so that the sound [r] is now very frequently inserted before a word beginning with a vowel : *I'd no idea*-r-*of this*, *a drama*-r-*of Ibsen* (many references MEG i. 13. 42). In French final *t* and *s* have become mute, but are retained before a vowel : *il est* [ɛ] *venu*, *il est* [ɛt] *arrivé* ; *les* [le] *femmes*, *les* [lez] *hommes* ; and now vulgar speakers will insert [t] or [z] in the wrong place between vowels : *pa-t assez*, *j'allai-t écrire*, *avant-z-hier*, *moi-z-aussi* ; this is called ' cuir ' or ' velours.'

In course of time a ' phonetic law ' may undergo a kind of metamorphosis, being extended to a greater and greater number of combinations. As regards recent times we are sometimes able to trace such a gradual development. A case in point is the dropping of [j] in [ju·] after certain consonants in English [see MEG i. 13, 7). It began with *r* as in *true*, *rude* ; next came *l* when preceded by a consonant, as in *blue*, *clue* ; in these cases

[j] is never heard.　But after *l* not preceded by another consonant there is a good deal of vacillation, thus in *Lucy, absolute* ; after [s, z] as in *Susan, resume* there is a strong tendency to suppress [j], though this pronunciation has not yet prevailed,[1] and after [t, d, n], as in *tune, due, new*, the suppression is in Britain only found in vulgar speakers, while in some parts of the United States it is heard from educated speakers as well.　In the speech of these the sound law may be said to attack any [juˑ] after any point consonant, while it will have to be formulated in various less comprehensive terms for British speakers belonging to older or younger generations. It is extremely difficult, not to say impossible, to reconcile such occurrences with the orthodox ' young grammarian ' theory of sound changes being due to a shifting of the organic feeling or motor sensation (verschiebung des bewegungsgefühls) which is supposed to have necessarily taken place wherever the same sound was under the same phonetic conditions.　For what are here the same phonetic conditions ?　The position after *r*, after *l* combinations, after *l* even when standing alone, after all point consonants ?　Each generation of English speakers will give a different answer to this question.　Now, it is highly probable that many of the comprehensive prehistoric sound changes, of which we see only the final result, while possible intermediate stages evade our inquiry, have begun in the same modest way as the transition from [juˑ] to [uˑ] in English : with regard to them we are in exactly the same position as a man who had heard only such speakers as say consistently [truˑ, ruˑd, bluˑ, luˑsi, suˑzn, ri'zuˑm, tuˑn, duˑ, nuˑ] and who would then naturally suppose that [j] in the combination [juˑ] had been dropped all at once after any point consonant.

XV.—§ 11. Spreading of Sound Change.

Sound laws (to retain provisionally that firmly established term) have by some linguists, who rightly reject the comparison with natural laws (e.g. Meringer), been compared rather with the ' laws ' of fashion in dress.　But I think it is important to make a distinction here : the comparison with fashions throws no light whatever on the question how sound changes *originate*—it can tell us nothing about the first impulse to drop [j] in certain positions before [uˑ] ; but the comparison is valid when we come to consider the question how such a change when first begun in one individual *spreads to other individuals*.　While the former question has been

---

[1] Some speakers will say [suˑ] in *Susan, supreme, superstition*, but will take care to pronounce [sjuˑ] in *suit, sue*.　Others are more consistent one way or the other.

dealt with at some length in the preceding investigation, it now remains for us to say something about the latter. The spreading of phonetic change, as of any other linguistic change, is due to imitation, conscious and unconscious, of the speech habits of other people. We have already met with imitation in the chapters dealing with the child and with the influence exerted by foreign languages. But man is apt to imitate throughout the whole of his life, and this statement applies to his language as much as to his other habits. What he imitates, in this as in other fields, is not always the best; a real valuation of what would be linguistically good or preferable does not of course enter the head of the ' man in the street.' But he may imitate what he thinks pretty, or funny, and especially what he thinks characteristic of those people whom for some reason or other he looks up to. Imitation is essentially a social phenomenon, and if people do not always imitate the best (the best thing, the best pronunciation), they will generally imitate ' their betters,' i.e. those that are superior to them—in rank, in social position, in wealth, in everything that is thought enviable. What constitutes this superiority cannot be stated once for all; it varies according to surroundings, age, etc. A schoolboy may feel tempted to imitate a rough, swaggering boy a year or two older than himself rather than his teachers or parents, and in later life he may find other people worthy of imitation, according to his occupation or profession or individual taste. But when he does imitate he is apt to imitate everything, even sometimes things that are not worth imitating. In this way Percy, in *Henry IV, Second Part*, II. 3. 24—

> was indeed the glasse
> Wherein the noble youth did dresse themselues.
> He had no legges, that practic'd not his gate,
> And *speaking thicke* [1] (*which Nature made his blemish*)
> *Became the accents of the valiant.*
> *For those that could speake low and tardily,*
> *Would turne their owne perfection to abusce,*
> *To seeme like him. So that in speech,* in gate . . .
> He was the marke, and glasse, coppy, and booke,
> That fashion'd others.

The spreading of a new pronunciation through imitation must necessarily take some time, though the process may in some instances be fairly rapid. In some historical instances we are able to see how a new sound, taking its rise in some particular part of a country, spreads gradually like a wave, until finally it has pervaded the whole of a linguistic area. It cannot become universal all at once; but it is evident that the more natural a new

---

[1] I.e. " With confused and indistinct articulation; also, with a husky or hoarse voice "—NED.

mode of pronunciation seems to members of a particular speech community, the more readily will it be accepted and the more rapid will be its diffusion. Very often, both when the new pronunciation is easier and when there are special psychological inducements operating in one definite direction, the new form may originate independently in different individuals, and that of course will facilitate its acceptation by others. But as a rule a new pronunciation does not become general except after many attempts : it may have arisen many times and have died out again, until finally it finds a fertile soil in which to take firm root. It may not be superfluous to utter a warning against a fallacy which is found now and then in linguistic works : when some Danish or English document, say, of the fifteenth century contains a spelling indicative of a pronunciation which we should call 'modern,' it is hastily concluded that people in those days spoke in that respect exactly as they do now, whatever the usual spelling and the testimony of much later grammarians may indicate to the contrary. But this is far from certain. The more isolated such a spelling is, the greater is the probability that it shows nothing but an individual or even momentary deviation from what was then the common pronunciation—the first swallow ' who found with horror that he'd not brought spring.'

XV.—§ 12. Reaction.

Even those who have no linguistic training will have some apperception of sounds as such, and will notice regular correspondences, and even occasionally exaggerate them, thereby producing those ' hypercorrect ' forms which are of specially frequent occurrence when dialect speakers try to use the ' received standard ' of their country. The psychology of this process is well brought out by B. I. Wheeler, who relates (*Transact. Am. Philol. Ass*. 32. 14, 1901 ; I change his symbols into my own phonetic notation) : " In my own native dialect I pronounced *new* as [nu·]. I have found myself in later years inclined to say [nju·], especially when speaking carefully and particularly in public ; so also [tju·zdi] *Tuesday*. There has developed itself in connexion with these and other words a dual sound-image [u· : ju·] of such validity that whenever [u·] is to be formed after a dental [alveolar] explosive or nasal, the alternative [ju·] is likely to present itself and create the effect of momentary uncertainty. Less frequently than in *new, Tuesday*, the [j] intrudes itself in *tune, duty, due, dew, tumour, tube, tutor*, etc. ; but under special provocation I am liable to use it in any of these, and have even caught myself, when in a mood of uttermost precision, passing beyond the bounds of the imitative adoption of the new sound into self-annexed territory, and creating [dju·] *do* and [tju·] *two*." One more instance from America may be given : " In the dialect of Missouri and the neighbouring States, final *a* in such words as *America, Arizona, Nevada* becomes *y—Americy, Arizony, Nevady.* All educated people in that region carefully correct this vulgarism out of their speech ; and many of them carry the correction too far and say *Missoura, praira,* etc." (Sturtevant, LCH 79). Similarly, many Irish people, noticing that refined English has [i·] in many cases where they have [e·] (*tea, sea, please,* etc.) adopt [i·] in these words, and transfer it erroneously to words like *great, pear, bear,* etc. (MEG i. 11. 73) ; they may also, when correcting their own *ar* into *er*, in such words as *learn*, go too far and speak of *derning* a stocking (Joyce, *English as we speak it in Ireland*, 93). Cf. from England such forms as *ruing, certing,* for *ruin, certain.*

From Germany I may mention that Low German speakers desiring to talk High German are apt to say *zeller* instead of *teller*, because High German in many words has *z* for their *t* (*zahl, zahm*, etc.), and that those who in their native speech have *j* for *g* (Berlin, etc., *eine jute jebratene jans ist eine jute jabe jottes*) will sometimes, when trying to talk correctly, say *getzt, gahr* for *jetzt, jahr*.[1]

It will be easily seen that such hypercorrect forms are closely related to those ' spelling pronunciations ' which become frequent when there is much reading of a language whose spelling is not accurately phonetic ; the nineteenth century saw a great number of them, and their number is likely to increase in this century— especially among social upstarts, who are always fond of showing off their new-gained superiority in this and similar ways. But they need not detain us here, as being really foreign to our subject, the natural development of speech sounds. I only wish to point out that many forms which are apparently due to influence from spelling may not have their origin *exclusively* from that source, but may be genuine archaic forms that have been preserved through purely oral tradition by the side of more worn-down forms of the same word. For it must be admitted that two or three forms of the same word may coexist and be used according to the more or less solemn style of utterance employed. Even

---

[1] Even in speaking a foreign language one may unconsciously apply phonetic correspondences ; a countryman of mine thus told me that he once, in his anger at being charged an exorbitant price for something, exclaimed : " Das sind doch *unblaue* preise ! "—coining in the hurry the word *unblaue* for the Danish *ublu* (shameless), because the negative prefix *un-* corresponds to Dan. *u-*, and *au* very often stands in German where Dan. has *u* (*haus = hus*, etc.). On hearing his own words, however, he immediately saw his mistake and burst out laughing

among savages, who are unacquainted with the art of writing, we are told that archaic forms of speech are often kept up and remembered as parts of old songs only, or as belonging to solemn rites, cults, etc.

XV.—§ 13. Sound Laws and Etymological Science.

In this and the preceding chapter I have tried to pass in review the various circumstances which make for changes in the phonetic structure of languages. My treatment is far from exhaustive and may have other defects; but I want to point out the fact that nowhere have I found any reason to accept the theory that sound changes always take place according to rigorous or 'blind' laws admitting no exceptions. On the contrary, I have found many indications that complete consistency is no more to be expected from human beings in pronunciation than in any other sphere.

It is very often said that if sound laws admitted of exceptions there would be no possibility of a science of etymology. Thus Curtius wrote as early as 1858 (as quoted by Oertel 259): "If the history of language really showed such sporadic aberrations, such pathological, wholly irrational phonetic malformations, we should have to give up all etymologizing. For only that which is governed by law and reducible to a coherent system can form the object of scientific investigation; whatever is due to chance may at best be guessed at, but will never yield to scientific inference." In his practice, however, Curtius was not so strict as his followers. Leskien, one of the recognized leaders of the 'young grammarians,' says (Deklination, xxvii): "If exceptions are admitted at will (abweichungen), it amounts to declaring that the object of examination, language, is inaccessible to scientific comprehension." Since then, it has been repeated over and over again that without strict adherence to phonetic laws etymological science is a sheer impossibility, and sometimes those who have doubted the existence of strict laws in phonology have been looked upon as obscurantists adverse to a scientific treatment of language in general, although, of course, they did not believe that everything is left to chance or that they were free to put forward purely arbitrary exceptions.

There are, however, many instances in which it is hardly possible to deny etymological connexion, though 'the phonetic laws are not observed.' Is not Gothic azgo with its voiced consonants evidently 'the same word' as E. ash, G. asche, Dan. aske, with their voiceless consonants ? G. neffe with short vowel must nevertheless be identical with MHG. neve, OHG. nevo ; E. pebble with OE. papol ; rescue with ME. rescowe ; flagon with Fr. flacon, though each of these words contains deviations from what we find in other cases. It is hard to keep apart two similar forms for 'heart,' one with initial *gh* in Skt. *hrd* and Av. *zered-*, and another with initial *k* in Gr. *kardía*, *kēr*, Lat. *cor*, Goth. *haírto*, etc. The Greek ordinals *hébdomos*, *ógdoos* have voiced consonants over against the voiceless combinations in *heptá*, *oktṓ*, and yet cannot be separated from them. All this goes to show (and many more cases might be instanced) that there are in every language words so similar in sound and signification that they cannot be separated, though they break the 'sound laws': in such cases, where etymologies are too palpable, even the strictest scholars momentarily forget their strictness, maybe with great reluctance and in the secret hope that some day the reason for the deviation may be discovered and the principle thus be maintained.

Instead of exacting strict adherence to sound laws everywhere as the basis of any etymologizing, it seems therefore to be in better agreement with common sense to say : whenever an etymology is not palpably evident, whenever there is some difficulty because the compared words are either too remote in sound or in sense or belong to distant periods of the same language or to remotely related languages, your etymology cannot be reckoned as *proved* unless you have shown by other strictly parallel cases that the sound in question has been treated in exactly the same way in the same language. This, of course, applies more to old than to modern periods, and we thus see that while in living languages accessible to direct observation we do not find sound laws observed without exceptions, and though we must suppose that, on account of the essential similarity of human psychology, conditions have been the same at all periods, it is not unreasonable, in giving etymologies for words from old periods, to act as if sound changes followed strict laws admitting no exceptions ; this is simply a matter of proof, and really amounts to this : where the matter is doubtful, we must require a great degree of probability in that field which allows of the simplest and most easily controllable formulas, namely the phonetic field. For here we have comparatively definite phenomena and are consequently able with relative ease to compute the possibilities of change, while this is infinitely more difficult in the field of significations. The possibilities of semantic change are so manifold that the only thing generally required when the change is not obvious is to show some kind of parallel change, which need not even have taken place in the same language or group of languages, while with regard to sounds the corresponding changes must have occurred in the same language and at the same period in order for the evidence to be sufficient to establish the etymology in question.

It would perhaps be best if linguists entirely gave up the habit of speaking about phonetic 'laws,' and instead used some such expression as phonetic formulas or rules. But if we are to keep the word 'law,' we may with some justice think of the use of that word in juridical parlance. When we read such phrases as : this assumption is against phonetic laws, or, phonetic laws do not allow us this or that etymology, or, the writer of some book under review is guilty of many transgressions of established phonetic laws, etc., such expressions cannot help suggesting the idea that phonetic laws resemble paragraphs of some criminal law. We may formulate the principle in something like the following way : If in the etymologies you propose you do not observe these rules, if, for instance, you venture to make Gr. *kaléo* = E. *call* in spite of the fact that Gr. *k* in other words corresponds to E. *h*, then you incur the severest punishment of science, your etymology is rejected, and you yourself are put outside the pale of serious students.

In another respect phonetic laws may be compared with what we might call a Darwinian law in zoology, such as this : the fore-limbs of the common ancestor of mammals have developed into flippers in whales and into hands in apes and men. The similarity between both kinds of laws is not inconsiderable. A microscopic examination of whales, even an exact investigation by means of the eye alone, will reveal innumerable little deviations : no two flippers are exactly alike. And in the same way no two persons speak in exactly the same way. But the fact that we cannot in detail account for each of these *nuances* should not make us doubt that they are developed in a perfectly natural way, in accordance with the great law of causality, nor should we despair of the possibility of scientific treatment, even if some of the flippers and some of the sounds are not exactly what we should expect. A law of fore-limb development can only be deduced through such observation of many flippers as will single out what is typical of whales' flippers, and then a comparison with the typical fore-limbs of their ancestors or of their congeners among existing mammals. And in the same way we do not find laws of phonetic development until, after leaving what can be examined as it were microscopically, we go on telescopically to examine languages which are far removed from each other in space or time : then small differences disappear, and we discover nothing but the great lines of a regular evolution which is the outcome of an infinite number of small movements in many different directions.

XV.—§ 14. Conclusion.

It has been one of the leading thoughts in the two chapters devoted to the causes of linguistic change that phonetic changes, to be fully understood, should not be isolated from other changes, for in actual linguistic life we witness a constant interplay of sound and sense. Not only should each sound change be always as far as possible seen in connexion with other sound changes going on in the same period in the same language (as in the great vowel-raising in English), but the effects on the speech material as a whole should in each case be investigated, so as to show what homophones (if any) were produced, and what danger they entailed to the understanding of natural sentences. Sounds should never be isolated from the words in which they occur, nor words from sentences. No hard-and-fast boundary can be drawn between phonetic and non-phonetic changes. The psychological motives for both kinds of changes are the same in many cases, and the way in which both kinds spread through imitation is absolutely identical : what was said on this subject above (§ 11) applies without the least qualification to any linguistic change, whether in sounds, in grammatical forms, in syntax, in the signification of words, or in the adoption of new words and dropping of old ones.

We shall here finally very briefly consider something which plays a certain part in the development of language, but which has not been adequately dealt with in what precedes, namely, the desire to play with language. We have already met with the effects of playfulness in one of the chapters devoted to children (p. 148) : here we shall see that the same tendency is also powerful in the language of grown-up people, though most among young people. There is a certain exuberance which will not rest contented with traditional expressions, but finds amusement in the creation and propagation of new words and in attaching new meanings to old words : this is the exact opposite of that linguistic poverty which we found was at the bottom of such minimum languages as Pidgin-English. We find it in the wealth of pet-names which lovers have for each other and mothers for their children, in the nicknames of schoolboys and of ' pals ' of later life, as well as in the perversions of ordinary words which at times become the fashion among small sets of people who are constantly thrown together and have plenty of spare time ; cf. also the ' little language ' of Swift and Stella. Most of these forms of speech have a narrow range and have only an ephemeral existence, but in the world of *slang* the same tendencies are constantly at work. Slang words are often confused with vulgarisms, though the

two things are really different. The vulgar tongue is a class
dialect, and a vulgarism is an element of the normal speech of
low-class people, just as ordinary dialect words are elements of
the natural speech of peasants in one particular district ; slang
words, on the other hand, are words used in conscious contrast
to the natural or normal speech : they can be found in all classes
of society in certain moods, and on certain occasions when a speaker
wants to avoid the natural or normal word because he thinks it
too flat or uninteresting and wants to achieve a different effect
by breaking loose from the ordinary expression. A vulgarism is
what will present itself at once to the mind of a person belonging
to one particular class ; a slang word is something that is wilfully
substituted for the first word that will present itself. The distinction will perhaps appear most clearly in the case of grammar :
if a man says *them boys* instead of *those boys*, or *knowed* instead of
knew, these are the normal forms of his language, and he knows
no better, but the educated man looks down upon these forms
as vulgar. Inversely, an educated man may amuse himself now
and then by using forms which he perfectly well knows are not
the received forms, thus *wunk* from *wink*, *collode* from *collide*,
praught from *preach* (on the analogy of *taught*) ; " We handshook
and *candlestuck*, as somebody said, and went to bed " (H. James).
But, of course, slang is more productive in the lexical than in the
grammatical portion of language. And there is something that
makes it difficult in practice always to keep slang and vulgar speech
apart, namely, that when a person wants to leave the beaten path
of normal language he is not always particular as to the source
whence he takes his unusual words, and he may therefore sometimes take a vulgar word and raise it to the dignity of a slang word.

A slang word is at first individual, but may through imitation
become fashionable in certain sets ; after some time it may either
be accepted by everybody as part of the normal language, or else,
more frequently, be so hackneyed that no one finds pleasure in
using it any longer.

Slang words may first be words from the ordinary language
used in a different sense, generally metaphorically. Sometimes
we meet with the same figurative expression in the slang of various
countries, as when the ' head ' is termed *the upper story* (*upper
loft, upper works*) in English, *øverste etage* in Danish, and *oberstübchen*
in German ; more often different images are chosen in different
languages, as when for the same idea we have *nut* or *chump* in
English and *pære* (' pear ') in Danish, *coco* or *ciboule* (or *boule*) in
French. Slang words of this character may in some instances give
rise to expressions the origin of which is totally forgotten. In old
slang there is an expression for the tongue, *the red rag* ; this is

shortened into *the rag*, and I suspect that the verb *to rag*, ' to scold, rate, talk severely to ' (" of obscure origin," NED), is simply from this substantive (cf. *to jaw*).

Secondly, slang words may be words of the normal language used in their ordinary signification, but more or less modified in regard to form. Thus we have many shortened forms, *exam, quad, pub*, for *examination, quadrangle, public-house*, etc. Not unfrequently the shortening process is combined with an extension, some ending being more or less arbitrarily substituted for the latter part of the word, as when *football* becomes *footer*, and *Rugby football* and *Association football* become *Rugger* and *Socker*, or when at Cambridge a freshman is called a *fresher* and a bedmaker a *bedder*.

In schoolboys' slang (Harrow) there is an ending *-agger* which may be added instead of the latter part of any word ; about 1885 Prince Albert Victor when at Cambridge was nicknamed *the Pragger* ; an Agnostic was called a *Nogger*, etc. I strongly suspect that the word *swagger* is formed in the same way from *swashbuckler*. Another schoolboys' ending is *-g* : *fog, seg, lag*, for ' first, second, last,' *gag* at Winchester for ' gathering ' (a special kind of Latin exercise). Charles Lamb mentions from Christ's Hospital *crug* for ' a quarter of a loaf,' evidently from *crust* ; *sog* = sovereign, *snag* = snail (old), *swig* = swill ; words like *fag, peg away*, and others are perhaps to be explained from the same tendency. Arnold Bennett in one of his books says of a schoolboy that his vocabulary comprised an extraordinary number of words ending in *gs* : *foggs, seggs*, for first, second, etc. It is interesting to note that in French argot there are similar endings added to more or less mutilated words : *-aque, -èque, -oque* (Sainéan, *L'Argot ancien*, 1907, 50 and especially 57).

There is also a peculiar class of roundabout expressions in which the speaker avoids the regular word, but hints at it in a covert way by using some other word, generally a proper name, which bears a resemblance to it or is derived from it, really or seemingly. Instead of saying ' I want to go to bed,' he will say, ' I am for Bedfordshire,' or in German ' Ich gehe nach Bethlehem ' or ' nach Bettingen,' in Danish ' gå til Slumstrup, Sovstrup, Hvilsted.' Thus also ' send a person to Birching-lane,' i.e. to whip him, ' he has been at Hammersmith,' i.e. has been beaten, thrashed ; ' you are on the highway to Needham,' i.e. on the high-road to poverty, etc. (Cf. my paper on " Punning or Allusive Phrases " in *Nord. Tidsskr. f. Fil.* 3 r. 9. 66.)

The language of poetry is closely related to slang, in so far as both strive to avoid commonplace and everyday expressions. The difference is that where slang looks only for the striking or unexpected expression, and therefore often is merely eccentric or funny (sometimes only would-be comic), poetry looks higher and craves abiding beauty—beauty in thought as well as beauty in form, the latter obtained, among other things, by rhythm, alliteration, rime, and harmonious variety of vowel sounds.

In some countries these forms tend to become stereotyped, and then may to some extent kill the poetic spirit, poetry becoming artificiality instead of art; the later Skaldic poetry may serve as an illustration. Where there is a strong literary tradition—and that may be found even where there is no written literature—veneration for the old literature handed down from one's ancestors will often lead to a certain fossilization of the literary language, which becomes a shrine of archaic expressions that no one uses naturally or can master without great labour. If this state of things persists for centuries, it results in a cleavage between the spoken and the written language which cannot but have the most disastrous effects on all higher education : the conditions prevailing nowadays in Greece and in Southern India may serve as a warning. Space forbids me more than a bare mention of this topic, which would deserve a much fuller treatment; for details I may refer to K. Krumbacher, *Das Problem der neugriechischen Schriftsprache*, Munich, 1902 (for the other side of the case see G. N. Hatzidakis, *Die Sprachfrage in Griechenland*, Athens, 1905) and G. V. Ramamurti, *A Memorandum on Modern Telugu* Madras, 1913.

BOOK IV

THE DEVELOPMENT OF LANGUAGE

CHAPTER XVI

ETYMOLOGY

§ 1. Achievements. § 2. Doubtful Cases. § 3. Facts, not Fancies. § 4. Hope.
§ 5. Requirements. § 6. Blendings. § 7. Echo Words. § 8. Some
Conjunctions. § 9. Object of Etymology. § 10. Reconstruction.

XVI.—§ 1. Achievements.

FEW things have been more often quoted in works on linguistics
than Voltaire's *mot* that in etymology vowels count for nothing
and consonants for very little. But it is now said just as often
that the satire might be justly levelled at the pseudo-scientific
etymology of the eighteenth century, but has no application to our
own times, in which etymology knows how to deal with both
vowels and consonants, and—it should be added, though it is
often forgotten—with the meanings of words. One often comes
across outbursts of joy and pride in the achievements of modern
etymological science, like the following, which is quoted here *instar
omnium* : " Nowadays etymology has got past the period of more
or less ' happy thoughts ' (glücklichen einfälle) and has developed
into a science in which, exactly as in any other science, serious
persevering work must lead to reliable results " (H. Schröder,
Ablautstudien, 1910, X; cf. above, Max Müller and Whitney, p. 89).

There is no denying that much has been achieved, but it is
equally true that a skeptical mind cannot fail to be struck with
the uncertainty of many proposed explanations : very often
scholars have not got beyond ' happy thoughts,' many of which
have not even been happy enough to have been accepted by
anybody except their first perpetrators. From English alone,
which for twelve hundred years has had an abundant written
literature, and which has been studied by many eminent linguists,
who have had many sister-languages with which to compare it, it would be an easy matter to compile a long list of
words, well-known words of everyday occurrence, which etymologists have had to give up as beyond their powers of solution
(*fit, put, pull, cut, rouse, pun, fun, job*). And equally perplexing
are many words now current all over Europe, some of them
comparatively recent and yet completely enigmatic : *race, baron,
baroque, rococo, zinc.*

XVI.—§ 2. Doubtful Cases.

Or let us take a word of that class which forms the staple subject of etymological disquisitions, one in which the semantic side is literally as clear as sunshine, namely the word for ' sun.' Here we have, among others, the following forms : (1) *sun*, OE. *sunne*, Goth. *sunno* ; (2) Dan., Lat. *sol*, Goth. *sauil*, Gr. *hélios* ; (3) OE. *sigel*, *sœgl*, Goth. *sugil* ; (4) OSlav. *slŭnĭce*, Russ. *solnce* (now with mute *l*). That these forms are related cannot be doubted, but their mutual relation, and their relation to Gr. *selénē*, which means ' moon,' and to OE. *swegel* ' sky,' have never been cleared up. Holthausen derives *sunno* from the verb *sinnan* ' go ' and OE. *sigel* from the verb *sigan* ' descend, go down '—but is it really probable that our ancestors should have thought of the sun primarily as the one that goes, or that sets ? The word *south* (orig. **sunþ*; the *n* as in OHG. *sund* is still kept in Dan. *sønden*) is generally explained as connected with *sun*, and the meaning ' sunny side ' is perfectly natural ; but now H. Schröder thinks that it is derived from a word meaning ' right ' (OE. *swiðre*, orig. ' stronger,' a comparative of the adj. found in G. *geschwind*), and he says that the south is to the right when you look at the sun at sunrise—which is perfectly true, but why should people have thought of the south as being to the right when they wanted to speak of it in the afternoon or evening ?

Let me take one more example to show that our present methods, or perhaps our present data, sometimes leave us completely in the lurch with regard to the most ordinary words. We have a series of words which may all, without any formal difficulties, be referred to a root-form *seqw-*. Their significations are, respectively—

(1) ' say,' E. *say*, OE. *secgan*, ON. *segja*, G. *sagen*, Lith. *sakýti*. To this is referred Gr. *énnepe*, *enispein*, Lat. *inseque* and possibly *inquam*.

(2) ' show, point out,' OSlav. *sočiti*, Lat. *signum*.

(3) ' see,' E. *see*, OE. *seon*, Goth. *saihwan*, G. *sehen*, etc.

(4) ' follow,' Lat. *sequor*, Gr. *hépomai*, Skr. *sácate*. Here belongs Lat. *socius*, OE. *secg* ' man,' orig. ' follower.'

Now, are these four groups ' etymologically identical ' ? Opinions differ widely, as may be seen from C. D. Buck, " Words of Speaking and Saying " (*Am. Journ. of Philol.* 36. 128, 1915). They may be thus tabulated, a comma meaning supposed identity and a dash the opposite :

1, 2–3, 4 Kluge, Falk, Torp.

1, 2, 3–4 Brugmann.

1, 2, 3, 4 Wood, Buck.[1]

---

[1] With regard to Lat. *signum* it should be noted that it is by others explained as coming from Lat. *secare* and as meaning a notch.

For the transition in meaning from 'see' to 'say' we are referred to such words as *observe, notice*, G. *bemerkung*, while in G. *anweisen*, and still more in Lat. *dico*, there is a similar transition from 'show' to 'say.' Wood derives the signification 'follow' from 'point out,' through 'show, guide, attend.' With regard to the relation between 3 and 4, it has often been said that to see is to follow with the eyes. In short, it is possible, if you take some little pains, to discover notional ties between all four groups which may not be so very much looser than those between other words which everybody thinks related. And yet ? I cannot see that the knowledge we have at present enables us, or can enable us, to do more than leave the mutual relation of these groups an open question. One man's guess is just as good as another's, or one man's yes as another man's no—if the connexion of these words is 'science,' it is, if I may borrow an expression from the old archæologist Samuel Pegge, *scientia ad libitum*. Personal predilection and individual taste have not been ousted from etymological research to the extent many scholars would have us believe.

Or we may perhaps say that among the etymologies found in dictionaries and linguistic journals some are solid and firm as rocks, but others are liquid and fluctuate like the sea ; and finally not a few are in a gaseous state and blow here and there as the wind listeth. Some of them are no better than poisonous gases, from which may Heaven preserve us ! [1]

XVI.—§ 3. Facts, not Fancies.

As early as 1867 Michel Bréal, in an excellent article (reprinted in M 267 ff.), called attention to the dangers resulting from the general tendency of comparative linguists to " jump intermediate steps in order at once to mount to the earliest stages of the language," but his warning has not taken effect, so that etymologists in dealing with a word found only in comparatively recent times will often try to reconstruct what might have been its Proto-Aryan form and compare that with some word found in some other language. Thus, Falk and Torp refer G. *krieg* to an Aryan primitive form **grêigho-, *grîgho-*, which is compared with Irish

---

[1] It is, of course, impossible to say how great a proportion of the etymologies given in dictionaries should strictly be classed under each of the following heads : (1) certain, (2) probable, (3) possible, (4) improbable, (5) impossible—but I am afraid the first two classes would be the least numerous. Meillet (Gr 59) has some excellent remarks to the same effect ; according to him, " pour une étymologie sûre, les dictionnaires en offrent plus de dix qui sont douteuses et dont, en appliquant une méthode rigoureuse, on ne saurait faire la preuve."

brig 'force.' But the German word is not found in use till the middle period; it is peculiar to German and unknown in related languages (for the Scandinavian and probably also the Dutch words are later loans from Germany). These writers do not take into account how improbable it is that such a word, if it were really an old traditional word for this fundamental idea, should never once have been recorded in any of the old documents of the whole of our family of languages. What should we think of the man who would refer *boche*, the French nickname for 'German' which became current in 1914, and before that time had only been used for a few years and known to a few people only, to a Proto-Aryan root-form? Yet the method in both cases is identical; it presupposes what no one can guarantee, that the words in question are of those which trot along the royal road of language for century after century without a single side-jump, semantic or phonetic. Such words are the favourites of linguists because they have always behaved themselves since the days of Noah; but others are full of the most unexpected pranks, which no scientific ingenuity can discover if we do not happen to know the historical facts. Think of *grog*, for example. Admiral Vernon, known to sailors by the nickname of " Old Grog " because he wore a cloak of grogram (this, by the way, from Fr. *gros grain*), in 1740 ordered a mixture of rum and water to be served out instead of pure rum, and the name was transferred from the person to the drink. If it be objected that such leaps are found only in slang, the answer is that slang words very often become recognized after some time, and who knows but that may have been the case with *krieg* just as well as with many a recent word?

At any rate, facts weigh more than fancies, and whoever wants to establish the etymology of a word must first ascertain all the historical facts available with regard to the place and time of its rise, its earliest signification and syntactic construction, its diffusion, the synonyms it has ousted, etc. Thus, and thus only, can he hope to rise above loose conjectures. Here the great historical dictionaries, above all the Oxford *New English Dictionary*, render invaluable service. And let me mention one model article outside these dictionaries, in which Hermann Möller has in my opinion given a satisfactory solution of the riddle of G. *ganz*: he explains it as a loan from Slav *konici* 'end,' used especially adverbially (perhaps with a preposition in the form *v-konec* or *v-konc*) ' to the end, completely'; Slav c = G. z, Slav k pronounced essentially as South G. g; the gradual spreading and various significations and derived forms are accounted for with very great learning (*Zs. f. D. Alt.* 36. 326 ff.). It is curious that this article should have been generally overlooked or neglected, though the writer seems to have met all the legitimate requirements of a scientific etymology.

XVI.—§ 4. Hope.

I have endeavoured to fulfil these requirements in the new explanation I have given of the word *hope* (Dan. *håbe*, Swed. *hoppas*, G. *hoffen*), now used in all Gothonic tongues in exactly the same signification. Etymologists are at variance about this word. Kluge connects it with the OE. noun *hyht*, and from that form infers that Gothonic **hopôn* stands for **huqôn*, from an Aryan root *kug*; he says that a connexion with Lat. *cupio* is scarcely possible. Walde likewise rejects connexion between *cupio* and either *hope* or Goth. *hugjan*. To Falk and Torp *hope* has probably nothing to do with *hyht*, but probably with *cupio*, which is derived from a root **kup = kvap*, found in Lat. *vapor* ' steam,' and with a secondary form **kub*, in *hope*, and **kvab* in Goth. *af-hwapjan* ' choke '—a wonderful medley of significations. H. Möller (*Indoeur.-Semit. sammenlignende Glossar* 63), in accordance with his usual method, establishes an Aryo-Semitic root **k̂-u̯-*, meaning ' ardere ' and transferred to ' ardere amore, cupiditate, desiderio,' the root being extended with *b-* : *p-* in *hope* and *cupio*, with *gh-* in Goth. *hugs*, and with *ĝ-* in OE. *hyht*. Surely a typical example of the perplexity of our etymologists, who disagree in everything except just in the one thing which seems to me extremely doubtful, that *hope* with the present spiritual signification goes back to common Aryan. Now, what are the real facts of the matter ? Simply these, that the word *hope* turns up at a comparatively late date in historical times at one particular spot, and from there it gradually spreads to the neighbouring countries. In Denmark (*håb, håbe*) and in Sweden (*hopp, hoppas*) it is first found late in the Middle Ages as a religious loan from Low German *hope, hopen*. High German *hoffen* is found very rarely about 1150, but does not become common till a hundred years later ; it is undoubtedly taken (with sound substitution) from Low German and moves in Germany from north to south. Old Saxon has the subst. *tō-hopa*, which has probably come from OE., where we have the same form for the subst., *tō-hopa*. This is pretty common in religious prose, but in poetry it is found only once (Boet.)—a certain indication that the word is recent. The subst. without *tō* is comparatively late (Ælfric, ab. 1000). The verb is found in rare instances about a hundred years earlier, but does not become common till later. Now, it is important to notice that the verb in the old period never takes a direct object, but is always connected with the preposition *tō* (compare the subst.), even in modern usage we have *to hope to, for, in*. Similarly in G., where the phrase was *auf etwas hoffen* ; later the verb took a genitive, then a pronoun in the accusative, and finally an ordinary object ; in biblical language we find also *zu gott hoffen*. Now, I would connect our word with the form *hopu*, found twice as part of a compound in *Beowulf* (450 and 764), where 'refuge' gives good sense : *hopan to*, then, is to 'take one's refuge to,' and *to-hopa* 'refuge.' This verb I take to be at first identical with *hop* (the only OE. instance I know of this is Ælfric, *Hom.* 1. 202 : *hoppode ongean his drihten*). We have also one instance of a verb *onhupian* (*Cura Past.* 441) 'draw back, recoil,' which agrees with ON. *hopa* 'move backwards' (to the quotations in Fritzner may be added Laxd. 49, 15, þeir Osvígssynir hopudu undan).[1] The original meaning seems to have been 'bend, curb, bow, stoop,' either in order to leap, or to flee, from something bad, or towards something good ; cf. the subst. *hip*, OE. *hype*, Goth. *hups*, Dan. *hofte*, G. *hüfte*, Lat. *cubitus*, etc. (Holthausen, *Anglia Beibl.*, 1904, 350, deals with these words, but does not connect them with *hop*, *-hopu*, or *hope*.) The transition from bodily movement to the spiritual 'hope' may have been favoured by the existence of the verb OE. *hogian* 'think,' but is not in itself more difficult than with, e.g., Lat. *ex(s)ultare* 'leap up, rejoice,' or Dan. *lide på* 'lean to, confide in, trust,' *tillid* 'confidence, reliance' ; and a new word for 'hope' was required because the old *wen* (Goth. *wens*), vb. *wenan*, had at an early age acquired a more general meaning 'opinion, probability,' vb. 'suppose, imagine.' The difficulty that the word for 'hope' has single or short *p* (in Swed., however, *pp*), while *hop*, OE. *hoppian*, has double or long *p*, is no serious hindrance to our etymology, because the gemination may easily be accounted for on the principle mentioned below (Ch. XX § 9), that is, as giving a more vivid expression of the rapid action.

XVI.—§ 5. Requirements.

It is, of course, impossible to determine once for all by hard-and-fast rules how great the correspondence must be for us to recognize two words as 'etymologically identical,' nor to say to which of the two sides, the phonetic and the semantic, we should attach the greater importance. With the rise of historical phonology the tendency has been to require exact correspondence in the former respect, and in semantics to be content with more or less easily found parallels. One example will show how

[1] Westphalian also has *hoppen* 'zurückweichen,' ESt. 54. 88.

particular many scholars are in matters of sound. The word *nut* (OE. *hnutu*, G. *nuss*, ON. *hnot*, Dan. *nød*) is by Paul declared " not related to Lat. *nux* " and by Kluge " neither originally akin with nor borrowed from Lat. *nux*," while the NED does not even mention *nux* and thus must think it quite impossible to connect it with the English word. We have here in two related languages two words resembling each other not only in sound, but in stem-formation and gender, and possessing exactly the same signification, which is as concrete and definite as possible. And yet we are bidden to keep them asunder ! Fortunately I am not the first to protest against such barbarity : H. Pedersen (KZ n.f. 12. 251) explains both words from **dnuk-*, which by metathesis has become **knud-*; while Falk and Torp as well as Walde think the latter form the original one, which in Latin has been shifted into **dnuk-*. Which of these views is correct (both may be wrong) is of less importance than the victory of common sense over phonological pedantry.

There are two explanations which have had very often to do duty where the phonological correspondence is not exact, namely root-variation (root-expansion with determinatives) and apophony (ablaut). Of the former Uhlenbeck (PBB 30. 252) says : " The theory of root determinatives no doubt contains a kernel of truth, but it has only been fatal to etymological science, as it has drawn the attention from real correspondences between well-substantiated words to delusive similarities between hypothetical abstractions." Apophony inspires more confidence, and in many cases offers fully reliable explanations ; but this principle, too, has been often abused, and it is difficult to find its true limitations. Many special applications of it appear questionable ; thus, when G. *stumm*, Dan. *stum*, is explained as an apophonic form of the adj. *stam*, Goth. *stamms*, from which we have the verb *stammer*, G. *stammeln*, Dan. *stamme* : is it really probable that the designation of muteness should be taken from the word for stammering ? This appears especially improbable when we consider that at the time when the new word *stumm* made its appearance there was already another word for ' mute,' namely *dumm*, *dumb*, the word which has been preserved in English. I therefore propose a new etymology : *stumm* is a blending of the two synonyms *still(e)* and *dum(b)*, made up of the beginning of the one and the ending of the other word ; through adopting the initial *st-* the word was also associated with *stump*, and we get an exact correspondence between *dumm*, *dum*, *stumm*, *stum*, applied to persons, and *dumpf*, *stumpf*, Dan. *dump*, *stump*, applied to things. Note that in those languages (G., Dan.) in which the new word *stum(m)* was used, the unchanged *dum(m)* was free to develop the new sense ' stupid ' (or was the creation of *stum* occasioned by the old word tending already to acquire this secondary meaning ?), while *dumb* in English stuck to the old signification.

XVI.—§ 6. Blendings.

Blendings of synonyms play a much greater rôle in the development of language than is generally recognized. Many instances may be heard in everyday life, most of them being immediately corrected by the speaker (see above, XV § 4), but these momentary lapses cannot be separated from other instances which are of more permanent value because they are so natural that they will occur over and over again until speakers will hardly feel the blend as anything else than an ordinary word. M. Bloomfield (IF 4. 71) says that he has been many years conscious of an irrepressible desire to assimilate the two verbs *quench* and *squelch* in both directions by forming *squench* and *quelch*, and he has found the former word in a negro story by Page. The expression ' irrepressible desire ' struck me on reading this, for I have myself in my Danish speech the same feeling whenever I am to speak of tending a patient, for I nearly always say *plasse* as a result of wavering between *pleje* [*plaiə*] and *passe*. Many examples may be found in G. A. Bergström, *On Blendings of Synonymous or Cognate Expressions in English*, Lund, 1906, and Louise Pound, *Blends, Their Relation to English Word Formation*, Heidelberg, 1914. But neither of these two writers has seen the full extent of this principle of formation, which explains many words of greater importance than those nonce words which are found so plentifully in Miss Pound's paper. Let me give some examples, some of them new, some already found by others :

> *blot* = *bl*emish, *bl*ack + sp*ot*, p*l*ot, d*ot* ; there is also an obsolete sp*l*ot.
>
> *blunt* = *bl*ind + s*t*unt.
>
> *crouch* = *cr*inge, *cr*ook, *cr*awl, †*crouk* + *couch*.
>
> *flush* = *fl*ash + b*lush*.
>
> *frush* = *fr*og + th*rush* (all three names of the same disease in a horse's foot).
>
> *glaze* (Shakespeare) = *gl*are + *gaze*.
>
> *good-bye* = *good*-night, *good*-morning + *godbye* (God be with ye).
>
> *knoll* = *kn*ell + *toll*.
>
> *scroll* = *scrow* + *roll*.
>
> *slash* = *sl*ay, *sl*ing, *sl*at + *gash*, d*ash*.
>
> *slender* ⇐ *sl*ight (*sl*im) + *tender*.

Such blends are especially frequent in words expressive of sounds or in some other way symbolical, as, for instance :

flurry = *fl*ing, *fl*ow and many other *fl*-words + *hurry* (note also *scurry*).

gruff = *gru*m, *gri*m + *rough*.

slide = *sli*p + *glide*.

troll = *tri*ll + *roll* (in some senses perhaps rather from *tread*, *trundle* + *roll*).

twirl = *twi*st + *whirl*.

In slang blends abound, e.g. :

tosh   (Harrow) = *tu*b + *wash*. (Sometimes explained as *toe-wash*.)

blarmed = *blamed*, *blessed* and other *bl*-words + *darned* (damned).

be danged = *da*mned + *hanged*.

I swow = *swe*ar + *vow*.

brunch = *br*eakfast + *lunch* (so also, though more rarely *brupper* (. . . + *supper*), *tunch* (*tea* + *lunch*), *tupper* = *tea* + *supper*).[1]

XVI.—§ 7. Echo-words.

Most etymologists are very reluctant to admit echoism ; thus Diez rejects onomatopœic origin of It. *pisciare*, Fr. *pisser*—an echo-word if ever there was one—and says, " One can easily go too far in supposing onomatopœia : as a rule it is more advisable to build on existing words " ; this he does by deriving this verb from a non-existing *pipisare, *pipsare*, from *pipa* ' pipe, tube.' Falk and Torp refer *dump* (Dan. *dumpe*) to Swed. *dimpa*, a Gothonic root *demp*, supposed to be an extension of an Aryan root *dhen* : thus they are too deaf to hear the sound of the heavy fall expressed by *um*(*p*), cf. Dan. *bumpe*, *bums*, *plumpe*, *skumpe*, *jumpe*, and similar words in other languages.

It may be fancy, but I think I hear the same sound in Lat. *plumbum*, which I take to mean at first not the metal, but the plummet that was dumped or plumped into the water and was denominated from the sound ; as this was generally made of lead, the word came to be used for the metal. Most etymologists take it for granted that *plumbum* is a loan-word, some being honest enough to confess that they do not know from what language, while others without the least scruple or hesitation say that it was taken from Iberian : our ignorance of that language is so

---

[1] Lewis Carrol's ' portmanteau words ' are, of course, famous.

deep that no one can enter an expert's protest against such a supposition.[1] But if my hypothesis is right, the words *plummet* (from OFr. *plommet*, a diminutive of *plomb*) as well as the verb Fr. *plonger*, whence E. *plunge*, from Lat. **plumbicare*, are not only derivatives from *plumbum* (the only thing mentioned by other scholars), but also echo-words, and they, or at any rate the verb, must to a great extent owe their diffusion to their felicitously symbolic sound. In a novel I find : "Plump went the lead "— showing how this sound is still found adequate to express the falling of the lead in sounding. The NED says under the verb *plump* : "Some have compared L. *plumbare* . . . to throw the lead-line . . . but the approach of form between *plombar* and the LG. *plump-plomp* group seems merely fortuitous" (!). I see sound symbolism in *all* the words *plump*, while the NED will only allow it in the most obvious cases. From the sound of a body plumping into the water we have interesting developments in the adverb, as in the following quotations : I said, *plump* out, that I couldn't stand any more of it (Bernard Shaw) | The famous diatribe against Jesuitism points *plumb* in the same direction (Morley) | fall *plum* into the jaws of certain critics (Swift) | Nollie was a *plumb* little idiot (Galsworthy). In the last sense ' entirely ' it is especially frequent in America, e.g. They lost their senses, *plumb* lost their senses (Churchill) | she's *plum* crazy, it's *plum* bad, etc. Related words for fall, etc., are *plop*, *plout*, *plunk*, *plounce*. Much might also be said in this connexion of various *pop* and *bob* words, but I shall refrain.

XVI.—§ 8. Some Conjunctions.

Sometimes obviously correct etymologies yet leave some psychological points unexplained. One of my pet theories concerns some adversative conjunctions. Lat. *sed* has been supplanted by *magis* : It. *ma*, Sp. *mas*, Fr. *mais*. The transition is easily accounted for ; from ' more ' it is no far cry to ' rather ' (cf. G. *vielmehr*), which can readily be employed to correct or gainsay what has just been said. The Scandinavian word for ' but ' is *men*, which came into use in the fifteenth century and is explained as a blending

---

[1] Speculation has been rife, but without any generally accepted results, as to the relation between *plumbum* and words for the same metal in cognate languages : Gr. *molibos*, *molubdos* and similar forms, Ir. *luaide*, E. *lead* (G. *lot*, ' plummet, half an ounce '), Scand. *bly*, OSlav. *olovo*, OPruss. *alwis* ; see Curtius, Prellwitz, Boisacq, Hirt Idg. 686, Schrader *Sprachvergl. u. Urgesch.*, 3d. ed., ii. 1. 95 ; Herm. Möller, *Sml. Glossar* 87, says that *molibos* and *plumbum* are extensions of the root *m-l* ' mollis esse ' and explains the difference between the initial sounds by referring to *multum* : comp. *plus*—certainly most ingenious, but not convincing. Some of these words may originally have been echo-words for the plumping plummet.

of *meden* in its shortened form *men* (now *mens*) ' while ' and Low
German *men* ' but,' which stands for older *niwan*, from the negative
ni and *wan* ' wanting ' ; the meaning has developed through that
of ' except ' and the sound is easily understood as an instance of
assimilation. The same phonetic development is found in Dutch
maar, OFris. *mar*, from *en ware* ' were not,' the same combination
which has yielded G. *nur*. Thus we have four different ways of
getting to expressions for ' but,' none of which presents the least
difficulty to those familiar with the semantic ways of words. But
why did these various nations seize on new words ? Weren't the
old ones good enough ?

Here I must call attention to two features that are common
to these new conjunctions, first their syntactic position, which
is invariably in the beginning of the sentence, while such synonymous words as Lat. *autem* and G. *aber* may be placed after one
or more words ; then their phonetic agreement in one point : *magis*,
men, *maar* all begin with *m*. Now, both these features are found
in two words for ' but,' about whose etymological origin I can
find no information, Finnic *mutta* and Santal *menkhan*, as well as
in *me*, which is used in the *Ancrene Riwle* and a few other early
Middle English texts and has been dubiously connected with the
Scandinavian (and French ?) word. How are we to explain these
curious coincidences ? I think by the nature of the sound [m],
which is produced when the lips are closed while the tongue rests
passively and the soft palate is lowered so as to allow air to escape
through the nostrils—in short, the position which is typical of
anybody who is quietly thinking over matters without as yet
saying anything, with the sole difference that in his case the vocal
chords are passive, while they are made to vibrate to bring forth
an *m*.

Now, it very often happens that a man wants to say something,
but has not yet made up his mind as to *what* to say ; and in this
moment of hesitation, while thoughts are in the process of conception, the lungs and vocal chords will often be prematurely
set going, and the result is [m] (sometimes preceded by the corresponding voiceless sound), often written *hm* or *h'm*, which thus
becomes the interjection of an unshaped contradiction. Not
infrequently this [m] precedes a real word ; thus *M'yes* (written
in this way by Shaw, *Misalliance* 154, and Merrick, *Conrad* 179)
and Dan. *mja*, to mark a hesitating consent.

This will make it clear why words beginning with *m* are so
often chosen as adversative conjunctions : people begin with this
sound and go on with some word that gives good sense and which
happens to begin with *m* : *mais*, *maar*. The Dan. *men* in the
mouth of some early speakers is probably this [m], sliding into

the old conjunction *en*, just as *myes* is *m* + *yes* ; while other original users of *men* may have been thinking of *men* = *meden*, and others again of Low German *men* : these three etymologies are not mutually destructive, for all three origins may have concurrently contributed to the popularity of *men*. Modern Greek and Serbian *ma* are generally explained as direct loans from Italian, but may be indigenous, as may also dialectal Rumanian *ma* in the same sense, for in the hesitating [m] as the initial sound of objections we have one of those touches of nature which make the whole world kin.[1]

XVI.—§ 9. Object of Etymology.

What is the object of etymological science ? "To determine the true signification of a word," answers one of the masters of etymological research (Walde, *Lat. et. Wörterb.* xi). But surely in most cases that can be achieved without the help of etymology. We know the true sense of hundreds of words about the etymology of which we are in complete ignorance, and we should know exactly what the word *grog* means, even if the tradition of its origin had been accidentally lost. Many people still believe that an account of the origin of a name throws some light on the essence of the thing it stands for ; when they want to define say ' religion ' or ' civilization,' they start by stating the (real or supposed) origin of the name—but surely that is superstition, though the first framers of the name ' etymology ' (from Gr. *etumon* ' true ') must have had the same idea in their heads. Etymology tells us nothing about the things, nor even about the present meaning of a word, but only about the way in which a word has come into existence. At best, it tells us not what *is* true, but what *has been* true.

The overestimation of etymology is largely attributable to the "conviction that there can be nothing in language that had not an intelligible purpose, that there is nothing that is now irregular that was not at first regular, nothing irrational that was not originally rational " (Max Müller)—a conviction which is still found to underlie many utterances about linguistic matters, but which readers of the present volume will have seen is erroneous in many ways. On the whole, Max Müller naïvely gives expression to what is unconsciously at the back of much that is said and believed about language ; thus, when he says (L 1. 44) : " I must ask you at present to take it for granted that everything in language had originally a meaning. As language can have no other object but to express our meaning, it might seem to follow almost by

---

[1] I have discussed this more in detail and added other *m*-words of a somewhat related character in *Studier tillegnade E. Tegnér*, 1918, p. 49 ff.

necessity that language should contain neither more nor less than
what is required for that purpose." Yes, so it would if language
had been constructed by an omniscient and omnipotent being,
but as it was developed by imperfect human beings, there is every
possibility of their having failed to achieve their purpose and
having done either more or less than was required to express
their meaning. It would be wrong to say that language (i.e.
speaking man) created first what was strictly necessary, and afterwards what might be considered superfluous ; but it would be
equally wrong to say that linguistic luxuries were always created
before necessaries ; yet that view would probably be nearer the
truth than the former. Much of what in former ages was felt
to be necessary to express thoughts was afterwards felt as pedantic
crisscross and gradually eliminated ; but at all times many things
have been found in language that can never have been anything
else but superfluous, exactly as many people use a great many
superfluous gestures which are not in the least significant and in
no way assist the comprehension of their intentions, but which
they somehow feel an impulse to perform. In language, as in
life generally, we have too little in some respects, and too much
in others.

XVI.—§ 10. Reconstruction.

Kluge somewhere (PBB 37. 479, 1911) says that the establishment of the common Aryan language is the chief task of our
modern science of linguistics (to my mind it can never be more
than a fragment of that task, which must be to understand the
nature of language), and he thinks optimistically that "reconstructions with their reliable methods have taken so firm root
that we are convinced that we know the common Aryan *grund-
sprache* just as thoroughly as any language that is more or less
authenticated through literature." This is a palpable exaggeration, for no one nowadays has the courage of Schleicher to print
even the smallest fable in Proto-Aryan, and if by some miraculous
accident we were to find a text written in that language we may
be sure it would puzzle us just as much as Tokharian does.

Reconstruction has two sides, an outer and an inner. With
regard to sounds, it seems to me that very often the masters of
linguistics treat us to reconstructed forms that are little short
of impossible. This is not the place to give a detailed criticism
of the famous theory of 'nasalis sonans,' but I hope elsewhere
to be able to state why I think this theory a disfiguring excrescence on linguistic science : no one has ever been able to find
in any existing language such forms as *mnto* with stressed syllabic

[n], given as the old form of our word *mouth* (Falk and Torp even give *stmnto* in order to connect the word with Gr. *stóma*), or as *dkmtóm* (whence Lat. *centum*, etc.) or *bhrghnties* or *gumskete* (Brugmann). Not only are these forms phonetically impossible, but the theory fails to explain the transitions to the forms actually existing in real languages, and everything is much easier if we assume forms like [ʌm, ʌn] with some vowel like that of E. *un-*. The use in Proto-Aryan reconstructions of non-syllabic *i* and *u* also in some respects invites criticism, but it will be better to treat these questions in a special paper.

Semantic reconstruction calls for little comment here. It is evident from the nature of the subject that no such strict rules can be given in this domain as in the domain of sound ; but nowadays scholars are more realistic than formerly. Most of them will feel satisfied when *moon* and *month* are associated with words having the same two significations in related languages, without indulging in explanations of both from a root *me* ' to measure ' ; and when our *daughter* has been connected with Gr. *thugáter*, Skt. *duhitár* and corresponding words in other languages, no attempt is made to go beyond the meaning common to these words ' daughter ' and to speculate what had induced our ancestors to bestow that word on that particular relation, as when Lassen derived it from the root *duh* ' to milk ' and pictured an idyllic family life, in which it was the business of the young girls to milk the cows, or when Fick derived the same word from the root *dheugh* ' to be useful ' (G. *taugen* : ' wie die *magd, maid* von *mögen* '), as if the daughters were the only, or the most, efficient members of the family. Unfortunately, such speculations are still found lingering in many recent handbooks of high standing : Kluge hesitates whether to assign the word *mutter, mother*, to the root *ma* in the sense ' mete out ' or in the sense found in Sanskrit ' to form,' used of the fœtus in the womb. A resigned acquiescence in inevitable ignorance and a sense of reality should certainly be characteristics of future etymologists.

CHAPTER XVII

PROGRESS OR DECAY?

§ 1. Linguistic Estimation.   § 2. Degeneration ?   § 3. Appreciation of Modern
Tongues.   § 4. The Scientific Attitude.   § 5. Final Answer.   § 6.
Sounds.   § 7. Shortenings.   § 8. Objections.   Result.   § 9. Verbal
Forms.   § 10. Synthesis and Analysis.   § 11. Verbal Concord.

XVII.—§ 1. Linguistic Estimation.

THE common belief of linguists that one form or one expression
is just as good as another, provided they are both found in actual
use, and that each language is to be considered a perfect vehicle
for the thoughts of the nation speaking it, is in some ways the
exact counterpart of the conviction of the Manchester school of
economics that everything is for the best in the best of all possible
worlds if only no artificial hindrances are put in the way of free
exchange, for demand and supply will regulate everything better
than any Government would be able to.   Just as economists were
blind to the numerous cases in which actual wants, even crying
wants, were not satisfied, so also linguists were deaf to those instances which are, however, obvious to whoever has once turned
his attention to them, in which the very structure of a language
calls forth misunderstandings in everyday conversation, and in
which, consequently, a word has to be repeated or modified or
expanded or defined in order to call forth the idea intended by
the speaker : he took his stick—no, not John's, but *his own*;
or : I mean *you* in the plural (or, you all, or you girls) ; no, a
box on the ear ; un dé à jouer, non pas un dé à coudre ; nein, ich
meine *Sie persönlich* (with very strong stress on *Sie*), etc.   Every
careful writer in any language has had the experience that on
re-reading his manuscript he has discovered that a sentence which
he thought perfectly clear when he wrote it lends itself to misunderstanding and has to be put in a different way ; sometimes
he has to add a clarifying parenthesis, because his language is
defective in some respect, as when Edward Carpenter (*Art of
Creation* 171), in speaking of the deification of the Babe, writes :
" It is not likely that Man—the human male—left to himself
would have done this ; but to woman it was natural," thus avoiding
the misunderstanding that he was speaking of the whole species,

comprising both sexes. Herbert Spencer writes : "Charles had recently obtained—a post in the Post Office I was about to say, but the cacophony stopped me ; and then I was about to say, an office in the Post Office, which is nearly as bad ; let me say— a place in the Post Office" (*Autobiogr.* 2. 73—but of course the defect is not really one of sound, as implied by the expression 'cacophony,' but one of signification, as both words *post* and *office* are ambiguous, and the attempted collocation would therefore puzzle the reader or hearer, because the same word would have to be apprehended in two different senses in close succession). Similar instances might be alleged from any language.

No language is perfect, but if we admit this truth (or truism), we must also admit by implication that it is not unreasonable to investigate the relative value of different languages or of different details in languages. When comparative linguists set themselves against the narrowmindedness of classical scholars who thought Latin and Greek the only worthy objects of study, and emphasized the value of all, even the least literary languages and dialects, they were primarily thinking of their value to the scientist, who finds something of interest in each of them, but they had no idea of comparing the relative value of languages from the point of view of their users—and yet the latter comparison is of much greater importance than the former.

XVII.—§ 2. Degeneration ?

People will often use the expressions ' evolution ' and ' development ' in connexion with language, but most linguists, when taken to task, will maintain that these expressions as applied to languages should be used without the implication which is commonly attached to them when used of other objects, namely, that there is a progressive tendency towards something better or nearer perfection. They will say that ' evolution ' means here simply changes going on in languages, without any judgment as to the value of these changes.

But those who do pronounce such a judgment nearly always take the changes as a retrogressive rather than a progressive development : "Tongues, like governments, have a natural tendency to degeneration," said Dr. Samuel Johnson in the Preface to his Dictionary, and the same lament has been often repeated since his time. This is quite natural : people have always had a tendency to believe in a golden age, that is, in a remote past gloriously different to the miserable present. Why not, then, have the same belief with regard to language, the more so because one cannot fail to notice things in contemporary speech which (superficially at any rate) look like corruptions of the 'good old' forms ? Everything 'old' thus comes to be considered 'good.' Lowell and others think they have justified many of the commonly reviled Americanisms if they are able to show them to have existed in England in the sixteenth century, and similar considerations are met with everywhere. The same frame of mind finds support in the usual grammar-school admiration for the two classical languages and their literatures. People were taught to look down upon modern languages as mere dialects or *patois* and to worship Greek and Latin ; the richness and fullness of forms found in those languages came naturally to be considered the very *beau idéal* of linguistic structure. Bacon gives a classical expression to this view when he declares " ingenia priorum seculorum nostris fuisse multo acutiora et subtiliora " (*De augm. scient.*[1]). To men fresh from the ordinary grammar-school training, no language would seem really respectable that had not four or five distinct cases and three genders, or that had less than five tenses and as many moods in its verbs. Accordingly, such poor languages as had either lost much of their original richness in grammatical forms (*e.g.* French, English, or Danish), or had never had any, so far as one knew (*e.g.* Chinese), were naturally looked upon with something of the pity bestowed on relatives in reduced circumstances, or the contempt felt for foreign paupers. It is well known how in West-European languages, in English, German, Danish, Swedish, Dutch, French, etc., obsolete forms were artificially kept alive and preferred to younger forms by most grammarians ; but we see exactly the same point of view in such a language as Magyar, where, under the influence of the historical studies of the grammarian Révai, the belief in the excellence of the 'veneranda antiquitas' as compared with the corruption of the modern language has been prevalent in schools and in literature. (See Simonyi US 259; cf. on Modern Greek and Telugu above, p. 301.)

Comparative linguists had one more reason for adopting this manner of estimating languages. To what had the great victories won by their science been due ? Whence had they got the material for that magnificent edifice which had proved spacious enough to hold Hindus and Persians, Lithuanians and Slavs, Greeks, Romans, Germans and Kelts ? Surely it was neither from Modern English nor Modern Danish, but from the oldest stages of each linguistic group. The older a linguistic document was, the

---

[1] Quoted here from John Wilkins, *An Essay towards a Real Character and a Philosophical Language*, 1668, p. 448 : Wilkins there subjects Bacon's saying to a crushing criticism, laying bare a great many radical deficiencies in Latin to bring out the logical advantages of his own artificial 'philosophical' language.

more valuable it was to the first generation of comparative linguists. An English form like *had* was of no great use, but Gothic *habaide-deima* was easily picked to pieces, and each of its several elements lent itself capitally to comparison with Sanskrit, Lithuanian and Greek. The linguist was chiefly dependent for his material on the old and archaic languages; his interest centred round their fuller forms : what wonder, then, if in his opinion those languages were superior to all others ? What wonder if by comparing *had* and *habaidedeima* he came to regard the English form as a mutilated and worn-out relic of a splendid original ? or if, noting the change from the old to the modern form, he used strong language and spoke of degeneration, corruption, depravation, decline, phonetic decay, etc. ?

The view that the modern languages of Europe, Persia and India are far inferior to the old languages, or the one old language, from which they descend, we have already encountered in the historical part of this work, in Bopp, Humboldt, Grimm and their followers. It looms very large in Schleicher, according to whom the history of language is all a Decline and Fall, and in Max Müller, who says that " on the whole, the history of all the Aryan languages is nothing but a gradual process of decay." Nor is it yet quite extinct.

XVII.—§ 3. Appreciation of Modern Tongues.

Some scholars, however, had an indistinct feeling that this unconditional and wholesale depreciation of modern languages could not contain the whole truth, and I have collected various passages, nearly always of a perfunctory or incidental character, in which these languages are partly rehabilitated. Humboldt (Versch 284) speaks of the modern use of auxiliary verbs and prepositions as a convenience of the intellect which may even in some isolated instances lead to greater definiteness. On Grimm see above, p. 62. Rask (SA 1. 191) says that it is possible that the advantages of simplicity may be greater than those of an elaborate linguistic structure. Madvig turns against the uncritical admiration of the classical languages, but does not go further than saying that the modern analytical languages are just as good as the old synthetic ones, for thoughts can be expressed in both with equal clearness. Kräuter (*Archiv f. neu. spr.* 57. 204) says : " That decay is consistent with clearness and precision is shown by French ; that it is not fatal to poetry is seen in the language of Shakespeare." Osthoff (*Schriftspr. u. Volksmundart*, 1883, 13) protests against a one-sided depreciation of the language of Lessing and Goethe in favour of the language of Wulfila or

Otfried, or vice versa : a language possesses an inestimable charm if its phonetic system remains unimpaired and its etymologies are transparent ; but pliancy of the material of language and flexibility to express ideas is really no less an advantage ; everything depends on the point of view : the student of architecture has one point of view, the people who are to live in the house another.

Among those who thus half-heartedly refused to accept the downhill theory to its full extent must be mentioned Whitney, many passages in whose writings show a certain hesitation to make up his mind on this question. When speaking of the loss of old forms he says that " some of these could well be spared, but others were valuable, and their relinquishment has impaired the power of expression of the language." To phonetic corruption we owe true grammatical forms, which make the wealth of every inflective language ; but it is also destructive of the very edifice which it has helped to build. He speaks of " the legitimate tendency to neglect and eliminate distinctions which are practically unnecessary," and will not admit " that we can speak our minds any less distinctly than our ancestors could, with all their apparatus of inflexions " ; gender is a luxury which any language can well afford to dispense with, but language is impoverished by the obliteration of the subjunctive mood.   The giving up of grammatical endings is akin to wastefulness, and the excessive loss in English makes truly for decay (L 31, 73, 74, 76, 77, 84, 85 ; G 51, 105, 104).

XVII.—§ 4. The Scientific Attitude.

Why are all such expressions either of depreciation or of partial appreciation of the modern languages so utterly unsatisfactory ? One reason is that they are so vague and dependent on a general feeling of inferiority or the reverse, instead of being based on a detailed comparative estimation of real facts in linguistic structure. If, therefore, we want to arrive at a scientific answer to the question " Decay or progress ? " we must examine actual instances of changes, but must take particular care that these instances are not chosen at random, but are typical and characteristic of the total structure of the languages concerned. What is wanted is not a comparison of isolated facts, but the establishment of general laws and tendencies, for only through such can we hope to decide whether or no we are justified in using terms like ' development ' and ' evolution ' in linguistic history.

The second reason why the earlier pronouncements quoted above do not satisfy us is that their authors nowhere raise the question of the method by which linguistic value is to be measured, by what standard and what tests the comparative merits of languages or of forms are to be ascertained. Those linguists who looked upon language as a product of nature were by that very fact precluded from establishing a rational basis for determining linguistic values ; nor is it possible to find one if we look at things from the one-sided point of view of the linguistic historian. An almost comical instance of this is found when Curtius (*Sprachwiss. u. class. phil.* 39) says that the Greek accusative *póda* is better than Sanskrit *padam,* because it is possible at once to see that it belongs to the third declension. What is to be taken into account is of course the interests of the speaking community, and if we consistently consider language as a set of human actions with a definite end in view, namely, the communication of thoughts and feelings, then it becomes easy to find tests by which to measure linguistic values, for from that point of view it is evident that THAT LANGUAGE RANKS HIGHEST WHICH GOES FARTHEST IN THE ART OF ACCOMPLISHING MUCH WITH LITTLE MEANS, OR, IN OTHER WORDS, WHICH IS ABLE TO EXPRESS THE GREATEST AMOUNT OF MEANING WITH THE SIMPLEST MECHANISM.

The estimation has to be thoroughly and frankly *anthropocentric.* This may be a defect in other sciences, in which it is a merit on the part of the investigator to be able to abstract himself from human considerations ; in linguistics, on the contrary, on account of the very nature of the object of study, one must constantly look to the human interest, and judge everything from that, and from no other, point of view. Otherwise we run the risk of going astray in all directions.

It will be noticed that my formula contains two requirements : it demands a maximum of efficiency and a minimum of effort. Efficiency means expressiveness, and effort means bodily and mental labour, and thus the formula is simply one of modern energetics. But unfortunately we are in possession of no method by which to measure either expressiveness or effort exactly, and in cases of conflict it may be difficult to decide to which of the two sides we are to attach the greater importance, how great a surplus of efficiency is required to counterbalance a surplus of exertion, or inversely. Still, in many cases no doubt can arise, and we are often able to state progress, because there is either a clear gain in efficiency or a diminution of exertion, or both.

There is one objection which is likely to present itself to many of my readers, namely, that natives handle their language without the least exertion or effort (cf. XIV § 6, p. 262). Madvig (1857, 73 ff.=Kl 260 ff.) admits that a simplification in linguistic structure will make the language easier to learn for foreigners, but denies that it means increased ease for the native. Similarly Wechssler (L 149) says that "der begriff der schwierigkeit und unbequemheit für die einheimischen nicht existiert." I might quote against him his countryman Gabelentz, who expressly says that the difficulties of the German languages are felt by natives, a view that is endorsed by Schuchardt in various places.[1] To my mind there is not the slightest doubt that different languages differ very much in easiness even to native speakers. In the chapters devoted to children we have already seen that the numerous mistakes made by them in every possible way testify to the labour involved in learning one's own language. This labour must naturally be greater in the case of a highly complicated linguistic structure with many rules and still more exceptions to the rules, than in languages constructed simply and regularly.

Nor is the difficulty of correct speech confined to the first mastering of the language. Even to the native who has spoken the same language from a child, its daily use involves no small amount of exertion. Under ordinary circumstances he is not conscious of any exertion in speaking ; but such a want of conscious feeling is no proof that the exertion is absent. And it is a strong argument to the contrary that it is next to impossible for you to speak correctly if you are suffering from excessive mental work ; you will constantly make slips in grammar and idiom as well as in pronunciation ; you have not the same command of language as under normal conditions. If you have to speak on a difficult and unfamiliar subject, on which you would not like to say anything but what is to the point or strictly justifiable, you will sometimes find that the thoughts themselves claim so much mental energy that there is none left for speaking with elegance, or even with complete regard to grammar : to your own vexation you will have a feeling that your phrases are confused and your language incorrect. A pianist may practise a difficult piece of music so as to have it "at his fingers' ends " ; under ordinary circumstances he will be able to play it quite mechanically, without ever being conscious of effort ; but, nevertheless, the effort is there. How great the effort is appears when some day or other the musician is 'out of humour,' that is, when his brain is at work on other subjects or is not in its usual working order. At once his execution will be stumbling and faulty.

[1] Cf. also what Paul says (P 144) about one point in German grammar (strong and weak forms of adjectives) : "But the difficulty of the correct maintenance of the distinction is shown in numerous offences made by writers against the rules of grammar "—of course, not only by writers, but by ordinary speakers as well.

XVII.—§ 5. Final Answer.

I may here anticipate the results of the following investigation and say that in all those instances in which we are able to examine the history of any language for a sufficient length of time, we find that languages have a progressive tendency. But if languages progress towards greater perfection, it is not in a bee-line, nor are all the changes we witness to be considered steps in the right direction. The only thing I maintain is that *the sum total of these changes, when we compare a remote period with the present time, shows a surplus of progressive over retrogressive or indifferent changes,* so that the structure of modern languages is nearer perfection than that of ancient languages, if we take them as wholes instead of picking out at random some one or other more or less significant detail. And of course it must not be imagined that progress has been achieved through deliberate acts of men conscious that they were improving their mother-tongue. On the contrary, many a step in advance has at first been a slip or even a blunder, and, as in other fields of human activity, good results have only been won after a good deal of bungling and 'muddling along.' [1] My attitude towards this question is the same as that of Leslie Stephen, who writes in a letter (*Life* 454): "I have a perhaps unreasonable amount of belief, not in a millennium, but in the world on the whole blundering rather forwards than backwards."

Schleicher on one occasion used the fine simile : "Our words, as contrasted with Gothic words, are like a statue that has been rolling for a long time in the bed of a river till its beautiful limbs have been worn off, so that now scarcely anything remains but a polished stone cylinder with faint indications of what it once was" (D 34). Let us turn the tables by asking : Suppose, however, that it would be quite out of the question to place the statue on a pedestal to be admired ; what if, on the one hand, it was not ornamental enough as a work of art, and if, on the other hand, human well-being was at stake if it was not serviceable in a rolling-mill : which would then be the better—a rugged and unwieldy statue, making difficulties at every rotation, or an even, smooth, easygoing and well-oiled roller ?

After these preliminary considerations we may now proceed to a comparative examination of the chief differences between ancient and modern stages of our Western European languages.

---

[1] It has often been pointed out how Great Britain has 'blundered' into creating her world-wide Empire, and Gretton, in *The King's Government* (1914), applies the same view to the development of governmental institutions.

XVII.—§ 6. Sounds.

The student who goes through the chapters devoted to sound
changes in historical and comparative grammars will have great
difficulty in getting at any great lines of development or general
tendencies : everything seems just haphazard and fortuitous ; a
long *i* is here shortened and there diphthongized or lowered into *e*,
etc. The history of sounds is dependent on surroundings in many,
though not in all circumstances, but surroundings do not always
act in the same way ; in short, there seem to be so many conflicting tendencies that no universal or even general rules can be
evolved from all these 'sound laws.' Still less would it seem
possible to state anything about the comparative value of the
forms before and after the change, for it does not seem to matter
a bit for the speaking community whether it says *stān* as in Old
English or *stone* as now, and thus in innumerable cases. Nay,
from one point of view it may seem that any change militates
against the object of language (cf. Wechssler L 28), but this is
true only of the very moment when the change sets in while people
are accustomed to the old sound (or the old signification), and
even then the change is only injurious provided it impedes understanding or renders understanding less easy, which is far from
always being the case.

There is one scholar who has asserted the existence of a universal progressive tendency in languages, or, as he calls it, a
humanization of language, namely Baudouin de Courtenay (*Ver-
menschlichung der Sprache*, 1893). He is chiefly thinking of the
sound system,[1] and he maintains that there is a tendency towards
eliminating the innermost articulations and using instead sounds
that are formed nearer to the teeth and lips. Thus some back
(postpalatal, velar) consonants become *p*, *b*, while others develop
into *s* sounds ; cf. Slav *slovo* 'word' with Lat. *cluo*, etc. Baudouin
also mentions the frequent palatalization of back consonants, as in
French and Italian *ce*, *ci*, *ge*, *gi*, but as this is due to the influence
of the following front vowel, it should not perhaps be mentioned
as a universal tendency of human language. It is further said
that throat sounds, which play such a great rôle in Semitic languages,
have been discarded in most modern languages. But it may be
objected that sometimes throat sounds do develop in modern
periods, as in the Danish 'stød' and in English dialectal *bu'er* for

[1] In the realm of significations he sees the 'humanization' of language
exclusively in the development of abstract terms. An important point
of disagreement between Baudouin and myself is in regard to morphology,
where he sees only 'oscillations' in historical times, in which he is unable
to discover a continuous movement in any definite direction, while I maintain that languages here manifest a definite progressive tendency.

butter, etc. A universal tendency of sounds to move away from
the throat cannot be said to be firmly established ; but for our
purpose it is more important to say that even were it true, the
value of such a tendency for the speaking community would not
be great enough to justify us in speaking of progress towards a
truly ' human ' language as opposed to the more beastlike language
of our primeval ancestors. It is true that Baudouin (p. 25) says
that it is possible to articulate in the front and upper part with
less effort and with greater precision than in the interior and
lower parts of the speaking apparatus, but if this is true with regard
to the mouth proper, it cannot be maintained with regard to the
vocal chords, where very important effects may be produced in the
most precise way by infinitely little exertion. Thus in no single
point can I see that Baudouin de Courtenay has made out a strong
case for *his* conception of ' humanization of language.'

XVII.—§ 7. Shortenings.

But there is another phonetic tendency which is much more
universal and infinitely more valuable than the one asserted by
Baudouin de Courtenay, namely, the tendency to shorten words.
Words get shorter and shorter in consequence of a great many
of those changes that we see constantly going on in all languages :
vowels in weak syllables are pronounced more and more indistinctly and finally disappear altogether, as when OE. *lufu, stānas,
sende*, through ME. *luve, stanes, sende* with pronounced *e*'s, have
become our modern monosyllables *love, stones, send*, or when
Latin *bonum, homo, viginti* have become Fr. *bon, on, vingt*, and
Lat. *bona, hominem*, Fr. *bonne, homme*, where the vowel was kept,
because it was *a* or protected by the consonant group, but has
now also disappeared in normal pronunciation. Final vowels
have been dropped extensively in Danish and German dialects,
and so have the *u*'s and *i*'s in Russian, which are now kept in the
spelling merely as signs of the quality of the preceding consonant.
It would be easy to multiply instances. Nor are the consonants
more stable ; the dropping of final ones is seen most easily in
Modern French, because they are retained in spelling, as in *tout,
vers, champ, chant*, etc. In the two last examples two consonants have disappeared, the *m* and *n*, however, leaving a trace
in the nasalized pronunciation of the vowel, as also in *bon, nom*,
etc. Final *r* and *l* often disappear in Fr. words like *quatre, simple*,
and medial consonants have been dropped in such cases as *côte*
from *coste*, *bête* from *beste*, *sauf* [so·f] from *salvo*, etc. We have
corresponding omissions in English, where in very old times *n*
was dropped in such cases as *us, five, other*, while the German

forms *uns, fünf, ander* have kept the old consonants ; in more
recent times *l* was dropped in *half, calm,* etc., *gh* [x] in *light, bought,*
etc., and *r* in the prevalent pronunciation of *warm, part,* etc. Initial
consonants are more firmly fixed in many languages, yet we see
them lost in the E. combinations *kn, gn, wr,* where *k, g, w* used to
be sounded, e.g. in *know, gnaw, wrong.* Consonant assimilation
means in most cases the same thing as dropping of one consonant,
for no trace of the consonant is left, at any rate after the compen-
sating lengthening has been given up, as is often the case, e.g. in
E. *cupboard, blackguard* [kʌbəd, blæga·d].

So far we have given instances of what might be called the most
regular or constant types of phonetic change leading to shorter
forms ; but the same result is the natural outcome of a process
which occurs more sporadically. This is haplology, by which one
sound or one group of sounds is pronounced once only instead of
twice, the hearer taking it through a kind of acoustic delusion as
belonging both to what precedes and to what follows. Examples
are *a goo(d) deal, wha(t) to do, nex(t) time, simp(le)ly, England*
from *Englaland, eighteen* from OE. *eahtatiene, honesty* from
honestete, Glou(ce)ster, Worcester [wustə], familiarly *pro(ba)bly,*
vulgarly *lib(ra)ry, Febr(uar)y.* From other languages may be
quoted Fr. *cont(re)rôle, ido(lo)lâtre, Neu(ve)ville,* Lat. *nu(tri)trix,*
sti(pi)pendium, It. qual(che)cosa, cosa for *che cosa,* etc. (Cf. my
LPh 11. 9.)

The accumulation through centuries of such influences results
in those instances of seemingly violent contractions with
which every student of historical linguistics is familiar. One
classical example has already been mentioned above, E. *had,*
corresponding to Gothic *habaidedeima* ; other examples are *lord,*
with its three or four sounds, which was formerly *laverd,* and in
Old English *hláford ;* the old Gothonic form of the same word
contained indubitably as many as twelve sounds ; Latin *augustum*
has in French through *aoust* become *août,* pronounced [au] or even
[u] ; Latin *oculum* has shrunk into four sounds in Italian *occhio,*
three in Spanish *ojo,* and two in Fr. *œil ;* It. *medesimo,* Sp. *mismo*
and Fr. *même* represent various stages of the shrinking of
Lat. *metipsimum* ; cf. also Fr. *ménage* from *mansion-* + *-aticum*
Primitive Norse *ne veit ek hvat* 'not know I what' has
become Dan. *noget* 'something,' often pronounced [no·ð] or
[nɔ·ð].

In all these cases the shortening process has taken centuries,
but we have other instances in which it has come about quite
suddenly, without any intermediate stages, namely, in those
stump-words which we have already considered (Ch. IX § 7 ; cf.
XIV § 12 on corresponding syntactical shortenings).

XVII.—§ 8. Objections. Result.

There cannot therefore be the slightest doubt that the general tendency of all languages is towards shorter and shorter forms : the ancient languages of our family, Sanskrit, Zend, etc., abound in very long words ; the further back we go, the greater the number of *sesquipedalia*. It cannot justly be objected that we see sometimes examples of phonetic lengthenings, as in E. *sound* from ME. *soun*, Fr. *son*, E. *whilst, amongst* from ME. *whiles, amonges* ; a similar excrescence of *t* after *s* is seen in G. *obst, pabst*, Swed. *eljest* and others ; after *n, t* is added in G. *jemand, niemand* (two syllables, while there is nothing added to the trisyllabic *jedermann*)—for even if such instances might be multiplied, their number and importance is infinitely smaller than those in the opposite direction. (On the seeming insertion of *d* in *ndr*, see p. 264, note). In some cases we witness a certain reaction against word forms that are felt to be too short and therefore too indistinct (see Ch. XV § 1, XX § 9), but on the whole such instances are few and far between : the prevailing tendency is towards shorter forms.

Another objection must be dealt with here. It is said that it is only the purely phonetic development that tends to make words shorter, but that in languages as wholes words do not become shorter, because non-phonetic forces counteract the tendency. In modern languages we thus have some analogical formations which are longer than the forms they have supplanted, as when *books* has one sound more than OE. *bēc*, or when G. *bewegte* takes the place of *bewog*. Further, we have in modern languages many auxiliary words (prepositions, modal verbs) in places where they were formerly not required. That this objection is not valid if we take the whole of the language into consideration may perhaps be proved statistically if we compute the length of the same long text in various languages : the Gospel of St. Matthew contains in Greek about 39,000 syllables, in Swedish about 35,000, in German 33,000, in Danish 32,500, in English 29,000, and in Chinese only 17,000 (the figures for the Authorized English Version and for Danish are my own calculation ; the other figures I take from Tegnér SM 51, Hoops in *Anglia, Beiblatt* 1896, 293, and Sturtevant LCh 175). In comparing these figures it should even be taken into consideration that translations naturally tend to be more long-winded and verbose than the original, so that the real gain in shortness may be greater than indicated.[1]

---

[1] On the other hand, it is not, perhaps, fair to count the number of *syllables*, as these may vary very considerably, and some languages favour syllables with heavy consonant groups unknown in other tongues. The most rational measure of length would be to count the numbers of distinct (not sounds, but) articulations of separate speech organs—but that task is at any rate beyond *my* powers.

Next, we come to consider the question whether the tendency towards shorter forms is a valuable asset in the development of languages or the reverse. The answer cannot be doubtful. Take the old example, English *had* and Gothic *habaidedeima* : the English form is preferable, on the principle that anyone who has to choose between walking one mile and four miles will, other things being equal, prefer the shorter cut. It is true that if we take words to be self-existing natural objects, *habaidedeima* has the air of a giant and *had* of a mere pigmy : this valuation lies at the bottom of many utterances even by recent linguistic thinkers, as when Sweet (H 10) speaks of the vanishing of sounds as " a purely destructive change." But if we adopt the anthropocentric standard which has been explained above, and realize that what we call a word is really and primarily the combined action of human muscles to produce an audible effect, we see that the shortening of a form means a diminution of effort and a saving of time in the communication of our thoughts. If, as it is said, *had* has suffered from wear and tear in the long course of time, this means that the wear and tear of people now using this form in their speech is less than if they were still encumbered with the old giant *habaidedeima*. Voltaire was certainly very wide of the mark when he wrote : " C'est le propre des barbares d'abréger les mots "— long and clumsy words are rather to be considered as signs of barbarism, and short and nimble ones as signs of advanced culture.

Though I thus hold that the development towards shorter forms of expression is *on the whole* progressive, i.e. beneficial, I should not like to be too dogmatic on this point and assert that it is *always* beneficial : shortness may be carried to excess and thus cause obscurity or difficulty of understanding. This may be seen in the telegraphic style as well as in the literary style of some writers too anxious to avoid prolixity (some of Pope's lines might be quoted in illustration of the classical : brevis esse laboro, obscurus fio). But in the case of the language of a whole community the danger certainly is very small indeed, for there will always be a natural and wholesome reaction against such excessive shortness. There is another misunderstanding I want to guard against when saying that the shortening makes on the whole for progress. It must not be thought that I lay undue stress on this point, which is after all chiefly concerned with a greater or smaller amount of physical or muscular exertion : this should neither be underrated nor overrated ; but it will be seen that neither in my former work nor in this does the consideration of this point of mere shortness or length take up more than a fraction of the space allotted to the more psychical sides of the question, to which we shall now turn our attention and to which I attach much more importance.

XVII.—§ 9. Verbal Forms.

We may here recur to Schleicher's example, E. *had* and Gothic *habaidedeima*. It is not only in regard to economy of muscular exertion that the former carries the day over the latter. *Had* corresponds not only to *habaidedeima*, but it unites in one short form everything expressed by the Gothic *habaida, habaides, habaidedu, habaideduts, habaidedum, habaidedup, habaidedun, habaidedjau, habaidedeis, habaidedi, habaidedeiwa, habaidedeits, habaidedeima, habaidedeip, habaidedeina*—separate forms for two or three persons in three numbers in two distinct moods ! It is clear, therefore, that the English form saves a considerable amount of brainwork to all English-speaking people—not only to children, who have fewer forms to learn, but also to adults, who have fewer forms to choose between and to keep distinct whenever they open their mouths to speak. Someone might, perhaps, say that on the other hand English people are obliged always to join personal pronouns to their verbal forms to indicate the person, and that this is a drawback counterbalancing the advantage, so that the net result is six of one and half a dozen of the other. This, however, would be a very superficial objection. For, in the first place, the personal pronouns are the same for all tenses and moods, but the endings are not. Secondly, the possession of endings does not exempt the Goths from having separate personal pronouns ; and whenever these are used, as is very often the case in the first and second persons, those parts of the verbal endings which indicate persons are superfluous. They are no less superfluous in those extremely numerous cases in which the subject is either separately expressed by a noun or is understood from the preceding proposition, thus in the vast majority of the cases of the third person. If we compare a few pages of Old English prose with a modern rendering we shall see that in spite of the reduction in the latter of the person-indicating endings, personal pronouns are not required in any great number of sentences in which they were dispensed with in Old English. So that, altogether, the numerous endings of the older languages must be considered uneconomical.

If Gothic, Latin and Greek, etc., burden the memory by the number of their flexional endings, they do so even more by the many irregularities in the formation of these endings. In all the languages of this type, anomaly and flexion invariably go together. The intricacies of verbal flexion in Latin and Greek are well known, and it requires no small amount of mental energy to master the various modes of forming the present stems in Sanskrit—to take only one instance. Many of these irregularities disappear in course of time, chiefly, but not exclusively, through analogical formations, and though it is true that a certain number of new irregularities may come into existence, their number is relatively small when compared with those that have been removed. Now, it is not only the forms themselves that are irregular in the early languages, but also their uses : logical simplicity prevails much more in Modern English syntax than in either Old English or Latin or Greek. But it is hardly necessary to point out that growing regularity in a language means a considerable gain to all those who learn it or speak it.

It has been said, however, by one of the foremost authorities on the history of English, that "in spite of the many changes which this system [i.e. the complicated system of strong verbs] has undergone in detail, it remains just as intricate as it was in Old English" (Bradley, *The Making of English* 51). It is true that the way in which vowel change is utilized to form tenses is rather complicated in Modern English (*drink drank*, *give gave*, *hold held*, etc.), but otherwise an enormous simplification has taken place. The personal endings have been discarded with the exception of -*s* in the third person singular of the present (and the obsolete ending -*est* in the second person, and then this has been regularized, *thou sangest* having taken the place of *þu sunge*) ; the change of vowel in *ic sang*, *þu sunge*, *we sungon* in the indicative and *ic sunge*, *we sungen* in the subjunctive has been given up, and so has the accompanying change of consonant in many cases. Thus, instead of the following forms, *cēosan*, *cēose*, *cēoseþ*, *cēosaþ*, *cēosen*, *cēas*, *curon*, *cure*, *curen*, *coren*, we have the following modern ones, which are both fewer in number and less irregular : *choose*, *chooses*, *chose*, *chosen*—certainly an advance from a more to a less intricate system (cf. GS § 178).

An extreme, but by no means unique example of the simplification found in modern languages is the English *cut*, which can serve both as present and past tense, both as singular and plural, both in the first, second and third persons, both in the infinitive, in the imperative, in the indicative, in the subjunctive, and as a past (or passive) participle ; compare with this the old languages with their separate forms for different tenses, moods, numbers and persons ; and remember, moreover, that the identical form, without any inconvenience being occasioned, is also used as a noun (*a cut*), and you will admire the economy of the living tongue. A characteristic feature of the structure of languages in their early stages is that each form contains in itself several minor modifications which are often in the later stages expressed separately

by means of auxiliary words. Such a word as Latin *cantavisset*
unites into one inseparable whole the equivalents of six ideas :
(1) 'sing,' (2) pluperfect, (3) that indefinite modification of the
verbal idea which we term subjunctive, (4) active, (5) third person,
and (6) singular.

XVII.—§ 10. Synthesis and Analysis.

Such a form, therefore, is much more concrete than the forms
found in modern languages, of which sometimes two or more
have to be combined to express the composite notion which was
rendered formerly by one. Now, it is one of the consequences
of this change that it has become easier to express certain minute,
but by no means unimportant, shades of thought by laying extra
stress on some particular element in the speech-group. Latin
cantaveram amalgamates into one indissoluble whole what in E.
I had sung is analysed into three components, so that you can at
will accentuate the personal element, the time element or the
action. Now, it is possible (who can affirm and who can deny it ?)
that the Romans could, if necessary, make some difference in
speech between *cántaveram* (non saltaveram) 'I had *sung*,' and
cantavorám (non cantabam), 'I *had* sung '; but even then, if it
was the personal element which was to be emphasized, an *ego*
had to be added. Even the possibility of laying stress on the
temporal element broke down in forms like *scripsi, minui, sum,
audiam*, and innumerable others. It seems obvious that the
freedom of Latin in this respect must have been inferior to that of
English. Moreover, in English, the three elements, 'I,' 'had,' and
'sung,' can in certain cases be arranged in a different order, and
other words can be inserted between them in order to modify
and qualify the meaning of the sentence. Note also the concise-
ness of such answers as "Who had sung ? " "I had." "What
had you done ? " "Sung." "I believe he has enjoyed himself."
"I know he has." And contrast the Latin "Cantaveram et
saltaveram et luseram et riseram " with the English "I had sung
and danced and played and laughed." What would be the Latin
equivalent of "Tom never *did* and never *will* beat me " ?

In such cases, analysis means suppleness, and synthesis means
rigidity ; in analytic languages you have the power of kaleidosco-
pically arranging and rearranging the elements that in synthetic
forms like *cantaveram* are in rigid connexion and lead a Siamese-
twin sort of existence. The synthetic forms of Latin verbs remind
one of those languages all over the world (North America, South
America, Hottentot, etc.) in which such ideas as 'father' or
'mother' or 'head' or 'eye' cannot be expressed separately,

but only in connexion with an indication of *whose* father, etc.,
one is speaking about : in one language the verbal idea (in the
finite moods), in the other the nominal idea, is necessarily fused
with the personal idea.

XVII.—§ 11. Verbal Concord.

This formal inseparability of subordinate elements is at the
root of those rules of concord which play such a large rôle in the
older languages of our Aryan family, but which tend to disappear
in the more recent stages. By concord we mean the fact that a
secondary word (adjective or verb) is made to agree with the
primary word (substantive or subject) to which it belongs. Verbal
concord, by which a verb is governed in number and person by
the subject, has disappeared from spoken Danish, where, for
instance, the present tense of the verb meaning ' to travel ' is
uniformly *rejser* in all persons of both numbers ; while the written
language till towards the end of the nineteenth century kept up
artificially the plural *rejse*, although it had been dead in the spoken
language for some three hundred years. The old flexion is an
article of luxury, as a modification of the idea belonging properly
to the subject is here transferred to the predicate, where it has
no business ; for when we say ' mændene rejse ' (die männer reisen),
we do not mean to imply that they undertake several journeys
(cf. Madvig Kl 28, *Nord. tsk. f. filol.*, n.r. 8. 134).

By getting rid of this superfluity, Danish has got the start
of the more archaic of its Aryan sister-tongues. Even English,
which has in most respects gone farthest in simplifying its flexional
system, lags here behind Danish, in that in the present tense of
most verbs the third person singular deviates from the other
persons by ending in -*s*, and the verb *be* preserves some other
traces of the old concord system, not to speak of the form in -*st*
used with *thou* in the language of religion and poetry. Small
and unimportant as these survivals may seem, still they are in
some instances impediments to the free and easy expression of
thought. In Danish, for instance, there is not the slightest difficulty in saying ' enten du eller jeg har uret,' as *har* is used both
in the first and second persons singular and plural. But when
an Englishman tries to render the same simple sentiment he is
baffled ; ' either you or I *are* wrong ' is felt to be incorrect, and
so is ' either you or I *am* wrong ' ; he might say ' either you are
wrong, or I,' but then this manner of putting it, if grammatically
admissible (with or without the addition of *am*), is somewhat stiff
and awkward ; and there is no perfectly natural way out of the
difficulty, for Dean Alford's proposal to say ' either you or I *is*

wrong' (*The Queen's Engl.* 155) is not to be recommended. The advantage of having verbal forms that are no respecters of persons is seen directly in such perfectly natural expressions as ' either you or I must be wrong,' or ' either you or I may be wrong,' or ' either you or I began it '—and indirectly from the more or less artificial rules of Latin and Greek grammars on this point ; in the following passages the Gordian knot is cut in different ways :

Shakespeare *LLL* v. 2. 346 Nor God, nor I, *delights* in perjur'd men | id. *As* I. 3. 99 Thou and I *am* one | Tennyson *Poet. W.* 369 For whatsoever knight against us came Or I or he *have* easily overthrown | Galsworthy *D* 30 *Am* I and all women really what they think us ? | Shakespeare *H4B* IV. 2. 121 Heauen, and not wee, *haue* safely fought to day (Folio, where the Quarto has : God, and not wee, *hath.* . . .)

The same difficulty often appears in relative clauses ; Alford (l.c. 152) calls attention to the fact of the Prayer Book reading " Thou art the God that *doeth.* wonders," whereas the Bible version runs " Thou art the God that *doest* wonders." Compare also :

Shakespeare *As* III. 5. 55 'Tis not her glasse, but you that *flatters* her | id. *Meas.* II. 2. 80 It is the law, not I, *condemne* your brother | Carlyle *Fr. Rev.* 38, There is none but you and I that *has* the people's interest at heart (translated from : Il n'y a que vous et moi qui *aimions* le peuple).

In all such cases the construction in Danish is as easy and natural as it generally is in the English preterit : " It was not her glass, but you that flattered her." The disadvantage of having verbal forms which enforce the indication of person and number is perhaps seen most strikingly in a French sentence like this from Romain Rolland's *Jean Christophe* (7. 221) : " Ce mot, naturellement, ce n'est ni toi, ni moi, qui *pouvons* le dire "—the verb agrees with that which *cannot* be the subject (we) ! For what is meant is really : ' celui qui peut le dire, ce n'est ni moi ni toi.'

PROGRESS

XVIII.—§ 1. Nominal Forms.

IN the flexion of substantives and adjectives we see phenomena corresponding to those we have just been considering in the verbs. The ancient languages of our family have several forms where modern languages content themselves with fewer ; forms originally kept distinct are in course of time confused, either through a phonetic obliteration of differences in the endings or through analogical extension of the functions of one form. The single form *good* is now used where OE. used the forms *god, godne, gode, godum, godes, godre, godra, goda, godan, godena* ; Ital. *uomo* or French *homme* is used for Lat. *homo, hominem, homini, homine* —nay, if we take the spoken form into consideration, Fr. [ɔm] corresponds not only to these Latin forms, but also to *homines, hominibus*. Where the modern language has one or two cases, in an earlier stage it had three or four, and still earlier seven or eight. The difficulties inherent in the older system cannot, however, be measured adequately by the number of forms each word is susceptible of, but are multiplied by the numerous differences in the formation of the same case in different classes of declension; sometimes we even find anomalies which affect one word only.

Those who would be inclined to maintain that new irregularities may and do arise in modern languages which make up for whatever earlier irregularities have been discarded in the course of the historical development will do well to compile a systematic list of *all* the flexional forms of two different stages of the same languages, arranged exactly according to the same principles : this is the only way in which it is possible really to balance losses and profits in a language. This is what I have done in my *Progress in Language* § 111 ff. (reprinted in ChE § 9 ff.), where I have contrasted the case systems of Old and Modern English :

the result is that the former system takes 7 (+ 3) pages, and the latter only 2 pages. Those pages, with their abbreviations and tabulations, do not, perhaps, offer very entertaining reading, but I think they are more illustrative of the real tendencies of language than either isolated examples or abstract reasonings, and they cannot fail to convince any impartial reader of the enormous gain achieved through the changes of the intervening nine hundred years in the general structure of the English language.

For our general purposes it will be worth our while here to quote what Friedrich Müller (Gr i. 2. 7) says about a totally different language : " Even if the Hottentot distinguishes ' he,' ' she ' and ' it,' and strictly separates the singular from the plural number, yet by his expressing ' he ' and ' she ' by one sound in the third person, and by another in the second, he manifests that he has no perception at all of our two grammatical categories of gender and number, and consequently those elements of his language that run parallel to our signs of gender and number must be of an entirely different nature." Fr. Müller should not perhaps throw too many stones at the poor Hottentots, for his own native tongue is no better than a glass house, and we might with equal justice say, for instance : " As the Germans express the plural number in different manners in words like *gott—götter*, *hand—hände*, *vater—väter*, *frau—frauen*, etc., they must be entirely lacking in the sense of the category of number." Or let us take such a language as Latin ; there is nothing to show that *dominus* bears the same relation to *domini* as *verbum* to *verba*, *urbs* to *urbes*, *mensis* to *menses*, *cornu* to *cornua*, *fructus* to *fructūs*, etc. ; even in the same word the idea of plurality is not expressed by the same method for all the cases, as is shown by a comparison of *dominus—domini*, *dominum—dominos*, *domino—dominis*, *domini—dominorum*. Fr. Müller is no doubt wrong in saying that such anomalies preclude the speakers of the language from conceiving the notion of plurality ; but, on the other hand, it seems evident that a language in which a difference so simple even to the understanding of very young children as that between one and more than one can only be expressed by a complicated apparatus must rank lower than another language in which this difference has a single expression for all cases in which it occurs. In this respect, too, Modern English stands higher than the oldest English, Latin or Hottentot.

XVIII.—§ 2. Irregularities Original.

It was the belief of the older school of comparativists that each case had originally one single ending, which was added to all nouns indifferently (e.g. -*as* for the genitive sg.), and that the irregularities found in the existing oldest languages were of later growth ; the actually existing forms were then derived from the supposed unity form by all kinds of phonetic tricks and dodges. Now people have begun to see that the primeval language cannot have been quite uniform and regular (see, for instance, Walde in Streitberg's *Gesch.*, 2. 194 ff.). If we look at facts, and not at imagined or reconstructed forms, we are forced to acknowledge that in the oldest stages of our family of languages not only did the endings present the spectacle of a motley variety, but the kernel of the word was also often subject to violent changes in different cases, as when it had in different forms different accentuation and (or) different apophony, or as when in some of the most frequently occurring words some cases were formed from one ' stem ' and others from another, for instance, the nominative from an *r* stem and the oblique cases from an *n* stem. In the common word for ' water ' Greek has preserved both stems, nom. *hudōr*, gen. *hudatos*, where *a* stands for original [ən]. Whatever the origin of this change of stems, it is a phenomenon belonging to the earlier stages of our languages, in which we also sometimes find an alteration between the *r* stem in the nominative and a combination of the *n* and the *r* stems in the other cases, as in Lat. *jecur* ' liver,' *jecinoris* ; *iter* ' voyage,' *itineris*, which is supposed to have supplanted *itinis*, formed like *feminis* from *femur*. In the later stages we always find a simplification, one single form running through all cases ; this is either the nominative stem, as in E. *water*, G. *wasser* (corresponding to Gr. *hudōr*), or the oblique case-stem, as in the Scandinavian forms, Old Norse *vatn*, Swed. *vatten*, Dan. *vand* (corresponding to Gr. *hudat-*), or finally a contaminated form, as in the name of the Swedish lake *Vättern* (Noreen's explanation), or in Old Norse and Dan. *skarn* ' dirt,' which has its *r* from a form like the Gr. *skōr*, and its *n* from a form like the Gr. genitive *skatos* (older [skəntos]). The simplification is carried furthest in English, where the identical form *water* is not only used unchanged where in the older languages different case forms would have been used (' the water is cold,' ' the surface of the water,' ' he fell into the water,' ' he swims in the water '), but also serves as a verb (' did you water the flowers ? '), and as an adjunct as a quasi-adjective (' a water melon,' ' water plants ').

In most cases irregularities have been done away with in the way here indicated, one of the forms (or stems) being generalized ; but in other cases it may have happened, as Kretschmer supposes (in Gercke and Nolde, *Einleit. in die Altertumswiss.*, I, 501) that irregular flexion caused a word to go out of use entirely ; thus in Modern Greek *hêpar* was supplanted by *sukŏti*,[1] *phréar* by *pēgadi*, *húdōr* by *neró*, *oûs* by *aphtí* (= *ōtíon*), *kúōn* by *skullí ;* this possibly also accounts for *commando* taking the place of Lat. *jubeo*.

Some scholars maintain that the medieval languages were more regular than their modern representatives ; but if we look more closely into what they mean, we shall see that they are not speaking of any regularity in the sense in which the word has here been used—the only regularity which is of importance to the speakers of the language—but of the regular correspondence of a language with some earlier language from which it is derived. This is particularly the case with E. Littré, who, in his essays on *L'Histoire de la Langue Française*, was full of enthusiasm for Old French, but chiefly for the fidelity with which it had preserved some features of Latin. There was thus the old distinction of two cases : nom. sg. *murs*, acc. sg. *mur*, and in the plural inversely nom. *mur* and acc. *murs*, with its exact correspondence with Latin *murus*, *murum*, pl. *muri*, *muros*. When this ' règle de *l*'s ' was discovered, and the use or omission of *s*, which had hitherto been looked upon as completely arbitrary in Old French, was thus accounted for, scholars were apt to consider this as an admirable trait in the old language which had been lost in modern French, and the same view obtained with regard to the case distinction found in other words, such as OFr. nom. *maire*, acc. *majeur*, or nom. *emperere*, acc. *emperëur*, corresponding to the Latin forms with changing stress, *májor*, *majórem*, *imperátor*, *imperatórem*, etc. But, however interesting such things may be to the historical linguist, there is no denying that to the users of French the modern simpler flexion is a gain as compared with this more complex system. " Des sprachhistorikers freud ist des sprachbrauchers leid," as Schuchardt somewhere shrewdly remarks.

XVIII.—§ 3. Syntax.

There were also in the old languages many irregularities in the syntactic use of the cases, as when some verbs governed the genitive and others the dative, etc. Even if it may be possible in many instances to account historically for these uses, to the speakers of the languages they must have appeared to be mere caprices which had to be learned separately for each verb, and it is therefore a great advantage when they have been gradually done away with, as has been the case, to a great extent, even in a language like German, which has retained many old case forms. Thus verbs like *entbehren*, *vergessen*, *bedürfen*, *wahrnehmen*, which formerly took the genitive, are now used more and more with the

---

[1] Thus also the corresponding Lat. *jecur* by *ficatum*, Fr. *foie*.

simple accusative—a simplification which, among other things,
makes the construction of sentences in the passive voice easier
and more regular.

The advantage of discarding the old case distinctions is seen
in the ease with which English and French speakers can say,
e.g., ' with or without my hat,' or ' in and round the church,'
while the correct German is ' mit meinem hut oder ohne denselben '
and ' in der kirche und um dieselbe '; Wackernagel writes :
" Was in ihm und um ihn und über ihm ist." When the prepositions are followed by a single substantive without case distinction,
German, of course, has the same simple construction as English,
e.g. ' mit oder ohne geld,' and sometimes even good writers will
let themselves go and write ' um und neben dem hochaltare '
(Goethe), or ' Ihre tochter wird meine frau mit oder gegen ihren
willen ' (these examples from Curme, *German Grammar* 191).
Cf. also : ' Ich kann deinem bruder nicht helfen und ihn unter-
stützen.'

Many extremely convenient idioms unknown in the older
synthetic languages have been rendered possible in English through
the doing away with the old case distinctions, such as : Genius,
demanding bread, is given a stone after its possessor's death (Shaw)
(cf. my ChE § 79) | he was offered, and declined, the office of
poet-laureate (Gosse) | the lad was spoken highly of | I love, and
am loved by, my wife | these laws my readers, whom I consider
as my subjects, are bound to believe in and to obey (Fielding) |
he was heathenishly inclined to believe in, or to worship, the
goddess Nemesis (id.) | he rather rejoiced in, than regretted, his
bruise (id.) | many a dun had she talked to, and turned away
from her father's door (Thackeray) | their earthly abode, which
has seen, and seemed almost to sympathize in, all their honour
(Ruskin).

XVIII.—§ 4. Objections.

Against my view of the superiority of languages with few
case distinctions, Arwid Johannson, in a very able article (in
IF I, see especially p. 247 f.), has adduced a certain number of
ambiguous sentences from German :

> Soweit die deutsche zunge klingt und *gott* im himmel
> lieder singt (is *gott* nominative or dative ?) | Seinem landsmann,
> dem er in seiner ganzen bildung ebensoviel verdankte, wie
> *Goethe* (nominative or dative ?) | Doch würde die gesellschaft
> *der Indierin* (genitive or dative ?) lästig gewesen sein | Dar-
> in hat Caballero wohl nur einen konkurrenten, die Eliot,
> *welche* freilich *die spanische dichterin* nicht ganz erreicht | Nur

Diopeithes feindet insgeheim dich an und *die schwester* des Kimon und *dein weib* Telesippa. (In the last two sentences what is the subject, and what the object ?)

According to Johannson, these passages show the disadvantages of doing away with formal distinctions, for the sentences would have been clear if each separate case had had its distinctive sign ; "the greater the wealth of forms, the more intelligible the speech." And they show, he says, that such ambiguities will occur, even where the strictest rules of word order are observed. I shall not urge that this is not exactly the case in the last sentence if *die schwester* and *dein weib* are to be taken as accusatives, for then *an* should have been placed at the very end of the sentence ; nor that, in the last sentence but one, the mention of George Eliot as the 'konkurrent' of Fernan Caballero seems to show a partiality to the Spanish authoress on the part of the writer of the sentence, so that the reader is prepared to take *welche* as the nominative case ; *freilich* would seem to point in the same direction. But these, of course, are only trifling objections ; the essential point is that we must grant the truth of Johannson's contention that we have here a flaw in the German language ; the defects of its grammatical system may and do cause a certain number of ambiguities. Neither is it difficult to find the reasons of these defects by considering the structure of the language in its entirety, and by translating the sentences in question into a few other languages and comparing the results.

First, with regard to the formal distinctions between cases, the really weak point cannot be the fewness of these endings, for in that case we should expect the same sort of ambiguities to be very common in English and Danish, where the formal case distinctions are considerably fewer than in German ; but as a matter of fact such ambiguities are more frequent in German than in the other two languages. And, however paradoxical it may seem at first sight, one of the causes of this is the greater wealth of grammatical forms in German. Let us substitute other words for the ambiguous ones, and we shall see that the amphibology will nearly always disappear, because most other words will have different forms in the two cases, e.g. :

Soweit die deutsche zunge klingt und *dem allmächtigen* (or, *der allmächtige*) lieder singt | Seinem landsmann, dem er ebensoviel verdankte, wie *dem grossen dichter* (or, *der grosse dichter*) | Doch würde die gesellschaft *des Indiers* (or, *dem Indier*) lästig gewesen sein | Darin hat Calderon wohl nur einen konkurrenten, Shakespeare, *welcher* freilich *den span-*

ischen dichter nicht erreicht (or, *den* . . . *der spanische dich-ter* . . .) | Nur Diopeithes feindet dich insgeheim an, und *der bruder* des Kimon und *sein freund* T. (or, *den bruder* . . . *seinen freund*).

It is this very fact that countless sentences of this sort are perfectly clear which leads to the employment of similar construc-tions even where the resulting sentence is by no means clear ; but if all, or most, words were identical in the nominative and the dative, like *gott*, or in the dative and genitive, like *der Indierin*, constructions like those used would be impossible to imagine in a language meant to be an intelligible vehicle of thought. And so the ultimate cause of the ambiguities is the inconsistency in the formation of the several cases. But this inconsistency is found in all the old languages of the Aryan family : cases which in one gender or with one class of stems are kept perfectly distinct, are in others identical. I take some examples from Latin, because this is perhaps the best known language of this type, but Gothic or Old Slavonic would show inconsistencies of the same kind. *Domini* is genitive singular and nominative plural (corresponding to, e.g., *verbi* and *verba*) ; *verba* is nominative and accusative pl. (corresponding to *domini* and *dominos*) ; *domino* is dative and ablative ; *dominæ* gen. and dative singular and nominative plural ; *te* is accusative and ablative ; *qui* is singular and plural ; *quæ* singular fem. and plural fem. and neuter, etc. Hence, while *patres filios amant* or *patres filii amant* are perfectly clear, *patres consules amant* allows of two interpretations ; and in how many ways cannot such a proposition as *Horatius et Virgilius poetæ Varii amici erant* be construed ? *Menenii patris munus* may mean ' the gift of father Menenius,' or ' the gift of Menenius's father ' ; *expers illius periculi* either ' free from that danger ' or ' free from (sharing) that person's danger ' ; in an infinitive construction with two accusatives, the only way to know which is the subject and which the object is to consider the context, and that is not always decisive, as in the oracular response given to the Æacide Pyrrhus, as quoted by Cicero from Ennius : " Aio *te*, Æacida, *Romanos* vincere posse." Such drawbacks seem to be inseparable from the structure of the highly flexional Aryan languages ; although they are not logical consequences of a wealth of forms, yet his-torically they cling to those languages which have the greatest number of grammatical endings. And as we are here concerned not with the question how to construct an artificial language (and even there I should not advise the adoption of many case distinctions), but with the valuation of natural languages as actually existing in their earlier and modern stages, we cannot accept Johannson's verdict : " The greater the wealth of forms, the more intelligible the speech."

XVIII.—§ 5. Word Order.

If the German sentences quoted above are ambiguous, it is not only on account of the want of clearness in the forms employed, but also on account of the German rules of word order. One rule places the verb last in subordinate sentences, and in two of the sentences there would be no ambiguity in principal sentences : Die deutsche zunge klingt und *singt gott* im himmel lieder ; or, Die deutsche zunge klingt, und *gott im himmel singt* lieder | *Sie erreicht* freilich nicht die spanische dichterin ; or, Die spanische dichterin *erreicht sie* freilich nicht. In one of the remaining sentences the ambiguity is caused by the rule that the verb must be placed immediately after an introductory subjunct : if we omit *doch* the sentence becomes clear : Die *gesellschaft der Indierin würde* lästig gewesen sein, or, *Die gesellschaft würde der Indierin* lästig gewesen sein. Here, again we see the ill consequences of inconsistency of linguistic structure ; some of the rules for word position serve to show grammatical relations, but in certain cases they have to give way to other rules, which counteract this useful purpose. If you change the order of words in a German sentence, you will often find that the meaning is not changed, but the result will be an unidiomatic construction (bad grammar) ; while in English a transposition will often result in perfectly good grammar, only the meaning will be an entirely different one from the original sentence. This does not amount to saying that the German rules of position are useless and the English ones all useful, but only to saying that in English word order is utilized to express difference of meaning to a far greater extent than in German.

One critic cites against me " one example, which figures in almost every Rhetoric as a violation of clearness : *And thus the son the fervid sire address'd*," and he adds : " The use of a separate form for nominative and accusative would clear up the ambiguity immediately." The retort is obvious : no doubt it would, but so would the use of a natural word order. Word order is just as much a part of English grammar as case-endings are in other languages ; a violation of the rules of word order may cause the same want of intelligibility as the use of *dominum* instead of *dominus* would in Latin. And if the example is found in almost every English Rhetoric, I am glad to say that equally ambiguous sentences are very rare indeed in other English books. Even in poetry, where there is such a thing as poetic licence, and where the exigencies of rhythm and rime, as well as the fondness for archaic and out-of-the-way expressions, will often induce deviations from the word order of prose, real ambiguity will very seldom arise on that account. It is true that it has been disputed which is the subject in Gray's line :

> And all the air a solemn stillness holds,

but then it does not matter much, for the ultimate understanding of the line must be exactly the same whether the air holds stillness or stillness holds the air. In ordinary language we may find similar collocations, but it is worth saying with some emphasis that there can never be any doubt as to which is the subject and which the object. The ordinary word order is, Subject-Verb-Object, and where there is a deviation there must always be some special reason for it. This may be the wish, especially for the sake of some contrast, to throw into relief some member of the sentence. If this is the subject, the purpose is achieved by stressing it, but the word order is not affected. But if it is the object, this may be placed in the very beginning of the sentence, but in that case English does not, like German and Danish, require inversion of the verb, and the order consequently is, Object-Subject-Verb, which is perfectly clear and unambiguous. See, for instance, Dickens's sentence : "*Talent, Mr. Micawber* has; *capital, Mr. Micawber* has not," and the following passage from a recent novel : " Even Royalty had not quite their glow and glitter ; *Royalty you* might see any day, driving, bowing, smiling. The Queen had a smile for every one ; but *the Duchess no one, not even Lizzie,* ever saw." Thus, also, in Shakespeare's :

> *Things base and vilde,* holding no quantity,
> *Loue* can transpose to forme and dignity (*Mids.* i. 1. 233),

and in Longfellow's translation from Logau :

> A blind man is a poor man, and blind a poor man is ;
> For the former seeth no man, and *the latter no man* sees.

The reason for deviating from the order, Subject-Verb-Object, may again be purely grammatical : a relative or an interrogative pronoun must be placed first ; but here, too, English grammar precludes ambiguity, as witness the following sentences : This picture, which surpasses Mona Lisa | This picture, which Mona Lisa surpasses | What picture surpasses Mona Lisa ? | What picture does not Mona Lisa surpass ? In German (dieses bild, welches die M. L. übertrifft, etc.) all four sentences would be ambiguous, in Danish the two last would be indistinguishable ; but English shows that a small number of case forms is not incompatible with perfect clearness and perspicuity. If the famous oracular answer (*Henry VI, 2nd Part*, I. 4. 33), "The Duke yet liues, that Henry shall depose," is ambiguous, it is only because it is in verse, where you expect inversions : in ordinary prose it could be understood only in one way, as the word order would be reversed if *Henry* was meant as the object.

XVIII.—§ 6. Gender.

Besides case distinctions the older Aryan languages have a rather complicated system of gender distinctions, which in many instances agrees with, but in many others is totally independent of, and even may be completely at war with, the natural distinction between male beings, female beings and things without sex. This grammatical gender is sometimes looked upon as something valuable for a language to possess ; thus Schroeder (*Die formale Unterscheidung* 87) says : "The formal distinction of genders is decidedly an enormous advantage which the Aryan, Semitic and Egyptian languages have before all other languages." Aasen (*Norsk Grammatik* 123) finds that the preservation of the old genders gives vividness and variety to a language ; he therefore, in constructing his artificial Norwegian 'landsmaal,' based it on those dialects which made a formal distinction between the masculine and feminine article. But other scholars have recognized the disadvantages accruing from such distinctions ; thus Tegnér (SM 50) regrets the fact that in Swedish it is impossible to give such a form to the sentence ' sin make må man ej svika ' as to make it clear that the admonition is applicable to both husband and wife, because *make*, ' mate,' is masculine, and *maka* feminine. In Danish, where *mage* is common to both sexes, no such difficulty arises. Gabelentz (Spr 234) says : "Das grammatische geschlecht bringt es weiter mit sich dass wir deutschen nie eine frauensperson als einen menschen und nicht leicht einen mann als eine person bezeichnen."

As a matter of fact, German gender is responsible for many difficulties, not only when it is in conflict with natural sex, as when one may hesitate whether to use the pronoun *es* or *sie* in reference to a person just mentioned as *das mädchen* or *das weib*, or *er* or *sie* in reference to *die schildwache*, but also when sexless things are concerned, and *er* might be taken as either referring to the man or to *der stuhl* or to *der wald* just mentioned, etc. In France, grammarians have disputed without end as to the propriety or not of referring to the (feminine) word *personnes* by means of the pronoun *ils* (see Nyrop, *Kongruens* 24, and Gr. iii. § 712) : "Les personnes que vous attendiez sont *tous logés* ici." As a negative pronoun *personne* is now frankly masculine : ' personne n'est mal-

heureux.' With *gens* the old feminine gender is still kept up when
an adjective precedes, as in *les bonnes gens*, thus also *toutes les
bonnes gens*, but when the adjective has no separate feminine
form, schoolmasters prefer to say *tous les honnêtes gens*, and the
masculine generally prevails when the adjective is at some distance
from *gens*, as in the old school-example, *Instruits par l'expérience,
toutes les vieilles gens sont soupçonneux*. There is a good deal of
artificiality in the strict rules of grammarians on this point, and
it is therefore good that the Arrêté ministériel of 1901 tolerates
greater liberty; but conflicts are unavoidable, and will rise quite
naturally, in any language that has not arrived at the perfect
stage of complete genderlessness (which, of course, is not identical
with inability to express sex-differences).

Most English pronouns make no distinction of sex : *I, you,
we, they, who, each, somebody*, etc. Yet, when we hear that
Finnic and Magyar, and indeed the vast majority of languages
outside the Aryan and Semitic world, have no separate forms
for *he* and *she*, our first thought is one of astonishment; we fail
to see how it is possible to do without this distinction. But if
we look more closely we shall see that it is at times an inconvenience
to have to specify the sex of the person spoken about. Coleridge
(*Anima Poetæ* 190) regretted the lack of a pronoun to refer to
the word *person*, as it necessitated some stiff and strange construction like ' not letting the person be aware wherein offence had
been given,' instead of ' wherein he or she has offended.' It
has been said that if a genderless pronoun could be substituted
for *he* in such a proposition as this : ' It would be interesting if
each of the leading poets would tell us what he considers his best
work,' ladies would be spared the disparaging implication that
the leading poets were all men. Similarly there is something
incongruous in the following sentence found in a German review
of a book : "Was Maria und Fritz so zueinander zog, war, dass
jeder von ihnen *am anderen* sah, wie *er* unglücklich war." Anyone who has written much in Ido will have often felt how convenient
it is to have the common-sex pronouns *lu* (he or she), *singlu, altru*,
etc. It is interesting to see the different ways out of the difficulty
resorted to in actual language. First the cumbrous use of *he
or she*, as in Fielding *TJ* 1. 174, the reader's heart (if he or she
have any) | Miss Muloch *H*. 2. 128, each one made his or her
comment.[1] Secondly, the use of *he* alone : If anybody behaves
in such and such a manner, he will be punished (cf. the wholly

---

[1] This ungainly repetition is frequent in the Latin of Roman law, e.g.
Digest. IV. 5. 2, *Qui quæve . . .* capite *diminuti diminutæ* esse dicentur,
in *eos easve . . .* iudicium dabo. | XLIII. 30, *Qui quæve* in potestate Lucii
Titii est, si *is eave* apud te est, dolove malo tuo factum est quominus apud

unobjectionable, but not always applicable, formula : Whoever behaves in such and such a manner will be punished). This use of *he* has been legalized by the Act 13 and 14 Vict., cap. 21. 4 : " That in all acts words importing the masculine gender shall be deemed and taken to include females." Third, the sexless but plural form *they* may be used. If you try to put the phrase, ' Does anybody prevent you ? ' in another way, beginning with ' Nobody prevents you,' and then adding the interrogatory formula, you will perceive that ' does he ' is too definite, and ' does he or she ' too clumsy ; and you will therefore naturally say (as Thackeray does, *P* 2. 260), " Nobody prevents you, do they ? " In the same manner Shakespeare writes (*Lucr.* 125) : " Everybody to rest themselves betake." The substitution of the plural for the singular is not wholly illogical ; for *everybody* is much the same thing as ' all men,' and *nobody* is the negation of ' all men ' ; but the phenomenon is extended to cases where this explanation will not hold good, as in G. Eliot, *M*. 2. 304, I shouldn't like to punish any one, even if *they'd* done me wrong. (For many examples from good writers see my MEG. ii. 5, 56.)

The English interrogative *who* is not, like the *quis* or *quæ* of the Romans, limited to one sex and one number, so that our question ' Who did it ? ' to be rendered exactly in Latin, would require a combination of the four : *Quis hoc fecit? Quæ hoc fecit? Qui hoc fecerunt? Quæ hoc fecerunt?* or rather, the abstract nature of *who* (and of *did*) makes it possible to express such a question much more indefinitely in English than in any highly flexional language ; and indefiniteness in many cases means greater precision, or a closer correspondence between thought and expression.

XVIII.—§ 7. Nominal Concord.

We have seen in the case of the verbs how widely diffused in all the old Aryan languages is the phenomenon of Concord. It is the same with the nouns. Here, as there, it consists in secondary words (here chiefly adjectives) being made to agree with principal words, but while with the verbs the agreement was in number and person, here it is in number, case and gender. This is well known in Greek and Latin ; as examples from Gothic may here be given Luk. 1. 72, *gamunan triggwos weihaizos seinaizos*, ' to remember

te esset, ita *eum eamve* exhibeas. | XI. 3, Qui *servum servam alienum alienam* recepisse persuasisseve quid ei dicitur dolo malo, quo *eum eam* deteriorem faceret, in eum, quanti ea res erit, in duplum iudicium dabo. I owe these and some other Latin examples to my late teacher, Dr. O. Siesbye. From French, Nyrop (*Kongruens*, p. 12) gives some corresponding examples : *tous ceux et toutes celles* qui, ayant été orphelins, avaient eu une enfance malheureuse (Philippe), and from Old French : Lors donna congié à *ceus et à celes* que il avoit rescous (Villehardouin).

His holy covenant,' and 1. 75, *allans dagans unsarans*, ' all our days.' The English translation shows how English has discarded this trait, for there is nothing in the forms of (*his*), *holy*, *all* and *our*, as in the Gothic forms, to indicate what substantive they belong to.

Wherever the same adjectival idea is to be joined to two substantives, the concordless junction is an obvious advantage, as seen from a comparison of the English ' my wife and children ' with the French ' ma femme et mes enfants,' or of ' the *local* press and committees ' with ' *la* presse *locale* et *les* comités *locaux*.' Try to translate exactly into French or Latin such a sentence as this : " What are the present state and wants of mankind ? " (Ruskin).   Cf. also the expression ' a verdict of wilful murder against *some* person or persons *unknown*,' where *some* and *unknown* belong to the singular as well as to the plural forms ; Fielding writes (*TJ* 3. 65) : " *Some particular* chapter, or perhaps chapters, *may be obnoxious.*" Where an English editor of a text will write : " Some (indifferently singular and plural) word or words wanting here," a Dane will write : " Et (sg.) eller flere (pl.) ord (indifferent) mangler her." These last examples may be taken as proof that it might even in some cases be advantageous to have forms in the substantives that did not show number ; still, it must be recognized that the distinction between one and more than one rightly belongs to substantival notions, but logically it has as little to do with adjectival as with verbal notions (cf. above, Ch. XVII § 11).   In ' black spots ' it is the spots, but not the qualities of black, that we count.   And in ' two black spots ' it is of course quite superfluous to add a dual or plural ending (as in Latin *duo*, *duæ*) in order to indicate once more what the word *two* denotes sufficiently, namely, that we have not to do with a singular. Compare, finally, E. *to the father and mother*, Fr. *au père et à la mère*, G. *zu dem vater und der mutter* (*zum vater und zur mutter*).

If it is admitted that it is an inconvenience whenever you want to use an adjective to have to put it in the form corresponding in case, number and gender to its substantive, it may be thought a redeeming feature of the language which makes this demand that, on the other hand, it allows you to place the adjective at some distance from the substantive, and yet the hearer or reader will at once connect the two together.   But here, as elsewhere in ' energetics,' the question is whether the advantage counterbalances the disadvantage ; in other words, whether the fact that you are free to place your adjective where you will is worth the price you pay for it in being always saddled with the heavy apparatus of adjectival flexions.   Why should you want to remove the adjective from the substantive, which naturally must be in your

thought when you are thinking of the adjective ? There is one
natural employment of the adjective in which it has very often
to stand at some distance from the substantive, namely, when it
is predicative ; but then the example of German shows the needless-
ness of concord in that case, for while the adjunct adjective is
inflected (ein *guter* mensch, eine *gute* frau, ein *gutes* buch, *gute*
bücher) the predicative is invariable like the adverb (der mensch
ist *gut*, die frau ist *gut*, das buch ist *gut*, die bücher sind *gut*). It
is chiefly in poetry that a Latin adjective is placed far from its
substantive, as in Vergil : " Et bene apud memores veteris stat
gratia facti " (*Æn.* IV. 539), where the form shows that *veteris*
is to be taken with *facti* (but then, where does *bene* belong ? it
might be taken with *memores*, *stat* or *facti*). In Horace's well-
known aphorism : " Æquam memento rebus in arduis servare
mentem," the flexional form of *æquam* allows him to place it first,
far from *mentem*, and thus facilitates for him the task of building
up a perfect metrical line ; but for the reader it would certainly
be preferable to have had *æquam mentem* together at once, instead
of having to hold his attention in suspense for five words, till
finally he comes upon a word with which to connect the adjective.
There is therefore no economizing of the energy of reader or hearer.
Extreme examples may be found in Icelandic skaldic poetry, in
which the poets, to fulfil the requirements of a highly complicated
metrical system, entailing initial and medial rimes, very often
place the words in what logically must be considered the worst
disorder, thereby making their poem as difficult to understand
as an intricate chess-problem is to solve—and certainly coming
short of the highest poetical form.

XVIII.—§ 8. The English Genitive.

If we compare a group of Latin words, such as *opera virorum
omnium bonorum veterum*, with a corresponding group in a few other
languages of a less flexional type : OE. *ealra godra ealdra manna
weorc* ; Danish *alle gode gamle mænds værker* ; Modern English
all good old men's works, we perceive by analyzing the ideas expressed by the several words that the Romans said really : ' work,'
plural, nominative or accusative + ' man,' plural, masculine,
genitive + ' all,' plural, genitive + ' good,' plural, masculine,
genitive + ' old,' plural, masculine, genitive. Leaving *opera* out
of consideration, we find that plural number is expressed four
times, genitive case also four times, and masculine gender twice ; [1]

[1] If instead of *omnium veterum* I had chosen, for instance, *multorum
antiquorum*, the meaning of masculine gender would have been rendered
four times : for languages, especially the older ones, are not distinguished
by consistency.

in Old English the signs of number and case are found four times each, while there is no indication of gender ; in Danish the plural number is marked four times and the case once. And finally, in Modern English, we find each idea expressed once only ; and as nothing is lost in clearness, this method, as being the easiest and shortest, must be considered the best. Mathematically the different ways of rendering the same thing might be represented by the formulas : $anx + bnx + cnx = (an + bn + cn)x = (a+b+c)nx$.

This unusual faculty of ' parenthesizing ' causes Danish, and to a still greater degree English, to stand outside the definition of the Aryan family of languages given by the earlier school of linguists, according to which the Aryan substantive and adjective can never be without a sign indicating case. Schleicher (NV 526) says : " The radical difference between Magyar and Indo-Germanic (Aryan) words is brought out distinctly by the fact that the post-positions belonging to co-ordinated nouns can be dispensed with in all the nouns except the last of the series, e.g. *a jó embernek*, ' dem guten menschen ' (*a* for *az*, demonstrative pronoun, article ; *jó*, good ; *ember*, man, *-nek*, *-nak*, postposition with pretty much the same meaning as the dative case), for *az-nak* (annak) *jó-nak ember-nek*, as if in Greek you should say το ἀγαθο ἀνθρώπῳ. An attributive adjective preceding its noun always has the form of the pure stem, the sign of plurality and the postposition indicating case not being added to it. Magyars say, for instance, *Hunyady Mátyás magyar király-nak* (to the Hungarian king Mathew Hunyady), *-nak* belonging here to all the preceding words. Nearly the same thing takes place where several words are joined together by means of ' and.' "

Now, this is an exact parallel to the English group genitive in cases like ' all good old men's works,' ' the King of England's power,' ' Beaumont and Fletcher's plays,' ' somebody else's turn,' etc. The way in which this group genitive has developed in comparatively recent times may be summed up as follows (see the detailed exposition in my ChE ch. iii.) : In the oldest English *-s* is a case-ending, like all others found in flexional languages ; it forms together with the body of the noun one indivisible whole, in which it is sometimes impossible to tell where the kernel of the word ends and the ending begins (compare *endes* from *ende* and *heriges* from *here*) ; only some words have this ending, and in others the genitive is indicated in other ways. As to syntax, the meaning or function of the genitive is complicated and rather vague, and there are no fixed rules for the position of the genitive in the sentence.

In course of time we witness a gradual development towards greater regularity and precision. The partitive, objective, descriptive and some other functions of the genitive become obsolete; the genitive is invariably put immediately before the word it belongs to; irregular forms disappear, the *s* ending alone surviving as the fittest, so that at last we have one definite ending with one definite function and one definite position.

In Old English, when several words belonging together were to be put in the genitive, each of them had to take the genitive mark, though this was often different in different words, and thus we had combinations like *anes reades mannes*, ' a red man's ' | *þære godlican lufe*, ' the godlike love's ' | *ealra godra ealdra manna weorc*, etc. Now the *s* used everywhere is much more independent, and may be separated from the principal word by an adverb like *else* or by a prepositional group like *of England*, and one *s* is sufficient at the end even of a long group of words. Here, then, we see in the full light of comparatively recent history a giving up of the old flexion with its inseparability of the constituent elements of the word and with its strictness of concord; an easier and more regular system is developed, in which the ending leads a more independent existence and may be compared with the ' agglutinated ' elements of such a language as Magyar or even with the ' empty words ' of Chinese grammar. The direction of this development is the direct opposite of that assumed by most linguists for the development of languages in prehistoric times.

XVIII.—§ 9. Bantu Concord.

One of the most characteristic traits of the history of English is thus seen to be the gradual getting rid of concord as of something superfluous. Where concord is found in our family of languages, it certainly is an heirloom from a primitive age, and strikes us now as an outcome of a tendency to be more explicit than to more advanced people seems strictly necessary. It is on a par with the ' concord of negatives,' as we might term the emphasizing of the negative idea by seemingly redundant repetitions. In Old English it was the regular idiom to say: *n*an man *n*yste *n*an þing, ' no man not-knew nothing '; so it was in Chaucer's time: he *n*euere yet *n*o vileynye *n*e sayde In all his lyf unto *n*o manner wight; and it survives in the vulgar speech of our own days: there was *n*iver *n*obody else gen (gave) me nothin' (George Eliot); whereas standard Modern English is content with one negation: no man knew anything, etc. That concord is really a primitive trait (though not, of course, found equally distributed among all ' primitive peoples ') will be seen also by a rapid glance at the structure of the South African group of languages called Bantu, for here we find not only repetition of negatives, but also other phenomena of concord in specially luxuriant growth.

I take the following examples chiefly from W. H. I. Bleek's excellent, though unfortunately unfinished, *Comparative Grammar*, though I am well aware that expressions like *si-m-tanda* (we love him) "are never used by natives with this meaning without being determined by some other expression" (Torrend, p. 7). The Zulu word for ' man ' is *umuntu*; every word in the same or a following sentence having any reference to that word must begin with something to remind you of the beginning of *umuntu*. This will be, according to fixed rules, either *mu* or *u*, or *w* or *m*. In the following sentence, the meaning of which is ' our handsome man (or woman) appears, we love him (or her),' these reminders (as I shall term them) are printed in italics:

*umu*ntu	*w*etu	*omu*chle *u*yabonakala,	sim*tanda* (1)
man	ours	handsome appears,	we love.

If, instead of the singular, we take the corresponding plural *abantu*, ' men, people ' (whence the generic name of Bantu), the sentence looks quite different:

*aba*ntu *b*etu *aba*chle *ba*yabonakala, si*ba*tanda (2).

In the same way, if we successively take as our starting-point *ilizwe*, ' country,' the corresponding plural *amazwe*, ' countries,' *isizwe*, ' nation,' *izizwe*, ' nations,' *intombi*, ' girl,' *izintombi*, ' girls,' we get:

*ili*zwe	*l*etu	*eli*chle	*li*yabonakala,	si*li*tanda	(5)
*ama*zwe	*e*tu	*ama*chle	*a*yabonakala,	si*wa*tanda	(6)
*isi*zwe	*s*etu	*esi*chle	*si*yabonakala,	si*si*tanda	(7)
*izi*zwe	*z*etu	*ezi*chle	*zi*yabonakala,	si*zi*tanda	(8)
*in*tombi	*y*etu	*en*chle	*i*yabonakala,	si*yi*tanda	(9)
*izin*tombi	*z*etu	*ezin*chle	*zi*yabonakala,	si*zi*tanda	(10)
(girls)	our	handsome	appear,	we love.[1]	

In other words, every substantive belongs to one of several classes, of which some have a singular and others a plural meaning; each of these classes has its own prefix, by means of which the concord of the parts of a sentence is indicated. (An inhabitant

---

[1] The change of the initial sound of the reminder belonging to the adjective is explained through composition with a ' relative particle ' *a*; *au* becoming *o*, and *ai*, *e*. The numbers within parentheses refer to the numbers of Bleek's classes. Similar sentences from Tonga are found in Torrend's *Compar. Gr.* p. 6 f.

of the country of *U*ganda is called *mu*ganda, pl. *ba*ganda or *wa*ganda ; the language spoken there is *lu*ganda.)

It will be noticed that adjectives such as ' handsome ' or ' ours ' take different shapes according to the word to which they refer ; in the Zulu Lord's Prayer ' thy ' is found in the following forms : *l*ako (referring to *i*gama, ' name,' for *ili*gama, 5), *b*ako, (*ubu*kumkani, ' kingdom,' 14), *y*ako (*in*tando, ' will,' 9). So also the genitive case of the same noun has a great many different forms, for the genitive relation is expressed by the reminder of the governing word + the ' relative particle ' *a* (which is combined with the following sound) ; take, for instance, *inkosi*, ' chief, king ' :

> *umu*ntu *w*enkosi, ' the king's man ' (1 ; *we* for *w* + *a* + *i*).
> *aba*ntu *b*enkosi, ' the king's men ' (2).
> *ili*zwe *l*enkosi, ' the king's country ' (5).
> *ama*zwe *e*nkosi, ' the king's countries ' (6).
> *isi*zwe *s*enkosi, ' the king's nation ' (7).
> *uku*tanda *kw*enkosi, ' the king's love ' (15).

Livingstone says that these apparently redundant repetitions "impart energy and perspicuity to each member of a proposition, and prevent the possibility of a mistake as to the antecedent." These prefixes are necessary to the Bantu languages ; still, Bleek is right as against Livingstone in speaking of the repetitions as cumbersome, just as the endings of Latin *multorum virorum antiquorum* are cumbersome, however indispensable they may have been to the contemporaries of Cicero.

These African phenomena have been mentioned here chiefly to show to what lengths concord may go in the speech of some primitive peoples. The prevalent opinion is that each of these prefixes (*umu, aba, ili*, etc.) was originally an independent word, and that thus words like *umuntu, ilizwe*, were at first compounds like E. *steamship*, where it would evidently be possible to imagine a reference to this word by means of a repeated *ship* (our ship, which ship is a great ship, the ship appears, we love the ship) ; but at any rate the Zulus extend this principle to cases that would be parallel to an imagined repetition of *friendship* by means of the same *ship*, or to referring to *steamer* by means of the ending *er* (Bleek 107). Bleek and others have tried to find out by an analysis of the words making up the different classes what may have been the original meaning of the class-prefix, but very often the connecting tie is extremely loose, and in many cases it seems that a word might with equal right have belonged to another class than the one to which it actually belongs. The connexion also frequently seems to be a derived rather than an original one,

and much in this class-division is just as arbitrary as the reference
of Aryan nouns to each of the three genders. In several of the
classes the words have a definite numerical value, so that they go
together in pairs as corresponding singular and plural nouns ; but
the existence of a certain number of exceptions shows that these
numerical values cannot originally have been asscciated with the
class prefixes, but must be due to an extension by analogy
(Bleek 140 ff.). The starting-point may have been substantives
standing to each other in the relation of ' person ' to ' people,'
' soldier ' to ' army,' ' tree ' to ' forest,' etc. The prefixes of
such words as the latter of each of these pairs will easily acquire
a certain sense of plurality, no matter what they may have meant
originally, and then they will lend themselves to forming a kind
of plural in other nouns, being either put instead of the prefix
belonging properly to the noun (*amazwe*, ' countries,' 6 ; *ilizwe*,
' country,' 5), or placed before it (*ma-luto*, ' spoons,' 6, *luto*,
' spoon,' 11).

In some of the languages "the forms of some of the prefixes
have been so strongly contracted as almost to defy identification."
(Bleek 234). All the prefixes probably at first had fuller forms
than appear now. Bleek noticed that the *ma-* prefix never, except
in some degraded languages, had a corresponding *ma-* as particle,
but, on the contrary, is followed in the sentence by *ga-*, *ya-*, or
a-, and *mu-* (3) generally has a corresponding particle *gu-*. Now,
Sir Harry Johnston (*The Uganda Protectorate*, 1902, 2. 891) has
found that on Mount Eldon and in Kavirondo there are some very
archaic forms of Bantu languages, in which *gumu-* and *gama-*
are the commonly used forms of the *mu-* and *ma-* prefixes, as well
as *baba-* and *bubu-* for ordinary *ba-*, *bu-* ; he infers that the original
forms of *mu-*, *ma-* were *ngumu-*, *ngama-*. I am not so sure that
he is right when he says that these prefixes were originally "words
which had a separate meaning of their own, either as directives
or demonstrative pronouns, as indications of sex, weakness, little-
ness or greatness, and so on "—for, as we shall see in a subsequent
chapter, such grammatical instruments may have been at first
inseparable parts of long words—parts which had no meaning
of their own—and have acquired some more or less vague grammatical meaning through being extended gradually to other words
with which they had originally nothing to do. The actual
irregularity in their distribution certainly seems to point in that
direction.

XVIII.—§ 10. Word Order Again.

Mention has already been made here and there of word order
and its relation to the great question of simplification of gram-

matical structure ; but it will be well in this place to return to the subject in a more comprehensive way. The theory of word order has long been the Cinderella of linguistic science : how many even of the best and fullest grammars are wholly, or almost wholly, silent about it ! And yet it presents a great many problems of high importance and of the greatest interest, not only in those languages in which word order has been extensively utilized for grammatical purposes, such as English and Chinese, but in other languages as well.

In historical times we see a gradual evolution of strict rules for word order, while our general impression of the older stages of our languages is that words were often placed more or less at random. This is what we should naturally expect from primitive man, whose thoughts and words are most likely to have come to him rushing helter-skelter, in wild confusion. One cannot, of course, apply so strong an expression to languages such as Sanskrit, Greek or Gothic ; still, compared with our modern languages, it cannot be denied that there is in them much more of what from one point of view is disorder, and from another freedom.

This is especially the case with regard to the mutual position of the subject of a sentence and its verb. In the earliest times, sometimes one of them comes first, and sometimes the other. Then there is a growing tendency to place the subject first, and as this position is found not only in most European languages but also in Chinese and other languages of far-away, the phenomenon must be founded in the very nature of human thought, though its non-prevalence in most of the older Aryan languages goes far to show that this particular order is only natural to *developed* human thought.

Survivals of the earlier state of things are found here and there ; thus, in German ballad style : " Kam ein schlanker bursch gegangen." But it is well worth noticing that such an arrangement is generally avoided, in German as well as in the other modern languages of Western Europe, and in those cases where there is some reason for placing the verb before the subject, the speaker still, as it were, satisfies his grammatical instinct by putting a kind of sham subject before the verb, as in E. *there* comes a time when . . ., Dan. *der* kommer en tid da . . ., G. *es* kommt eine zeit wo . . ., Fr. *il* arrive un temps où . . .

In Keltic the habitual word order placed the verb first, but little by little the tendency prevailed to introduce most sentences by a periphrasis, as in ' (it) is the man that comes,' and as that came to mean merely ' the man comes,' the word order Subject-Verb was thus brought about circuitously.

Before this particular word order, Subject-Verb, was firmly established in modern Gothonic languages, an exception obtained wherever the sentence began with some other word than the subject; this might be some important member of the proposition that was placed first for the sake of emphasis, or it might be some unimportant little adverb, but the rule was that the verb should at any rate have the second place, as being felt to be in some way the middle or central part of the whole, and the subject had then to be content to be placed after the verb. This was the rule in Middle English and in Old French, and it is still strictly followed in German and Danish: Gestern *kam das schiff* | Pigen *gav jeg kagen, ikke drengen.* Traces of the practice are still found in English in parenthetic sentences to indicate who is the speaker ('Oh, yes,' said he), and after a somewhat long subjunct, if there is no object ('About this time died the gentle Queen Elizabeth'), where this word order is little more than a stylistic trick to avoid the abrupt effect of ending the sentence with an isolated verb like *died.* Otherwise the order Subject-Verb is almost universal in English.

XVIII.—§ 11. Compromises.

The inverted order, Verb-Subject, is used extensively in many languages to express questions, wishes and invitations. But, as already stated, this order was not originally peculiar to such sentences. A question was expressed, no matter how the words were arranged, by pronouncing the whole sentence, or the most important part of it, in a peculiar rising tone. This manner of indicating questions is, of course, still kept up in modern speech, and is often the only thing to show that a question is meant ('John?' | 'John is here?'). But although there was thus a natural manner of expressing questions, and although the inverted word order was used in other sorts of sentences as well, yet in course of time there came to be a connexion between the two things, so that putting the verb before the subject was felt as implying a question. The rising tone then came to be less necessary, and is much less marked in inverted sentences like 'Is John here?' than in sentences with the usual word order: 'John is here?'

Now, after this method of indicating questions had become comparatively fixed, and after the habit of thinking of the subject first had become all but universal, these two principles entered into conflict, the result of which has been, in English, Danish and French, the establishment in some cases of various kinds of compromise, in which the interrogatory word order has formally carried the day, while really the verb, that is to say the verb which means something, is placed after its subject. In English, this is attained by means of the auxiliary *do* : instead of Shakespeare's " Came he not home to-night ? " (*Ro.* II. 4. 2) we now say, " Did he not (or, Didn't he) come home to-night ? " and so in all cases where a similar arrangement is not already brought about by the presence of some other auxiliary, 'Will he come ? ', 'Can he come ? ', etc. Where we have an interrogatory pronoun as a subject, no auxiliary is required, because the natural front position of the pronoun maintains the order Subject-Verb (Who came ? | What happened ?). But if the pronoun is not the subject, *do* is required to establish the balance between the two principles (Who(m) did you see ? | What does he say ?).

In Danish, the verb *mon*, used in the old language to indicate a weak necessity or a vague futurity, fulfils to a certain extent the same office as the English *do* ; up to the eighteenth century *mon* was really an auxiliary verb, followed by the infinitive : 'Mon han komme ? ' ; but now the construction has changed, the indicative is used with *mon* : 'Mon han kommer ? ', and *mon* is uo longer a verb, but an interrogatory adverb, which serves the purpose of placing the subject before the verb, besides making the qnestion more indefinite and vague : 'Kommer han ? ' means 'Does he come ? ' or 'Will he come ? ' but 'Mon han kommer ? ' means ' Does he come (Will he come), do you think ? '

French, finally, has developed two distinct forms of compromise between the conflicting principles, for in ' Est-ce que Pierre bat Jean ? ' *est-ce* represents the interrogatory and *Pierre bat* the usual word order, and in ' Pierre bat-il Jean ? ' the real subject is placed before and the sham subject after the verb. Here also, as in Danish, the ultimate result is the creation of 'empty words,' or interrogatory adverbs : *est-ce-que* in every respect except in spelling is one word (note that it does not change with the tense of the main verb), and thus is a sentence prefix to introduce questions ; and in popular speech we find another empty word, namely *ti* (see, among other scholars, G. Paris, *Mélanges ling.* 276). The origin of this *ti* is very curious. While the *t* of Latin *amat*, etc., coming after a vowel, disappeared at a very early period of the French language, and so produced *il aime*, etc., the same *t* was kept in Old French wherever a consonant protected it,[1] and so gave the forms *est*, *sont*, *fait* (from *fact*, for *facit*), *font*, *chantent*, etc. From *est-il*, *fait-il*, etc., the *t* was then by analogy reintroduced in *aime-t-il*, instead of the earlier *aime il*. Now, towards the end of the Middle Ages, French final consonants were as a rule

---

[1] This protecting consonant was dropped in pronunciation at a later period.

dropped in speech, except when followed immediately by a word beginning with a vowel. Consequently, while *t* is mute in sentences like ' Ton frère *dit* | Tes frères *disent*,' it is sounded in the corresponding questions, ' Ton frère *dit-il* ? Tes frères *disent-ils* ? ' As the final consonants of *il* and *ils* are also generally dropped, even by educated speakers, the difference between interrogatory and declarative sentences in the spoken language depends solely on the addition of *ti* to the verb : written phonetically, the pairs will be :

[tɔ̃ frɛ·r di — tɔ̃ frɛ·r di ti]
[te frɛ·r diˑz — te frɛ·r diˑz ti].

Now, popular instinct seizes upon this *ti* as a convenient sign of interrogative sentences, and, forgetting its origin, uses it even with a feminine subject, turning ' Ta sœur di(t) ' into the question ' Ta sœur di ti ? ', and in the first person : ' Je di ti ? ' ' Nous dison ti ? ' ' Je vous fais-ti tort ? ' (Maupassant). In novels this is often written as if it were the adverb *y* : C'est-y pas vrai ? | Je suis t'y bête ! | C'est-y vous le monsieur de l'Académie qui va avoir cent ans ? (Daudet). I have dwelt on this point because, besides showing the interest of many problems of word order, it also throws some light on the sometimes unexpected ways by which languages must often travel to arrive at new expressions for grammatical categories.

It was mentioned above that the inverted order, Verb-Subject, is used extensively, not only in questions, but also to express wishes and invitations. Here, too, we find in English compromises with the usual order, Subject-Verb. For, apart from such formulas as ' Long live the King ! ' a wish is generally expressed by means of *may*, which is placed first, while the real verb comes after the subject : ' May she be happy ! ', and instead of the old ' Go we ! ' we have now ' Let us go ! ' with *us*, the virtual subject, placed before the real verb. When a pronoun is wanted with an imperative, it used to be placed after the verb, as in Shakespeare : ' *Stand thou* forth ' and ' *Fear* not *thou*,' or in the Bible : ' *Turn ye* unto him,' but now the usual order has prevailed : ' *You try !* ' ' *You take* that seat, and *somebody fetch* a few more chairs ! ' But if the auxiliary *do* is used, we have the compromise order : ' *Don't you stir !* '

XVIII.—§ 12. Order Beneficial ?

I have here selected one point, the place of the subject, to illustrate the growing regularity in word order ; but the same tendency is manifested in other fields as well : the place of the object (or of two objects, if we have an indirect besides a direct object), the place of the adjunct adjective, the place of a sub-ordinate adverb, which by coming regularly before a certain case may become a preposition 'governing' that case, etc. It cannot be denied that the tendency towards a more regular word order is universal, and in accordance with the general trend of this inquiry we must next ask the question : Is this tendency a beneficial one ? Does the more regular word order found in recent stages of our languages constitute a progress in linguistic structure ? Or should it be deplored because it hinders freedom of movement ?

In answering this question we must first of all beware of letting our judgment be run away with by the word 'freedom.' Because freedom is desirable elsewhere, it does not follow that it should be the best thing in this domain ; just as above we did not allow ourselves to be imposed on by the phrase 'wealth of forms,' so here we must be on our guard against the word 'free' : what if we turned the question in another way : Which is preferable, order or disorder ? It may be true that, viewed exclusively from the standpoint of the speaker, freedom would seem to be a great advantage, as it is a restraint to him to be obliged to follow strict rules ; but an orderly arrangement is decidedly in the interest of the hearer, as it very considerably facilitates his understanding of what is said ; it is therefore, though indirectly, in the interest of the speaker too, because he naturally speaks for the purpose of being understood. Besides, he is soon in his turn to become the hearer : as no one is exclusively hearer or speaker, there can be no real conflict of interest between the two.

If it be urged in favour of a free word order that we owe a certain regard to the interests of poets, it must be taken into con-sideration, first, that we cannot all of us be poets, and that a regard to all those of us who resemble Molière's M. Jourdain in speaking prose without being aware of it is perhaps, after all, more important than a regard for those very few who are in the enviable position of writing readable verse ; secondly, that a statistical investigation would, no doubt, give as its result that those poets who make the most extensive use of inversions are not among the greatest of their craft ; and, finally, that so many methods are found of neutralizing the restraint of word order, in the shape of particles, passive voice, different constructions of sentences, etc., that no artist in language need despair.

So far, we have scarcely done more than clear the ground before answering our question. And now we must recognize that there are some rules of word order which cannot be called beneficial in any way ; they are like certain rules of etiquette, in so far as one can see no reason for their existence, and yet one is obliged to bow to them. Historians may, in some cases, be able to account for their origin and show that they had a *raison d'être* at some remote period ; but the circumstances that called them into existence then have passed away, and they are now felt to be restraints with no concurrent advantage to reconcile us to their observance. Among rules of this class we may reckon those for placing the French pronouns now before, and now after, the verb, now with the dative and now with the accusative first, ' elle *me le* donne | elle *le lui* donne | donnez-*le moi* | ne *me le* donnez pas.' And, again, the rules for placing the verb, object, etc., in German subordinate clauses otherwise than in main sentences. That the latter rules are defective and are inferior to the English rules, which are the same for the two kinds of sentences, was pointed out before, when we examined Johannson's German sentences (p. 341), but here we may state that the real, innermost reason for condemning them is their inconsistency : the same rule does not apply in all cases. It seems possible to establish the important principle that the more consistent a rule for word order is, the more useful it is in the economy of speech, not only as facilitating the understanding of what is said, but also as rendering possible certain thorough-going changes in linguistic structure.

XVIII.—§ 13. Word Order and Simplification.

This, then, is the conclusion I arrive at, that as simplification of grammatical structure, abolition of case distinctions, and so forth, always go hand in hand with the development of a fixed word order, this cannot be accidental, but there must exist a relation of cause and effect between the two phenomena. Which, then, is the *prius* or cause ? To my mind undoubtedly the fixed word order, so that the grammatical simplification is the *posterius* or effect. It is, however, by no means uncommon to find a half-latent conception in people's minds that the flexional endings were first lost ' by phonetic decay,' or ' through the blind operation of sound laws,' and that then a fixed word order had to step in to make up for the loss of the previous forms of expression. But if this were true we should have to imagine an intervening period in which the mutual relations of words were indicated in neither way ; a period, in fact, in which speech was unintelligible and consequently practically useless. The theory is therefore untenable. It follows that a fixed word order must have come in first : it would come quite gradually as a natural consequence of greater mental development and general maturity, when the speaker's ideas no longer came into his mind helter-skelter, but in orderly sequence. If before the establishment of some sort of fixed word order any tendency to slur certain final consonants or vowels of grammatical importance had manifested itself, it could not have become universal, as it would have been constantly checked by the necessity that speech should be intelligible, and that therefore those marks which showed the relation of different words should not be obliterated. But when once each word was placed at the exact spot where it properly belonged, then there was no longer anything to forbid the endings being weakened by assimilation, etc., or being finally dropped altogether.

To bring out my view I have been obliged in the preceding paragraph to use expressions that should not be taken too literally; I have spoken as if the changes referred to were made ' in the lump,' that is, as if the word order was first settled in every respect, and after that the endings began to be dropped. The real facts are, of course, much more complicated, changes of one kind being interwoven with changes of the other in such a way as to render it difficult, if not impossible, in any particular case to discover which was the *prius* and which the *posterius*. We are not able to lay our finger on one spot and say : Here final *m* or *n* was dropped, because it was now rendered superfluous as a case-sign on account of the accusative being invariably placed after the verb, or for some other such reason. Nevertheless, the essential truth of my hypothesis seems to me unimpeachable. Look at Latin final *s*. Cicero (*Orat.* 48. 161) expressly tells us, what is corroborated by a good many inscriptions, that there existed a strong tendency to drop final *s* ; but the tendency did not prevail. The reason seems obvious ; take a page of Latin prose and try the effect of striking out all final *s*'s, and you will find that it will be extremely difficult to determine the meaning of many passages ; a consonant playing so important a part in the endings of nouns and verbs could not be left out without loss in a language possessing so much freedom in regard to word position as Latin. Consequently it was kept, but in course of time word position became more and more subject to laws ; and when, centuries later, after the splitting up of Latin into the Romanic languages, the tendency to slur over final *s* knocked once more at the door, it met no longer with the same resistance : final *s* disappeared, first in Italian and Rumanian, then in French, where it was kept till about the end of the Middle Ages, and it is now beginning to sound a retreat in Spanish ; see on Andalusian Fr. Wulff, *Un Chapitre de Phonétique Andalouse*, 1889.

The main line of development in historical times has, I take it, been the following : first, a period in which words were placed somewhere or other according to the fancy of the moment, but many of them provided with signs that would show their mutual relations ; next, a period with retention of these signs, combined with a growing regularity in word order, and at the same time in many connexions a more copious employment of prepositions ; then an increasing indistinctness and finally complete dropping of the endings, word order (and prepositions) being now sufficient to indicate the relations at first shown by endings and similar means.

Viewed in this light, the transition from freedom in word position to greater strictness must be considered a beneficial change, since it has enabled the speakers to do away with more circumstantial and clumsy linguistic means. Schiller says :

> Jeden anderen meister erkennt man an dem, was er ausspricht ;
> Was er weise verschweigt, zeigt mir den meister des stils.

(Every other master is known by what he says, but the master of style by what he is wisely silent on.) What style is to the individual, the general laws of language are to the nation, and we must award the palm to that language which makes it possible " to be wisely silent " about things which in other languages have to be expressed in a troublesome way, and which have often to be expressed over and over again (vir*orum* omni*um* bon*orum* veter*um*, eal*ra* god*ra* eald*ra* mann*a*). Could any linguistic expedient be more worthy of the genus *homo sapiens* than using for different purposes, with different significations, two sentences like ' John beats Henry ' and ' Henry beats John,' or the four Danish ones, ' Jens slaar Henrik—Henrik slaar Jens—slaar Jens Henrik ?—slaar Henrik Jens ? ' (John beats Henry—H. beats J.—does J. beat H. ?—does H. beat J. ?), or the Chinese use of *či* in different places (Ch. XIX § 3) ? Cannot this be compared with the ingenious Arabic system of numeration, in which 234 means something entirely different from 324, or 423, or 432, and the ideas of " tens " and " hundreds " are elegantly suggested by the order of the characters, not, as in the Roman system, ponderously expressed ?

Now, it should not be forgotten that this system, " where more is meant than meets the ear," is not only more convenient, but also clearer than flexions, as actually found in existing languages, for word order in those languages which utilize it grammatically is used much more consistently than any endings have ever been in the old Aryan languages. It is not true, as Johannson would have us believe, that the dispensing with old flexional endings was too dearly bought, as it brought about increasing possibilities of misunderstandings ; for in the evolution of languages the discarding of old flexions goes hand in hand with the development of simpler and more regular expedients that are rather less liable than the old ones to produce misunderstandings. Johannson writes : " In contrast to Jespersen I do not consider that the masterly expression is the one which is ' wisely silent,' and consequently leaves the meaning to be partly guessed at, but the one which is able to impart the meaning of the speaker or writer clearly and perfectly "—but here he seems rather wide of the mark. For, just as in reading the arithmetical symbol 234 we are perfectly sure that two hundred and thirty-four is meant, and not three hundred and forty-two, so in reading and hearing ' The boy hates the girl ' we cannot have the least doubt who hates whom. After all, there is less guesswork in the grammatical understanding of English than of Latin ; cf. the examples given above, Ch. XVIII § 4, p. 343.

The tendency towards a fixed word order is therefore a progressive one, directly as well as indirectly. The substitution of word order for flexions means a victory of spiritual over material agencies.

XVIII.—§ 14. Summary.

We may here sum up the results of our comparison of the main features of the grammatical structures of ancient and modern languages belonging to our family of speech. We have found certain traits common to the old stages and certain others characteristic of recent ones, and have thus been enabled to establish some definite tendencies of development and to find out the general direction of change ; and we have shown reasons for the conviction that this development has on the whole and in the main been a beneficial one, thus justifying us in speaking about ' progress in language.' The points in which the superiority of the modern languages manifested itself were the following :

(1) The forms are generally shorter, thus involving less muscular exertion and requiring less time for their enunciation.

(2) There are not so many of them to burden the memory.

(3) Their formation is much more regular.

(4) Their syntactic use also presents fewer irregularities.

(5) Their more analytic and abstract character facilitates expression by rendering possible a great many combinations and constructions which were formerly impossible or unidiomatic.

(6) The clumsy repetitions known under the name of concord have become superfluous.

(7) A clear and unambiguous understanding is secured through a regular word order.

These several advantages have not been won all at once, and languages differ very much in the velocity with which they have been moving in the direction indicated ; thus High German is in many respects behindhand as compared with Low German ;

European Dutch as compared with African Dutch ; Swedish as compared with Danish ; and all of them as compared with English ; further, among the Romanic languages we see considerable variations in this respect. What is maintained is chiefly that there is a general tendency for languages to develop along the lines here indicated, and that this development may truly, from the anthropocentric point of view, which is the only justifiable one, be termed a progressive evolution.

But is this tendency really general, or even universal, in the world of languages ? It will easily be seen that my examples have in the main been taken from comparatively few languages, those with which I myself and presumably most of my readers are most familiar, all of them belonging to the Gothonic and Romanic branches of the Aryan family. Would the same theory hold good with regard to other languages ? Without pretending to an intimate knowledge of the history of many languages, I yet dare assert that my conclusions are confirmed by all those languages whose history is accessible to us. Colloquial Irish and Gaelic have in many ways a simpler grammatical structure than the Oldest Irish. Russian has got rid of some of the complications of Old Slavonic, and the same is true, even in a much higher degree, of some of the other Slavonic languages ; thus, Bulgarian has greatly simplified its nominal and Serbian its verbal flexions. The grammar of spoken Modern Greek is much less complicated than that of the language of Homer or of Demosthenes. The structure of Modern Persian is nearly as simple as English, though that of Old Persian was highly complicated. In India we witness a constant simplification of grammar from Sanskrit through Prakrit and Pali to the modern languages, Hindi, Hindostani (Urdu), Bengali, etc. Outside the Aryan world we see the same movement : Hebrew is simpler and more regular than Assyrian, and spoken Arabic than the old classical language, Koptic than Old Egyptian. Of most of the other languages we are not in possession of written records from very early times ; still, we may affirm that in Turkish there has been an evolution, though rather a slow one, of a similar kind ; and, as we shall see in a later chapter, Chinese seems to have moved in the same direction, though the nature of its writing makes the task of penetrating into its history a matter of extreme difficulty. A comparative study of the numerous Bantu languages spoken all over South Africa justifies us in thinking that their evolution has been along the same lines : in some of them the prefixes characterizing various classes of nouns have been reduced in number and in extent (cf. above, § 9). Of one of them we have a grammar two hundred years old, by Brusciotto à Vetralla (re-edited by H. Grattan Guinness, London, 1882). A comparison of his description with the language now spoken in the same region (Mpongwe) shows that the class signs have dwindled down considerably and the number of the classes has been reduced from 16 to 10. In short, though we can only prove it with regard to a minority of the multitudinous languages spoken on the globe, this minority embraces *all* the languages known to us for so long a period that we can talk of their history, and we may, therefore, confidently maintain that what may be briefly termed the tendency towards grammatical simplification is a universal fact of linguistic history.

That this simplification is progressive, i.e. beneficial, was overlooked by the older generation of linguistic thinkers, because they saw a kosmos, a beautiful and well-arranged world, in the old languages, and missed in the modern ones several things that they had been accustomed to regard with veneration. To some extent they were right : every language, when studied in the right spirit, presents so many beautiful points in its systematic structure that it may be called a ' kosmos.' But it is not in every way a kosmos ; like everything human, it presents fine and less fine features, and a comparative valuation, such as the one here attempted, should take both into consideration. There is undoubtedly an exquisite beauty in the old Greek language, and the ancient Hellenes, with their artistic temperament, knew how to turn that beauty to the best account in their literary productions ; but there is no less beauty in many modern languages —though its appraisement is a matter of taste, and as such evades scientific inquiry. But the æsthetic point of view is not the decisive one : language is of the utmost importance to the whole practical and spiritual life of mankind, and therefore has to be estimated by such tests as those applied above ; if that is done, we cannot be blind to the fact that modern languages as wholes are more practical than ancient ones, and that the latter present so many more anomalies and irregularities than our present-day languages that we may feel inclined, if not to apply to them Shakespeare's line, " Misshapen chaos of well-seeming forms," yet to think that the development has been from something nearer chaos to something nearer kosmos.

CHAPTER XIX

ORIGIN OF GRAMMATICAL ELEMENTS

XIX.—§ 1. The Old Theory.

WHAT has been given in the last two chapters to clear up the problem " Decay or progress ? " has been based, as will readily be noticed, exclusively on easily controllable facts of linguistic history. So far, then, it has been very smooth sailing. But now we must venture out into the open sea of prehistoric speculations. Our voyage will be the safer if we never lose sight of land and have a reliable compass tested in known waters.

In our historical survey of linguistic science we have already seen that the prevalent theory concerning the prehistoric development of our speech is this : an originally isolating language, consisting of nothing but formless roots, passed through an agglutinating stage, in which formal elements had been developed, although these and the roots were mutually independent, to the third and highest stage found in flexional languages, in which formal elements penetrated the roots and made inseparable unities with them. We shall now examine the basis of this theory.

In the beginning was the root. This is " the result of strict and careful induction from the facts recorded in the dialects of the different members of the family " (Whitney L 260). " The firm foundation of the theory of roots lies in its logical necessity as an inference from the doctrine of the historical growth of grammatical apparatus " (Whitney G 200). " An instrumentality cannot but have had rude and simple beginnings, such as, in language, the so-called roots . . . such imperfect hints of expression as we call roots " (Whitney, *Views of L.* 338). These are really three different statements : induction from the facts, a logical inference from the doctrine about grammatical apparatus (i.e. the usually accepted doctrine, but on what is that built up except on the root theory ?), and the *a priori* argument that an 'instrumentality' must have simple beginnings. Even granted that these three arguments given at different times, each of them in turn as the sole argument, must be taken as supplementing each other, the three-legged stool on which the root theory is thus made to sit is a very shaky one, for none of the three legs is very solid, as we shall soon have occasion to see.

XIX.—§ 2. Roots.

In the beginning was the root—but what was it like ? Bopp took over the conception of root from the Indian grammarians, and like them was convinced that roots were all monosyllabic, and that view was accepted by his followers. These latter at times attributed other phonetic qualities to these roots, e.g. that they always had a short vowel (Curtius C 22). I quote from a very recent treatise (Wood, "Indo-European Root-formation," *Journal of Germ. Philol.* 1. 291) : "I range myself with those who believe that IE. roots were monosyllabic . . . these roots began, for the most part, with a vowel. The vowels certainly were the first utterances,[1] and though we cannot make the beginning of IE. speech coeval with that of human speech, we may at least assume that language, at that time, was in a very primitive state."

The number of these roots was not very great (Curtius, l.c. ; Wood 294). This seems a natural enough conclusion when we picture the earliest speech as the most meagre thing possible.

These few short monosyllabic roots were real words—this is a necessary assumption if we are to imagine a root stage as a real language, and it is often expressly stated ; Curtius, for instance, insists that roots are real and independent words (C 22, K 132) ; cf. also Whitney, who says that the root *VAK* "had also once an independent status, that it was a word " (L 255). We shall see afterwards that there is another possible conception of what a ' root ' is ; but let us here grant that it is a real word. The question whether a language is possible which contains nothing but such root words was always answered affirmatively by a reference to Chinese—and it will therefore be well here to give a short sketch of the chief structural features of that language.

[1] Why so ? Did sheep and cows also begin with vowels only, adding *b* and *m* afterwards to make up their *bah* and *moo* ?

XIX.—§ 3. Structure of Chinese.

Each word consists of one syllable, neither more nor less. Each of these monosyllables has one of four or five distinct musical tones (not indicated here). The parts of speech are not distinguished : *ta* means, according to circumstances, great, much, magnitude, enlarge. Grammatical relations, such as number, person, tense, case, etc., are not expressed by endings and similar expedients ; the word in itself is invariable. If a substantive is to be taken as plural, this as a rule must be gathered from the context ; and it is only when there is any danger of misunderstanding, or when the notion of plurality is to be emphasized, that separate words are added, e.g. *ki* 'some,' *šu* 'number.' The most important part of Chinese grammar is that dealing with word order : *ta kuok* means 'great state(s),' but *kuok ta* 'the state is great,' or, if placed before some other word which can serve as a verb, 'the greatness (size) of the state'; *tsĭ niu* 'boys and girls,' but *niu tsĭ* 'girl (female child),' etc. Besides words properly so called, or as Chinese grammarians call them 'full words,' there are several 'empty words' serving for grammatical purposes, often in a wonderfully clever and ingenious way. Thus *či* has besides other functions that of indicating a genitive relation more distinctly than would be indicated by the mere position of the words ; *min* (people) *lik* (power) is of itself sufficient to signify 'the power of the people,' but the same notion is expressed more explicitly by *min či lik*. The same expedient is used to indicate different sorts of connexion : if *či* is placed after the subject of a sentence it makes it a genitive, thereby changing the sentence into a kind of subordinate clause : *wang pao min* = 'the king protects the people'; but if you say *wang či pao min yeu* (is like) *fu* (father) *či pao tsĭ*, the whole may be rendered, by means of the English verbal noun, 'the king's protecting the people is like the father's protecting his child.' Further, it is possible to change a whole sentence into a genitive ; for instance, *wang pao min či tao* (manner) *k'o* (can) *kien* (see, be seen), 'the manner in which the king protects (the manner of the king's protecting) his people is to be seen'; and in yet other positions *či* can be used to join a word-group consisting of a subject and verb, or of verb and object, as an adjunct (attribute) to a noun ; we have participles to express the same modification of the idea : *wang pao či min* 'the people protected by the king'; *pao min či wang* 'a king protecting the people.' Observe here the ingenious method of distinguishing the active and passive voices by strictly adhering to the natural order and placing the subject before and the object after the verb. If we put *i* before, and *ku* after, a single word, it means ' on account of, because of ' (cf. E. for . . . 's sake); if we place a whole sentence between these ' brackets,' as we might term them, they are a sort of conjunction, and must be translated ' because.' [1]

XIX.—§ 4. History of Chinese.

These few examples will give some faint idea of the Chinese language, and—if the whole older generation of scholars is to be trusted—at the same time of the primeval structure of our own language in the root-stage. But is it absolutely certain that Chinese has retained its structure unchanged from the very first period ? By no means. As early as 1861, R. Lepsius, from a comparison of Chinese and Tibetan, had derived the conviction that " the monosyllabic character of Chinese is not original, but is a lapse (!) from an earlier polysyllabic structure." J. Edkins, while still believing that the structure of Chinese represents " the speech first used in the world's grey morning " (*The Evolution of the Chinese Language*, 1888), was one of the foremost to examine the evidence offered by the language itself for the determination of its earlier pronunciation. This, of course, is a much more complicated problem in Chinese than in our alphabetically written languages ; for a Chinese character, standing for a complete word, may remain unchanged while the pronunciation is changed indefinitely. But by means of dialectal pronunciations in our own day, of remarks in old Chinese dictionaries, of transcriptions of Sanskrit words made by Chinese Buddhists, of rimes in ancient poetry, of phonetic or partly phonetic elements in the word-characters, etc., is has been possible to demonstrate that Chinese pronunciation has changed considerably, and that the direction of change has been, here as elsewhere, towards shorter and easier word-forms. Above all, consonant groups have been simplified.

In 1894 I ventured to offer my mite to these investigations by suggesting an explanation of one phenomenon of pronunciation in present-day Chinese. I refer to the change sometimes wrought in the meaning of a word by the adoption of a different tone. Thus *wang* with one tone is ' king,' with another ' to become king '; *lao* with one is ' work,' with another ' pay the work '; *tsung* with one tone means ' follow,' with another ' follower,' and with a third ' footsteps '; *tshi* with one tone is ' wife,' with another ' marry '; *haò* is ' good,' and *haó* is ' love.' Nay, meanings so different as ' acquire ' and ' give ' (*sheu*) or ' buy ' and ' sell ' (*mai*) are only distinguished by the tones. Edkins and V. Henry

[1] The examples taken from Gabelentz's *Grammar* and an article in Techmer's *Internat. Zeitschrift* I.

(*Le Muséon*, Louvain, 1882, i. 435) have attempted to explain this from gestures ; but this is palpably wrong. In the Danish dialect spoken in Sundeved, in southernmost Jutland, two tones are distinguished, one high and one low (see articles by N. Andersen and myself in *Dania*, vol. iv.). Now, these tones often serve to keep words or forms of words apart that but for the tone, exactly as in Chinese, would be perfect homophones. Thus *na* with the low tone is ' fool,' but with the high tone it is either the plural ' fools ' or else a verb ' to cheat, hoax ' ; *ri* ' ride ' is imperative or infinitive according to the tone in which it is uttered ; *jem* in the low tone is ' home ' and in the high ' at home ' ; and so on in a great many words. There is no need, however, in this language to resort to gestures to explain these tonic differences : the low tone is found in words originally monosyllabic (compare standard Danish *nar, rid, hjem*), and the high tone in words originally dissyllabic (compare Danish *narre, ride, hjemme*). The tones belonging formerly to two syllables are now condensed on one syllable. Although, of course, Chinese tones cannot in every respect be paralleled with Scandinavian ones, we may provisionally conjecture that the above-mentioned pairs of Chinese words were formerly distinguished by derivative syllables or flexional endings (see below, p. 373) which have now disappeared without leaving any traces behind them except in the tones. This hypothesis is perhaps rendered more probable by what seems to be an established fact—that one of the tones has arisen through the dropping of final stopped consonants (*p, t, k*).

However this may be, the death-blow was given to the dogma of the primitiveness of Chinese speech by Ernst Kuhn's lecture *Ueber Herkunft und Sprache der Transgangetischen Völker* (Munich, 1883). He compares Chinese with the surrounding languages of Tibet, Burmah and Siam, which are certainly related to Chinese and have essentially the same structure ; they are isolating, have no flexion, and word order is their chief grammatical instrument. But the laws of word order prove to be different in these several languages, and Kuhn draws the incontrovertible conclusion that it is impossible that any one of these laws of word position should have been the original one ; for that would imply that the other nations have changed it without the least reason and at a risk of terrible confusion. The only likely explanation is that these differences are the outcome of a former state of greater freedom. But if the ancestral speech had a free word order, to be at all intelligible it must have been possessed of other grammatical appliances than are now found in the derived tongues ; in other words, it must have indicated the relations of words to each other by something like our derivatives or flexions.

To the result thus established by Kuhn, that Chinese cannot have had a fixed word order from the beginning, we seem also to be led if we ask the question, Is primitive man likely to have arranged his words in this way ? A Chinese sentence, according to Gabelentz (Spr 426), is arranged with the same logical precision as the direction on an English envelope, where the most specific word is placed first, and each subsequent word is like a box comprising all that precedes—only that a Chinaman would reverse the order, beginning with the most general word and then in due order specializing. Now, is it probable that primitive man, that unkempt, savage being, who did not yet deserve the proud generic name of *homo sapiens*, but would be better termed, if not *homo insipiens*, at best *homo incipiens*—is it probable that this *urmensch*, who was little better than an *unmensch*, should have been able at once to arrange his words, or, what amounts to the same thing, his thoughts, in such a perfect order ? I incline to believe rather that logical, orderly thinking and speaking have only been attained by mankind after a long and troublesome struggle, and that the grammatical expedient of a fixed word order has come to Chinese as to European languages through a gradual development in which other, less logical and more material grammatical appliances have in course of time been given up.

We have thus arrived at a conception of Chinese which is *toto cælo* removed from the view formerly current. The Chinese language can no longer be adduced in support of the hypothesis that our Aryan languages, or all human languages, started at first as a grammarless speech consisting of monosyllabic root-words.

XIX.—§ 5. Recent Investigations.

I have reprinted the above sketch of Chinese, with a few very insignificant verbal changes, as I wrote it about thirty years ago, because I think that the main reasoning is just as valid now as then, and because everything I have since then read about this interesting language has only confirmed the opinion I ventured to express after what was certainly a very insufficient study. Chinese pronunciation, including its tones, may now be studied in two excellent books, dealing with two different dialects—Daniel Jones and Kwing Tong Woo, *A Cantonese Phonetic Reader*, London, 1912, and Bernhard Karlgren, *A Mandarin Phonetic Reader in the Pekinese Dialect*, Upsala, Leipzig and Paris, 1917 (Archives d'Études Orientales, vol. 13). Karlgren is also the author of *Études sur la Phonologie Chinoise* (ib. vol. 15, 1915–19), in which he deals with the history of Chinese sounds and the reconstruction of the old pronunciation in a thoroughly scholarly manner on the basis of an intimate knowledge of spoken and written Chinese, and in *Ordet och pennan i mittens rike* (Stockholm, 1918), he has given a masterly popular sketch of the structure of the Chinese language and its system of writing.

Of the greatest importance for our purposes is the same scholar's recent brilliant discovery of a real case distinction in the oldest Chinese. In classical Chinese there are four pronouns of the first person (I, we) which have always been considered as absolutely synonymous. But Karlgren shows that the two of them which occur as the usual forms in Confucius's conversations are so far from being used indiscriminately that one is nearly always a nominative and the other an objective case; the exceptions are not numerous and are easily explained. The present Mandarin pronunciation of the first is [u], of the second either [uo] or [ηo]. But if we go back to the sixth century of our era we are able with certainty to say that the pronunciation of the former was [ηuo], and of the latter [ηa]. This, then, constitutes a real declension. Now, in the second person Karlgren is also able to point out a distinction of two pronouns, though not quite so clearly marked as in the first person, the objective showing here a greater tendency to encroach on the nominative (Karlgren here ingeniously adduces the parallel from our languages that the first person has retained the suppletive system *ego* : *me*, while the second uses the same stem *tu* : *te*). The oldest Chinese thus has the following case flexion :

	1st Per.	2nd Per.
Nom.	ηuo	nżiwo
Obj.	ηa	nżia

(See " Le Proto-chinois, langue flexionnelle," *Journal Asiatique*, 1920, 205 ff.).[1]

XIX.—§ 6. Roots Again.

To return to roots. The influence of Indian grammar on European linguists with regard to the theory of roots extended also to the meanings assigned to roots, which were all of them

---

[1] I must also mention A. Conrady, *Eine indochinesische Causativ-denominativ-bildung* (Leipzig, 1896), in which Lepsius's theory is carried a great step further and it is demonstrated with very great learning that many of the tone relations (as well as modifications of initial sounds) of Chinese and kindred languages find their explanation in the previous existence of prefixes which are now extinct, but which can still be pointed out in Tibetan. Though I ought, therefore, to have spoken of prefixes instead of ' flexional endings ' above, p. 371, the essence of the contention that prehistoric Chinese must have had a polysyllabic and non-isolating structure is thus borne out by the researches of competent specialists in this field.

of verbal character, and nearly always highly general or abstract, such as ‘ breathe, move, be sharp or quick, blow, go,’ etc. The impossibility of imagining anybody expressing himself by means of a language consisting exclusively of such abstracts embarrassed people much less than one would expect : Chinese, of course, has plenty of words for concrete objects.

The usual assumption was that there was one definite root period in which all the roots were created, and after which this form of activity ceased. But Whitney demurred to this (M 36), saying that E. *preach* and *cost* may be considered new roots, though ultimately coming from Lat. *præ-dicare* and *con-stare* : these old compounds are felt as units, “ reducing to the semblance of roots elements that are really derivative or compound.” As Whitney goes no further than to establish the *semblance* of new roots, he might be taken as an adherent rather than as an opponent of the theory he objects to. But, as a matter of fact, new words *are* created in modern languages, and if they form the basis of derived words, we may really speak of new roots (*pun—punning*, *punster* ; *fun—funny* ; etc.). Why not say that we have a French root *roul* in *rouler, roulement, roulage, roulier, rouleau, roulette, roulis* ? This only becomes unjustifiable if we think that the establishment of this root gives us the ultimate explanation of these words ; for then the linguistic historian steps in with the objection that the words have been formed, not from a root, but from a real word, which is not even in itself a primary word, but a derivative, Lat. *rotula*, a diminutive of *rota* ‘ wheel.’ (I take this example from Bréal M 407). To the popular instinct *sorrow* and *sorry* are undoubtedly related to one another, and we may say that they contain a root *sorr-* ; but a thousand years ago they had nothing to do with one another, and belonged to different roots : OE. *sorg* ‘ care ’ and *sārig* ‘ wounded, afflicted.’ If all traces of Latin and Greek were lost, a linguist would have no more scruples about connecting *scene* with *see* than most illiterate Englishmen have now. Who will vouch that many Aryan roots may not have originated at various times through similar processes as these new roots *preach, cost, roul, sorr, see* ?

The proper definition of a root seems to be : what is common to a certain number of words felt by the popular instinct of the speakers as etymologically belonging together. In this sense we may of course speak of roots at any stage of any language, and not only at a hypothetical initial stage. In some cases these roots may be used as separate words (E. *preach, fun*, etc., Fr. *roul* = what is spelt *roule, roules, roulent*) ; in other cases this is impossible (Lat. *am* in *amo, amor, amicus* ; E. *sorr*) ; in many cases because the common element cannot, for phonetic reasons, be easily pronounced, as when E. *drink, drank, drunk* or *sit, sat, seat, set* are naturally felt to belong together, though it is impossible to state the root except in some formula like *dr.nk, s.t,* where the dot stands for some vowel. Similar considerations may be adduced with regard to the consonants if we want to establish what is felt to be common in *give* and *gift* (*gi* + labiodental spirant) or in *speak* and *speech,* etc.; but this need not detain us here.

In my view, then, the root is something real and important, though not always tangible. And as its form is not always easy to state or pronounce, so must its meaning, as a rule, be somewhat vague and indeterminate, for what is common to several ideas must of course be more general and abstract than either of the more special ideas thus connected ; it is also natural that it will often be necessary to state the signification of a root in terms of verbal ideas, for these are more general and abstract than nominal ideas. But roots thus conceived belong to any and all periods, and we must cease to speak of the earliest period of human speech as ' the root period.'

XIX.—§ 7. The Agglutination Theory.

According to the received theory (see above, § 1) some of the roots became gradually attached to other roots and lost their independence, so as to become finally formatives fused with the root. This theory, generally called the agglutination theory, contains a good deal of truth ; but we can only accept it with three important provisos, namely, first, that there has never been one definite period in which those languages which are now flexional were wholly agglutinative, the process of fusion being liable to occur at any time ; second, that the component parts which become formatives are not at first roots, but real words ; and third, that this process is not the only one by which formatives may develop : it may be called the rectilinear process, but by the side of that we have also more circuitous courses, which are no less important in the life of languages for being less obvious.

In the process of coalescence or integration there are many possible stages, with may be denominated figuratively by such expressions as that two words are placed together (that is—in non-figurative language—pronounced after one another), tied together, knit together, glued together (' agglutinated '), soldered together, welded together, fused together or amalgamated. What is really the most important part of the process is the degree in which one of the components loses its independence, phonetically and semantically.

As 'agglutination' is thus only one intermediate stage in a continuous process, it would be better to have another name for the whole theory of the origin of formatives than 'the agglutination theory,' and I propose therefore to use the term 'coalescence theory.' The usual name also fixes the attention too exclusively on the so-called agglutinative languages, and if we take the formatives of such a language as Turkish, as in *sev-mek* 'to love,' *sev-il-mek* 'to be loved,' *sev-dir-mek* 'to cause to love,' *sev-dir-il-mek* 'to be made to love,' *sev-ish-mek* 'to love one another,' *sev-ish-dir-il-mek* 'to be made to love one another'—who will vouch that these formatives were all of them originally independent words ? Those who are most competent to have an opinion on the matter seem nowadays inclined to doubt it and to reject much of what was current in the description of these languages given by the earlier scholars ; see, especially, the interesting final chapter of V. Grønbech, *Forstudier til tyrkisk lydhistorie* (København, 1902).

XIX.—§ 8. Coalescence.

The various degrees of coalescence, and the coexistence at the same linguistic period of these various degrees, may be illustrated by the old example, English *un-tru-th-ful-ly*, and by German *un-be-stimm-bar-keit*. Let us look a little at each of these formatives. The only one that can still be used as an independent word is *ful*(l). From the collocation in ' I have my hand full of peas ' the transition is easy to ' a handful of peas,' where the accentual subordination of *full* to *hand* paves the way for the combination becoming one word instead of two : this is not accomplished till it becomes possible to put the plural sign at the end (*handfuls*, thus also *basketfuls* and others), while in less familiar combinations the *s* is still placed in the middle (*bucketsful*, two *donkeysful* of children, see MEG ii. 2. 42). In these substantives -*ful* keeps its full vowel [u]. But in adjectival compounds, such as *peaceful*, *awful*, there is a colloquial pronunciation with obscured or omitted vowel [-fəl, -fl], in which the phonetic connexion with the full word is thus weakened ; the semantic connexion, too, is loosened when it becomes possible to form such words as *dreadful*, *bashful*, in which it is not possible to use the definition ' full of . . .' Here, then, the transition from a word to a derivative suffix is complete.

English -*hood*, -*head* in *childhood*, *maidenhead* also is originally an independent word, found in OE. and ME. in the form *had*, meaning ' state, condition,' Gothic *haidus*. In German it has two forms, -*heit*, as in *freiheit*, and -*keit*, whose *k* was at first the final sound of the adjective in *ewigkeit*, MHG. *ewecheit*, but was later felt as part of the suffix and then transferred to cases in which the stem had no *k*, as in *tapferkeit, ehrbarkeit*.

The suffix *-ly* is from *lik*, which was a substantive meaning 'form, appearance, body' ('a dead body' in Dan. *lig*, E. *lich* in *lichgate*); *manlik* thus is 'having the form or appearance of a man'; the adjective *like* originally was *ge-lic* 'having the same appearance with' (as in Lat. *con-form-is*). In compounds *-lik* was shortened into *-ly*: in some cases we still have competing forms like *gentlemanlike* and *gentlemanly*. The ending was, and is still, used extensively in adjectives; if it is now also used to turn adjectives into adverbs, as in *truthful-ly, luxurious-ly*, this is a consequence of the two OE. forms, adj. *-lic* and adv. *-lice*, having phonetically fallen together.

It may perhaps be doubtful whether the G. suffix *-bar* (OHG. *-bari*, OE. *bære*) was ever really an independent word, but its connexion with the verb *beran*, E. *bear*, cannot be doubted: *fruchtbar* is what bears fruit (cf. OE. *æppelbære* 'bearing apples'), but the connexion was later loosened, and such adjectives as *ehrbar, kostbar, offenbar* have little or nothing left of the original meaning of the suffix. The two prefixes in our examples, *un-* and *be-*, are differentiated forms of the old negative *ne* and the preposition *by*, and the only affix in our two long words which is thus left unexplained is *-th*, which makes *true* into *truth* and is found also in *length, health*, etc.

XIX.—§ 9. Flexional Endings.

There can be no doubt, therefore, that some at any rate of our suffixes and prefixes go back to independent words which have been more or less weakened to become derivative formatives. But does the same hold good with those endings which we are accustomed to term flexional endings? The answer certainly must be in the affirmative—with regard to *some* endings.

Thus the Scandinavian passive originates in a coalescence of the active verb and the pronoun *sik*: Old Norse (*þeir*) *finna sik* ('they find themselves' or 'each other'), gradually becomes one word (*þeir*) *finnask*, later *finnast, finnaz*, Swedish (*de*) *finnas*, Dan. (*de*) *findes* 'they are found.' In Old Icelandic the pronoun is still to some extent felt as such, though formally an indistinguishable part of the verb; thus combinations like the following are very frequent: *Bolli kvaz þessu ráða vilja = kvað sik vilja*; "Bolli dixit se velle: B. said that he would have his own way" (Laxd. 55). In Danish a distinction can sometimes be made between a reflexive and a purely passive employment: *de slås* with a short vowel is 'they fight (one another),' but with a long vowel 'they are beaten.'

A similar coalescence is taking place in Russian, where *sja* ' himself '
(myself, etc.) dwindles down to a suffixed *s* : *kazalos* 'it showed itself,
turned out.'

A similar case is the Romanic future : It. *finiro*, Sp. *finire*,
Fr. *finirai*, from *finire habeo* (*finir ho*, etc.), originally ' I have to
finish.' Before the coalescence was complete, it was possible to
insert a pronoun, Old Sp. *cantar-te-hé* ' I shall sing to you.'

A third case in point is the suffixed definite article, if we are
allowed to consider that as a kind of flexion : Old Norse *mannenn*
(*manninn*) accusative ' the man,' *landet* (*landit*) ' the land ' ; Dan.
manden, landet, from *mann, land* + the demonstrative pronoun *enn*,
neuter *et*. Rumanian *domnul* ' the lord,' from Lat. *dominu(m)*
illu(m), is another example.

XIX.—§ 10. Validity of the Theory.

Now, does this kind of explanation admit of universal application—in other words, were all our derivative affixes and flexional
endings originally independent words before they were ' glued '
to or fused with the main word ?   This has been the prevalent, one
might almost say the orthodox, view of all the leading linguists,
who may be mustered in formidable array in defence of the
agglutination theory.[1]

Against the universality of this origin for formatives I adduced
in my former work (1894, p. 66 f., cf. *Kasus*, 1891, p. 36) four
reasons, which I shall here restate in a different order and in a
fuller form.

(1) Nothing can be proved with regard to the ultimate genesis
of flexion in general from the adduced examples, for in all of them
the elements were already fully flexional before the coalescence
(cf. ON. *finnask, fannsk* ; It. *finirð, finirai, finira* ; ON. *maðrenn*,
mannenn, mansens, etc.).   What they show, then, is really nothing
but the growth of new flexional formations on an old flexional
soil, and it might be imagined that the fusion would not have taken
place, or not so completely, if the minds of the speakers had not
been already prepared to accept formations of this character.
I do not, however, attach much importance to this argument, and
turn to those that are more cogent.

(2) The number of actual forms proved beyond a doubt to

[1] Madvig Kl 170, Max Müller L 1. 271, Whitney OLS 1. 283, G 124, Paul
P 1st ed. 181, repeated in the following editions, see 4th, 1909, 350 and 347,
349 ; Brugmann VG 1889, 2. 1 (but in 2nd ed. this has been struck out in
favour of hopeless skepticism), Schuchardt, *Anlass d. Volapüks* 11, Gabelentz
Spr 189, Tegnér SM 53, Sweet, *New Engl. Gr.* § 559, Storm, *Engl. Phil.* 673,
Rozwadowski, *Wortbildung u. Wortbed.*, Uhlenbeck, *Karakt. d. bask. Gramm.*
24, Sütterlin WGS 1902, 122, Porzezinski, Spr 1910, 229.

have originated through coalescence is comparatively small. It is true that not a few derivative syllables were originally independent; still, if we compare them with the number of those for which no such origin has been proved or even proposed, we find that the proportion is very small indeed. In the list of English suffixes enumerated in Sweet's *Grammar*, only eleven can be traced back to independent words, while 74 are not thus explicable. Anyone going through the countless suffixes enumerated in the second volume of Brugmann's *Vergleichende Grammatik* will, I think, be struck with the impossibility of any great number of them being traced back to words in the same way as *hood*, etc., above: their forms and, still more, their vague spheres of meaning, and on the whole their manner of application, distinctly speak against such an origin.

As to real flexional endings traceable to words, their number is even comparatively smaller than that of derivative suffixes; the three or four instances named above are everywhere appealed to, but are there so many more than these ? And are they numerous enough to justify so general an assertion ? My impression is that the basis for the induction is very far from sufficient.

(3) This argument is strengthened when we are able to point out instances in which, as a matter of fact, flexional endings have arisen in a way that is totally opposed to the agglutinative, which then must renounce all claims to be the *only* possible way for a language to arrive at flexional formatives. See below (§ 13) on Secretion.

(4) Assuming the theory to be true, we should expect much greater regularity, both in formal (morphological) and in semantic (syntactic) respect than we actually find in the old Aryan languages ; for if one definite element was added to signify one definite modification of the idea, we see no reason why it should not have been added to all words in the same way. As a matter of fact, the Romanic future, the Scandinavian passive voice and definite article present much greater regularity than is found in the flexion of nouns and verbs in old Aryan.

XIX.—§ 11. Irregularity Original.

It will be objected that the irregularity which we find in these old languages is of later growth, and that, in fact, flexion, as Schuchardt says, is "anomal gewordene agglutination." Whitney said that " each suffix has its distinct meaning and office, and is applied in a whole class of analogous words " (L. 254), and in reading Schleicher's *Compendium* one gains the impression that the old Aryan sounds and forms were like a regiment of well-trained soldiers marching along in the best military style, while all irregularities were the result of later decay in each language separately. But the trend of the whole scientific development of the last fifty years has been in the direction of demonstrating more and more irregularity in the original forms : where formerly only one ending was assumed for the same case, etc., now several are assumed. (See, e.g., Walde in Streitberg's *Gesch.*, 2. 194, Thumb, ib. 2. 69.) And as with the forms, so also with the meanings and applications of the forms. Madvig as early as 1857 (p. 27, Kl 202) had seen that the signification of the grammatical forms must originally have been extremely vague and fluctuating, but most scholars went on imagining that each case, each tense, each mood had originally stood for something quite settled and definite, until gradually the progress of linguistics made away with that conception point by point. In place of the belief that the original Aryan verb had a definite system of tense forms, it is now generally assumed that different 'aspects' ('aktionsarten'), somewhat like those of Slav verbs, were indicated, and that the notion of 'time' differences was only afterwards developed out of the notion of aspect : but if we compare the divisions and definitions of these aspects given by various scholars, we see how essentially vague this notion is ; instead of being a model system of nice logical distinctions, the original condition must rather have been one in which such notions as duration, completion, result, beginning, repetition were indistinctly found as germs, from which such ideas as perfect and imperfect, past and present, were finally evolved with greater and greater clearness.

Similar remarks apply to moods. All attempts at finding out, deductively or inductively, the fundamental notion (grundbegriff) attached to such a mood as the subjunctive have failed : it is impossible to establish one original, sharply circumscribed sphere of usage, from which all the various, partly conflicting, usages in the actually existing languages can be derived. The usual theory is that there existed one true subjunctive, characterized by long thematic vowels $-\bar{e}-$, $-\bar{a}-$, $-\bar{o}-$, and distinct from that an optative, characterized by a formative $-i\bar{e}-$: $-\bar{\imath}-$,[1] and that these two were fused in Latin. But, as Oertel and Morris have shown in their valuable article " An Examination of the Theories regarding the Nature and Origin of Indo-European Inflection " (*Harvard Studies in Classical Philol.* XVI, 1905) it is probably safer to assume for the Indo-European period substantial identity of meaning

---

[1] Two explanations of this formative element were given by the old school : according to Schleicher Ć § 290, it was the root *ja* of the relative pronoun ; according to Curtius and others it was the root *i* ' to go,' Greek *fer-o-i-mi* being analyzed as ' I go to bear,' whence, by an easy (?) transition, ' I should like to bear,' etc.

in the modal formatives *iě* : *i* and the long thematic vowels -*ě*-, -*ā*-, -*ō*-, which were then continued undifferentiated in Latin, while on the one hand the Germanic branch has practically discarded the forms with long thematic vowel and confined itself to the *i* suffix, and on the other hand two branches, Greek and Indo-Iranic, have availed themselves of the formal difference and separated a 'subjunctive' and an 'optative' mood.

XIX.—§ 12. Coalescence Theory dropped.

In the historical part I have already mentioned some instances of coalescence explanations of Aryan forms which have been abandoned by most scholars, such as the theory that the *r* of the Latin passive is a disguised *se*, which would agree very well with the Scandinavian passive, but falls to the ground when one remembers that corresponding forms are found in Keltic, where the transition from *s* to *r* is otherwise unknown : these forms are now believed to be related to some *r* forms found in Sanskrit, but there not possessed of any passive signification, this latter being thus a comparatively late acquisition of Keltic and Italic : these two branches turning an existing, non-meaning consonant to excellent use in their flexional system and generalizing it in the new application.[1]

The explanation of the 'weak' Gothonic preterit from a coalescence of *did* (*loved = love did*) was long one of the strongholds of the agglutination theory, Bopp's original collocation of these forms with other forms which could not be thus explained (see above 51) having passed into oblivion. Now we have Collitz's comprehensive book *Das schwache Präteritum*, 1912, in which the formative consonant is shown to have been Aryan *t*, and the close correspondence not only with the passive participle, but also with the verbal nouns in -*ti* is duly emphasized.

The impossibility of explaining the Latin perfect in -*vi* from composition with *fui* has been demonstrated by Mcrguet (see Walde in Streitberg's *Gesch.*, 2. 220). Instead of this rectilinear explanation, scholars now incline to assume an intricate play of various analogical influences starting from a pre-ethnic perfect in *w* in isolated instances.

Many have explained the case ending -*s* as a coalesced demonstrative pronoun *sa* or, as it is now given, *so* ; the difficulty that the same *s* denotes now the nominative and now the genitive was got over

[1] Cf. Sommer, Lat. 528, and on Armenian and Tokharian *r* forms MSL 18. 10 ff. and Feist KI 455. But it must not be overlooked that H. Pedersen (KZ 40. 166 ff.) has revived and strengthened the old theory that *r* in Italic and Keltic is an original *se*.

by Curtius (C 12) by the assumption that *sa* was added at two distinct periods, and that each period made a different use of the addition, though Curtius does not tell us how one or the other function could be evolved from such a pronoun.   The latest attempt at explanation, which reaches me as I am writing this chapter, is by Hermann Möller (KZ 49. 219) : according to him the common Aryan and Semitic nominative ended in *o* and the genitive in *e*, but to this was added in the masculine, and more rarely in the feminine, the pronoun *s* as a definite article, so that the primitive form corresponding to Lat. *lupus* meant ' the wolf ' and *lupu* ' (a) wolf ' ; later the *s*-less form was given up, and *lupus* came to be used for both ' the wolf ' and ' wolf ' (similarly presumably in the genitive, if we translate the presumed original forms into Latin *lupis* ' the wolf's ' and *lupi* ' (a) wolf's,' later *lupi* in both functions).   In Semitic, inversely, an element *m*, corresponding to the Aryan accusative ending, was added as an *in*definite article, the *m*-less form thus becoming definite, but in the oldest Babylonian-Assyrian the distinction has been given up, and the form in *m* is (like the Latin form in *s*) used both definitely and indefinitely.   Ingenious as these constructions are, the whole theory seems to me highly artificial, and it is difficult to imagine that both Aryans and Semites, after having evolved such a valuable distinction as that between ' the wolf ' and ' a wolf,' expressed by simple means, should have wilfully given it up—to evolve it again in a later period.[1]   Fortunately one is allowed to confess one's ignorance of the origin of the case endings *s* and *m*, but if I were on pain of death to choose between Möller's hypothesis and the suggestion thrown out by Humboldt (Versch 129), that the light (high-pitched) *s* symbolized the living (personal) and active (the subject), and the dark (low-pitched) *m* the lifeless (neutral) and passive (the object), I should certainly prefer the latter explanation.

Hirt (GDS 37) also thinks that the *s* found in Aryan cases is an originally independent word, only he thinks that this *se*, *so* was not originally a demonstrative pronoun, but the particle, which with the extension *i* is found in Gothic *sai* ' ecce,' and as it can thus be compared with the particle *c* in Lat. *hic*, it is clear that it might be added in all cases—and as a matter of fact Hirt finds it in six different cases in the singular and in all cases in the plural except the genitive.   Hirt makes no attempt at explaining how these various case-forms have come to acquire the signification (function) with which we find them in the oldest documents ; " the *s* element had nothing to do with the denotation of any case, number or gender, and only after it had been added to some cases

---

[1] If *s* was a definite article, why should it be used only with some stems and not with others ?   Why should neuters never require a definite article ?

and not to others could it come to be distinctive of cases " (p. 39).
In other words, his explanation explains just nothing at all. The
same is true with regard to the ' particles ' *om* or *em, e, o, i*, which
he thinks were added in other cases, and when he ends (p. 42)
by saying that " this must be sufficient to give a glimpse of the
way in which Aryan flexion originated," the only thing we have
really seen is the haphazard way in which this flexion is formed,
and the impossibility at present of arriving at a fully satisfactory
explanation of these things. I should especially demur to the two
suppositions underlying Hirt's theory that Aryan had at one
period a completely flexionless structure, and that the same sound
when occurring in various cases must have had the same origin :
it seems much more probable to me that the *s* of the nominative
and the *s* of the genitive were not at first identical.[1]

That item of the coalescence theory which probably appealed
most to the fancy of scholars and laymen alike was the explanation
of the personal endings in the verbs from the personal pronouns :
we have an *m* in the first person of the *mi*-verbs (*esmi*) and in the
pronoun *me*, etc., and we have a *t* in the third person (*esti*) and
in a third-person pronoun or demonstrative (*to*) ; it is, therefore,
quite natural to think that *esmi* is simply the root *es* ' to be ' + the
pronoun *mi* ' I,' and *esti es* + the other pronoun, and to extend
this view to the other persons. And yet not even this has been
allowed to stand unchallenged by later disrespectful linguists,
headed by A. H. Sayce (Techmer's *Zeitschr. f. allg. Sprwiss.* i. 22)
and Hirt. As a matter of fact, the theory is based exclusively
on the above-mentioned correspondence in the first and third
persons singular, while the dual and plural endings do not at all
agree with the corresponding personal pronouns and the endings
of the second person can only be compared with the pronoun
through the employment of phonological tricks unworthy of a
scientific linguist. Even in the first person the correspondence
is not complete, for besides -*mi* we have other endings : -*m*, which
cannot be very well considered a shortened -*mi* (and which agrees,

[1] While it is difficult to see the relation between a demonstrative pronoun
or a deictic particle and genitival function, it would be easy enough to understand the latter if we started from a possessive pronoun (ejus, suus), and,
curiously enough, we find this very sound *s* used as a sign for the genitive
in two independent languages, starting from that notion. In Indo-Portuguese
we have *gobernadors casa* ' governor's house,' from *gobernador su casa* (above,
Ch. XI § 12, p. 213), and in the South-African ' Taal ' the usual expression
for the genitive is by means of *syn*, which is generally shortened into *se* (*s*)
and glued enclitically to the substantive, even to feminines and plurals :
Marie-se boek ' Maria's book,' *di gouweneur se hond* ' the governor's dog '
(H. Meyer, *Die Sprache der Buren*, 1901, p. 40, where also the confusion
with the adjective ending -*s*, in Dutch spelt -*sch*, is mentioned. For the
construction compare G. *dem vater sein hut* and others from various languages ;
cf. the appendix on E. *Bill Stumps his mark* in ChE 182 f.).

as Sayce remarks, much more closely with the accusative ending of nouns), -o and -a, neither of which can be explained from any known pronoun. There is thus nothing for it except to say, as Brugmann does (KG § 770) : "The origin of the personal endings is not clear"; cf. also Misteli 47 : "The relations between personal endings and the independent personal pronouns must be much more evident to justify this view. . . . The Aryan language offers direct evidence against the assumption that a sentence has been thus drawn together, because it uses in the verbal forms of the first and third person sg. pronominal stems which are otherwise employed only as objects, and, moreover, would here place the subject after the predicate, though in sentences it observes the opposite order." Meillet expresses himself very categorically (*Bulletin de la Soc. de Ling.* 1911, 143) : "Scarcely any linguist who has studied Aryan languages would venture to affirm that **-mi* of the type Gr. *fēmi* is an old personal pronoun."

The impression left on us by all these cases is that many of the earlier explanations by agglutination have proved unsatisfactory, and that linguists are nowadays inclined either to leave the forms entirely unexplained or else to admit less rectilinear developments, in which we see the speakers of the old languages groping tentatively after means of expression and finding them only by devious and circuitous courses. It is, of course, difficult to classify such explanations, and the agglutination or coalescence theory has to be supplemented by various other kinds of explanation; but I think one of these, which has not received its legitimate share of attention, is important and distinctive enough to have its own name, and I propose to term it the 'secretion' theory.

XIX.—§ 13. Secretion.

By secretion I understand the phenomenon that one integral portion of a word comes to acquire a grammatical signification which it had not at first, and is then felt as something added to the word itself. Secretion thus is a consequence of a 'metanalysis' (above, Ch. X § 2); it shows its full force when the element thus secreted comes to be added to other words not originally possessing this element.

A clear instance is offered in the history of some English possessive pronouns. In Old English *min* and *þin* the *n* is kept throughout as part and parcel of the words themselves, the other cases having such forms as *mine, minum, minre*, exactly as in German *mein, meine, meinem, meiner*, etc. But in Middle English the endings were gradually dropped, and *min* and *þin* for a short time became the only forms. Soon, however, *n* was dropped before substantives beginning with a consonant, but was retained in other positions (*my* father—*mine* uncle, it is *mine*); then the former form was transferred also to those cases in which the pronoun was used (as an adjunct) before words beginning with vowels (*my* father, *my* uncle—it is *mine*). The distinction between *my* and *mine*, *thy* and *thine*, which was originally a purely phonetic one, exactly like that between *a* and *an* (*a* father, *an* uncle), gradually acquired a functional value, and now serves to distinguish an adjunct from a principal (or, to use the terms of some grammars, a conjoint from an absolute form); *my* came to be looked upon as the proper form, while the *n* of *mine* was felt as an ending serving to indicate the function as a principal word. That this is really the instinctive feeling of the people is shown by the fact that in dialectal and vulgar speech the same *n* is added to *his, her, your* and *their*, to form the new pronouns *hisn, hern, yourn, theirn*: " He that prigs what isn't hisn, when he's cotch'd, is sent to prison. She that prigs what isn't hern, At the treadmill takes a turn."

Another instance of secretion is *-en* as a plural ending in E. *oexn*, G. *ochsen*, etc. Here originally *n* belonged to the word in all cases and all numbers, just as much as the preceding *s*; *ox* was an *n* stem in the same way as, for instance, Lat. (homo), hom*in*em, hom*in*is, etc., or Gr. ku*ō*n, ku*n*a, ku*n*os, etc., are *n* stems. In Gothic *n* is found in most of the cases of similar *n* stems. In OE. the nom. is *oxa*, the other cases in the sg. *oxan*, pl. *oxan* (*oxen*), *oxnum, oxena*, but in ME. the *n*-less form is found throughout the singular (gen. analogically *oxes*), and the plural only kept *-n*. Thus also a great many other words, e.g. (I give the plural forms) *apen, haren, sterren* (stars), *tungen, siden, eyen*, which all of them belonged to the *n* declension in OE. When *-en* had thus become established as a plural sign, it was added analogically to words which were not originally *n* stems, e.g. ME. *caren, synnen, treen* (OE. *cara, synna, treow*), and this ending even seemed for some time destined to be the most usual plural ending in the South of England, until it was finally supplanted by *-s*, which had been the prevalent ending in the North ; *eyen, foen, shoen* were for a time in competition with *eyes, foes, shoes*, and now *-n* is only found in *oxen* (and *children*). In German to-day things are very much as they were in Southern ME. : *-en* is kept extensively in the old *n* stems and is added to some words which had formerly other endings, e.g. *hirten, soldaten, thaten*. The result is that now plurality is indicated by an ending which had formerly no such function (which, indeed, had no function at all) ; for if we look upon the actual language, *oxen* (G. *ochsen*) is = *ox* (*ochs*) singular + the plural ending *-en*;

only we must not on any account imagine that the form was originally thus welded together (agglutinated)—and if in G. *soldaten* we may speak of *-en* being glued on to *soldat*, this ending is not, and has never been, an independent word, but is an originally insignificative part secreted by other words.

A closely similar case is the plural ending *-er*. The consonant originally was *s*, as seen, for instance, in the Gr. and Lat. nom. *genos*, *genus*, gen. Gr. *gene(s)os*, *genous*, Lat. *generis* for older *genesis*. In Gothonic languages *s*, in accordance with a regular sound shift in this case, became *r* (through *z*) whenever it was retained, but in the nom. sg. it was dropped, and thus we have in OE. sg. *lamb*, *lambe*, *lambes*, but in the pl. *lambru*, *lambrum*, *lambra*. In English only few words show traces of this flexion, thus OE. *cild*, pl. *cildru*, ME. *child*, *childer*, whence, with an added *-en*, our modern *children*. But in German the class had much more vitality, and we have not only words belonging to it of old, like *lamm*, pl. *lämmer*, *rind*, *rinder*, but also gradually more and more words which originally belonged to other classes, but adopted this ending after it had become a real sign of the plural number, thus *wörter*, *bücher*.

There is one trait that should be noticed as highly characteristic of these instances of secretion, that is, that the occurrence of the endings originating in this way seems from the first regulated by the purest accident, seen from the point of view of the speakers : they are found in some words, but not in others, whereas the endings treated of under the heading Coalescence are added much more uniformly to the whole of the vocabulary. But as a similarly irregular or arbitrary distribution is met with in the case of nearly all flexional endings in the oldest stages of languages belonging to our family of speech, the probability is that most of those endings which it is impossible for us to trace back to their first beginnings have originated through secretion or similar processes, rather than through coalescence of independent words or roots.

XIX.—§ 14. Extension of Suffixes.

A special subdivision of secretion comprises those cases in which a suffix takes over some sound or sounds from words to which it was added. Clear instances are found in French, where in consequence of the mutescence of a final consonant some suffixes to the popular instinct must seem to begin with a consonant, though originally this did not belong to the suffix. Thus *laitier*, at first formed from *lait* + *ier*, now came to be apprehended as = *lai(t)* + *tier*, and *cabaretier* as *cabare(t)* + *tier*, and the new suffix was then used to form such new words as *bijoutier, ferblantier, cafetier* and others. In the same way we have *tabatière*, where we should expect *tabaquière*, and the predilection for the extended form of the suffix is evidently strengthened by the syllable division in frequent formations like *ren-tier, por-tier, por-tière, charpen-tier*. In old Gothonic we have similar extensions of suffixes, when instead of *-ing* we get *-ling*, starting from words like OHG. *ediling* from *edili*, ON. *vesling* from *vesall*, OE. *lytling* from *lytel*, etc. Consequently we have in English quite a number of words with the extended ending : *duckling, gosling, hireling, underling*, etc. In Gothic some words formed with *-assus*, such as *þiudin-assus* 'kingdom,' were apprehended as formed with *-nassus*, and in all the related languages the suffix is only known with the initial *n*; thus in E. *-ness* : *hardness, happiness, eagerness*, etc.; G. *-keit* with its *k* from adjectives in *-ic* has already been mentioned (376). From *criticism, Scotticism*, we have *witti-cism*, and Milton has *witticaster* on the analogy of *criticaster*, where the suffix of course is *-aster*, as in *poetaster*. Instead of *-ist* we also find in some cases *-nist* : *tobacconist, lutenist* (cf. *botan-ist, mechan-ist*).

To form a new word it is often sufficient that some existing word is felt in a vague way to be made up of something + an ending, the latter being subsequently added on to another word. In Fr. *mérovingien* the *v* of course is legitimate, as the adjective is derived from Mérovée, Merowig, but this word was made the starting-point for the word designating the succeeding dynasty : *carlovingien*, where *v* is simply taken over as part of the suffix ; nowadays historians try to be more ' correct ' and prefer the adjective *carolingien*, which was unknown to Littré. *Oligarchy* is *olig* + *archy*, but for the opposite notion the word *poligarchy* or *polygarchy* was framed from *poly* and the last two syllables of *oli-garchy*, and though now scholars have made *polyarchy* the usual form, the word with the intrusive *g* was the common form two hundred years ago in English, and corresponding forms are found in French, Spanish and other languages. *Judgmatical* is made on the pattern of *dogmatical*, though there the stem is *dogmat-*. In jocular German *schwachmatikus* ' valetudinarian,' we have the same suffix with a different colouring, taken from *rheumatikus* (thus also Dan. *svagmatiker*). Swift does not hesitate to speak of a *sextumvirate*, which suggests *triumvirate* better than *sexvirate* would have done ; and Bernard Shaw once writes " his equipage (or autopage) "— evidently starting from the popular, but erroneous, belief that *equipage* is derived from Lat. *equus* and then dividing the word *equi* + *page*. Cf. *Scillonian* from *Scilly* on account of *Devonian* as if this were *Dev* + *onian* instead of *Devon* + *ian*.

XIX.—§ 15. Tainting of Suffixes.

It will be seen that in some of these instances the suffix has appropriated to itself not only part of the sound of the stem, but also part of its signification. This is seen very clearly in the case of *chandelier*, in French formed from *chandelle* ' candle ' with the suffix *-ier*, of rather vague signification, ' anything connected with, or having to do with '; in English the word is used for a hanging branched frame to hold a number of lights ; consequently a similar apparatus for gas-burners was denominated *gaselier* (*gasalier*, *gasolier*), and with the introduction of electricity the formation has even been extended to *electrolier*. *Vegetarian* is from the stem *veget-* with added *-ari-an*, which ending has no special connexion with the notion of eating or food, but recently we have seen the new words *fruitarian* and *nutarian*, meaning one whose food consists (exclusively or chiefly) in fruits and nuts. Cf. *solemncholy*, which according to Payne is in use in Alabama, framed evidently on *melancholy*, analyzed in a way not approved by Greek scholars. The whole ending of *septentrionalis* (from the name of the constellation *Septem triones*, the seven oxen) is used to form the opposite : *meridi-onalis*.

A similar case of ' tainting ' is found in recent English. The NED, in the article on the suffix *-eer*, remarks that " in many of the words so formed there is a more or less contemptuous implication," but does not explain this, and has not remarked that it is found only in words ending in *-teer* (from words in *-t*). I think this contemptuous implication starts from *garreteer* and *crotcheteer* (perhaps also *pamphleteer* and *privateer*); after these were formed the disparaging words *sonneteer, pulpiteer*. During the war (1916, I think) the additional word *profiteer* [1] came into use, but did not find its way into the dictionaries till 1919 (Cassell's). And only the other day I read in an American publication a new word of the same calibre : " Against *patrioteering*, against fraud and violence ... Mr. Mencken has always nobly and bravely contended."

XIX.—§ 16. The Classifying Instinct.

Man is a classifying animal : in one sense it may be said that the whole process of speaking is nothing but distributing phenomena,

---

[1] Cf. Lloyd George's speech at Dundee (*The Times*, July 6, 1917): " The Government will not permit the burdens of the country to be increased by what is called ' profiteering.' Although I have been criticized for using that word, I believe on the whole it is a rather good one. It is *profiteer-ing* as distinguished from *profit-ing*. Profiting is fair recompense for services rendered, either in production or distribution ; profiteering is an extravagant recompense given for services rendered. I believe that unfair in peace. In war it is an outrage."

of which no two are alike in every respect, into different classes on the strength of perceived similarities and dissimilarities. In the name-giving process we witness the same ineradicable and very useful tendency to see likenesses and to express similarity in the phenomena through similarity in name. Professor Hempl told me that one of his little daughters, when they had a black kitten which was called *Nig* (short for Nigger), immediately christened a gray kitten *Grig* and a brown one *Brownig*. Here we see the genesis of a suffix through a natural process, which has little in common with the gradual weakening of an originally independent word, as in *-hood* and the other instances mentioned above. In children's speech similar instances are not unfrequent (cf. Ch. VII § 5); Meringer L 148 mentions a child of 1.7 who had the following forms : *augn, ogn, agn,* for ' augen, ohren, haare.' How many words formed or transformed in the same way must we require in order to speak of a suffix ? Shall we recognize one in Romanic *leve, greve* (cf. Fr. *grief*), which took the place of *leve, grave* ? Here, as Schuchardt aptly remarks, it was not only the opposite signification, but also the fact that the words were frequently uttered shortly after one another, that made one word influence the other.

The classifying instinct often manifests itself in bringing words together in form which have something in common as regards signification. In this way we have smaller classes and larger classes, and sometimes it is impossible for us to say in what way the likeness in form has come about : we can only state the fact that at a given time the words in question have a more or less close resemblance. But in other cases it is easy to see which word of the group has influenced the others or some other. In the examples I am about to give, I have been more concerned to bring together words that exhibit the classifying tendency than to try to find out the impetus which directed the formation of the several groups.

In OE. we have some names of animals in *-gga : frogga, stagga, docga, wicga,* now *frog, stag, dog, wig. Savour* and *flavour* go together, the latter (OFr. *flaur*) having its *v* from the former. *Groin,* I suppose, has its diphthong from *loin*; the older form was *grine, grynd(e). Claw, paw* (earlier *powe,* OFr. *pol*). *Rim, brim. Hook, nook. Gruff, rough (tough, bluff, huff—miff, tiff, whiff). Fleer, leer, jeer. Twig, sprig. Munch, crunch (lunch). Without uttering or muttering a word. The trees were lopped and topped.* In old Gothonic the word for ' eye ' has got its vowel from the word for ' ear,' with which it was frequently collocated : *augo(n), auso(n),* but in the modern languages the two words have again been separated in their phonetic development. In French I suspect that popular instinct will class the words *air, terre, mer* together as names of what used to be termed the ' elements,' in spite of the different spelling and origin of the sounds. In Russian *kogot'* 'griffe' (claw), *nogot'* 'ongle' (fingernail), and *lokot'* 'coude' (elbow), three names of parts of the body, go together in flexion and accent (Boyer et Speranski, *Manuel de la l. russe* 33). So do in Latin *culex* 'gnat' and *pulex* 'flea.' *Atrox, ferox.* A great many examples have been collected by M. Bloomfield, "On Adaptation of Suffixes in Congeneric Classes of Substantives" (*Am. Journal of Philol.* XII, 1891), from which I take a few. A considerable number of designations of parts of the body were formed with heteroclitic declension as *r-n* stems (cf. above, XVIII § 2): 'liver,' Gr. *hēpar, hēpatos,* 'udder,' Gr. *outhar, outhatos,* 'thigh,' Lat. *femur, feminis,* further Aryan names for blood, wing, viscera, excrement, etc. Other designations of parts of the body were partly assimilated to this class, having also *n* stems in the oblique cases, though their nominative was formed in a different way. Words for 'right' and 'left' frequently influence one another and adopt the same ending, and so do opposites generally : Bloomfield explains the *t* in the Gothonic word corresponding to E. *white,* where from Sanskr. we should expect *th, çveta,* as due to the word for 'black'; Goth. *hweits, swarts,* ON. *hvîtr, svartr,* etc. A great many names of birds and other animals appear with the same ending, Gr. *glaux* 'owl,' *kokkux* 'cuckoo,' *korax* 'crow,' *ortux* 'quail,' *aix* 'goat,' *alopex* 'fox,' *bombux* 'silkworm,' *lunx* 'lynx' and many others, also some plant-names. Names for winter, summer, day, evening, etc., also to a great extent form groups. In a subsequent article (in IF vi. 66 ff.) Bloomfield pursues the same line of thought and explains likenesses in various words of related signification, in direct opposition to the current explanation through added root-determinatives, as due to blendings (cf. above, Ch. XVII § 6). In Latin the inchoative value of the verbs in *-esco* is due to the accidentally inherent continuous character of a few verbs of the class : *adolesco, senesco, cresco* ; but the same suffix is also found in the oldest words for 'asking, wishing, searching,' retained in E. *ask, wish,* G. *forschen,* which thus become a small group linked together by form and meaning alike.

XIX.—§ 17. Character of Suffixes.

There seems undoubtedly to be something accidental or haphazard in most of these transferences of sounds from one word to another through which groups of phonetically and semantically similar words are created ; the process works unsystematically, or rather, it consists in spasmodic efforts at regularizing something which is from the start utterly unsystematic. But where conditions are favourable, i.e. where the notional connexion is patent and the phonetic element is such that it can easily be added to many words, the group will tend constantly to grow larger within the natural boundaries given by the common resemblance in signification.

I have no doubt that the vast majority of our formatives, such as suffixes and flexional endings, have arisen in this way through transference of some part, which at first was unmeaning in itself, from one word to another in which it had originally no business, and then to another and another, taking as it were a certain colouring from the words in which it is found, and gradually acquiring a more or less independent signification or function of its own. In long words, such as were probably frequent in primitive speech, and which were to the minds of the speakers as unanalyzable as *marmalade* or *crocodile* is to Englishmen nowadays, it would be perhaps most natural to keep the beginning unchanged and to modify the final syllable or syllables to bring about conformity with some word with which it was associated ; hence the prevalence of suffixes in our languages, hence also the less systematic character of these suffixes as compared with the prefixes, most of which have originated in independent words, such as adverbs. What is from the merely phonetic point of view the ' same ' suffix, in different languages may have the greatest variety of meaning, sometimes no discernible meaning at all, and it is in many cases utterly impossible to find out why in one particular language it can be used with one stem and not with another. Anyone going through the collections in Brugmann's great *Grammar* will be struck with this purely accidental character of the use of most of the suffixes—a fact which would be simply unthinkable if each of them had originally one definite, well-determined signification, but which is easy to account for on the hypothesis here adopted. And then many of them are not added to ready-made words or ' roots,' but form one indivisible whole with the initial part of the word ; cf., for instance, the suffix *-le* in English *squabble, struggle, wriggle, babble, mumble, bustle*, etc.

XIX.—§ 18. Brugmann's Theory of Gender.

As I have said, man is a classifying animal, and in his language tends to express outwardly class distinctions which he feels more or less vaguely. One of the most important of these class divisions, and at the same time one of the most difficult to explain, is that of the three ' genders ' in our Aryan languages. If we are to believe Brugmann, we have here a case of what I have in this work termed secretion.   In his well-known paper, " Das Nominalgeschlecht in den indogermanischen Sprachen " (in Techmer's *Zs. f. allgem. Sprachwissensch.* 4. 100 ff., cf. also his reply to Roethe's criticism,

PBB 15. 522) he puts the question : How did it come about that
the old Aryans attached a definite gender (or sex, geschlecht) to
words meaning foot, head, house, town, Gr. *pous*, for instance,
being masculine, *kephalē* feminine, *oikos* masculine, and *polis*
feminine ?   The generally accepted explanation, according to which
the imagination of mankind looked upon lifeless things as living
beings, is, Brugmann says, unsatisfactory ; the masculine and
feminine of grammatical gender are merely unmeaning forms and
have nothing to do with the ideas of masculinity and femininity ;
for even where there exists a natural difference of sex, language
often employs only one gender.   So in German we have *der hase*,
die maus, and *der weibliche hase* is not felt to be self-contradictory.
Again, in the history of languages we often find words which change
their gender exclusively on account of their form.   Thus, in German,
many words in -*e*, such as *traube*, *niere*, *wade*, which were formerly
masculine, have now become feminine, because the great majority
of substantives in -*e* are feminine (*erde*, *ehre*, *farbe*, etc.).   Nothing
accordingly hinders us from supposing that grammatical gender
originally had nothing at all to do with natural sex.   The question,
therefore, according to Brugmann, is essentially reduced to this :
How did it come to pass that the suffix -*a* was used to designate
female beings ?   At first it had no connexion with femininity, witness Lat. *aqua* ' water ' and hundreds of other words ; but among
the old words with that ending there happened to be some denoting
females : *mama* ' mother ' and *gena* ' woman ' (compare E. *quean*,
queen).   Now, in the history of some suffixes we see that, without
any regard to their original etymological signification, they may
adopt something of the radical meaning of the words to which
they are added, and transfer that meaning to new formations.   In
this way *mama* and *gena* became the starting-point for analogical
formations, as if the idea of female was denoted by the ending,
and new words were formed, e.g. Lat. *dea* ' goddess ' from *deus*
' god,' *equa* ' mare ' from *equus* ' horse,' etc.   The suffix -*iē-* or -*ī-*
probably came to denote feminine sex by a similar process, possibly
from Skr. *strī* ' woman,' which may have given a fem. **u̯l̥qī* ' she-
wolf ' to **u̯l̥qos* ' wolf.'   The above is a summary of Brugmann's
reasoning ; it may interest the reader to know that a closely similar
point of view had, several years previously, been taken by a far-
seeing scholar in respect to a totally different language, namely
Hottentot, where, according to Bleek, CG 2. 118-22, 292–9, a
class division which had originally nothing to do with sex has
been employed to distinguish natural sex.   I transcribe a few of
Bleek's remarks : " The apparent sex-denoting character which
the classification of the nouns now has in the Hottentot language
was evidently imparted to it after a division of the nouns into

classes [1] had taken place. It probably arose, in the first instance, from the possibly accidental circumstance that the nouns indicating (respectively) man and woman were formed with different derivative suffixes, and consequently belonged to different classes (or genders) of nouns, and that these suffixes thus began to indicate the distinction of sex in nouns where it could be distinguished " (p. 122). " To assume, for example, that the suffix of the m. sg. (-p) had originally the meaning of ' man,' or the fem. sg. (-s) that of ' woman,' would in no way explain the peculiar division of the nouns into classes as we find it in Hottentot, and would be opposed to all that is probable regarding the etymology of these suffixes, and also to the fact that so many nouns are included in the sex-denoting classes to which the distinction of sex can only be applied by a great effort. . . . If the word for ' man ' were formed with one suffix (-p), and the word indicating ' woman ' (be it accidentally or not) by another (-s), then other nouns would be formed with the same suffixes, in analogy with these, until the majority of the nouns of each sex were formed with certain suffixes which would thus assume a sex-denoting character " (p. 298).

Brugmann's view on Aryan gender has not been unchallenged. The weakest points in his arguments are, of course, that there are so few old naturally feminine words in -a and -i to take as starting-points for such a thoroughgoing modification of the grammatical system, and that Brugmann was unable to give any striking explanation of the concord of adjectives and pronouns with words that had not these endings, but which were nevertheless treated as masculines and feminines respectively   It would lead us too far here to give any minute account of the discussion which arose on these points ; [2] one of the most valuable contributions seems to me Jacobi's suggestion (Compositum u. Nebensatz, 1897, 115 ff.) that the origin of grammatical gender is not to be sought in the noun, but in the pronoun (he finds a parallel in the Dravidian languages)—but even he does not find a fully satisfactory explanation, and the Aryan gender distinction reaches back to so remote an antiquity, thousands of years before any literary tradition, that we shall most probably never be able to fathom all its mysteries. Of late years less attention has been given to the problem of the feminine, which presented itself to Brugmann, than to the distinction between two classes, one of which was characterized by the

---

[1] Bleek is here thinking of classes like those of the Bantu languages, which have nothing to do with sex.

[2] For bibliography and criticism see Wheeler in *Journ. of Germ. Philol.* 2. 528 ff., and especially Josselin de Jong in *Tijdschr. v. Ned. Taal- en Letterk.* 29. 21 ff., and the same writer's thesis *De Waardeeringsonderscheiding van levend en levenloos in het Indogermaansch vergel. m. hetzelfde verschijnsel in Algonkin-talen* (Leiden, 1913). Cf. also Hirt GDS 45 ff.

use of a nominative in -*s*, which is now looked upon as a 'transitive-active' case, and the other by no ending or by an ending -*m*, which is the same as was used as the accusative in the first class (an 'intransitive-passive' case), and an attempt has been made to see in the distinction something analogous to the division found in Algonkin languages between a class of 'living' and another of 'lifeless' things—though these two terms are not to be taken in the strictly scientific sense, for primitive men do not reason in the same way as we do, but ascribe or deny 'life' to things according to criteria which we have great difficulty in apprehending. This would mean a twofold division into one class comprising the historical masculines and feminines, and another comprising the neuters.

As to the feminine, we saw two old endings characterizing that gender, *a* and *i*. With regard to the latter, I venture to throw out the suggestion that it is connected with diminutive suffixes containing that vowel in various languages : on the whole, the sound [i] has a natural affinity with the notion of small, slight, insignificant and weak (see Ch. XX § 8). In some African languages we find two classes, one comprising men and big things, and the other women and small things (Meinhof, *Die Sprachen der Hamiten* 23), and there is nothing unnatural in the supposition that similar views may have obtained with our ancestors. This would naturally account for Skr. *vṛk-ī* 'she-wolf' (orig. little wolf, 'wolfy') from Skr. *vṛkas*, *napt-ī*, Lat. *neptis*, G. *nichte*, Skr. *dēv-ī* 'goddess,' etc. But the feminine -*a* is to me just as enigmatic as, say, the *d* of the old ablative

XIX.—§ 19. Final Considerations.

The ending -*a* serves to denote not only female beings, but also abstracts, and if in later usage it is also applied to males, as in Latin *nauta* 'sailor,' *auriga* 'charioteer,' this is only a derived use of the abstracts denoting an activity, sailoring, driving, etc., just as G. *die wache*, besides the activity of watching, comes to mean the man on guard, or as *justice* (Sp. *el justicia*) comes to mean 'judge.' The original sense of *Antonius collega fuit Ciceronis* was 'A. was the co-election of C.' (Osthoff, *Verbum in d. Nominalcompos.*, 1878, 263 ff., Delbrück, *Synt. Forsch.* 4. 6).

The same -*a* is finally used as the plural ending of most neuters, but, as is now universally admitted (see especially Johannes Schmidt, *Die Pluralbildungen der indogerm. Neutra*, 1889), the ending here was originally neither neuter nor plural, but, on the contrary, feminine and singular. The forms in -*a* are properly collective formations like those found, for instance, in Lat. *opera*, gen. *operæ*,

' work,' comp. *opus* ' (a piece of) work '; Lat. *terra* ' earth,' comp.
Oscan *terum* ' plot of ground '; *pugna* ' boxing, fight,' comp.
pugnus ' fist.' This explains among other things the peculiar
syntactic phenomenon, which is found regularly in Greek and
sporadically in Sanskrit and other languages, that a neuter plural
subject takes the verb in the singular. Greek *toxa* is often used
in speaking of a single bow ; and the Latin poetic use of *guttura*,
colla, ora, where only one person's throat, neck or face is meant,
points similarly to a period of the past when these words did not
denote the plural. We can now see the reason of this -*a* being
in some cases also the plural sign of masculine substantives :
Lat. *loca* from *locus, joca* from *jocus,* etc. ; Gr. *sita* from *sitos.*
Joh. Schmidt refers to similar plural formations in Arabic ; and as
we have seen (Ch. XIX § 9), the Bantu plural prefixes had probably
a similar origin. And we are thus constantly reminded that languages must often make the most curious *détours* to arrive at a
grammatical expression for things which appear to us so self-evident
as the difference between he and she, or that between one and
more than one. Expressive simplicity in linguistic structure
is not a primitive, but a derived quality.

CHAPTER XX

SOUND SYMBOLISM

§ 1. Sound and Sense. § 2. Instinctive Feeling. § 3. Direct Imitation. § 4. Originator of the Sound. § 5. Movement. § 6. Things and Appearances. § 7. States of Mind. § 8. Size and Distance. § 9. Length and Strength of Words and Sounds. § 10. General Considerations. § 11. Importance of Suggestiveness. § 12. Ancient and Modern Times.

XX.—§ 1. Sound and Sense.

THE idea that there is a natural correspondence between sound and sense, and that words acquire their contents and value through a certain sound symbolism, has at all times been a favourite one with linguistic dilettanti, the best-known examples being found in Plato's *Kratylos*. Greek and Latin grammarians indulge in the wildest hypotheses to explain the natural origin of such and such a word, as when Nigidius Figulus said that in pronouncing *vos* one puts forward one's lips and sends out breath in the direction of the other person, while this is not the case with *nos*. With these early writers, to make guesses at sound symbolism was the only way to etymologize ; no wonder, therefore, that we with our historical methods and our wider range of knowledge find most of their explanations ridiculous and absurd. But this does not justify us in rejecting any idea of sound symbolism : abusus non tollit usum !

Humboldt (Versch 79) says that " language chooses to designate objects by sounds which partly in themselves, partly in comparison with others, produce on the ear an impression resembling the effect of the object on the mind ; thus *stehen, stätig, starr*, the impression of firmness, Sanskrit *li* ' to melt, diverge,' that of liquidity or solution (des zerfliessenden). . . . In this way objects that produce similar impressions are denoted by words with essentially the same sounds, thus *wehen, wind, wolke, wirren, wunsch*, in all of which the vacillating, wavering motion with its confused impression on the senses is expressed through . . . *w*." Madvig's objection (1842, 13 = Kl 64) that we need only compare four of the words Humboldt quotes with the corresponding words in the very nearest sister-language, Danish *blæse, vind, sky, ønske*, to see how wrong this is, seems to me a little cheap : Humboldt himself expressly assumes that much of primitive sound symbolism may have disappeared in course of time and warns us against making this kind of explanation a 'constitutive principle,' which would lead to great dangers ("so setzt man sich grossen gefabren aus und verfolgt einen in jeder rücksicht schlüpfrigen pfad "). Moreover *blœse* (E. *blow*, Lat. *flare*) is just as imitative as *wind, vind* : no one of course would pretend that there was only one way of expressing the same sense perception. Among Humboldt's examples *wolke* and *wunsch* are doubtful, but I do not see that this affects the general truth of his contention that there is something like sound symbolism in *some* words.

Nyrop in his treatment of this question (Gr IV § 545 f.) repeats Madvig's objection that the same name can denote various objects, that the same object can be called by different names, and that the significations of words are constantly changing ; further, that the same group of sounds comes to mean different things according to the language in which it occurs. He finally exclaims : "How to explain [by means of sound symbolism] the difference in signification between *murus, nurus, durus, purus,* etc. ? "

XX.—§ 2. Instinctive Feeling.

Yes, of course it would be absurd to maintain that all words at all times in all languages had a signification corresponding exactly to their sounds, each sound having a definite meaning once for all. But is there really much more logic in the opposite extreme, which denies any kind of sound symbolism[1] (apart from the small class of evident echoisms or 'onomatopœia') and sees in our words only a collection of wholly accidental and irrational associations of sound and meaning ? It seems to me that the conclusion in this case is as false as if you were to infer that because on one occasion X told a lie, he therefore never tells the truth. The correct conclusion would be : as he has told a lie once, we cannot always trust him ; we must be on our guard with him— but sometimes he may tell the truth. Thus, also, sounds may in some cases be symbolic of their sense, even if they are not so in all words. If linguistic historians are averse to admitting sound symbolism, this is a natural consequence of their being chiefly occupied with words which have undergone regular changes in sound and sense ; and most of the words which form the staple of linguistic books are outside the domain of sound symbolism.

[1] "Inner and essential connexion between idea and word . . . there is none, in any language upon earth," says Whitney L 32.

There is no denying, however, that there are words which we feel instinctively to be adequate to express the ideas they stand for, and others the sounds of which are felt to be more or less incongruous with their signification. Future linguists will have to find out in detail what domains of human thought admit, and what domains do not admit, of congruous expression through speech sounds, and further what sounds are suitable to express such and such a notion, for though it is clear—to take only a few examples—that there is little to choose between *apple* and *pomme*, or between *window* and *fenster*, as there is no sound or sound group that has any natural affinity with such thoroughly concrete and composite ideas as those expressed by these words, yet on the other hand everybody must feel that the word *roll, rouler, rulle, rollen* is more adequate than the corresponding Russian word *katat', katit'*.

It would be an interesting task to examine in detail and systematically what ideas lend themselves to symbolic presentation and what sounds are chosen for them in different languages. That, however, could only be done on the basis of many more examples than I can find space for in this work, and I shall, therefore, only attempt to give a preliminary enumeration of the most obvious classes, with a small fraction of the examples I have collected.[1]

XX.—§ 3. Direct Imitation.

The simplest case is the direct imitation of the sound, thus *clink, clank, ting, tinkle* of various metallic sounds, *splash, bubble, sizz, sizzle* of sounds produced by water, *bow-wow, bleat, roar* of sounds produced by animals, and *snort, sneeze, snigger, smack, whisper, grunt, grumble* of sounds produced by human beings. Examples might easily be multiplied of such 'echoisms' or 'onomatopœia' proper. But, as our speech-organs are not capable of giving a perfect imitation of all 'unarticulated' sounds, the choice of speech-sounds is to a certain extent accidental, and different nations have chosen different combinations, more or less conventionalized, for the same sounds; thus *cock-a-doodle-doo*, Dan. *kykeliky*, Sw. *kukeliku*, G. *kikeriki*, Fr. *coquelico*, for the sound of a cock; and for *whisper*: Dan. *hviske*, ON. *kvisa*, G. *flüstern*, Fr. *chuchoter*, Sp. *susurar*. The continuity of a sound is frequently indicated by *l* or *r* after a stopped consonant: *rattle, rumble, jingle, clatter, chatter, jabber*, etc.

[1] I have learnt very little from the discussion which followed Wundt's remarks on the subject (S 1. 312–347); see Delbrück Grfr 78 ff., Sütterlin WSG 29 ff., Hilmer Sch 10 ff.

XX.—§ 4. Originator of the Sound.

Next, the echoic word designates the being that produces the sound, thus the birds *cuckoo* and *peeweet* (Dan. *vibe*, G. *kibitz*, Fr. pop. *dix-huit*).

A special subdivision of particular interest comprises those names, or nicknames, which are sometimes popularly given to nations from words continually occurring in their speech. Thus the French used to call an Englishman a *god-damn* (*godon*), and in China an English soldier is called *a-says* or *I-says*. In Java a Frenchman is called *orang-deedong* (*orang* ' man '), in America *ding-dong*, and during the Napoleonic wars the French were called in Spain *didones*, from *dis-donc* ; another name for the same nation is *wi-wi* (Australia), *man-a-wiwi* (in Beach-la-mar), or *oui-men* (New Caledonia). In Eleonore Christine's *Jammersminde* 83 I read, " Ich habe zwei *parle mi franço* gefangen," and correspondingly Goldsmith writes (Globe ed. 624) : " Damn the French, the *parle vous*, and all that belongs to them. What makes the bread rising ? the *parle vous* that devour us." In Rovigno the surrounding Slavs are called *čuje* from their exclamation *čuje* ' listen, I say,' and in Hungary German visitors are called *vigéc* (from *wie geht's ?*), and customs officers *vartapiszli* (from *wart' a bissl*). Round Panama everything native is called *spiggoty*, because in the early days the Panamanians, when addressed, used to reply, " No spiggoty [speak] Inglis." In Yokohama an English or American sailor is called *Damuraïsu H'to* from ' Damn your eyes ' and Japanese H'to ' people.' [1]

XX.—§ 5. Movement.

Thirdly, as sound is always produced by some movement and is nothing but the impression which that movement makes on the ear, it is quite natural that the movement itself may be expressed by the word for its sound : the two are, in fact, inseparable. Note, for instance, such verbs as *bubble, splash, clash, crack, peck*. Human actions may therefore be denoted by such words as to *bang* the door, or (with slighter sounds) to *tap* or *rap* at a door. Hence also the substantives a *tap* or a *rap* for the action, but the substantive may also come to stand for the implement, as when from the verb to *hack*, ' to cut, chop off, break up hard earth,' we have the noun *hack*, ' a mattock or large pick.'

Then we have words expressive of such movements as are not to the same extent characterized by loud sounds ; thus a great

[1] Schuchardt, KS 5. 12, *Zs. f. rom. Phil.* 33. 458, Churchill B 53, Sandfeld-Jensen, *Nationalfølelsen* 14, Lentzner, *Col.* 87, Simonyi US 157, *The Outlook*, January 1910, *New Quarterly Mag.*, July 1879.

many words beginning with *l*-combinations, *fl-* : *flow*, *flag* (Dan. *flagre*), *flake*, *flutter*, *flicker*, *fling*, *flit*, *flurry*, *flirt* ; *sl-* : *slide*, *slip*, *slive* ; *gl-* : *glide*. Hence adjectives like *fleet*, *slippery*, *glib*. Sound and sight may have been originally combined in such expressions for an uncertain walk as *totter*, *dodder*, dialectical *teeter*, *titter*, *dither*, but in cases of this kind the audible element may be wanting, and the word may come to be felt as symbolic of the movement as such. This is also the case with many expressions for the sudden, rapid movement by which we take hold of something ; as a short vowel, suddenly interrupted by a stopped consonant, serves to express the sound produced by a very rapid striking movement (*pat*, *tap*, *knock*, etc.), similar sound combinations occur frequently for the more or less noiseless seizing of a thing (with the teeth or with the hand) : *snap*, *snack*, *snatch*, *catch*, Fr. *happer*, *attraper*, *gripper*, E. *grip*, Dan. *hapse*, *nappe*, Lat. *capio*, Gr. *kaptō*, Armenian *kap* ' I seize,' Turk *kapmak* (*mak* infin. ending), etc. (I shall only mention one derivative meaning that may develop from this group : E. *snack* ' a hurried meal,' in Swift's time called a *snap* (*Journ. to Stella* 270) ; cf. G. *schnapps*, Dan. *snaps* ' glass of spirits.') E. *chase* and *catch* are both derived from two dialectically different French forms, ultimately going back to the same late Latin verb *captiare*, but it is no mere accident that it was the form ' catch ' that acquired the meaning ' to seize,' not found in French, for it naturally associated itself with *snatch*, and especially with the now obsolete verb *latch* ' to seize.'

There is also a natural connexion between action and sound in the word to *tickle*, G. *kitzeln*, ON. *kitla*, Dan. *kilde* (*d* mute), Nubian *killi-killi*, and similar forms (Schuchardt, *Nubisch. u. Bask.* 9), Lat. *titillare* ; cp. also the word for the kind of laughter thus produced : *titter*, G. *kichern*.

XX.—§ 6. Things and Appearances.

Further, we have the extension of symbolical designation to things ; here, too, there is some more or less obvious association of what is only visible with some sound or sounds. This has been specially studied by Hilmer, to whose book (Sch) the reader is referred for numerous examples, e.g. p. 237 ff., *knap* ' a thick stick, a knot of wood, a bit of food, a protuberance, a small hill ; *knop* ' a boss, stud, button, knob, a wart, pimple, the bud of a flower, a promontory,' with the variants *knob*, *knup*. . . . Hilmer's word-lists from German and English comprise 170 pages !

There is also a natural association between high tones (sounds with very rapid vibrations) and light, and inversely between low tones and darkness, as is seen in the frequent use of adjectives

like ' light ' and ' dark ' in speaking of notes.   Hence the vowel
[i] is felt to be more appropriate for light, and [u] for dark, as
seen most clearly in the contrast between *gleam, glimmer, glitter*
on the one hand and *gloom* on the other (Zangwill somewhere
writes : " The gloom of night, relieved only by the gleam from
the street-lamp ") ; the word *light* itself, which has now a diphthong
which is not so adequate to the meaning, used to have the vowel
[i] like G. *licht* ; for the opposite notions we have such words as
G. *dunkel*, Dan. *mulm*, Gr. *amolgós, skótos*, Lat. *obscurus*, and with
another ' dark ' vowel E. *murky*, Dan. *mörk*.

XX.—§ 7. States of Mind.

From this it is no far cry to words for corresponding states
of mind : to some extent the very same words are used, as *gloom*
(Dowden writes : " The good news was needed to cast a gleam
on the gloom that encompassed Shelley ") ; hence also *glum,
glumpy, glumpish, grumpy, the dumps, sulky*.   If E. *moody* and
sullen have changed their significations (OE. *modig* ' high-spirited,'
ME. *solein* ' solitary '), sound symbolism, if I am not mistaken,
counts for something in the change ; the adjectives now mean
exactly the same as Dan. *mut, but*.

If *grumble* comes to mean the expression of a mental state of
dissatisfaction, the connexion between the sound of the word and
its sense is even more direct, for the verb is imitative of the sound
produced in such moods, cf. *mumble* and *grunt, gruntle*.   The
name of Mrs. *Grundy* is not badly chosen as a representative of
narrow-minded conventional morality.

A long list might be given of symbolic expressions for dislike,
disgust, or scorn ; here a few hints only can find place.   First we
have the same dull or dump (back) vowels as in the last paragraph :
*blunder, bungle, bung, clumsy, humdrum, humbug, strum, slum,
slush, slubber, sloven, muck, mud, muddle, mug* (various words,
but all full of contempt), *juggins* (a silly person), *numskull* (old
numps, nup, nupson), *dunderhead, gull, scug* (at Eton a dirty or
untidy boy). . . .   Many words begin with *sl-* (we have already
seen some) : *slight, slim, slack, sly, sloppy, slipslop, slubby, slattern,
slut, slosh*. . . .   Initial labials are also frequent.[1]   After the
vowel we have very often the sound [ʃ] or [tʃ], as in *trash, tosh,
slosh, botch, patch* ; cf. also G. *kitsch* (bad picture, smearing),
patsch(e) (mire, anything worthless), *quatsch* (silly nonsense),
putsch (riot, political *coup de main*).   E. *bosh* (nonsense) is said
to be a Turkish loan-word ; it has become popular for the same

[1] *F*, for instance, in *fop, foozy, fogy, fogram* (old), all of them more or
less variants of *fool*.

reason for which the French nickname *boche* for a German was widely used during the World War. Let me finally mention the It. derivative suffix *-accio*, as in *poveraccio* (miserable), *acquaccia* (bad water), and *-uccio*, as in *cavalluccio* (vile horse).

XX.—§ 8. Size and Distance.

The vowel [i], especially in its narrow or thin variety, is particularly appropriate to express what is small, weak, insignificant, or, on the other hand, refined or dainty. It is found in a great many adjectives in various languages, e.g. *little, petit, piccolo, piccino,* Magy. *kis,* E. *wee, tiny* (by children often pronounced *teeny* [*ti·ni*]), *slim,* Lat. *minor, minimus,* Gr. *mikros ;* further, in numerous words for small children or small animals (the latter frequently used as endearing or depreciative words for children), e.g. *child* (formerly with [i·] sound), G. *kind,* Dan. *pilt,* E. *kid, chit, imp, slip, pigmy, midge,* Sp. *chico,* or for small things : *bit, chip, whit,* Lat. *quisquiliæ, mica,* E. *tip, pin, chink, slit. . . .* The same vowel is found in diminutive suffixes in a variety of languages, as E. *-y, -ie* (*Bobby, baby, auntie, birdie*), Du. *-ie, -je* (*koppie* ' little hill '), Gr. *-i-* (*paid-i-on* ' little boy '), Goth. *-ein,* pronounced [i·n] (*gumein* ' little man '), E. *-kin, -ling,* Swiss German *-li,* It. *-ino,* Sp. *-ico, -ito, -illo. . . .*

As smallness and weakness are often taken to be characteristic of the female sex, I suspect that the Aryan feminine suffix *-i,* as in Skr. *vṛkī* ' she-wolf,' *naptī* ' niece,' originally denotes smallness (' wolfy '), and in the same way we find the vowel *i* in many feminine suffixes ; thus late Lat. *-itta* (*Julitta,* etc., whence Fr. *-ette, Henriette,* etc.), *-ina* (*Carolina*), further G. *-in* (*königin*), Gr. *-issa* (*basilissa* ' queen '), whence Fr. *-esse,* E. *-ess.*

The same vowel [i] is also symbolical of a very short time, as in the phrases *in a jiff, jiffy,* Sc. *in a clink,* Dan. *i en svip ;* and correspondingly we have adjectives like *quick, swift, vivid* and others. No wonder, then, that the Germans feel their word for ' lightning,' *blitz,* singularly appropriate to the effect of light and to the shortness of duration.[1]

It has often been remarked [2] that in corresponding pronouns and adverbs the vowel *i* frequently indicates what is nearer, and other vowels, especially *a* or *u,* what is farther off ; thus Fr. *ci, là,*

---

[1] The preceding paragraphs on the symbolic value of *i* are an abstract of a paper which will be printed in *Philologica,* vol. i.

[2] Benfey Gesch 791, Misteli 539, Wundt S 1. 331 (but his examples from out-of-the-way languages must be used with caution, and curiously enough he thinks that the phenomenon is limited to primitive languages and is not found in Semitic or Aryan languages), GRM 1. 638, Simonyi US 255, Meinhof, Ham 20.

E. *here*, *there*, G. *dies*, *das*, Low G. *dit*, *dat*, Magy. *ez*, *emez* ' this,'
az, *amaz* ' that,' *itt* ' here,' *ott* ' there,' Malay *iki* ' this,' *ika* ' that,
a little removed,' *iku* ' yon, farther away.' In Hamitic languages
i symbolizes the near and *u* what is far away. We may here
also think of the word *zigzag* as denoting movement in alternate
turns here and there ; and if in the two E. pronouns *this* and *that*
the old neuter forms have prevailed (OE. m. þes, *se*, f. þeos, *seo*,
n. þis, þæt) the reason (or one of the reasons) may have been that
a characteristic difference of vowels in the two contrasted pronouns
was thus secured.

XX.—§ 9. Length and Strength of Words and Sounds.

Shorter and more abrupt forms are more appropriate to certain
states of mind, longer ones to others. An imperative may be
used both for command and for a more or less humble appeal or
entreaty ; in Magyar dialects there are short forms for command :
irj, dolgozz ; long for entreaty : *irjál, dolgozzál* (Simonyi US 359, 214).
Were Lat. *dic, duc, fac, fer* used more than other imperatives in
commands ? The fact that they alone lost *-e* might indicate that
this was so. On the other hand the imperatives *es, este* and *i* had
to yield to the fuller (and more polite) *esto, estote, vade*, and
scito is always said instead of *sci* (Wackernagel, *Gött. Ges. d.
Wiss.*, 1906, 182, on the avoidance of too short forms in general).
Other languages, which have only one form for the imperative,
soften the commanding tone by adding some word like *please,
bitte*.

An emotional effect is obtained in some cases by lengthening
a word by some derivative syllables, in themselves unmeaning ;
thus in Danish words for ' lengthy ' or ' tiresome ' : *langsommelig,
kedsommelig, evindelig* for *lang(som), kedelig, evig*. (Cf. Ibsen,
Når vi døde vågner 98 : Du er kanske ble't ked af dette evige
samliv med mig.—Evige ? Sig lige så godt : evindelige.) In the
same way the effect of *splendid* is strengthened in slang : *splen-
diferous, splendidous, splendidious, splendacious*. A long word like
aggravate is felt to be more intense than *vex* (Coleman)—and that
may be the reason why the long word acquires a meaning that is
strange to its etymology. And " to disburden one's self of a sense
of contempt, a robust full-bodied detonation, like, for instance,
platitudinous, is, unquestionably, very much more serviceable
than any evanescing squib of one or two syllables " (Fitzedward
Hall). Cf. also *multitudinous, multifarious*.

We see now the emotional value of some ' mouth-filling ' words,
some of which may be considered symbolical expansions of existing
words (what H. Schröder terms ' streckformen '), though others

cannot be thus explained; not unfrequently the effect of length is combined with some of the phonetic effects mentioned above. Such words are, e.g., *slubberdegullion* 'dirty fellow,' *rumbustious* 'boisterous,' *rumgumption, rumfustian, rumbullion* (cf. *rum-puncheon* 'cask of rum' as a term of abuse in Stevenson, *Treas. Isl.* 48, "the cowardly son of a rum-puncheon"), *rampallion* 'villain,' *rapscallion, ragamuffin*; *sculduddery* 'obscenity'; *cantankerous* 'quarrelsome,' U.S. also *rantankerous* (cf. *cankerous, rancorous*); *skilligalee* 'miserable gruel,' *flabbergast* 'confound,' *catawampous* (or *-ptious*) 'fierce' ("a high-sounding word with no very definite meaning," NED); Fr. *hurluberlu* 'crazy' and the synonymous Dan. *tummelumsk*, Norw. *tullerusk*.

In this connexion one may mention the natural tendency to lengthen and to strengthen single sounds under the influence of strong feeling and in order to intensify the effect of the spoken word; thus, in 'it's very cold' both the diphthong [ou] and the [l] may be pronounced extremely long, in 'terribly dull' the [l] is lengthened, in 'extremely long' either the vowel [ɔ] or the [ŋ] (or both) may be lengthened. In Fr. 'c'était horrible' the trill of the [r] becomes very long and intense (while the same effect is not generally possible in the corresponding English word, because the English [r] is not trilled, but pronounced by one flap of the tip). In some cases a lengthening due to such a psychological cause may permanently alter a word, as when Lat. *totus* in It. has become *tutto* (Fr. *tout, toute* goes back to the same form, while Sp. *todo* has preserved the form corresponding to the Lat. single consonant). An interesting collection of such cases from the Romanic tongues has been published by A. J. Carnoy (*Mod. Philol.* 15. 31, July 1917), who justly emphasizes the symbolic value of the change and the special character of the words in which it occurs (pet-names, children's words, ironic or derisive words, imitative words . . .). He says : "While to a phonetician the phenomenon would seem capricious, its apportionment in the vocabulary is quite natural to a psychologist. In fact, reduplication, be it of syllables or of consonants, generally has that character in languages. One finds it in perfective tenses, in intensive or frequentative verbs, in the plural, and in collectives. In most cases it is a reduplication of syllables, but a lengthening of vowels is not rare and the reinforcement of consonants is also found. In Chinook, for instance, the emotional words, both diminutive and augmentative, are expressed by increasing the stress of consonants. It is, of course, also well known that in Semitic the intensive radical of verbs is regularly formed by a reduplication of consonants. To a stem *qatal*, e.g., answers an intensive : Eth. *qattala*, Hebr. *qittel*. Cf. Hebr. *shibbar* 'to cut in small pieces' [cf. below], *hillech* ' to walk,' *qibber* ' to bury many,' etc.   Cf. Brockelmann, *Vergl. Gramm.*, p. 244."

I add a few more examples from Misteli (428 f.) of this Semitic strengthening : the first vowel is lengthened to express a tendency or an attempt : *qatala jaqtulu* ' kill ' (in the third person masc., the former in the prefect-aorist, the latter in the imperfect-durative, where *ja*, *ju* is the sign of the third person m.), *qātala juqātilu* ' try to kill, fight '; *faXara jufXaru* ' excel in fame,' *fāXara jufāXiru* ' try to excel, vie.' Through lengthening (doubling) of a consonant an intensification of the action is denoted : Hebr. *šāβar jišbōr* ' zerbrechen,' *šibbēr ješabbēr* ' zerschmettern,' Arab. *ḍaraba jaḍrubu* ' strike,' *ḍarraba juḍarribu* ' beat violently, or repeatedly '; sometimes the change makes a verb into a causative or transitive, etc.

I imagine that we have exactly the same kind of strengthening for psychological (symbolical) reasons in a number of verbs where Danish has *pp*, *tt*, *kk* by the side of *b*, *d*, *g* (spirantic) : *pippe pibe*, *stritte stride*, *snitte snide*, *skøtte skøde*, *splitte splide*, *skrikke skrige*, *lukke luge*, *hikke hige*, *sikke sige*, *kikke kige*, *prikke prige* (cf. also *sprække sprænge*). Some of these forms are obsolete, others dialectal, but it would take us too far in this place to deal with the words in detail. It is customary to ascribe this gemination to an old *n* derivative (see, e.g., Brugmann VG 1. 390, Streitberg Urg pp. 135, 138, Noreen UL 154), but it does not seem necessary to conjure up an *n* from the dead to make it disappear again immediately, as the mere strengthening of the consonant itself to express symbolically the strengthening of the action has nothing unnatural in it. Cf. also G. *placken* by the side of *plagen*. The opposite change, a weakening, may have taken place in E. *flag* (cf. OFr. *flaquir*, to become flaccid), *flabby*, earlier *flappy*, *drib* from *drip*, *slab*, if from OFr. *esclape*, *clod* by the side of *clot*, and possibly *cadge*, *bodge*, *grudge*, *smudge*, which had all of them originally *-tch*. But the common modification in sense is not so easily perceived here as in the cases of strengthening.

I may here, for the curiosity of the thing, mention that in a ' language ' coined by two English children (a vocabulary of which was communicated to me by one of the inventors through Miss I. C. Ward, of the Department of Phonetics, University College, London) there was a word *bal* which meant ' place,' but the bigger the place the longer the vowel was made, so that with three different quantities it meant ' village,' ' town ' and ' city ' respectively. The word for ' go ' was *dudu*, " the greater the speed of the going, the more quickly the word was said—[dœˑdœˑ] walk slowly." Cf. Humboldt, ed. Steinthal 82 : " In the southern dialect of the Guarani language the suffix of the perfect *yma* is pronounced more or less slowly according to the more or less remoteness of the past to be indicated."

XX.—§ 10. General Considerations.

Sound symbolism, as we have considered it in this chapter, has a very wide range of application, from direct imitation of perceived natural sounds to such small quantitative changes of existing non-symbolic words as may be used for purely grammatical purposes. But in order to obtain a true valuation of this factor in the life of language it is of importance to keep in view the following considerations :

(1) No language utilizes sound symbolism to its full extent, but contains numerous words that are indifferent to or may even jar with symbolism. To express smallness the vowel [i] is most adequate, but it would be absurd to say that that vowel always implies smallness, or that smallness is always expressed by words containing that vowel : it is enough to mention the words *big* and *small*, or to point to the fact that *thick* and *thin* have the same vowel, to repudiate such a notion.

(2) Words that have been symbolically expressive may cease to be so in consequence of historical development, either phonetic or semantic or both. Thus the name of the bird *crow* is not now so good an imitation of the sound made by the bird as OE. *crawe* was (Dan. *krage*, Du. *kraai*). Thus, also, the verbs *whine, pipe* were better imitations when the vowel was still [iˑ] (as in Dan. *hvine, pibe*). But to express the sound of a small bird the latter word is still pronounced with the vowel [i] either long or short (*peep, pip*), the word having been constantly renewed and as it were reshaped by fresh imitation ; cf. on Irish *wheen* and dialectal *peep*, XV § 8. Lat. *pipio* originally meant any ' peeping bird,' but when it came to designate one particular kind of birds, it was free to follow the usual trend of phonetic development, and so has become Fr. *pigeon* [piӡɔ̃], E. *pigeon* [pidӡin]. E. *cuckoo* has resisted the change from [u] to [ʌ] as in *cut*, because people have constantly heard the sound and fashioned the name of the bird from it. I once heard a Scotch lady say [kʌkuˑ], but on my inquiry she told me that there were no cuckoos in her native place ; hence the word had there been treated as any other word containing the short [u]. The same word is interesting in another way ; it has resisted the old Gothonic consonant-shift, and thus has the same consonants as Skt. *kōkiláḥ*, Gr. *kókkux*, Lat. *cuculus*. On the general preservation of significative sounds, cf. Ch. XV § 8.

(3) On the other hand, some words have in course of time become more expressive than they were at first ; we have some-

thing that may be called secondary echoism or secondary symbolism.
The verb *patter* comes from *pater* (= *paternoster*), and at first meant
to repeat that prayer, to mumble one's prayers ; but then it was
associated with the homophonous verb *patter* ' to make a rapid
succession of *pats* ' and came under the influence of echoic words
like *prattle, chatter, jabber* ; it now, like these, means ' to talk rapidly
or glibly ' and is to all intents a truly symbolical word; cf. also the
substantive *patter* ' secret lingo, speechifying, talk.' *Husky* may
at first have meant only " full of husks, of the nature of a husk "
(NED), but it could not possibly from that signification have
arrived at the now current sense ' dry in the throat, hoarse ' if it
had not been that the sound of the adjective had reminded one
of the sound of a hoarse voice. Dan. *pöjt* ' poor drink, vile stuff '
is now felt as expressive of contempt, but it originates in *Poitou*,
an innocent geographical name of a kind of wine, like *Bordeaux* ;
it is now connected with other scornful words like *spröjt* and *döjt*.

In E. *little* the symbolic vowel *i* is regularly developed from
OE. *y*, *lytel*, whose *y* is a mutated *u*, as seen in OSax. *luttil* ; *u* also
appears in other related languages, and the word thus originally
had nothing symbolical about it. But in Gothic the word is *leitils*
(*ei*, sounded [i·]) and in ON. *litinn*, and here the vowel is so difficult
to account for on ordinary principles that the NED in despair
thinks that the two words are " radically unconnected." I have
no hesitation in supposing that the vowel *i* is due to sound symbolism, exactly as the smaller change introduced in modern E.
' leetle,' with narrow instead of wide (broad) [i]. In the word
for the opposite meaning, *much*, the phonetic development may
also have been influenced by the tendency to get an adequate
vowel, for normally we should expect the vowel [i] as in Sc. *mickle*,
from OE. *micel*. In E. *quick* the vowel best adapted to the idea
has prevailed instead of the one found in the old nom. forms
cwucu, cucu from *cwicu* (inflected *cwicne, cwices*, etc.), while in the
word *widu, wudu*, which is phonetically analogous, there was no
such inducement, and the vowel [u] has been preserved : *wood*.
The same prevalence of the symbolic *i* is noticed in the Dan. adj.
kvik, MLG. *quik*, while the same word as subst. has become Dan.
kvæg, MLG. *quek*, where there was no symbolism at work, as it
has come to mean ' cattle.' I even see symbolism in the preservation of the *k* in the Dan. adj. (as against the fricative in *kvæg*),
because the notion of ' quick ' is best expressed by the short [i],
interrupted by a stop ; and may not the same force have been
at work in this adjective at an earlier period ? The second *k* in
OE. *cwicu*, ON. *kvikr* as against Goth. *qius*, Lat. *vivus*, has not
been sufficiently explained. An [i], symbolic of smallness, has been
introduced in some comparatively recent E. words : *tip* from *top*,

trip ' small flock ' from *troop, sip* ' drink in small quantities ' from *sup, sop.*

Through changes in meaning, too, some words have become symbolically more expressive than they were formerly ; thus the agreement between sound and sense is of late growth in *miniature,* which now, on account of the *i,* has come to mean ' a small picture,' while at first it meant ' image painted with minium or vermilion,' and in *pittance,* now ' a scanty allowance,' formerly any pious donation, whether great or small. Cf. what has been said above of *sullen, moody, catch.*

XX.—§ 11. Importance of Suggestiveness.

The suggestiveness of some words as felt by present-day speakers is a fact that must be taken into account if we are to understand the realities of language. In some cases it may have existed from the very first : these words sprang thus into being because that shape at once expressed the idea the speaker wished to communicate. In other cases the suggestive element is not original : these words arose in the same way as innumerable others whose sound has never carried any suggestion. But if the sound of a word of this class was, or came to be, in some way suggestive of its signification—say, if a word containing the vowel [i] in a prominent place meant ' small ' or something small—then the sound exerted a strong influence in gaining popular favour to the word ; it was an inducement to people to choose and to prefer that particular word and to cease to use words for the same notion that were not thus favoured. Sound symbolism, we may say, makes some words more fit to survive and gives them considerable help in their struggle for existence. If we want to denote a little child by a word for some small animal, we take some word like *kid, chick, kitten,* rather than *bat* or *pug* or *slug,* though these may in themselves be smaller than the animal chosen.

It is quite true that Fr. *rouler,* our *roll,* is derived from Lat. *rota* ' wheel ' + a diminutive ending *-ul-,* but the word would never have gained its immense popularity, extending as it does through English, Dutch, German and the Scandinavian languages, if the sound had not been eminently suggestive of the sense, so suggestive that it seems to us now *the* natural expression for that idea, and we have difficulty in realizing that the word has not existed from the very dawn of speech. Or let me take another example, in which the connexion between sound and sense is even more ' fortuitous.' About a hundred years ago a member of Congress, Felix Walker, from Buncombe County, North Carolina, made a long and tedious speech. '' Many members left the hall.

Very naïvely he told those who remained that they might go too ; he should speak for some time, but ' he was only talking for Buncombe,' to please his constituents." Now *buncombe* (*buncome*, *bunkum*) has become a widely used word, not only in the States, but all over the English-speaking world, for political speaking or action not resting on conviction, but on the desire of gaining the favour of electors, or for any kind of empty ' clap-trap ' oratory ; but does anybody suppose that the name of Mr. Walker's constituency would have been thus used if he had happened to hail from Annapolis or Philadelphia, or some other place with a name incapable of tickling the popular fancy in the same way as *Buncombe* does ? (Cf. above, p. 401 on the suggestiveness of the short *u*.) In a similar way *hullaballoo* seems to have originated from the Irish village *Ballyhooly* (see P. W. Joyce, *English as we speak it in Ireland*) and to have become popular on account of its suggestive sound.

In loan-words we can often see that they have been adopted less on account of any cultural necessity (see above, p. 209) than because their sound was in some way or other suggestive. Thus the Algonkin (Natick) word for ' chief,' *mugquomp*, is used in the United States in the form of *mugwump* for a ' great man ' or ' boss,' and especially, in political life, for a man independent of parties and thinking himself superior to parties. Now, no one would have thought of going to an Indian language to express such a notion, had not an Indian word presented itself which from its uncouth sound lent itself to purposes of ridicule. Among other words whose adoption has been favoured by their sounds I may mention *jungle* (from Hindi *jangal*, associated more or less closely with *jumble*, *tumble*, *bundle*, *bungle*); *bobbery*, in slang ' noise, squabble,' " the Anglo-Indian colloquial representation of a common exclamation of Hindus when in surprise or grief—*Bap-rē !* or *Bap-rē Bap* ' O Father ! ' " (Hobson-Jobson); *amuck* ; and U.S. *bunco* ' swindling game, to swindle,' from It. *banco*.

XX.—§ 12. Ancient and Modern Times.

It will be seen that our conception of echoism and related phenomena does not carry us back to an imaginary primitive period : these forces are vital in languages as we observe them day by day. Linguistic writers, however, often assume that sound symbolism, if existing at all, must date back to the earliest times, and therefore can have no reality nowadays. Thus Benfey (Gesch 288) turns upon de Brosse, who had found rudeness in Fr. *rude* and gentleness in Fr. *doux*, and says : " As if the sounds of such words, which are distant by an infinite length of time from

the time when language originated, were able to contribute ever
so little to explain the original designation of things." (But
Benfey is right in saying that the impression made by those two
French words may be imaginary ; as examples they are not particularly well chosen.) Sütterlin (WW 14) says : " It is bold to
search for such correspondence as still existing in detail in the
language of our own days. For words like *liebe*, *süss* on the one
hand, and *zorn*, *hass*, *hart* on the other, which are often alleged
by dilettanti, prove nothing to the scholar, because their form
is young and must have had totally different sounds in the period
when language was created."

Similarly de Saussure (LG 104) gives as one of the main principles of our science that the tie between sound and sense is
arbitrary or rather motiveless (immotivé), and to those who would
object that onomatopoetic words are not arbitrary he says that
" they are never organic elements of a linguistic system. Besides,
they are much less numerous than is generally supposed. Such
words as Fr. *fouet* and *glas* may strike some ears with a suggestive
ring ; [1] but they have not had that character from the start, as is
sufficiently proved if we go back to their Latin forms (*fouet* derived
from *fagus* ' beech,' *glas* = *classicum*) ; the quality possessed by,
or rather attributed to, their actual sounds is a fortuitous result
of phonetic development."

Here we see one of the characteristics of modern linguistic
science : it is so preoccupied with etymology, with the origin of
words, that it pays much more attention to what words have
come from than to what they have come to be. If a word has
not always been suggestive on account of its sound, then its actual
suggestiveness is left out of account and may even be declared
to be merely fanciful. I hope that this chapter contains throughout
what is psychologically a more true and linguistically a more
fruitful view.

Though some echo words may be very old, the great majority
are not ; at any rate, in looking up the earliest ascertained date
of a goodly number of such words in the NED, I have been struck
by the fact of so many of them being quite recent, not more than
a few centuries old, and some not even that. To some extent

---

[1] I must confess that I find nothing symbolical in *glas* and very little
in *fouet* (though the verb *fouetter* has something of the force of E. *whip*).
On the whole, much of what people ' hear ' in a word appears to me fanciful
and apt to discredit reasonable attempts at gaining an insight into the
essence of sound symbolism ; thus E. Lerch's ridiculous remark on G. *loch*
in GRM 7. 101 : " *loch* malt die bewegung, die der anblick eines solchen
im beschauer auslöst, durch eine entsprechende bewegung der sprachwerk-
zeuge, beginnend mit der liquida zur bezeichnung der rundung und endend
mit dem gutturalen *ch* tief hinten in der gurgel."

their recent appearance in writing may be ascribed to the general character of the old literature as contrasted with our modern literature, which is less conventional, freer in many ways, more true to life with its infinite variety and more true, too, to the spoken language of every day. But that cannot account for everything, and there is every probability that this class of words is really more frequent in the spoken language of recent times than it was formerly, because people speak in a more vivid and fresh fashion than their ancestors of hundreds or thousands of years ago. The time of psychological reaction is shorter than it used to be, life moves at a more rapid rate, and people are less tied down to tradition than in former ages, consequently they are more apt to create and to adopt new words of this particular type, which are felt at once to be significant and expressive. In all languages the creation and use of echoic and symbolic words seems to have been on the increase in historical times. If to this we add the selective process through which words which have only secondarily acquired symbolical value survive at the cost of less adequate expressions, or less adequate forms of the same words, and subsequently give rise to a host of derivatives, then we may say that languages in course of time grow richer and richer in symbolic words. So far from believing in a golden primitive age, in which everything in language was expressive and immediately intelligible on account of the significative value of each group of sounds, we arrive rather, here as in other domains, at the conception of a slow progressive development towards a greater number of easy and adequate expressions—expressions in which sound and sense are united in a marriage-union closer than was ever known to our remote ancestors.

CHAPTER XXI

THE ORIGIN OF SPEECH

XXI.—§ 1. Introduction.

MUCH of what is contained in the last chapters is preparatory
to the theme which is to occupy us in this chapter, the ultimate
origin of human speech. We have already seen the feeling with
which this subject has often been regarded by eminent linguists,
the feeling which led to an absolute taboo of the question in the
French Société de linguistique (p. 96). One may here quote
Whitney : " No theme in linguistic science is more often and
more voluminously treated than this, and by scholars of every
grade and tendency ; nor any, it may be added, with less profitable
result in proportion to the labour expended ; the greater part of
what is said and written upon it is mere windy talk, the assertion
of subjective views which commend themselves to no mind save
the one that produces them, and which are apt to be offered with
a confidence, and defended with a tenacity, that are in inverse
ratio to their acceptableness. This has given the whole question
a bad repute among sober-minded philologists " (OLS 1. 279).

Nevertheless, linguistic science cannot refrain for ever from
asking about the whence (and about the whither) of linguistic
evolution. And here we must first of all realize that man is not
the only animal that has a ' language,' though at present we know
very little about the real nature and expressiveness of the languages
of birds and mammals or of the signalling system of ants, etc.
The speech of some animals may be more like our language than
most people are willing to admit—it may also in some respects
be even more perfect than human language precisely because it
is unlike it and has developed along lines about which we can know
nothing; but it is of little avail to speculate on these matters. What
is certain is that no race of mankind is without a language which

in everything essential is identical in character with our own, and that there are a certain number of circumstances which have been of signal importance in assisting mankind in developing language (cf. Gabelentz Spr 294 ff.).

First of all, man has an upright gait ; this gives him two limbs more than the dog has, for instance : he can carry things and yet jabber on ; he is not reduced to defending himself by biting, but can use his mouth for other purposes. Feeding also takes less time in his case than in that of the cow, who has little time for anything else than chewing and a *moo* now and then. The sexual life of man is not restricted to one particular time of the year, the two sexes remain together the whole year round, and thus sociability is promoted ; the helplessness of babies works in the same direction through necessitating a more continuous family life, in which there is also time enough for all kinds of sports, including play with the vocal organs. Thus conditions have been generally favourable for the development of singing and talking, but the problem is, how could sounds and ideas come to be connected as they are in language ?

What method or methods have we for the solution of this question ? With very few exceptions those who have written about our subject have conjured up in their imagination a primitive era, and then asked themselves : How would it be possible for men or manlike beings, hitherto unfurnished with speech, to acquire speech as a means of communication of thought ? Not only is this method followed, so to speak, instinctively by investigators, but we are even positively told (by Marty) that it is the only method possible. In direct opposition to this assertion, I think that it is chiefly and principally due to this method and to this way of putting the question that so little has yet been done to solve it. If we are to have any hope of success in our investigation we must try new methods and new ways—and fortunately there *are* ways which lead us to a point from which we may expect to see the world of primitive language revealed to us in a new light. But let us first cast a rapid glance at those theories which have been advanced by followers of the speculative or *a priori* method.

XXI.—§ 2. Former Theories.

One theory is that primitive words were imitative of sounds : man copied the barking of dogs and thereby obtained a natural word with the meaning of ' dog ' or ' bark.' To this theory, nicknamed the *bow-wow* theory, Renan objects that it seems rather absurd to set up this chronological sequence : first the lower animals are original enough to cry and roar ; and then comes man, making a language for himself by imitating his inferiors. But surely man would imitate not only the cries of inferior animals, but also those of his fellow-men, and the salient point of the theory is this : sounds which in one creature were produced without any meaning, but which were characteristic of that creature, could by man be used to designate the creature itself (or the movement or action productive of the sound). In this way an originally unmeaning sound could in the mouth of an imitator and in the mind of someone hearing that imitation acquire a real meaning. In the chapter on Sound Symbolism I have tried to show how from the rudest and most direct imitations of this kind we may arrive through many gradations at some of the subtlest effects of human speech, and how imitation, in the widest sense we can give to this word— a wider sense than most advocates of the theory seem able to imagine—is so far from belonging exclusively to a primitive age that it is not extinct even yet. There is not much of value in Max Müller's remark that " the onomatopœic theory goes very smoothly as long as it deals with cackling hens and quacking ducks ; but round that poultry-yard there is a high wall, and we soon find that it is behind that wall that language really begins " (*Life* 2. 97), or in his other remark that " words of this kind (*cuckoo*) are, like artificial flowers, without a root. They are sterile, and unfit to express anything beyond the one object which they imitate " (ib. 1. 410). But *cuckoo* may become *cuckold*(Fr. *cocu*), and from *cock* are derived the names Müller himself mentions, Fr. *coquet, coquetterie, cocart, cocarde, coquelicot*. . . . Echoic words may be just as fertile as any other part of the vocabulary.

Another theory is the interjectional, nicknamed the *pooh-pooh*, theory : language is derived from instinctive ejaculations called forth by pain or other intense sensations or feelings. The adherents of this theory generally take these interjections for granted, without asking about the way in which they have come into existence. Darwin, however, in *The Expression of the Emotions*, gives purely physiological reasons for some interjections, as when the feeling of contempt or disgust is accompanied by a tendency " to blow out of the mouth or nostrils, and this produces sounds like *pooh* or *pish*." Again, " when anyone is startled or suddenly astonished, there is an instantaneous tendency, likewise from an intelligible cause, namely, to be ready for prolonged exertion, to open the mouth widely, so as to draw a deep and rapid inspiration. When the next full expiration follows, the mouth is slightly closed, and the lips, from causes hereafter to be discussed, are somewhat protruded ; and this form of the mouth, if the voice be at all exerted, produces . . . the sound of the vowel *o*. Certainly a deep sound of a prolonged *Oh !* may be heard from a whole crowd of people immediately after witnessing any astonishing spectacle. If, together with surprise, pain be felt, there is a tendency to contract all the muscles of the body, including those of the face, and the lips will then be drawn back ; and this will perhaps account for the sound becoming higher and assuming the character of *Ah !* or *Ach !* "

To the ordinary interjectional theory it may be objected that the usual interjections are abrupt expressions for sudden sensations and emotions ; they are therefore isolated in relation to the speech material used in the rest of the language. " Between interjection and word there is a chasm wide enough to allow us to say that the interjection is the negation of language, for interjections are employed only when one either cannot or will not speak " (Benfey Gesch 295). This ' chasm ' is also shown phonetically by the fact that the most spontaneous interjections often contain sounds which are not used in language proper, voiceless vowels, inspiratory sounds, clicks, etc., whence the impossibility properly to represent them by means of our ordinary alphabet : the spellings *pooh, pish, whew, tut* are very poor renderings indeed of the natural sounds. On the other hand, many interjections are now more or less conventionalized and are learnt like any other words, consequently with a different form in different languages : in pain a German and a Seelander will exclaim *au*, a Jutlander *aus*, a Frenchman *ahi* and an Englishman *oh*, or perhaps *ow*. Kipling writes in one of his stories : " That man is no Afghan, for they weep ' Ai ! Ai ! ' Nor is he of Hindustan, for they weep ' Oh ! Ho ! ' He weeps after the fashion of the white men, who say, ' Ow ! Ow ! ' ' "

A closely related theory is the nativistic, nicknamed the *ding-dong*, theory, according to which there is a mystic harmony between sound and sense : " There is a law which runs through nearly the whole of nature, that everything which is struck rings. Each substance has its peculiar ring." Language is the result of an instinct, a " faculty peculiar to man in his primitive state, by which every impression from without received its vocal expression from within "—a faculty which " became extinct when its object was fulfilled." This theory, which Max Müller propounded and afterwards wisely abandoned, is mentioned here for the curiosity of the matter only.

Noiré started a fourth theory, nicknamed thē *yo-he-ho* : under any strong muscular effort it is a relief to the system to let breath come out strongly and repeatedly, and by that process to let the vocal chords vibrate in different ways ;. when primitive acts were performed in common, they would, therefore, naturally be accompanied with some sounds which would come to be associated with the idea of the act performed and stand as a name for it ; the

first words would accordingly mean something like ' heave ' or
' haul.'

Now, these theories, here imperfectly reproduced each in a few
lines, are mutually antagonistic : thus Noiré thinks it possible to
explain the origin of speech without sound imitation. And yet
what should prevent our combining these several theories and using
them concurrently ? It would seem to matter very little whether
the first word uttered by man was *bow-wow* or *pooh-pooh*, for the
fact remains that he said both one and the other. Each of the three
chief theories enables one to explain *parts of language*, but still
only parts, and not even the most important parts—the main
body of language seems hardly to be touched by any of them.
Again, with the exception of Noiré's theory, they are too
individualistic and take too little account of language as a
means of human intercourse. Moreover, they all tacitly assume
that up to the creation of language man had remained mute or
silent ; but this is most improbable from a physiological point
of view. As a rule we do not find an organ already perfected
on the first occasion of its use ; it is only by use that an organ
is developed.

XXI.—§ 3. Method.

So much for the results of the first method of approaching
the question of the origin of speech, that of trying to picture to
oneself a speechless mankind and speculating on the way in which
language could then have originated. We shall now, as hinted
above (p. 413), indicate the ways in which it is possible to supplement, and even in some measure to supplant, this speculative
or deductive method by means of inductive reasonings. These
can be based on three fields of investigation, namely :

(1) The language of children ;
(2) The language of primitive races, and
(3) The history of language.

Of these, the third is the most fruitful source of information.

First, as to the language of children. Some biologists maintain
that the development of the individual follows on the whole the
same course as that of the race ; the embryo, before it arrives at
full maturity, will have passed through the same stages of development which in countless generations have led the whole species
to its present level. It has, therefore, occurred to many that the
acquisition by mankind at large of the faculty of speech may
be mirrored to us in the process by which any child learns to
communicate its thoughts by means of its vocal organs. Accord-

ingly, children's language has often been invoked to furnish illustrations and parallels of the process gone through in the formation of primitive language. But many writers have been guilty of an erroneous inference in applying this principle, inasmuch as they have taken all their examples from a child's acquisition of an already existing language. The fallacy will be evident if we suppose for a moment the case of a man endeavouring to arrive at the evolution of music from the manner in which a child is nowadays taught to play on the piano. Manifestly, the modern learner is in quite a different position to primitive man, and has quite a different task set him : he has an instrument ready to hand, and melodies already composed for him, and finally a teacher who understands how to draw these tunes forth from the instrument. It is the same thing with language : the task of the child is to learn an existing language, that is, to connect certain sounds heard on the lips of others with the same ideas that the speakers associate with them, but not in the least to frame anything new. No ; if we are seeking some parallel to the primitive acquisition of language, we must look elsewhere and turn to baby language as it is spoken in the first year of life, before the child has begun to ' notice ' and to make out what use is made of language by grown-up people. Here, in the child's first purposeless murmuring, crowing and babbling, we have real nature sounds ; here we may expect to find some clue to the infancy of the language of the race. And, again, we must not neglect the way children have of creating new words never heard before, and often of attaching a sense to originally meaningless conglomerations of sound.

As for the languages of contemporary savages, we may in some instances take them as typical of more primitive languages than those of civilized nations, and therefore as illustrating a linguistic stage that is nearer to that in which speech originated. Still, inferences from such languages should be used with great caution, for it should never be forgotten than even the most backward race has many centuries of linguistic evolution behind it, and that the conditions therefore may, or must, be very different from those of primeval man. The so-called primitive languages will therefore in the following sections be only invoked to corroborate conclusions at which it is possible to arrive from other data.

The third and most fruitful source from which to gather information of value for our investigation is the history of language as it has been considered in previous chapters of this work. While the propounders of the theories of the origin of speech mentioned above made straight for the front of the lion's den, we are like the fox in the fable, who noticed that all the traces led into the den and not a single one came out ; we will therefore try and steal into the den from behind. They thought it logically correct, nay necessary, to begin at the beginning; let us, for variety's sake, begin with languages accessible at the present day, and let us attempt from that starting-point step by step to trace the backward path. Perhaps in this way we may reach the very first beginnings of speech.

The method I recommend, and which I think I am the first to employ consistently, is to trace our modern twentieth-century languages as far back in time as history and our materials will allow us; and then, from this comparison of present English with Old English, of Danish with Old Norse, and of both with ' Common Gothonic,' of French and Italian with Latin, of modern Indian dialects with Sanskrit, etc., to deduce definite laws for the development of languages in general, and to try and find a system of lines which can be lengthened backwards beyond the reach of history. If we should succeed in discovering certain qualities to be generally typical of the earlier as opposed to the later stages of languages, we shall be justified in concluding that the same qualities obtained in a still higher degree in the earliest times of all; if we are able within the historical era to demonstrate a definite direction of linguistic evolution, we must be allowed to infer that the direction was the same even in those primeval periods for which we have no documents to guide us. But if the change witnessed in the evolution of modern speech out of older forms of speech is thus on a larger scale projected back into the childhood of mankind, and if by this process we arrive finally at uttered sounds of such a description that they can no longer be called a real language, but something antecedent to language—why, then the problem will have been solved; for transformation is something we can understand, while a creation out of nothing can never be comprehended by human understanding.

This, then, will be the object of the following rapid sketch: to search the several departments of the science of language for general laws of evolution—most of them have already been discussed at some length in the preceding chapters—then to magnify the changes observed, and thus to form a picture of the outer and inner structure of some sort of speech more primitive than the most primitive language accessible to direct observation.

XXI.—§ 4. Sounds.

First, as regards the purely phonetic side of language, we observe everywhere the tendency to make pronunciation more easy, so as to lessen the muscular effort; difficult combinations of sounds are discarded, those only being retained which are pronounced with ease (see Ch. XIV § 6 ff.). Modern research has shown that the Proto-Aryan sound-system was much more complicated than was imagined in the reconstructions of the middle of the nineteenth century. In most languages now only such sounds are used as are produced by expiration, while inbreathed sounds and clicks or suction-stops are not found in connected speech. In civilized languages we meet with such sounds only in interjections, as when an inbreathed voiceless *l* (generally with rhythmic variations of strength and corresponding small movements of the tongue) is used to express delight in eating and drinking, or when the click inadequately spelt *tut* is used to express impatience. In some very primitive South African languages, on the other hand, clicks are found as integral parts of words ; and Bleek has rendered it probable that in former stages of these languages they were in more extensive use than now. We may perhaps draw the conclusion that primitive languages in general were rich in all kinds of difficult sounds.

The following point is of more far-reaching consequence. In some languages we find a gradual disappearance of tone or pitch accent ; this has been the case in Danish, whereas Norwegian and Swedish have kept the old tones ; so also in Russian as compared with Serbo-Croatian. In the works of old Indian, Greek and Latin grammarians we have express statements to the effect that pitch accent played a prominent part in those languages, and that the intervals used must have been comparatively greater than is usual in our modern languages. In modern Greek and in the Romanic languages the tone element has been obscured, and now 'stress' is heard on the syllable where the ancients noted only a high or a low tone. About the languages spoken nowadays by savage tribes we have generally very little information, as most of those who have made a first-hand study of such languages have not been trained to observe and to describe these delicate points ; still, there is of late years an increasing number of observations of tone accents, for instance in African languages, which may justify us in thinking that tone plays an important part in many primitive languages.[1]

[1] It may not be superfluous expressly to point out that there is no contradiction between what is said here on the disappearance of tones and the remarks made above (Ch. XIX § 4) on Chinese tones. There the change wrought in the meaning of a word by a mere change of tone was explained on the principle that the difference of meaning was at an earlier stage expressed by affixes, the tone that is now concentrated on one syllable belonging formerly to two syllables or perhaps more. But this evidently presupposes that each syllable had already some tone of its own—and that is what in this chapter is taken to be the primitive state. Word-tones were originally frequent, but meaningless ; afterwards they were dropped in some languages, while in others they were utilized for sense-distinguishing purposes.

So much for word tones ; now for the sentence melody. It is a well-known fact that the modulation of sentences is strongly influenced by the effect of intense emotions in causing stronger and more rapid raisings and sinkings of the tone. " All passionate language does of itself become musical—with a finer music than the mere accent ; the speech of a man even in zealous anger becomes a chant, a song " (Carlyle). "The sounds of common conversation have but little resonance ; those of strong feeling have much more. Under rising ill-temper the voice acquires a metallic ring. . . . Grief, unburdening itself, uses tones approaching in *timbre* to those of chanting ; and in his most pathetic passages an eloquent speaker similarly falls into tones more vibratory than those common to him. . . . While calm speech is comparatively monotonous, emotion makes use of fifths, octaves, and even wider intervals " (H. Spencer).

Now, it is a consequence of advancing civilization that passion, or, at least, the expression of passion, is moderated, and we must therefore conclude that the speech of uncivilized and primitive men was more passionately agitated than ours, more like music or song. This conclusion is borne out by what we hear about the speech of many savages in our own days. European travellers very often record their impression of the speech of different tribes in expressions like these : " pronouncing whatever they spoke in a very singing manner," " the singing tone of voice, in common conversation, was frequent," " the speech is very much modulated and resembles singing," " highly artificial and musical," etc.

These facts and considerations all point to the conclusion that there once was a time when all speech was song, or rather when these two actions were not yet differentiated ; but perhaps this inference cannot be established inductively at the present stage of linguistic science with the same amount of certainty as the statements I am now going to make as to the nature of primitive speech.

As we have seen above (Ch. XVII § 7), a great many of the changes going on regularly from century to century, as well as some of the sudden changes which take place now and then in the history of each language, result in the shortening of words. This is seen everywhere and at all times, and in consequence of this universal tendency we find that the ancient languages of our family, Sanskrit, Zend, etc., abound in very long words ; the further back we go, the greater the number of *sesquipedalia*. We have seen also how the current theory, according to which every language started with monosyllabic roots, fails at every point to account for actual facts and breaks down before the established truths of linguistic history. Just as the history of religion does not pass from the belief in one god to the belief in many gods, but inversely from polytheism towards monotheism, so language proceeds from original polysyllabism towards monosyllabism : if the development of language took the same course in prehistoric as in historic times, we see, by projecting the teaching of history on a larger scale back into the darkest ages, that early words must have been to present ones what the plesiosaurus and gigantosaurus are to present-day reptiles. The outcome of this phonetic section is, therefore, that we must imagine primitive language as consisting (chiefly at least) of very long words, full of difficult sounds, and sung rather than spoken.

XXI.—§ 5. Grammar.

Can anything be stated about the grammar of primitive languages ? Yes, I think so, if we continue backwards into the past the lines of evolution resulting from the investigations of previous chapters of this volume. Ancient languages have more forms than modern ones ; forms originally kept distinct are in course of time confused, either phonetically or analogically, alike in substantives, adjectives and verbs.

A characteristic feature of the structure of languages in their early stages is that each form of a word (whether verb or noun) contains in itself several minor modifications which, in the later stages, are expressed separately (if at all), that is, by means of auxiliary verbs or prepositions. Such a word as Latin *cantavisset* unites in one inseparable whole the equivalents of six ideas : (1) ' sing,' (2) pluperfect, (3) that indefinite modification of the verbal idea which we term subjunctive, (4) active, (5) third person, and (6) singular. The tendency of later stages is towards expressing such modifications analytically ; but if we accept the terms ' synthesis ' and ' analysis ' for ancient and recent stages, we must first realize that there exist many gradations of both : in no single language do we find either synthesis or analysis carried out with absolute purity and consistency. Everywhere we find a more or less. Latin is synthetic in comparison with French, French analytic in comparison with Latin ; but if we were able to see the direct ancestor of Latin, say two thousand years before the earliest inscriptions, we should no doubt find a language so synthetic that in comparison with it Cicero's would have to be termed highly analytic.

Secondly, we must not from the term ' synthesis,' which etymologically means ' composition ' or ' putting together,' draw the conclusion that synthetic forms, such as we find, for instance, in Latin, consist of originally independent elements put together and thus in their turn presuppose a previous stage of analysis. Whoever does not share the usual opinion that all flexional forms have originated through coalescence of separate words, but sees as we have seen (in Ch. XIX) also the reverse process of inseparable portions of words gaining greater and greater independence, will perhaps do well to look out for a better and less ambiguous word than *synthesis* to describe the character of primitive speech. What in the later stages of languages is analyzed or dissolved, in the earlier stages was unanalyzable or indissoluble ; ' entangled ' or ' complicated ' would therefore be better renderings of our impression of the first state of things.

XXI.—§ 6. Units.

But are the old forms really less dissoluble than their modern equivalents ? This is repeatedly denied even by recent writers, on· whom my words in *Progress*, p. 117, cannot have made much impression, if they have read them at all ; and it will therefore be necessary to take up this cardinal point. Let me begin with quoting what others have said. " Historically considered, the Latin *amat* is really two words, as much as its English representative, the final *t* being originally a pronoun signifying ' he,' ' she ' or ' it,' and it is only reasons of practical convenience that prevent us from writing *am at* or *ama t* as two and *heloves* as one word. . . . The really essential difference between *amat* and *he loves* is that in the former the pronominal element is expressed by a suffix, in the latter by a prefix " (Sweet PS 274, 1899). " It is purely accidental that the Latin form is not written *am-av-it*. To the unsophisticated Frenchman *il a aimé* is neither less nor more one unit than *amavit* to a Roman. . . . When the locution *il a aimé* sprang up, each element of it was still to some extent felt separately ; but after it had become a fixed formula the elements were fused together into one whole. As a matter of fact, uneducated French people have not the least idea whether it is one or three words they speak " (Sütterlin WGS 11, 1902). " In some modern languages the personal pronoun is, just as in archaic Greek, beginning to be amalgamated with verbs so as to become a mere termination (*sic* : *désinence* ; prefix must be what is meant) : Fr. *j'don'*, *tu-don'*, *il-don'* (je donne, tu donnes, il donne) and E. *i-giv'*, *we giv'*, *you-giv'*, *they-giv'*, correspond exactly to Gr. *dido-mi*, *dido-si*, *dido-ti*, only that the personal particle is in a different place " (Dauzat V 155, 1910). " If French were a savage language not yet reduced to writing, a travelling linguist, hearing the present tense of the verb *aimer* pronounced by the natives, would transcribe it in the following way : *jèm, tu èm, ilèm, nouzémon, vouzémé, ilzèm*. He would be

struck particularly with the agglutination of the pronominal
subject and the verb, and would never feel tempted to draw up
a paradigm without pronouns : *aime, aimes, aime, aimons*, etc.,
in which traditional spelling makes us believe. . . . He would
even, through a comparison of *ilèm* and *ilzèm*, be led to establish
a tendency to incorporation, as the only sign of the plural is a *z*
infixed in the verbal complex " (Bally LV 43, 1913).

In these utterances two questions are really mixed together,
that of the origin of Aryan flexional forms and that of the actual
status of some forms in various languages. As to the former
question, we have seen (p. 383) how very uncertain it is that *amat*
and *didosi*, etc., contain pronouns. As to the latter question,
it is quite true that we should not let the usual spelling be decisive
when it is asked whether we have one or two or three words ; but
all these writers strangely overlook the really important criteria
which we possess in this matter. Bally's traveller could only have
arrived at his result by listening to grammar lessons in which the
three persons of the verb were rattled off one after the other, for
if he had taken his forms from actual conversation he would have
come across numerous instances in which the forms occurred
without pronouns, first in the imperative, *aime, aimons, aimez*, then
in collocations like *celui qui aime, ceux qui aiment*, in which there
is no infix to denote the plural ; in *le mari aime, les maris aiment*,
and innumerable similar groups there is neither pronoun nor infix.
If he were at first inclined to take *ilaaimé* as one word, he would
on further acquaintance with the language discover that the elements were often separated : *il n'a pas aimé, il nous a toujours
aimés*, etc. Similarly with the English forms adduced : *I never
give, you always give*. This is the crucial point : the French and
English combinations are two (three) words because the elements
are not always placed together ; Lat. *amat, amavit*, are each of
them only one word because they can never be divided, and in the
same way we never find anything placed between *am* and *o* in
the first person, *amo*. These forms are as inseparable as E. *loves*,
but E. *heloves* is separable because both *he* and *loves* can stand
alone, and can also, in certain combinations, though now rarely,
be transposed : *loves he*. Some writers would compare French
combinations like *il te le disait* with verbal forms in certain Amerindian languages, in which subject and direct and indirect object
are alike 'incorporated' in a 'polysynthetic' verbal form ; it is
quite true that these French pronominal forms can never be used
by themselves, but only in conjunction with a verb ; still, the French
pronouns are more independent of each other than the elements
of some other more primitive languages. In the first place, this
is shown by the possibility of varying the pronunciation : *il te*

le disait may be either [itlədizɛ] or [itəldizɛ] or even more solemnly [iltələdizɛ] ; secondly, by the regularity of these joined pronominal forms, for they are always the same, whatever the verb may be ; and lastly, by their changing places in certain cases : *te le disait-il ? dis-le-lui*, etc.

Nor can it be said that English forms like *he's = he is* (or *he has*), *I'd = I had* (or *I would*), *he'll = he will* show a tendency towards 'entangling,' for however closely together these forms are generally pronounced, each of them must be said to consist of two words, as is shown by the possibility of transposition (Is he ill ?) and of intercalation of other words (I never had) ; it is also noteworthy that the same short forms of the verbs can be added to all kinds of words (the water'll be . . ., the sea'd been calm). In the forms *don't, won't, can't* there is something like amalgamation of the verbal with the negative idea. Still, it is important to notice that the amalgamation only takes place with a few verbs of the auxiliary class. In saying ' I don't write ' the full verb is not touched by the fusion, and is even allowed to be unchanged in cases where it would have been inflected if no auxiliary had been used ; compare *I write, he writes, I wrote* with the negative *I don't write, he doesn't write, I didn't write.* It will be seen, especially if we take into account the colloquial or vulgar form for the third person, *he don't write*, that the general movement here as elsewhere is really rather in the direction of ' isolation ' than of fusion ; for the verbal form *write* is stripped of all signs of person and tense, the person being indicated separately (if at all), and the tense sign being joined to the negation. So also in interrogative sentences ; and if that tendency which can be observed in Elizabethan English had prevailed by using the combination *I do write* in positive statements, even where no special emphasis is intended, English verbs (except a few auxiliaries) would have been entirely stripped of those elements which to most grammarians constitute the very essence of a verb, namely, the marks of person, number, tense and mood, *write* being the universal form, besides the quasi-nominal forms *writing* and *written.*

Now, it is often said that the history of language shows a sort of gyration or movement in spirals, in which synthesis is followed by analysis, this by a new synthesis (flexion), and this again by analysis, and so forth. Latin *amabo* (which according to the old theory was once *ama* + some auxiliary) has been succeeded by *amare habeo*, which in its turn is fused into *amerò, aimerai*, and the latter form is now to some extent giving way to *je vais aimer.* But this pretended law of rotation is only arrived at by considering a comparatively small number of phenomena, and not by viewing the successive stages of the same language as wholes and drawing general inferences as to their typically distinctive characters (cf. above, p. 337). If for every two instances of new flexions springing up we see ten older ones discarded in favour of analysis or isolation, are we not entitled to the generalization that flexion or indissolubility tends to give way to analysis ? We should beware of being under the same delusion as a man who, in walking over a mountainous country, thinks that he goes down just as many and just as long hills as he goes up, while on the contrary each ascent is higher than the preceding descent, so that finally he finds himself unexpectedly many thousand feet above the level from which he started.

The direction of movement is towards flexionless languages (such as Chinese, or to a certain extent Modern English) with freely combinable elements ; the starting-point was flexional languages (such as Latin or Greek) ; at a still earlier stage we must suppose a language in which a verbal form might indicate not only six things, like *cantavisset*, but a still larger number, in which verbs were perhaps modified according to the gender (or sex) of the subject, as they are in Semitic languages, or according to the object, as in some Amerindian languages, or according to whether a man, a woman, or a person who commands respect is spoken to, as in Basque. But that amounts to the same thing as saying that the border-line between word and sentence was not so clearly defined as in more recent times ; *cantavisset* is really nothing but a sentence-word, and the same holds good to a still greater extent of the sound conglomerations of Eskimo and some other North American languages. Primitive linguistic units must have been much more complicated in point of meaning, as well as much longer in point of sound, than those with which we are most familiar.

XXI.—§ 7. Irregularities.

Another point of great importance is this : in early languages we find a far greater number of irregularities, exceptions, anomalies, than in modern ones. It is true that we not unfrequently see new irregularities spring up, where the formations were formerly regular ; but these instances are very far from counterbalancing the opposite class, in which words once irregularly inflected become regular, or are given up in favour of regularly inflected words, or in which anomalies in syntax are levelled. The tendency is more and more to denote the same thing by the same means in every case, to extend the ending, or whatever it is, that is used in a large class of words to express a certain modification of the central idea, until it is used in all other words as well.

Comparative linguistics did not attain a scientific character till the principle was established that the relationship of two languages had to be determined by a thoroughgoing conformity in the most necessary parts of language, namely (besides grammar proper) pronouns and numerals and the most indispensable of nouns and verbs. But if this domain of speech, by preserving religiously, as it were, the old tradition, affords infallible criteria of the near or remote relationship of different languages, may we not reasonably expect to find in the same domain some clue to the oldest grammatical system used by our ancestors ? What sort of system, then, do we find there ? We see such a declension as *I, me, we, us* : the several forms of the ' paradigm ' do not at all resemble each other, as they do in more recently developed declensions. We find masculines and feminines, such as *father, mother, man, wife, bull, cow* ; while such methods of derivation as are seen in *count, countess, he-bear, she-bear*, belong to a later time. We meet with degrees of comparison like *good, better, ill, worse*, while regular forms like *happy, happier, big, bigger*, prevail in all the younger strata of languages. We meet with verbal flexion such as appears in *am, is, was, been*, which forms a striking contrast to the more modern method of adding a mere ending while leaving the body of the word unchanged. In an interesting book, *Vom Suppletivwesen der indogermanischen Sprachen* (1899), H. Osthoff has collected a very great number of examples from the old Aryan languages of different stems supplementing each other, and has pointed out that this phenomenon is characteristic of the most necessary ideas occurring every moment in ordinary conversation : I take at random a few of the best-known of his examples : Fr. *aller, je vais, j'irai*, Lat. *fero, tuli*, Gr. *horaō, opsomai, eidon*, Lat. *bonus, melior, optimus*. Osthoff fully agrees with me that we have here a trait of primitive psychology : our remote ancestors were not able to see and to express what was common to these ideas ; their minds were very unsystematic, and separated in their linguistic expressions things which from a logical point of view are closely related : much of their grammar, therefore, was really of a lexical character.

XXI.—§ 8. Savage Tribes.

If now it is asked whether the conclusions we have thus arrived at are borne out by a consideration of the languages of savage or primitive races nowadays, the answer is that these cannot be lumped together; there are among them many different types, even with regard to grammatical structure. But the more these languages are studied and the more accurately their structure is described, the more also students perceive intricacies and anomalies in their grammar, Gabelentz (Spr 386) says that the casual observer has no idea how manifold and how nicely circumscribed grammatical categories can be, even in the seemingly crudest languages, for ordinary grammars tell us nothing about that. P. W. Schmidt (*Die Stellung der Pygmäenvölker*, 1910, 129) says that whoever, from the low culture of the Andamanese, would expect to find their language very simple and poor in expressions would be strangely deceived, for its mechanism is highly complicated, with many prefixes and suffixes, which often conceal the root itself. Meinhof (MSA 136) mentions the multiplicity of plural formations in African languages. Vilhelm Thomsen, in speaking of the Santhal (Khervarian) language, says that its grammar is capable of expressing a multiplicity of *nuances* which in other languages must be expressed by clumsy circumlocutions; the native speakers go beyond what is necessary through requiring expressions for many subordinate notions, the language having, so to speak, only one fine gold-balance, on which everything, even the simplest and commonest things, must be weighed by the adding-up of a whole series of minutiæ. Curr speaks about the erroneous belief in the simplicity of Australian languages, which on the contrary have a great number of conjugations, etc. The extreme difficulty and complex structure of Eskimo and of many Amerindian languages is so notorious that no words need be wasted on them here. And the forms of the Basque verb are so manifold and intricate that we understand how Larramendi, in his legitimate pride at having been the first to reduce them to a system, called his grammar *El Imposible Vencido*, 'The Impossible Overcome.' At Béarn they have the story that the good God, wishing to punish the devil for the temptation of Eve, sent him to the Pays Basque with the command that he should remain there till he had mastered the language. At the end of seven years God relented, finding the punishment too severe, and called the devil to him. The devil had no sooner crossed the bridge of Castelondo than he found he had forgotten all that he had so hardly learned.

What is here said about the languages of wild tribes (and of the Basques, who are not exactly savages, but whose language is generally taken to have retained many primeval traits) is in exact keeping with everything that recent study of primitive man has brought to light : the life of the savage is regulated to the minutest details through ceremonies and conventionalities to be observed on every and any occasion; he is restricted in what he may eat and drink and when and how ; and all these, to our mind, irrational prescriptions and innumerable prohibitions have to be observed with the most scrupulous, nay religious, care : it is the same with all the meticulous rules of his language.

XXI.—§ 9. Law of Development.

So far, then, from subscribing to Whitney's dictum that " the law of simplicity of beginnings applies to language not less naturally and necessarily than to other instrumentalities " (G 226), we are drawn to the conclusion that primitive language had a superabundance of irregularities and anomalies, in syntax and word-formation no less than in accidence.   It was capricious and fanciful, and displayed a luxuriant growth of forms, entangled one with another like the trees in a primeval forest.   " Rien n'entre mieux dans les esprits grossiers que les subtilités des langues " (Tarde, *Lois de l'imitation* 285).   Human minds in the early times disported themselves in long and intricate words as in the wildest and most wanton play.   Nothing could be more beside the mark than to suppose that grammatical and logical categories were in primitive languages generally in harmony (as is supposed, e.g., by Sweet, *New Engl. Grammar* § 543) : primitive speech cannot have been distinguished for logical consistency ; nor, so far as we can judge, was it simple and facile : it is much more likely to have been extremely clumsy and unwieldy.   Renan rightly reminds us of Turgot's wise saying : " Des hommes grossiers ne font rien de simple.   Il faut des hommes perfectionnés pour y arriver."

We have seen in earlier chapters that the old theory of the three stages through which human language was supposed always to proceed, isolation, agglutination and flexion, was built up on insufficient materials ; but while we feel tempted totally to reverse this system, we must be on our guard against establishing too rigid and too absolute a system ourselves.   It would not do simply to reverse the order and say that flexion is the oldest stage, from which language tends through an agglutinative stage towards complete isolation, for flexion, agglutination and isolation do not include all possible structural types of speech.   The possibilities of development are so manifold, and there are such innumerable ways of arriving at more or less adequate expressions for human thought, that it is next to impossible to compare languages of different families.   Even, therefore, if it is probable that English, Finnish and Chinese are all simplifications of more complex languages, we cannot say that Chinese, for instance, at one time resembled English in structure and at some other time Finnish. English was once a flexional language, and is still so in some respects, while in others it is agglutinative, and in others again isolating, or nearly so.   But we may perhaps give the following formula of what is our total impression of the whole preceding inquiry :

THE EVOLUTION OF LANGUAGE SHOWS A PROGRESSIVE TEN-
DENCY FROM INSEPARABLE IRREGULAR CONGLOMERATIONS TO
FREELY AND REGULARLY COMBINABLE SHORT ELEMENTS.

The old system of historical linguistics may be likened to an
enormous pyramid ; only it is a pity that it should have as its
base the small, square, strong, smart root word, and suspended
above it the unwieldy, lumbering, ill-proportioned, flexion-encum-
bered sentence-vocable. Structures of this sort may with some
adroitness be made to stand ; but their equilibrium is unstable,
and sooner or later they will inevitably tumble over.

XXI.—§ 10. Vocabulary.

On the lexical side of language we find a development parallel
to that noticed in grammar ; and, indeed, if we go deep enough
into the question, we shall see that it is really the very same
movement that has taken place. The more advanced a language
is, the more developed is its power of expressing abstract or
general ideas. Everywhere language has first attained to expressions for the concrete and special. In accounts of the languages
of barbarous races we constantly come across such phrases as
these : " The aborigines of Tasmania had no words representing
abstract ideas ; for each variety of gum-tree and wattle-tree,
etc., they had a name ; but they had no equivalent for the
expression ' a tree ' ; neither could they express abstract qualities,
such as ' hard, soft, warm, cold, long, short, round ' " ; or,
The Mohicans have words for cutting various objects, but none
to convey *cutting* simply. The Zulus have no word for ' cow,'
but words for ' red cow,' ' white cow,' etc. (Sayce S 2. 5, cf.
1. 121). In Bakaïri (Central Brazil) "each parrot has its special
name, and the general idea ' parrot ' is totally unknown, as well
as the general idea ' palm.' But they know precisely the qualities
of each subspecies of parrot and palm, and attach themselves so
much to these numerous particular notions that they take no interest
in the common characteristics. They are choked in the abundance
of the material and cannot manage it economically. They have
only small coin, but in that they must be said to be excessively
rich rather than poor " (K. v. d. Steinen, *Unter den Naturvölkern
Brasiliens*, 1894, 81). The Lithuanians, like many primitive
tribes, have many special, but no common names for various
colours : one word for gray in speaking about wool and geese,
one about horses, one about cattle, one about the hair of men and
some animals, and in the same way for other colours (J. Schmidt,
Kritik d. Sonantentheorie 37). Many languages have no word
for ' brother,' but words for ' elder brother ' and ' younger brother ' ;

others have different words according to whose (person and number) father or brother it is (see, e.g., the paradigm in Gabelentz Spr 421), and the same applies in many languages to names for various parts of the body. In Cherokee, instead of one word for ' washing ' we find different words, according to what is washed : *kutuwo* ' I wash myself,' *kulestula* ' I wash my head,' *tsestula* ' I wash the head of somebody else,' *kukuswo* ' I wash my face,' *tsekuswo* ' I wash the face of somebody else,' *takasula* ' I wash my hands or feet,' *takunkela* ' I wash my clothes,' *takutega* ' I wash dishes,' *tsejuwu* ' I wash a child,' *kowela* ' I wash meat ' (see, however, the criticism of Hewitt, *Am. Anthropologist*, 1893, 398). Primitive man did not see the wood for the trees.[1]

In some Amerindian languages there are distinct series of numerals for various classes of objects ; thus in Kwakiatl and Tsimoshian (Sapir, *Language and Environment* 239) ; similarly the Melanesians have special words to denote a definite number of certain objects, e.g. *a buku niu* ' two coconuts,' *a buru* ' ten coconuts,' *a koro* ' a hundred coconuts,' *a selavo* ' a thousand coconuts,' *a uduudu* ' ten canoes,' *a bola* ' ten fishes,' etc. (Gabelentz, *Die melan. Spr.* 1. 23). In some languages the numerals are the same for all classes of objects counted, but require after them certain class-denoting words varying according to the character of the objects (in some respects comparable to the English twenty *head* of cattle, Pidgin *piecey* ; cf. Yule and Burnell, Hobson-Jobson s.v. Numerical Affixes). This reminds one of the systems of weights and measures, which even in civilized countries up to a comparatively recent period varied not only from country to country, sometimes even from district to district, but even in the same country according to the things weighed or measured (in England *stone* and *ton* still vary in this way).

In old Gothonic poetry we find an astonishing abundance of words translated in our dictionaries by ' sea,' ' battle,' ' sword,' ' hero,' and the like : these may certainly be considered as relics of an earlier state of things, in which each of these words had its separate shade of meaning, which was subsequently lost and which it is impossible now to determine with certainty. The nomenclature of a remote past was undoubtedly constructed upon similar principles to those which are still preserved in a word-group like *horse, mare, stallion, foal, colt*, instead of he-horse, she-horse, young horse, etc. This sort of grouping has only survived in a few cases in which a lively interest has been felt in the objects or animals concerned. We may note, however, the different terms employed

[1] On the lack of abstract and general terms in savage languages, see also Ginneken LP 108 and the works there quoted.

for essentially the same idea in a *flock* of sheep, a *pack* of wolves, a *herd* of cattle, a *bevy* of larks, a *covey* of partridges, a *shoal* of fish. Primitive language could show a far greater number of instances of this description, and, so far, had a larger vocabulary than later languages, though, of course, it lacked names for a great number of ideas that were outside the sphere of interest of uncivilized people.

There was another reason for the richness of the vocabulary of primitive man : his superstition about words, which made him avoid the use of certain words under certain circumstances— during war, when out fishing, during the time of the great cultic festivals, etc.—because he feared the anger of gods or demons if he did not religiously observe the rules of the linguistic tabu. Accordingly, in many cases he had two or more sets of words for exactly the same notions, of which later generations as a rule preserved only one, unless they differentiated these words by utilizing them to discriminate objects that were similar but not identical.

XXI.—§ 11. Poetry and Prose.

On the whole the development of languages, even in the matter of vocabulary, must be considered to have taken a beneficial course ; still, in certain respects one may to some extent regret the consequences of this evolution. While our words are better adapted to express abstract things and to render concrete things with definite precision, they are necessarily comparatively colourless. The old words, on the contrary, spoke more immediately to the senses—they were manifestly more suggestive, more graphic and pictorial : while to express one single thing we are not unfrequently obliged to piece the image together bit by bit, the old concrete words would at once present it to the hearer's mind as a whole ; they were, accordingly, better adapted to poetic purposes. Nor is this the only point in which we see a close relationship between primitive words and poetry.

If by a mental effort we transport ourselves to a period in which language consisted solely of such graphic concrete words, we shall discover that, in spite of their number, they would not suffice, taken all together, to cover everything that needed expression ; a wealth in such words is not incompatible with a certain poverty. They would accordingly often be required to do service outside of their proper sphere of application. That a figurative or metaphorical use of words is a factor of the utmost importance in the life of all languages is indisputable ; but I am probably right in thinking that it played a more prominent part in old times than now. In the course of ages a great many metaphors have lost their freshness and vividness, so that nobody feels them to be metaphors any longer. Examine closely such a sentence as this : " He *came* to *look upon* the low *ebb* of morals as an *outcome* of bad *taste*," and you will find that nearly every word is a dead metaphor.[1] But the better stocked a language is with those ex-metaphors which have become regular expressions for definite ideas, the less need there is for going out of one's way to find new metaphors. The expression of thought therefore tends to become more and more mechanical or prosaic.

Primitive man, however, on account of the nature of his language, was constantly reduced to using words and phrases figuratively : he was forced to express his thoughts in the language of poetry. The speech of modern savages is often spoken of as abounding in similes and all kinds of figurative phrases and allegorical expressions.   Just as in the literature transmitted to us poetry is found in every country to precede prose, so poetic language is on the whole older than prosaic language ; lyrics and cult songs come before science, and Oehlenschläger is right when he sings (in N. Møller's translation) :

> Thus Nature drove us ; warbling rose
> Man's voice in verse before he spoke in prose.

XXI.—§ 12. Emotional Songs.

If we now try to sum up what has been inferred about primitive speech, we see that by our backward march we arrived at a language whose units had a very meagre substance of thought, and this as specialized and concrete as possible ; but at the same time the phonetic body was ample ; and the bigger and longer the words, the thinner the thoughts ! Much cry and little wool ! No period has seen less taciturn people than the first framers of speech ; primitive speakers were not reticent and reserved beings, but youthful men and women babbling merrily on, without being so very particular about the meaning of each word. They did not narrowly weigh every syllable—what were a couple of syllables more or less to them ? They chattered away for the mere pleasure of chattering, resembling therein many a mother of our own time, who will chatter away to baby without measuring her words or looking too closely into the meaning of each ; nay, who is not a bit troubled by the consideration that the little deary does not understand a single word of her affectionate eloquence. But

---

[1] Of course, if instead of *look upon* and *outcome* we had taken the corresponding terms of Latin root, *consider* and *result*, the metaphors would have been still more dead to the natural linguistic instinct.

primitive speech—and we return here to an idea thrown out above—still more resembles the speech of little baby himself, before he begins to frame his own language after the pattern of the grown-ups ; the language of our remote forefathers was like that ceaseless humming and crooning with which no thoughts are as yet connected, which merely amuses and delights the little one. Language originated as play, and the organs of speech were first trained in this singing sport of idle hours.

Primitive language had no great store of ideas, and if we consider it as an instrument for expressing thoughts, it was clumsy, unwieldy and ineffectual ; but what did that matter ? Thoughts were not the first things to press forward and crave for expression ; emotions and instincts were more primitive and far more powerful. But what emotions were most powerful in producing germs of speech ? To be sure not hunger and that which is connected with hunger : mere individual self-assertion and the struggle for material existence. This prosaic side of life was only capable of calling forth short monosyllabic interjections, howls of pain and grunts of satisfaction or dissatisfaction ; but these are isolated and incapable of much further development ; they are the most immutable portions of language, and remain now at essentially the same standpoint as thousands of years ago.

If after spending some time over the deep metaphysical speculations of a number of German linguistic philosophers you turn to men like Madvig and Whitney, you are at once agreeably impressed by the sobriety of their reasoning and their superior clearness of thought. But if you look more closely, you cannot help thinking that they imagine our primitive ancestors after their own image as serious and well-meaning men endowed with a large share of common-sense. By their laying such great stress on the communication of thought as the end of language and on the benefit to primitive man of being able to speak to his fellow-creatures about matters of vital importance, they leave you with the impression that these " first framers of speech " were sedate citizens with a strong interest in the purely business and matter-of-fact side of life ; indeed, according to Madvig, women had no share in the creating of language.

In opposition to this rationalistic view I should like, for once in a way, to bring into the field the opposite view : the genesis of language is not to be sought in the prosaic, but in the poetic side of life ; the source of speech is not gloomy seriousness, but merry play and youthful hilarity. And among the emotions which were most powerful in eliciting outbursts of music and of song, love must be placed in the front rank. To the feeling of love, which has left traces of its vast influence on countless points in the evolution of organic nature, are due not only, as Darwin has shown, the magnificent colours of birds and flowers, but also many of the things that fill us with joy in human life ; it inspired many of the first songs, and through them was instrumental in bringing about human language. In primitive speech I hear the laughing cries of exultation when lads and lasses vied with one another to attract the attention of the other sex, when everybody sang his merriest and danced his bravest to lure a pair of eyes to throw admiring glances in his direction. Language was born in the courting days of mankind ; the first utterances of speech I fancy to myself like something between the nightly love-lyrics of puss upon the tiles and the melodious love-songs of the nightingale.[1]

XXI.—§ 13. Primitive Singing.

Love, however, was not the only feeling which tended to call forth primitive songs. Any strong emotion, and more particularly any pleasurable excitement, might result in song. Singing, like any other sort of play, is due to an overflow of energy, which is discharged in "unusual vivacity of every kind, including vocal vivacity." Out of the full heart the mouth sings ! Savages will sing whenever they are excited : exploits of war or of the chase, the deeds of their ancestors, the coming of a fat dog, any incident " from the arrival of a stranger to an earthquake " is turned into a song ; and most of these songs are composed extem-

---

[1] From the experience I had with my previous book, *Progress,* from which this chapter has, with some alterations and amplifications, passed into this volume, I feel impelled here to warn those critics who do me the honour to mention my theory of the origin of language, not to look upon it as if it were contained simply in my remarks on primitive love-songs, etc., and as if it were based on *a priori* considerations, like the older speculative theories. What I may perhaps claim as my original contribution to the solution of this question is the *inductive* method based on the three sources of information indicated on p. 416, and especially on the ' backward ' consideration of the history of language. Some critics think they have demolished my view by simply representing it as a romantic dream of a primitive golden age in which men had no occupation but courting and singing. I have never believed in a far-off golden age, but rather incline to believe in a progressive movement from a very raw and barbarous age to something better, though it must be said that our own age, with its national wars, world wars and class wars, makes one sometimes ashamed to think how little progress our so-called civilization has made. But primitive ages were probably still worse, and the only thing I have felt bold enough to maintain is that in those days there were some moments consecrated to youthful hilarity, and that this gave rise, among other merriment, to vocal play of such a character as closely to resemble what we may infer from the known facts of linguistic history to have been a stage of language earlier than any of those accessible to us. There is no ' romanticism ' (in a bad sense) in such a theory, and it can only be refuted by showing that the view of language and its development on which it is based is erroneous from beginning to end.

pore. "When rowing, the Coast negroes sing either a description of some love intrigue or the praise of some woman celebrated for her beauty." The Malays beguile all their leisure hours with the repetition of songs, etc. "In singing, the East African contents himself with improvising a few words without sense or rime and repeats them till they nauseate." (These quotations, and many others, are found in Herbert Spencer's *Essay on the Origin of Music*, with his Postscript.) The reader of Karl Bücher's painstaking work *Arbeit und Rhythmus* (2te aufl. 1899) will know from his numerous examples and illustrations what an enormous rôle rhythmic singing plays in the daily life of savages all over the world, how each kind of work, especially if it is done by many jointly, has its own kind of song, and how nothing is done except to the sound of vocal music. In many instances savages are mentioned as very expert in adapting the subjects of their songs to current events. Nor is this sort of singing on every and any occasion confined to savages ; it is found wherever the indoor life of civilization has not killed all open-air hilarity ; formerly in our Western Europe people sang much more than they do now. The Swedish peasant Jonas Stolt (ab. 1820) writes : "I have known a time when young people were singing from morning till eve. Then they were carolling both out- and indoors, behind the plough as well as at the threshing-floor and at the spinning-wheel. This is all over long ago : nowadays there is silence everywhere ; if someone were to try and sing in our days as we did of old, people would term it bawling."

The first things that were expressed in song were, to be sure, neither deep nor wise ; how could you expect it ? Note the frequency with which we are told that the songs of savages consist of or contain totally meaningless syllables. Thus we read about American Indians that "the native word which is translated 'song' does not suggest any use of words. To the Indian, the music is of primal importance ; words may or may not accompany the music. When words are used in song, they are rarely employed as a narrative, the sentences are not apt to be complete " (Louise Pound, Mod. Lang. Ass. 32. 224), and similarly : "Even where the slightest vestiges of epic poetry are missing, lyric poetry of one form or another is always present. It may consist of the musical use of meaningless syllables that sustain the song ; or it may consist largely of such syllables, with a few interspersed words suggesting certain ideas and certain feelings ; or it may rise to the expression of emotions connected with warlike deeds, with religious feeling, love, or even to the praise of the beauties of nature " (Boas, *International Journ. Amer. Ling.* 1. 8). The magic incantations of the Greenland Eskimo, according to

W. Thalbitzer, contain many incomprehensible words never used outside these songs (but have they ever been real words ?), and the same is said about the mystic religious formulas of Maoris and African negroes and many other tribes, as well as about the old Roman hymns of the Arval Brethren. The mere joy in sonorous combinations here no doubt counts for very much, as in the splendid but meaningless metrical lists of names in the Old Norse Edda, and in many a modern refrain, too. Let me give one example of half (or less than half) understood strings of syllables from "The Oath of the Canting Crew" (1749, Farmer's *Musa Pedestris*, 51):

> No dimber, dambler, angler, dancer,
> Prig of cackler, prig of prancer ;
> No swigman, swaddler, clapper-dudgeon,
> Cadge-gloak, curtal, or curmudgeon ;
> No whip-jack, palliard, patrico ;
> No jarkman, be he high or low ;
> No dummerar or romany . . .
> Nor any other will I suffer.

In the cultic and ceremonial songs of savage tribes in many parts of the world this is a prominent trait : it seems, indeed, to be universal. Even with us the thoughts associated with singing are generally neither very clear nor very abstruse ; like humming or whistling, singing is often nothing more than an almost automatic outcome of a mood ; and " What is not worth saying can be sung." Besides, it has been the case at all times that things transient and trivial have found readier expression than Socratic wisdom. But the frivolous use tuned the instrument, and rendered it little by little more serviceable to a multiplicity of purposes, so that it became more and more fitted to express everything that touched human souls.

Men sang out their feelings long before they were able to speak their thoughts. But of course we must not imagine that " singing " means exactly the same thing here as in a modern concert hall. When we say that speech originated in song, what we mean is merely that our comparatively monotonous spoken language and our highly developed vocal music are differentiations of primitive utterances, which had more in them of the latter than of the former. These utterances were at first, like the singing of birds and the roaring of many animals and the crying and crooning of babies, exclamative, not communicative—that is, they came forth from an inner craving of the individual without any thought of any fellow-creatures. Our remote ancestors had not the slightest notion that such a thing as communicating ideas and feelings to someone else was possible. They little suspected that in singing

as nature prompted them they were paving the way for a
language capable of rendering minute shades of thought; just
as they could not suspect that out of their coarse pictures of
men and animals there should one day grow an art enabling men
of distant countries to speak to one another. As is the art of
writing to primitive painting, so is the art of speaking to primitive
singing. And the development of the two vehicles of communication of thought presents other curious and instructive
parallels. In primitive picture-writing, each sign meant a whole
sentence or even more—the image of a situation or of an incident
being given as a whole; this developed into an ideographic
writing of each word by itself; this system was succeeded by
syllabic methods, which had in their turn to give place to alpha-
betic writing, in which each letter stands for, or is meant to
stand for, one sound. Just as here the advance is due to a further
analysis of language, smaller and smaller units of speech being
progressively represented by single signs, in an exactly similar
way, though not quite so unmistakably, the history of language
shows us a progressive tendency towards analyzing into smaller
and smaller units that which in the earlier stages was taken as an
inseparable whole.

One point must be constantly kept in mind. Although we
now regard the communication of thought as the main object
of speaking, there is no reason for thinking that this has always
been the case; it is perfectly possible that speech has developed
from something which had no other purpose than that of exercising
the muscles of the mouth and throat and of amusing oneself and
others by the production of pleasant or possibly only strange
sounds. The motives for uttering sounds may have changed
entirely in the course of centuries without the speakers being at any
point conscious of this change within them.

XXI.—§ 14. Approach to Language.

We get the first approach to language proper when com-
municativeness takes precedence of exclamativeness, when sounds
are uttered in order to 'tell' fellow-creatures something, as
when birds warn their young ones of some imminent danger. In
the case of human language, communication is infinitely more
full and rich and elaborate; the question therefore is a very
complex one: How did the association of sound and sense come
about? How did that which originally was a jingle of meaningless
sounds come to be an instrument of thought? How did man
become, as Humboldt has somewhere defined him, "a singing
creature, only associating thoughts with the tones"?

In the case of an onomatopoetic or echo-word like *bow-wow* and an interjection like *pooh-pooh* the association was easy and direct ; such words were at once employed and understood as signs for the corresponding idea. But this was not the case with the great bulk of language. Here association of sound with sense must have been arrived at by devious and circuitous ways, which to a great extent evade inquiry and make a detailed exposition impossible. But this is in exact conformity with very much that has taken place in recent periods ; as we have learnt in previous chapters, it is only by indirect and roundabout ways that many words and grammatical expedients have acquired the meanings they now have, or have acquired meaning where they originally had none. Let me remind the reader of the word *grog* (p. 308), of interrogative particles (p 358), of word order (p. 356), of many endings (Ch. XIX § 13 ff.), of tones (Ch. XIX § 5), of the French negative *pas*, of vowel-alternations like those in *drink, drank, drunk*, or in *foot, feet*, etc. Language is a complicated affair, and no more than most other human inventions has it come about in a simple way : mankind has not moved in a straight line towards a definitely perceived goal, but has muddled along from moment to moment and has thereby now and then stumbled on some happy expedient which has then been retained in accordance with the principle of the survival of the fittest.

We may perhaps succeed in forming some idea of the most primitive process of associating sound and sense if we call to mind what was said above on the signification of the earliest words, and try to fathom what that means. The first words must have been as concrete and specialized in meaning as possible. Now, what are the words whose meaning is the most concrete and the most specialized ? Without any doubt proper names—that is, of course, proper names of the good old kind, borne by and denoting only one single individual. How easily might not such names spring up in a primitive state such as that described above ! In the songs of a particular individual there would be a constant recurrence of a particular series of sounds sung with a particular cadence ; no one can doubt the possibility of such individual habits being contracted in olden as well as in present times. Suppose, then, that " in the spring time, the only pretty ring time " a lover was in the habit of addressing his lass " with a hey, and a ho, and a hey nonino." His comrades and rivals would not fail to remark this, and would occasionally banter him by imitating and repeating his " hey-and-a-ho-and-a-hey-nonino." But when once this had been recognized as what Wagner would term a person's ' leitmotiv,' it would be no far cry from mimicking it to using the " hey-and-a-ho-and-a-hey-nonino " as a sort of nickname for the man concerned ; it might be employed, for instance, to signal his arrival. And when once proper names had been bestowed, common names (or nouns) would not be slow in following ; we see the transition from one to the other class in constant operation, names originally used exclusively to denote an individual being used metaphorically to connote that person's most characteristic peculiarities, as when we say of one man that he is a ' Crœsus ' or a ' Vanderbilt ' or ' Rockefeller,' and of another that he is ' no Bismarck.' A German schoolboy in the 'eighties said in his history lesson that Hannibal swore he would always be a *Frenchman* to the Romans. This is, at least, one of the ways in which language arrives at designations of such ideas as ' rich,' ' statesman ' and ' enemy.' From the proper name of *Cæsar* we have both the Russian *tsar'* and the German *kaiser*, and from *Karol* (Charlemagne) Russian *korol'* ' king ' (also in the other Slav languages) and Magyar *király*. Besides being designations for persons, proper names may also in some cases come to mean tools or other objects, originally in most cases probably as a term of endearment, as when in thieves' slang a crowbar or lever is called a *betty* or *jemmy* ; E. *derrick* and *dirk*, as well as G. *dietrich*, Dan. *dirk*, Swed. *dyrk*, is nothing but *Dietrich (Derrick, Theodoricus)*, and thus in innumerable instances. In the École polytechnique in Paris there are many words of the same character : *bacha* ' cours d'allemand ' from a teacher, M. Bacharach, *borius* ' bretelles ' from General Borius, *malo* ' éperon ' from Captain Malo, etc. (MSL 15. 179). *Pamphlet* is from Pamphilet, originally *Pamphilus seu de Amore*, the name of a popular booklet on an erotic subject. Compare also the history of the words *bluchers, jack* (boot-jack, jack for turning a spit, a pike, etc., also *jacket*), *pantaloon, hansom, boycott, to burke*, to name only a few of the best-known examples.

XXI.—§ 15. The Earliest Sentences.

Again, we saw above that the further back we went in the history of known languages, the more the sentence was one indissoluble whole, in which those elements which we are accustomed to think of as single words were not yet separated. Now, the idea that language began with sentences, not with words, appears to Whitney (*Am. Journ. of Philol.* 1. 338) to be, " if capable of any intelligent and intelligible statement, *a fortiori*, too wild and baseless to deserve respectful mention " (cf. also Madvig Kl 85). But the absurdity appears only if we think of sentences like those found in our languages, consisting of elements (words) capable of being used in other combinations and there forming other

sentences : this seems to be what Gabelentz (Spr 351) imagines ;
but it is not so wild to imagine as the first beginning something
which can be *translated* into our languages by means of a sentence,
but which is not 'articulated' in the same way as such a sentence ;
we translate or explain the dental click ('*tut*') by means of the
sentence 'that is a pity,' but the interjection is not in other
respects a grammatical 'sentence.' Or we may take an illustration
from the modern use of a telegraphic code : if *suzaw* means 'I
have not received your telegram,' or *sempo* 'reserve one single
room and bath at first-class hotel '—we have unanalyzable wholes
capable of being rendered in complete sentences, but not in every
way analogous to these sentences.

Now, it is just units of this character (though not, of course,
with exactly the same kind of meaning as the two code words)
whose genesis we can most easily imagine on the supposition of
a primitive period of meaningless singing. If a certain number
of people have together witnessed some incident and have
accompanied it with some sort of impromptu song or refrain, the
two ideas are associated, and later on the same song will tend to
call forth in the memory of those who were present the idea of the
whole situation. Suppose some dreaded enemy has been defeated
and slain ; the troop will dance round the dead body and strike
up a chant of triumph, say something like 'Tarara-boom-de-ay !'
This combination of sounds, sung to a certain melody, will now
easily become what might be called a proper name for that particular
event ; it might be roughly translated, 'The terrible foe from
beyond the river is slain,' or 'We have killed the dreadful man
from beyond the river,' or, 'Do you remember when we killed
him ?' or something of the same sort. Under slightly altered
circumstances it may become the proper name of the man who
slew the enemy. The development can now proceed further by
a metaphorical transference of the expression to similar situations
('There is another man of the same tribe : let us kill him as we
did the first !') or by a blending of two or more of these proper-
name melodies. How this kind of blending may lead to the development of something like derivative affixes may be gathered
from our chapter on Secretion ; it may also result in parts of
the whole melodic utterance being disengaged as something more
like our 'words.' From the nature of the subject it is impossible
to give more than hints, but I seem to see ways by which primitive
'lieder ohne worte ' may have become, first, indissoluble rigmaroles,
with something like a dim meaning attached to them, and then
gradually combinations of word-like smaller units, more and more
capable of being analyzed and combined with others of the same
kind. Anyhow, this theory seems to explain better than any

other the great part which fortuitous coincidence and irregularity always play in that part of any language which is not immediately intelligible, thus both in lexical and grammatical elements.

Primitive man came to attach meaning to what were originally rambling sequences of syllables in pretty much the same way as the child comes to attach a meaning to many of the words he hears from his elders, the whole situation in which they are heard giving a clue to their interpretation. The difference is that in the latter case the speaker has already associated a meaning with the sound ; but from the point of view of the hearer this is comparatively immaterial : the savage of a far-distant age hearing some syllables for the first time and the child hearing them nowadays are in essentially the same position as to their interpretation. Parallels are also found in the words of the *mamma* class (Ch. VIII § 9), in which hearers give a signification to something pronounced unintentionally, the same syllables being then capable of serving afterwards as real words. If one of our forebears on some occasion accidentally produced a sequence of sounds, and if the people around him were seen (or heard) to respond appreciatively, he would tend to settle on the same string of sounds and repeat it on similar occasions, and in this way it would gradually become ' conventionalized ' as a symbol of what was then foremost in his and in their minds. As in agriculture primitive man reaped before he sowed, so also in his vocal outbursts he first reaped understanding, and then discovered that by intentionally sowing the same seed he was able to call forth the same result. And as with corn, he would slowly and gradually, by weeding out (i.e. by not using) what was less useful to him, improve the quality, till finally he had come into possession of the marvellous, though far from perfect, instrument which we now call our language. The development of our ordinary speech has been largely an intellectualization, and the emotional quality which played the largest part in primitive utterances has to some extent been repressed ; but it is not extinct, and still gives a definite colouring to all passionate and eloquent speaking and to poetic diction. Language, after all, is an art—one of the finest of arts.

XXI.—§ 16. Conclusion.

Language, then, began with half-musical unanalyzed expressions for individual beings and solitary events. Languages composed of, and evolved from, such words and quasi-sentences are clumsy and insufficient instruments of thought, being intricate, capricious and difficult. But from the beginning the tendency has been one of progress, slow and fitful progress, but still progress towards greater and greater clearness, regularity, ease and pliancy. No one language has arrived at perfection; an ideal language would always express the same thing by the same, and similar things by similar means; any irregularity or ambiguity would be banished; sound and sense would be in perfect harmony; any number of delicate shades of meaning could be expressed with equal ease; poetry and prose, beauty and truth, thinking and feeling would be equally provided for: the human spirit would have found a garment combining freedom and gracefulness, fitting it closely and yet allowing full play to any movement.

But, however far our present languages are from that ideal, we must be thankful for what has been achieved, seeing that—

> Language is a perpetual orphic song,
> Which rules with Dædal harmony a throng
> Of thoughts and forms, which else senseless and shapeless were.

INDEX